ETHICAL LAWYERING

LEGAL AND PROFESSIONAL RESPONSIBILITIES IN THE PRACTICE OF LAW

Second Edition

By

Paul T. Hayden

Professor of Law
and Jacob J. Becker Fellow
Loyola Law School, Los Angeles

THOMSON

WEST

Mat #40384169

American Casebook Series and West Group are trademarks registered in the U.S. Patent and Trademark Office.

© West, a Thomson business, 2003
© 2007 Thomson/ West
      610 Opperman Drive
      P.O. Box 64526
      St. Paul, MN 55164–0526
      1–800–328–9352

Printed in the United States of America

ISBN: 978–0–314–16225–0

 TEXT IS PRINTED ON 10% POST CONSUMER RECYCLED PAPER

For Diane

*

Preface

The course in professional responsibility is one of the most interesting and complex in the entire law school curriculum. It has been a continuing mystery to me, in almost two decades of teaching the subject at three different law schools and in four very different formats, why so many students and professors apparently think otherwise. Learning and teaching this subject should be both fun and invigorating. This casebook reflects that perspective.

I was in my second year of law teaching at Indiana University School of Law in Indianapolis when I first offered to take on the professional responsibility course. The Associate Dean was by all accounts quite pleased. I was a popular young professor, and he told me that the class could use more teachers like me. But he warned me that I could expect my usually high student evaluations to dip or even plunge.

Happily, that did not happen, and my enthusiasm for teaching this subject has never waned over the years. Perhaps it is because I have taught the course as if it were any other upper-division course, rather than as something uniquely difficult to sell to students. In all such classes, I have focused on the law and used cases as the primary teaching vehicle. Students in my basic ethics course do not bog down in repetitious parsing of the rules of professional conduct (which is about as interesting as a forced march through the Administrative Procedure Act); neither do they spend hour after hour on sociological or philosophical materials. The doctrine in the course provides an excellent jumping-off point for non-doctrinal flights, since (as in any other course) the law itself is merely a first step toward deeper analysis of core issues.

I make no apologies for this doctrinal focus. The body of law and rules governing lawyers is as intricate and challenging as any, drawing on the law of agency, trusts, contracts, torts, procedure, evidence and constitutional law, among other subjects. This doctrine is also alive, applied every day to real people in real situations. To capture some of the life of these rules and law, this book is structured around cases, rather than hypothetical problems or academic readings. The facts in these reported cases are typically not edited heavily, to preserve the complexity that only real life can provide. Cases have been chosen either because of their intrinsic importance in the field, or because of the quality of their illumination of the legal or ethical rules at issue, or both. Where possible I have chosen recent cases with interesting and memorable facts. Notes after each case ask questions and provide more details, often through more cases, about the issues raised in the primary case. The facts of these cases, of course, focus on lawyers—and here is a difference between this course and others in the curriculum. The lawyer is always at the center of the picture in this class. While you may never represent a criminal defendant, or prepare an income tax return, you will be a lawyer and the law and rules that we look at in this class will apply to you and your clients from the first day you practice.

Many of the issues raised in this book are quite long-lived, even timeless. Others are distinctly current, although I have attempted to avoid a focus on the "flavor of the month" approach, giving only brief attention to issues that appear to be of fleeting rather than lasting importance.

The book begins with a long look at what it means to be a "professional." Why are lawyers different from other people who work for a living? We see in Chapter One cases and textual materials that raise these issues provocatively, ranging from portions of cases involving lawyer advertising, to materials on legal education and bar admission, to cases on the unauthorized practice of law. Chapter Two, titled "Incompetence and Its Consequences," stresses the duty of competence that all lawyers owe to clients, and examines the contours of civil liability for legal malpractice and the constitutional claim of ineffective assistance of counsel. Chapter Three explores a lawyer's duty of confidentiality, as found both in the law of evidence and in the rules of ethics. Chapter Four is at the center of the book and of the course, examining several aspects of the creation, maintenance and termination of the client-lawyer relationship. This chapter includes readings (and cases) on the importance of effective interviewing and counseling of clients, reflecting my own experience as a lawyer and a teacher of those skills for the last several years. Chapter Five deals with fees. Chapter Six, on conflicts of interest, addresses several kinds of conflicts, from doing business with clients, to representing one client against another, to the problems raised when lawyers change firms. Conflicts of interest are frequently litigated these days, and the length and detail of Chapter Six reflects its real-world importance. Chapter Seven focuses on special rules that apply to litigators. Chapter Eight covers advertising and solicitation, and contains some of the most important U.S. Supreme Court opinions in this area of law. Finally, the course ends with a look at some key issues about the law and ethics of judging.

A word on editing conventions. As mentioned above, I have not edited cases too heavily, in general, to preserve factual detail and the kinds of policy asides that add richness to otherwise dry legal analysis. But of course most cases are edited somewhat. Deletions are indicated by an ellipsis. Some portions of cases contain my own summaries of points made by the court; that is indicated by the use of brackets. Internal citations within primary cases may be edited or omitted entirely without any indication at all. Footnotes in cases may also be omitted without any indication. Footnotes that appear in cases are those of the court unless otherwise indicated, and retain their original numbering.

Some sources are cited repeatedly. The Restatement of the Law Governing Lawyers, published by the American Law Institute in 2000, is referenced simply as "the Restatement." Other Restatements (such as Torts and Agency) are specifically identified as such. The Model Rules of Professional Conduct is usually referred to collectively as "the Model Rules" and individual rules may be cited with the predicate "MR" before the relevant rule number. The older set of ABA model ethics rules, known as the Model Code of Professional Responsibility, is usually referred to as "the Model Code" and individual rules may be cited with the predicate "DR" (for "Disciplinary Rule") or "EC" (for "Ethical Consideration") before the relevant rule number. Citations to state versions of ethics rules are largely self-explanatory, but another word of explanation is probably in order. I frequently cite in notes not only to the relevant Model Rule, which usually is the majority rule in the United States, but also to the rules of California and New York, our two largest states, neither of which presently follows the Model Rules. In the interests of full disclosure, I must admit to having worked for New York City law firm for two years after college and to being a 23-year member of the California State Bar. But my decision to cite those two states' rules in many places in this book derives mainly from my desire to offer a comparison to the ABA Model Rules on many points, rather than from my large-state parochialism. I have spent over half of my life as a citizen of three much smaller states.

I hope students and teachers will enjoy using this book and that it will facilitate learning and teaching this wonderful subject. I welcome your suggestions and comments, which will be considered for future editions. I may be reached by email at Paul.Hayden@lls.edu.

PAUL T. HAYDEN

Los Angeles, California
October, 2006

*

Acknowledgments

Even a book with a single author's name on the cover cannot be written alone, and this one is no exception. I could not have produced this book without the support and assistance of my family, my friends, my colleagues and my institution. More broadly, I would never have been in the position to take on this project at all without the guidance and advice of the many highly ethical lawyers, law professors and judges with whom I have been associated over the last quarter century.

Specifically, I owe a tremendous debt of gratitude to my wife Diane Leiserson Hayden, without whom I could accomplish very little. My two youngest daughters, Dorothy Jean Hayden and Rose Alice Hayden, have been patient during the drafting process and have become experts at telling junk callers that I am not available.

My friend and co-author on another casebook, Dan B. Dobbs, deserves special recognition. Dan not only read portions of the original manuscript and made detailed comments, but also provided invaluable advice on how to write a casebook—something at which he is a true master. Perhaps even more importantly, Dan is always ready with words of encouragement as I struggle with this or that.

I am blessed to have a number of outstanding colleagues at Loyola Law School who share my enthusiasm for this subject. Several of them use this casebook and have given me invaluable suggestions for this Second Edition. Thanks to Susan Smith Bakhshian, Sascha Benzinger, Barbara Blanco, Bob Brain, Sande Buhai, Dan Martin, and Arnie Siegel. Thanks also to my students through the years, especially those recent ones who studied from the First Edition and asked many of the great questions that caused me to make revisions in this edition. Thanks to colleagues at other schools who adopted the First Edition and sent me comments about their experiences using the book in their classes. And thanks to Loyola Law School itself, and to my dean David W. Burcham, for generous financial support.

I must also thank some of the people who helped intensify my continuing interest in this subject. In law school I took classes from Murray Schwartz, Carrie Menkel-Meadow, and David Mellinkoff, all giants in this field. After graduation I clerked for two exemplary judges, Dorothy W. Nelson of the U.S. Court of Appeals for the Ninth Circuit (after whom my second daughter is named), and J. Spencer Letts of the U.S. District Court for the Central District of California, both of whom taught me a great deal about personal integrity on and off the bench, and both of whom helped me to secure an academic position some years later. In law practice I was surrounded by excellent lawyers of unimpeachable character, from whom I also learned much. Before coming to Loyola, I benefitted from teaching alongside Bill Hodes, Norman Lefstein, and David Ray Papke (at Indiana University School of Law at Indianapolis) and Cruz Reynoso (at UCLA School of Law). They all helped me find my voice. Any wrong notes in this book, of course, are entirely my own.

P.T.H.

————————

Certain materials have been quoted herein with the continuing permission of the copyright holders, as follows:

ABA Model Rules of Professional Conduct. Copyright © 2002 by the American Bar Association. All rights reserved. Reprinted by Permission.

ABA Standards Relating to the Administration of Criminal Justice: The Prosecution Function. Copyright © 1992, American Bar Association. Reprinted by Permission.

ABA Standards Relating to the Administration of Criminal Justice: The Defense Function. Copyright © 1991, American Bar Association. Reprinted by Permission.

ABA Model Rules for Lawyer Disciplinary Enforcement. Copyright © 1999 by the American Bar Association. All rights reserved. Reprinted by Permission.

ABA Model Code of Judicial Conduct. Copyright © 2002 by the American Bar Association. All rights reserved. Reprinted by Permission.

ABA Formal Ethics Opinion 01–421 (2001). Copyright © 2001 by the American Bar Association. Reprinted by Permission.

Robert E. Shapiro, "Advance Sheet," Litigation, Vol. 28, No. 3 (Spring 2002). Copyright © 2002 by the American Bar Association. All rights reserved. Reprinted by Permission.

ABA Section of Litigation, Ethical Guidelines for Settlement Negotiations (August 2002). Copyright © 2002 by the American Bar Association. Reprinted by Permission.

ABA Commission on Billable Hours Report, 2001–2002. Copyright © 2002 by the American Bar Association. Reprinted by Permission.

Restatement of the Law Governing Lawyers. Copyright © 2000 by the American Law Institute. All rights reserved. Reprinted with permission.

Lon L. Fuller & John D. Randall, Professional Responsibility: Report of the Joint Conference, 44 American Bar Association Journal 1159 (1958). Copyright © 1958 by the ABA Journal. Reprinted by permission of the ABA Journal.

Marvin E. Frankel, The Search for Truth: An Umpireal View, 123 University of Pennsylvania Law Review 1031 (1975). Copyright © 1975, University of Pennsylvania Law Review. Reprinted with permission.

William H. Simon, The Belated Decline of Literalism in Professional Responsibility Doctrine: Soft Deception and the Rule of Law, 70 Fordham Law Review 1881 (2002). Copyright © 2002 Fordham Law Review. Reprinted with permission.

*

Summary of Contents

Table of Contents

*

Table of Cases

The principal cases are in bold type. Cases cited or discussed in the text are roman type. References are to pages. Cases cited in principal cases and within other quoted materials are not included.

*

Table of Authorities

where is ref. to FRCPs? / statutes?

ETHICAL LAWYERING

LEGAL AND PROFESSIONAL RESPONSIBILITIES IN THE PRACTICE OF LAW

Second Edition

*

Chapter 1

PROFESSIONALISM AND
THE PRACTICE OF LAW

---

§ 1.   THE CONCEPT OF "PROFESSIONALISM"

Everyone knows that lawyers are "professionals." So are doctors, teachers, and members of the clergy. But what does it mean to be a professional? And what does "professionalism" itself mean? As we will see, there is no simple answer to these questions; professionalism means different things to different people. As a 1986 American Bar Association commission report put it, professionalism is an "elastic concept, the meaning and application of which are hard to pin down."

Roscoe Pound, in his landmark book The Lawyer from Antiquity to Modern Times (1953), wrote that the term professional "refers to a group . . . pursuing a learned art as a common calling in the spirit of public service—no less a public service because it may incidentally be a means of livelihood. Pursuit of the learned art in the spirit of public service is the primary purpose." Another scholar has identified four key "elements" of a profession as follows: (1) its practice requires substantial intellectual training and the use of complex judgments; (2) clients must trust those they consult, since they cannot adequately evaluate the quality of the professional's work; (3) self-interest is sublimated to the client's interest and the public good; and (4) it is self-regulating.

Even if we accept the brief definitions of a profession as fitting the calling of lawyers, the devil is in the details. How do we separate "professional" from "unprofessional" *behavior*? It is certainly true that a member of a professional group can act in an "unprofessional" manner. But sometimes, what is considered "unprofessional" conduct by one person will be viewed as perfectly appropriate by another. The boundaries of "professionalism," and sometimes its core, remain fuzzy and elusive the harder we look.

In many ways, though, defining the appropriate boundaries of professional behavior is at the core of ethical lawyering. Admitted-

1

ly, the impossibility of reaching a consensus definition of "professionalism" perforce means that there will be disagreement about whether or not certain kinds of lawyer conduct are ethically proper. Some of these disagreements are temporal, primarily; that is, earlier views of what was appropriate or inappropriate have changed with the times. Lawyer advertising, once banned, is in this category, at least for now. Other disagreements rage today. Is it professionally acceptable to join in a partnership with non-lawyers to provide more complete "one-stop" service to clients? Or to take a start-up business client's stock in lieu of cash for legal fees? Or to divulge client confidences to prevent financial harm to third parties? Rules of professional conduct may appear on their surface to "resolve" these disagreements; an exclusive focus on current model rules can produce such an illusion. But the reality is that the "rules" of proper lawyering are as disparate, contradictory and fluid as the "rules" of tort law, contract law, or property law. Different states adopt differing approaches to particular issues. Thus it is fair to say that on many discrete topics we will study in this class, there is not a single "correct" or "professional" course of action. Rather, there is a range of such courses, with boundaries. Forming your own vision of "professionalism" involves recognizing where the present boundaries are, along with—perhaps more importantly—developing a framework for deciding what kind of lawyer you want to be.

Leaders of the organized bar have for several decades exhorted lawyers to uphold professionalism while lamenting its deterioration. Not so long ago, lawyer advertising produced a heated argument within our highest court about the contours of professionalism and its importance to the bar.

BATES v. STATE BAR OF ARIZONA

Supreme Court of the United States, 1977.
433 U.S. 350, 97 S.Ct. 2691, 53 L.Ed.2d 810.

[Two Arizona lawyers were disciplined by the bar for running a newspaper advertisement for their "legal clinic," which said they were offering "legal services at very reasonable fees," and listed their fees for certain routine services. Arizona ethics rules banned all lawyer advertising. The Supreme Court held that such ads, if not false, deceptive or misleading, were protected by the First Amendment, and therefore that the state bar rules were unconstitutional. The Court addressed one of the State Bar's key arguments in support of the advertising prohibition, as follows.]

Mr. Justice BLACKMUN delivered the opinion of the Court.

The key to professionalism, it is argued, is the sense of pride that involvement in the discipline generates. It is claimed that price advertising will bring about commercialization, which will undermine the attorney's sense of dignity and self-worth. The hustle of the marketplace will adversely affect the profession's service orientation, and irreparably damage the delicate balance between the lawyer's need to earn and his obligation selflessly to serve. Advertising is also said to erode the client's trust in his attorney: Once the client perceives that the lawyer is motivated by profit, his confidence that the attorney is acting out of a commitment to the client's welfare is jeopardized. And advertising is said to tarnish the dignified public image of the profession.

We recognize, of course, and commend the spirit of public service with which the profession of law is practiced and to which it is dedicated.... But we find the postulated connection between advertising and the erosion of true professionalism to be severely strained. At its core, the argument presumes that attorneys must conceal from themselves and from their clients the real-life fact that lawyers earn their livelihood at the bar. We suspect that few attorneys engage in such self-deception. And rare is the client, moreover, even one of the modest means, who enlists the aid of an attorney with the expectation that his services will be rendered free of charge....

Moreover, the assertion that advertising will diminish the attorney's reputation in the community is open to question. Bankers and engineers advertise, and yet these professions are not regarded as undignified. In fact, it has been suggested that the failure of lawyers to advertise creates public disillusionment with the profession. The absence of advertising may be seen to reflect the profession's failure to reach out and serve the community: Studies reveal that many persons do not obtain counsel even when they perceive a need because of the feared price of services or because of an inability to locate a competent attorney. Indeed, cynicism with regard to the profession may be created by the fact that it long has publicly eschewed advertising, while condoning the actions of the attorney who structures his social or civic associations so as to provide contacts with potential clients.

Mr. Justice POWELL, with whom Mr. Justice STEWART joins, concurring in part and dissenting in part.

... I cannot join the Court's holding that under the First Amendment 'truthful' newspaper advertising of a lawyer's prices for 'routine legal services' may not be restrained. Although the Court appears to note some reservations ... , it is clear that within undefined limits today's decision will effect profound changes in the practice of law, viewed for centuries as a learned profession. The supervisory power of the courts over members of the bar, as officers of the courts, and the authority of the respective States to oversee the regulation of the profession have been weakened. Although the Court's opinion professes to be framed narrowly, and its reach is subject to future clarification, the holding is explicit and expansive with respect to the advertising of undefined 'routine legal services.' In my view, this result is neither required by the First Amendment, nor in the public interest.

[Legal services are unique, and vastly unlike fungible commodities.] The average lay person simply has no feeling for which services are included in [an advertised service for "routine" legal work], and thus no capacity to judge the nature of the advertised product. As a result, the type of advertisement before us inescapably will mislead many who respond to it. In the end, it will promote distrust of lawyers and disrespect for our own system of justice. . . .

The Court emphasizes the need for information that will assist persons desiring legal services to choose lawyers. Under our economic system, advertising is the most commonly used and useful means of providing information as to goods and other services, but it generally has not been used with respect to legal and certain other professional services. Until today, controlling weight has been given to the danger that general advertising of such services too often would tend to mislead rather than inform. Moreover, there has been the further concern that the characteristics of the legal profession thought beneficial to society a code of professional ethics, an imbued sense of professional and public responsibility, a tradition of self-discipline, and duties as officers of the courts would suffer if the restraints on advertising were significantly diluted. . . .

The area into which the Court now ventures has, until today, largely been left to self-regulation by the profession within the framework of canons or standards of conduct prescribed by the respective States and enforced where necessary by the courts. The problem of bringing clients and lawyers together on a mutually fair basis, consistent with the public interest, is as old as the profession itself. It is one of considerable complexity, especially in view of the constantly evolving nature of the need for legal services. The problem has not been resolved with complete satisfaction despite diligent and thoughtful efforts by the organized bar and others over a period of many years, and there is no reason to believe that today's best answers will be responsive to future needs.

In this context, the Court's imposition of hard and fast constitutional rules as to price advertising is neither required by precedent nor likely to serve the public interest. One of the great virtues of federalism is the opportunity it affords for experimentation and innovation, with freedom to discard or amend that which proves unsuccessful or detrimental to the public good. The constitutionalizing—indeed the affirmative encouraging—of competitive price advertising of specified legal services will substantially inhibit the experimentation that has been underway and also will limit the control heretofore exercised over lawyers by the respective States.

I am apprehensive, despite the Court's expressed intent to proceed cautiously, that today's holding will be viewed by tens of thousands of lawyers as an invitation—by the public-spirited and the selfish lawyers alike—to engage in competitive advertising on an escalating basis. Some lawyers may gain temporary advantages; others will suffer from the economic power of stronger lawyers, or by the subtle deceit of less scrupulous lawyers. Some members of the public may benefit marginally, but the risk is that many others will be victimized by simplistic price advertising of professional services 'almost infinite in variety and nature … '. Until today, in the long history of the legal profession, it was not thought that this risk of public deception was required by the marginal First Amendment interests asserted by the Court.

Notes

1.   The American Bar Association promulgated its first set of professional ethics rules, the Canons of Professional Ethics, in 1908. The Canons remained in place, as amended from time to time, for over six decades, and were widely adopted by the states as the disciplinary rules for lawyers within their particular jurisdictions. (The development of these various sets of ethics rules receives more detailed treatment in the next section of this Chapter.) Canon 27 stated: "It is unprofessional to solicit professional employment by circulars, advertisements, through touters or by personal communications or interviews not warranted by personal relations." Even "indirect advertisements" such as the self-laudatory act of "furnishing or inspiring newspaper comments" were condemned as "reprehensible" on the ground that they "offend the traditions and lower the tone of our profession." Later codes carried forward this ban on advertising and solicitation, checked only by the line of constitutional decisions that began with *Bates*.

2.   Justice Rehnquist dissented in *Bates* on an even stronger ground than did Justice Powell: commercial speech has no First Amendment protection at all. He said: "While I agree with my Brother Powell that the effect of today's opinion on the professions is both unfortunate and not required by the First and Fourteenth Amendments, I cannot join the implication in his opinion that some forms of legal advertising may be constitutionally protected." In other words, Justice Rehnquist took the position that the state could constitutionally ban all lawyer advertising.

3.   Do you agree with Justice Powell that many lawyer advertisements are misleading to consumers? Why might that be true?

4.   Does the majority opinion in *Bates* blur the lines between law as a *business* and law as a *profession*? Does constitutionally protecting

lawyer advertising make the practice of law look like something it is not? Or does it recognize it for what it is?

5. Both the majority and the dissent appear to be concerned with the public image of lawyers and how advertising might affect it. Do lawyers who advertise strike you as less "professional" than lawyers who do not?

6. At a broader level, is the public image of lawyers even a relevant concern? Why might it be? Does the public image of lawyers affect their "professionalism?" How?

7. Justice Powell also asserts that recognizing a constitutional protection for lawyer advertising undermines state regulation of lawyers. How would this be so? If true, why would this be problematic?

8. In his dissent in *Bates*, Justice Powell noted as "highly relevant" the opinion in *Semler v. Oregon State Board of Dental Examiners*, 294 U.S. 608, 55 S.Ct. 570, 79 L.Ed. 1086 (1935), which upheld state restriction of advertising by dentists. Chief Justice Hughes wrote in that case that professions "demand[] different standards of conduct from those which are traditional in the competition of the market place. The [professional] community is concerned with the maintenance of professional standards which will insure not only competency in individual practitioners, but protection against those who would prey upon a public peculiarly susceptible to imposition through alluring promises of physical relief. And the community is concerned in providing safeguards not only against deception, but against practices which would tend to demoralize the profession by forcing its members into an unseemly rivalry which would enlarge the opportunities of the least scrupulous. What is generally called the 'ethics' of the profession is but the consensus of expert opinion as to the necessity of such standards."

Does the *Bates* majority reject the notion that the "community" of lawyers has a legitimate interest in avoiding being forced into an "unseemly rivalry" for clients? Or is the interest simply not proven to be "substantial?"

SHAPERO v. KENTUCKY BAR ASS'N

Supreme Court of the United States, 1988.
486 U.S. 466, 108 S.Ct. 1916, 100 L.Ed.2d 475.

[A Kentucky Supreme Court Rule, patterned after the ABA's Model Rule of Professional Conduct 7.3, prohibited lawyers from soliciting legal business for pecuniary gain by sending even truthful and nondeceptive letters to potential clients known to face particular legal problems. A Kentucky lawyer applied to that state's Attorneys Advertising Commission for advance approval of a letter that he proposed to send "to potential clients who have had a foreclosure suit filed against them," which, *inter alia,* advised the client that "you may be about to lose your home," that "[f]ederal law may allow you to ... *ORDE[R]* your creditor to *STOP*," that "you may call my office ... for *FREE* information," and that "[i]t may surprise you what I may be able to do for you." On the basis of the Kentucky Supreme Court Rule, the Commission declined to approve of the letter's content. The lawyer challenged this decision and the underlying rule on First Amendment grounds. Writing for the Court, Justice Brennan held that such advertising is constitutionally protected commercial speech, subject to restriction only in the service of a substantial governmental interest, and only through means that directly advance that interest. Justice O'Connor filed a dissent, excerpted below.]

O'CONNOR, dissenting:

... Attorney advertising generally falls under the rubric of "commercial speech." ... A standardized legal test has been devised for commercial speech cases. Under that test, such speech is entitled to constitutional protection only if it concerns lawful activities and is not misleading; if the speech is protected, government may still ban or regulate it by laws that directly advance a substantial governmental interest and are appropriately tailored to that purpose. See *Central Hudson Gas & Electric Corp. v. Public Service Comm'n of New York*, 447 U.S. 557, 566, 100 S.Ct. 2343, 2351, 65 L.Ed.2d 341 (1980). Applying that test to attorney advertising, it is clear to me that the States should have considerable latitude to ban advertising that is "*potentially* or demonstrably misleading," *as well as* truthful advertising that undermines the substantial governmental interest in promoting the high ethical standards that are necessary in the legal profession....

... Applying the *Central Hudson* test to the regulation at issue today ... , I think it clear that Kentucky has a substantial interest in preventing the potentially misleading effects of targeted, direct-mail advertising as well as the corrosive effects that such advertising can have on appropriate professional standards. Soliciting business from strangers who appear to need particular legal services, when a significant motive for the offer is the lawyer's pecuniary gain, always has a tendency to corrupt the solicitor's professional judgment. This is especially true when the solicitation includes the offer of a "free sample," as petitioner's proposed letter does. I therefore conclude that American Bar Association Model Rule of Professional Conduct 7.3 (1984) sweeps no more broadly than is necessary to advance a substantial governmental interest. The Kentucky Supreme Court correctly found that petitioner's letter could permissibly be banned under Rule 7.3, and I dissent from the Court's decision to reverse that judgment.

The roots of the error in our attorney advertising cases are a defective analogy between professional services and standardized consumer products and a correspondingly inappropriate skepticism about the States' justifications for their regulations.... [T]he *Bates* majority simply insisted on concluding that the benefits of advertising outweigh its dangers. In my view, that policy decision was not derived from the First Amendment, and it should not have been used to displace a different and no less reasonable policy decision of the State whose regulation was at issue....

Even if I agreed that this Court should take upon itself the task of deciding what forms of attorney advertising are in the public interest, I would not agree with what it has done. The best arguments in favor of rules permitting attorneys to advertise are founded in elementary economic principles. Restrictions on truthful advertising, which artificially interfere with the ability of suppliers to transmit price information to consumers, presumably reduce the efficiency of the mechanisms of supply and demand.... Assuming, *arguendo,* that the removal of advertising restrictions should lead in the short run to increased efficiency in the provision of legal services, I would not agree that we can safely assume the same effect in the long run. The economic argument against these restrictions ignores the delicate role they may play in preserving the norms of the legal profession. While it may be difficult to defend this role with precise economic logic, I believe there is a powerful argument in favor of restricting lawyer advertising and that this argument is at the very least not easily refuted by economic analysis.

One distinguishing feature of any profession, unlike other occupations that may be equally respectable, is that membership entails an ethical obligation to temper one's selfish pursuit of economic success by adhering to standards of conduct that could not be enforced either by legal fiat or through the discipline of the market. There are sound reasons to continue pursuing the goal that is implicit in the traditional view of professional life. Both the special privileges incident to membership in the profession and the advantages those privileges give in the necessary task of earning a living are means to a goal that transcends the accumulation of wealth. That goal is public service, which in the legal profession can take a variety of familiar forms. This view of the legal profession need not be rooted in romanticism or self-serving sanctimony, though of course it can be. Rather, special ethical standards for lawyers are properly understood as an appropriate means of restraining lawyers in the exercise of the unique power that they inevitably wield in a political system like ours.

It is worth recalling why lawyers are regulated at all, or to a greater degree than most other occupations, and why history is littered with failed attempts to extinguish lawyers as a special class. See generally R. Pound, The Lawyer from Antiquity to

Modern Times (1953). Operating a legal system that is both reasonably efficient and tolerably fair cannot be accomplished, at least under modern social conditions, without a trained and specialized body of experts. This training is one element of what we mean when we refer to the law as a "learned profession." Such knowledge by its nature cannot be made generally available, and it therefore confers the power and the temptation to manipulate the system of justice for one's own ends. Such manipulation can occur in at least two obvious ways. One results from overly zealous representation of the client's interests; abuse of the discovery process is one example whose causes and effects (if not its cure) is apparent. The second, and for present purposes the more relevant, problem is abuse of the client for the lawyer's benefit. Precisely because lawyers must be provided with expertise that is both esoteric and extremely powerful, it would be unrealistic to demand that clients bargain for their services in the same arm's-length manner that may be appropriate when buying an automobile or choosing a dry cleaner. Like physicians, lawyers are subjected to heightened ethical demands on their conduct towards those they serve. These demands are needed because market forces, and the ordinary legal prohibitions against force and fraud, are simply insufficient to protect the consumers of their necessary services from the peculiar power of the specialized knowledge that these professionals possess.

Imbuing the legal profession with the necessary ethical standards is a task that involves a constant struggle with the relentless natural force of economic self-interest. It cannot be accomplished directly by legal rules, and it certainly will not succeed if sermonizing is the strongest tool that may be employed. Tradition and experiment have suggested a number of formal and informal mechanisms, none of which is adequate by itself and many of which may serve to reduce competition (in the narrow economic sense) among members of the profession. A few examples include the great efforts made during this century to improve the quality and breadth of the legal education that is required for admission to the bar; the concomitant attempt to cultivate a subclass of genuine scholars within the profession; the development of bar associations that aspire to be more than trade groups; strict disciplinary rules about conflicts of interest and client abandonment; and promotion of the expectation that an attorney's history of voluntary public service is a relevant factor in selecting judicial candidates.

Restrictions on advertising and solicitation by lawyers properly and significantly serve the same goal. Such restrictions act as a concrete, day-to-day reminder to the practicing attorney of why it is improper for any member of this profession to regard it as a trade or occupation like any other. There is no guarantee, of course, that the restrictions will always have the desired effect,

NOTE: FIGHTING BIAS AND PREJUDICE

In 2005, the high court of Maryland adopted a new disciplinary rule which states that it is professional misconduct for a lawyer to:

> knowingly manifest by words or conduct when acting in a professional capacity bias or prejudice based upon race, sex, religion, national origin, disability, age, sexual orientation or socioeconomic status when such action is prejudicial to the administration of justice, provided, however that legitimate advocacy is not a violation of this paragraph.

Md. Rule 8.4 (c). A handful of other states (including Colorado, Minnesota, Nebraska, New Jersey, Ohio and Texas) have adopted similar provisions in their state disciplinary rules for lawyers. Some states make explicit reference to anti-discrimination laws in disciplinary provisions that require lawyers to obey the law. See, e.g., Iowa Rule 8.4(g); Minn. Rule 8.4(h); N.Y. DR 1–102(A)(6); Cal. Rule 2–400(B).

While several committees within the ABA have tried through the years to get the ABA's governing body to insert a specific anti-bias provision in the Model Rules, that has not happened. The sole specific reference to bias or prejudice in the Model Rules, inserted in 1998, appears as a Comment rather than in the black-letter. See MR 8.4, comment [3] (providing that knowingly manifesting bias or prejudice in the course of representing a client constitutes a violation of the rule, if such actions are prejudicial to the administration of justice).

Should more states adopt a rule making it a disciplinary offense to manifest bias or prejudice when acting in a professional capacity? One principled objection is the very one stated by the ABA Standing Committee on Ethics and Professional Responsibility in 1998 when it decided against proposing such a rule: some bias and prejudice will be manifested in statements, and some of those statements may well be protected by the First Amendment. Apart from that objection, some in the legal profession, while not bigoted themselves, may believe that the profession is largely free of prejudice and that any such rule is therefore unnecessary. After all, they may think, women now occupy half the seats in law schools, and people of color are actively recruited by elite law schools, corporations and law firms. The reality, however, is not that rosy. Studies consistently show that bias and discrimination remain severe, if sometimes closeted, problems for the legal profession, as for society at large.

In a 2005 report titled "Miles to Go: Progress of Minorities in the Legal Profession," the ABA Commission on Racial and Ethnic

Diversity in the Legal Profession found that the legal profession lags behind other key professions in minority representation. For example, while almost a quarter of all physicians and surgeons are members of a racial minority group, less than ten percent of all lawyers are. The Commission also found that minorities remain grossly under-represented at the highest levels of the profession, such as law firm partnership and corporate general counsel positions. And, while the number of women in the legal profession has continued to grow—for example, the percentage of women in medium and large-sized law firms tripled between 1975 (14 percent) to 2002 (40 percent)—gender bias in law firms and in the courtroom has certainly not disappeared. The same is true of bias and prejudice against the disabled and lesbian, gay, bisexual or transsexual persons. A 2001 report of a subcommittee of the California Judicial Council's Access and Fairness Advisory Committee reported that over half of the gay or lesbian lawyers and court employees surveyed had experienced or observed biased acts or comments toward gays or lesbians. Twenty percent of court employees questioned in the same survey reported hearing derogatory comments or jokes about gays or lesbians in open court. See Krista Glaser & Jose D. Alarcon, *Bias in the Courtroom*, California Bar Journal 10 (Aug. 2005).

Perhaps the worst abuses of this kind are sufficiently covered by existing rules. Clearly, if a lawyer engages in discrimination or sexual harassment in contravention of federal or state anti-discrimination statutes, that lawyer will have violated one or more provisions of any state's ethics rules and may be disciplined for that. See, e.g., *In re Tenenbaum*, 880 A.2d 1025 (Del. 2005) (three year suspension for lawyer who sexually harassed female clients and members of his law office staff over a five- to ten-year period). Lawyers have also been disciplined for such things as moving for a mistrial, then for a new trial, on the ground that a judge's disabled law clerk was in the courtroom during a personal-injury case involving the lawyer's less-disabled client, supposedly making the jury less sympathetic to the client's plight. *In re Panel Case No. 15976*, 653 N.W.2d 452 (Minn. 2002). See also *In re Panel File 98–26*, 597 N.W.2d 563 (Minn. 1999) (disciplining a prosecutor for making a motion to exclude a public defender from trying a case, solely on the basis of his race).

On a broader level, though, we are examining here what it means to be a professional; our focus at this point should not be narrowly doctrinal. Is a lawyer who exhibits bias in subtler ways than a rule would proscribe nonetheless acting unprofessionally? Is a lawyer who does not actively fight bias and discrimination acting unprofessionally? Do lawyers, as compared to other professionals, have heightened duties in this area? If so, why?

§ 2. SOURCES OF REGULATION OF LAWYERS

Law is a heavily regulated profession, and much of its regulation is self-imposed. (Indeed, self-regulation is another hallmark of a "profession.") We will see many sources of regulation in this course. The most important ones are described briefly below.

A. Rules of Professional Conduct

1. History and Main Characteristics of Rules

Rules of professional conduct, often called "ethics rules," are designed to provide a basis for the discipline of lawyers. This is an important function, but these rules are certainly not all-encompassing. For one thing, discipline is only one sanction to which lawyers are subject; as we will see, in certain contexts, discipline is not a particularly significant sanction. For another, the rules of professional conduct cover only a fraction of the subject of "ethical lawyering." While the rules are a key component of this course, then, it would be a grave error to see them as the *whole* course.

Discipline of lawyers, including the adoption of the disciplinary rules themselves, is a matter largely left to the states. Each state determines its own rules of professional responsibility and what sanctions to impose for violations. Generally, this state power resides in the state's highest court, although it may be delegated. For the last century, however, a private, national group of lawyers—the American Bar Association—has provided the states with "model" rules which have then been voluntarily adopted by most states. (States need not adopt the entire model set, but may instead "pick and choose" as they see fit.) While there remain significant state-to-state variations in certain rules, the ABA's role has produced a far greater standardization of state ethics rules than would have occurred without its contribution.

The ABA itself was founded in 1878 by an elite group of white male lawyers, during a time of rapid increases in lawyer numbers and changes in demographics. The men who formed the ABA were not only aware of these trends, they were alarmed by them. Their new association had the stated objective to "uphold the honor of the profession of law." The ABA leaders, in other words, were centrally concerned about "professionalism," a concern which continues to this day, albeit usually in more egalitarian forms.

In 1905, the ABA appointed a five-member committee to study the drafting of a "code of professional ethics." The Report of the Committee on Code of Professional Ethics, delivered to the ABA in St. Paul in the summer of 1906, stressed the need for a clear, uniform set of rules that could be used to discipline unethical lawyers of perceived low character who continued to join the ranks at an ever-burgeoning pace. "We cannot be blind," said the report, "to the fact that, however high may be the motives of some, the trend of many is away from the ideals of the past and the tendency more and more to reduce our high calling to the level of a trade. . . . " The report spoke of "changed conditions" in the bar due to "the influx of increasing numbers, who seek admission to the profession mainly for its emoluments." It lamented the new world in which "the shyster, the barratrously inclined, the ambulance chaser, the member of the Bar with a system of runners, pursue their nefarious methods with no check save the rope of sand of moral suasion . . . so long as they violate no criminal law." Lawyers, the report continued, should serve only during good behavior—and " 'good behavior' should not be a vague, meaningless or shadowy term devoid of practical application." Rather, standards of ethics should be "crystallized into a written code" that could be used to exclude a lawyer who violates its provisions from practicing or retaining membership in voluntary professional organizations such as the ABA.

Despite this practical goal, the resulting Canons of Ethics as adopted by the ABA in 1908 tended more toward moral exhortation than rigid rule, and was thereby limited as an effective disciplinary code. The Canons drew heavily on the Alabama Bar Association's Code of Ethics (1887), which was itself based largely on two mid-century works, George Sharswood's Professional Ethics (1854) and David Hoffman's A Course of Legal Study (2d ed. 1836). The Canons' drafters expressly disclaimed that they comprised a *complete* set of ethics rules, recognizing in the Preamble that "No code or set of rules can be framed, which will particularize all the duties of the lawyer. . . . [T]he enumeration of particular duties should not be construed as a denial of the existence of others equally imperative, though not specifically mentioned." These limitations prompted Supreme Court Justice Harlan Fiske Stone to describe the Canons in 1934 as "for the most part generalizations designed for an earlier era." Despite such critiques, the Canons were widely adopted and followed in most states for over six decades.

By the mid–1960s, bar leaders recognized the need for a more effective ethics code. ABA President Lewis Powell, later a Supreme Court justice, appointed a committee to amend the Canons in 1964. This era witnessed the first waves of what would become an enormous new explosion in the number of lawyers, and clear signs of a coming radical shift in who those new lawyers were— that is, the same sort of situation that had helped inspire the drafting of the Canons over a half century before. Between 1963 and 1973, total law school enrollment went from 49,552 to 106,-102, and new admissions to the bar more than doubled. The percentage of female law school students—for decades stuck in the three- to four-percent range, had begun to climb in 1967–68, and reached 20 percent in 1974–75. Between 1972 and 1973 alone, there was a 37.8 percent increase of women in first year law school classes. In the midst of these changes, the bar's elite came to the obvious conclusion that legal ethics could no longer be simply part of an unwritten "gentlemen's code," enforced by the informal sanction of shame. Rules of conduct had to become more and more formal.

So work began on drafting a new kind of ethics code, one tighter and more definite than the Canons had been. The final product, approved in 1969 by the ABA and promulgated in 1970, contained legally-binding norms in the form of Disciplinary Rules, while also retaining something of the tone of the Canons in Ethical Considerations. Most states quickly adopted them, following a highly organized campaign by the ABA to achieve that goal.

The Code itself was soon criticized on a number of grounds, and threats of an antitrust action by the U.S. Department of Justice prompted the ABA to begin a wholesale revision of the Code just seven years after its promulgation. The ABA's Kutak Commission (named after its chair, Omaha lawyer Robert Kutak) began its work in 1977 and within two years drafts were circulating. The Model Rules that finally emerged (as promulgated by the ABA in 1983) look much like a Restatement of the Law in format, with black-letter rules followed by often-lengthy Comments designed to provide lawyers with guidance in complying with the rules. As with the Canons and the Model Code, the ABA's Model Rules were just that—*model rules* with no legal effect whatsoever until adopted by state authorities. Most state authorities quickly did adopt these rules, however, as they had their predecessor models–although there were several state variations on key rules, most notably confidentiality.

In the decades since the Model Rules were first promulgated, the ABA has continued its periodic revision process. In the early 2000's, the Model Rules underwent a substantial overhaul, although the ABA retained the Rules' basic format and title. Almost every state has now voluntarily adopted most of the Model Rules, although it is common to find state-to-state variation in particular rules (often the most important ones, as we'll see). California and New York have never adopted the Model Rules at all, and thus follow their own unique rules, although both states may be close adopting the Model Rules format and much of its substance.

The Model Rules have largely completed what the Model Code had started in 1969, transforming the rules of legal ethics into positive doctrine. With each successive set of ethics rules, from the Canons to the Code to the Rules, the ABA has offered ever more concrete statements of lawyers' obligations that must be obeyed lest the lawyer risk discipline. While this movement towards the "legalization" of ethics rules has been criticized, it has by any estimate flourished in recent decades.

2. Sanctions for Rule Violations

As we have seen, just as each state determines its own rules, each state also determines for itself what sanctions may be imposed for violations of those rules. As with the rules themselves, however, there is significant (although certainly not complete) national standardization, due in large part to the ABA's promulgation in 1986 of model guidelines for this purpose. These ABA Standards for Imposing Lawyer Sanctions have now been adopted in whole or part by the majority of states. Another set of widely-adopted ABA rules, the Model Rules for Lawyer Disciplinary Enforcement, first promulgated in 1989, also contain some recommendations about sanctions, although they primarily deal with procedure.

Who may be subject to discipline by a particular state's authorities? Model Rule 8.5(a) provides that any lawyer admitted in a jurisdiction is subject to that jurisdiction's disciplinary authorities, no matter where the misconduct occurs. For example, a lawyer who is admitted to practice in both Wisconsin and Michigan may be disciplined by Wisconsin for behavior that occurred in a Michigan courtroom in violation of Michigan rules. See *In re Disciplinary Proceedings Against Marks*, 265 Wis.2d 1, 665 N.W.2d 836 (2003). Further, Rule 8.5 provides that a lawyer who is not admitted in a particular jurisdiction is nonetheless subject to that jurisdiction's authority "if the lawyer provides or offers to provide any legal services" in that jurisdiction. This means that if a lawyer admitted only in Nebraska lawyer engages in misconduct while working temporarily on a legal matter in Arkansas, he could also be disciplined by the Arkansas authorities for the same conduct. Rule 8.5(b) sets forth choice of law guidelines for such situations.

In all states, and pursuant to the ABA Standards, the precise sanction imposed in any case depends ultimately on the facts of the case. Specifically, pursuant to the ABA's model framework, the disciplinary body first determines the type of lawyer misconduct involved by looking at what ethical duty was violated, the lawyer's mental state, and the extent of the actual or potential injury caused by the violation. Next, the body determines the recommended sanction. The ABA Standards, 4.0 through 8.0, set forth such recommendations for a number of specific rule violations, under certain generic circumstances. For example, the Standards recommend the most severe sanction where a lawyer knowingly reveals confidential information with the intent to benefit the lawyer or another and the client is actually or potentially injured. Standard 4.21. Where the lawyer reveals confidential information negligently, causing little or no harm, however, the recommended sanction is minimal. Standard 4.24. The final step in the decisional process is for the body to consider any aggravating or mitigating factors, which may result in increasing or decreasing the sanction. Typically available sanctions, from most to least severe, are (1) disbarment; (2) suspension; (3) public reprimand; (4) private reprimand; and (5) probation.

● *Disbarment* takes away the lawyer's status as a lawyer. Contrary to popular belief, disbarment is not permanent in most states. Rather, the disbarred lawyer can apply for readmission, usually after five years. The ABA Standards recommend that to be readmitted, a disbarred lawyer must prove by clear and convincing evidence that he is rehabilitated and has complied with all disciplinary orders or rules, such as completion of the bar exam.

● *Suspension* takes away the lawyer's ability to practice law, usually for a definite time. The states vary in the length of time suspensions may run; the ABA recommends that this sanction run between six months and three years. The ABA further recommends that suspended lawyers should be allowed to return to practice only upon showing rehabilitation, compliance with disciplinary body orders, and fitness to practice law. If a suspended lawyer fails to prove fitness to practice, the suspension may extend indefinitely and become tantamount to disbarment. See, e.g., *In re Stanton*, 860 A.2d 369 (D.C. 2004)(denying petitioner's fifth petition for reinstatement in 21 years, following suspension in 1983).

● *Public reprimand*, also called censure or public censure, is a declaration that the lawyer's conduct was improper, without restricting the right to practice law. The ABA Standards explain that a public reprimand "serves the useful purpose of identifying lawyers who have violated ethical standards, and, if accompanied by a published opinion, educates members of the bar as to these standards." A reprimand may be accompanied by some additional conditions, such as a requirement that the reprimanded lawyer submit to monitoring by the bar, or take continuing legal education courses.

● *Private reprimand*, also called admonition, is a formal sanction in which the lawyer is told that his or her conduct was wrongful, but the public is not informed of the lawyer's identity. The ABA takes the position that this sanction should be used "only when the lawyer is negligent, when the ethical violation results in little or no injury to a client, the public, the legal system, or the profession, and when there is little or no likelihood of repetition."

Private reprimands have often been criticized as too weak. But does private always mean "private?" In *Mack v. State Bar of California*, 92 Cal.App.4th 957, 112 Cal.Rptr.2d 341 (2001), an attorney stipulated to a private reprimand in 1995. Four years later he learned that the State Bar had posted the fact that he had been disciplined on the State Bar's internet website. In a section on that site called "Member Records Online" was the lawyer's name, bar number, and a notation that he "has a public record of discipline." Mack sued the State Bar for breaching the stipulation. Affirming the trial court's ruling for the Bar, the appeals court reasoned that the record of even private reprimands are a matter of public record under California Bus. & Prof. Code § 6086.1(a), and therefore that a lawyer's private sanction could be disclosed in response to public inquiries. The lawyer's contention that the Bar could not also post the information on its website was labeled "a Luddite's argument," since the internet simply allows the Bar to respond "much the same as it would to a telephone caller" who asks about a lawyer's disciplinary record.

● *Probation* may be imposed as a stand-alone sanction; in conjunction with a public or private reprimand or suspension; or as a condition of reinstatement. A lawyer on probation can practice, but under specified conditions, such as supervision by a disciplinary committee member; periodic audits; attendance at continuing legal education classes; or passing the bar examination or the professional responsibility portion thereof. Probation typically ends when the lawyer has fully complied with all of the conditions of probation. If a lawyer violates probation, the disciplinary body may impose a more severe sanction. According to the ABA, "Probation is appropriate for conduct which may be corrected, *e.g.*, improper maintenance of books and records, lack of timely communication with clients, failure to file income tax returns, or alcohol and chemical dependency."

How common is discipline? According to recent data compiled by the ABA, there are about 1.3 million lawyers in active practice in the United States today. In 2003, there were over 119,000 complaints against lawyers filed with various state bar disciplinary authorities. Only a small percentage of these complaints (6,000) resulted in discipline, about evenly divided between public and private forms. Each year in the United States about 1,000 lawyers are disbarred. Two main areas of misconduct lead most often to serious discipline: money violations, such as commingling or misappropriating client funds, and repeated failures to communicate with clients or to perform work competently. Data consistently show that lawyers in small-firm and solo practice are disciplined more frequently than lawyers in other settings.

NOTE: RECIPROCAL DISCIPLINE

A court's ruling in a disciplinary matter is entitled to full faith and credit in other jurisdictions. The ABA's Model Rules for Disciplinary Enforcement, Rule 22, reflects this, providing that a final adjudication that a lawyer has violated a disciplinary rule "shall establish conclusively" the lawyer's misconduct in other states. The same Rule establishes a presumption of reciprocal discipline: After notice to one state that a lawyer subject to its jurisdiction has been disciplined by another, that state "shall impose the identical discipline" unless the imposition of the identical discipline would be inappropriate for any one of a number of listed reasons, including problems with the first state's adjudicative process; that "grave injustice" would result; or "the misconduct established warrants substantially different discipline in this state." This rule prevents a lawyer who has been disbarred in one state from freely practicing in another. It also allows, where an exception overcomes the presumption, one state to impose a greater sanction than another imposed earlier. For example, in *In re Krouner*, 748 A.2d 924 (D.C.App.2000), a New York lawyer who was also a member of the D.C. Bar was censured in New York after being convicted of theft of services and other offenses. The Board of Professional Responsibility of the District of Columbia recommended that Krouner be given a stronger sanction, suspension, within that jurisdiction. The D.C. court agreed with the Board on the ground that had Krouner committed the same offense in the District of Columbia, he would have received a minimum sanction of a 30–day suspension, and thus that his misconduct warrants "substantially different discipline" in D.C. than was meted out by New York. See also *The Florida Bar v. Karahalis*, 780 So.2d 27 (Fla. 2001)(upholding Florida's disbarment of lawyer for bribery after Massachusetts had only suspended him for the same conduct). Some states have read Rule 22 more restrictively, holding that harsher reciprocal discipline is rarely, if ever, appropriate. See *In re Welker*, 100 P.3d 1197 (Utah 2004)(Utah could not disbar lawyer who had been merely suspended by California for the same misconduct).

3. Disciplinary Powers and Procedure

State court power. Ultimate authority for disciplining lawyers resides in the highest court of each state. Indeed, in most states, the power to regulate lawyers is vested *entirely* in the courts, a concept known as the inherent-powers doctrine. Pursuant to this doctrine, state legislatures cannot regulate lawyers at all, at least not in a manner inconsistent with judicial regulation, without running afoul of the separation of powers provisions of the applicable state constitution. See, e.g., *Cripe v. Leiter*, 184 Ill.2d 185, 234 Ill.Dec. 488, 703 N.E.2d 100 (1998)(state consumer fraud statute held not to apply to claim that lawyer charged excessive fees); *In re Petition of the Judicial Conduct Committee*, 151 N.H. 123, 855 A.2d 535 (2004) (state legislature lacks constitutional authority to tell state judiciary how and when to discipline judges). New York and California allow greater legislative involvement in lawyer regulation than do other states; we will see some examples of this in this course. The California legislature, in fact, maintains a quite pervasive role in lawyer regulation and one cannot understand California's ethics rules without reference to legislative provisions governing lawyers.

Federal court. There are no uniform rules of ethics (or disciplinary procedure) in federal court. Each district is able to define its own rules and determine its own sanctions for misconduct that occurs in connection with its proceedings. Most federal courts have voluntarily adopted the disciplinary rules of the states in which they sit. A federal statute, 28 U.S.C. § 530B, applies state ethics standards to federal government lawyers. That is, while a federal court has the power and responsibility to determine the discipline that will be meted out to a lawyer in practice before that court, the rules used to make that determination are most often the very same rules that have been adopted for state discipline by the supreme court in that state. Because of the Supremacy Clause of the U.S. Constitution, state courts and disciplinary authorities have no power to restrict federal courts and agencies in promulgating and enforcing rules concerning lawyers engaged in practice before federal courts and agencies. See, e.g., *Surrick v. Killion*, 449 F.3d 520 (3d Cir. 2006) (state court could not prevent a lawyer, not admitted to practice in Pennsylvania, from opening an office in Pennsylvania to practice federal law exclusively).

State procedure. With respect to the procedures used by the states to discipline attorneys, there is a good deal of similarity among the states, at least at the broad level. The ABA Model Rules for Lawyer Disciplinary Enforcement provides a model for such proceedings and has proved influential. Both this model, and actual state processes, are quite complex in their details, but a brief summary is possible here. Disciplinary procedures are *sui generis*, although some states accurately label them "quasi-criminal." Under the model disciplinary rules, and in most states, the state court performs investigatory, prosecutorial and adjudicative functions, delegating these functions to other bodies for all steps prior to final adjudication. Specifically, the state high court appoints a Disciplinary Board, which is empowered to perform appellate adjudicatory functions and to make recommendations to the high court about disciplinary rules. The Board in turn appoints hearing committees, whose job it is to conduct hearings into formal charges of lawyer misconduct. The high court also appoints a full-time disciplinary counsel, who also appoints a staff, whose job it is to investigate and prosecute.

The disciplinary counsel investigates all matters brought to his or her attention by way of a complaint about a lawyer's alleged misconduct or incapacity. Most complaints come from dissatisfied clients, although a court can initiate disciplinary proceedings on its own motion, pursuant to its inherent powers. See, e.g., *In re Disciplinary Action Against Dvorak*, 611 N.W.2d 147 (N.D.2000) (lawyer attempted to intimidate a witness in a divorce case). Complaints may also come from fellow lawyers, who in most states are under a mandatory duty, within the rules of client confidentiality, to inform the disciplinary authorities if they have knowledge that another lawyer has violated the ethics rules in a way that raises "a substantial question as to that lawyer's honesty, fitness, truthworthiness or fitness as a lawyer in other respects." MR 8.3(a). Complaints also come from judges, who are placed under a similar duty as lawyers to report lawyer misconduct. ABA Model Code of Judicial Conduct Canon 3D(2) (2005).

If the allegation against the lawyer, even if true, would not constitute misconduct or incapacity, the matter will be dismissed by disciplinary counsel at this early stage. At the conclusion of any investigation, disciplinary counsel may also decide to dismiss. The complaining party may appeal this dismissal. If dismissal is not warranted, written notice and an opportunity to be heard must be provided to the lawyer under investigation. If formal charges against the lawyer are made, disciplinary counsel serves the lawyer with a copy of the charges and files those charges in writing with the Disciplinary Board. The lawyer is given a reasonable time to file a written response to the charges. If any matters are disputed, a hearing is held (either before the Board itself or before a hearing committee to which the Board has delegated power). At this hearing, the lawyer may be represented by counsel, may cross-examine witnesses, and may introduce evidence. Disciplinary counsel acts as prosecutor. The complaining party may make a statement about the lawyer's misconduct and the harm it caused, but is not otherwise centrally involved in the prosecution.

Some states restrict the complaining party, or the lawyer being charged, or both, from publicly revealing or commenting on the charges as they are being adjudicated. A number of state courts have determined that such restrictions violate the First Amendment. See *R.M. v. Supreme Court*, 185 N.J. 208, 883 A.2d 369 (2005); *Doe v. Doe*, 127 S.W.3d 728 (Tenn. 2004).

After the hearing is completed and a decision rendered, either the lawyer or the disciplinary counsel may appeal. This, too, is a formal hearing process. Ultimately, the state's high court may review a disciplinary matter if either the lawyer or the Disciplinary Board seeks such review. The court will then issue a written opinion.

Constitutional challenges to state disciplinary processes that follow this general model (other than those with a "gag rule" as referenced above) have usually failed. For example, in *Goldstein v. Commission on Practice of the Supreme Court*, 297 Mont. 493, 995 P.2d 923 (2000), lawyers challenged the structure and function of the Montana disciplinary body. Specifically, the lawyer plaintiffs alleged that their rights to due process were violated because both investigatory and initial adjudicatory functions are vested in the

Commission. Rejecting this challenge, the Supreme Court stressed that the Commission only makes recommendations to the Court. Because the Court retains the sole authority for the final adjudication of ethical violations and for determining sanctions, due process is not violated.

Lawyers under investigation by the state disciplinary authorities have a mandatory duty to cooperate with that investigation. A lawyer who breaches that duty may be disciplined for not cooperating. See MR 8.1(b); see, e.g., *State ex rel. Oklahoma Bar Ass'n v. Simank*, 19 P.3d 860 (Okla.2001) (lawyer publicly reprimanded for failure to respond to 15 letters from Oklahoma State Bar requesting information about three grievances filed against him). A lawyer may, however, invoke a constitutional privilege (such as the Fifth Amendment) without being subject to discipline for non-cooperation simply on that basis. See, e.g, *Spevack v. Klein*, 385 U.S. 511, 87 S.Ct. 625, 17 L.Ed.2d 574 (1967) (lawyer could not be disbarred for refusing on Fifth Amendment self-incrimination grounds to provide evidence to disciplinary authorities).

B. Ethics Opinions

While the ethics rules themselves comprise a body of substantive law pursuant to which lawyers may be disciplined, they may also serve to guide proper lawyer behavior (although, remember, they do not purport to be exhaustive). To this end, designated groups within the bar issue both formal and informal opinions interpreting these rules under hypothetical facts. These opinions are advisory only and do not adjudicate actual disputes or serve as binding precedent, but they do offer helpful interpretive guidance. At the national level, the ABA's ten-member Standing Committee on Ethics and Professional Responsibility periodically issues such interpretations, either in response to questions or on its own initiative. These opinions, both "formal" and "informal," are influential and often cited by courts and scholars examining the meaning of various Model Rules. Even though these model rules have no legal status until adopted by states, remember that most states have done so with most rules. Thus many state ethics authorities rely on the ABA Ethics Committee's interpretations. See Lawrence K. Hellman, *When "Ethics Rules" Don't Mean What They Say: The Implications of Strained ABA Ethics Opinions*, 10 Geo. J. Legal Ethics 317 (1997) (noting some shortcomings in many of the interpretations). Advisory ethics opinions are also issued by many state and local bar associations, generally interpreting not the ABA Models but rather the actual state rules.

Can a lawyer be sanctioned for engaging in conduct that an ethics opinion has labeled wrongful, even though the professional conduct rules themselves are not so clear? See *In re Admonition Issued in Panel File No. 99–42*, 621 N.W.2d 240 (Minn.2001) (no;

lawyers are not subject to discipline simply for violating an ethics opinion issued by the state's lawyer disciplinary board).

C. Other Law

1. The Connection to the Disciplinary Process

It is crucial to recognize that the text of the Model Rules does not provide a complete picture of ethical lawyering any more than the Code or the Canons did. The drafters never believed otherwise. The Model Rules' Preamble states that while "[m]any of a lawyer's professional responsibilities are prescribed in the Rules," substantive and procedural law outside the rules as well as "personal conscience and the approbation of professional peers" also defines proper lawyer behavior. Further, the Scope section recognizes that "The Rules presuppose a larger legal context shaping the lawyer's role. That context includes court rules and statutes ... and substantive and procedural law in general."

This means that even if one focuses solely on the discipline of lawyers by state authorities—certainly not the only sanction available against lawyers, as we will soon see—the rules themselves are not self-contained. Rather, they incorporate by reference a good deal of the general substantive law. Model Rule 8.4, for example, labels as "professional misconduct" the commission of a "criminal act that reflects adversely on the lawyer's honesty, trustworthiness or fitness as a lawyer in other respects," or engaging in conduct involving "dishonesty, fraud, deceit or misrepresentation." This means that lawyers can be disciplined for conduct that has nothing whatsoever to do with practicing law. See, e.g., *In re Caldwell*, 27 A.D.3d 154, 809 N.Y.S.2d 59 (2006) (3–year suspension for failure to pay 167 parking tickets); *The Florida Bar v. Bartholf*, 775 So.2d 957 (Fla.2000) (lawyer placed on probation by state bar for threatening another golfer with a golf club and trying to run over him with a golf cart).

California provides for "summary disbarment" for attorneys convicted of certain felonies involving moral turpitude. Cal. Bus. & Prof. Code § 6102(c). Disbarment is required in California where an element of the felony is the specific intent to deceive, defraud, steal or make or suborn a false statement, or if it involves moral turpitude. In virtually all states, even if a lawyer is *acquitted* in a criminal case involving non-lawyer-related conduct, he may still be subject to discipline. For example, in *Attorney Grievance Comm'n of Maryland v. Childress*, 364 Md. 48, 770 A.2d 685 (2001), a lawyer's felony conviction for traveling interstate with the intent to commit a sexual act with a minor was reversed, yet his suspension from the bar was upheld. In other words, a lawyer must obey the "regular" law just as non-lawyer must, and is also subject to bar discipline for violating any such law, at least if the violative conduct reflects adversely on fitness to practice law.

2. *Relevance Outside the Disciplinary Context*

With a few exceptions, a lawyer is subject to the same kinds of civil liability and criminal penalties as any non-lawyer who commits the same acts. Tax law, tort law, contract law, property law, and criminal law, for example, apply to lawyers with the same force as they apply to anyone else. (One noteworthy exception is that a litigator is accorded an absolute privilege to defame others in connection with litigation, a point we will see in Chapter 7.) Indeed, because lawyers are so often "on the inside" of transactions and complex dealings, lawyers are often more exposed than non-lawyers to such liability and sanction. See, e.g., *U.S. v. Ryan–Webster*, 353 F.3d 353 (4th Cir. 2003) (lawyer convicted for forging signatures on immigration documents for her clients). Because lawyers are so closely aligned with their clients, when a client is liable under criminal or civil law, the lawyer may also be implicated. Also, as we will see, lawyers assume significant duties simply by acting as lawyers, and can be sued for breaching those duties. They may owe duties not only to clients, but also to third parties. Many of these duties arise under the common law and are enforced through lawsuits brought by the aggrieved parties.

While this "other law" is spread throughout many sources—in pre-computer days we would say it could be found all over the law library—much of the most directly-relevant doctrinal material is now covered in the American Law Institute's Restatement of the Law Governing Lawyers ("The Restatement"), promulgated in 1998. For example, the Restatement contains sections on civil liability of lawyers, the attorney-client privilege, and the formation of the lawyer-client relationship—areas expressly not addressed by the Model Rules.

In addition to the laws that apply to everyone, a number of statutes apply with special force to lawyers. For example, the Fair Debt Collection Practices Act, 15 U.S.C. § 1692, was held to apply to lawyers who "regularly engage in consumer-debt collection activity, even when that activity consists of litigation," in *Heintz v. Jenkins*, 514 U.S. 291, 115 S.Ct. 1489, 131 L.Ed.2d 395 (1995). The FDCPA prohibits "debt collectors" from making false or misleading representations and from engaging in various abusive and unfair debt collection practices. Those who violate the Act are subject to civil liability to those they treat unfairly. The plaintiff in *Heintz* defaulted on a car loan from Gainer Bank. The Bank sued to recover the balance. The lawyer who was held to be subject to the Act represented the Bank in the case, and had written a letter to the plaintiff's lawyer in an attempt to settle the case, making a monetary demand that arguably violated the Act since it was an amount not authorized by the loan agreement. Since the *Heintz* decision, many lawyers have been held liable under the FDCPA. See, e.g., *Piper v. Portnoff Law Associates, Ltd.*, 396 F.3d 227 (3d Cir. 2005); *Fields v. Wilber Law Firm, P.C.*, 383 F.3d 562 (7th Cir. 2004).

Many rules of procedure and statutes apply to lawyers in litigation. We will see a number of them in Chapter 7.

§ 3. LEGAL EDUCATION AND BAR ADMISSION

A. The Evolution of Legal Education in the United States

Recall that, as Roscoe Pound put it, a professional is a member of a group pursuing a "learned art." Lawyers, then, are supposed to be "learned." But legal education as we know it is a fairly recent phenomenon. As late as 1891, only one of every five lawyers admitted to practice in the United States was a law school graduate. Most lawyers apprenticed in law offices. They "read the law" rather than going though a formal educational process. Until the late Nineteenth century, there were only a handful of law schools in this country—fewer than two dozen at mid-century—and none resembled a modern law school.

The ABA was founded in 1878 in part to address the perceived shortcomings of new lawyers' preparation to practice, and from its very beginnings took the position that all lawyers should be law school graduates. The ABA's Section of Legal Education and Admission to the Bar, created in 1893, was dedicated to provide an opportunity for focused study and discussion of legal education. The Section began to take the leadership role in developing law school standards; in 1896 the Section adopted a resolution that the ABA should formally adopt such standards.

In 1900 the Section on Legal Education created the Association of American Law Schools to assist with its goal of improving (and standardizing) law schools. Two decades later, in 1921, the ABA adopted its first Standards for Legal Education under the leadership of Elihu Root, a former U.S. Secretary of War, Secretary of State, Senator, and winner of the 1912 Nobel Peace Prize. Root's committee's motion for the adoption of these standards was seconded by William Howard Taft, the Chief Justice of the United States and the former President. This event marked the beginnings of the ABA as a law school accrediting agency, even though the ABA at that time did not have any formal enforcement powers. Shortly thereafter the ABA issued its first list of approved law schools (made up of schools that complied with its Standards).

During this period, the number of law schools grew dramatically, attributable in large part to the creation of new part-time programs. Further, the part-time programs tended to have more students than their full-time counterparts, coupled with much higher teacher-student ratios. And often, the students at these part-time schools were the sons of new immigrants, or Catholics or Jews excluded from the full-time schools. Through the 1920s, the ABA and the AALS worked closely together to develop new regulations for law schools, including minimum teacher-student ratios, library volumes, and pre-law school educational experience for students. But in 1921–22, only 31 of the 148 American law schools were in compliance with the ABA's new standards. The ABA hoped, according to one scholar, that once its standards became entrenched, "deviant institutions would simply vanish." Richard L. Abel, AMERICAN LAWYERS 46 (1989).

To that end the ABA pushed the states to restrict bar admission to only those applicants who had graduated from ABA-approved law schools. About half of the states now have such a restriction. See, e.g., *Florida Board of Bar Examiners ex rel. Barry University School of Law*, 821 So.2d 1050 (Fla.2002); *In re Bar Admission of Petrie v. Board of Bar Examiners*, 216 Wis.2d 640, 575 N.W.2d 266 (1998); *Bring v. North Carolina State Bar*, 348 N.C. 655, 501 S.E.2d 907 (1998). Some of the other states allow those who have graduated from unaccredited schools to take the bar exam if they prove that their law school's course of study was "substantially equivalent" to that provided by accredited schools within the state of application. See, e.g., *In re Lewis*, 86 S.W.3d 419 (Ky.2002). Only a few states, California among them, engage in separate state accreditation of law schools and then allow graduates of those schools—even if non-ABA accredited—to sit for the bar exam. Still others allow a person to take the bar exam without attending (or in some cases completing) law school, a method commonly known as "reading the law." Both California and New York allow this—New York requires one year of law school study—but very few applicants make the attempt.

B. The Bar Examination

Almost all jurisdictions require new lawyers-to-be (that is, ones not already admitted elsewhere) to take and pass a bar examination. Perhaps the most common rationale for such an exam is that it helps insure that only those competent to practice law obtain a license do so, which protects future clients from harm at the hands of the unqualified. Another frequently-heard justification is that the exam holds law schools accountable for the quality of their programs and students. Many states at one time granted a "diploma privilege" to graduates of its own state's law schools—not requiring such graduates to pass the bar exam—but only one state (Wisconsin) maintains this system.

In most states, the bar exam consists of essays on substantive law and a set of multiple-choice questions called the Multistate Bar Examination (MBE). A number of states augment this with some form of "practical" section in which applicants are asked to take a set of provided materials and write a lawyerly document such as a memorandum, client letter or negotiation plan. Additionally, the Multistate Professional Responsibility Examination (MPRE) must be passed separately in almost all jurisdictions, as well. It is a test of competence with respect to legal ethics and the law of lawyering, but within a limited scope. It is a multiple-choice test, first given in 1980, that has been described by the National Council of Bar Examiners (the group that developed the MBE and the MPRE) as "an awareness test," whose "goal is to make the applicant acutely mindful that the profession considers ethics a matter of the highest priority in the practice of law." (The MPRE was patterned after a similar multiple-choice test, the California Professional Responsibility Examination, first given to applicants in that state in 1975.)

Model Rule 8.1 prohibits an applicant for admission to the bar from knowingly making a false statement of material fact, or failing to disclose a fact necessary to correct a factual misapprehension. The comment to this rule explains that violation of this provision "may be the basis for subsequent disciplinary action if the person is admitted." MR 8.1, comment [1]. In *In re Moore*, 442 Mass. 285, 812 N.E.2d 1197 (2004), a lawyer had been duly admitted to practice in Connecticut but was disciplined there (for forging documents and impersonating a court clerk) and resigned. He sought reinstatement some years later but his petition was denied. Over a decade after that, he sat for and passed the Massachusetts bar exam, on his second try. Later, it was discovered that he failed to disclose numerous things—including the Connecticut discipline—and affirmatively misrepresented many things on his bar application. Massachusetts bar authorities sought his disbarment; the Massachusetts Supreme Judicial Court ordered a two-year suspension.

States determine for themselves whether to give a bar exam at all, as well as the format and content of that exam. Bar examinations of any kind were rare in our nation's early history. In the Colonial Period, admission to practice was most frequently accomplished by motion to the court after the applicant had served a long apprenticeship in a law office, or by proof to the court of prior membership in one of the English Inns of Court. Oral bar examinations were sometimes given; New Jersey required an oral exam as early as 1755. After the Revolution, these practices continued until the 1830s when, in the Jacksonian era, some states offered bar admission without any examination or other qualification whatsoever. The most noteworthy example was Indiana, whose 1851 Constitution provided that "Every person of good moral character who is a voter is entitled to practice law in any of the courts of this state." This provision was not repealed until 1932.

In most states, the oral bar examination tradition continued well into the Nineteenth century, with the applicant typically being questioned in open court by judges. As the number of bar applicants grew, the oral examination fell increasingly to lawyers appointed to ask the questions and evaluate the responses. (Abraham Lincoln served as an Illinois bar examiner before becoming President.) These oral bar exams were usually short and focused on rote formalities such as time limits and forms of pleading, but they were anything but standardized. Different examiners would ask entirely different questions and evaluate the responses in different ways.

It was largely in response to these shortcomings that written bar exams developed in the latter part of the Nineteenth century. The first written exam was given in Massachusetts in 1855, although only those candidates who could not demonstrate that they had three years of legal study had to pass it, and this experiment lasted only until 1859. Sporadic revivals of a written examination requirement surfaced from time to time until a genuine movement gained momentum late in the century. The New York Supreme Court began to require written examinations in 1877, and by 1914, most states required written bar exams.

Criticisms of bar exams abound. Some argue that the exams fail to test on many skills lawyers need to know; this criticism has led to the adoption in some states of a "practical" portion of the exam, in which students write a memorandum or client letter using materials in a closed file—although this does not entirely address the criticism. Others say that the exam is biased against minority applicants. And some thoughtful commentators assert that the existence of the bar exam impacts negatively, in various ways, on the law school experience. Despite these criticisms, no state is seriously considering doing away with the bar exam as a gateway to entering the legal profession. Proposed alternatives exist, however. For example, a joint committee of the New York State and New York City Bar Associations proposed in 2002 a "Public Service Alternative Bar Exam" that envisions a limited number of law school graduates gaining admission by apprenticing for three months with the New York State court system, being supervised by court attorneys. Students admitted to the bar through this process would agree to perform 150 hours of pro bono work for the court system. The program has not been implemented as of this writing (October 2006). New Hampshire has recently embarked on a pilot alternative-admission program for selected students from its only law school, Franklin Pierce, under which students participate in clinics or externships and complete a series of written assignments which are then reviewed by the state Board of Bar Examiners. An applicant may be admitted to the bar if the written work satisfies the Board that the applicant demonstrates sufficient legal skill and knowledge.

For critical discussions of these and other possible alternatives to the traditional bar exam, see the Articles collected in *Symposium: Rethinking the Licensing of New Attorneys: An Exploration of Alternatives to the Bar Exam,* 20:4 Ga. St. U. L. Rev. (2004).

Proponents of bar-exam reform must fight against a countervailing trend towards even greater standardization from state to state, an overt goal of the National Council of Bar Examiners. Is greater diversity in state bar exams desirable? Or does greater standardization encourage multi-jurisdictional practice?

C. Character and Fitness Certification

Graduating from an approved law school and passing the written bar examination does not guarantee admission to the bar. Applicants must also be certified as possessing the requisite "character and fitness" to be a lawyer. Such certification has been a constant requirement in this country. In earlier times, this requirement could be used effectively to keep out of the profession any person who was regarded as unseemly, perhaps because of race, gender or ethnicity. See, e.g., *Bradwell v. State,* 83 U.S. (16 Wall.) 130, 21 L.Ed. 442 (1872) (upholding Illinois bar's exclusion of a female applicant, Myra Bradwell, from admission solely on the ground that she was a married woman).

The character and fitness hurdle also once blocked the admission of candidates whose political beliefs were found offensive. In 1971, the Supreme Court said that a bar committee cannot constitutionally inquire about "beliefs alone" without a compelling reason. See *Baird v. State Bar of Arizona,* 401 U.S. 1, 91 S.Ct. 702, 27 L.Ed.2d 639 (1971)(applicant could refuse to answer question about whether she had ever been a member of the Communist Party, where there was no evidence of her lack of character to practice law); *In re Stolar,* 401 U.S. 23, 91 S.Ct. 713, 27 L.Ed.2d 657 (1971) (unconstitutional to ask bar applicants to list all organizations to which they have ever belonged). However, in *Law Students Civil Rights Research Council, Inc. v. Wadmond,* 401 U.S. 154, 91 S.Ct. 720, 27 L.Ed.2d 749 (1971), the court upheld the right of New York bar authorities to ask whether an applicant was ever a "knowing member" of an organization which advocated the violent overthrow of the U.S. government. The court was badly divided in these cases and their contours are less than clear. In 1998, an Illinois character and fitness panel denied Matthew Hale's admission to the bar because he was an admitted white supremacist, despite the fact that he had not committed any crime and "had not yet threatened to exterminate anyone." Its conclusion was that "The Bar of Illinois cannot certify someone as having good moral character and general fitness to practice law who has dedicated his life to inciting racial hatred for the purpose of implementing those views." *In re Hale,* Comm. On Character and Fitness for the 3d Appellate Dist. of the Supreme Court of

Illinois (1998). The Illinois Supreme Court refused to hear the case, allowing the denial of admission to stand. See *In re Hale*, 723 N.E.2d 206, 243 Ill.Dec. 174 (1999) (Heiple, J., dissenting from the denial of Hale's petition for review) (arguing that "[t]he issues presented by Mr. Hale's petition are of such significant constitutional magnitude that they deserve a judicial review and determination by this court.") Hale was later convicted of soliciting an undercover FBI informant to murder a federal judge, and is now serving a 40–year prison sentence.

Today, state bar examiners or separate character committees typically conduct the inquiry into each applicant's character and fitness. Applicants to the bar are usually asked to fill out a detailed form when registering to take the bar exam; the form asks about employment history, prior convictions and other matters. Candidates are also asked to provide references, whom the committee can then ask about the candidate's character and fitness to practice law. Most litigated cases, such as the one below, involve denials of admission due to an applicant's behavior that calls into question his or her honesty or integrity.

IN RE APPLICATION OF CHAPMAN

Supreme Court of Ohio, 1994.
69 Ohio St.3d 17, 630 N.E.2d 322.

[Syllabus by the Court.]

Frank H. Chapman II applied for admission to the practice of law and to take the bar examination. Since his residence was in Portage County at the time of application, the Admissions Committee of the Portage County Bar Association conducted the investigation into his character, fitness, and moral qualifications for admission to the practice of law. On January 26, 1993, the committee filed its report recommending approval. Applicant took and passed the February 1993 bar examination.

[In March, 1993, the Admissions Office of the Supreme Court received a letter alleging that the applicant had been named as a defendant in a civil action filed by the Ohio Attorney General, involving deceptive and unconscionable sales practices by the applicant and his father in connection with the father's carpet and upholstery cleaning business. Two months later the Admissions Office received a letter and documents from the Ohio Attorney General's office which stated that the applicant had entered into a consent dismissal with the Attorney General and had agreed to testify against his father. An affidavit from the applicant was attached to this letter.]

In the affidavit, the applicant admitted that (1) he worked for his father's carpet and upholstery cleaning business periodically between 1983 and 1991; (2) he learned about, typed and taught new employees how to implement a sales plan used by his uncle, Don Chapman, in his Florida carpet and upholstery cleaning business; (3) under the plan, salespersons who increased the amount of a quoted price to perform a job received a twenty-eight percent commission on the increased price; (4) the plan directed salespersons to estimate customers' income for the purpose of setting a higher price and offered illusory discounts; (5) technicians routinely drycleaned fabrics that did not require drycleaning, in order to increase the contract price; (6) his personal expenses, including law school tuition, were paid by the business; (7) and he transferred motor vehicles used in the business and titled in his name to fictitious corporations.

[In the consent dismissal, the applicant did not admit any allegation in the complaint. He agreed, however, to a permanent injunction prohibiting him from engaging in deceptive consumer practices; to pay restitution; to pay civil penalties; and to testify in the civil proceeding.]

Thereafter, the Board of Commissioners on Character and Fitness *sua sponte* began an investigation pursuant to Gov.Bar R. I(9)(B)(2)(e) into the applicant's character and fitness and appointed a hearing panel, which held a hearing on September 17, 1993. At the hearing, the applicant admitted having taught techniques for selling unneeded services, never having received an Internal Revenue Service form W–2 or 1099 for working in the family business, and transferring title of motor vehicles from his name to fictitious companies. He also stated that in August or September 1992, he began to believe certain aspects of the business were wrong, and he sought to dissociate himself from the business after that time.

The panel found that the applicant had failed to sustain his burden of proving good character and fitness to be admitted to the practice of law. It found his 1992 conversion "from his previous pattern of highly questionable ethical and outright illegal behavior * * * too recent to be convincing." It recommended that he not be sworn in as a member of the Bar of Ohio "until he can demonstrate that he possesses the requisite character and fitness to be admitted to practice." It stated its belief that it would take at least two years for the applicant to demonstrate this.

The board considered the panel's report on October 1, 1993. It adopted the report by unanimous vote, except that it recommended that the applicant not be permitted to reapply for admission until February 1996, at which time he was to undergo further examination as to character, fitness, and moral qualifications.

The applicant filed objections to the findings and recommendations of the board, and a hearing was conducted before the court on February 1, 1994.

PER CURIAM.

The court accepts the findings of the panel and board, but modifies the board's recommendation to the extent that Frank H. Chapman II may not reapply for admission to the Bar of Ohio before May 1995. Upon reapplication he will undergo further investigation by the board, in order to determine whether he possesses the character, fitness and moral qualifications required for admission to the practice of law in Ohio.

Judgment accordingly.

Notes

1. The U.S. Supreme Court has held that "[a] State can require high standards of qualification, such as good moral character or proficiency in its law, before it admits an applicant to the bar, but any qualification must have a rational connection with the applicant's fitness or capacity to practice law." *Schware v. Board of Bar Examiners of New Mexico*, 353 U.S. 232, 239, 77 S.Ct. 752, 1 L.Ed.2d 796 (1957) (reversing state court's denial of admission merely on grounds of former Communist Party membership, where nothing in the record demonstrated acts on Schware's part that reflected adversely on his character).

2. In a character and fitness hearing, the burden of proof is usually on the applicant to prove good character; often the applicant must do so by "clear and convincing evidence." Why would this be? Should the bar authorities bear the burden of proving a *lack* of good character? Does the burden allocation keep some worthy candidates from becoming lawyers?

3. Some observers have concluded that state bars are stricter with bar applicants than they are with already-admitted lawyers; that is, that applicants are denied admission to the bar for conduct that might not be sanctioned severely if the offender was already a member of the bar. What would be the justification for such a situation?

4. *Law school behavior as a basis for denial.* Could an applicant's behavior during law school—behavior directly related to law school—disqualify him from bar admission? Yes. In *In re Application of Converse*, 258 Neb. 159, 602 N.W.2d 500 (1999), the applicant, while a law student, engaged in a series of bizarre confrontations with his law school dean, other administrators, professors and fellow students. The court concluded that the record showed that he "seeks to resolve disputes not in a peaceful manner, but by personally attacking those who oppose him in any way and then resorting to arenas outside the field of law to publicly humiliate and intimidate those opponents. Such a pattern of behavior is incompatible with what we have required to be obligatory conduct for attorneys, as well as for applicants to the bar." The applicant argued that much of the conduct that formed the basis of the negative finding was protected by the First Amendment. The court held in response that Supreme Court precedent "makes clear that a bar commission is allowed to consider speech and conduct in making determinations of an appli-

cant's character," even if such conduct was protected by the First Amendment.

IN RE HAMM

Supreme Court of Arizona, 2005.
211 Ariz. 458, 123 P.3d 652.

McGREGOR, Chief Justice. . . .

I.

[In 1974, Hamm and two accomplices committed two "execution style" murders of college students who had arranged to buy 20 pounds of marijuana from them. Hamm personally shot both victims, who were robbed of $1400. He was originally charged with two counts of first-degree murder and two counts of armed robbery, and pleaded guilty to one count of first-degree murder. Hamm was sentenced to life in prison with no possibility of parole for 25 years. Once in prison, Hamm "took advantage of any and every educational opportunity the prison system had to offer." Ultimately he graduated summa cum laude from Arizona State University though a prison study program. He met and married his second wife while in prison and with her founded a prisoner and prisoner family advocacy organization. Hamm was paroled in 1992, and while on parole graduated from Arizona State University College of Law. In July 1999, he passed the Arizona bar exam, but was denied admission by the Character and Fitness Committee.]

II.

. . . The Committee may recommend an applicant for admission only if that applicant, in addition to meeting other requirements, satisfies the Committee that he or she is of good moral character. . . . In determining whether an applicant's prior conduct indicates a lack of good moral character, the Committee must consider the following non-exhaustive list of factors:

A.   The applicant's age, experience and general level of sophistication at the time of the conduct

B.   The recency of the conduct

C.   The reliability of the information concerning the conduct

D.   The seriousness of the conduct

E.   Consideration given by the applicant to relevant laws, rules and responsibilities at the time of the conduct

F.   The factors underlying the conduct

G.   The cumulative effect of the conduct

H.   The evidence of rehabilitation

I.   The applicant's positive social contributions since the conduct

J.   The applicant's candor in the admissions process

K.   The materiality of any omissions or misrepresentations by the applicant.

. . . If the applicant fails to convince the Committee of his or her good moral character, the Committee has a *duty not to recommend* that person to this Court. After the Committee submits its report, an aggrieved applicant may petition this Court for review. This Court then independently determines whether the applicant possesses good moral character and, based upon that determination, grants or denies the candidate's application. . . . As Hamm asserts, the rules and standards governing admission to the practice of law in Arizona include no *per se* disqualifications. Instead, we consider each case on its own merits. In *Walker*, [539 P.2d 891 (Ariz. 1975)], we described the principles on which we rely as follows:

> 'Upright character' * * * is something more than an absence of bad character. * * * It means that he [an applicant for admission] must have conducted himself as a man of upright character ordinarily would, should, or does. Such character expresses itself not in negatives nor in following the line of least resistance, but quite often in the will to do the unpleasant thing if it is right, and the resolve not to do the pleasant thing if it is wrong.

We also agree with Hamm that, under the Rule applicable to Hamm's application, our concern must be with the applicant's present moral character. . . . Past misconduct, however, is not irrelevant. Rather, this Court must determine what past bad acts reveal about an applicant's current character.

III.

[The Committee conducted a formal hearing over two days in 2004. Testimony was adduced from Hamm and his wife and from three lawyers who had worked with Hamm and recommended his admission. A number of letters, pro and con, were also considered. The Committee concluded that Hamm had failed to meet his burden to establish that he "possesses the requisite character and fitness for admission to the Bar."]

. . . Hamm's past criminal conduct and the serious nature of that conduct affect the burden he must meet to establish good moral character. He must first establish rehabilitation from prior criminal conduct, a requirement that adds to his burden of showing current good moral character. . . . The added burden becomes greater as past unlawful conduct becomes more serious. . . . We agree with the New Jersey Supreme Court, which recognized that "in the case of extremely damning past misconduct, a showing of rehabilitation may be virtually impossible to make." *In re Matthews,* 94 N.J. 59, 462 A.2d 165, 176 (1983). Indeed, we are aware of no instance in which a person convicted of first-degree murder has been admitted to the practice of law.

To show rehabilitation, Hamm must show that he has accepted responsibility for his criminal conduct.... Hamm *says* he has done so, repeatedly and strongly, but some of his other statements indicate to the contrary. The inconsistencies among his various statements related to accepting responsibility are most evident when he discusses Staples' murder. Although he *told* the Committee that he accepts responsibility for Staples' murder, in fact he consistently assigns that responsibility to his accomplice....

We also give serious consideration to the Committee's finding that Hamm was not completely forthright in his testimony about the murders.[5] Hamm has insisted in his filings with this Court that he did not intend to kill, but only to rob, his victims. The agreed facts, however, lead directly to the inference that Hamm intended to kill.... The Committee observed Hamm testify and was able to judge the credibility of his testimony in light of uncontested facts. We agree that the record shows that Hamm, despite his current protestations to the contrary, intended to kill the victims. His failure to confront the fact that these murders were intentional undermines his statements that he fully accepts responsibility for his actions.

As did the Committee, we give substantial weight to Hamm's attempts at rehabilitation, [but] when an applicant has committed first-degree murder, a crime that demonstrates an extreme lack of good moral character, that applicant must make an extraordinary showing of present good moral character to establish that he or she is qualified to be admitted to the practice of law.... We conclude that Hamm failed to make that showing.

We share the Committee's deep concern about Hamm's longstanding failure to fulfill, or even address, his child support obligation to his son, born in 1969, four years before Hamm and his first wife separated. Not until he prepared his application for admission to the Bar in 2004 did Hamm make any effort to meet his responsibility to provide support for his son. During the Committee hearing, Hamm advanced several explanations for his failure to do so. Like the Committee, we find none of his explanations credible.... Hamm's failure to meet his parental obligation for nearly thirty years makes it more difficult for him to make the required extraordinary showing that he "has conducted himself as a man ordinarily would, should, or does."

---

5. Hamm's lack of candor on this question also impacts our analysis of whether he met his burden of showing present good moral character.

We also agree with the Committee that Hamm did not display honesty and candor in discussing his failure to pay child support with the Committee. Hamm testified both that his son told him personally that he had been adopted and that his son "adamantly refused" to accept interest payments on the unpaid child support. Hamm's son testified, however, that he had never been adopted, that prior to his contact with Hamm he had changed his name himself, and that he had not told Hamm he had been adopted.... Like the Committee, we find the testimony of his son to be more credible.

We further conclude that Hamm did not adequately explain his failure to disclose an incident involving him and his current wife, Donna, when he submitted his application to the Committee. In 1996, Hamm and Donna engaged in a physical altercation outside a convenience store.... Both called the police, who arrested neither Hamm nor Donna.... Nonetheless, when filling out his Character and Fitness Report, Hamm failed to disclose the incident to the Committee. Question 25 on the report asks specifically whether the applicant, among other things, has been "questioned" concerning any felony or misdemeanor. Hamm told the Committee that, in reading the application, he missed the word "questioned" in the list of encounters with law enforcement that Question 25 directs an applicant to report.... Hamm's explanation strains credulity.... [W]e infer from Hamm's knowledge of the law and his efforts in 1996 to document a defense for the domestic incident that he fully understood its importance and must have known that the incident would be of interest to the Committee. His failure to include it in his initial application further affects his ability to make the needed extraordinary showing of good moral character.

Hamm's actions during these proceedings also raise questions about his fitness to practice law. The introduction to Hamm's petition before this Court begins:

> The consequences of this case for Petitioner take it out of the ordinary realm of civil cases. If the Committee's recommendation is followed, it will prevent him from earning a living through practicing law. This deprivation has consequences of the greatest import for Petitioner, who has invested years of study and a great deal of financial resources in preparing to be a lawyer....

This language repeats nearly verbatim the language of the United States Supreme Court in *Konigsberg v. State Bar,* 353 U.S. 252, 77 S.Ct. 722, 1 L.Ed.2d 810 (1957), in which the Court wrote:

> While this is not a criminal case, its consequences for Konigsberg take it out of the ordinary run of civil cases. The Committee's action prevents him from earning a living by practicing law. This deprivation has grave con-

sequences for a man who has spent years of study and a great deal of money in preparing to be a lawyer.

If an attorney submits work to a court that is not his own, his actions may violate the rules of professional conduct. *Iowa Supreme Court Bd. of Prof'l Ethics & Conduct v. Lane,* 642 N.W.2d 296, 299 (Iowa 2002) ("[P]lagiarism constitute[s], among other things, a misrepresentation to the court. An attorney may not engage in conduct involving dishonesty, fraud, deceit, or misrepresentation."); *see also* Rule 42, ER 8.4(c) (defining professional misconduct as including "engag[ing] in conduct involving dishonesty, fraud, deceit or misrepresentation"). We are concerned about Hamm's decision to quote from the Supreme Court's opinion without attribution and are equally troubled by his failure to acknowledge his error. When the Committee's response pointed to Hamm's failure to attribute this language to *Konigsberg,* he avoided the serious questions raised and refused to confront or apologize for his improper actions.... Hamm apparently either does not regard his actions as improper or simply refuses to take responsibility. In either case, his actions here do not assist him in making the requisite showing of good moral character.

When Hamm committed first-degree murder in 1974, he demonstrated his extreme lack of good moral character. Although this Court has not adopted a *per se* rule excluding an applicant whose past includes such serious criminal misconduct, we agree with those jurisdictions that have held that an applicant with such a background must make an extraordinary showing of rehabilitation and present good moral character to be admitted to the practice of law. Perhaps such a showing is, in practical terms, a near impossibility. We need not decide that question today, however, because Hamm's lack of candor before the Committee and this Court, his failure to accept full responsibility for his serious criminal misconduct, and his failure to accept or fulfill, on a timely basis, his parental obligation of support for his son, all show that Hamm has not met the stringent standard that applies to an applicant in his position who seeks to show his present good moral character....

Because James Hamm has failed to meet his burden of proving that he is of good moral character, we deny his application for admission to the State Bar of Arizona.

Notes

1. *Criminal record as a basis for denial.* At one time, prior conviction of a crime, especially a felony, would automatically disqualify a candidate for admission. The trend today, however, is away from any bright-line test. Very few states today would bar an applicant solely on the basis of a prior criminal record. See Maureen M. Carr, *The Effect of*

Prior Criminal Conduct on the Admission to Practice Law: The Move to More Flexible Admission Standards, 8 Geo. J. Legal Ethics 367 (1995).

2. Should a person convicted of murder ever be admitted to the practice of law? In *Hamm*, the character and fitness committee and the reviewing court found several other reasons to conclude that the applicant had not met his burden of showing good character. Had those other reasons been absent, might Hamm have been successful? See *In re Dortch*, 199 W.Va. 571, 486 S.E.2d 311 (1997) (denying admission to an applicant who had graduated from law school after being paroled from prison on a second-degree murder charge).

3. *Effect of lack of candor in the bar application.* While a criminal record alone might not prevent certification to the bar, lying on the bar application form about a prior criminal record, on the other hand, would result in a denial of admission in most states today. Why would this be?

4. *Effect of lack of candor in the fitness hearing.* The court in *Hamm* made much of the applicant's lack of candor during the character and fitness hearing, pointing to such things as his testimony about his past crime, his statements about child support, and even his use of an unattributed almost-direct quote from a Supreme Court case. Why would such conduct be considered so problematic to judges determining fitness to practice law?

5. *Mental health history as a basis for denial.* Should character and fitness examiners be allowed to ask a bar applicant about previous counseling for emotional disorders? See *Clark v. Virginia Board of Bar Examiners*, 880 F.Supp. 430 (E.D.Va.1995). *Should* they ask, even if allowed to do so?

D. Admission Without Passing the Bar Exam

In addition to the Wisconsin "diploma privilege" mentioned above, there are two main ways a person can be admitted to practice in a state without taking the bar exam. In both cases, however, the person must already be a lawyer duly admitted in another state, and in the first case the admission is only temporary.

Pro hac vice admission. Litigators who enter a state in which they are not admitted for purposes of handling a particular lawsuit may ask the court to admit them *pro hac vice*. Most courts grant such requests liberally, although the lawyer seeking such admission must of course comply with the jurisdiction's rules. The most common rule is that the lawyer must associate local counsel.

California prohibits California residents who are not members of the California Bar from being admitted *pro hac vice* in California state courts. What is the point of that rule? Might it have something to do with the fact that California has a comparatively low pass rate on its bar examination? See *Paciulan v. George*, 229 F.3d 1226 (9th Cir.2000) (upholding the rule, finding that it

in the matter of infractions of the code of conduct which,
in the public interest, lawyers are bound to observe.

The Florida Bar as an agent of this Court, plays a large role
in the enforcement of court policies and rules and has been active
in regulating and disciplining unethical conduct by its members.
Because of the natural tendency of all professions to act in their
own self interest, however, this Court must closely scrutinize all
regulations tending to limit competition in the delivery of legal
services to the public, and determine whether or not such regulations are truly in the public interest. Indeed, the active role of
state supreme courts in the regulation of the practice of law (when
such regulation is subject to pointed reexamination by the state
court as policy maker) is accorded great deference and exemption
from federal interference under the Sherman Act. Bates v. State
Bar of Arizona, 433 U.S. 350, 97 S.Ct. 2691, 2698, 53 L.Ed.2d 810
(1977).

The United States Supreme Court has recently decided issues
which may drastically change the practice of law throughout the
country, especially with regards to advertising and price competition among attorneys. Bates v. State Bar of Arizona, supra;
Goldfarb, et al. v. Virginia State Bar, 421 U.S. 773, 95 S.Ct. 2004,
44 L.Ed.2d 572 (1975). In addition, the Supreme Court has
affirmed the fundamental constitutional right of all persons to
represent themselves in court proceedings, Faretta v. California,
422 U.S. 806, 95 S.Ct. 2525, 45 L.Ed.2d 562 (1975). In Faretta, the
Supreme Court emphasized that an attorney is merely an assistant who helps a citizen protect his legal rights and present his
case to the courts. A person should not be forced to have an
attorney represent his legal interests if he does not consent to
such representation. It is imperative for us to analyze these cases
and determine how their holdings and the policies behind them
affect our regulation of the legal profession in this state.

With regard to the charges made against Marilyn Brumbaugh, this Court appointed a referee to receive evidence and to
make findings of fact, conclusions of law, and recommendations as
to the disposition of the case. The referee found that respondent,
under the guise of a "secretarial" or "typing" service prepares,
for a fee, all papers deemed by her to be needed for the pleading,
filing, and securing of a dissolution of marriage, as well as detailed
instructions as to how the suit should be filed, notice served,
hearings set, trial conducted, and the final decree secured. The
referee also found that in one instance, respondent prepared a
quit claim deed in reference to the marital property of the parties.
The referee determined that respondent's contention that she
merely operates a typing service is rebutted by numerous facts in
evidence. Ms. Brumbaugh has no blank forms either to sell or to
fill out. Rather, she types up the documents for her customers
after they have asked her to prepare a petition or an entire set of

dissolution of marriage papers. Prior to typing up the papers, respondent asks her customers whether custody, child support, or alimony is involved. Respondent has four sets of dissolution of marriage papers, and she chooses which set is appropriate for the particular customer. She then types out those papers, filling in the blank spaces with the appropriate information. Respondent instructs her customers how the papers are to be signed, where they are to be filed, and how the customer should arrange for a final hearing.

Marilyn Brumbaugh, who is representing herself in proceedings before this Court, has made various objections to the procedure and findings of fact of the referee.... Respondent argues that she has never held herself out as an attorney, and has never professed to have legal skills. She does not give advice, but acts merely as a secretary. She is a licensed counselor, and asserts the right to talk to people and to let her customers make decisions for themselves. Finally, respondent contends that her civil rights have been violated, and that she has been denied the right to make an honest living.

This case does not arise out of a complaint by any of Ms. Brumbaugh's customers as to improper advice or unethical conduct. It has been initiated by members of The Florida Bar who believe her to be practicing law without a license. The evidence introduced at the hearing below shows that none of respondent's customers believed that she was an attorney, or that she was acting as an attorney in their behalf. Respondent's advertisements clearly addressed themselves to people who wish to do their own divorces. These customers knew that they had to have "some type of papers" to file in order to obtain their dissolution of marriage. Respondent never handled contested divorces. During the past two years respondent has assisted several hundred customers in obtaining their own divorces. The record shows that while some of her customers told respondent exactly what they wanted, generally respondent would ask her customers for the necessary information needed to fill out the divorce papers, such as the names and addresses of the parties, the place and duration of residency in this state, whether there was any property settlement to be resolved, or any determination as to custody and support of children. Finally, each petition contained the bare allegation that the marriage was irretrievably broken. Respondent would then inform the parties as to which documents needed to be signed, by whom, how many copies of each paper should be filed, where and when they should be filed, the costs involved, and what witness testimony is necessary at the court hearing. Apparently, Ms. Brumbaugh no longer informs the parties verbally as to the proper procedures for the filing of the papers, but offers to let them copy papers described as "suggested procedural education."

The Florida Bar argues that the above activities of respondent violate the rulings of this Court in The Florida Bar v. American Legal and Business Forms, Inc., 274 So.2d 225 (Fla.1973), and The Florida Bar v. Stupica, 300 So.2d 683 (Fla.1974). In those decisions we held that it is lawful to sell to the public printed legal forms, provided they do not carry with them what purports to be instructions on how to fill out such forms or how to use them. We stated that legal advice is inextricably involved in the filling out and advice as to how to use such legal forms, and therein lies the danger of injury or damage to the public if not properly performed in accordance with law. In Stupica, supra, this Court rejected the rationale of the New York courts in New York County Lawyers' Association v. Dacey, 28 A.D.2d 161, 283 N.Y.S.2d 984, reversed and dissenting opinion adopted 21 N.Y.2d 694, 287 N.Y.S.2d 422, 234 N.E.2d 459 (N.Y.1967), which held that the publication of forms and instructions on their use does not constitute the unauthorized practice of law if these instructions are addressed to the public in general rather than to a specific individual legal problem. The Court in Dacey stated that the possibility that the principles or rules set forth in the text may be accepted by a particular reader as solution to his problem, does not mean that the publisher is practicing law. Other states have adopted the principle of law set forth in Dacey, holding that the sale of legal forms with instructions for their use does not constitute unauthorized practice of law. However, these courts have prohibited all personal contact between the service providing such forms and the customer, in the nature of consultation, explanation, recommendation, advice, or other assistance in selecting particular forms, in filling out any part of the forms, suggesting or advising how the forms should be used in solving the particular problems.

Although persons not licensed as attorneys are prohibited from practicing law within this state, it is somewhat difficult to define exactly what constitutes the practice of law in all instances. This Court has previously stated that:

> ... if the giving of such advice and performance of such services affect important rights of a person under the law, and if the reasonable protection of the rights and property of those advised and served requires that the persons giving such advice possess legal skill and a knowledge of the law greater than that possessed by the average citizen, then the giving of such advice and the performance of such services by one for another as a course of conduct constitute the practice of law.

This definition is broad and is given content by this Court only as it applies to specific circumstances of each case. We agree that "any attempt to formulate a lasting, all encompassing definition of 'practice of law' is doomed to failure 'for the reason that under our system of jurisprudence such practice must necessarily change with the everchanging business and social order.' "

In determining whether a particular act constitutes the practice of law, our primary goal is the protection of the public. However, any limitations on the free practice of law by all persons necessarily affects important constitutional rights. Our decision here certainly affects the constitutional rights of Marilyn Brumbaugh to pursue a lawful occupation or business. Our decision also affects respondent's First Amendment rights to speak and print what she chooses. In addition, her customers and potential customers have the constitutional right of self representation, Faretta, supra, and the right of privacy inherent in the marriage relationship, Roe v. Wade, 410 U.S. 113, 93 S.Ct. 705, 35 L.Ed.2d 147 (1973); Boddie v. Connecticut, 401 U.S. 371, 91 S.Ct. 780, 28 L.Ed.2d 113 (1971). All citizens in our state are also guaranteed access to our courts by Article I, Section 21, Florida Constitution (1968). Although it is not necessary for us to provide affirmative assistance in order to ensure meaningful access to the courts to our citizens, as it is necessary for us to do for those incarcerated in our state prison system, Bounds v. Smith, 430 U.S. 817, 97 S.Ct. 1491, 52 L.Ed.2d 72 (1977), we should not place any unnecessary restrictions upon that right. We should not deny persons who wish to represent themselves access to any source of information which might be relevant in the preparation of their cases. There are numerous texts in our state law libraries which describe our substantive and procedural law, purport to give legal advice to the reader as to choices that should be made in various situations, and which also contain sample legal forms which a reader may use as an example. We generally do not restrict the access of the public to these law libraries, although many of the legal texts are not authored by attorneys licensed to practice in this state. These texts do not carry with them any guarantees of accuracy, and only some of them purport to update statements which have been modified by subsequently enacted statutes and recent case law.

The policy of this Court should continue to be one of encouraging persons who are unsure of their legal rights and remedies to seek legal assistance from persons licensed by us to practice law in this state. However, in order to make an intelligent decision as whether or not to engage the assistance of an attorney, a citizen must be allowed access to information which will help determine the complexity of the legal problem. Once a person has made the decision to represent himself, we should not enforce any unnecessary regulation which might tend to hinder the exercise of this constitutionally protected right. However, any restriction of constitutional rights must be "narrowly drawn to express only the legitimate state interests at stake." Roe v. Wade, supra, NAACP v. Button, 371 U.S. 415, 438, 83 S.Ct. 328, 340, 9 L.Ed.2d 405 (1963). And if there are other reasonable ways to achieve those goals with a lesser burden on constitutionally protected activity, a state may not choose the way of greater interference. If it acts at all, it must choose less drastic means.

It is also important for us to consider the legislative statute governing dissolution of marriage in resolving the question of what constitutes the practice of law in this area. Florida's "no fault" dissolution of marriage statute clearly has the remedial purpose of simplifying the dissolution of marriage whenever possible. Section 61.001, Florida Statutes (1975) states:

    (1) This chapter shall be liberally construed and applied to promote its purposes.

    (2) Its purposes are:

        (a) To preserve the integrity of marriage and to safeguard meaningful family relationships;

        (b) To promote the amicable settlement of disputes that have arisen between parties to a marriage;

        (c) To mitigate the potential harm to the spouses and their children caused by the process of legal dissolution of marriage.

Families usually undergo tremendous financial hardship when they decide to dissolve their marital relationships. The Legislature simplified procedures so that parties would not need to bear the additional burden of expensive legal fees where they have agreed to the settlement of their property and the custody of their children. This Court should not place unreasonable burdens upon the obtaining of such divorces, especially where both parties consent to the dissolution.

Present dissolution procedures in uncontested situations involve a very simplified method of asserting certain facts required by statute, notice to the other parties affected, and a simple hearing where the trial court may hear proof and make inquiries as to the facts asserted in those pleadings.

The legal forms necessary to obtain such an uncontested dissolution of marriage are susceptible of standardization. This Court has allowed the sale of legal forms on this and other subjects, provided that they do not carry with them what purports to be instructions on how to fill out such forms or how they are to be used. The Florida Bar v. American Legal and Business Forms, Inc., supra; The Florida Bar v. Stupica, supra. These decisions should be reevaluated in light of those recent decisions in other states which have held that the sale of forms necessary to obtain a divorce, together with any related textual instructions directed towards the general public, does not constitute the practice of law. The reasons for allowing the sale of such legal publications which contain sample forms to be used by individuals who wish to represent themselves are persuasive....

Although there is a danger that some published material might give false or misleading information, that is not a sufficient reason to justify its total ban. We must assume that our citizens will generally use such publications for what they are worth in the preparation of their cases, and further assume that most persons will not rely on these materials in the same way they would rely on the advice of an attorney or other persons holding themselves out as having expertise in the area. The tendency of persons seeking legal assistance to place their trust in the individual purporting to have expertise in the area necessitates this Court's regulation of such attorney-client relationships, so as to require that persons giving such advice have at least a minimal amount of legal training and experience. Although Marilyn Brumbaugh never held herself out as an attorney, it is clear that her clients placed some reliance upon her to properly prepare the necessary legal forms for their dissolution proceedings. To this extent we believe that Ms. Brumbaugh overstepped proper bounds and engaged in the unauthorized practice of law. We hold that Ms. Brumbaugh, and others in similar situations, may sell printed material purporting to explain legal practice and procedure to the public in general and she may sell sample legal forms. To this extent we limit our prior holdings in Stupica and American Legal and Business Forms, Inc. Further, we hold that it is not improper for Marilyn Brumbaugh to engage in a secretarial service, typing such forms for her clients, provided that she only copy the information given to her in writing by her clients. In addition, Ms. Brumbaugh may advertise her business activities of providing secretarial and notary services and selling legal forms and general printed information. However, Marilyn Brumbaugh must not, in conjunction with her business, engage in advising clients as to the various remedies available to them, or otherwise assist them in preparing those forms necessary for a dissolution proceeding. More specifically, Marilyn Brumbaugh may not make inquiries nor answer questions from her clients as to the particular forms which might be necessary, how best to fill out such forms, where to properly file such forms, and how to present necessary evidence at the court hearings. Our specific holding with regard to the dissolution of marriage also applies to other unauthorized legal assistance such as the preparation of wills or real estate transaction documents. While Marilyn Brumbaugh may legally sell forms in these areas, and type up instruments which have been completed by clients, she must not engage in personal legal assistance in conjunction with her business activities, including the correction of errors and omissions.

Accordingly, having defined the limits within which Ms. Brumbaugh and those engaged in similar activities may conduct their business without engaging in the unauthorized practice of law, the rule to show cause is dissolved.

It is so ordered.

KARL, Justice, concurring specially.

There is a popular notion that every attempt to define the practice of law and restrict the activities within the definition to those who are authorized to practice law is nothing more than a method of providing economic protection for lawyers. I recognize that a small number of attorneys who advocate a broad definition of the practice coupled with severe penalties for those who encroach are motivated by economic self-interest. Indeed, regardless of motive, any law or rule that stakes out an area "for lawyers only" will result in some incidental benefit to those who are authorized to practice law a form of serendipity for them.

What is often lost in the rush to condemn members of the legal profession for alleged selfishness is the existence of a genuine need to protect the public from those who are willing to give legal advice and render legal service, for their own profit, without being competent to do so and without being subject to restraint and punishment if they cause damage to some unsuspecting and uninformed persons in the process. Just as the public must be protected from physical harm inflicted by those who would prescribe drugs and perform surgery without proper training, so must we provide protection from financial and other damage inflicted by pseudo-lawyers.

We could develop a perfect set of disciplinary rules for attorneys and establish a procedure that quickly disbars and delicenses those who violate the rules, but if we should then permit nonmembers of the bar, including those who have been disbarred, to engage in the same activities as lawyers, we would have accomplished nothing. The members of the public would still be in serious jeopardy....

———

NOTE: DEFINING THE "PRACTICE OF LAW"

"It is not easy to define the practice of law." *Lowell Bar Ass'n v. Loeb*, 315 Mass. 176, 52 N.E.2d 27 (1943), quoted in *In re Chimko*, 444 Mass. 743, 831 N.E.2d 316 (2005). Still, most states have adopted a definition, either by statute, ethics rule, case law, or advisory opinion. An ABA commission recently attempted to draft a uniform definition, but abandoned the attempt after it came under fire from many groups that found the entire effort anti-competitive. Case law definitions of the "practice of law" often seem to beg the question rather than answering it. See, e.g., *State Bar of Arizona v. Arizona Land Title & Trust Co.*, 90 Ariz. 76, 366 P.2d 1 (1961) (defining practice of law as "those acts, whether performed in court or in the law office, which lawyers customarily have carried on from day to day through the centuries."). See also *Birbrower, infra.* Statutes usually tend toward greater precision. Georgia's statute, Ga. Code 15–19–50, for example, provides as follows:

The practice of law in this state is defined as:

(1) Representing litigants in court and preparing pleadings and other papers incident to any action or special proceedings in any court or other judicial body;

(2) Conveyancing;

(3) The preparation of legal instruments of all kinds whereby a legal right is secured;

(4) The rendering of opinions as to the validity or invalidity of titles to real or personal property;

(5) The giving of any legal advice; and

(6) Any action taken for others in any matter connected with the law.

Of course, even a statutory definition must be interpreted in each case in which a claim of "unauthorized practice" is made, and clauses such as paragraph (6) in the Georgia statute are quite open-ended.

Notes

1.　Most states have adopted unauthorized practice statutes. These statutes typically specify the remedies available against those who engage in unauthorized practice; these remedies include civil injunctions, civil contempt citations, civil fines, and restitution. A large number of the statutes also make engaging in unauthorized practice a crime, punishable by a fine or a jail term. In Pennsylvania, for example, the unauthorized practice of law is a misdemeanor of the third degree on the first violation, with every subsequent violation a misdemeanor of the first degree. 42 Pa. C.S.A. § 2524(a). A third-degree misdemeanor is punishable by up to one year of imprisonment, a first degree misdemeanor by up to five years. 18 Pa. C.S.A. §§ 106(b)(6) & (8). Florida's legislature amended its statute in 2004 to make the unauthorized practice of law a felony of the third degree, punishable by up to five years imprisonment and a fine of up to $5,000. Fla. Stat. Ann. § 454.23.

Should conduct like that engaged in by Ms. Brumbaugh be considered *criminal?*

2.　In 2003, the California legislature increased the statutory penalty for the unauthorized practice of law, partially in response to widespread abuses by non-lawyers purporting to provide "legal services" to new immigrants in the Asian and Latino communities. Often these non-lawyers claim to have "inside connections" with the Immigration and

Naturalization Service, and promise their customers that they can obtain "green cards" to work in the U.S. Outrageously high fees are often charged and green cards not obtained. Cal. Bar J., Oct. 2002, at 1, 18. The revised law provides that UPL is punishable by up to one year in county jail or a $1,000 fine or both, with subsequent convictions requiring a minimum 90–day jail sentence. Cal. Bus. & Prof. Code § 6126. In 2006, another new California law authorized the state bar to petition state superior courts to assume jurisdiction over the unauthorized practices of non-lawyers, and ultimately to shut them down, seize files, and return them to clients. Enforcement of UPL laws has greatly increased in the state as a result.

3.   Notice that none of Ms. Brumbaugh's customers complained about the nature or quality of her services. The court did not find this particularly relevant. Should this have been *determinative*? Why should the bar, or a member of the bar, have standing to complain if customers did not?

4.   Florida has the largest budget of all the states for enforcing its UPL laws, and it enforces the laws with vigor. *Brumbaugh* was hardly atypical. See, e.g., *The Florida Bar v. We The People Forms & Service Center*, 883 So.2d 1280 (Fla. 2004) (enjoining and fining a chain document-preparation service for engaging in nine separate acts of unauthorized practice).

5.   Don't many non-lawyers routinely engage in law-related work as part of their normal jobs? For example, don't real estate brokers, insurance agents, bankers and accountants work partially within a legal realm? Are they practicing law when they give advice to clients and prepare documents that have legal ramifications? Compare *Countrywide Home Loans, Inc. v. Kentucky Bar Ass'n*, 113 S.W.3d 105 (Ky. 2003) (non-lawyers may conduct real estate closings, but may not answer legal questions or offer legal advice) and *Perkins v. CTX Mortgage Co.*, 137 Wash.2d 93, 969 P.2d 93 (1999)(the selection and completion of mortgage documents is the practice of law, but merely entering data on a mortgage form is not), with *King v. First Capital Financial Servs. Corp.*, 215 Ill.2d 1, 293 Ill.Dec. 657, 828 N.E.2d 1155 (2005) (UPL for non-attorneys to prepare promissory notes and mortgage documents) and *Doe v. McMaster*, 355 S.C. 306, 585 S.E.2d 773 (2003) (performing a title search and preparing documents for a loan without direct attorney supervision is UPL).

Is it practical, or desirable, to restrict non-lawyers in these activities and force consumers to hire lawyers, often at much higher prices?

6.   Is it the unauthorized practice of law for a non-lawyer to take a fee for helping people file insurance claims arising from automobile accidents? What about negotiating with the insurance company about those claims? See *Cincinnati Bar Ass'n v. Cromwell*, 82 Ohio St.3d 255, 695 N.E.2d 243 (1998); *Bergantzel v. Mlynarik*, 619 N.W.2d 309 (Iowa 2000).

7. What if an insurance company gives third-party claimants a brochure that says "people who settle insurance claims without an attorney generally settle their claims more quickly than those who have hired attorneys" and that "[a]ttorneys often take up to one third of the settlement you receive." Is this engaging in the unauthorized practice of law? See *Allstate Ins. Co. v. West Virginia State Bar*, 998 F.Supp. 690 (S.D.W.Va.1998), *aff'd*, 233 F.3d 813 (4th Cir.2000).

8. *Software Programs.* As we saw in *Brumbaugh*, most states would not conclude that merely selling forms or do-it-yourself law kits is the "practice of law," as long as the sale was not linked to personalized advice on how to use the kits or fill out the forms. Should software programs be treated any differently? The Texas legislature amended its statute in 1999 to provide that the practice of law "does not include the design, creation, publication, distribution, display, or sale ... [of] computer software or similar products if the products clearly and conspicuously state that the products are not a substitute for the advice of an attorney." Tex. Gov't Code § 81.101. The legislature acted after a federal district court had held that the sale of Quicken Family Lawyer software constituted the unauthorized practice of law in Texas. *Unauthorized Practice of Law Committee v. Parsons Technology, Inc.*, 1999 WL 47235 (N.D.Tex.1999), *vacated*, 179 F.3d 956 (5th Cir.1999) (in light of the amended statute).

9. What about websites on which non-lawyers opine about legal issues, without giving particularized advice tailored to a specific person? Is that UPL? See *Office of Disciplinary Counsel v. Palmer*, 115 Ohio Misc.2d 70, 761 N.E.2d 716 (Ohio Bd. of Comm'rs on UPL 2001).

10. *Suspended or disbarred lawyers.* Obviously, a lawyer who has been suspended or disbarred can no longer legally practice as a lawyer while the sanction remains in place. Can such a lawyer (or ex-lawyer) work as a paralegal or lawyer's assistant? The states are split almost evenly on this point. See ABA Center for Professional Responsibility, 2004 Survey of Unauthorized Practice of Law Committees, Chart II, at 2. The National Federation of Paralegal Associations takes the position that suspended or disbarred lawyers should not be allowed to act as paralegals. Do you agree?

11. *Assisting UPL.* Remember that a lawyer who assists a non-lawyer in UPL thereby violates the ethics rules and may be disciplined. MR 5.5(b). Could a lawyer be disciplined for participating in estate-planning seminars during which a non-lawyer dispensed advice on how to settle an estate without a lawyer, and splitting seminar fees with the non-lawyer? See *In re Deddish*, 347 S.C. 614, 557 S.E.2d 655 (2001) (yes; held to be assisting UPL).

Note that a lawyer can assist a person who is representing himself *pro se,* without assisting UPL—since the *pro se* litigant himself is not engaged in UPL at all. MR 5.5, Comment [1].

12. A frail, 94–year old woman granted a durable power of attorney to her adult nephew, authorizing him to take charge of her affairs. Did

that legal document—giving the nephew the specific power to "compromise, settle and adjust all claims (including tax claims) in favor of or against me"—empower him (a non-lawyer) to prepare a complaint with a state tax agency contesting her real-estate property tax bill? Or was this the unauthorized practice of law? Should it matter that she would have had the right to prepare such a complaint herself? See *Fravel v. Stark County Bd. of Revision*, 88 Ohio St.3d 574, 728 N.E.2d 393 (2000).

13. *Non-lawyer representation before administrative agencies.* The Federal Administrative Procedure Act allows any person who is "compelled to appear in person before an agency or representative thereof ... to be accompanied, represented, and advised by counsel or, if permitted by the agency, by other qualified representative." 5 U.S.C. § 555(b). The same provision allows a party to appear in person "by or with counsel or other duly qualified representative in an agency proceeding." *Id.* This provision allows federal agencies to allow non-lawyers to represent clients in proceedings before them. Many do allow that. For example, non-lawyer representatives may appear on behalf of clients in Federal Tax Court, as long as the representative has passed an exam and paid a fee. Tax Court Rule 200 (a)(3) (2002). Non-lawyers may represent clients in IRS proceedings. 31 C.F.R. § 10.3 *et seq.* Non-lawyers are also allowed to prepare and prosecute patent applications. 37 C.F.R. § 1.31 (2004). See *Sperry v. Florida*, 373 U.S. 379, 83 S.Ct. 1322, 10 L.Ed.2d 428 (1967) (state could not enjoin non-lawyer from working on patent applications for clients, since federal patent law allows that and preempts state law.)

Many states have similar statutes, allowing non-lawyers to represent parties in administrative proceedings. See, e.g., Fla. Stat. Ann. § 120.62 (allowing any person who appears before an administrative agency "to be accompanied, represented, and advised by counsel or by other qualified representatives"); Md. Code, State Gov't, § 9–1607.1(a) (allowing "an individual who is not licensed to practice law in this State" to represent a party in certain enumerated types of administrative proceedings). Statutes such as this prevent a state bar from claiming successfully that an authorized person is engaged in UPL. See, e.g., *Cleveland Bar Ass'n v. CompManagement*, 104 Ohio St.3d 168, 818 N.E.2d 1181 (2004) (non-lawyer appearing on behalf of a client in a workers' comp proceeding was not engaged in UPL, since a resolution of the state Industrial Commission authorizes such appearances). Why would many states authorize these kinds of representations? Is this activity not "the practice of law?"

Is it the unauthorized practice of law for a non-lawyer to represent parties in securities arbitrations? See *Disciplinary Counsel v. Alexicole, Inc.*, 105 Ohio St.3d 52, 822 N.E.2d 348 (2004) (yes; evidence showed the respondent "regularly prepares statements of claims, conducts discovery, participates in prehearing conferences, negotiates settlements, and participates in mediation and arbitration hearings, all on behalf of Alexicole clients").

BIRBROWER, MONTALBANO, CONDON & FRANK, P.C. v. THE SUPERIOR COURT OF SANTA CLARA COUNTY

Supreme Court of California, 1998.
17 Cal.4th 119, 949 P.2d 1, 70 Cal.Rptr.2d 304.

CHIN, J.

Business and Professions Code section 6125 states: "No person shall practice law in California unless the person is an active member of the State Bar." We must decide whether an out-of-state law firm, not licensed to practice law in this state, violated section 6125 when it performed legal services in California for a California-based client under a fee agreement stipulating that California law would govern all matters in the representation. . . .

I. BACKGROUND

The facts with respect to the unauthorized practice of law question are essentially undisputed. Birbrower is a professional law corporation incorporated in New York, with its principal place of business in New York. During 1992 and 1993, Birbrower attorneys, defendants Kevin F. Hobbs and Thomas A. Condon (Hobbs and Condon), performed substantial work in California relating to the law firm's representation of ESQ. Neither Hobbs nor Condon has ever been licensed to practice law in California. None of Birbrower's attorneys were licensed to practice law in California during Birbrower's ESQ representation.

ESQ is a California corporation with its principal place of business in Santa Clara County. In July 1992, the parties negotiated and executed the fee agreement in New York, providing that Birbrower would perform legal services for ESQ, including "All matters pertaining to the investigation of and prosecution of all claims and causes of action against Tandem Computers Incorporated (Tandem)." The "claims and causes of action" against Tandem, a Delaware corporation with its principal place of business in Santa Clara County, California, related to a software development and marketing contract between Tandem and ESQ dated March 16, 1990 (Tandem Agreement). The Tandem Agreement stated that "The internal laws of the State of California (irrespective of its choice of law principles) shall govern the validity of this Agreement, the construction of its terms, and the interpretation and enforcement of the rights and duties of the parties hereto." Birbrower asserts, and ESQ disputes, that ESQ knew Birbrower was not licensed to practice law in California.

While representing ESQ, Hobbs and Condon traveled to California on several occasions. In August 1992, they met in California with ESQ and its accountants. During these meetings, Hobbs and Condon discussed various matters related to ESQ's dispute with Tandem and strategy for resolving the dispute. They made recommendations and gave advice. During this California trip, Hobbs and Condon also met with Tandem representatives on four or five occasions during a two-day period. At the meetings, Hobbs and Condon spoke on ESQ's behalf. Hobbs demanded that Tandem pay ESQ $15 million. Condon told Tandem he believed that damages would exceed $15 million if the parties litigated the dispute.

Around March or April 1993, Hobbs, Condon, and another Birbrower attorney visited California to interview potential arbitrators and to meet again with ESQ and its accountants. Birbrower had previously filed a demand for arbitration against Tandem with the San Francisco offices of the American Arbitration Association (AAA). In August 1993, Hobbs returned to California to assist ESQ in settling the Tandem matter. While in California, Hobbs met with ESQ and its accountants to discuss a proposed settlement agreement Tandem authored. Hobbs also met with Tandem representatives to discuss possible changes in the proposed agreement. Hobbs gave ESQ legal advice during this trip, including his opinion that ESQ should not settle with Tandem on the terms proposed.

[ESQ and Tandem settled their dispute before the matter ever went to arbitration. ESQ then sued Birbrower in California state court for legal malpractice. Birbrower removed the case to federal court and filed a counterclaim for attorneys fees. After a remand to state court, ESQ moved for partial summary judgment, arguing that Birbrower was engaged in the unauthorized practice of law in violation of section 6125, rendering the fee agreement unenforceable. The Superior court granted ESQ's motion. The Court of Appeal affirmed, and this appeal ensued.]

II. DISCUSSION

A. *The Unauthorized Practice of Law*

The California Legislature enacted section 6125 in 1927 as part of the State Bar Act (the Act), a comprehensive scheme regulating the practice of law in the state. (*J.W. v. Superior Court* (1993) 17 Cal.App.4th 958, 965 [22 Cal.Rptr.2d 527].) Since the Act's passage, the general rule has been that, although persons may represent themselves and their own interests regardless of State Bar membership, no one but an active member of the State Bar may practice law for another person in California. The prohibition against unauthorized law practice is within the state's police power and is designed to ensure that those performing legal services do so competently.

A violation of section 6125 is a misdemeanor. (§ 6126.) Moreover, "No one may recover compensation for services as an attorney at law in this state unless [the person] was at the time the services were performed a member of The State Bar."

[handwritten: can't collect $]

Although the Act did not define the term "practice law," case law explained it as " 'the doing and performing services in a court of justice in any matter depending therein throughout its various stages and in conformity with the adopted rules of procedure.' " (*People v. Merchants Protective Corp.* (1922) 189 Cal. 531, 535 [209 P. 363].) *Merchants* included in its definition legal advice and legal instrument and contract preparation, whether or not these subjects were rendered in the course of litigation. (*Ibid.*; see *People v. Ring* (1937) 26 Cal.App.2d. Supp. 768, 772–773 [70 P.2d 281].) *Ring* later determined that the Legislature "accepted both the definition already judicially supplied for the term and the declaration of the Supreme Court [in *Merchants*] that it had a sufficiently definite meaning to need no further definition. The definition . . . must be regarded as definitely establishing, for the jurisprudence of this state, the meaning of the term 'practice law.' "

In addition to not defining the term "practice law," the Act also did not define the meaning of "in California." In today's legal practice, questions often arise concerning whether the phrase refers to the nature of the legal services, or restricts the Act's application to those out-of-state attorneys who are physically present in the state.

Section 6125 has generated numerous opinions on the meaning of "practice law" but none on the meaning of "in California." In our view, the practice of law "in California" entails sufficient contact with the California client to render the nature of the legal service a clear legal representation. In addition to a quantitative analysis, we must consider the nature of the unlicensed lawyer's activities in the state. Mere fortuitous or attenuated contacts will not sustain a finding that the unlicensed lawyer practiced law "in California." The primary inquiry is whether the unlicensed lawyer engaged in sufficient activities in the state, or created a continuing relationship with the California client that included legal duties and obligations.

[handwritten left margin: Rule/ interp of "in CA"]

[handwritten right margin: Issue in this case — did they practice law "in california"]

[handwritten right margin: (def of "in CA")]

Our definition does not necessarily depend on or require the unlicensed lawyer's physical presence in the state. Physical presence here is one factor we may consider in deciding whether the unlicensed lawyer has violated section 6125, but it is by no means exclusive. For example, one may practice law in the state in violation of section 6125 although not physically present here by advising a California client on California law in connection with a California legal dispute by telephone, fax, computer, or other modern technological means. Conversely, although we decline to provide a comprehensive list of what activities constitute sufficient contact with the state, we do reject the notion that a person *automatically* practices law "in California" whenever that person practices California law anywhere, or "virtually" enters the state by telephone, fax, e-mail, or satellite. (See e.g., *Baron v. City of Los Angeles* (1970) 2 Cal.3d 535, 543 [86 Cal.Rptr. 673, 469 P.2d 353, 42 A.L.R.3d 1036] (*Baron*) ["practice law" does not encompass all professional activities].) Indeed, we disapprove *Ring, supra,* 26 Cal.App.2d Supp. 768, and its progeny to the extent the cases are inconsistent with our discussion. We must decide each case on its individual facts.

This interpretation acknowledges the tension that exists between interjurisdictional practice and the need to have a state-regulated bar. As stated in the American Bar Association Model Code of Professional Responsibility, Ethical Consideration EC 3–9, "Regulation of the practice of law is accomplished principally by the respective states. Authority to engage in the practice of law conferred in any jurisdiction is not per se a grant of the right to practice elsewhere, and it is improper for a lawyer to engage in practice where he is not permitted by law or by court order to do so. However, the demands of business and the mobility of our society pose distinct problems in the regulation of the practice of law by the states. In furtherance of the public interest, the legal profession should discourage regulation that unreasonably imposes territorial limitations upon the right of a lawyer to handle the legal affairs of his client or upon the opportunity of a client to obtain the services of a lawyer of his choice in all matters including the presentation of a contested matter in a tribunal before which the lawyer is not permanently admitted to practice." *Baron* implicitly agrees with this canon. (*Baron, supra,* 2 Cal.3d at p. 543.) . . .

Exceptions to section 6125 do exist, but are generally limited to allowing out-of-state attorneys to make brief appearances before a state court or tribunal. They are narrowly drawn and strictly interpreted. For example, an out-of-state attorney not licensed to practice in California may be permitted, *by consent of a trial judge*, to appear in California in a particular pending action.

In addition, with the permission of the California court in which a particular cause is pending, out-of-state counsel may appear before a court as counsel pro hac vice. (Cal. Rules of Court, rule 983.) A court will approve a pro hac vice application only if the out-of-state attorney is a member in good standing of another state bar and is eligible to practice in any United States court or the highest court in another jurisdiction. (Cal. Rules of Court, rule 983(a).) The out-of-state attorney must also associate an active member of the California Bar as attorney of record and is subject to the Rules of Professional Conduct of the State Bar. . . .

Rule 988

Finally, California Rules of Court, rule 988, permits the State Bar to issue registration certificates to foreign legal consultants who may advise on the law of the foreign jurisdiction where they are admitted. These consultants may not, however, appear as attorneys before a California court or judicial officer or otherwise prepare pleadings and instruments in California or give advice on the law of California or any other state or jurisdiction except those where they are admitted.

The Legislature has recognized an exception to section 6125 in international disputes resolved in California under the state's rules for arbitration and conciliation of international commercial disputes. (Code Civ. Proc., § 1297.11 et seq.) This exception states that in a commercial conciliation in California involving international commercial disputes, "The parties may appear in person or be represented or assisted by any person of their choice. A person assisting or representing a party need not be a member of the legal profession or licensed to practice law in California." (Code Civ. Proc., § 1297.351.) Likewise, the Act does not apply to the preparation of or participation in labor negotiations and arbitrations arising under collective bargaining agreements in industries subject to federal law.

check quote

B.   *The Present Case*

The undisputed facts here show that neither *Baron's* definition nor our "sufficient contact" definition of "practice law in California" would excuse Birbrower's extensive practice in this state. Nor would any of the limited statutory exceptions to section 6125 apply to Birbrower's California practice. As the Court of Appeal observed, Birbrower engaged in unauthorized law practice *in California* on more than a limited basis, and no firm attorney engaged in that practice was an active member of the California State Bar. As noted, in 1992 and 1993, Birbrower attorneys traveled to California to discuss with ESQ and others various matters pertaining to the dispute between ESQ and Tandem. Hobbs and Condon discussed strategy for resolving the dispute and advised ESQ on this strategy. Furthermore, during California meetings with Tandem representatives in August 1992, Hobbs demanded Tandem pay $15 million, and Condon told Tandem he believed damages in the matter would exceed that amount if the parties proceeded to litigation. Also in California, Hobbs met with ESQ for the stated purpose of helping to reach a settlement agreement and to discuss the agreement that was eventually proposed. Birbrower attorneys also traveled to California to initiate arbitration proceedings before the matter was settled. As the Court of Appeal concluded, " ... the Birbrower firm's in-state activities clearly constituted the [unauthorized] practice of law" *in California.*

holding affirmed

Birbrower contends, however, that section 6125 is not meant to apply to *any* out-of-state *attorneys*. Instead, it argues that the statute is intended solely to prevent nonattorneys from practicing law. This contention is without merit because it contravenes the plain language of the statute. Section 6125 clearly states that *no person* shall practice law in California unless that person is a member of the State Bar. The statute does not differentiate between attorneys or nonattorneys, nor does it excuse a person who is a member of another state bar. . . .

Birbrower next argues that we do not further the statute's intent and purpose—to protect California citizens from incompetent attorneys—by enforcing it against out-of-state attorneys. Birbrower argues that because out-of-state attorneys have been licensed to practice in other jurisdictions, they have already demonstrated sufficient competence to protect California clients. But Birbrower's argument overlooks the obvious fact that other states' laws may differ substantially from California law. Competence in one jurisdiction does not necessarily guarantee competence in another. By applying section 6125 to out-of-state attorneys who engage in the extensive practice of law in California without becoming licensed in our state, we serve the statute's goal of assuring the competence of all attorneys practicing law in this state.

California is not alone in regulating who practices law in its jurisdiction. Many states have substantially similar statutes that serve to protect their citizens from unlicensed attorneys who engage in unauthorized legal practice. Like section 6125, these other state statutes protect local citizens "against the dangers of legal representation and advice given by persons not trained, examined and licensed for such work, whether they be laymen or lawyers from other jurisdictions." (*Spivak v. Sachs* (1965) 16 N.Y.2d 163 [263 N.Y.S.2d 953, 211 N.E.2d 329, 331].) Whether an attorney is duly admitted in another state and is, in fact, competent to practice in California is irrelevant in the face of section 6125's language and purpose. (See *Ranta v. McCarney* (N.D.1986) 391 N.W.2d 161, 163 (*Ranta*) [noting that out-of-state attorney's competence is irrelevant because purpose of North Dakota law against unauthorized law practice is to assure competence *before* attorney practices in state].) Moreover, as the North Dakota Supreme Court pointed out in *Ranta*: "It may be that such an [out-of-state attorney] exception is warranted, but such a plea is more properly made to a legislative committee considering a bill enacting such an exception or to this court in its rule-making function than it is in a judicial decision." Similarly, a decision to except out-of-state attorneys licensed in their own jurisdictions from section 6125 is more appropriately left to the California Legislature.

Assuming that section 6125 does apply to out-of-state attorneys not licensed here, Birbrower alternatively asks us to create an exception to section 6125 for work incidental to private arbitration or other alternative dispute resolution proceedings.... We decline Birbrower's invitation to craft an arbitration exception to section 6125's prohibition of the unlicensed practice of law in this state. Any exception for arbitration is best left to the Legislature, which has the authority to determine qualifications for admission to the State Bar and to decide what constitutes the practice of law....

Finally, Birbrower urges us to adopt an exception to section 6125 based on the unique circumstances of this case. Birbrower notes that "Multistate relationships are a common part of today's society and are to be dealt with in commonsense fashion." (*In re Estate of Waring* (1966) 47 N.J. 367 [221 A.2d 193, 197].) In many situations, strict adherence to rules prohibiting the unauthorized practice of law by out-of-state attorneys would be " 'grossly impractical and inefficient.' "

Although ... we recognize the need to acknowledge and, in certain cases, to accommodate the multistate nature of law practice, the facts here show that Birbrower's extensive activities within California amounted to considerably more than any of our state's recognized exceptions to section 6125 would allow. Accordingly, we reject Birbrower's suggestion that we except the firm from section 6125's rule under the circumstances here....

III. Disposition

We conclude that Birbrower violated section 6125 by practicing law in California. To the extent the fee agreement allows payment for those illegal local services, it is void, and Birbrower is not entitled to recover fees under the agreement for those services....

KENNARD, J., dissenting.

... The majority focuses its attention on the question of whether the New York lawyers had engaged in the practice of law *in California*, giving scant consideration to a decisive preliminary inquiry: whether, through their activities here, the New York lawyers had engaged in the practice of law *at all*. In my view, the record does not show that they did. In reaching a contrary conclusion, the majority relies on an overbroad definition of the term "practice of law." I would adhere to this court's decision in *Baron v. City of Los Angeles*, more narrowly defining the practice of law as the representation of another in a judicial proceeding or an activity requiring the application of that degree of legal knowledge and technique possessed only by a trained legal mind. Under this definition, this case presents a triable issue of material fact as to whether the New York lawyers' California activities constituted the practice of law. . . .

Pursuant to its inherent authority to define and regulate the practice of law, this court in 1922 defined the practice of law as follows: " '[A]s the term is generally understood, the practice of the law is the doing and performing services in a court of justice in any matter depending therein throughout its various stages and in conformity with the adopted rules of procedure. But in a larger sense it includes legal advice and counsel and the preparation of legal instruments and contracts by which the legal rights are secured although such matter may or may not be depending in a court.' " (*People v. Merchants Protective Corp.* (1922)) 189 Cal. 531, 535 [209 P. 363]. . . .

In 1970, in *Baron v. City of Los Angeles,* this court reiterated the *Merchants* court's definition of the term "practice of law." We were quick to point out in *Baron,* however, that "ascertaining whether a particular activity falls within this general definition may be a formidable endeavor." *Baron* emphasized "that it is not the whole spectrum of professional services of lawyers with which the State Bar Act is most concerned, but rather it is the smaller area of activities defined as the 'practice of law.' " It then observed: "In close cases, the courts have determined that the resolution of legal questions for another by advice and action is practicing law 'if difficult or doubtful legal questions are involved which, to safeguard the public, reasonably demand the application of a *trained legal mind.*' " *Baron* added that "if the application of legal knowledge and technique is *required*, the activity constitutes the practice of law. . . . " This definition is quite similar to that proposed by Cornell Law School Professor Charles Wolfram, the chief reporter for the American Law Institute's Restatement of the Law Governing Lawyers: "The correct form of the test [for the practice of law] should inquire whether the matter handled was of such complexity that only a person trained as a lawyer should be permitted to deal with it." (Wolfram, Modern Legal Ethics (1986) p. 836.) . . .

Applying that definition here, I conclude that the trial court should not have granted summary adjudication for plaintiffs based on the Birbrower lawyers' California activities. That some or all of those activities related to arbitration does not necessarily establish that they constituted the practice of law. . . . [U]nder this court's decisions, arbitration proceedings are not governed or constrained by the rule of law; therefore, representation of another in an arbitration proceeding, including the activities necessary to prepare for the arbitration hearing, does not necessarily require a trained legal mind.

Commonly used arbitration rules further demonstrate that legal training is not essential to represent another in an arbitration proceeding. Here, for example, Birbrower's clients agreed to resolve any dispute arising under their contract with Tandem using the American Arbitration Association's rules, which allow any party to be "represented by counsel *or other authorized representative.*" (Am. Arbitration Assn., Com. Arbitration Rules (July 1, 1996) § 22, italics added.) Rules of other arbitration organizations also allow for representation by nonattorneys. . . .

In this case, plaintiffs have not identified any specific California activities by the New York lawyers of the Birbrower firm that meet the narrow definition of the term "practice of law" as articulated by this court in *Baron*. Accordingly, I would reverse the judgment of the Court of Appeal and direct it to remand the matter to the trial court with directions to vacate its order granting plaintiff's motion for summary adjudication and to enter a new order denying that motion.

Notes

1. After *Birbrower* was decided, the California legislature amended its Civil Procedure Code to allow lawyers admitted in other states to represent clients in arbitral proceedings in California. Cal. Code Civ. Proc. § 1282.4. The remainder of the opinion, however, remains good law.

2. The lawyers involved in *Birbrower* were duly licensed in New York, and had represented their California client for many years. What, then, is the court's concern about their representation in this case? Is it a legitimate concern? Who was the California Supreme Court protecting with its ruling? The California clients? California lawyers?

3. Does Justice Kennard have a good point when she argues that the Birbrower lawyers were not engaged in the "practice of law" at all in their California activities? Would a tighter and more uniform definition of the "practice of law" solve some UPL issues?

4. *Sanctions for UPL.* A variety of sanctions are possible when a lawyer engages in law practice within a state in violation of that state's UPL rules. A fee may be lost, as we saw in *Birbrower*. Legal work that a lawyer performs may be deemed to be null and void, causing great harm to the lawyer's client. See, e.g., *Preston v. University of Arkansas for Medical Sciences*, 354 Ark. 666, 128 S.W.3d 430 (2003) (a complaint filed in an Arkansas court by two lawyers admitted in Oklahoma but not Arkansas was a nullity, since the lawyers were engaged in UPL; the client's claim was held time-barred because the invalid filing did not toll the statute of limitations).

5. *Lawyers on inactive status.* Many states allow lawyers to go on "inactive" status, usually offering greatly reduced bar dues while on that status; lawyers can then "reactivate" their status simply by paying a fee. But a lawyer on inactive status cannot practice law, and doing so is UPL. See, e.g., *In re Disciplinary Proceedings Against Bolte*, 285 Wis.2d 569,

699 N.W.2d 914 (2005) (lawyer on inactive status in Wisconsin gave legal advice in Colorado; UPL in both states).

Perhaps most drastically, a lawyer who is found to have engaged in UPL in one state may be disbarred by the state in which he is admitted, as a reciprocal sanction. See *In re Barneys*, 861 A.2d 1270 (D.C. 2004) (lawyer was admitted in New York, Connecticut and D.C., and opened an office in Maryland without seeking admission there; lawyer was held to have committed UPL in Maryland and was disbarred in D.C.). Cf. *In re Application of Jackman*, 165 N.J. 580, 761 A.2d 1103 (2000) (delaying for 18 months the certification of admission to practice of a lawyer licensed in Massachusetts who practiced as an associate in a firm in New Jersey for several years before taking the New Jersey bar exam).

NOTE: THE EVOLVING RULES ON MULTIJURISDICTIONAL PRACTICE

1. *Birbrower* is just part of a long and heated dispute about the wisdom of the strict regulation of practice across state lines. The Restatement flatly rejects *Birbrower* as "unduly restrictive," providing that a lawyer admitted to the bar of one state may practice within another jurisdiction "to the extent that the lawyer's activities in the matter arise out of or are otherwise reasonably related to the lawyer's practice" in his or her home state. Restatement § 3.

In 2002, the ABA Commission on Multijurisdictional Practice issued an influential report after two years of work. That report contained nine specific recommendations, including proposals to amend Model Rules 5.5 (on unauthorized practice and multijurisdictional practice) and 8.5 (on disciplinary authority and choice of law). The ABA approved all of these recommendations in the summer of 2002. The revised version of MR 5.5 (c) provides that lawyers admitted in one state may practice temporarily in another state in a number of different circumstances, including representing clients in ADR proceedings such as arbitration and mediation, so long as the services arise out of or are reasonably related to the lawyer's practice in a state in which the lawyer is admitted–in other words, a flat rejection of *Birbrower*. Another subsection of the same rule allows lawyers to provide legal services on a temporary basis in any matter that arises out of or is reasonably related to the lawyer's practice in a state in which the lawyer is admitted. MR 5.5(c)(4).

Each state must now decide whether to adopt the ABA's revised version. Not surprisingly, a growing number have done so, with a very small number (Connecticut, so far) refusing to go along with the trend. Does the new MR 5.5 undercut state regulation of lawyers? Is that a good thing?

MR 5.5(d)

2. *In-house counsel.* Model Rule 5.5(d) provides that a lawyer who is providing legal services to "the lawyer's employer or its organizational affiliates" may provide such services without being admitted in the state in which the services are provided, as long as the lawyer is admitted in another U.S. jurisdiction. Is this a good rule, or should in-house counsel for a corporation have to be admitted in whatever state he or she works in?

3. *Lawyers in purely federal practice.* Model Rule 5.5(d) also provides that a lawyer can provide services "authorized by federal or other law" without being admitted to practice in the state in which the services are provided. Case law virtually uniformly holds that states have no power to require lawyers to be members of their state bars in order to practice exclusively federal law, if federal law contains no such requirement. This is a matter of constitutional dimension: the Supremacy Clause makes federal law supreme over state law. As one court put it, "When state licensing laws purport to prohibit lawyers from doing that which federal law entitles them to do, the state law must give way." *In re Desilets*, 291 F.3d 925 (6th Cir. 2002). See also *Augustine v. Dept. of Veterans Affairs*, 429 F.3d 1334 (Fed. Cir. 2005) (state had no power to require a lawyer practicing exclusively before a federal agency in that state to obtain a state license to practice). But see *Office of Disciplinary Counsel v. Marcone*, 579 Pa. 1, 855 A.2d 654 (2004) (lawyer suspended from practice in Pennsylvania may not maintain an office in Pennsylvania, even if limited to federal practice), called into question by *Surrick v. Killion*, 449 F.3d 520 (3d Cir. 2006) (on similar facts, opining that *Marcone* was incorrectly decided as a matter of constitutional law).

QUOTE

new cases?

Lawyers engaged in purely federal practice who are guilty of professional misconduct may be disciplined by the authorities of the state in which the practice takes place. See MR 5.5, comment [19]; *Gadda v. Ashcroft*, 377 F.3d 934 (9th Cir. 2004).

MR 5.5 CASE

4. *Foreign lawyers.* In 1994, the United States joined the World Trade Organization. One of the international trade agreements annexed to the WTO is the General Agreement on Trade in Services, commonly known as GATS. GATS requires member countries to publish their rules on practice by foreign lawyers working within their geographic boundaries. This poses quite a challenge for the United States, since—as we have seen—each state has its own rules on who may practice law within that state. Experts predict that GATS may result in the easing of restrictions both on foreign lawyers practicing temporarily in the United States, and on U.S. lawyers practicing in other states and other countries. See Laurel S. Terry, *GATS' Applicability to Transnational Lawyering and Its Potential Impact on U.S. State Regulation of Lawyers*, 34 Vand. J. Transnat'l L. 989 (2001) and *Author Corrections*, 35 Vand. J. Transnat'l L. 1387 (2002); Martha Neil, *Gearing Up for GATS*, A.B.A.J. 18 (Sept. 2003). The ABA main-

Scholarly source

tains a web page on GATS at www.abanet.org/cpr/gats, which provides up-to-date information on the progress of negotiations.

Roughly half of the states now allow "foreign legal consultants" to practice within their borders, although the authorization to practice is limited. Florida's rule is typical (based on an ABA model), requiring that a person seeking to be licensed as a foreign legal consultant must have been licensed and practicing as an attorney or the equivalent in their home country for five of the past seven years. Practice is then limited to services "regarding the laws of the foreign country in which such person is admitted to practice." Rules Regulating the Fla. Bar, Foreign Legal Consultancy Rule 16–1. Additionally, some states have amended their version of Rule 5.5 to allow temporary practice by foreign lawyers (defined as those who are members of a legal profession in a foreign jurisdiction that has effective regulation and disciplinary processes) on terms basically equivalent to that which domestic lawyers are allowed to do. See, e.g, Ga.Rule 5.5(e). This is sometimes called a "fly-in, fly-out" rule. See Robert E. Lutz, *et al., Transnational Legal Practice Developments*, 39 Int'l Law. 619 (2005).

Chapter 2

INCOMPETENCE
AND ITS CONSEQUENCES

Lawyers owe clients a duty to perform competently. As Model Rule 1.1 puts it, "Competent representation requires the legal knowledge, skill, thoroughness and preparation reasonably necessary for the representation." Failure to fulfill this duty may cause significant harm to clients or other people. When such harm occurs, what recourse exists? What must be proved to get a remedy? Are there differences between civil and criminal cases?

§ 1. THE EFFECT OF LAWYER ERROR OR MISCONDUCT

BAILEY v. ALGONQUIN GAS TRANSMISSION CO.

Supreme Court of Rhode Island, 2002.
788 A.2d 478.

FLANDERS, Justice.

This is another inglorious chapter in a long-running series of civil cases in which, regrettably, the sins of the lawyer as agent are visited upon the client as principal.

The defendant-client, Maguire Group, Architects, Engineers, Planners, Ltd. (Maguire), appeals from a Superior Court order denying its motion to vacate a default judgment that entered against it on August 6, 1999, in the amount of $458,533.69, including interest and costs. The court entered the default judgment because Maguire's lawyer, John Coffey, Jr. (Coffey), inexcusably had failed to respond to a request for production of documents and then inexcusably failed to respond to a series of follow-up motions and conditional court orders compelling Maguire to produce the requested documents. Despite proper service of these documents on Coffey, both his and Maguire's stony silence eventually culminated in the entry of a default judgment against Ma-

67

guire for the amount of the plaintiffs' damages and prejudgment interest.

The plaintiffs alleged that they suffered personal injuries while they were excavating a trench and laying a gas line in East Providence, and that defendants' negligence caused these injuries. Although Maguire filed an answer denying these allegations, its later default mooted whatever defenses it may have possessed to its asserted liability on these claims. But when plaintiffs attempted to execute on the default judgment, Maguire learned for the first time of its lawyer's malfeasance and sought to vacate the judgment. The motion justice refused to do so, however, finding no manifest injustice in holding Maguire's feet to the fire lit by its own lawyer's inexcusable neglect. Because we are unable to conclude that the motion justice abused his discretion in denying the motion to vacate the default judgment, we affirm for the reasons amplified below.

Facts and Travel

. . . In March 1997, during pretrial discovery, plaintiffs propounded a request to Maguire for the production of relevant documents, to which Maguire failed to respond. There followed, in due course, a motion and an order compelling Maguire to produce the requested documents, a conditional default order, the entry of a default, a hearing on damages, and, finally, a default judgment, in August 1999. Despite proper service of these court papers on Maguire's lawyer and his receipt of several commendable letters from plaintiffs' lawyer entreating him to comply, Coffey failed to respond to any of them. Ultimately, an execution on the judgment issued on September 7, 1999, and plaintiffs caused it to be duly served on Maguire soon thereafter. Finally waking up to the fact that its own lawyer had been asleep at the switch while this train wreck of a default was occurring, Maguire engaged new counsel who, in October 1999, filed a motion to vacate the judgment. The court denied the motion and Maguire then appealed to this Court.

Before representing Maguire on this particular case, for many years Coffey had handled various types of legal work for this same client, mostly of the corporate variety. During 1999, when this lawsuit was pending in the Superior Court, Maguire was providing Coffey with an office, absorbing certain of his administrative expenses, and paying him a retainer of $15,500 per month. At quarterly meetings he attended with officers of the company, Coffey would report to Maguire on the status of this case and on the various other legal matters for which Maguire had engaged him to represent the company. Although Coffey recalled receiving in the mail a request for document production in this case, he testified he did not inform anyone at Maguire about it. He admitted that he did not respond to the request for production or to the motion to compel that followed soon thereafter. He also acknowledged that, during the 1997–1998 period, he had received several items of mail in connection with this case; and that he had opened and looked at some but not all of these court documents that were mailed to him. Instead of responding to the requests and to the orders of the court, however, he would "just stack it [the mail] someplace and ultimately I would throw it away." When Maguire asked him about this case at its quarterly meetings, Coffey testified, he would tell his client that nothing was happening. He conceded that he had done nothing in the case from the time he first had received the request for production in March 1997, up to the time he received the notice of execution on the default judgment in September 1999. Apparently, Coffey considered the case to be one of relative low priority compared with the other legal matters he was handling for Maguire.

Neither Coffey nor Maguire offered any explanation to the motion justice for his total inaction in the case, other than referring to the fact that Coffey was imbibing heavily during this time by consuming eight to ten glasses of wine per day, beginning at lunch (after leaving Maguire's premises for the day) and ending when he went to bed at night. Ultimately, Coffey had himself checked into Butler Hospital in September 1999, where he was treated for alcoholism. Coffey believed that his consumption of alcohol had affected his handling of this case by impairing his judgment. He stated: "I think it was a pattern that had developed of making bad judgments that sort of steam roll you, and this just happened to be there. And I have no—I can't explain it myself."

Maguire based its motion to vacate the default judgment on Rule 60(b)(1) and (6) of the Superior Court Rules of Civil Procedure. Rule 60(b)(1) provides that a party may be relieved from a final judgment for "mistake, inadvertence, surprise, or excusable neglect." Rule 60(b)(6) allows relief for "any *other* reason justifying relief from the operation of the judgment." (Emphasis added.) The motion justice denied the motion on both grounds. He determined, first, that there was no causal connection between Coffey's tippling and his failure to handle this case properly, noting that Coffey had competently managed various other legal matters for Maguire during the same period he was ignoring the discovery requirements in this case.... The motion justice next concluded that Coffey's failure to respond to plaintiffs' document requests did not constitute excusable neglect, but rather it was the result of either unexplained or willful conduct. On appeal, Maguire does not challenge the motion justice's findings with respect to Rule 60(b)(1), but it contends that its motion to vacate should have been granted under Rule 60(b)(6)....

Analysis

We will not disturb a trial court's ruling on a motion to vacate a judgment absent a showing of abuse of discretion or error of law. Maguire argues that it should not be held liable for the actions of its attorney because the evidence showed that Coffey was grossly negligent in his handling of this case. Even though the motion justice found that Coffey's negligence was inexcusable, Maguire argues, he should have granted Maguire relief from the judgment under Rule 60(b)(6) because its attorney was not merely negligent, but grossly so and his malfeasance included misrepresentations that led Maguire to believe nothing was happening in the case. The plaintiffs respond that this interpretation of Rule 60(b)(6) would eviscerate the excusable-neglect standard of Rule 60(b)(1) and result in the granting of nearly all motions to vacate based upon the attorney's negligent conduct. Indeed, the more inexcusable and reprehensible the attorney's neglect, the more likely the client would be entitled to relief under Rule 60(b)(6) but not under 60(b)(1).

Under Rule 60(b)(1), unexplained neglect, standing alone, whether by counsel or a party, will not excuse a party's noncompliance with orderly procedural requirements, such as compliance with deadlines for responding to discovery requests and the court's compliance orders. In *King v. Brown,* 103 R.I. 154, 235 A.2d 874 (1967), this Court held that a party was not entitled to relief from a default judgment resulting from the failure of his counsel to comply with procedural requirements unless it is first established that the attorney's neglect was occasioned by some extenuating circumstances of sufficient significance to render it excusable. A Rule 60(b)(6) motion can be granted only for some "other reason justifying relief" than the reasons specified in Rule 60(b)(1) through (5) and "only in unique circumstances to prevent manifest injustice." It might be argued that "inexcusable neglect" is indeed an "other reason justifying relief" under Rule 60(b)(6) because "excusable neglect" is required to justify relief under Rule 60(b)(1). But if the neglect is inexcusable, thereby precluding any relief under Rule 60(b)(1), then that same inexcusable neglect cannot constitute the "other grounds" required to obtain relief under Rule 60(b)(6) unless other extraordinary and unusual factors also are present that would justify granting such relief. Thus, in *Bendix Corp. v. Norberg,* 122 R.I. 155, 404 A.2d 505 (1979), this Court noted that Rule 60(b)(6) was not intended to constitute a "catchall" and it quoted Professor Kent's treatise in stating that "circumstances must be extraordinary to justify relief [under Rule 60(b)(6)]." *Id.* at 158 (quoting 1 Kent, *R.I. Civ.Prac.* § 60.08 at 456 (1969)).

Maguire maintains that this case presented the very type of extraordinary and unusual circumstances that cried out for relief under Rule 60(b)(6). It argues that it should not be held accountable for the gross negligence of its attorney in ignoring the document requests and the court order directing its compliance....

Holding the client responsible for the lawyer's inexcusable neglect may seem to constitute a harsh result in these circumstances, but it comports with the agency principles that control in this area of the law. As the United States Supreme Court has stated:

> [W]e have held that clients must be held accountable for the acts and omissions of their attorneys. In *Link v. Wabash R. Co.*, 370 U.S. 626, 82 S.Ct. 1386, 8 L.Ed.2d 734 (1962), we held that a client may be made to suffer the consequence of dismissal of its lawsuit because of its attorney's failure to attend a scheduled pretrial conference. In so concluding, we found 'no merit to the contention that dismissal of petitioner's claim because of his counsel's unexcused conduct imposes an unjust penalty on the client.' *Id.*, at 633, 82 S.Ct. at 1390. To the contrary, the Court wrote: 'Petitioner voluntarily chose this attorney as his representative in the action, and he cannot now avoid the consequences of the acts or omissions of this freely selected agent. Any other notion would be wholly inconsistent with our system of representative litigation, in which each party is deemed bound by the acts of his lawyer-agent and is considered to have 'notice of all facts, notice of which can be charged upon the attorney.' *Id.* at 633–634, 82 S.Ct. at 1390 (quoting *Smith v. Ayer,* 101 U.S. 320, 326, 25 L.Ed. 955 (1880)). * * * This principle applies with equal force here and requires that respondents be held accountable for the acts and omissions of their chosen counsel. . . .

Maguire also cites to cases from other jurisdictions in support of its position that it should not have to suffer the consequences of its attorney's gross negligence. Although some courts appear to agree with this proposition,[3] the United States Supreme Court has indicated that, as a general rule, clients are responsible for the acts and omissions of their attorneys in the course of representing their clients in civil litigation. . . .

. . . Maguire contends that the motion justice overlooked the stipulation that it was not negligent in this case, and that, through no fault of its own, it was misled by its grossly negligent attorney. This argument, however, fails to recognize the "fundamental of agency law which imputes the neglect of an attorney in professional matters to his client and considers the omissions of the attorney as though they were the neglect of the client himself." That fundamental law of agency does not mutate merely because the viral strain of legal misconduct in a particular case has become so virulent as to constitute "gross" negligence. . . .

---

3. *See* Annot. 64 A.L.R. 4th § 4(b) (1988) for a collection of cases that recognize an exception to the general rule imputing an attorney's negligence to the client when the attorney is guilty of gross negligence.

The inexcusable neglect evident in this situation—though we hope and believe it does not represent the usual case of this ilk— still does not present conditions that are so extraordinary and so unusual in circumstances accompanying failures to comply with the rules that a motion justice would abuse his or her discretion by denying a motion to vacate the default judgment that had entered in the case. Unfortunately, the cases are legion in which the client's attorney was too busy, too distracted, or too unconscientious to bother responding to discovery requests or to other rule-based filing requirements, or to follow-on motions to compel, conditional orders of default, or default judgments. And, most regrettably, it is not unusual for the lawyer to attempt to cover up his or her wrongdoing by failing to report or misrepresenting the true status of the case to the client. Yet such inexcusable misconduct does not thereby morph into "reasons other than those set out in the first five clauses of the rule" for the purpose of granting relief under Rule 60(b)(6)....

Maguire also maintains that the motion justice ignored the relative prejudice to the parties in the present case. Maguire asserts that it will be greatly prejudiced if it is denied an opportunity to defend this lawsuit, whereas plaintiffs will suffer no significant prejudice if the case is allowed to proceed to trial.... Here, as plaintiffs point out, because this is an attorney-neglect case, the issue of prejudice to the opposing party was irrelevant under Rule 60(b)(1). In *Astors' Beechwood v. People Coal Co.*, 659 A.2d 1109 (R.I.1995), we indicated that the issue of prejudice should not even be addressed in such excusable-neglect cases. "Rather, the rules focus on the movant's reasons for missing the deadline, not on the effect of missing the deadline upon the opposing party." *Id.* at 1116.

Although prejudice to the opposing party can and should be considered under Rule 60(b)(6), it should not be the sole criterion and need not be the dispositive factor in deciding whether to vacate default judgments, especially in light of the strong countervailing principles favoring finality-of-judgments and attribution of the lawyer's agency status to the client that weigh against the granting of such relief....

The final issue raised by Maguire concerns the motion justice's comment at the end of his decision to the effect that Maguire may well possess a malpractice cause of action against Coffey for negligence or breach of contract. Although some legal authority supports the proposition advanced by Maguire—namely, that the client's proper recourse for an attorney's *ordinary* negligence causing a default judgment to enter is the filing of a malpractice suit against the attorney, but that the attorney's *gross* negligence can justify the granting a motion to vacate a default judgment, *see Resolution Trust Corp. v. Ferri*, 120 N.M. 320, 901 P.2d 738, 743 (1995)—Maguire cites no Rhode Island cases that adopt this line of reasoning. Consequently, we decline to second guess the motion justice's discretionary call in this case. Even though it may be possible in some truly unusual circumstances—despite an attorney's gross and inexcusable negligence—for a client whose own conduct has been faultless to obtain relief under Rule 60(b)(6), we are still not persuaded that the motion justice abused his discretion in this case when he declined to grant that relief.

[Affirmed.]

Notes

1.   Binding a client to the lawyer's errors reflects the agency nature of the client-lawyer relationship. The general rule of agency is axiomatic: A principal is bound by the neglect or mistakes of the agent, with only narrow exceptions. As one court put it succinctly, "A client is ordinarily chargeable with his counsel's negligent acts." *Community Dental Services v. Tani*, 282 F.3d 1164 (9th Cir. 2002). To quote another, "Under general rules of agency, which apply to the attorney-client relationship, the neglect of the attorney is equivalent to the neglect of the client himself when the attorney is acting within the scope of his authority." *Panzino v. City of Phoenix*, 196 Ariz. 442, 999 P.2d 198 (2000). The very concept of agency "posits a consensual relationship in which one person . . . acts on behalf of another person with power to affect the legal rights and duties of the other person." Restatement (Third) of Agency § 1.01, comment c (2006).

2.   Rhode Island Rule 60(b) is that state's counterpart to Rule 60(b) of the Federal Rules of Civil Procedure, and the *Bailey* court's construction reflects the majority approach of the federal courts. Virtually all states have a similar, if not identical, procedural rule. As you can see, relief from a final judgment is not easily obtained. Incompetent lawyering in the litigation setting, then, creates genuine problems for the client.

3.   The first listed ground for relief in Rule 60(b) is "excusable neglect." The precise meaning of this phrase is impossible to pin down; clearly it means that where neglect is "inexcusable," relief won't be granted, but beyond that courts decide cases based on their facts. The leading case is *Pioneer Investment Services Co. v. Brunswick Assocs. Ltd. Partnership*, 507 U.S. 380, 113 S.Ct. 1489, 123 L.Ed.2d 74 (1993), which sets up a four-part balancing test to determine whether a party moving for relief on that ground should prevail: (1) the danger of prejudice to the non-moving party; (2) the length of delay and its potential impact on judicial proceedings; (3) the reason for the delay, including whether it was within the reasonable control of the movant, and (4) whether the moving party's conduct was in good faith. The Court noted that "inadvertence, ignorance of the rules, or mistakes construing the rules do not usually constitute 'excusable' neglect."

4. Courts in some jurisdictions have granted clients relief from judgments where the lawyer has completely abandoned the client, which may be seen either as a complete severing of the agency relationship or as the commission of a fraud on the client. This is unusual, however—and courts usually look for literal abandonment as opposed to anything less severe. See, e.g., *Amco Builders & Developers, Inc. v. Team Ace Joint Venture*, 469 Mich. 90, 666 N.W.2d 623 (2003). Cf. Cal. Code Civ. Proc. § 473.1 (authorizing court to grant relief when the movant's lawyer was disbarred, suspended, or otherwise incapacitated, and that caused the abandonment).

5. The *Bailey* court recognizes that a few jurisdictions allow relief where the lawyer was guilty of "gross negligence." See, e.g., *Community Dental Services*, supra Note 1 (finding support for that position in the case law of three other circuits). Is that a good idea? A leading authority, quoted by the court in an omitted portion of the opinion, criticizes that approach as "illogical, in that the opponent is made to bear the brunt of unacceptable conduct by an attorney while the party that hired the attorney obtains relief." 12 Moore's Federal Practice § 60.48[4][b] (3d Ed. 2001).

6. Some states have construed their state statutes and rules to allow for relief under "extraordinary circumstances," an obviously fact-centered inquiry. See, e.g., *Tischler v. Watts*, 177 N.J. 243, 827 A.2d 1036 (2003) (lawyer's sudden onset of cancer, and "the immediate and debilitating effects of her aggressive radiation and chemotherapy treatments," warranted relief from dismissal for failure to file a required document); *Barr v. MacGugan*, 119 Wash.App. 43, 78 P.3d 660 (2003) (severe clinical depression of lawyer was an "extraordinary circumstance" justifying granting relief from order dismissing a case as a sanction for violation of a discovery order); *Martinelli v. Farm–Rite, Inc.*, 345 N.J.Super. 306, 785 A.2d 33 (2001) (computer malfunction of lawyer not an "extraordinary circumstance").

7. California's statute allows a court to grant relief "upon any terms as may be just" within six months of the entry of a default judgment or dismissal caused by the lawyer's "mistake, inadvertence, surprise or excusable neglect." Cal. Code Civ. Proc. § 473(b). To obtain such relief, the lawyer must attest to his or her mistake, inadvertence or neglect in a sworn affidavit. Further, "the court shall, whenever relief is granted based on an attorney's affidavit of fault, direct the attorney to pay reasonable compensatory legal fees and costs to opposing counsel or parties," and may order the offending attorney to pay additional monetary penalties of up to $2,000. *Id.*, § 473(c).

8. Federal Rule of Appellate Procedure 4(a)(1)(a) allows a 30–day time period in which to file a notice of appeal from a federal trial court's judgment. The trial court can grant an extension if a party shows it missed the deadline because of "excusable neglect or good cause." In one widely-publicized case, the court in *Pincay v. Andrews*, 389 F.3d 853 (9th Cir. 2004)(en banc), upheld a trial judge's discretionary grant of an

extension based on a paralegal's erroneous calendaring of the filing deadline. The court noted that it was "a lawyer's nightmare": the case had been litigated for 15 years and "any lawyer or paralegal should have been able to read the rule correctly." But in part because of the narrow standard of review (abuse of discretion), the court affirmed the grant of relief: "Had the district court declined to permit the filing of the notice [of appeal], we would be hard pressed to find any rationale requiring us to reverse." Three judges dissented. "At bottom," they said, "what the sophisticated calendaring system excuse comes down to is that the lawyer didn't bother to read the rule; instead, he relied on what a calendaring clerk told him. While delegation may be a necessity in modern law practice, it can't be a level for ratcheting down the standard for professional competence." *Id.* (Kozinski, J., dissenting).

9. A lawyer usually acts with actual authority, based on the creation of a client-lawyer relationship—usually by express contract. But would a lawyer's errors or misdeeds bind a client when the lawyer *lacked* actual authority, but some third person reasonably believed that such authority exists? Agency law provides the answer here, too. Even where actual authority has been terminated, an agent may still be cloaked in apparent authority. Restatement (Third) of Agency § 3.11 (2006). And apparent authority is authority. As the Agency Restatement puts it, "Apparent authority is the power held by an agent or other actor to affect a principal's legal relations with third parties when a third party reasonably believes the actor has authority to act on behalf of the principal and that belief is traceable to the principal's manifestations." Id., § 2.03. Apparent authority ends only when "it is no longer reasonable for the third party with whom an agent deals to believe that the agent continues to act with actual authority." Such a third party might be an adversary in litigation or another party to a transaction. Either way, a lawyer usually binds the client by acting on the client's behalf, either in actuality or apparently. See Restatement (Third) of the Law Governing Lawyers §§ 26 (lawyer's actual authority) and 27 (apparent authority).

10. *Settling a claim without express authority.* What if a lawyer enters into a settlement of a matter with a client's adversary in a litigated matter, and the client subsequently argues that the lawyer lacked the authority to do that? Is the client still bound by the lawyer's "misdeed" if in fact there was no actual authority? Most jurisdictions hold that a lawyer cannot bind a client to a settlement without express authority, since the decision whether to settle is the client's alone. See Luethke v. Suhr, 264 Neb. 505, 650 N.W.2d 220 (2002) (collecting cases). Other jurisdictions say that if a lawyer has apparent authority, the client will be bound by the settlement. See *Makins v. District of Columbia*, 861 A.2d 590 (D.C. 2004). Of course, if a client later ratifies a previously-unauthorized settlement, the client will be bound by that ratification—and such ratification may even bar a suit for legal malpractice alleging the settlement was insufficient or ill-advised. See *Puder v. Buechel*, 183

N.J. 428, 874 A.2d 534 (2005) (client told the judge in open court that the settlement was acceptable and fair).

11.   All of this means that when a lawyer acts incompetently (or worse), a client can rarely "undo" the problem that the lawyer has created. That is, as against a third party (an adversary in litigation, or someone across the table in a transaction), the deal is done. What, then, can the client do about it? Where the agent's errors bind the principal to the principal's detriment, the principal's remedy lies against the agent. We see those remedies, as they pertain to clients and lawyers, in the rest of this Chapter.

§ 2.   LEGAL MALPRACTICE IN CIVIL MATTERS

A.   The Prima Facie Case

1.   Duty

TOGSTAD v. VESELY, OTTO, MILLER & KEEFE

Supreme Court of Minnesota, 1980.
291 N.W.2d 686.

PER CURIAM.

This is an appeal by the defendants from a judgment of the Hennepin County District Court involving an action for legal malpractice. The jury found that the defendant attorney Jerre Miller was negligent and that, as a direct result of such negligence, plaintiff John Togstad sustained damages in the amount of $610,500 and his wife, plaintiff Joan Togstad, in the amount of $39,000. Defendants (Miller and his law firm) appeal to this court from the denial of their motion for judgment notwithstanding the verdict or, alternatively, for a new trial. We affirm.

In August 1971, John Togstad began to experience severe headaches and on August 16, 1971, was admitted to Methodist Hospital where tests disclosed that the headaches were caused by a large aneurism on the left internal carotid artery. The attending physician, Dr. Paul Blake, a neurological surgeon, treated the problem by applying a Selverstone clamp to the left common carotid artery. The clamp was surgically implanted on August 27, 1971, in Togstad's neck to allow the gradual closure of the artery over a period of days....

In the early morning hours of August 29, 1971, a nurse observed that Togstad was unable to speak or move. At the time, the clamp was one-half (50%) closed. Upon discovering Togstad's condition, the nurse called a resident physician, who did not adjust the clamp. Dr. Blake was also immediately informed of Togstad's condition and arrived about an hour later, at which time he opened the clamp. Togstad is now severely paralyzed in his right arm and leg, and is unable to speak....

About 14 months after her husband's hospitalization began, plaintiff Joan Togstad met with attorney Jerre Miller regarding her husband's condition. Neither she nor her husband was personally acquainted with Miller or his law firm prior to that time. John Togstad's former work supervisor, Ted Bucholz, made the appointment and accompanied Mrs. Togstad to Miller's office. Bucholz was present when Mrs. Togstad and Miller discussed the case.

Mrs. Togstad had become suspicious of the circumstances surrounding her husband's tragic condition due to the conduct and statements of the hospital nurses shortly after the paralysis occurred. One nurse told Mrs. Togstad that she had checked Mr. Togstad at 2 a.m. and he was fine; that when she returned at 3 a.m., by mistake, to give him someone else's medication, he was unable to move or speak; and that if she hadn't accidentally entered the room no one would have discovered his condition until morning. Mrs. Togstad also noticed that the other nurses were upset and crying, and that Mr. Togstad's condition was a topic of conversation.

Mrs. Togstad testified that she told Miller "everything that happened at the hospital," including the nurses' statements and conduct which had raised a question in her mind. She stated that she "believed" she had told Miller "about the procedure and what was undertaken, what was done, and what happened." She brought no records with her. Miller took notes and asked questions during the meeting, which lasted 45 minutes to an hour. At its conclusion, according to Mrs. Togstad, Miller said that "he did not think we had a legal case, however, he was going to discuss this with his partner." She understood that if Miller changed his mind after talking to his partner, he would call her. Mrs. Togstad "gave it" a few days and, since she did not hear from Miller, decided "that they had come to the conclusion that there wasn't a case." No fee arrangements were discussed, no medical authorizations were requested, nor was Mrs. Togstad billed for the interview.

Mrs. Togstad denied that Miller had told her his firm did not have expertise in the medical malpractice field, urged her to see another attorney, or related to her that the statute of limitations for medical malpractice actions was two years. She did not consult another attorney until one year after she talked to Miller. Mrs. Togstad indicated that she did not confer with another attorney earlier because of her reliance on Miller's "legal advice" that they "did not have a case."

On cross-examination, Mrs. Togstad was asked whether she went to Miller's office "to see if he would take the case of (her) husband * * *." She replied, "Well, I guess it was to go for legal advice, what to do, where shall we go from here? That is what we went for." Again in response to defense counsel's questions, Mrs. Togstad testified as follows:

> Q. And it was clear to you, was it not, that what was taking place was a preliminary discussion between a prospective client and lawyer as to whether or not they wanted to enter into an attorney-client relationship?

> A. I am not sure how to answer that. It was for legal advice as to what to do.

> Q. And Mr. Miller was discussing with you your problem and indicating whether he, as a lawyer, wished to take the case, isn't that true?

> A. Yes.

On re-direct examination, Mrs. Togstad acknowledged that when she left Miller's office she understood that she had been given a "qualified, quality legal opinion that (she and her husband) did not have a malpractice case."

Miller's testimony was different in some respects from that of Mrs. Togstad. Like Mrs. Togstad, Miller testified that Mr. Bucholz arranged and was present at the meeting, which lasted about 45 minutes. According to Miller, Mrs. Togstad described the hospital incident, including the conduct of the nurses. He asked her questions, to which she responded. Miller testified that "(t)he only thing I told her (Mrs. Togstad) after we had pretty much finished the conversation was that there was nothing related in her factual circumstances that told me that she had a case that our firm would be interested in undertaking."

Miller also claimed he related to Mrs. Togstad "that because of the grievous nature of the injuries sustained by her husband, that this was only my opinion and she was encouraged to ask another attorney if she wished for another opinion" and "she ought to do so promptly." He testified that he informed Mrs. Togstad that his firm "was not engaged as experts" in the area of medical malpractice, and that they associated with the Charles Hvass firm in cases of that nature. Miller stated that at the end of the conference he told Mrs. Togstad that he would consult with Charles Hvass and if Hvass's opinion differed from his, Miller would so inform her. Miller recollected that he called Hvass a "couple days" later and discussed the case with him. It was Miller's impression that Hvass thought there was no liability for malpractice in the case. Consequently, Miller did not communicate with Mrs. Togstad further.

On cross-examination, Miller testified as follows:

> Q. Now, so there is no misunderstanding, and I am reading from your deposition, you understood that she was consulting with you as a lawyer, isn't that correct?

A.   That's correct.

Q.   That she was seeking legal advice from a professional attorney licensed to practice in this state and in this community?

A.   I think you and I did have another interpretation or use of the term "Advice". She was there to see whether or not she had a case and whether the firm would accept it.

Q.   We have two aspects; number one, your legal opinion concerning liability of a case for malpractice; number two, whether there was or wasn't liability, whether you would accept it, your firm, two separate elements, right?

A.   I would say so.

Q.   Were you asked on page 6 in the deposition, folio 14, "And you understood that she was seeking legal advice at the time that she was in your office, that is correct also, isn't it?" And did you give this answer, "I don't want to engage in semantics with you, but my impression was that she and Mr. Bucholz were asking my opinion after having related the incident that I referred to." The next question, "Your legal opinion?" Your answer, "Yes." Were those questions asked and were they given?

MR. COLLINS: Objection to this, Your Honor. It is not impeachment.

THE COURT: Overruled.

THE WITNESS: Yes, I gave those answers. Certainly, she was seeking my opinion as an attorney in the sense of whether or not there was a case that the firm would be interested in undertaking.

Kenneth Green, a Minneapolis attorney, was called as an expert by plaintiffs. He stated that in rendering legal advice regarding a claim of medical malpractice, the "minimum" an attorney should do would be to request medical authorizations from the client, review the hospital records, and consult with an expert in the field. John McNulty, a Minneapolis attorney, and Charles Hvass testified as experts on behalf of the defendants. McNulty stated that when an attorney is consulted as to whether he will take a case, the lawyer's only responsibility in refusing it is to so inform the party. He testified, however, that when a lawyer is asked his legal opinion on the merits of a medical malpractice claim, community standards require that the attorney check hospital records and consult with an expert before rendering his opinion.

Hvass stated that he had no recollection of Miller's calling him in October 1972 relative to the Togstad matter. He testified that ... if he were consulted for a "legal opinion" regarding medical malpractice and 14 months had expired since the incident in question, "ordinary care and diligence" would require him to inform the party of the two-year statute of limitations applicable to that type of action.

This case was submitted to the jury by way of a special verdict form. The jury found that Dr. Blake and the hospital were negligent and that Dr. Blake's negligence (but not the hospital's) was a direct cause of the injuries sustained by John Togstad; that there was an attorney-client contractual relationship between Mrs. Togstad and Miller; that Miller was negligent in rendering advice regarding the possible claims of Mr. and Mrs. Togstad; that, but for Miller's negligence, plaintiffs would have been successful in the prosecution of a legal action against Dr. Blake; and that neither Mr. nor Mrs. Togstad was negligent in pursuing their claims against Dr. Blake. The jury awarded damages to Mr. Togstad of $610,500 and to Mrs. Togstad of $39,000....

In a legal malpractice action of the type involved here, four elements must be shown: (1) that an attorney-client relationship existed; (2) that defendant acted negligently or in breach of contract; (3) that such acts were the proximate cause of the plaintiffs' damages; (4) that but for defendant's conduct the plaintiffs would have been successful in the prosecution of their medical malpractice claim.

This court first dealt with the element of lawyer-client relationship in the decision of Ryan v. Long, 35 Minn. 394, 29 N.W. 51 (1886). The Ryan case involved a claim of legal malpractice and on appeal it was argued that no attorney-client relation existed. This court, without stating whether its conclusion was based on contract principles or a tort theory, disagreed:

> [I]t sufficiently appears that plaintiff, for himself, called upon defendant, as an attorney at law, for "legal advice," and that defendant assumed to give him a professional opinion in reference to the matter as to which plaintiff consulted him. Upon this state of facts the defendant must be taken to have acted as plaintiff's legal adviser, at plaintiff's request, and so as to establish between them the relation of attorney and client.

More recent opinions of this court, although not involving a detailed discussion, have analyzed the attorney-client consideration in contractual terms.... The trial court here ... applied a contract analysis in ruling on the attorney-client relationship question....

We believe it is unnecessary to decide whether a tort or contract theory is preferable for resolving the attorney-client relationship question raised by this appeal. The tort and contract analyses are very similar in a case such as the instant one,[4] and we conclude that under either theory the evidence shows that a lawyer-client relationship is present here. The thrust of Mrs. Togstad's testimony is that she went to Miller for legal advice, was told there wasn't a case, and relied upon this advice in failing to pursue the claim for medical malpractice. In addition, according to Mrs. Togstad, Miller did not qualify his legal opinion by urging her to seek advice from another attorney, nor did Miller inform her that he lacked expertise in the medical malpractice area. Assuming this testimony is true, as this court must do . . . we believe a jury could properly find that Mrs. Togstad sought and received legal advice from Miller under circumstances which made it reasonably foreseeable to Miller that Mrs. Togstad would be injured if the advice were negligently given. Thus, under either a tort or contract analysis, there is sufficient evidence in the record to support the existence of an attorney-client relationship.

Defendants argue that even if an attorney-client relationship was established the evidence fails to show that Miller acted negligently in assessing the merits of the Togstads' case. They appear to contend that, at most, Miller was guilty of an error in judgment which does not give rise to legal malpractice. However, this case does not involve a mere error of judgment. The gist of plaintiffs' claim is that Miller failed to perform the minimal research that an ordinarily prudent attorney would do before rendering legal advice in a case of this nature. The record, through the testimony of Kenneth Green and John McNulty, contains sufficient evidence to support plaintiffs' position.

In a related contention, defendants assert that a new trial should be awarded on the ground that the trial court erred by refusing to instruct the jury that Miller's failure to inform Mrs. Togstad of the two-year statute of limitations for medical malpractice could not constitute negligence. . . . The defect in defendants' reasoning is that there is adequate evidence supporting the claim that Miller was also negligent in failing to advise Mrs. Togstad of the two-year medical malpractice limitations period and thus the trial court acted properly in refusing to instruct the jury in the manner urged by defendants. One of defendants' expert witnesses, Charles Hvass, testified [that in his opinion "ordinary care and

---

4. Under a negligence approach it must essentially be shown that defendant rendered legal advice (not necessarily at someone's request) under circumstances which made it reasonably foreseeable to the attorney that if such advice was rendered negligently, the individual receiving the advice might be injured thereby. See, e. g., Palsgraf v. Long Island R. Co., 248 N.Y. 339, 162 N.E. 99, 59 A.L.R. 1253 (1928). Or, stated another way, under a tort theory,

"(a)n attorney-client relationship is created whenever an individual seeks and receives legal advice from an attorney in circumstances in which a reasonable person would rely on such advice." 63 Minn.L.Rev. 751, 759 (1979). A contract analysis requires the rendering of legal advice pursuant to another's request and the reliance factor, in this case, where the advice was not paid for, need be shown in the form of promissory estoppel.

diligence" would require a lawyer to inform a client of the statute of limitations in the situation presented here.]

Consequently, based on the testimony of Mrs. Togstad, i.e., that she requested and received legal advice from Miller concerning the malpractice claim, and the above testimony of Hvass, we must reject the defendants' contention, as it was reasonable for a jury to determine that Miller acted negligently in failing to inform Mrs. Togstad of the applicable limitations period. . . .

There is also sufficient evidence in the record establishing that, but for Miller's negligence, plaintiffs would have been successful in prosecuting their medical malpractice claim. Dr. Woods, in no uncertain terms, concluded that Mr. Togstad's injuries were caused by the medical malpractice of Dr. Blake. Defendants' expert testimony to the contrary was obviously not believed by the jury. Thus, the jury reasonably found that had plaintiff's medical malpractice action been properly brought, plaintiffs would have recovered.

Based on the foregoing, we hold that the jury's findings are adequately supported by the record. Accordingly we uphold the trial court's denial of defendants' motion for judgment notwithstanding the jury verdict. . . .

Affirmed.

Notes

1. *Elements.* While there is state-to-state variation, most courts list the elements of a legal malpractice claim in much the same way as does the *Togstad* court. See Restatement §§ 48–53. The first element, the existence of duty, is established if a client-lawyer relationship exists.

2. *Standard of care.* Most courts say that the standard of care for a lawyer is that degree of care, skill, diligence and knowledge commonly possessed and exercised by a reasonable, careful and prudent lawyer in the practice of law in the jurisdiction, under the same or similar circumstances.

3. Do you agree that a client-lawyer relationship was created in this brief meeting? Why was it not determinative that Miller never billed Mrs. Togstad for his services? See Restatement § 14.

4. If Miller believed that he and Mrs. Togstad were *not* forming a client-lawyer relationship, what might he have done differently to avoid this situation? See *Camarillo v. Vaage*, 105 Cal.App.4th 552, 130 Cal. Rptr.2d 26 (2003).

5. Even if Mrs. Togstad never became a "client," do you think Miller still erred in not telling her about the statute of limitations? See Restatement § 15(1)(c). Does he risk forming a relationship with her if he goes beyond that?

6. *Malpractice insurance.* Another significant barrier to a successful malpractice action against a lawyer is that malpractice liability insurance is mandatory in only one state, Oregon. Ore. Rev. Stat. § 752.035 (1999). Thus an aggrieved client may have a strong case on the merits only to be told by her new lawyer that there is no point in bringing the case because only a small recovery could be obtained from the uninsured lawyer. Should malpractice insurance be mandatory?

A growing number of states now require lawyers to inform either the client or the state bar whether the lawyer carries malpractice insurance. The ABA passed a Model Court Rule on Insurance Disclosure in 2004 that requires a lawyer to disclose each year to the highest court of the state whether the lawyer is currently covered by professional liability insurance and whether the lawyer intends to maintain that insurance, and to notify the court in writing if the insurance policy lapses or terminates for any reason. The Model Court Rule further provides that a lawyer who fails to comply with these provisions may be suspended from practice until such time as the lawyer complies. Should all states have such a requirement? Is it enough to inform the state bar, or should lawyers be required to inform clients? In Ohio, for example, a lawyer must inform a client in writing at the time of engagement if the lawyer does not have malpractice insurance coverage of at least $100,000 per occurrence and $300,000 in the aggregate. Is this a better rule than making insurance mandatory?

7. Clearly, a lawyer owes a duty of care to clients and will be liable to clients in the event a breach of duty causes harm. In Chapter 4, we will see more details on the issue of when a client-lawyer relationship exists. But a lawyer might also owe a duty of care to certain non-clients. Consider the next case.

LEAK-GILBERT v. FAHLE
Supreme Court of Oklahoma, 2002.
55 P.3d 1054.

KAUGER, J: . . .

This cause concerns a dispute over the will of a widower, Edward Leak (Mr. Leak/decedent), which was executed in Taloga, Oklahoma, on February 4, 1997. In early 1997, Mr. Leak hired the defendant, Pauline Fahle (Fahle/lawyer) to update his will. According to the lawyer, Mr. Leak gave her a copy of his existing will. He told her that he wanted to change his personal representative to his daughter-in-law, Jolene Leak, the wife of his deceased son, and that he also wanted her to receive his gun collection.

The lawyer insists that Mr. Leak identified his only heirs as the children of his deceased son (Alvin Troy Leak), Alvin James Leak, and the plaintiffs, Aleecia Leak–Gilbert and Dolcie Leak (beneficiaries). Mr. Leak also informed the lawyer that he wanted to disinherit the grandson. Consequently, the lawyer prepared a will, made Mr. Leak's requested changes and left the grandson one dollar and gave the granddaughters equal shares of the remainder of his estate.

After the Mr. Leak died in December of 1999, the will was submitted for probate. The probate proceeding revealed that Mr. Leak had four additional grandchildren by another deceased son, Clifford Wayne Leak, who were not mentioned in Mr. Leak's will. Consequently, the probate court treated the grandchildren as unintentionally omitted heirs, and it divided the estate among the grandchildren as if the decedent had died intestate.[2]

On June 22, 2001, the beneficiaries filed a legal malpractice action in federal district court against Fahle, asserting that she was negligent, and that she had breached the contract with the decedent because she failed to properly prepare his will according to his intentions. The beneficiaries allege that Fahle did not complete an investigation into the existence of the decedent's children or grandchildren. They insist that Fahle should have reviewed all of the files of her sister—the lawyer who had probated decedent's wife's will in 1989 which would have disclosed the omitted grandchildren.

[The lawyer moved for summary judgment. The federal trial court certified questions to the Oklahoma Supreme Court which are answered here.]

I.

. . . The lawyer does not dispute that the drafter of a will has a duty, absent a specific request by the client, to inquire, explain, or advise a client regarding heirs at law. Rather, she argues that the lawyer has no duty to confirm the client's information by conducting an independent investigation into the client's heirs. . . .

Lawyers are required to exercise ordinary professional skill and diligence in rendering their professional services. Accompanying every contract is a common-law duty to perform with care, skill, reasonable experience and faithfulness the thing agreed to be done. Duty of care is a question of law described as the total of policy considerations which lead to the conclusion that the plaintiff is entitled to protection. If a duty exists, the trier of fact then determines whether a violation of that duty has occurred.

---

2. Title 84 O.S.2001 § 132 provides:

"When any testator omits to provide in his will for any of his children, or for the issue of any deceased child unless it appears that such omission was intentional, such child, or the issue of such child, must have the same share in the estate of the testator, as if he had died intestate, and succeeds thereto as provided in the preceding section."

[The court examined two cases cited by the lawyer, one from Connecticut and one from Washington, in support of her argument that she owed no duty to investigate the testator's heirs on these facts.] The reasoning behind [these two cases] applies here, where it appears that the attorney may have been given incomplete or inaccurate information. We agree with the beneficiaries that when an attorney is hired to prepare a will, the attorney's obligation is to: 1) inquire into the client's heirs at law; 2) offer a proper explanation; 3) advise the client as to what is meant by heirs at law; 4) explain the significance of including all heirs at law in a will; and 5) prepare a will according to the client's directions.

[handwritten margin note: attorney's obligation in prepping a will]

However, to hold that an attorney has a duty to confirm heir information by conducting an investigation into a client's heirs independent of, or in addition to, the information provided by the client, even when not requested to do so, would expand the obligation of the lawyer beyond reasonable limits. The duty between an attorney and third persons affected by the attorney-client agreement should not be any greater than the duty between the attorney and the client. Although some exceptional circumstances might exist which would give rise to such a duty, none are present here. Consequently, we hold that, unless the client requests such an investigation, when an attorney is retained to draft a will, the attorney's duty to prepare a will according to the testator's wishes does not include the duty to investigate into a client's heirs independent of, or in addition to, the information provided by the client.

[handwritten margin note: duty too expansive]

[handwritten margin note: exceptions? such as]

II.

The beneficiaries argue that: 1) liability for legal malpractice should extend to intended beneficiaries of a will when the will does not carry out the testator's expressed intent and does not identify all of the decedent's heirs; and 2) Oklahoma should follow the majority rule allowing intended beneficiaries to assert malpractice claims based on contract or tort theories of recovery....

This Court has previously addressed the extension of an attorney's liability, in the absence of privity, to third party, non-client, will beneficiaries in *Hesser v. Central National Bank & Trust Co. of Enid,* 1998 OK 15, 956 P.2d 864. In *Hesser,* we held that a will beneficiary could maintain a negligence action against an attorney for failure to have the will properly executed.

Hesser involved an attorney who prepared a will for a client and then failed to properly execute the will. In the probate proceeding, the heirs at law contested the will, arguing that it was not properly executed. Subsequently, the matter was settled by agreement. Nevertheless, one of the beneficiaries under the will brought a legal malpractice action, asserting that the attorney was negligent in failing to properly execute the will. It was uncontested that the plaintiff was a third-party beneficiary to the agreement.

The *Hesser* Court recognized that: 1) as part of the agreement to prepare the will, the attorney was under a common law duty to perform with care, skill, reasonable expediency and faithfulness to properly execute the will; and 2) a duty created by a contract may be extended to a third party when the contract is made expressly for the benefit of a third-party, non-client beneficiary and the harm to the beneficiary is foreseeable. The Court determined that intended beneficiaries of a will could maintain an action against the lawyer because, as a matter of law, it was foreseeable that an intended beneficiary under the terms of a will could be harmed by an attorney's failure to have the will properly executed.

A few jurisdictions refuse to allow non-client, intended beneficiaries to bring such malpractice actions. However, our decision in *Hesser* is in accord with the majority of jurisdictions which recognize that intended beneficiaries harmed by a lawyer's malpractice may maintain a cause of action against lawyers who draft testamentary documents even though no attorney-client relationship exists. Some of these courts have recognized such actions as negligence actions, while others have determined that in an intended will beneficiary may proceed under either negligence or contract theories. Those allowing an intended beneficiary of a will to assert a third party breach of contract theory generally recognize that when such a breach occurs, named intended beneficiaries of a will also hold third party beneficiary status under the agreement between the testator and the attorney to draft a will according to the testator's wishes.

We have not previously determined whether a non-client, third party, such as an intended beneficiary of a will, is limited to asserting a legal malpractice action based on a negligence theory of recovery or whether breach of a third party intended beneficiary contract theory may alternatively be asserted. However, in *Great Plains Federal Savings and Loan Association v. Dabney,* 1993 OK 4, 846 P.2d 1088, we addressed third party beneficiary breach of contract actions in the context of an attorney and a non-client. *Dabney* involved a bank which asserted that its mortgagee had allegedly contracted with an attorney to search records of the county clerk and that it was a third party beneficiary of the contract. When it was discovered that the attorney breached the contract, the bank brought a third party breach of contract action against the attorney. The Court determined if an attorney breaches a contract with a client by failing to perform a specific, contracted for obligation, a third party, non-client may assert a breach of contract action against the attorney if the non-client can show third party beneficiary status.

Hesser teaches that when a lawyer undertakes to fulfill the testamentary instructions of a client, the lawyer must be aware that any consequences flowing from the lawyer's negligence will have an impact on the named beneficiaries. The failure of a testamentary scheme deprives the intended beneficiaries of their bequests. If the failure is due to substandard professional performance, it is reasonable to conclude that the injured parties should recover against the lawyer who caused their harm. *Dabney* teaches that when a third party, non-client is the person specifically intended to be benefitted by the legal services, the non-client may assert a breach of contract action against the lawyer.

Our decisions in *Hesser* and *Dabney* are consistent with those jurisdictions which allow intended will beneficiaries to assert malpractice claims. Consequently, we hold that an intended will beneficiary may maintain a legal malpractice action under negligence or contract theories against an attorney when the will fails to identify all of the decedent's heirs as a result of the attorney's substandard professional performance. . . .

Notes

1.   Until fairly recently, only a client could assert a malpractice claim against a lawyer. The first case to depart from this rule was *Lucas v. Hamm*, 56 Cal.2d 583, 15 Cal.Rptr. 821, 364 P.2d 685 (1961), which allowed the intended beneficiary of a will to sue the testator's lawyer for malpractice in drafting the will. As the Oklahoma Court points out above, most states now allow a malpractice action on those facts. Does that create too great a potential exposure for lawyers who draft wills for a living?

2.   Do you agree that a lawyer should owe a duty to intended beneficiaries of a client's will? Does imposing such a duty risk creating a conflict with the lawyer's duty to the client? See *Boranian v. Clark*, 123 Cal.App.4th 1012, 20 Cal.Rptr.3d 405 (2004) (lawyer's primary duty is owed to the client, so an intended beneficiary cannot sue a lawyer for failing to ascertain the client's intent or capacity).

3.   Some states allow a non-client to sue a lawyer for malpractice if the client's purpose in retaining the lawyer was to provide a direct benefit to the non-client. See, e.g., *Francis v. Piper*, 597 N.W.2d 922 (Minn.App.1999). This is sometimes called the "primary beneficiary" doctrine. See Restatement § 51 (3). While it may often overlap with the will–beneficiary rule, it potentially goes beyond it. Here, too, courts extending a duty to non-client primary beneficiaries must take care not to create conflicts with the lawyer's primary duties to the client. See *In re Estate of Drwenski*, 83 P.3d 457 (Wyo. 2004) (daughter was not an intended beneficiary of her father's retention of defendant attorney to handle his divorce, and so could not sue the lawyer for malpractice); *Hall v. Superior Court*, 108 Cal.App.4th 706, 133 Cal.Rptr.2d 806 (2003) (estranged husband of woman who hired defendant attorney to bring a

wrongful death claim based on the death of their child was not an intended beneficiary of the lawyer's work, and so could not sue the lawyer for malpractice).

4. What if a lawyer knows or should know that a non-client will rely on the lawyer's actions, and such reliance occurs to the non-client's detriment? Should a duty arise then? See, e.g., *Cowan Liebowitz & Latman, P.C. v. Kaplan*, 902 So.2d 755 (Fla. 2005) (creditors could sue lawyers who produced private placement memoranda for sale of corporate shares); *Petrillo v. Bachenberg*, 139 N.J. 472, 655 A.2d 1354 (1995) (allowing claim for negligent misrepresentation in opinion letter given to non-client); *Prudential Ins. Co. v. Dewey, Ballantine, Bushby, Palmer & Wood*, 80 N.Y.2d 377, 590 N.Y.S.2d 831, 605 N.E.2d 318 (1992) (lender could sue borrower's attorney for negligently preparing an opinion letter, where the relationship between the borrower and the lawyer "approach[ed] that of privity"); *Greycas v. Proud*, 826 F.2d 1560 (7th Cir. 1987) (negligent misrepresentation, for representing in client's loan application that there were no liens on property). Restatement §§ 51(2) & 95 (evaluation undertaken for a third person).

2. Breach of Duty

EQUITANIA INSURANCE CO. v. SLONE & GARRETT, P.S.C.

Supreme Court of Kentucky, 2006.
191 S.W.3d 552.

WINTERSHEIMER, Justice.

This appeal is from an opinion of the Court of Appeals which affirmed a judgment of the circuit court based on a summary judgment/jury verdict that rejected the claim of the Equitania Insurance Company and its Vimont shareholder group for legal malpractice against Garrett and her law firm. . . .

Two groups of shareholders, the Vimont group, composed of four of the shareholders, and the Pavenstedt group, composed of a group of shareholders led by Johann Pavenstedt began to vie for control of Equitania, an insurance company which provided insurance for horse owners. After the Vimont group bought out the Pavenstedt group, the company continued to decline in its efforts to return a profit. Vimont eventually entered an agreement to sell the book of business to Markel Insurance Company. That deal was closed in January 1995. In March of that year, the Vimont group filed a civil action in circuit court, seeking to rescind the agreement between them and the Pavenstedt group. That case was assigned to Fayette Circuit Judge Gary Payne. A judgment was rendered against the Vimont group and it was upheld by the Court of Appeals in an unpublished opinion.

Laurel Garrett and the law firm of Slone & Garrett represented the Vimont group in its attempt to gain control of the company prior to Vimont buying the shares of Pavenstedt. As a result of that representation, Vimont filed a civil action against Garrett in circuit court in February of 1997, alleging legal malpractice by Garrett in connection with her representation. That case was assigned to Fayette Circuit Judge John R. Adams and it is the principal subject of this appeal. Judge Adams ruled against Vimont and the Court of Appeals upheld that decision. This appeal followed.

This case is a complex legal malpractice claim brought by Vimont against Garrett alleging that she negligently advised them during the midst of the shareholder dispute. They claim that Garrett negligently failed to properly advise them as to how to retain control of the corporation; that the methods she advised violated the insurance code; violated a fiduciary duty to shareholders; was unethical, and was substantially more expensive. The circuit judge granted Garrett a partial summary judgment based on his interpretation of the contract which was different from the interpretation made by the circuit judge in the earlier civil case. The other portion of the claim was resolved in favor of Garrett by a jury verdict. The Court of Appeals upheld the decision of the circuit court, and this Court granted discretionary review.

[The major issue on appeal is whether the circuit court's jury instructions correctly stated the law concerning breach of duty.] Correct instructions are absolutely essential to an accurate jury verdict. The fundamental function of instructions is to tell the jury what it must believe from the evidence in order to resolve each dispositive factual issue in favor of the party who has the burden of proof on that issue.... We should note it is well recognized that the function of instructions is only to state what the jury must believe from the evidence. There should not be an abundance of detail but the jury instructions should provide only the "bare bones" of the question for the jury. *Hamby v. University of Kentucky Medical Center*, 844 S.W.2d 431 (Ky.App.1992). The bare bones may then be fleshed out by counsel during closing argument.

The jury instructions given by the trial court over the objection by Vimont were not an accurate statement of the law regarding legal malpractice in Kentucky. Vimont objected to the instructions and tendered instructions of their own which were not used. The instructions given follow:

Instruction No. 2: It was the duty of Defendant, Laurel Garrett, in undertaking the legal representation of the plaintiffs, to possess to an ordinary extent the technical knowledge commonly possessed in her profession, to exercise that degree of care and skill which an ordinary, reasonably competent lawyer would exercise under the same or similar circumstances. Provided, however, a lawyer cannot be held responsible for errors in judgment or for advising a course of action even if that course of action ultimately proves to be unsuccessful.

The given instructions were incorrect for several reasons.... Kentucky law does not provide for an exception for attorney liability for errors in judgment. A case relied on by the Court of Appeals, *Daugherty v. Runner,* 581 S.W.2d 12 (Ky.App.1978), stated that misjudgment of the law will generally not render a lawyer liable. However, *Daugherty, supra,* did not state that a lawyer can never be held liable for an error in judgment. The tendered instructions did not advise the jury that it had to be an error of law which precluded liability, nor did it inform the jury that there are circumstances in which misjudgment of the law could be a basis for liability. There can be many circumstances in which lawyers can commit errors of judgment which deviate from the standard of care. Whether an error of judgment is legal malpractice is a question of fact for the jury.

Vimont offered an expert, Manning Warren, to evaluate the methods undertaken by Garrett to assist the company in its shareholders dispute. Specifically, Warren testified that Garrett should have pursued an administrative process with the Department of Insurance to join the Vimont group to the Pavenstedt agreement which, if successful, would have resulted in the shareholders maintaining control of Equitania and would have resolved the issue. This would have avoided a prolonged battle with Pavenstedt and would have avoided spending over two million dollars by buying the stock. They also would have avoided the issues with the Department of Insurance regarding change of control as a result of their purchase. It was their conclusion that Garrett committed ongoing malpractice by failing to advise them of change of control issues. Warren further testified that it was a deviation to fail to pursue this option. However, it is apparently undisputed that the Department of Insurance would not have approved a Pavenstedt sale even if it had been properly submitted.

Kentucky should not allow lawyers to avoid liability for committing errors in judgment which the average reasonably prudent lawyer would not commit. Any avoidance of liability should only be allowed for errors of judgment made in absolute good faith.

Here, Garrett failed to plead or present evidence regarding her alleged errors in judgment so as to justify her decision. The error in judgment instruction indirectly required the jury to define and understand abstract legal principles. The jury could not have reasonably understood the distinction between errors in judgment and legal malpractice....

The proper jury instruction must follow a form similar to that in Palmore, 2 *Kentucky Instructions to Juries* § 21.01 (4th Ed.1989):

It was the duty of Defendant in undertaking the legal representation of Plaintiff to exercise the degree of care and skill expected of a reasonably competent lawyer acting under similar circumstances. If you are satisfied from the evidence that Defendant failed to comply with this duty and that such failure was a substantial factor causing the loss, you will find for Plaintiff; otherwise you will find for Defendant.

This instruction form contains the elements prescribed in *Daugherty* without requiring the jury to understand abstract legal principles. The jury is able to determine from the evidence whether there was a breach of duty and whether that breach caused the loss. . . .

Consequently, under the circumstances regarding the instructions, this matter is reversed and remanded. The decisions of the Court of Appeals and the trial court are reversed and this matter is remanded to the trial court for a jury determination as to all factual issues. . . .

Notes

1. The second element of a legal malpractice case, breach of duty, requires proof by the plaintiff that the lawyer's conduct fell below the standard of care. As is true with negligence cases generally, this is a question of fact for the jury unless reasonable people cannot differ about it. The factfinder's job is to determine whether a reasonable and prudent lawyer, under the same or similar circumstances that the defendant was in at the time, would have acted differently. This is a "foresight" test, meaning that the focus is on "what a [reasonable] lawyer would have done at the time, excluding the benefit of hindsight." *Hopp & Flesch, LLC v. Backstreet*, 123 P.3d 1176 (Colo. 2005).

2. Most courts would agree that "[i]t is *prima facie* negligent conduct for an attorney to misadvise a client on . . . a settled point of law that can be looked up by the means of ordinary research techniques." *Lopez v. Clifford Law Offices, P.C.*, 362 Ill.App.3d 969, 841 N.E.2d 465, 299 Ill.Dec. 53 (2005). Not surprisingly, then, lawyers sued for malpractice based on allegedly poor legal advice sometimes argue that the law in the area of their advice was "unsettled." Should a lawyer escape liability as a matter of law for that reason? Or is this argument essentially like the "judgment" argument made by the lawyer in *Equitania*? See, e.g., *Jerry's Enterprises, Inc. v. Larkin, Hoffman, Daly & Lindgren, Ltd.*, 711 N.W.2d 811 (Minn. 2006); *Oxley v. Lenn*, 819 N.E.2d 851 (Ind. App. 2004).

3. Should violation of one or more rules of professional conduct be considered breach in and of itself (*i.e.*, negligence per se)? See MR Scope; Cal. Rule 1–100A. Should the fact that a lawyer's conduct violates one or more rules of professional conduct be relevant in a legal malpractice

action? Why or why not? See, e.g., *Archuleta v. Hughes*, 969 P.2d 409 (Utah 1998); *Orsini v. Larry Moyer Trucking, Inc.*, 310 Ark. 179, 833 S.W.2d 366 (1992); *Day v. Rosenthal*, 170 Cal.App.3d 1125, 217 Cal.Rptr. 89 (1985).

NOTE: BREACH OF FIDUCIARY DUTY

A lawyer is a fiduciary to the client. This is so because the client places trust in the lawyer in circumstances that usually make close supervision impossible. See Restatement § 16, comment, par. b. It also means that a lawyer can be liable to the client for breach of fiduciary duty if the lawyer violates that trust, such as by engaging in self-dealing, violating client confidences, or representing conflicting interests without the client's consent. See Restatement § 49.

Breach of fiduciary duty and legal malpractice are separate legal theories. As the court explained in *Beverly Hills Concepts, Inc. v. Schatz and Schatz, Ribicoff & Kotkin*, 247 Conn. 48, 717 A.2d 724 (1998), "Professional negligence implicates a duty of care, while breach of a fiduciary duty implicates a duty of loyalty and honesty." Where the two claims are not duplicative—that is, when the two claims are based on separate facts or separate misdeeds—a lawyer can be sued on both theories. See, e.g., *Martinez v. Badis*, 842 P.2d 245 (Colo.1992). Note, however, that a breach of fiduciary duty claim will probably not be available for mere lawyer incompetence. The duty of loyalty and fidelity must be implicated as well. See, e.g., *American Airlines, Inc. v. Sheppard, Mullin, Richter & Hampton*, 96 Cal.App.4th 1017, 117 Cal.Rptr.2d 685 (2002) (representation of conflicting interests, where duty of confidentiality could be compromised, held to establish breach of fiduciary duty as a matter of law).

Why would a plaintiff sue for breach of fiduciary duty in a legal malpractice case? The short answer is that it is a separate tort, which may have a different statute of limitations and will often offer additional remedial options, such as the imposition of a constructive trust or other forms of restitution, without "case within a case" proof of damages. See, e.g., *In re Estate of Corriea*, 719 A.2d 1234 (D.C.1998) (plaintiff's inability to quantify damages did not prevent court from ordering disgorgement of ill-gotten profits). A lawyer who breaches a fiduciary duty to a client may be required to forfeit all or part of his fee, even if the breach caused the client no actual damages. See *Rwanda v. Johnson*, 409 F.3d 368 (D.C. Cir. 2005) (lawyer whose conduct breached fiduciary duty owed to client by engaging in unauthorized work cannot receive any profit from that transaction); *Burrow v. Arce*, 997

S.W.2d 229 (Tex.1999) (tracing such a rule to the law of trusts and agency; fees at issue in the case totaled $60 million).

Not all malpractice constitutes a breach of fiduciary duty, however, and where both claims are brought in a complaint but there is no evidence that the lawyer's misdeeds "resulted from an improper motive, a conflict of interest, or any other consideration beyond carelessness and lack of attention," the fiduciary duty claim is duplicative and will be subject to dismissal. *Moguls of Aspen, Inc. v. Faegre & Benson*, 956 P.2d 618 (Colo.App.1997). As the court said in *Calhoun v. Rane*, 234 Ill.App.3d 90, 95, 175 Ill.Dec. 304, 307, 599 N.E.2d 1318, 1321 (1992), "A fiduciary relationship exists as a matter of law between an attorney and his client. Thus, in effect any alleged malpractice by an attorney also evidences a simultaneous breach of trust; however, that does not mean every cause of action for professional negligence also sets forth a separate and independent cause of action for breach of fiduciary duty.... A duplicative count may be properly dismissed."

A lawyer may owe fiduciary duties to persons other than clients. For example, in *Johnson v. Brewer & Pritchard, P.C.*, 73 S.W.3d 193 (Tex.2002), an associate in a law firm was held to have breached a fiduciary duty to the firm by referring a legal matter to another law firm, for a fee, without his firm's permission. And if a lawyer represents a client who acts as a fiduciary to others, the lawyer may owe a duty of care to those others to protect them from the client's breaches of fiduciary duty. See, e.g, *Wolf v. Mitchell*, 76 Cal.App.4th 1030, 90 Cal.Rptr.2d 792 (1999); *Arpadi v. First MSP Corp.*, 68 Ohio St.3d 453, 628 N.E.2d 1335 (1994); *Pierce v. Lyman*, 1 Cal.App.4th 1093, 3 Cal.Rptr.2d 236 (1991); *see also* Restatement § 51(4). But see *Reynolds v. Schrock*, 341 Or. 338, 142 P.3d 1062 (2006) (lawyer has a qualified privilege against third-party claim that the lawyer assisted a client in breaching a fiduciary duty owed to the third party). Does one co-counsel owe the other a fiduciary duty not to commit legal malpractice, thus reducing or eliminating the lawyer's chance to earn a fee from the co-representation? See *Beck v. Wecht*, 28 Cal.4th 289, 48 P.3d 417, 121 Cal.Rptr.2d 384 (2002) (no; to recognize such a duty would interfere with fiduciary duties owed to the client).

3. Causation of Harm

TIG INSURANCE CO. v. GIFFIN WINNING COHEN & BODEWES, P.C.

United States Court of Appeals, Seventh Circuit, 2006.
444 F.3d 587.

EVANS, Circuit Judge.

TIG Insurance Company appeals the dismissal of its malpractice case against the Giffin Winning law firm and one of its attorneys, Carol Hansen Posegate.

To explain the malpractice claim we must reach back to the underlying lawsuit, in which Giffin Winning, at least for a time, represented Illinois State University (ISU) in a class-action, gender-discrimination lawsuit brought by several female professors. In the suit, *Varner v. Illinois State University,* which was assigned to District Judge Michael M. Mihm, the plaintiffs contended that they were being paid less than male professors and that ISU retaliated against female professors who complained about the discrimination. Their attorney was Joel Bellows. TIG was ISU's liability insurer at the time and it paid the attorney fees which are at the heart of the present malpractice action; TIG, in turn, was reimbursed by its reinsurers.

The malpractice alleged in the present case arose out of discovery problems in the *Varner* case. The major problem involved Giffin Winning's failure to produce three documents called gender equity studies (two of which are at issue here) in their response to a discovery request. The response was signed in October 1996. A month later the *Varner* case was stayed. Soon thereafter, the law firm of Latham & Watkins filed an appearance on behalf of ISU and essentially took control of ISU's defense, though Giffin Winning remained of record. Latham had an attorney-client relationship with ISU's insurer TIG. Giffin Winning did not.

The facts show that Giffin Winning received two gender equity studies from ISU in 1994—while the *Varner* case was still pending before the Equal Employment Opportunity Commission. Two years later, when the law firm received the second request for documents, the subject of the October 1996 response at issue here, they routed the request to William Gorrell, the former executive director for Information Systems and the head of the Planning Policy department at ISU. He did not at that time forward the studies to Giffin Winning for production and the law firm did not produce them on its own. On this point, Judge Mihm later said that Gorrell was the one who "dropped the ball entirely."

During the stay in the *Varner* case, Bellows talked with Gorrell, who by then was no longer employed by ISU and had his own lawsuit pending against the school for wrongful termination. He independently provided Bellows with the gender equity studies. He also executed an affidavit detailing particulars of a "planning policy database" on which he said the studies were based.

Once the stay was lifted, Bellows confronted Latham with the studies. (The Latham firm was now representing ISU). Bellows demanded that ISU turn over the database on which he alleged the studies were based. Apparently thinking the best defense is a good offense, Latham's first response apparently was to point fingers, saying Bellows had also not adequately complied with discovery requests. Also at this time, Latham began preparing a motion to disqualify Bellows for improperly soliciting privileged information from Gorrell.

For his part, Bellows filed a motion for sanctions against both ISU and Giffin Winning, in part based on the failure to produce the gender equity studies. As relevant here, Bellows' contention in his motion for sanctions was not simply that the studies were not produced. After all, he now had the studies. Rather, he claimed that the gender equity studies were not produced because of a conspiracy to hide the "Planning Policy database." To have produced the studies, he argued, "would have alerted the *Varner* plaintiffs to the existence of the databases. . . . "

We now arrive at the essence of the case—the pivotal facts about the database. At a 4–day hearing on the pending motions, Gorrell testified that the database contained variables relevant to the issue of gender equity and was maintained in a format which enabled a user to prepare comparative studies. He testified that the gender equity studies were prepared from this database. He said he had done one of the studies himself, though he also said he had never personally accessed the database. The actual data processing, he said, was done by his research assistant, Anna Wells, and her preparation of the data for his 1994 study would have taken her no more than a day or two using the database. . . . That apparently was news to Wells. She testified that she did not use any database in compiling the data. . . . Why? Because, as Judge Mihm found, there was no database and never had been. . . .

Nevertheless, Judge Mihm sanctioned Giffin Winning $10,000 for discovery lapses, a sanction which was later vacated. Judge Mihm, however, wisely denied Bellows' request for a default judgment based on the failure to produce the gender equity studies. . . . In addition, although he denied Latham's motion to disqualify Bellows because of his contact with Gorrell, Judge Mihm sanctioned Bellows $10,000 as well. Ultimately, the *Varner* case was settled; mercifully, we think.

We now get to the present malpractice action that TIG filed against Giffin Winning in which the damages TIG alleges are the attorney fees it paid Latham to defend against the sanction motion—a whopping $1.2 million, give or take, for the work of 27 attorneys and various paralegals. It seems that when Latham said it took the motion seriously, it meant it. As we said, TIG paid the bill and was subsequently reimbursed by its reinsurers.

Several issues swirl around in this appeal from the district court's grant of summary judgment for Giffin Winning. . . . Our focus will be on the issue of causation.... The elements of a legal malpractice action in Illinois are well-settled. They are: "(1) the existence of an attorney-client relationship that establishes a duty on the part of the attorney; (2) a negligent act or omission constituting a breach of that duty; (3) proximate cause; and (4) damages." *Lopez v. Clifford Law Offices,* 362 Ill.App.3d 969, 299 Ill.Dec. 53, 841 N.E.2d 465, 470–471 (2005), citing cases.

A legal malpractice case is similar to any other negligence claim, and traditional principles apply. Proximate cause describes two distinct requirements—cause in fact and legal cause. Cause in fact exists only if the defendant's conduct was a "material element and a substantial factor in bringing about the injury." Legal cause, on the other hand, is largely a question of foreseeability. The relevant inquiry is whether "the injury is of a type that a reasonable person would see *as a likely result* of his or her conduct." The occurrence must have been "reasonably" foreseeable: "Not what actually happened, but what the reasonably prudent person would then have foreseen as likely to happen, is the key to the question of reasonableness." *Cunis v. Brennan,* 56 Ill.2d 372, 308 N.E.2d 617, 619 (1974), quoting 2 Law of Torts (1956), sec. 16.9 at 929....

Proximate cause is the issue on which this case falters. Having said that, we recognize that the Illinois courts indicate that proximate cause should ordinarily be decided not as a matter or law, but by a trier of fact. However, in a situation in which it is clear as a matter of law that the injury could not have been foreseeable, Illinois courts have upheld summary judgment on the issue. The situation before us is such a case.

The fundamental negligence allegedly committed by Giffin Winning in the *Varner* case was a failure to produce documents—especially gender equity studies—pursuant to a discovery request. The attorneys had routed the request to Gorrell, who was at that point still employed by ISU. He did not forward the studies to the attorneys. However, the attorneys had copies of the studies, which they also failed to produce. This is a clear breakdown of the discovery process, which we infer was not going at all smoothly on either side of this case.

In this all-too-common situation, the question for us is whether it would be reasonably foreseeable that a failure to produce these documents would result in the injury alleged here. Could the attorneys foresee that Gorrell, who failed to produce the documents when they turned the request over to him, would then, after he became disgruntled with ISU, independently provide the documents to Bellows? Beyond that, would reasonable people foresee that Gorrell would mislead Bellows about a database which did not exist? Would reasonable people then think that, upon hearing Gorrell's story, Bellows' first impulse would be to move for sanctions including default judgment in the case? Would reasonable people foresee that, next, a large law firm, apparently thinking of Judge Mihm as a bit trigger-happy, would jump into high gear out of fear of default judgment and launch an army of 27 attorneys, plus paralegals, to defend against the possibility that Judge Mihm might grant default judgment on the basis of an alleged conspiracy to hide something which does not exist? In other words, was the *Latham* response to a failure to produce documents and the resulting injury foreseeable?

We think it was not as a matter of law. Our point can be illustrated by a very different sort of negligence action. In *Abrams v. City of Chicago*, 211 Ill.2d 251, 285 Ill.Dec. 183, 811 N.E.2d 670 (2004), the city failed to send an ambulance for a woman, Abrams (of course), who was in labor. A friend, who then drove her to the hospital, ran a red light and collided with a car driven by a drug-and-alcohol-impaired driver with a suspended license. Abrams was seriously injured and spent 2 weeks in a coma; sadly, her baby died. The court found, however, that as a matter of law there was no proximate cause. The city could not have foreseen the situation that unfolded. Perhaps a bit callously, the court remarked that "[m]illions of women in labor make it safely to the hospital each year by private transportation."

It is also true—though less tragically so—that countless failures to produce documents occur in the federal courts every year. That is not a good thing. But we are not at a point at which it is foreseeable that such a failure will spawn a million-dollar bill for attorney fees. If it were, litigation would become more of a blood sport than it already is. Lawyers would be even more obsessive about irrelevant and tedious details. No good could come of it.

There is, in fact, nothing which distinguishes the failure to produce in this case with countless others. Judge Mihm himself made this point in response to Bellows' argument that this was the worst discovery abuse he had ever seen. Judge Mihm said: "But you said in your 34 years of practice this was the most shocking thing you had ever seen in terms of this discovery issue. I wonder what kind of practice you've had if that's the case because, boy, in the scheme of things, I've seen things 50 times worse than this."

What is foreseeable as a result of a failure to produce documents is the reasonable procedure set out in Civil Rule of Civil Procedure 37, which provides for sanctions only after other reasonable efforts to work out disagreements fail. It may be that, as Judge Mihm also said, that did not happen enough in this case. But ISU and Giffin Winning could hardly be expected to foresee all this trouble over a phantom database. Why would they? It was ISU's alleged database and Giffin Winning was representing ISU at the time. They knew of no database; they were hiding no

database; there was no database. For Giffin Winning's carelessness in failing to produce documents (which Bellows had in his
possession), the sanction of $10,000 might well have been sus-
tained on appeal. But as a matter of law, the injury alleged here
was not reasonably foreseeable.

Accordingly, the judgment of the district court dismissing this
case is AFFIRMED.

Notes

1. In order to establish a prima facie case, a plaintiff must prove
that the lawyer's breach of duty was both an actual cause (a "but for"
cause, usually), and a proximate cause of legally-cognizable harm.

2. Actual causation is a more common, and often more straightforward, issue. A case fails on actual cause grounds where even if, hypothet-
ically, the lawyer had not acted negligently, the harm to the plaintiff
would have occurred anyway. For example, in *Fang v. Bock*, 305 Mont.
322, 28 P.3d 456 (2001), Fang, a Chinese citizen and lawful permanent
resident of the United States, had been arrested for domestic violence.
He was advised by lawyer Bock to plead guilty, but in giving that advice
Bock did not realize that under federal law domestic violence convictions
are deportable offenses. Several weeks after pleading guilty, Fang was
notified by the INS that he was subject to deportation. He hired new
counsel and withdrew his guilty plea, then pleaded guilty to a lesser
offense. Based on the new conviction, the INS ordered him deported. He
sued Bock for malpractice. The court assumed for the sake of argument
that Bock's advice was negligent. But, said the court, "her advice did not
lead to his current predicament.... Fang's situation regarding deportation is a result of the conduct he has admitted, and is the same following
correct legal advice as it was from following Bock's advice. Therefore,
Fang cannot prove that 'but for' negligent legal advice he could have
avoided deportation...."

3. In a transactional matter, the plaintiff is required to prove that
had the lawyer acted non-negligently, a better deal would have been
struck. See *Viner v. Sweet*, 30 Cal.4th 1232, 135 Cal.Rptr.2d 629, 70 P.3d
1046 (2003). Or, as another court put it, "in cases involving transactional legal malpractice, there must be evidence to establish that the negligence was a substantial factor in bringing about the loss of a gain or a
benefit from the transaction.... [T]he plaintiff must present evidence
that, ... in the absence of negligence by the attorney, the other parties
to the transaction would have recognized plaintiff's interest and plaintiff
would have derived a benefit from it." *Froom v. Perel*, 377 N.J.Super.
298, 872 A.2d 1067 (2005).

4. Proximate cause, as the *TIG* case explains, is about the reasonable foreseeability of the type of harm. That is, in accord with normal
negligence rules, a negligent act is a proximate cause of harm only where
the harm that occurred is of a type that a reasonable person would have

foreseen as a likely result of his or her conduct. See *Andrews v. Saylor*, 134 N.M. 545, 80 P.3d 482 (App. 2003); *First Springfield Bank & Trust v. Galman*, 188 Ill.2d 252, 242 Ill.Dec. 113, 720 N.E.2d 1068 (1999). In most legal malpractice cases, it is not a disputed issue, since most often lawyer malpractice causes monetary losses that are clearly of a foreseeable type. But the issue does sometimes arise, as you can see in *TIG*, when the plaintiff alleges some loss beyond the norm. See also, e.g., *Worsham v. Nix*, 145 P.3d 1055 (Okla. 2006) (widow sued lawyer for causing her husband's suicide, which she claimed occurred as a result of the firm's negligence in handling husband's legal claims against his employer).

5. Courts often say that proof of malpractice causation in a litigated matter requires that the plaintiff prove that had the lawyer acted properly, the client would have won the case. While these are often the facts (*i.e.*, that because of malpractice a case was lost—or, as in *Togstad*, never brought) the statement is not always literally true. What if a lawyer, through incompetence, advises a defendant not to settle a claim for $50,000, and the case later settles for $850,000. In neither case could the client have "won." But should the lawyer nonetheless be liable for malpractice? See *California State Auto. Ass'n Inter–Ins. Bureau v. Parichan, Renberg, Crossman & Harvey*, 84 Cal.App.4th 702, 101 Cal.Rptr.2d 72 (2000). On the flip side, what if a lawyer negligently advises a plaintiff to accept a small settlement when a competent lawyer would have obtained many times that amount? See *White v. Jungbauer*, 128 P.3d 263 (Colo. App. 2005); *Garcia v. Kozlov, Seaton, Romanini & Brooks, P.C.*, 179 N.J. 343, 845 A.2d 602 (2004). In both situations the client "won." Should the lawyer nonetheless be liable for malpractice? Do you see any problems for a plaintiff in proving that a better settlement would have been obtained but for the lawyer's malpractice? See *Merritt v. Hopkins Goldenberg, P.C.*, 362 Ill.App.3d 902, 841 N.E.2d 1003, 299 Ill.Dec. 271 (2005) (holding that plaintiffs' proof was insufficient as a matter of law, reversing a $675,000 jury verdict).

6. Must a plaintiff in a malpractice action prove that the economic loss caused by the lawyer's negligence in a litigated matter was actually collectable? Most courts have said yes, a plaintiff must prove that had the defendant performed adequately "the plaintiff would have succeeded on the merits in the underlying case and would have succeeded in collecting on the resulting judgment, because only then would plaintiff have proven that the lawyer's malfeasance was the proximate cause of plaintiff's loss." *Smith v. Haden*, 868 F.Supp. 1 (D.D.C. 1994). A growing number of jurisdictions, however, place the burden of proving non-collectability on the lawyer. See *Carbone v. Tierney*, 151 N.H. 521, 864 A.2d 308 (2004) (collecting cases); *Lindenman v. Kreitzer*, 7 A.D.3d 30, 775 N.Y.S.2d 4 (2004).

7. What if a client, recognizing the lawyer's malpractice before it really messes things up, expends money to avoid its effects. Can that count as legally-cognizable harm, to support a legal malpractice claim, or is the case not "ripe"? That is, can a plaintiff prove that negligence

caused harm on such facts? See *Porter v. Ogden, Newell & Welch*, 241 F.3d 1334 (11th Cir.2001).

8. Can a client claim as an element of compensatory damages in a malpractice case the amount of lost punitive damages in the underlying action that a non-negligent attorney would have obtained? Courts have split on this issue. Compare *Tri-G, Inc. v. Burke, Bosselman & Weaver*, 222 Ill.2d 218, 856 N.E.2d 389 (2006); *Ferguson v. Lieff, Cabraser, Heimann & Bernstein, LLP*, 30 Cal.4th 1037, 69 P.3d 965, 135 Cal. Rptr.2d 46 (2003) and *Summerville v. Lipsig*, 270 A.D.2d 213, 704 N.Y.S.2d 598 (2000) (not allowing), with *Haberer v. Rice*, 511 N.W.2d 279 (S.D. 1994); *Elliott v. Videan*, 164 Ariz. 113, 791 P.2d 639 (1989); *Hunt v. Dresie*, 241 Kan. 647, 740 P.2d 1046 (1987) (allowing).

9. What if a lawyer negligently fails to make a timely jury request in a trial and the case goes forward before a judge. Can the client sue for legal malpractice? What would the "harm" be in such a situation? Consider the next case.

JONES MOTOR CO. v. HOLTKAMP, LIESE, BECKEMEIER & CHILDRESS, P.C.

United States Court of Appeals, Seventh Circuit, 1999.
197 F.3d 1190.

POSNER, Chief Judge.

The plaintiffs in this legal malpractice suit appeal from its dismissal on the defendants' motion for summary judgment, raising a novel issue concerning the law of legal malpractice. The issue, which arises when as in this case the plaintiff is complaining that his lawyer booted a procedural entitlement, such as the right to a jury trial, is whether the plaintiff must show that his lawyer's negligence not only caused him to lose but brought about an unjust result—the wrong party won. The plaintiffs are the Jones Motor Company, a trucker, and its insurer. The defendants are lawyers who represented Jones in a personal injury lawsuit brought against it by Elston Cannon. Federal jurisdiction is based on diversity of citizenship; and the applicable law, the parties agree, is Illinois's common law of malpractice.

The underlying suit had been filed in a state court in St. Clair County and assigned to a judge who we are told, and accept for purposes of deciding this appeal, has the reputation of favoring plaintiffs in personal injury suits. Jones's lawyers negligently failed to make a timely *effective* request for a jury because they failed to accompany the request with payment of the fee for a jury trial. As a result the case was tried to the judge, who entered a judgment of $2.8 million for the plaintiff; the suit was then settled for $2.5 million. In the present case, the malpractice case, Jones tendered the opinion of an experienced lawyer in St. Clair County that had the case been tried to a jury, the verdict would have been in the neighborhood of $500,000. Jones and its insurer, which paid a part of the $2.5 million settlement, are suing for the $2 million difference. . . .

Issue

[T]he most important issue . . . is whether, and if so when, the loss of a procedural advantage can give rise to a malpractice suit even if the advantage was not essential to the protection of the client's substantive rights. Through the defendants' negligence Jones and its insurer lost their right to a jury trial and were forced to submit to a bench trial—which means they got a trial before an authorized tribunal. They allege no error in the conduct of the trial by the judge whom they did not want to try the case, and they did not appeal from the judgment that he rendered, large as it was. The plaintiffs thus got a fair trial and there is no basis for supposing that the judgment was excessive, albeit it may have been higher than it would have been had Jones's lawyers not thrown away their client's right to a jury trial. Some Illinois cases say or imply that you cannot get a judgment for malpractice against a lawyer unless you can show that you had a meritorious claim (or defense, when the client had been a defendant rather than a plaintiff), and Jones's lawyers argue correctly that their client had no entitlement not to be mulcted by a judgment of $2.8 million.

But we think the real thrust of these cases is that a malpractice plaintiff cannot prevail merely by showing that his claim which his lawyer booted, though baseless, had some nuisance value. Imagine a situation in which a class action is brought and is thrown out as a result of a negligent mistake by the lawyer for the class, who is then sued for tens or hundreds of millions of dollars in another class action, in which it is argued that although the suit was frivolous it is well known that frivolous class actions can sometimes extort sizeable settlements from the defendants, as we pointed out in *In re Rhone–Poulenc Rorer Inc.*, 51 F.3d 1293, 1298 (7th Cir. 1995). To impose malpractice liability for booting a nuisance suit would—like deeming a plaintiff who obtains a nuisance settlement a prevailing party for purposes of entitlement to an award of attorneys' fees, which courts also refuse to do—simply encourage nuisance suits, of which we have enough already.

nuisance suits?

But to say that the plaintiff's loss of a nuisance suit is not a ground for the plaintiff's suing his lawyer is not the same thing as saying that the plaintiff must prove that had it not been for his lawyer's negligence he would have won the suit for sure. Take the classic case of legal malpractice in litigation—failure to file suit before the statute of limitations expires. If the suit thus aborted had only nuisance value, then, as we have just said, the lawyer's negligence would not support a malpractice suit. But if as with most suits the probability of a successful outcome was less than 100 percent, the plaintiff in the malpractice suit could not "prove" that he would have won. The outcome of the suit (had there been no malpractice) might have turned on which of two witnesses the jury would have believed, and if there were a reasonable probability that the defendant would have won the swearing contest then it could not be said that a loss of the case by the plaintiff could only have reflected injustice. Such possibilities do not defeat malpractice liability. *Nicolet Instrument Corp. v. Lindquist & Vennum*, 34 F.3d 453, 455 (7th Cir.1994); 2 Ronald E. Mallen & Jeffrey M. Smith, *Legal Malpractice* § 19.3, p. 600 (4th ed.1996).

There is a difference, however, between saying that a claim can be meritorious without its being certain to prevail at trial and saying that one of the parties would have done better than the other, had it not been for the negligence of his lawyer, regardless of the relative merits of the parties' positions. And that is (at most) this case. Although the judge who tried the case against Jones may have a reputation of being more liberal in personal-injury suits than the average jury in his county, it is impossible to infer from this that the $2.8 million judgment that he rendered against Jones was too high; the average jury verdict in such a case might be too low. Of course if this judge were *prejudiced* against motor carriers, or litigants named Jones, or defendants in personal injury cases, there would be a basis for inferring that the negligence of Jones's lawyer had cost Jones a shot *to which Jones was entitled* at a lower damages award, albeit an entitlement not certain to be enforced even by a jury; but of this there is no evidence.

Yet this analysis is not satisfactory either. We must ask why Illinois allows a defendant in a civil suit to elect to be tried by a jury even though the plaintiff would prefer a bench trial. The answer must be that *each* party is deemed entitled to seek the "protection" of the jury against being tried by a judge. That entitlement, a real legal entitlement and not just a tactical opportunity to obtain a more favorable tribunal, was worth something to Jones, and it was kicked away by the defendants' negligence. The only reason for treating it differently from other entitlements, such as the entitlement to introduce evidence or to enforce a substantive right, is practical; it is the difficulty of valuing its loss. The difficulty becomes impossibility in a case (which is not this case, however) in which, at the time the right to a jury trial is forfeited, the identity of the judge who will try the case in lieu of the jury is not known. There is variance among judges as well as among juries, and it is very hard to say that the average jury is likely to be more favorable to a defendant than the average judge. Hence the foreseeable loss in such a case would be extremely hard to estimate.

What is true, but not helpful to Jones, is that a defendant who has a very *weak* case—a case he deserves to lose—will prefer a jury trial. The reason is that there is greater variance (implying less accuracy) in jury verdicts and therefore a greater chance that a weak case will convince a jury than that it will convince a judge. The fact that Jones wanted a jury instead of a judge would ordinarily signal a weak rather than a strong case, but the inference is countered here by the argument that even with a strong case a defendant might prefer a jury to a judge known to favor plaintiffs in personal-injury suits.

Partly because the precise issue has never arisen before, so far as the parties' research or our own discloses, either in Illinois or in any other jurisdiction, we hesitate to rule out the possibility of convincing an Illinois court to allow a malpractice suit to go forward on the basis of an argument that the plaintiff lost a procedural entitlement even though it was not an entitlement necessary to avert an unjust outcome. But given the uncertainty of harm we think the plaintiff in such a case must do more than the plaintiffs have done here to show that they can prove damages to a reasonable certainty. Some degree of speculation is permissible in computing damages, because reasonable doubts as to remedy ought to be resolved against the wrongdoer; but there are limits. Although there is plenty of evidence that the defendant in any personal-injury case assigned to the judge who presided at *Cannon v. Jones Motor Group, Inc.* would want a jury rather than this judge to determine damages, there is no credible evidence of what a jury might have awarded. The principal evidence is the opinion of the lawyer who thought Cannon's case worth to a jury in the range of $500,000, but this was offered as a bare conclusion without data of actual verdicts in St. Clair County in comparable cases from which some reasonable confidence interval, some range in which any jury verdict would be quite likely to lie, might have been computed. No reasonable trier of fact could have been allowed to award damages to Jones and its insurer on the basis of such unsubstantiated expert testimony.

The plaintiffs argue that the way to compute damages in this case is simply to try the malpractice claim to a jury. That is a bad suggestion quite apart from the fact that a jury in a federal district court is not drawn from the same pool as the jury in a state court. The suggestion overlooks the fact that given the variance among juries, it would be necessary to try the malpractice claim a number of times in order to get a sense of the *average* performance of a jury in this case, and it is the difference between the judge's judgment and the judgment that Jones could have *expected* from a jury, which would be an average jury performance, that is the measure of what Jones lost as a result of its lawyers' negligence. So the suit was rightly dismissed after all.

AFFIRMED.

Notes

1. The normal rule, that damages cannot be recovered when they are too speculative, applies in legal malpractice as well. Was that the plaintiff's problem in *Jones Motor Co.*, or was the problem a matter of the proof adduced? Is there a difference?

2. Is the court's final paragraph an indictment of the "case within a case" requirement? Is the court saying that a plaintiff in a legal malpractice case should have try the "case within a case" numerous times in order to prove damages with the requisite degree of certainty? Would that be a good rule?

3. What if a client suffers mental anguish as a result of economic losses caused by a lawyer's negligence. Is the mental anguish compensable? See *Douglas v. Delp*, 987 S.W.2d 879 (Tex.1999) (no). Could a lawyer's negligent conduct constitute "outrageous" conduct so as to allow a claim for intentional infliction of emotional distress? See *Bennett v. Jones, Waldo, Holbrook & McDonough*, 70 P.3d 17 (Utah 2003) (allegation of improper filing of a lawsuit does not allege outrageousness, as a matter of law); *Ross v. Creel Printing & Pub. Co.*, 100 Cal.App.4th 736, 122 Cal.Rptr.2d 787 (2002) (mere violation of an ethical rule is not outrageous, as a matter of law).

4. What if the mental distress the client suffers is due to a protracted period of pre-trial incarceration, caused by his lawyer's negligent ten-day delay in securing his release from jail? Should that be recoverable? See *Rowell v. Holt*, 850 So.2d 474 (Fla. 2003).

B. Proving a Legal Malpractice Claim

VANDERMAY v. CLAYTON

Supreme Court of Oregon, En Banc, 1999.
328 Or. 646, 984 P.2d 272.

LEESON, J.

In this legal malpractice action, the question is whether the trial court erred in granting defendant's motion for a directed verdict on the ground that, without expert testimony, the jury could not have found that defendant had been negligent. The Court of Appeals held that expert testimony was not necessary and reversed the trial court. For the reasons that follow, we affirm.

... Plaintiff worked for a major oil company for many years in a variety of capacities, including as a dealer representative, training instructor, and territory manager. While working for that company in California, plaintiff and Bob Wester decided that they would like to buy an oil company in Oregon. In 1977, they formed the VanWest Oil Company (VanWest) and negotiated the purchase of Macklin Oil Company (Macklin) in Tillamook. After they had made a tentative agreement for the purchase of Macklin, plaintiff and Wester employed defendant, a Eugene lawyer and Wester's brother-in-law, to "[handle] the legalese with the Macklins' attorney and put the deal together." In addition to buying Macklin, which consisted of two bulk oil plants and several service stations, VanWest leased several other service stations and entered into several supply contracts to deliver gasoline and petroleum products in the area.

After the purchase of Macklin, plaintiff and his wife moved to Tillamook. Defendant served as plaintiff's corporate and personal lawyer from 1977 until March 1990, and plaintiff relied on defendant's legal advice. During plaintiff's ownership of VanWest, the corporation acquired additional service stations and entered into more supply agreements. In 1983, Wester sold his shares in VanWest to plaintiff, and defendant represented both parties in that transaction.

In 1986, plaintiff decided to sell VanWest, and he listed it with a real estate company in Lake Oswego. Three years later, VanWest still was on the market, and plaintiff continued to operate and expand its business. By the end of 1989, VanWest had doubled in size from what it was in 1977, and plaintiff had made improvements at several of its properties, including upgrading tanks and lines, adding car washes at service stations, and putting in a new fuel island at one of the service stations. In the spring or summer of 1989, plaintiff was planning to tear down and replace a service station and add a convenience store on West Marine Drive in Astoria (Astoria site). Those plans included applying for a loan of over $400,000 to finance the project and working with City of Astoria planning and zoning staff to acquire the necessary permits.

By the end of the 1980s, environmental rules affecting underground storage tanks were being implemented at both the national and state levels. Plaintiff realized that the bank loan for the Astoria site upgrade would not be approved without an environmental assessment. Consequently, in October 1989, he hired a company to conduct soil tests at the Astoria site. Those tests revealed soil contamination at depths of five, ten, and fifteen feet. Plaintiff believed that the contamination had been caused by small spills from storage tank filling over the years and that it would not cost much to clean it up. Plaintiff did not report the results of the soil tests to the Department of Environmental Quality (DEQ).

In October 1989, David Harris expressed an interest in buying VanWest. He submitted a written offer to plaintiff on December 19. Paragraph 11 of the offer included an indemnification provision requiring plaintiff to hold Harris harmless "against any claims, environmental or otherwise" existing before the sale. The indemnification provision also stated that Harris would accept the 1989 soil test report that showed some contamination at the Astoria site and that, regarding that site, plaintiff's "indemnity under this paragraph will apply to the contamination conditions described therein."

Negotiations for the sale of VanWest continued for several weeks after Harris submitted his written offer, and defendant represented plaintiff in those negotiations. In January 1990, plaintiff learned that his loan application for the Astoria site upgrade had been rejected. Plaintiff also learned that there was contamination at a VanWest bulk plant site, but he had insurance coverage for any environmental contamination there, subject to a $25,000 deductible. Plaintiff was concerned about the continuing liability that he might face at the Astoria site because he knew that, under paragraph 11 of Harris's offer to purchase VanWest, Harris refused to be responsible for any cleanup at that site. Plaintiff estimated that it would cost about $2,500 to clean up the contamination that was discovered at the Astoria site in 1989. However, to "make the deal fly" with Harris, plaintiff agreed that he would pay up to $5,000 to clean up that site. Plaintiff was not willing to be responsible for more than $5,000 for that cleanup. He instructed defendant to draft a separate indemnity agreement for the sale of VanWest that limited his liability to $5,000 for cleaning up the Astoria site.

Consistent with plaintiff's instructions, on February 26, 1990, defendant submitted to Harris an indemnity agreement that provided, in part:

> "Notwithstanding that Harris Enterprise, Inc. has accepted the environmental report concerning [the Astoria site], the indemnification agreement contained in Paragraph 11 shall apply to any cleanup costs or costs of remediation of the condition existing therein, * * * in an amount up to, but not exceeding, the sum of $5,000.00."

The sale of VanWest to Harris closed on March 1, 1990. The transaction included the sale of most of VanWest's holdings, but it also included some lease-backs to VanWest, an employment contract for plaintiff, a noncompetition agreement, and an indemnity agreement. Because of the large number of documents that had to be signed, the closing lasted for more than two hours. During the closing, Harris informed plaintiff that the indemnity agreement that defendant had drafted was unacceptable to Harris. Plaintiff gave no indication to defendant that, in light of Harris's rejection of that indemnity agreement, plaintiff was willing to be responsible for more than $5,000 to clean up the Astoria site. Harris had his lawyer prepare a different indemnity agreement covering both the bulk site where contaminates had been discovered and the Astoria site. That agreement provided:

"The parties further understand that there is no insurance coverage available for the costs of any cleanup and remedial action at the Astoria site. As between the parties hereto, it is agreed that VanWest shall not be required to expend more than the sum of $5,000 for any costs of cleanup and remedial action at the Astoria site; provided, however, it is understood and agreed that VanWest may be liable for such costs in excess of $5,000 under applicable environmental federal and state laws."

Plaintiff read the agreement and saw that "it said $5,000 liability." He testified that he looked down the table at defendant, who indicated, apparently by the nod of his head, that it was "okay for [plaintiff] to sign it." Plaintiff signed the new indemnity agreement and the other documents, thereby completing the sale of VanWest to Harris. Plaintiff testified that he would not have proceeded with the sale of VanWest if he had known that he would be liable for "something much greater" than $5,000 to clean up the Astoria site.[2]

In October 1990, additional soil tests at the Astoria site revealed substantial contamination. In December, petroleum fumes were detected in an apartment building adjacent to the Astoria site. At that time, under one of the agreements that the parties had signed as part of the sale of VanWest, Harris employed plaintiff as an environmental control officer. Plaintiff began an investigation and soon discovered that the contamination at the Astoria site was extensive. The DEQ informed plaintiff that he should have reported the soil contamination that was discovered in 1989, and it ordered both plaintiff and Harris to clean up the site.

In subsequent litigation between plaintiff and Harris, plaintiff contended that his liability for cleaning up the Astoria site was limited to $5,000, and Harris contended that plaintiff's liability was unlimited. The trial court found that the indemnity agreement that Harris's lawyer had drafted, which plaintiff and Harris signed on March 1, 1990, was ambiguous. Ultimately, plaintiff and Harris settled their litigation, agreeing to share equally the costs of cleaning up the Astoria site. Plaintiff's share of the cost was over $585,000.

Plaintiff brought this action against defendant, alleging legal malpractice and seeking $585,895.02 in damages. At trial, plaintiff

2. Defendant gave a substantially different account of what transpired between him and plaintiff at the closing meeting. According to defendant, he and plaintiff "talked about what the differences were in the form [defendant] had proposed and the form that was actually revised at [the] closing [meeting] and what that meant from the standpoint of potential exposure down the road." Defendant also testified that he told plaintiff that the indemnity agreement that Harris presented at the closing [meeting] "was not an absolute $5,000 limit." However, as noted at the outset of this opinion, we view the facts in the light most favorable to plaintiff and do not seek to resolve conflicts in the parties' testimony.

called one expert witness, a lawyer who, at that time, had specialized in environmental law for over 25 years at a large law firm in Portland. Plaintiff asked the expert if he had an opinion about what a lawyer in defendant's position, exercising due care, skill, and diligence in representing his client, would have done regarding the indemnity agreement that Harris presented to plaintiff on March 1, 1990. Defendant objected to that question on the ground that plaintiff had failed to lay an adequate foundation. According to defendant, plaintiff had failed to establish whether the expert was familiar with the quality of care that ordinarily is exercised by general practitioners in small law firms. The trial court excused the jury and conducted a hearing ... to determine whether an adequate foundation existed for the expert's opinion testimony.

In that hearing, the expert testified that he did not know the standard of care that would apply to a practitioner in defendant's circumstances but that there were others in his firm who did business with small firm practitioners. Plaintiff did not make an offer of proof regarding the expert's opinion about whether defendant's conduct breached the applicable standard of care.

The trial court concluded that the foundation for the expert's testimony was inadequate, because the expert was not personally aware of the standard of care applicable to general practitioners who provide advice in circumstances like those presented in this case. The court therefore sustained defendant's objection. Plaintiff then rested his case.

Defendant moved for a directed verdict ... arguing that, without expert testimony on whether defendant had breached the standard of care, plaintiff had failed to present sufficient evidence. Plaintiff responded that no expert testimony was required because defendant's negligence was a simple matter of defendant's failure to secure an indemnity agreement that limited plaintiff's liability for cleaning up the Astoria site to $5,000. The trial court granted defendant's motion. It held that expert testimony was required, because it is not within the common knowledge of jurors what a lawyer in defendant's position should have done in the circumstances presented by this case.

On plaintiff's appeal, the Court of Appeals ... held that any error in excluding the expert's testimony would not justify reversal. However, the Court of Appeals agreed with plaintiff that, in this case, expert testimony was not required, because defendant "either did or did not comply" with plaintiff's specific instructions to draft an indemnity agreement that would limit plaintiff's liability at the Astoria site to $5,000. The Court of Appeals therefore reversed the trial court....

This court has not addressed whether expert testimony is required in legal malpractice actions to establish breach of the standard of care. However, this court has held that, "in most charges of negligence against professional persons, expert testimony is required to establish what the reasonable practice is in the community." *Getchell v. Mansfield,* 260 Or. 174, 179, 489 P.2d 953 (1971). Specifically, expert testimony is required if the issues are not within the knowledge of the ordinary lay juror. Expert testimony is not required if, without an expert's opinion, the jury is capable of deciding whether the professional's conduct was reasonable.

With respect to the need for expert witness testimony, legal malpractice actions are no different from other professional malpractice actions. Whether expert testimony is necessary to establish that a defendant's conduct fell below the standard of care is a legal question that the court must determine by examining the particular malpractice issues that the case presents.

Viewed in the light most favorable to plaintiff, the evidence in this case is that plaintiff told defendant that he wanted to limit his liability to $5,000 for cleaning up the contamination at the Astoria site, and he instructed defendant to prepare an indemnity agreement to accomplish that goal. Defendant understood that a limit on plaintiff's liability for cleaning up that site was a critical condition that plaintiff had placed on the sale of VanWest to Harris. Viewing the evidence in the light most favorable to plaintiff, plaintiff would not have sold VanWest if he had understood that he would be liable after the sale for substantially more money to clean up the Astoria site. Harris rejected the indemnity agreement that defendant had drafted at plaintiff's request and submitted another indemnity agreement at the closing meeting, but those facts did not alter plaintiff's directives to defendant to obtain the indemnification that plaintiff requested. Although defendant knew or should have known that the indemnity agreement drafted by Harris's lawyer did not limit plaintiff's liability for cleaning up the Astoria site to $5,000, defendant instructed plaintiff to sign that agreement nonetheless.

The facts surrounding the sale of VanWest were complicated, because the sale involved many agreements, there were disputes over which indemnity agreement would be acceptable to the parties, and both plaintiff and Harris were aware of the implications of environmental contamination. Nonetheless, whether defendant failed to warn plaintiff that the indemnification agreement that plaintiff was signing did not contain the protections that plaintiff insisted on is straightforward. If defendant failed to do so, then he breached the standard of care he owed to his client. A lay jury is capable of making that determination without expert testimony. The trial court therefore erred in granting defendant's motion for a directed verdict on the ground that, without expert testimony, plaintiff failed to present evidence from which the jury could find that defendant breached the standard of care.

The decision of the Court of Appeals is affirmed. The judgment of the circuit court is reversed, and the case is remanded to the circuit court for further proceedings.

Notes

1. Bringing a legal malpractice claim is expensive, in part because an expert is usually needed to testify about the standard of care, whether it was breached, and often whether that breach caused harm. See, e.g., *Kaempe v. Myers*, 367 F.3d 958 (D.C. Cir. 2004) (failure to present expert testimony on the standard of care in a patent suit precluded malpractice claims); *Barth v. Reagan*, 139 Ill.2d 399, 564 N.E.2d 1196, 151 Ill.Dec. 534 (1990) (reversing jury verdict for plaintiff on the ground that she did not call an expert to testify in case involving a lawyer's negligence in defending foreclosure actions); *Johnson v. Carleton*, 765 A.2d 571 (Me. 2001) (lawyer entitled to summary judgment in a legal malpractice case because of the client-plaintiff's failure to timely designate an expert witness on causation issue); *Carbone v. Tierney*, 151 N.H. 521, 864 A.2d 308 (2004) (expert testimony required on causation); *Alexander v. Turtur & Assocs., Inc.*, 146 S.W.3d 113 (Tex. 2004) (expert testimony required on causation).

2. The *Vandermay* court, in accord with most others, draws a parallel between legal malpractice and medical malpractice. Most of us would probably agree that non-doctors lack an adequate understanding of medical procedures to reach a reasoned conclusion without the aid of expert testimony as to whether a doctor has committed medical malpractice. But is that equally true with legal work? Or is it just that the "common understanding" exception to the expert rule will probably apply more often in legal malpractice cases than it does in medical malpractice cases? See, e.g., *Zok v. Collins*, 18 P.3d 39 (Alaska 2001) (lawyer's failure to oppose several defense motions at trial were "so obviously a breach of an attorney's duty to his client that the average juror untrained in the law would be able to make a finding of negligence"); *Baiko v. Mays*, 140 Ohio App.3d 1, 746 N.E.2d 618 (2000) (lawyer's failure to review records and financial books of dental practice that plaintiff/client was purchasing was an allegation of malpractice within the ordinary understanding of a lay jury).

3. Is the expert witness requirement the same in a jury trial and a bench trial? That is, can a trial judge's knowledge of the standard of care, and what constitutes breach, obviate the need for the plaintiff to present expert testimony on those matters? See *Dubreuil v. Witt*, 80 Conn.App. 410, 835 A.2d 477 (2003), *aff'd*, 271 Conn. 782, 860 A.2d 698 (2004).

4. *Geographic scope.* Many courts regard the relevant jurisdiction for purposes of the lawyer standard of care—and thus for the testifying expert—as the state, not the particular locality. See, e.g, *Brett v. Berkowitz*, 706 A.2d 509 (Del.1998); *Moore v. Lubnau*, 855 P.2d 1245 (Wyo.1993) (adopting a statewide standard of care, which rendered an expert affida-

vit insufficient because it spoke only to the standard of care in the county); see also *Kellos v. Sawilowsky*, 254 Ga. 4, 325 S.E.2d 757 (1985). Many other courts do not draw any rigid geographical boundaries, saying that the fact that the testifying expert is not admitted in the same state as the lawyer-defendant goes to the weight of the testimony, not its admissibility. See, e.g., *Smith v. Haynsworth, Marion, McKay & Geurard*, 322 S.C. 433, 472 S.E.2d 612 (1996); *Walker v. Bangs*, 92 Wash.2d 854, 601 P.2d 1279 (1979). Why might the state, as opposed to the particular town or county, be considered the relevant jurisdiction for malpractice purposes? Would a national standard make sense?

5. *Specialists*. Specialist lawyers are usually held to the standard of care of other lawyers in the same speciality. Thus a plaintiff suing a specialist for malpractice must generally retain an expert from the same speciality. Not all courts agree, however, holding that such matters go only to weight, not admissibility.

6. Could a party in a malpractice case call the actual judge from the underlying case to testify about what he or she would have done if particular actions had been taken by the lawyer? Is the real question in the case what the actual judge would have done, or is it something else? See *Marrs v. Kelly*, 95 S.W.3d 856 (Ky. 2003).

C. Defenses

1. Contributory Negligence

CLARK v. ROWE

Supreme Judicial Court of Massachusetts, 1998.
428 Mass. 339, 701 N.E.2d 624.

WILKINS, Chief Justice.

The plaintiff sustained losses in real estate investments that she attributed to the fault of the defendant Harvey Rowe, who was her lawyer, and to the fault of the defendant Shawn Potter, who was her banker.

After a trial of her various claims, judgment was entered for each defendant. The trial judge directed a verdict for Potter. In a special verdict, the jury decided certain claims in favor of Rowe, but also answered that Rowe, as lawyer for the plaintiff, was negligent in representing her in connection with the refinancing of a loan secured by property in Haverhill. That negligence, the jury found, was a substantial contributing cause of certain of the plaintiff's substantial losses. The jury also found, however, that the plaintiff was negligent in connection with that refinancing and that seventy per cent of all the negligence was hers and thirty per cent was Rowe's. The judge ordered the entry of judgment for Rowe, applying principles of comparative negligence to deny the plaintiff recovery for Rowe's malpractice in the refinancing of the Haverhill property. The plaintiff's principal contention in her appeal, which we transferred here on our own motion, is that comparative fault is inapplicable to her claim against Rowe. We affirm the judgments for Rowe and Potter.

We turn first to the question of the appropriateness of the entry of judgment in favor of Rowe notwithstanding the jury's special verdict in favor of the plaintiff. In her appeal, the plaintiff does not argue, as she did below, that the evidence was insufficient to submit the question of her contributory fault to the jury. There was evidence that she had substantial experience in real estate matters and was a sophisticated business person.

[The plaintiff failed to object appropriately to the judge's jury instruction on comparative negligence.] Although the issue was not preserved for appellate review, the question whether comparative fault can properly be considered in a malpractice action against a lawyer is unanswered in this Commonwealth. The issue is fully briefed and likely to arise in other cases. We choose in our discretion to discuss the issue....

The fact that a malpractice claim against a lawyer may be viewed as an action in contract does not make contributory fault automatically irrelevant. The standard of care normally applied is whether the lawyer failed to exercise reasonable care and skill in handling the client's matter, a classical tort negligence standard. A malpractice claim does not sound exclusively in either contract or tort. A lawyer's negligence may constitute a violation of an implied condition of the contractual relationship between lawyer and client but that does not foreclose the application of contributory fault principles to the client's claim....

The plaintiff makes a persuasive argument that our comparative negligence statute does not apply to an action based on a claim of financial loss caused by a lawyer's negligence. That statute, G.L. c. 231, § 85 ... concerns recovery of damages for negligence "resulting in death or in injury to person or property." The quoted language is a limitation on the word "damages." If the injury to "property" included economic loss, little would be left of the limitation in § 85 that concerns property. Moreover, cases have suggested that pecuniary loss is not injury or damage to property.

The inapplicability of § 85 to claims of legal malpractice does not dispose of the matter. The question remains whether we would apply the public policy considerations underlying § 85 to support a common law rule of comparative negligence in a case such as this. Many courts in jurisdictions having a comparative negligence statute similar to ours ("damages ... resulting in ... injury to ... property") have, expressly or implicitly, without even referring to the statute, recognized that contributory fault properly may apply in a malpractice action against a lawyer. We recognize the doctrine of comparative negligence in medical malpractice actions, and there is no reason not to do so in legal malpractice actions. See *Theobald v. Byers,* 193 Cal.App.2d 147, 150, 13 Cal.Rptr. 864 (1961) ("Doctors and dentists are held to this higher standard of care and their services can also be said to be of a fiduciary and confidential nature. Hence it would seem clear that similar rules of law would be applicable to all three professions"); *Lyle, Siegel, Croshaw & Beale, P.C. v. Tidewater Capital Corp.,* 249 Va. 426, 432, 457 S.E.2d 28 (1995) ("With respect to contributory negligence, we discern no logical reason for treating differently legal malpractice and medical malpractice actions."); *Cicorelli v. Capobianco,* 90 A.D.2d 524, 524, 453 N.Y.S.2d 21 (N.Y.App.Div. 1982), aff'd. 59 N.Y.2d 626, 463 N.Y.S.2d 195, 449 N.E.2d 1273 (1983) ("[T]he courts of this State have recognized that both physicians and attorneys may plead subsequent negligence by other parties as a mitigating factor"). Cf. *Somma v. Gracey,* 15 Conn.App. 371, 378, 544 A.2d 668 (1988) ("[w]e see no basis for distinguishing between actions for legal malpractice and other claims sounding in negligence"); Restatement (Third) of The Law Governing Lawyers § 76, Comment d (Tent. Draft No. 8, 1997).

Comparative fault appropriately applies to a client's claim of malpractice by a lawyer. See *Pinkham v. Burgess,* 933 F.2d 1066, 1073 (1st Cir.1991) ("[a]ll of the courts that have considered the issue have held that the defense of contributory negligence applies in legal malpractice actions, despite the fiduciary nature of the attorney-client relationship"). The limitations on recovery stated in G.L. c. 231, § 85, appropriately guide us to adopt them as a common law rule. Because the plaintiff's negligence exceeded that of the defendant Rowe, the judge was correct in entering judgment for Rowe on the count alleging malpractice. . . .

We add that there are bases for the civil liability of a lawyer apart from a claim of malpractice. Intentional breaches of fiduciary duties, such as the misappropriation of funds, surely can be a basis for attorney liability. Breaches of client confidences, inappropriate conflicts of interest, and the use of advantages arising out of the client-lawyer relationship may be intentional wrongs or may be negligent acts depending on the circumstances. If a breach of one of these fiduciary duties is a substantial cause of injury to the client, the lawyer could be liable to the client. We need not decide the extent to which, if at all, the client's negligence in particular circumstances would reduce or eliminate the client's right to recover damages for the lawyer's breach of fiduciary duty. . . .

Judgments affirmed.

Notes

1.   Most courts allow a client's contributory negligence to be used as a defense in a legal malpractice suit. There are three main approaches

to contributory negligence. About a dozen states follow a "pure" form of comparison, in which a plaintiff's fault will reduce recovery in the percentage of fault found by the jury, but will not bar recovery. Four states follow the older rule that a plaintiff's negligence bars a claim entirely. The majority of states (Massachusetts is in this category) bar recovery only if the plaintiff's negligence is found to be greater than or equal to that of the defendant; otherwise the plaintiff's recovery is reduced by the percentage of the plaintiff's fault.

2. Is it good policy to allow a lawyer to defend a malpractice claim by raising the client's contributory negligence? In *Stroud v. Arthur Andersen & Co.*, 37 P.3d 783 (Okla.2001), the court held that an accounting firm could not attempt to excuse its own misconduct by blaming the plaintiff's negligence, unless that negligence interfered with the accountants' ability to perform their job. In such a situation, the plaintiff's actions, not the accountants', caused the harm. The court concluded that "to hold otherwise would render illusory the notion that an accounting firm is negligent when its performance breaches the duty of care it owes as a professional to the public and causes injury." The court asserted that its holding applies to "all professionals." Does this ruling represent good policy?

3. In *Lopez v. Clifford Law Offices, P.C.*, 362 Ill.App.3d 969, 841 N.E.2d 465, 299 Ill.Dec. 53 (2005), the court said, "It is axiomatic, as one court aptly put it, that the duty of an attorney encompasses protecting a client 'from self-inflicted harm.'" (Quoting *Conklin v. Hannoch Weisman*, 145 N.J. 395, 678 A.2d 1060 (1996).) Might that be taken to mean that a lawyer should not be able to use his client's negligence as a defense—since the lawyer's duty is to protect the client from his own negligence?

4. What if a client signs a settlement stipulation prepared by a lawyer without reading it first, then sues the lawyer for negligently drafting the document? Can the client maintain a legal malpractice action? See *Arnav Industries, Inc. Retirement Trust v. Brown, Raysman, Millstein, Felder & Steiner, L.L.P.*, 96 N.Y.2d 300, 751 N.E.2d 936, 727 N.Y.S.2d 688 (2001) (yes, where the lawyer had misrepresented the document's contents).

5. Look back at *Vandermay* in subsection B above. Could the lawyer in that case have argued that the plaintiff-client was contributorily negligent in signing the indemnification agreement?

6. A client discharges a lawyer, then hires a new lawyer who acts negligently, then sues both lawyers for malpractice. Can the first lawyer escape liability (entirely even if negligent) on the ground that the second lawyer's negligence is a superseding cause of harm? Or can the first lawyer base a defense of comparative negligence on the malpractice of the second lawyer? See *Andrews v. Saylor*, 134 N.M. 545, 80 P.3d 482 (App. 2003).

7. Some jurisdictions have applied the doctrine of *in pari delicto* ("in equal fault"), commonly called "unclean hands," to bar a plaintiff's

malpractice suit entirely where the client has engaged in dishonest or immoral practices in the matter. See *Choquette v. Isacoff*, 65 Mass.App. Ct. 1, 836 N.E.2d 329 (2005); *Evans v. Cameron*, 121 Wis.2d 421, 360 N.W.2d 25 (1985); *Robins v. Laskey*, 123 Ill.App.3d 194, 78 Ill.Dec. 655, 462 N.E.2d 774 (1984).

2.　*Statute of Limitations*

SHUMSKY v. EISENSTEIN

Court of Appeals of New York, 2001.
96 N.Y.2d 164, 750 N.E.2d 67, 726 N.Y.S.2d 365.

LEVINE, J.

In April 1993, plaintiffs David Shumsky and Marjorie Scheiber retained defendant Paul Eisenstein, an attorney, for the specific purpose of commencing an action against Charles Fleischer, a home inspector, for breach of contract. Defendant did not contact plaintiffs to keep them informed and, in fact, avoided plaintiffs' inquiries regarding the status of the matter.

In response to a formal disciplinary grievance plaintiffs filed against him in September of 1997, defendant admitted that he had failed to commence the action against Fleischer before the Statute of Limitations had expired in March of 1994 and stated that, after two years, when his clients finally contacted him, he was "too embarrassed to discuss the matter and put it off."* Thereafter, on December 5, 1997, plaintiffs commenced this legal malpractice action against defendant, sounding in both contract and tort. Defendant moved for summary judgment dismissing the complaint on the ground that plaintiffs' action was barred by the three-year Statute of Limitations, since the malpractice occurred in March 1994 when defendant failed to commence the action against Fleischer. Supreme Court denied defendant's motion, concluding that the continuous representation doctrine tolled the limitations period at least until defendant finally revealed, in 1997, that he had failed to timely commence plaintiffs' action against the home inspector.

The Appellate Division reversed, granted defendant's motion and dismissed the complaint. The court held that, on these facts, the doctrine of continuous representation was not applicable to toll the limitations period. Because plaintiffs' contract action was never commenced and defendant " 'did nothing to foster the impression or to lull [the] plaintiff into believing that the action [against Fleischer] was proceeding,' " the Appellate Division held that defendant was not representing plaintiffs in their contract

---

* In September 1998, the Grievance Committee for the Tenth Judicial District concluded that defendant's actions constituted a breach of the Code of Professional Responsibility and issued a Letter of Admonition to the attorney.

action against Fleischer [brackets in original]. We granted leave to appeal and now reverse.

An action to recover damages for legal malpractice accrues when the malpractice is committed (*see, Glamm v. Allen,* 57 N.Y.2d 87, 93, 453 N.Y.S.2d 674, 439 N.E.2d 390). "What is important is when the malpractice was committed, not when the client discovered it" (*id.*, at 95, 453 N.Y.S.2d 674, 439 N.E.2d 390). Here, plaintiffs' legal malpractice cause of action against defendant accrued in March of 1994, when the Statute of Limitations had expired on the underlying breach of contract action plaintiffs retained defendant to commence.... Because plaintiffs did not commence this action until December 5, 1997, ... plaintiffs' action is time-barred unless the continuous representation doctrine is available and applies to these facts.

The continuous representation doctrine, like the continuous treatment rule, its counterpart with respect to medical malpractice claims, "recognizes that a person seeking professional assistance has a right to repose confidence in the professional's ability and good faith, and realistically cannot be expected to question and assess the techniques employed or the manner in which the services are rendered" (*Greene v. Greene,* 56 N.Y.2d 86, 94, 451 N.Y.S.2d 46, 436 N.E.2d 496). The doctrine also appreciates the client's dilemma if required to sue the attorney while the latter's representation on the matter at issue is ongoing:

> "Neither is a person expected to jeopardize his pending case or his relationship with the attorney handling that case during the period that the attorney continues to represent the person. Since it is impossible to envision a situation where commencing a malpractice suit would not affect the professional relationship, the rule of continuous representation tolls the running of the Statute of Limitations on the malpractice claim until the ongoing representation is completed" (*Glamm v. Allen, supra,* 57 N.Y.2d, at 94, 453 N.Y.S.2d 674, 439 N.E.2d 390).

Application of the continuous representation or treatment doctrine is nonetheless generally limited to the course of representation concerning a specific legal matter or of treatment of a specific ailment or complaint; "[t]he concern, of course, is whether there has been continuous treatment, and not merely a continuing relation between physician and patient" (*McDermott v. Torre,* 56 N.Y.2d 399, 405, 452 N.Y.S.2d 351, 437 N.E.2d 1108). Thus, the doctrine is not applicable to a client's or patient's continuing general relationship with a lawyer or physician involving only routine contact for miscellaneous legal representation or medical care, unrelated to the matter upon which the allegations of malpractice are predicated. Instead, in the context of a legal malpractice action, the continuous representation doctrine tolls

RULE

not just a general cont. relationship

the Statute of Limitations only where the continuing representation pertains specifically to the matter in which the attorney committed the alleged malpractice.

Case

While it is true that this Court and others have held that a professional's failure to take action or provide services necessary to protect a client's or patient's interests does not, standing alone, constitute representation or treatment for purposes of tolling the Statute of Limitations, we reject defendant's contention, and the Appellate Division's conclusion, that the instant matter falls within that category of cases. The court below relied on *Ashmead v. Groper* (*supra*), a case in which the plaintiff retained the defendant attorney in 1981 to represent him in his pursuit of workers' compensation benefits. Shortly after the attorney had been retained, the plaintiff received an award based upon an established average weekly wage and, in May of 1984, the case was closed by the Workers' Compensation Board. In 1995 the plaintiff commenced a legal malpractice action alleging negligence in establishing plaintiff's average weekly wage. The timeliness of that action turned on whether the continuous representation doctrine tolled the applicable limitations period from May of 1984 until September 1992, when plaintiff had obtained another lawyer. In concluding that the doctrine did not apply to toll the limitations period, the Appellate Division noted that because "plaintiff was unaware of the need for any further legal services in connection with his workers' compensation claim, he was not faced with the dilemma that gave rise to the continuous treatment/representation doctrine."

Case

Similarly, *Young v. New York City Health & Hosps. Corp.* [,91 N.Y.2d 291, 670 N.Y.S.2d 169, 693 N.E.2d 196] involved a malpractice suit alleging failure to timely diagnose and treat plaintiff's breast cancer. There, a mammogram report had recommended a biopsy to rule out any malignancy but that recommendation was never communicated to plaintiff, even upon her return visits for treatment of an unrelated condition. Looking to the underlying purpose behind the continuous treatment doctrine—to avoid undermining the continuing trust developing between a professional and his or her client or patient—this Court determined that the doctrine was not applicable in the absence of contemplated subsequent treatment because "a patient who is not aware of the need for further treatment of a condition is not faced with the dilemma that the doctrine is designed to prevent." Even in *Young*, however, this Court did recognize that treatment does not "necessarily terminate upon a patient's last visit if further care or monitoring of the condition is 'explicitly anticipated by both physician and patient'."

d.quote

This case is distinguishable from both *Ashmead* and *Young*. In those cases, the plaintiffs were unaware of any need for further legal services or medical treatment, and there was no mutual understanding with the professional that further services were needed in connection with the specific subject matter out of which the malpractice arose. By contrast, plaintiffs here were acutely aware of such need for further representation on the specific subject matter underlying the malpractice claim and there was a mutual understanding to that effect. Moreover, the record indisputably established that plaintiffs were left with the reasonable impression that defendant was, in fact, actively addressing their legal needs. . . .

By a parity of reasoning, "continuous representation" in the context of a legal malpractice action does not automatically come to an end where, as here, pursuant to a retainer agreement, an attorney and client both explicitly anticipate continued representation. Plaintiffs retained defendant for the sole purpose of pursuing their specific contract claim. Thus, upon signing the retainer agreement, plaintiffs and the defendant reasonably intended that their professional relationship of trust and confidence—focused entirely upon the very matter in which the alleged malpractice was committed—would continue. Indeed, even in his letter to the Grievance Committee, defendant acknowledged that his services had been retained specifically to "investigate, research and *prosecute* their claim against Fleischer"—the equivalent of a "course of treatment" in the [medical] malpractice context. Moreover, . . . plaintiffs' attempt to contact defendant on at least one occasion, in October of 1996, inquiring about the status of their case and requesting a letter in response, confirms this understanding and supports application of the doctrine here. Accordingly, this case appears to fall well within that realm of *continuous* professional services already recognized by this Court in the medical malpractice context.

Of course, even when further representation concerning the specific matter in which the attorney allegedly committed the complained of malpractice is needed and contemplated by the client, the continuous representation toll would nonetheless end once the client is informed or otherwise put on notice of the attorney's withdrawal from representation. Here, at the earliest, plaintiffs may have received reasonable notice of defendant's withdrawal from representation upon defendant's interminable failure to respond to their telephone inquiries of October 18, 1996. We thus conclude that, on these facts, defendant was continuously representing plaintiffs at least until, after his extended failure to return their telephone inquiries of October 1996, they may have been put on sufficient notice that the representation had ceased. Even calculating the limitations period from that time, this action, brought just under 14 months from that date, was still timely.

Accordingly, the order of the Appellate Division should be reversed, with costs, and defendant's motion for summary judgment denied.

Notes

1. "Decisions on the statute of limitations in lawyer malpractice claims are quite diverse if not actually chaotic." Dan B. Dobbs, The Law of Torts § 491 (2000). Some courts say that a claim accrues at the time the harm occurs, even if the plaintiff was not aware of it at the time. There is a more modern trend (reflecting a larger trend in tort law generally) towards the "discovery rule," pursuant to which the malpractice claim accrues only when the plaintiff discovers or should reasonably have discovered the lawyer's negligence and the harm it caused. See, e.g., *Watkins v. Hedman, Hileman & Lacosta*, 321 Mont. 419, 91 P.3d 1264 (2004). Some states have adopted a discovery rule, but bar claims that occur more than a certain number of years after the harm has occurred. See, e.g., Cal. Civ. Proc. Code § 340.6 (limitations period is one year after plaintiff discovers or should have discovered "the facts constituting the wrongful act or omission," but not more than four years from the date of occurrence). In *Samuels v. Mix*, 22 Cal.4th 1, 989 P.2d 701, 91 Cal.Rptr.2d 273 (1999), the court held that the defendant has the burden of proof on the issue of whether the plaintiff should have discovered the malpractice within the one-year period.

2. The continuous representation rule, applied above in *Shumsky*, is growing in popularity and is now followed in a majority of states. See, e.g., *Biomet, Inc. v. Barnes & Thornburg*, 791 N.E.2d 760 (Ind.App. 2003); *Bailey v. Tucker*, 533 Pa. 237, 621 A.2d 108 (1993). Some states have adopted it by statute. See, e.g., Cal. Code Civ. Proc. § 340.6(a)(2) (tolling the SOL during the time "the attorney continues to represent the plaintiff regarding the specific subject matter in which the alleged wrongful act or omission occurred"). Is the continuous representation rule a good one? Do the rationales behind it seem sound?

3. The continuous representation rule applies only when the continuous representation concerns the very same matter that is the subject of the malpractice claim. A factual issue might arise if it is not clear when the representation ended. See *Gonzalez v. Kalu*, 140 Cal.App.4th 21, 43 Cal.Rptr.3d 866 (2006) (question of fact presented where client believed lawyer was working on case when he was not); *DeLeo v. Nusbaum*, 263 Conn. 588, 821 A.2d 744 (2003) (client's sending a letter to his former wife complaining of lawyer's representation was not de facto termination of client-lawyer relationship). What if the case in which the lawyer committed malpractice is over, but the same lawyer briefly reopens the matter in an attempt to correct an error in his representation. Does the reopening of the closed case "restart" the statute of limitations period? See *Bauer v. Ferriby & Houston, P.C.*, 235 Mich.App. 536, 599 N.W.2d 493 (1999).

4. Under the continuous representation rule (or an extension of it), should the statute of limitations be tolled after the client has fired the defendant lawyer and hired another lawyer who is trying to reverse or

mitigate the harm? See *VanSickle v. Kohout*, 215 W.Va. 433, 599 S.E.2d 856 (2004).

5. Does the continuous representation rule mean that the client's negligence in continuing the relationship is excused? In *Frederick Road Ltd. Partnership v. Brown & Sturm*, 360 Md. 76, 756 A.2d 963 (2000), the court reversed a summary judgment for the lawyer-defendants, saying, "A relationship which is built on trust and confidence generally gives the confiding party the right to relax his or her guard and rely on the good faith of the other party so long as the relationship continues to exist." This is not absolute, the court said; if "something occurs to make him or her suspicious," the client would then have a duty to investigate the quality of services received. The statute of limitations would begin to run "from the time the confiding party receives actual notice of the facts which placed him or her upon inquiry notice." What if the lawyer assures the client that everything is all right and that all problems will be fixed if the client will just be patient? See also *Supik v. Bodie, Nagle, Dolina, Smith & Hobbs, P.A.*, 152 Md.App. 698, 834 A.2d 170 (2003) (reasonableness of client's reliance on law firm's advice a question of fact going to continuous representation rule's application).

6. *Accrual of claim in litigation malpractice.* If a plaintiff discovers malpractice during a trial, does the statute of limitations begin to run at that time, or when appeals have been exhausted? Compare *Wettanen v. Cowper*, 749 P.2d 362 (Alaska 1988) (statute begins to run upon discovery) with *Pedigo v. Breen*, 169 S.W.3d 831 (Ky. 2004) (statute begins to run when the underlying litigation is final); *Apex Towing Co. v. Tolin*, 41 S.W.3d 118 (Tex.2001) (same); and *Fremont Indemnity Co. v. Carey, Dwyer, Eckhart, Mason & Spring, P.A.*, 796 So.2d 504 (Fla.2001) (same, which in this case was 12 years after the lawyer's error). Which is the better rule, and why?

3. Immunities

Lawyers performing certain roles may be immune from malpractice suits. For example, a lawyer appointed by a court to represent the rights of a child in a marital dissolution matter may be held to be immune from a malpractice suit on the rationale that the lawyer is performing a "judicial function." See *Carrubba v. Moskowitz*, 274 Conn. 533, 877 A.2d 773 (2005). Granting such immunity will depend on particular state statutes covering particular appointments. See *Fox v. Wills*, 390 Md. 620, 890 A.2d 726 (2006) (determining that Maryland statutes do not provide for any immunity for a lawyer appointed by a judge to represent a minor child in a divorce proceeding, rejecting analogies to other states' case law interpreting different state statutes).

Lawyers may also be able to escape malpractice liability in some situations because a federal law preempts state malpractice law. For example, lawyers retained to represent a labor union to perform services related to a collective bargaining agreement are immune from being sued for malpractice by individual union members, because of the preclusive effect of Labor Management Relations Act § 301(b). See, e.g., *Carino v. Stefan,* 376 F.3d 156 (3d Cir. 2004); *Dahl v. Rosenfeld,* 316 F.3d 1074 (9th Cir. 2003); *Waterman v. Transport Workers' Union Local 100,* 176 F.3d 150 (2d Cir. 1999); *Arnold v. Air Midwest, Inc.,* 100 F.3d 857 (10th Cir. 1996); *Peterson v. Kennedy,* 771 F.2d 1244 (9th Cir. 1985). This malpractice immunity was extended to a lawyer employed by a union of state employees, governed by state labor laws, in *Weiner v. Beatty,* 121 Nev. 243, 116 P.3d 829 (2005). The aggrieved client's exclusive remedy, held the court, was to file a claim against the union for breach of the duty of fair representation.

§ 3. INEFFECTIVE ASSISTANCE OF COUNSEL

STRICKLAND v. WASHINGTON

Supreme Court of the United States, 1984.
466 U.S. 668, 104 S.Ct. 2052, 80 L.Ed.2d 674.

Justice O'CONNOR delivered the opinion of the Court.

This case requires us to consider the proper standards for judging a criminal defendant's contention that the Constitution requires a conviction or death sentence to be set aside because counsel's assistance at the trial or sentencing was ineffective.

I

A

During a 10–day period in September 1976, respondent planned and committed three groups of crimes, which included three brutal stabbing murders, torture, kidnaping, severe assaults, attempted murders, attempted extortion, and theft. After his two accomplices were arrested, respondent surrendered to police and voluntarily gave a lengthy statement confessing to the third of the criminal episodes. The State of Florida indicted respondent for kidnaping and murder and appointed an experienced criminal lawyer to represent him.

Counsel actively pursued pretrial motions and discovery. He cut his efforts short, however, and he experienced a sense of hopelessness about the case, when he learned that, against his specific advice, respondent had also confessed to the first two murders. By the date set for trial, respondent was subject to indictment for three counts of first-degree murder and multiple counts of robbery, kidnaping for ransom, breaking and entering and assault, attempted murder, and conspiracy to commit robbery. Respondent waived his right to a jury trial, again acting against counsel's advice, and pleaded guilty to all charges, including the three capital murder charges.

In the plea colloquy, respondent told the trial judge that, although he had committed a string of burglaries, he had no significant prior criminal record and that at the time of his criminal spree he was under extreme stress caused by his inability to support his family. He also stated, however, that he accepted responsibility for the crimes. The trial judge told respondent that he had "a great deal of respect for people who are willing to step forward and admit their responsibility" but that he was making no statement at all about his likely sentencing decision.

Counsel advised respondent to invoke his right under Florida law to an advisory jury at his capital sentencing hearing. Respondent rejected the advice and waived the right. He chose instead to be sentenced by the trial judge without a jury recommendation.

In preparing for the sentencing hearing, counsel spoke with respondent about his background. He also spoke on the telephone with respondent's wife and mother, though he did not follow up on the one unsuccessful effort to meet with them. He did not otherwise seek out character witnesses for respondent. Nor did he request a psychiatric examination, since his conversations with his client gave no indication that respondent had psychological problems.

Counsel decided not to present and hence not to look further for evidence concerning respondent's character and emotional state. That decision reflected trial counsel's sense of hopelessness about overcoming the evidentiary effect of respondent's confessions to the gruesome crimes. It also reflected the judgment that it was advisable to rely on the plea colloquy for evidence about respondent's background and about his claim of emotional stress: the plea colloquy communicated sufficient information about these subjects, and by forgoing the opportunity to present new evidence on these subjects, counsel prevented the State from cross-examining respondent on his claim and from putting on psychiatric evidence of its own.

Counsel also excluded from the sentencing hearing other evidence he thought was potentially damaging. He successfully moved to exclude respondent's "rap sheet." Because he judged that a presentence report might prove more detrimental than helpful, as it would have included respondent's criminal history and thereby would have undermined the claim of no significant history of criminal activity, he did not request that one be prepared.

At the sentencing hearing, counsel's strategy was based primarily on the trial judge's remarks at the plea colloquy as well as on his reputation as a sentencing judge who thought it important for a convicted defendant to own up to his crime. Counsel argued that respondent's remorse and acceptance of responsibility justified sparing him from the death penalty. Counsel also argued that respondent had no history of criminal activity and that respondent committed the crimes under extreme mental or emotional disturbance, thus coming within the statutory list of mitigating circumstances. He further argued that respondent should be spared death because he had surrendered, confessed, and offered to testify against a codefendant and because respondent was fundamentally a good person who had briefly gone badly wrong in extremely stressful circumstances. The State put on evidence and witnesses largely for the purpose of describing the details of the crimes. Counsel did not cross-examine the medical experts who testified about the manner of death of respondent's victims. . . .

[T]he trial judge found numerous aggravating circumstances and no (or a single comparatively insignificant) mitigating circumstance. . . . He therefore sentenced respondent to death on each of the three counts of murder and to prison terms for the other crimes. The Florida Supreme Court upheld the convictions and sentences on direct appeal.

B

Respondent subsequently sought collateral relief in state court on numerous grounds, among them that counsel had rendered ineffective assistance at the sentencing proceeding. Respondent challenged counsel's assistance in six respects. He asserted that counsel was ineffective because he failed to move for a continuance to prepare for sentencing, to request a psychiatric report, to investigate and present character witnesses, to seek a presentence investigation report, to present meaningful arguments to the sentencing judge, and to investigate the medical examiner's reports or cross-examine the medical experts. In support of the claim, respondent submitted 14 affidavits from friends, neighbors, and relatives stating that they would have testified if asked to do so. . . .

C

[The trial court denied relief on the ground that the outcome would not have been any different no matter what Washington's lawyer had done. Petitioner then filed a writ of habeas corpus in the federal trial court. Denying relief, that court held that although trial counsel "made errors in judgment in failing to investigate nonstatutory mitigating evidence further than he did, no prejudice to respondent's sentence resulted from any such error in judgment." The Fifth Circuit, sitting en banc, reversed and remanded. The Supreme Court granted certiorari "to consider the standards by which to judge a contention that the Constitution requires that a criminal judgment be overturned because of the actual ineffective assistance of counsel."]

II

[handwritten margin note: support cases]

In a long line of cases that includes Powell v. Alabama, 287 U.S. 45, 53 S.Ct. 55, 77 L.Ed. 158 (1932), Johnson v. Zerbst, 304 U.S. 458, 58 S.Ct. 1019, 82 L.Ed. 1461 (1938), and Gideon v. Wainwright, 372 U.S. 335, 83 S.Ct. 792, 9 L.Ed.2d 799 (1963), this Court has recognized that the Sixth Amendment right to counsel exists, and is needed, in order to protect the fundamental right to a fair trial. The Constitution guarantees a fair trial through the Due Process Clauses, but it defines the basic elements of a fair trial largely through the several provisions of the Sixth Amendment, including the Counsel Clause:

[handwritten margin note: def of fair trial (d-quote)]

> "In all criminal prosecutions, the accused shall enjoy the right to a speedy and public trial, by an impartial jury of the State and district wherein the crime shall have been committed, which district shall have been previously ascertained by law, and to be informed of the nature and cause of the accusation; to be confronted with the witnesses against him; to have compulsory process for obtaining witnesses in his favor, and to have the Assistance of Counsel for his defence."

Thus, a fair trial is one in which evidence subject to adversarial testing is presented to an impartial tribunal for resolution of issues defined in advance of the proceeding. The right to counsel plays a crucial role in the adversarial system embodied in the Sixth Amendment, since access to counsel's skill and knowledge is necessary to accord defendants the "ample opportunity to meet the case of the prosecution" to which they are entitled.

Because of the vital importance of counsel's assistance, this Court has held that, with certain exceptions, a person accused of a federal or state crime has the right to have counsel appointed if retained counsel cannot be obtained. That a person who happens to be a lawyer is present at trial alongside the accused, however, is not enough to satisfy the constitutional command. The Sixth Amendment recognizes the right to the assistance of counsel because it envisions counsel's playing a role that is critical to the ability of the adversarial system to produce just results. An accused is entitled to be assisted by an attorney, whether retained or appointed, who plays the role necessary to ensure that the trial is fair.

[handwritten margin note: type of attorney assistance that the accused has a right to]

For that reason, the Court has recognized that "the right to counsel is the right to the effective assistance of counsel." Government violates the right to effective assistance when it interferes in certain ways with the ability of counsel to make independent decisions about how to conduct the defense. See, e.g., Geders v. United States, 425 U.S. 80, 96 S.Ct. 1330, 47 L.Ed.2d 592 (1976) (bar on attorney-client consultation during overnight recess); Herring v. New York, 422 U.S. 853, 95 S.Ct. 2550, 45 L.Ed.2d 593

(1975) (bar on summation at bench trial); Brooks v. Tennessee, 406 U.S. 605, 612–613, 92 S.Ct. 1891, 1895, 32 L.Ed.2d 358 (1972) (requirement that defendant be first defense witness); Ferguson v. Georgia, 365 U.S. 570, 593–596, 81 S.Ct. 756, 768–770, 5 L.Ed.2d 783 (1961) (bar on direct examination of defendant). Counsel, however, can also deprive a defendant of the right to effective assistance, simply by failing to render "adequate legal assistance," Cuyler v. Sullivan, 446 U.S., at 344, 100 S.Ct., at 1716. Id., at 345–350, 100 S.Ct., at 1716–1719 (actual conflict of interest adversely affecting lawyer's performance renders assistance ineffective).

The Court has not elaborated on the meaning of the constitutional requirement of effective assistance in the latter class of cases—that is, those presenting claims of "actual ineffectiveness." In giving meaning to the requirement, however, we must take its purpose—to ensure a fair trial—as the guide. The benchmark for judging any claim of ineffectiveness must be whether counsel's conduct so undermined the proper functioning of the adversarial process that the trial cannot be relied on as having produced a just result.

[margin note: standard]

The same principle applies to a capital sentencing proceeding such as that provided by Florida law. . . .

III

A convicted defendant's claim that counsel's assistance was so defective as to require reversal of a conviction or death sentence has two components. First, the defendant must show that counsel's performance was deficient. This requires showing that counsel made errors so serious that counsel was not functioning as the "counsel" guaranteed the defendant by the Sixth Amendment. Second, the defendant must show that the deficient performance prejudiced the defense. This requires showing that counsel's errors were so serious as to deprive the defendant of a fair trial, a trial whose result is reliable. Unless a defendant makes both showings, it cannot be said that the conviction or death sentence resulted from a breakdown in the adversary process that renders the result unreliable.

[margin note: How D can show:]

[margin note: rule]

A

As all the Federal Courts of Appeals have now held, the proper standard for attorney performance is that of reasonably effective assistance. . . . When a convicted defendant complains of the ineffectiveness of counsel's assistance, the defendant must show that counsel's representation fell below an objective standard of reasonableness.

[margin note: standard = reasonably effective assistance]

More specific guidelines are not appropriate. The Sixth Amendment refers simply to "counsel," not specifying particular requirements of effective assistance. It relies instead on the legal profession's maintenance of standards sufficient to justify the law's presumption that counsel will fulfill the role in the adversary process that the Amendment envisions. The proper measure of attorney performance remains simply reasonableness under prevailing professional norms.

Representation of a criminal defendant entails certain basic duties. Counsel's function is to assist the defendant, and hence counsel owes the client a duty of loyalty, a duty to avoid conflicts of interest. From counsel's function as assistant to the defendant derive the overarching duty to advocate the defendant's cause and the more particular duties to consult with the defendant on important decisions and to keep the defendant informed of important developments in the course of the prosecution. Counsel also has a duty to bring to bear such skill and knowledge as will render the trial a reliable adversarial testing process.

These basic duties neither exhaustively define the obligations of counsel nor form a checklist for judicial evaluation of attorney performance. In any case presenting an ineffectiveness claim, the performance inquiry must be whether counsel's assistance was reasonable considering all the circumstances. Prevailing norms of practice as reflected in American Bar Association standards and the like . . . are guides to determining what is reasonable, but they are only guides. No particular set of detailed rules for counsel's conduct can satisfactorily take account of the variety of circumstances faced by defense counsel or the range of legitimate decisions regarding how best to represent a criminal defendant. Any such set of rules would interfere with the constitutionally protected independence of counsel and restrict the wide latitude counsel must have in making tactical decisions. Indeed, the existence of detailed guidelines for representation could distract counsel from the overriding mission of vigorous advocacy of the defendant's cause. Moreover, the purpose of the effective assistance guarantee of the Sixth Amendment is not to improve the quality of legal representation, although that is a goal of considerable importance to the legal system. The purpose is simply to ensure that criminal defendants receive a fair trial.

Judicial scrutiny of counsel's performance must be highly deferential. It is all too tempting for a defendant to second-guess counsel's assistance after conviction or adverse sentence, and it is all too easy for a court, examining counsel's defense after it has proved unsuccessful, to conclude that a particular act or omission of counsel was unreasonable. A fair assessment of attorney performance requires that every effort be made to eliminate the distorting effects of hindsight, to reconstruct the circumstances of counsel's challenged conduct, and to evaluate the conduct from counsel's perspective at the time. Because of the difficulties inherent in making the evaluation, a court must indulge a strong presumption that counsel's conduct falls within the wide range of reasonable professional assistance; that is, the defendant must overcome the presumption that, under the circumstances, the challenged action "might be considered sound trial strategy." There are countless ways to provide effective assistance in any given case. Even the best criminal defense attorneys would not defend a particular client in the same way.

The availability of intrusive post-trial inquiry into attorney performance or of detailed guidelines for its evaluation would encourage the proliferation of ineffectiveness challenges. Criminal trials resolved unfavorably to the defendant would increasingly come to be followed by a second trial, this one of counsel's unsuccessful defense. Counsel's performance and even willingness to serve could be adversely affected. Intensive scrutiny of counsel and rigid requirements for acceptable assistance could dampen the ardor and impair the independence of defense counsel, discourage the acceptance of assigned cases, and undermine the trust between attorney and client.

Thus, a court deciding an actual ineffectiveness claim must judge the reasonableness of counsel's challenged conduct on the facts of the particular case, viewed as of the time of counsel's conduct. A convicted defendant making a claim of ineffective assistance must identify the acts or omissions of counsel that are alleged not to have been the result of reasonable professional judgment. The court must then determine whether, in light of all the circumstances, the identified acts or omissions were outside the wide range of professionally competent assistance. In making that determination, the court should keep in mind that counsel's function, as elaborated in prevailing professional norms, is to make the adversarial testing process work in the particular case. At the same time, the court should recognize that counsel is strongly presumed to have rendered adequate assistance and made all significant decisions in the exercise of reasonable professional judgment.

These standards require no special amplification in order to define counsel's duty to investigate, the duty at issue in this case. . . . [S]trategic choices made after thorough investigation of law and facts relevant to plausible options are virtually unchallengeable; and strategic choices made after less than complete investigation are reasonable precisely to the extent that reasonable professional judgments support the limitations on investigation. In other words, counsel has a duty to make reasonable investigations or to make a reasonable decision that makes particular investigations unnecessary. In any ineffectiveness case, a particular decision not to investigate must be directly assessed for reasonableness in all the circumstances, applying a heavy measure of deference to counsel's judgments. . . .

B

An error by counsel, even if professionally unreasonable, does not warrant setting aside the judgment of a criminal proceeding if the error had no effect on the judgment. The purpose of the Sixth Amendment guarantee of counsel is to ensure that a defendant has the assistance necessary to justify reliance on the outcome of the proceeding. Accordingly, any deficiencies in counsel's perform-ance must be prejudicial to the defense in order to constitute ineffective assistance under the Constitution.

In certain Sixth Amendment contexts, prejudice is presumed. Actual or constructive denial of the assistance of counsel altogeth-er is legally presumed to result in prejudice. So are various kinds of state interference with counsel's assistance. See United States v. Cronic, 466 U.S., at 659, and n. 25, 104 S.Ct., at 2046–2047, and n. 25. Prejudice in these circumstances is so likely that case-by-case inquiry into prejudice is not worth the cost. Moreover, such circumstances involve impairments of the Sixth Amendment right that are easy to identify and, for that reason and because the prosecution is directly responsible, easy for the government to prevent.

One type of actual ineffectiveness claim warrants a similar, though more limited, presumption of prejudice. In Cuyler v. Sullivan, 446 U.S., at 345–350, 100 S.Ct., at 1716–1719, the Court held that prejudice is presumed when counsel is burdened by an actual conflict of interest. In those circumstances, counsel breach-es the duty of loyalty, perhaps the most basic of counsel's duties. Moreover, it is difficult to measure the precise effect on the defense of representation corrupted by conflicting interests. Given the obligation of counsel to avoid conflicts of interest and the ability of trial courts to make early inquiry in certain situations likely to give rise to conflicts, see, e.g., Fed.Rule Crim.Proc. 44(c), it is reasonable for the criminal justice system to maintain a fairly rigid rule of presumed prejudice for conflicts of interest. Even so, the rule is not quite the per se rule of prejudice that exists for the Sixth Amendment claims mentioned above. Prejudice is presumed only if the defendant demonstrates that counsel "actively repre-sented conflicting interests" and that "an actual conflict of inter-est adversely affected his lawyer's performance." Cuyler v. Sulli-van, supra, 446 U.S., at 350, 348, 100 S.Ct., at 1719, 1718 (footnote omitted).

Conflict of interest claims aside, actual ineffectiveness claims alleging a deficiency in attorney performance are subject to a general requirement that the defendant affirmatively prove preju-dice. The government is not responsible for, and hence not able to prevent, attorney errors that will result in reversal of a conviction or sentence. Attorney errors come in an infinite variety and are as likely to be utterly harmless in a particular case as they are to be prejudicial. They cannot be classified according to likelihood of causing prejudice. Nor can they be defined with sufficient precision to inform defense attorneys correctly just what conduct to avoid. Representation is an art, and an act or omission that is unprofessional in one case may be sound or even brilliant in another. Even if a defendant shows that particular errors of counsel were unreasonable, therefore, the defendant must show that they actually had an adverse effect on the defense.

must show actual effect

It is not enough for the defendant to show that the errors had some conceivable effect on the outcome of the proceeding. Virtually every act or omission of counsel would meet that test, and not every error that conceivably could have influenced the outcome undermines the reliability of the result of the proceeding. Respondent suggests requiring a showing that the errors "impaired the presentation of the defense." That standard, however, provides no workable principle. Since any error, if it is indeed an error, "impairs" the presentation of the defense, the proposed standard is inadequate because it provides no way of deciding what impairments are sufficiently serious to warrant setting aside the outcome of the proceeding.

why outcome determinative standard is NOT proper

On the other hand, we believe that a defendant need not show that counsel's deficient conduct more likely than not altered the outcome in the case. This outcome-determinative standard has several strengths. It defines the relevant inquiry in a way familiar to courts, though the inquiry, as is inevitable, is anything but precise. The standard also reflects the profound importance of finality in criminal proceedings. Moreover, it comports with the widely used standard for assessing motions for new trial based on newly discovered evidence. Nevertheless, the standard is not quite appropriate.

not appropriate

Even when the specified attorney error results in the omission of certain evidence, the newly discovered evidence standard is not an apt source from which to draw a prejudice standard for ineffectiveness claims. The high standard for newly discovered evidence claims presupposes that all the essential elements of a presumptively accurate and fair proceeding were present in the proceeding whose result is challenged. An ineffective assistance claim asserts the absence of one of the crucial assurances that the result of the proceeding is reliable, so finality concerns are somewhat weaker and the appropriate standard of prejudice should be somewhat lower. The result of a proceeding can be rendered unreliable, and hence the proceeding itself unfair, even if the errors of counsel cannot be shown by a preponderance of the evidence to have determined the outcome.

TEST

Accordingly, the appropriate test for prejudice [is this:] The defendant must show that there is a reasonable probability that, but for counsel's unprofessional errors, the result of the proceeding would have been different. A reasonable probability is a probability sufficient to undermine confidence in the outcome. . . .

The governing legal standard plays a critical role in defining the question to be asked in assessing the prejudice from counsel's errors. When a defendant challenges a conviction, the question is whether there is a reasonable probability that, absent the errors, the factfinder would have had a reasonable doubt respecting guilt. When a defendant challenges a death sentence such as the one at issue in this case, the question is whether there is a reasonable probability that, absent the errors, the sentencer—including an appellate court, to the extent it independently reweighs the evidence—would have concluded that the balance of aggravating and mitigating circumstances did not warrant death. . . .

IV

A number of practical considerations are important for the application of the standards we have outlined. Most important, in adjudicating a claim of actual ineffectiveness of counsel, a court should keep in mind that the principles we have stated do not establish mechanical rules. Although those principles should guide the process of decision, the ultimate focus of inquiry must be on the fundamental fairness of the proceeding whose result is being challenged. In every case the court should be concerned with whether, despite the strong presumption of reliability, the result of the particular proceeding is unreliable because of a breakdown in the adversarial process that our system counts on to produce just results.

To the extent that this has already been the guiding inquiry in the lower courts, the standards articulated today do not require reconsideration of ineffectiveness claims rejected under different standards. In particular, the minor differences in the lower courts' precise formulations of the performance standard are insignificant: the different formulations are mere variations of the overarching reasonableness standard. With regard to the prejudice inquiry, only the strict outcome-determinative test, among the standards articulated in the lower courts, imposes a heavier burden on defendants than the tests laid down today. The difference, however, should alter the merit of an ineffectiveness claim only in the rarest case.

Although we have discussed the performance component of an ineffectiveness claim prior to the prejudice component, there is no reason for a court deciding an ineffective assistance claim to approach the inquiry in the same order or even to address both components of the inquiry if the defendant makes an insufficient showing on one. In particular, a court need not determine whether counsel's performance was deficient before examining the prejudice suffered by the defendant as a result of the alleged deficiencies. The object of an ineffectiveness claim is not to grade counsel's performance. If it is easier to dispose of an ineffectiveness claim on the ground of lack of sufficient prejudice, which we expect will often be so, that course should be followed. Courts should strive to ensure that ineffectiveness claims not become so burdensome to defense counsel that the entire criminal justice system suffers as a result. . . .

V

Having articulated general standards for judging ineffectiveness claims, we think it useful to apply those standards to the facts of this case in order to illustrate the meaning of the general principles. . . .

The facts as described above . . . make clear that the conduct of respondent's counsel at and before respondent's sentencing proceeding cannot be found unreasonable. They also make clear that, even assuming the challenged conduct of counsel was unreasonable, respondent suffered insufficient prejudice to warrant setting aside his death sentence.

With respect to the performance component, the record shows that respondent's counsel made a strategic choice to argue for the extreme emotional distress mitigating circumstance and to rely as fully as possible on respondent's acceptance of responsibility for his crimes. Although counsel understandably felt hopeless about respondent's prospects, nothing in the record indicates, as one possible reading of the District Court's opinion suggests, that counsel's sense of hopelessness distorted his professional judgment. Counsel's strategy choice was well within the range of professionally reasonable judgments, and the decision not to seek more character or psychological evidence than was already in hand was likewise reasonable. . . .

With respect to the prejudice component, the lack of merit of respondent's claim is even more stark. The evidence that respondent says his trial counsel should have offered at the sentencing hearing would barely have altered the sentencing profile presented to the sentencing judge. As the state courts and District Court found, at most this evidence shows that numerous people who knew respondent thought he was generally a good person and that a psychiatrist and a psychologist believed he was under considerable emotional stress that did not rise to the level of extreme disturbance. Given the overwhelming aggravating factors, there is no reasonable probability that the omitted evidence would have changed the conclusion that the aggravating circumstances outweighed the mitigating circumstances and, hence, the sentence imposed. . . .

Failure to make the required showing of either deficient performance or sufficient prejudice defeats the ineffectiveness claim. Here there is a double failure. More generally, respondent has made no showing that the justice of his sentence was rendered unreliable by a breakdown in the adversary process caused by deficiencies in counsel's assistance. Respondent's sentencing proceeding was not fundamentally unfair.

We conclude, therefore, that the District Court properly declined to issue a writ of habeas corpus. The judgment of the Court of Appeals is accordingly

Reversed.

[The Opinions of Justice Brennan, concurring in part and dissenting in part, and Justice Marshall, dissenting, are omitted.]

Notes

1. *Strickland* is truly one of the landmark cases in the field of ethical lawyering. As of October, 2006, it has been cited in court opinions more than 100,000 times. Its rules govern ineffective assistance challenges in both federal and state courts.

2. Justice Marshall, in dissent, argued that the "deficient performance" part of the *Strickland* test was so malleable that it would lead to "excessive variation" in outcomes in the lower courts. "To tell lawyers and the lower courts that counsel for a criminal defendant must behave 'reasonably,'" he said, "is to tell them almost nothing. In essence, the majority has instructed judges ... to advert to their own intuitions regarding what constitutes 'professional' representation." Justice Marshall also found fault with the majority's failure to specify whether the "reasonably competent attorney" to be used as a standard is a "reasonably competent adequately paid retained lawyer or a reasonable competent appointed attorney." Should the Court have made its test of adequate lawyer performance more specific? Why or why not?

3. Justice Marshall also found fault with the majority's prejudice standard, on two grounds. First, he said, it is very difficult to ascertain whether the outcome of a trial was affected by counsel's deficient performance. Second, the guarantee of effective assistance of counsel does more than "reduce the chance that innocent persons will be convicted. In my view," he wrote, "the guarantee also functions to ensure that convictions are obtained only through fundamentally fair procedures.... A proceeding in which the defendant does not receive meaningful assistance in meeting the forces of the State does not, in my opinion, constitute due process." Do you think the majority is too "bottom-line" oriented in its test?

4. What do you think of the *Strickland* Court's statements that "judicial scrutiny of counsel's performance must be highly deferential" and "a court must indulge a strong presumption that counsel's conduct

falls within the wide range of reasonable professional assistance'"? What justification does the Court offer for this presumption? Is it convincing?

5. Should defense lawyers in capital cases be held to higher standards? Within the several years, a number of states have declared a moratorium on the death penalty, and many other states are reexamining their capital procedures, especially with respect to legal representation in cases involving indigent defendants. In 1997 the ABA House of Delegates voted to support a moratorium on executions until states implement policies to ensure that the risks of executing the innocent are minimized. The ABA has also published guidelines for lawyer performance in death penalty cases, and recommends that capital defendants be represented by two lawyers.

6. *Deficient performance.* Under *Strickland,* counsel's performance must fall below an objective standard of reasonableness to establish the first required prong of the two-part test. This can be a difficult standard to meet. See, e.g., *Florida v. Nixon,* 543 U.S. 175, 125 S.Ct. 551, 160 L.Ed.2d 565 (2004) (lawyer's failure to obtain defendant's express consent to a strategy of conceding guilt at the guilt phase of a capital case was a "strategic choice" that was not unreasonable).

7. *Prejudice.* Prejudice is established when counsel's performance deprived his client of a "substantive or procedural right to which the law entitled him." *Williams v. Taylor,* 529 U.S. 362, 120 S.Ct. 1495, 146 L.Ed.2d 389 (2000). Thus most courts have found prejudice (and deficient performance by counsel) where a lawyer fails to object on Fourth Amendment grounds to the admission of evidence that ultimately results in his client's conviction. See *Owens v. United States,* 387 F.3d 607 (7th Cir. 2004) (Posner, J.) (collecting cases). But, as the Court contemplated, most ineffective assistance claims fail on the "prejudice" prong of *Strickland.* See, e.g., *People v. McDonald,* 1 N.Y.3d 109, 802 N.E.2d 131, 769 N.Y.S.2d 781 (2003) (lawyer erroneously told client that his guilty plea would not subject him to deportation). *Davis v. Greiner,* 428 F.3d 81 (2d Cir. 2005) (lawyer unreasonably failed to tell client during plea negotiations that his statements could be used against him if he stood trial).

8. *Habeas cases: The AEDPA.* The Antiterrorism and Effective Death Penalty Act, 28 U.S.C. § 2254(d) ("AEDPA"), restricts the federal courts' role in reviewing state prisoner habeas corpus applications. When a defendant has been convicted in state court and, after exhausting state appeals, applies to the federal court for habeas relief (such as on grounds of ineffective assistance), the federal court is empowered to grant the relief only if the state court's decision was "contrary to" or involved an "unreasonable application of clearly established Federal law." § 2254(d)(1). The Court in *Williams v. Taylor,* 529 U.S. 362, 120 S.Ct. 1495, 146 L.Ed.2d 389 (2000), held that the AEDPA requires a federal court to find that one of two conditions is satisfied as a condition of granting federal habeas relief: (1) that the state court decision "was contrary to clearly established Federal law, as determined by the Su-

preme Court of the United States," or (2) that the state court decision "involved an unreasonable application of clearly established Federal law, as determined by the Supreme Court of the United States." Under the "contrary to" test, the federal court must find that the state court arrived at a conclusion opposite to that reached by the Supreme Court on a question of law, or that the state court decided a case differently than the Supreme Court has on a set of marginally-indistinguishable facts. Under the alternative "unreasonable application" test, the federal court must find that the state court identified the correct governing principle from Supreme Court decisions, but unreasonably applied that principle to the facts of the prisoner's case. *Id.*

9. *The AEDPA in application: a double layer of deference.* Congress intended the AEDPA to restrict federal courts in granting ineffective assistance relief to state-convicted prisoners, and that has been its effect. In *Bell v. Cone*, 535 U.S. 685, 122 S.Ct. 1843, 152 L.Ed.2d 914 (2002), Cone was convicted of murder in Tennessee state court and sentenced to death. He appealed his conviction in Tennessee appellate court, claiming ineffective assistance of counsel. His conviction was affirmed on the ground that he failed to prove entitlement under *Strickland*. Cone then appealed in federal court. The Supreme Court held, 8–1, (1) that the *Strickland* standard applied to his claim that his counsel's performance was deficient because he failed to adduce certain evidence during the sentencing, and waived closing argument, and (2) he failed to show that the Tennessee court "applied *Strickland* to the facts of his case in an objectively unreasonable manner." "It is not enough," wrote the Chief Justice, "to convince a federal habeas court that, in its independent judgment, the state-court decision applied *Strickland* incorrectly." This amounts to a double layer of deference, since under *Strickland,* the state court applied a "highly deferential" standard to counsel's performance. Cone's habeas petition was therefore denied.

See also *Yarborough v. Gentry*, 540 U.S. 1, 124 S.Ct. 1, 157 L.Ed.2d 1 (2003) (upholding conviction, concluding that counsel was entitled to a strong presumption that his decisions were tactical, and that the state court was entitled to deference under the AEDPA); *Abdur'Rahman v. Bell*, 226 F.3d 696 (6th Cir.2000) (reversing trial court's grant of habeas relief, concluding that the court failed to presume the correctness of state court findings of fact under 28 U.S.C § 2254(d); even though counsel failed to investigate or present mitigating evidence in the death penalty sentencing phase, no prejudice was shown).

10. *Failure to investigate.* One type of lawyer error has resulted in a number of high-profile grants of federal habeas relief in recent years: a lawyer's failure to investigate the facts about his client's case. In *Wiggins v. Smith*, 539 U.S. 510, 123 S.Ct. 2527, 156 L.Ed.2d 471 (2003), even a heavy measure to deference to counsel's strategic decisions did not stop the court from concluding that a lawyer's decision not to expand their investigation of their client's life history for mitigating evidence in a murder trial fell below prevailing professional standards. The client was convicted of murder in state court and sentenced to death. Because

of a virtually complete lack of investigation, counsel failed to learn of their client's troubled childhood while in the custody of his alcoholic, absentee mother, and that he had suffered physical torment, sexual molestation, and repeated rape during his years in foster care. There was a reasonable probability that but for counsel's errors the jury would have returned with a different sentence, and the state court's contrary conclusion was an objectively unreasonable application of Supreme Court precedent.

In *Rompilla v. Beard*, 545 U.S. 374, 125 S.Ct. 2456, 162 L.Ed.2d 360 (2005), the court again reversed a state court's imposition of the death penalty on ineffective assistance grounds for failure to investigate. After the client's conviction for murder, his public defenders failed to examine the file on defendant's prior conviction of rape and assault, which contained several potentially mitigating facts, including an abusive childhood, severe mental problems, and a third-grade level of cognition. Defense counsel knew that the prosecutor was going to rely on the past convictions to seek the death penalty, but did not even look at it until warned by the prosecutor that they should do so. Even then the lawyers did not read the entire file. "We hold," wrote Justice Souter for the 5–4 majority, "that even when a capital defendant's family members and the defendant himself have suggested that no mitigating evidence is available, his lawyer is bound to make reasonable efforts to obtain and review material that counsel knows the prosecution will probably rely on as evidence of aggravation at the sentencing phase of trial." The state court's contrary holding was an "unreasonable application" of prior Supreme Court precedent. In finding counsel's performance deficient, the Court relied in part on the ABA Standards for Criminal Justice, which provide:

> It is the duty of the lawyer to conduct a prompt investigation of the circumstances of the case and to explore all avenues leading to facts relevant to the merits of the case and the penalty in the event of conviction. The investigation should always include efforts to secure information in the possession of the prosecution and law enforcement authorities. The duty to investigate exists regardless of the accused admissions or statements to the lawyer of facts constituting guilt or the accused's stated desire to plead guilty.

1 ABA Standards for Criminal Justice 4–4.1 (2d Ed. 1982 Supp.), quoted in *Rompilla*, 545 U.S. at 387.

Not surprisingly, these decisions have grabbed the attention of appellate counsel retained to represent convicted clients. See, e.g., *Gersten v. Senkowski*, 426 F.3d 588 (2d Cir. 2005) (affirming trial court's grant of habeas petition where defense counsel failed to consult any medical or psychological expert witnesses, or to do research on scientific issues, in client's trial for first degree sexual abuse of a child); *Earp v. Ornoski*, 431 F.3d 1158 (9th Cir. 2005) (holding that the trial court should have granted an evidentiary hearing on state petitioner's ineffective assistance claim where he alleged counsel's failure to fully investigate mitigating evidence that could have been used at the sentencing phase of trial).

11.   *Conflicts of interest. Cuyler v. Sullivan*, discussed in *Strickland*, established an exception of sorts to the usual prejudice rule, in cases involving actual conflicts of interest by criminal defense lawyers. In *Mickens v. Taylor*, 535 U.S. 162, 122 S.Ct. 1237, 152 L.Ed.2d 291 (2002), the Court held that when a defendant's lawyer has a conflict of interest but the trial judge fails to inquire about it, the petitioner must establish that the conflict of interest adversely affected his counsel's performance. Mickens murdered Timothy Hall during or after a sex act. Mickens' lead trial attorney (appointed by the court) was Bryan Saunders. Unknown to Mickens, at the time of the murder Saunders was representing Hall, a juvenile, on assault and concealed-weapons charges. Indeed, the same state judge who had appointed Saunders to represent Mickens on April 6, 1992, had appointed Saunders to represent Hall on March 20, 1992. Saunders did not disclose his prior representation of the victim to his client, his co-counsel or the court, and the trial court did not make any inquiry about it. Mickens learned of this conflict of interest only during his federal appeals, after having been convicted and sentenced to death. Justice Scalia, writing for the majority rejected petitioner's argument that such facts should require automatic reversal without a showing of prejudice. Rather, "it was at least necessary, to void the conviction, for petitioner to establish that the conflict of interest adversely affected his counsel's performance." Since petitioner failed to do that, his conviction and death sentence were affirmed. Four justices (Stevens, Souter, Breyer and Ginsburg) dissented. Justice Breyer put his position succinctly: "Virginia seeks to put the petitioner, Walter Mickens, Jr., to death after having appointed to represent him as his counsel a lawyer who, at the time of the murder, was representing the very person Mickens was accused of killing.... In a case such as this once, a categorical approach is warranted and automatic reversal is required." To carry out a death sentence after such a process, Breyer argued, would "diminish that public confidence in the criminal justice system upon which the successful functioning of that system continues to depend."

For a state-court reversal of a murder conviction based on a conflict similar to the one in *Mickens*, see *State ex rel. S.G.*, 175 N.J. 132, 814 A.2d 612 (2003) (law firm represented both the criminal defendant and his shooting victim; law firm could not proceed with the defense even if the defendant purportedly consented).

12.   *Ineffective assistance claims and guilty pleas.* Where a defendant pleads guilty and then seeks to withdraw his plea based on ineffective assistance of counsel, courts have said that the prejudice prong of *Strickland* is met by showing that there is a reasonable probability that but for counsel's errors defendant would not have pleaded guilty, but would instead have insisted on going to trial. *Hill v. Lockhart*, 474 U.S. 52, 106 S.Ct. 366, 88 L.Ed.2d 203 (1985).

13. *Forfeiting the right to effective assistance of counsel.* A few courts have held that a criminal defendant, by engaging in "extremely serious misconduct" in connection with the proceedings, may forfeit entirely the right to effective assistance of counsel. See *United States v. Lamplugh*, 334 F.3d 294 (3d Cir. 2003) (defendant presented falsified copies of tax returns to her lawyer for use in her trial for failure to file tax returns); *United States v. Leggett*, 162 F.3d 237 (3d Cir. 1998) (defendant physically attacked his lawyer in full view of the trial court during the sentencing phase); *United States v. McLeod*, 53 F.3d 322 (11th Cir. 1995) (defendant was "repeatedly abusive, threatening and coercive" towards his lawyer during a hearing). Should such a remedy be granted absent a showing that lesser measures, such as warnings or physical restraint, will not be adequate to protect lawyers or the court? See *King v. Superior Court*, 107 Cal.App.4th 929, 132 Cal.Rptr.2d 585 (2003).

14. *The absent (or nearly absent) lawyer.* In a companion case to *Strickland*, the Court held that a defendant did not have to prove prejudice in cases where defense counsel is absent at critical stages of a defendant's trial. *United States v. Cronic*, 466 U.S. 648, 104 S.Ct. 2039, 80 L.Ed.2d 657 (1984). How far might this holding extend? Consider the next case.

$\downarrow$

BURDINE v. JOHNSON

United States Court of Appeals, Fifth Circuit, en banc, 2001.
262 F.3d 336.

BENAVIDES, Circuit Judge:

In this case we consider whether the district court properly granted a Petition for Writ of Habeas Corpus filed by Calvin Jerold Burdine based on state habeas court findings that Burdine's court-appointed attorney slept repeatedly throughout the guilt-innocence phase of his 1984 capital murder trial. The district court concluded "sleeping counsel is equivalent to no counsel at all" and granted relief pursuant to 28 U.S.C. § 2254. A divided panel of this Court reversed. . . .

I.

In January 1984, after a trial that included 12 hours and 51 minutes of total time before the jury over a period of six days, a Harris County, Texas jury convicted petitioner Burdine of capital murder in connection with the death of W.T. "Dub" Wise. Wise was killed in April 1983 during the course of a robbery committed by Douglas McCreight and Burdine. After the jury affirmatively answered the two special issues, the state trial court assessed punishment as death by legal injection in accordance with Texas law. The Texas Court of Criminal Appeals affirmed Burdine's conviction and sentence on direct appeal. Throughout his trial and direct appeal, Burdine's court-appointed counsel was Joe F. Cannon of Houston.

Burdine's initial state application for a writ of habeas corpus was denied on June 29, 1994. Burdine filed a second application in December 1994. In relation to that application, the state habeas court conducted an evidentiary hearing during which Burdine called eight witnesses, including three jurors from the capital murder trial and the clerk of the court in which the trial was held. These four neutral witnesses, which the state habeas court found highly credible, testified that Cannon repeatedly dozed or slept as the State questioned witnesses and presented evidence supporting its case against Burdine.

Daniel Strickland, the foreman of the jury, recalled seeing Cannon doze or nod off between two and five times while the prosecuting attorney questioned witnesses. Myra Davis remembered being struck by the spectacle of Cannon's sleeping on the second day of trial, the same day that trial judge Joseph Guarino had chastised her for tardiness. According to Davis, Cannon "would nod his head down on his chest" with his eyes closed during the questioning of witnesses. "I was thinking to myself, you know look at him and [Judge Guarino] calls me out [for tardiness] in front of all these people, . . . and look at what that man is doing." Like Davis, Craig Engelhardt related that Cannon "would nod his head down, bob it, with eyes closed during all this." Engelhardt recalled Cannon sleeping as many as ten times during the trial, at one point for "a good probably at least 10 minutes" as the prosecution questioned a witness.

The testimony of Rose Berry, the deputy clerk assigned to the trial court that conducted Burdine's trial, confirmed the jurors' recollections. Berry recalled "lots of incidents" of Cannon sleeping during the trial. Though Berry could not specify a proportion of the trial in which Cannon slept, she did "know that he fell asleep and that he was asleep for long periods of time during the questioning of witnesses." According to the state habeas court, Berry was "the most compelling witness" in the proceeding not only because of her neutrality, but also because she was not required to pay attention to witnesses or the prosecutor and thus had a better opportunity to observe Cannon's conduct.

Other witnesses at the hearing, including Judge Joseph Guarino, prosecutor Ned Morris, and Carolyn Bonnin, a juror, testified that they had not noticed Cannon asleep during the trial. The prosecutor's testimony was challenged by James Pillow, the court coordinator of the trial court at the time of Burdine's trial. Pillow recalled having a conversation with the prosecutor, in which the prosecutor questioned Cannon's competency to represent capital defendants and suggested that Cannon not be appointed counsel in future capital cases. Neither the prosecutor nor Judge Guarino recalled ever discussing this issue, but Pillow noted that Cannon was not appointed by Judge Guarino to represent capital defendants after Burdine's trial. Cannon himself testified he had a "habit" of closing his eyes and tilting his head forward while concentrating, but that he never slept during Burdine's trial. The state habeas court pointed out the inconsistency between Cannon's testimony and the descriptions of the four neutral witnesses that saw Cannon's head bobbing. Moreover, Cannon's testimony as to his concentration habit was impeached by Philip Scardino, an attorney who worked with Cannon on a different capital case. While Scardino did not recall Cannon concentrating with his eyes closed, he did observe Cannon dozing during the voir dire of witnesses.

On April 3, 1995, the state habeas court entered comprehensive findings of fact and conclusions of law. After detailing the evidence presented during the evidentiary hearing, the court entered "a finding that defense counsel dozed and actually fell asleep during portions of [Burdine's] trial on the merits, in particular the guilt-innocence phase when the State's solo prosecutor, was questioning witnesses and presenting evidence." Based on evidence that "defense counsel repeatedly dozed and/or actually slept during substantial portions of [Burdine's] capital murder trial so that defense counsel was, in effect, absent[,]" the habeas court concluded that a showing of prejudice in accordance with *Strickland v. Washington,* 466 U.S. 668, 104 S.Ct. 2052, 80 L.Ed.2d 674 (1984), was not required. Accordingly, the court recommended that habeas relief be granted on Burdine's claim of ineffective assistance of counsel. In a one-page, unsigned opinion, the Texas Court of Criminal Appeals agreed that "the trial court's findings of fact [regarding the sleeping of trial counsel] are supported by the record." The court nevertheless concluded that Burdine was not entitled to relief because "he failed to discharge his burden of proof under *Strickland.*"

Burdine then filed an application for a writ of habeas corpus in the federal district court for the Southern District of Texas pursuant to 28 U.S.C. § 2254. That court determined, on the basis of the factual findings made by the state habeas court and accepted by the Court of Criminal Appeals, that Cannon's unconsciousness during Burdine's capital murder trial amounted to constructive denial of counsel for substantial periods of that trial. *See Burdine v. Johnson,* 66 F.Supp.2d 854, 866 (S.D.Tex.1999). Consequently, the district court determined that prejudice should be presumed in accordance with the Supreme Court's analysis in *Strickland* and *United States v. Cronic,* 466 U.S. 648, 104 S.Ct. 2039, 80 L.Ed.2d 657 (1984). The State now appeals from this determination.

II.

This federal habeas proceeding turns on the effect of state court findings that counsel repeatedly slept "during portions of [Burdine's] trial on the merits, in particular during the guilt-innocence phase when the State's solo prosecutor was questioning witnesses and presenting evidence." Although the Texas Court of Criminal Appeals rejected Burdine's habeas application, it found that the record supported the habeas court's findings of fact. In this appeal, the State concedes that we are bound by the habeas court's findings of fact. Specifically, the State "does not dispute that [counsel] dozed and actually fell asleep intermittently during Burdine's capital murder trial." [The State argues that habeas relief is nevertheless inappropriate, in part on the ground that the facts of the case do not warrant a presumption of prejudice.]

The State's arguments fail to address the fundamental unfairness in Burdine's capital murder trial created by the consistent unconsciousness of his counsel. It is well established that a defendant "requires the guiding hand of counsel at every step in the proceedings against him." *Powell v. Alabama,* 287 U.S. 45, 69, 53 S.Ct. 55, 64, 77 L.Ed. 158 (1932). Moreover, both the Supreme Court and this Court have recognized that the absence of counsel at critical stages of a defendant's trial undermines the fairness of the proceeding and therefore requires a presumption that the defendant was prejudiced by such deficiency. *See United States v. Cronic,* 466 U.S. 648, 659, 104 S.Ct. 2039, 80 L.Ed.2d 657 (1984); *United States v. Russell,* 205 F.3d 768, 770–71 (5th Cir.2000). Applying this longstanding principle, we conclude that a defendant's Sixth Amendment right to counsel is violated when that defendant's counsel is repeatedly unconscious through not insubstantial portions of the defendant's capital murder trial. Under such circumstances, *Cronic* requires that we presume that the Sixth Amendment violation prejudiced the defendant. . . .

. . . The purpose of this Sixth Amendment guarantee was and "is to ensure that a defendant has the assistance necessary to justify reliance on the outcome of the proceeding." *Strickland v. Washington,* 466 U.S. 668, 689, 104 S.Ct. 2052, 2067, 80 L.Ed.2d 674 (1984); *Cronic,* 466 U.S. at 658, 104 S.Ct. at 2046 ("[T]he right to the effective assistance of counsel is recognized not for its own sake, but because of the effect it has on the ability of the accused to receive a fair trial"). Because the Sixth Amendment serves solely to ensure a fair and reliable trial, "any deficiencies in counsel's performance must be prejudicial to the defense in order to constitute ineffective assistance under the Constitution." *Id.* In *Cronic,* however, the Court recognized that some egregious circumstances "are so likely to prejudice the accused that the cost of litigating their effect in a particular trial is unjustified." *Cronic,* 466 U.S. at 658, 104 S.Ct. at 2046. Both in *Cronic* and in *Strickland,* the Supreme Court recognized that the absence or denial of counsel at a critical stage of a criminal proceeding represents one of the egregious circumstances that requires the presumption of prejudice. *See Cronic,* 466 U.S. at 659, 104 S.Ct. at 2047; *Strickland,* 466 U.S. at 692, 104 S.Ct. at 2067.[4] Burdine seeks an application of this rule to the facts of his case. He argues that he was repeatedly without counsel throughout the most critical part of his capital murder trial: the guilt-innocence phase. Because he was without counsel, Burdine argues that we should presume prejudice in accordance with *Cronic* and *Strickland*. We agree with Burdine. . . .

The State concedes that *Cronic* calls for the presumption of prejudice when, during a critical stage of trial, counsel is either (1) totally absent, or (2) present but prevented from providing effective assistance. *See Cronic* 466 U.S. at 659 n. 25, 104 S.Ct. at 2047 n. 25. The State argues that applying this rule to the facts of Burdine's case expands *Cronic's* holding. . . . Specifically, the State maintains that (1) *Cronic* calls for a presumption of prejudice relating to absence of counsel only when state action causes such absence, and (2) any absence by Burdine's attorney was not proven to have taken place during a "critical stage" of Burdine's trial, as such term was understood by the Court in *Cronic*. We disagree with the State's excessively narrow reading of *Cronic*.

Initially, we note that the State's proposed state action requirement does not flow from the language of *Cronic*. *Cronic* recognized that because our system of justice deems essential the assistance of counsel, "a trial is unfair if the accused is denied counsel at a critical stage of his trial." *Id*. In a footnote following this sentence, the Court explained that presumption of prejudice was appropriate "when counsel was either totally absent, or prevented from assisting the accused during a critical stage of the proceeding." Though the term "prevented from assisting the accused" suggests the existence of some indeterminate external force, no inference of a state action requirement is possible from the Court's language discussing the appropriateness of a presumption when counsel is "totally absent." Later in *Cronic* the Court more directly dispelled the State's proposed state action requirement when it dismissed the idea that *the cause* of a Sixth Amendment deficiency should control whether a presumption of prejudice was warranted. . . . We conclude that the Sixth Amendment principle animating *Cronic's* presumption of prejudice is the fun-

---

4. In addition to the absence of counsel during critical phases of trial, *Cronic* suggested three other circumstances in which a presumption of prejudice would be required to ensure the fairness of a proceeding: (1) "if counsel entirely fails to subject the prosecution's case to meaningful adversarial testing;" (2) "when although counsel is available during trial, the likelihood that any lawyer, even a fully competent one, could provide effective assistance is so small that a presumption of prejudice is appropriate without inquiry into the actual conduct of the trial;" and (3) "when counsel labors under an actual conflict of interest." *Cronic,* 466 U.S. at 659–60, 662 n. 31, 104 S.Ct. at 2047, 2048 n. 31.

damental idea that a defendant must have the actual assistance of counsel at every critical stage of a criminal proceeding for the court's reliance on the fairness of that proceeding to be justified. The Court in *Cronic* was not concerned with the cause of counsel's absence, but rather the effect of such absence on the fairness of the criminal proceeding. . . .

The State next argues that because Burdine cannot demonstrate precisely when Cannon slept during his trial, he cannot prove that Cannon slept during critical stages of his criminal proceeding. In this regard, the State asks more of Burdine than the Supreme Court or this Court has ever asked of a defendant attempting to show the absence of counsel during a critical stage of trial. To justify a particular stage as "critical," the Court has not required the defendant to explain how having counsel would have altered the outcome of his specific case. Rather, the Court has looked to whether "the substantial rights of a defendant may be affected" during that type of proceeding. . . . Burdine has alleged and the state court findings support the fact that Burdine's counsel was unconscious, and hence absent, repeatedly throughout the guilt-innocence phase of Burdine's trial as evidence was being produced against Burdine. . . . [T]his stage of Burdine's trial was "critical." . . .

B. Is Presumption of Prejudice Appropriate in Burdine's Case?

The State purports to accept the state trial court's findings that defense counsel slept during substantial portions of Burdine's trial. Nonetheless, the State painstakingly conducts a page-by-page analysis of the trial record in an apparent attempt to demonstrate that counsel was awake during significant portions of the trial.[8] Yet, once we have accepted as presumptively correct the state court's finding that counsel slept "during portions of [Burdine's] trial on the merits, in particular during the guilt-innocence phase when the State's solo prosecutor was questioning witnesses and presenting evidence," there is no need to attempt to further scrutinize the record. *See Javor v. United States,* 724 F.2d 831, 834 (9th Cir. 1984) (holding that "[w]hen a defendant's attorney is asleep during a substantial portion of his trial, the defendant has not received the legal assistance necessary to defend his interests at trial" and thus, prejudice must be presumed).

The factual findings made during Burdine's state habeas proceedings demonstrate that Burdine's counsel was repeatedly asleep, and hence unconscious, as witnesses adverse to Burdine

---

8. We note that simply because counsel orally responded when addressed during trial does not necessarily indicate that he had been awake and attentive immediately prior to the exchange on the record. At the 1995 state habeas evidentiary hearing, two witnesses testified that, on different occasions during trial, counsel was awakened when the trial court or the prosecutor addressed him. Also, on occasion, Cannon's response was somewhat delayed because he had been asleep immediately prior to being addressed.

were examined and other evidence against Burdine was introduced. This unconsciousness extended through a not insubstantial portion of the 12 hour and 51 minute trial. Unconscious counsel equates to no counsel at all. Unconscious counsel does not analyze, object, listen or in any way exercise judgment on behalf of a client. As recognized by the Second Circuit, "the buried assumption in our *Strickland* cases is that counsel is present and conscious to exercise judgment, calculation and instinct, for better or worse. But that is an assumption we cannot make when counsel is unconscious at critical times." *Tippins v. Walker,* 77 F.3d 682, 687 (2d Cir.1996). When we have no basis for assuming that counsel exercised judgment on behalf of his client during critical stages of trial, we have insufficient basis for trusting the fairness of that trial and consequently must presume prejudice.

The State suggests that because Cannon was physically present in the courtroom, his dozing constituted a form of performance that should be subjected to prejudice analysis. The State maintains that it is impossible to distinguish between sleeping counsel and other impairments that nevertheless have been subjected to prejudice analysis. We disagree. An unconscious attorney does not, indeed cannot, perform at all. This fact distinguishes the sleeping lawyer from the drunk or drugged one. Even the intoxicated attorney exercises judgment, though perhaps impaired, on behalf of his client at all times during a trial. Yet, the attorney that is unconscious during critical stages of a trial is simply not capable of exercising judgment. The unconscious attorney is in fact no different from an attorney that is physically absent from trial since both are equally unable to exercise judgment on behalf of their clients. Such absence of counsel at a critical stage of a proceeding makes the adversary process unreliable, and thus a presumption of prejudice is warranted pursuant to *Cronic.*

[W]e decline to adopt a per se rule that any dozing by defense counsel during trial merits a presumption of prejudice. Our holding, that the repeated unconsciousness of Burdine's counsel through not insubstantial portions of the critical guilt-innocence phase of Burdine's capital murder trial warrants a presumption of prejudice, is limited to the egregious facts found by the state habeas court in this case.

III.

Based on the state court's findings that have been accepted by all as presumptively correct, we affirm the district court's grant of federal habeas corpus relief and vacate Burdine's capital murder conviction. The State is free to retry Burdine for capital murder.

AFFIRMED.

[Concurring and dissenting opinions omitted.]

Notes

1. The United States Supreme Court denied certiorari in *Burdine* in 2002. The following year, Burdine pleaded guilty to Wise's murder, as well as to aggravated assault and being a felon in possession of a weapon. He was sentenced to three consecutive life terms.

2. Could Burdine have proved prejudice under *Strickland*? What would he have had to show to prevail if prejudice had not been presumed?

3. The court declined to adopt a per se rule that a sleeping lawyer during trial merits a presumption of prejudice. Do you agree with that limitation? Could a lawyer sleep through part of a criminal trial—especially a death penalty trial—without that being prejudicial to the defense? What is the test of prejudice under *Strickland*?

4. The court also draws a distinction between a sleeping lawyer, who is likened to an absent lawyer, and a lawyer who is "merely" drunk or drugged. Should courts presume prejudice if a criminal defendant's lawyer is provably impaired during the trial? Is having a drunk lawyer better or worse than having no lawyer at all?

5. Cases like Burdine's, while perhaps not common, are sadly not rare, either. In *Mayfield v. Woodford*, 270 F.3d 915 (9th Cir. 2001), Mayfield murdered a woman as revenge for her turning him in for stealing a car, then murdered another man who witnessed the first murder. He was convicted of the two murders and sentenced to death. Every court that reviewed his conviction and sentence upheld them, until an en banc panel of the Ninth Circuit reversed the sentence on ineffective assistance grounds. The evidence showed that Mayfield's lawyer, S. Donald Ames, spent only 40 hours preparing for the guilt and penalty phases of the case and presented no mitigating evidence at the penalty phase. Judge Susan Graber, concurring, said that Ames's performance was so horrendous that he was, in effect, working for the prosecution. She also pointed to evidence that Ames was a racist; Mayfield is black. Judge D. Michael Hawkins commented that it was "a painful truth of the death penalty process that these most serious cases sometimes draw the least adequate counsel." He added that the lawyer's representation was so deficient as to be "the functional equivalent of no counsel at all."

6. In *Nance v. Frederick*, 358 S.C. 480, 596 S.E.2d 62 (2004), the South Carolina Supreme Court reversed the defendant's multiple convictions (murder, criminal sexual conduct, and armed robbery, just to name a few) and death sentence on the ground that defense counsel's conduct, investigation, preparation and presentation failed to provide any "meaningful adversary challenge" to the prosecution, thus allowing for a presumption of prejudice on the defendant's ineffective assistance claim. The U.S. Supreme Court granted certiorari and vacated the opinion and remanded in light of *Florida v. Nixon* (cited *supra* in Note 6 after

Strickland), which had granted a heavy degree of deference to defense counsel's choices in holding his performance non-deficient. *Ozmint v. Nance*, 543 U.S. 1043, 125 S.Ct. 868, 160 L.Ed.2d 763 (2005). On remand, the South Carolina Supreme Court reiterated its position that prejudice should be presumed. *Nance v. Ozmint*, 367 S.C. 547, 626 S.E.2d 878 (2006). The defendant's appointed counsel, the court said, failed to provide an adversarial challenge to the state, even helping to bolster the prosecution's case by his unwise calling and questioning of adverse witnesses and his deficient opening and closing statements.

§ 4.   MALPRACTICE IN CRIMINAL MATTERS

WILEY v. COUNTY OF SAN DIEGO

Supreme Court of California, 1998.
19 Cal.4th 532, 966 P.2d 983, 79 Cal.Rptr.2d 672.

BROWN, Justice.

When a former criminal defendant sues for legal malpractice, is actual innocence a necessary element of the cause of action? For reasons of policy and pragmatism, we conclude the answer is yes.

FACTUAL AND PROCEDURAL BACKGROUND

. . . In September 1990, plaintiff Kelvin Eugene Wiley (Wiley) was arrested and charged with burglary and various assaultive crimes against Toni DiGiovanni, a former girlfriend with whom he had a stormy relationship. At arraignment, he denied the charges and Deputy Public Defender John Jimenez was appointed to represent him. Wiley claimed he had been at his apartment at the time of the alleged crimes, and Jimenez arranged for an investigator to contact witnesses and prepare a report. The investigator had only limited success in finding anyone to establish an alibi. In the meantime, Wiley took a polygraph test, which Jimenez was informed he "had not passed."

At trial, DiGiovanni, the only percipient witness, testified that after Wiley entered her condominium in a rage, he hit her repeatedly with a wrench, threatened to kill her, and strangled her with a belt until she lost consciousness. Her 11-year-old son, Eric, testified that he found his mother lying on the floor and that Wiley had physically abused her on prior occasions. He also stated he saw Wiley's truck drive into the cul-de-sac where they lived the morning of the alleged attack. Taking the stand in his own behalf, Wiley denied attacking DiGiovanni and said she had been following and harassing him because he wanted to break off their relationship. According to his landlord, Wiley's truck was parked outside his duplex early on the morning of the alleged assault, and he did not see Wiley enter or leave his residence. Numerous character witnesses also attacked DiGiovanni's credibility.

A jury convicted Wiley of battery causing serious bodily injury, but could not reach verdicts on the remaining counts, which the prosecutor dismissed. Wiley was sentenced to four years in state prison. While his appeal was pending, he filed a petition for writ of habeas corpus challenging Jimenez's representation as ineffective due to his inadequate investigation of the defense. In support of the petition, he submitted declarations from several of DiGiovanni's neighbors, none of whom had been contacted by the defense investigator. In sum, they stated they had seen DiGiovanni driving away from her residence early on the morning in question and later saw a man other than Wiley banging on her door and shouting, "Let me in." They noticed no signs of injury in the days following the incident. The trial court denied the petition, finding Wiley had failed to establish the investigation, preparation, or trial strategy had been inadequate.

A year later, Wiley filed a second habeas corpus petition. In addition to the previous declarations, he submitted evidence DiGiovanni's son had recanted his statement that Wiley's truck was at the condominium the morning of the alleged attack. The court granted the petition, finding that the son had lied at trial and that his testimony was crucial to the conviction. As a second basis for granting relief, the court determined Jimenez's inadequate investigation had deprived Wiley of exculpatory witnesses. The prosecutor later dismissed the case.

Wiley then filed the present legal malpractice action against Jimenez and the County of San Diego (defendants). Prior to trial, the court determined Wiley's innocence was not an issue and refused to require proof on the matter or submit the question to the jury. The jury found in favor of Wiley and awarded him $162,500. On appeal, defendants challenged, inter alia, the trial court's ruling on the issue of actual innocence. In support of their argument, they cited *Tibor v. Superior Court* (1997) 52 Cal. App.4th 1359, 61 Cal.Rptr.2d 326, in which the appellate court "concluded that, as a matter of sound public policy, a former criminal defendant, in order to establish proximate cause [in a legal malpractice action], must prove, by a preponderance of the evidence, not only that his former attorney was negligent in his representation, but that he (the plaintiff) was innocent of the criminal charges filed against him."

The Court of Appeal reversed the judgment because the trial court erroneously admitted the transcript of the second habeas corpus hearing and erroneously excluded certain evidence on which Jimenez based his trial strategy: the polygraph examination, a psychological evaluation of Wiley, and a prior domestic violence incident. Defendants' arguments on the question of actual innocence were rejected, however. The court acknowledged the "visceral appeal" of imposing such a requirement, but declined to do so for several reasons. First, "it is 'difficult to defend logically a rule that requires proof of innocence as a condition of recovery, especially if a clear act of negligence of defense counsel was obviously the cause of the defendant's conviction of a crime.' (*Glenn* [*v. Aiken* (1991)] 409 Mass. 699, 569 N.E.2d [783,] 787, fn. omitted.)" Second, creating a separate standard for clients represented in a criminal setting is "fundamentally incompatible" with the constitutional guaranty of effective assistance of counsel. Third, no empirical evidence supported the rationale, advanced by some courts, that the threat of malpractice claims would discourage representation of criminal defendants, particularly those who are indigent. Finally, an actual innocence requirement would create "rather artificial distinctions" between criminal defense attorneys and civil attorneys.

We granted review to resolve the conflict in the Courts of Appeal and settle an important issue of state law.

DISCUSSION

. . . [T]his court has yet to address any aspect of criminal malpractice, including the relevance of the plaintiff's actual innocence.

In civil malpractice cases, the elements of a cause of action for professional negligence are: "(1) the duty of the attorney to use such skill, prudence and diligence as members of the profession commonly possess; (2) a breach of that duty; (3) a proximate causal connection between the breach and the resulting injury; and (4) actual loss or damage." In criminal malpractice cases, the clear majority of courts that have considered the question also require proof of actual innocence as an additional element.[2] [Citing cases from Illinois, Kentucky, Massachusetts, New York, Pennsylvania, Idaho, Missouri, Oregon, Nevada and Virginia.]

Common to all these decisions are considerations of public policy: "[P]ermitting a convicted criminal to pursue a legal malpractice claim without requiring proof of innocence would allow the criminal to profit by his own fraud, or to take advantage of his own wrong, or to found [a] claim upon his iniquity, or to acquire property by his own crime. As such, it is against public policy for the suit to continue in that it would indeed shock the public conscience, engender disrespect for courts and generally discredit the administration of justice. [C]ourts will not assist the participant in an illegal act who seeks to profit from the act's commission."

Additionally, "allowing civil recovery for convicts impermissibly shifts responsibility for the crime away from the convict. This opportunity to shift much, if not all, of the punishment assessed

---

2. Many of these decisions further require that "the person's conviction has been reversed, . . . on appeal or through post-conviction relief, or the person otherwise has been exonerated." [Citing cases from Oregon, Nevada and Texas.]

against convicts for their criminal acts to their former attorneys, drastically diminishes the consequences of the convicts' criminal conduct and seriously undermines our system of criminal justice.'' ''[I]f plaintiffs engaged in the criminal conduct they are accused of, then they alone should bear full responsibility for the consequences of their acts, including imprisonment. Any subsequent negligent conduct by a plaintiff's attorney is superseded by the greater culpability of the plaintiff's criminal conduct.'' (*Shaw v. State, Dept. of Admin.* (Alaska 1993) 861 P.2d 566, 572.) Accordingly, ''[t]hese cases treat a defendant attorney's negligence as not the cause of the former client's injury as a matter of law, unless the plaintiff former client proves that he did not commit the crime.''

Notwithstanding these policy considerations, actual innocence is not a universal requirement. (See *Gebhardt v. O'Rourke* (1994) 444 Mich. 535, 510 N.W.2d 900; *Krahn v. Kinney* (1989) 43 Ohio St.3d 103, 538 N.E.2d 1058; see also *Silvers v. Brodeur* (Ind.Ct. App.1997) 682 N.E.2d 811.) Those courts declining to require such proof generally do not discuss the public policy implications but simply consider criminal malpractice as indistinguishable from civil malpractice. For example, in *Krahn v. Kinney, supra,* 43 Ohio St.3d 103, 538 N.E.2d 1058, defense counsel failed to convey a plea bargain offer and his client ultimately pled guilty to a more serious charge than offered. The reviewing court allowed the client's subsequent criminal malpractice action to proceed without proof of innocence, analogizing to what it considered comparable negligence in a civil context. ''The situation is like that in a civil action where the attorney fails to disclose a settlement offer. Such failure [exposes] the attorney to a claim of legal malpractice.''

We find these latter decisions unpersuasive. To begin, the public policy reasons articulated in favor of requiring proof of actual innocence are compelling. Our legal system is premised in part on the maxim, ''No one can take advantage of his own wrong.'' ... Regardless of the attorney's negligence, a guilty defendant's conviction and sentence are the direct consequence of his own perfidy. The fact that nonnegligent counsel ''could have done better'' may warrant postconviction relief, but it does not translate into civil damages, which are intended to make the plaintiff whole. While a conviction predicated on incompetence may be erroneous, it is not unjust....

Only an innocent person wrongly convicted due to inadequate representation has suffered a compensable injury because in that situation the nexus between the malpractice and palpable harm is sufficient to warrant a civil action, however inadequate, to redress the loss. In sum, ''the notion of paying damages to a plaintiff who actually committed the criminal offense solely because a lawyer negligently failed to secure an acquittal is of questionable public policy and is contrary to the intuitive response that damages should only be awarded to a person who is truly free from any criminal involvement.'' We therefore decline to permit such an action where the plaintiff cannot establish actual innocence. . . .

[The Court here stressed the constitutionally-mandated procedural protections afforded criminal defendants: proof beyond a reasonable doubt; a presumption of innocence; the prohibition of double jeopardy; and the exclusionary rule.] These and other constitutional protections are to safeguard against conviction of the wrongly accused and to vindicate fundamental values. They are not intended to confer any direct benefit outside the context of the criminal justice system. Thus, defense counsel's negligent failure to utilize them to secure an acquittal or dismissal for a guilty defendant does not give rise to civil liability. Rather, the criminal justice system itself provides adequate redress for any error or omission and resolves the apparent paradox noted in case and commentary. All criminal defendants have a Sixth Amendment right to effective assistance of counsel, that is, counsel acting reasonably '' 'within the range of competence demanded of attorneys in criminal cases.' '' (*Strickland v. Washington* (1984) 466 U.S. 668, 687, 104 S.Ct. 2052, 80 L.Ed.2d 674.) Not only does the Constitution guarantee this right, any lapse can be rectified through an array of postconviction remedies, including appeal and habeas corpus. Such relief is afforded even to those clearly guilty as long as they demonstrate incompetence and resulting prejudice, i.e., negligence and damages, under the same standard of professional care applicable in civil malpractice actions. . . .

In such instances of attorney negligence, postconviction relief will provide what competent representation should have afforded in the first instance: dismissal of the charges, a reduced sentence, an advantageous plea bargain. In the case of trial error, the remedy will be a new trial. If the defendant has in fact committed a crime, the remedy of a new trial or other relief is sufficient reparation in light of the countervailing public policies and considering the purpose and function of constitutional guaranties. . . . Given [the] availability [of these remedies], it is inimical to sound public policy to afford a civil remedy, which in some cases would provide a further boon to defendants already evading just punishment on ''legal technicalities.''

In contrast to the postconviction relief available to a criminal defendant, a civil matter lost through an attorney's negligence is lost forever. The litigant has no recourse other than a malpractice claim. The superficial comparison between civil and criminal malpractice is also faulty in other crucial respects. Tort damages are in most cases fungible in the sense that the plaintiff seeks in a malpractice action exactly what was lost through counsel's negligence: money. ''Damages'' in criminal malpractice are difficult to quantify under any circumstances. Calculating them when, for example, counsel's incompetence causes a longer sentence would be all the more perplexing.

Tort law also operates on very different legal principles from the constitutionally reinforced and insulated criminal justice system. "Tort law provides damages only for harms to the plaintiff's legally protected interests, [citation], and the liberty of a guilty criminal is not one of them. The guilty criminal may be able to obtain an acquittal if he is skillfully represented, but he has no right to that result (just as he has no *right* to have the jury nullify the law, though juries sometimes do that), and the law provides no relief if the 'right' is denied him." Moreover, "[t]he underpinnings of common law tort liability, compensation and deterrence, do not support a rule that allows recovery to one who is guilty of the underlying criminal charge. A person who is guilty need not be compensated for what happened to him as a result of his former attorney's negligence. There is no reason to compensate such a person, rewarding him indirectly for his crime."

Reinforcing this conclusion are the pragmatic difficulties that would arise from simply overlaying criminal malpractice actions with the civil malpractice template. In civil actions, carrying the burden on causation is relatively straightforward and comprehensible for the jury, even if it necessitates a "trial within a trial." The factual issues in the underlying action are resolved according to the same burden of proof, and the same evidentiary rules apply. Thus, it is reasonably possible for the malpractice jury to assess whether and to what extent counsel's professional lapse compromised a meritorious claim or defense.

By contrast, "the prospect of retrying a criminal prosecution [is] 'something one would not contemplate with equanimity.... '" "[T]he standard of proof will be a complex one, in essence, a standard within a standard. [Plaintiff] must prove by a preponderance of the evidence that, but for the negligence of his attorney, the jury could not have found him guilty beyond a reasonable doubt." ...

We would also anticipate attorneys might practice "defensive" law more frequently to insulate their trial court decisions. "[I]n our already overburdened system it behooves no one to encourage the additional expenditure [of] resources merely to build a record against a potential malpractice claim."

For the foregoing reasons, we hold that in a criminal malpractice action actual innocence is a necessary element of the plaintiff's cause of action. Therefore, on retrial Wiley will have to prove by a preponderance of the evidence that he did not commit battery with serious bodily injury.

[Affirmed.]

Notes

damages v. retrial

1. How does a legal malpractice claim against a criminal defense attorney differ from a claim of ineffective assistance of counsel? What remedy is being sought in each case?

check this

2. The majority of courts follow the "actual innocence" rule enunciated in *Wiley*. How convincing do you find the court's stated rationales for its position?

3. Look at the facts of *Krahn v. Kinney*, the Ohio decision discussed in *Wiley*. Should that kind of case be actionable? If not, why not? Is it that damages would be too speculative? Or that the plaintiff somehow has "unclean hands?" Or that such harm should not be considered "legally cognizable?"

where MP is allowed

4. What if a criminal defendant maintains his innocence throughout the proceedings, but pleads guilty to a lesser crime on the advice of counsel. Can that person sue his lawyer for malpractice? See *Falkner v. Foshaug*, 108 Wash.App. 113, 29 P.3d 771 (2001) (yes).

5. What if a criminal defendant pleads guilty without being given timely advice by his lawyer concerning the importance of cooperating with the Government as a way of reducing the sentence. Malpractice? The court in *United States v. Fernandez*, 2000 WL 534449 (S.D.N.Y.), said yes.

check stats

6. Most courts that have adopted the "actual innocence" requirement also require that the defendant obtain post-conviction relief—formal proof of actual innocence, that is—as a precondition to suing the lawyer for legal malpractice. See, e.g., *Therrien v. Sullivan*, 153 N.H. 211, 891 A.2d 560 (2006); *Ang v. Martin*, 154 Wash.2d 477, 114 P.3d 637 (2005); *Glaze v. Larsen*, 207 Ariz. 26, 83 P.3d 26 (2004); *Trobaugh v. Sondag*, 668 N.W.2d 577 (Iowa 2003); *Canaan v. Bartee*, 276 Kan. 116, 72 P.3d 911 (2003); *Noske v. Friedberg*, 670 N.W.2d 740 (Minn. 2003); *Coscia v. McKenna & Cuneo*, 25 Cal.4th 1194, 25 P.3d 670, 108 Cal. Rptr.2d 471 (2001). Some disagree. See, e.g., *Rantz v. Kaufman*, 109 P.3d 132 (Colo. 2005); *Ereth v. Cascade Cty.*, 318 Mont. 355, 81 P.3d 463 (2003). The majority approach is usually accepted on the reasoning that absent post-conviction relief, the former criminal defense client cannot, as a matter of law, establish either the causation or damages element of the malpractice claim, and that such a requirement conserves judicial resources.

rationale

accrual SOL on such claims

7. *Effect on accrual of the claim.* A state's position on the post-conviction relief requirement impacts on when a claim *must* be brought as well as on when it *can* be brought. In most states adopting the post-conviction relief requirement, the statute of limitations on the malpractice claim begins to run upon the obtaining of post-conviction relief. But in some, the statute of limitations is not tolled during the litigation of the post-conviction claims; instead the former client must file the malpractice suit within the regular rules (usually, within one to three years

from the date of discovery) and must then seek a stay of the civil case pending the outcome of the criminal appeals. See, e.g., *Coscia v. McKenna & Cuneo*, 25 Cal.4th 1194, 25 P.3d 670, 108 Cal.Rptr.2d 471 (2001). Some states commence the running of the statute of limitations when the client-lawyer relationship ends, or when the client discovers or should have discovered his lawyer's mistake, whichever occurs later. See *Smith v. Conley*, 109 Ohio St.3d 141, 846 N.E.2d 509 (2006).

8. *Breach of contract theory.* Might a former criminal-defense client, unable to prove his actual innocence in a state that requires such proof for a malpractice claim, bring a breach of contract claim against his former lawyer instead, seeking a refund of the fees he paid? See *Winniczek v. Nagelberg*, 394 F.3d 505 (7th Cir. 2005) (Posner, J.).

9. *Civil rights claims.* In *Polk County v. Dodson*, 454 U.S. 312, 102 S.Ct. 445, 70 L.Ed.2d 509 (1981), the Supreme Court held that a public defender's relationship with his client is substantially identical to that of a private attorney, except for how he gets paid; thus his malpractice, if any, may subject him to a state-law malpractice claim but is not "state action" for purposes of civil rights liability under 42 U.S.C. § 1983. Could the head of a county public defender office qualify as a state actor so as to make him liable on a § 1983 claim, based on an allegation that he implemented policies of assigning his office's least experienced attorneys to capital cases while refusing to provide any training to those attorneys? See *Miranda v. Clark County, Nevada*, 319 F.3d 465 (9th Cir. 2003) (en banc).

10. *Immunity.* If the criminal defense lawyer being sued is a public defender, should he or she be immune from suit? There is no absolute immunity for public defenders in federal court. *Ferri v. Ackerman*, 444 U.S. 193, 100 S.Ct. 402, 62 L.Ed.2d 355 (1979). Some states have passed statutes making state public defenders immune, however. *See, e.g.,* Ill. Comp. Stat. Ann. Ch. 745 § 19/5 (public defenders immune from malpractice actions except where they engage in "willful or wanton misconduct"). Absent such a statute, some state courts have held that a public defender is immune from suit under the state tort claims act on the same basis as is any other state actor. Other states have rejected such an immunity, sometimes by interpreting the tort claims statute's "discretionary function" or "basic policy immunity" provisions. See, e.g., *Barner v. Leeds*, 24 Cal.4th 676, 13 P.3d 704, 102 Cal.Rptr.2d 97 (2000) (because public defenders' actions in defending clients involve operational judgments rather than basic policy decisions, they can be sued to the same extent as private attorneys).

11. *Collateral estoppel.* Some courts have held that a criminal defendant who loses an ineffective assistance claim in a post-conviction relief proceeding cannot sue the same lawyer for legal malpractice, because the latter claim is barred by collateral estoppel on the causation issue. See, e.g., *Brewer v. Hagemann*, 771 A.2d 1030 (Me.2001); contra, *Rantz v. Kaufman*, 109 P.3d 132 (Colo. 2005).

§ 5.   OTHER CHECKS ON INCOMPETENCE

A.   Ethics Rules of General Applicability

1.   *Substantive Rules*

Many rules of professional responsibility place lawyers under a duty to behave competently in one respect or another. For example, MR 1.1 mandates "competent representation." MR 1.3 requires a lawyer to act with reasonable diligence and promptness. MR 1.4 mandates that the lawyer maintain reasonable lines of communication with the client during a representation. Lawyers are usually not disciplined for isolated violations of these rules, however; most cases involve repeated or aggravated instances of incompetence. See, e.g., *In re Disciplinary Proceedings Against Winter*, 187 Wis.2d 309, 522 N.W.2d 504 (1994) (lawyer suspended for, among other things, failing to return 50 phone calls from a client). California's rule is explicit on this point: a lawyer violates the rule against incompetent performance only by doing so "intentionally, recklessly, or repeatedly." Cal. Rule 3–110(A).

2.   *Remedies: Client Protection Funds and Restitution Systems*

One possible non-litigation remedy for lawyer incompetence that causes financial harm is recourse to the Client Protection Fund. Every jurisdiction has set up such a fund, designed to reimburse clients victimized by bad lawyering. But these funds vary widely in their effectiveness, and payouts are generally available only when the lawyer has committed especially egregious misconduct. In most states, the lawyer has to have been disbarred before the client can even apply to the fund for reimbursement of losses caused by the lawyer. Further, virtually all states cap the maximum payout per claim; for example, California's cap is $50,000, Illinois's is $10,000. See Elizabeth Amon, *An Empty Promise: How Client Protection Funds Betray Those They Were Designed to Protect*, Nat'l L.J., Aug. 28, 2000, at A1. Nationwide, these funds receive 4,700 claims per year. But they are "poorly endowed, stingy about payouts and virtually a secret, even to many lawyers, whose bar dues help finance them." *Id*. What this means, of course, is that even if state bars were to discipline lawyers for garden-variety incompetence (which they typically don't), the process would not provide adequate compensation to aggrieved clients.

In some states, clients can seek restitution from the lawyer in the same disciplinary proceeding determining whether the lawyer violated the rules of professional conduct. Should all states allow that? Would that result in fewer legal malpractice suits?

B. Ethics Rules on Law Firms and Associations

1. Duties of Supervisory Lawyers

Rules setting forth the duties of lawyers who supervise others in law firms also undergird the duty of competence. Model Rule 8.4 prohibits lawyers from knowingly assisting or inducing another lawyer to violate the rules. Under Model Rule 5.1(c), a lawyer who either orders a subordinate to violate the rules or who knows of a violation by a subordinate and fails to take remedial action is himself subject to discipline. Lawyers in supervisory positions (which includes partners in a general partnership) are not allowed to assume that subordinates will obey the rules. MR 5.1, comment [2]. Rather, a partner in a law firm must make "reasonable efforts" to see that the firm has procedures in place that will reasonably assure that the firm's lawyers obey the rules. MR 5.1(a). And a lawyer supervising another lawyer must make reasonable efforts to assure the other lawyer's compliance with the rules. MR 5.1(b). California's rules contain no special provision for supervisory lawyers, although the general rule on competence, Rule 3–110, has been used to discipline lawyers for failing to supervise both legal and non-legal personnel.

Some jurisdictions make supervisory lawyers responsible for a subordinate lawyer's misdeeds if the lawyer "knows or should know" of that conduct and fails to take reasonable remedial action. See, e.g., D.C. Rule 5.1(c)(2). In *In re Cohen*, 847 A.2d 1162 (D.C. 2004), a partner in a firm was suspended for 30 days for violating that rule, for failure to supervise adequately one of the firm's associates who himself violated rules on representing conflicting interests (Rule 1.7), failing to keep a client informed and to respond to requests for information (Rule 1.4), and failing to protect a client's interests after withdrawal from representation (Rule 1.16(d)). The partner conceded "that there was no system in place to impart rudimentary ethics training to lawyers in the firm, particularly the less experienced ones. Equally troubling was the lack of a review mechanism which allowed an associate's work to be reviewed and guided by a supervisory attorney." The partner argued, nonetheless, that he should not be held responsible for the conduct of a subordinate when he had no actual knowledge of the associate's offending conduct. Rejecting this contention in the face of the rule's clear language, the court said that D.C. Rule 5.1(c):

> reflects what this jurisdiction has determined to be a fair and necessary balance. On the one hand, it is not a rule of imputed liability for the underlying conduct.... On the other hand, Rule 5.1(c) (2) in this jurisdiction represents a judgment that attorneys supervising other lawyers must take reasonable steps to become knowledgeable about the actions of those attorneys in representing clients of the firm.... [T]he "reasonably know" provi-

sion was carefully crafted to encourage—indeed to require—supervising attorneys to reasonably monitor the
course of a representation such as respondent's firm had
undertaken on behalf of [the client here], denying them
the ostrich-like excuse of saying, in effect, "I didn't know
and I didn't want to know."

Model Rule 5.3 is a parallel provision to Rule 5.1, pertaining
to the supervision of non-lawyer assistants, such as secretaries,
investigators, paralegals, and law school student interns. See *In re
Comish*, 889 So.2d 236 (La. 2004) (three year suspension for
lawyer's failure to exercise sufficient supervisory oversight over
paralegal). Even if this rule did not exist, a lawyer whose supervision of non-legal staff members is shoddy or inattentive would
probably be subject to discipline under more general provisions on
competent representation. See, e.g., *Lorain Cty. Bar Ass'n v. Noll*,
105 Ohio St.3d 6, 821 N.E.2d 988 (2004) (applying Ohio disciplinary rules on neglecting legal matters, and on conduct that adversely reflects on a lawyer's fitness to practice, in case involving
inadequate supervision of paralegal; one-year suspension ordered).
Lawyers who supervise any such persons "shall make reasonable
efforts to ensure that the person's conduct is compatible with the
professional obligations of the lawyer," and will be responsible for
any such person's conduct "that would be a violation of the Rules
... if engaged in by a lawyer" on the same grounds as set forth
for lawyers in Rule 5.1(c). This means, among other things, a
lawyer cannot safely order a non-lawyer employee to engage in
conduct that would be unethical for the lawyer himself to engage
in. See, e.g., *Midwest Motor Sports v. Arctic Cat Sales, Inc.*, 347
F.3d 693 (8th Cir. 2003) (discovery misconduct).

2. *Duties of Subordinate Lawyers*

A lawyer being supervised by another lawyer—such as the
typical law firm associate—is bound by the rules even if directed
to take particular actions by a supervisory lawyer. MR 5.2(a).
However, where the supervisory lawyer makes a professional
judgment about an arguable issue of ethical propriety, the subordinate lawyer cannot be disciplined for acting in accordance with a
directive based on that judgment. MR 5.2(b). The comment to this
rule explains that if a particular question of professional duty
"can reasonably be answered only one way, the duty of both
lawyers is clear and they are equally responsible for fulfilling it."
Where a "question is reasonably arguable," however, the authority to resolve it "reposes in the supervisor, and a subordinate may
be guided accordingly." But where it is clear to the subordinate
that the supervisory lawyer is ordering the subordinate to engage
in conduct that would violate the ethics rules or other law, the
subordinate's proper course is to refuse the order. See, e.g.,
Kelley's Case, 137 N.H. 314, 627 A.2d 597 (1993) (subordinate

lawyer disciplined for representing conflicting interests on supervisory lawyer's orders). The subordinate might even be under a duty to report the supervisory lawyer's misconduct, as is explored in more detail below.

Does Rule 5.2's "safe harbor" provision strike the right balance, or should subordinate lawyers be liable for any misconduct even if they were following a supervisor's directions on an arguable point?

C. Reporting Professional Misconduct

In all but a few states (California, Georgia and Massachusetts), lawyers are placed under a limited, but mandatory, duty to report the misconduct of other lawyers to the proper authorities. As stated in Model Rule 8.3, this is indeed a limited duty: the duty to report depends on the lawyer's actual knowledge of the other lawyer's violation; the violation must raise a "substantial question as to that lawyer's honesty, trustworthiness or fitness as a lawyer in other respects"; and reporting is not required if it would require disclosure of information relating to the representation of a client and no exception to confidentiality applies. The ABA has opined that this reporting duty applies also to a lawyer who knows of another's mental impairment. ABA Formal Op. 03–431 (2003).

While discipline for failing to report other lawyers' misconduct or impairment is not common in Model Rule states, largely because of the "knowledge" requirement and the confidentiality exception, the universe is not entirely empty. In perhaps the most interesting case on the topic, *In re Riehlmann*, 891 So.2d 1239 (La. 2005), a criminal defense lawyer named Riehlmann met his close friend and law school classmate, a former prosecutor named Deegan, at a bar after work in April, 1994. Over drinks, Deegan told Riehlmann that he had just learned that he was dying of cancer. In the same conversation Deegan confessed that he had suppressed exculpatory blood evidence in a criminal case he had prosecuted years earlier. Riehlmann urged Deegan to "remedy the situation," but did not report Deegan's confession to anyone. Deegan died of cancer a few months later, having done nothing to remedy the situation.

Five years later, one of the defendants whom Deegan had prosecuted in 1985 was set to be executed by lethal injection. The lawyers for this defendant discovered a crime lab report that contained exculpatory blood evidence that proved their client's innocence. Riehlmann heard about this case, and immediately realized it was the case Deegan had told him about five years earlier. Riehlmann executed an affidavit for the defense lawyers in which he attested that in 1994 "the late Gerry Deegan said to me that he has intentionally suppressed blood evidence in the [case of the defendant] that in some way exculpated the defendant."

Shortly thereafter, Riehlmann reported Deegan's misconduct to state bar disciplinary authorities. He also testified in a hearing for a motion for new trial for the affected defendant.

Disciplinary authorities filed formal charges against Riehlmann for failing to report Deegan's misconduct earlier, in violation of Rules 8.3(a) (reporting misconduct) and 8.4(d) (engaging in conduct prejudicial to the administration of justice). Riehlmann claimed that he satisfied Rule 8.3 by reporting his conversation with Deegan to the defense attorneys, albeit years later. The disciplinary committee that first heard the case held that Riehlmann did not violate Rule 8.3 at all because "Mr. Deegan's statements at most suggested a *potential* violation of the ethical rules," and thus Riehlmann lacked "knowledge of a violation" that would trigger the reporting duty. On appeal to the next level of disciplinary authority, the hearing board reversed, finding a violation of Rule 8.3 and recommending a six month suspension. On final appeal, the Louisiana Supreme Court concluded that disciplinary counsel had proved a violation of Rule 8.3 by clear and convincing evidence. First, "absolute certainty of ethical misconduct is not required before the reporting requirement is triggered." The lawyer must have "more than a mere suspicion of ethical misconduct," but a report should be made if "a reasonable lawyer under the circumstances would form a firm belief that the [reportable] conduct in question had more likely than not occurred." Second, the rule requires "prompt" disclosure to bar disciplinary authorities, which was not done. Because Riehlmann lacked any "dishonest or selfish motive," however, the court ordered only a public reprimand.

The Model Code provision requiring reporting of other lawyers, DR 1–103(A), is stronger than its Model Rules counterpart, compelling reporting unless doing so would require the disclosure of information protected by the attorney-client privilege. Illinois, which still follows the Code, has a reporting requirement with real teeth. In *In re Himmel*, 125 Ill.2d 531, 127 Ill.Dec. 708, 533 N.E.2d 790 (1988), a lawyer was suspended for one year for failing to report to authorities his client's former lawyer's conversion of client funds. Discipline was ordered despite the fact that Himmel's client had directed him not to report her former lawyer, apparently on the belief that to do so would lessen her chances of getting her money back from him. See also *In re Anglin*, 122 Ill.2d 531, 120 Ill.Dec. 520, 524 N.E.2d 550 (1988) (denying petition for reinstatement by lawyer who refused to answer questions about another lawyer's misdeeds). Illinois' strict rule has influenced lawyers in that state to report other lawyers to the bar authorities almost 600 times per year, on average, since the *Himmel* decision. See Darryl Van Duch, *Partner Accused, Career Damaged*, Nat'l L. J., Mar. 15, 1999, at A1.

Is a reporting rule a good idea? Do you see it as part of the duty of a professional to help weed out bad colleagues? Do you think lawyers know of abuses that clients would not detect?

———

We saw in this chapter that a lawyer's incompetence will often bind the client to the poor result. We have also seen that winning a legal malpractice claim is no easy matter for a dissatisfied client. In the criminal setting, a lawyer's conduct must be beyond incompetent before a client can win either a malpractice suit or a reversal of the judgment based on ineffective assistance of counsel. If disciplinary enforcement is not particularly strict, either, what other forces push lawyers towards competent representation of clients? A sense of professionalism and pride in one's work, perhaps? Or does the market serve as the main deterrence to incompetence?

Chapter 3

THE DUTY OF CONFIDENTIALITY

Keeping clients' confidences is a fundamental duty of all lawyers, although this duty is subject to some well-recognized exceptions. The duty of confidentiality is embodied in two distinct doctrinal areas: (1) the law of evidence and (2) the rules of ethics, which in this instance derive primarily from the agency law. We will look at each of these areas in turn.

§ 1. ATTORNEY–CLIENT PRIVILEGE AND WORK–PRODUCT DOCTRINE

A. Purposes

The attorney-client privilege. Restatement § 68 provides that the attorney-client privilege may be invoked with respect to (1) a communication (2) made between privileged persons (3) in confidence (4) for the purpose of obtaining or providing legal assistance for the client. If a communication is ruled privileged, then it cannot be introduced into evidence in a legal proceeding, unless some exception applies or unless the privilege has been waived.

The privilege belongs to the client, not the lawyer. The client has the authority to decide whether to assert the privilege and whether to waive it. During a proceeding, if one party attempts to introduce into evidence or obtain discovery of a privileged communication, the lawyer of the client from whom the communication is sought must object and assert the privilege, unless the client has waived it or has authorized the lawyer to do so. Restatement § 86(1). The party asserting the privilege has the burden of proving each element of the privilege; a party asserting that the privilege has been waived or is subject to some exception bears that burden. Restatement §§ 86(2) & (3). A trial court's ruling on privilege is not usually immediately appealable, although some courts allow interlocutory appeals from such rulings. See *Ross v. City of Memphis*, 423 F.3d 596 (6th Cir. 2005) (following majority rule and noting contrary authority); Cf. *Will v. Hallock*, 546 U.S.

345, 126 S.Ct. 952, 163 L.Ed.2d 836 (2006) (describing collateral order doctrine generally).

Note that even though the privilege is the client's, the lawyer is allowed to reveal privileged communications in self-defense if the client sues the lawyer, or if the lawyer takes action to establish a right to attorney's fees the client refuses to pay. Restatement § 83. Situations under which the privilege may be waived are considered in Section D.

The work-product doctrine. Work product is tangible material that has been prepared by a party or a party's agent (such as a lawyer) in anticipation of litigation or for ongoing litigation. Such material is either: (a) "opinion" work product, which is material that reflects the lawyer's mental processes or opinions; or (b) "ordinary" work product, which is everything that is not "opinion" work product. See Restatement § 87. Opinion work product is usually completely immune from discovery, but there is only a qualified protection for ordinary work product. If the party asserting the work product immunity shows that the requested document or other tangible material qualifies as work product, then the party seeking discovery can overcome the immunity by showing "substantial need for the materials" and that the party "is unable without undue hardship to obtain the substantial equivalent of the materials by other means." FRCP 26(b)(3). Courts have split over who "owns" the work-product immunity, although most follow the rule that it belongs to the client, who has the authority to assert it or waive it. *Compare* Restatement § 90(1) (stating the majority rule) *with State Comp. Ins. Fund v. Superior Court*, 91 Cal.App.4th, 111 Cal.Rptr.2d (2001) (lawyer is the "exclusive holder" of the work product immunity).

All evidentiary privileges have the effect of withholding important information from the factfinder in a judicial proceeding. See *Fisher v. United States*, 425 U.S. 391, 96 S.Ct. 1569, 48 L.Ed.2d 39 (1976). What interests do the attorney-client privilege and work-product immunity protect? Are these interests sufficiently strong to warrant the costs these rules impose on the truth-seeking function of courts?

UPJOHN CO. v. UNITED STATES

Supreme Court of the United States, 1981.
449 U.S. 383, 101 S.Ct. 677, 66 L.Ed.2d 584.

Justice REHNQUIST delivered the opinion of the Court.

[After Upjohn's General Counsel was told that one of its foreign subsidiaries had made questionable payments to foreign government officials to secure government business, the company began an internal investigation. Upjohn lawyers sent a questionnaire to all foreign managers seeking detailed information about the payments, and the responses were returned to the General Counsel. The General Counsel and outside counsel also interviewed the recipients of the questionnaire and other Upjohn officers and employees. The Internal Revenue Service began its own investigation and sought production of the questionnaires and the memoranda and notes of the interviews. Upjohn refused to produce the documents, relying on the attorney-client and work product privileges. The trial court ordered production on the ground that the attorney-client privilege had been waived and that the IRS had made a sufficient showing of necessity to overcome the protection of the work-product doctrine. The Court of Appeals affirmed the order to produce, holding that while the attorney-client privilege had not been waived, it did not apply to communications that were made by officers and agents who were not in Upjohn's "control group"; that is, those officers who were responsible for directing Upjohn's actions in response to legal advice. The appeals court also held that the work-product doctrine did not apply to IRS summonses.]

. . . The attorney-client privilege is the oldest of the privileges for confidential communications known to the common law. Its purpose is to encourage full and frank communication between attorneys and their clients and thereby promote broader public interests in the observance of law and administration of justice. The privilege recognizes that sound legal advice or advocacy serves public ends and that such advice or advocacy depends upon the lawyer's being fully informed by the client. . . . "The lawyer-client privilege rests on the need for the advocate and counselor to know all that relates to the client's reasons for seeking representation if the professional mission is to be carried out." [T]he purpose of the privilege to be "to encourage clients to make full disclosure to their attorneys." This rationale for the privilege has long been recognized by the Court, see *Hunt v. Blackburn*, 128 U.S. 464, 470 (1888) (privilege "is founded upon the necessity, in the interest and administration of justice, of the aid of persons having knowledge of the law and skilled in its practice, which assistance can only be safely and readily availed of when free from the consequences or the apprehension of disclosure"). . . .

[T]he privilege exists to protect not only the giving of professional advice to those who can act on it but also the giving of information to the lawyer to enable him to give sound and informed advice. The first step in the resolution of any legal problem is ascertaining the factual background and sifting through the facts with an eye to the legally relevant. . . .

The communications at issue were made by Upjohn employees to counsel for Upjohn acting as such, at the direction of corporate superiors in order to secure legal advice from counsel. . . . The communications concerned matters within the scope of the employees' corporate duties, and the employees themselves were sufficiently aware that they were being questioned in order that the corporation could obtain legal advice.... Pursuant to explicit instructions from the Chairman of the Board, the communications were considered "highly confidential" when made, and have been kept confidential by the company. Consistent with the underlying purposes of the attorney-client privilege, these communications must be protected against compelled disclosure.

The Court of Appeals declined to extend the attorney-client privilege beyond the limits of the control group test for fear that doing so would entail severe burdens on discovery and create a broad "zone of silence" over corporate affairs. Application of the attorney-client privilege to communications such as those involved here, however, puts the adversary in no worse position than if the communications had never taken place. The privilege only protects disclosure of communications; it does not protect disclosure of the underlying facts by those who communicated with the attorney:

> "[T]he protection of the privilege extends only to *communications* and not to facts. A fact is one thing and a communication concerning that fact is an entirely different thing. The client cannot be compelled to answer the question, 'What did you say or write to the attorney?' but may not refuse to disclose any relevant fact within his knowledge merely because he incorporated a statement of such fact into his communication to his attorney." *Philadelphia v. Westinghouse Electric Corp.*, 205 F.Supp. 830, 831 (E.D.Pa.1962).

Here the Government was free to question the employees who communicated with Thomas and outside counsel. Upjohn has provided the IRS with a list of such employees, and the IRS has already interviewed some 25 of them. While it would probably be more convenient for the Government to secure the results of petitioner's internal investigation by simply subpoenaing the questionnaires and notes taken by petitioner's attorneys, such considerations of convenience do not overcome the policies served by the attorney-client privilege. As Justice Jackson noted in his concurring opinion in *Hickman v. Taylor*, 329 U.S., at 516: "Discovery was hardly intended to enable a learned profession to perform its functions ... on wits borrowed from the adversary." ...

Our decision that the communications by Upjohn employees to counsel are covered by the attorney-client privilege disposes of the case so far as the responses to the questionnaires and any notes reflecting responses to interview questions are concerned. The summons reaches further, however, and Thomas has testified that his notes and memoranda of interviews go beyond recording responses to his questions. To the extent that the material subject

to the summons is not protected by the attorney-client privilege as
disclosing communications between an employee and counsel, we
must reach the ruling by the Court of Appeals that the work-
product doctrine does not apply . . .

The Government concedes, wisely, that the Court of Appeals
erred and that the work-product doctrine does apply to IRS
summonses. This doctrine was announced by the Court over 30
years ago in *Hickman v. Taylor*, 329 U.S. 495 (1947). In that case
the Court rejected "an attempt, without purported necessity or
justification, to secure written statements, private memoranda
and personal recollections prepared or formed by an adverse
party's counsel in the course of his legal duties." The Court noted
that "it is essential that a lawyer work with a certain degree of
privacy" and reasoned that if discovery of the material sought
were permitted

> "much of what is now put down in writing would remain
> unwritten. An attorney's thoughts, heretofore inviolate,
> would not be his own. Inefficiency, unfairness and sharp
> practices would inevitably develop in the giving of legal
> advice and in the preparation of cases for trial. The effect
> on the legal profession would be demoralizing. And the
> interests of the clients and the cause of justice would be
> poorly served."

The "strong public policy" underlying the work-product doctrine . . . has been substantially incorporated in Federal Rule of
Civil Procedure 26(b)(3), [which] accords special protection to
work product revealing the attorney's mental processes. The Rule
permits disclosure of documents and tangible things constituting
attorney work product upon a showing of substantial need and
inability to obtain the equivalent without undue hardship. Rule 26
goes on, however, to state that "[i]n ordering discovery of such
materials when the required showing has been made, the court
shall protect against disclosure of the mental impressions, conclusions, opinions or legal theories of an attorney or other representative of a party concerning the litigation." Although this language does not specifically refer to memoranda based on oral
statements of witnesses, the *Hickman* court stressed the danger
that compelled disclosure of such memoranda would reveal the
attorney's mental processes. It is clear that this is the sort of
material the draftsmen of the Rule had in mind as deserving
special protection. . . .

The notes and memoranda sought by the Government here
. . . are work product based on oral statements. If they reveal
communications, they are, in this case, protected by the attorney-
client privilege. To the extent they do not reveal communications,
they reveal the attorneys' mental processes in evaluating the
communications. As Rule 26 and *Hickman* make clear, such work

product cannot be disclosed simply on a showing of substantial need and inability to obtain the equivalent without undue hardship.

While we are not prepared at this juncture to say that such material is always protected by the work-product rule, we think a far stronger showing of necessity and unavailability by other means than was made by the Government or applied by the [trial court] in this case would be necessary to compel disclosure....

[Reversed on the attorney-client issue; reversed and remanded on the work product issue.]

Notes

1. What would happen if there was no attorney-client privilege? Would a client speak freely to a lawyer, and vice versa? If not, why is that problematic? Wouldn't it be helpful for an adversary in litigation to know, for example, what the lawyer told the client about the strength of his case?

2. Why does a work-product immunity exist at all? Wouldn't allowing access even to notes reflecting lawyers' mental processes result in fewer frivolous lawsuits and faster (and more informed) settlements? Or does giving access to the adversary's lawyer's strategies run afoul of the accepted vision of "professionalism?"

3. *Sources of the law: the attorney-client privilege.* In cases to which federal law applies, the delineation of the contours of the attorney-client privilege, and the application of that privilege, is left to the common law process. Fed. R. Evid. 501 (questions of privilege "shall be governed by the principles of the common law"). When state law applies—either in state court, or in federal court when state law supplies the substantive applicable law—the rules setting out the contours of the privilege are most often found in a state statute, usually the state evidence code.

4. *Sources of the law: the work-product immunity.* As you can see from *Upjohn*, in cases to which federal law applies, the work-product doctrine is recognized both in a rule of federal civil procedure, and in the body of common law following *Hickman v. Taylor*. Most states have codified the work-product doctrine in state statutes or court rules for application in their own courts, although a few have only common-law rules on the subject. See Restatement § 87, comment e.

B.   Scope of Protection
1.   The Work–Product Doctrine

STEWART v. FALLEY'S, INC.
United States District Court, D. Kansas, 2001.
2001 WL 1318371.

KAREN M. HUMPHREYS, Magistrate Judge.

This employment discrimination action is before the court on plaintiff's motion to compel production of a memorandum created by defendant's employee. Defendant opposes the motion and argues that the memorandum was prepared in anticipation of litigation and should be protected under Fed.R.Civ.P. 26(b)(3). For the reasons stated below, the motion shall be denied.

The facts concerning creation of the memorandum are undisputed. On August 4, 1999, Beverly Broxterman, Falley's Human Resources Director, learned that plaintiff had made a report of sexual harassment on Falley's "Alert–Line." On August 5, Broxterman called plaintiff to inquire about the complaint and was told "talk to [my] lawyer." On the same day, plaintiff's attorney sent Broxterman a letter advising that plaintiff had filed a charge of discrimination with EEOC and that any future communications concerning plaintiff's termination should be directed to her counsel.

Broxterman commenced an investigation of plaintiff's sexual harassment claim based on counsel's notice of an EEOC charge and the "Alert Line" message. After interviewing several witnesses, Broxterman prepared a summary of her investigation and opinion about plaintiff's claims. During discovery the defendant provided plaintiff with the actual handwritten statements made by witnesses and plaintiff's motion seeks production of the memo containing Broxterman's summary and opinion....

Defendant contends that Rule 26(b)(3) protects Broxterman's memorandum from discovery. The Rule provides:

> [A] party may obtain discovery of documents and tangible things otherwise discoverable under subsection (b)(1) of this rule and prepared in anticipation of litigation or for trial by or for another party or by or for another party's representative (including the other party's attorney, consultant, surety, indemnitor, insurer, or agent) only upon a showing that the party seeking discovery has substantial need of the materials in the preparation of the party's case and that the party is unable without undue hardship to obtain the substantial equivalent of the materials by other means.

Fed.R.Civ.P. 26(b)(3)(emphasis added). The party opposing discovery must show (1) that the material is a document or tangible thing, (2) that the material was prepared in anticipation of litigation, and (3) that the material was prepared by or for a party or by or for the party's attorney. *Burton v. R.J. Reynolds Tobacco Co.*, 167 F.R.D. 134, 139 (D.Kan. 1996).

In this case, the first element (a document or tangible thing) has been clearly established because the discovery concerns a written memorandum. The second element (prepared in anticipation of litigation) has been satisfied by defendant's showing that the memorandum was prepared after notice that plaintiff was represented by counsel and had filed a discrimination claim. See e.g., *EEOC v. General Motors,* 1988 WL 170448 (D.Kan. August 23, 1988) (defendant justified in believing litigation imminent after charges filed with EEOC). The third element (by or for a party or by or for a party's representative) is established because Broxterman is defendant's employee and representative.

Although defendant has satisfied the three elements in Rule 26(b)(3), plaintiff argues that defendant must also show that the memorandum was prepared at the direction of an attorney. The court disagrees. The 1970 amendments to Rule 26 expressly extended the work product protection to documents prepared for litigation by the adverse party itself or its agent. 6 Wright, Miller & Marcus, Federal Practice and Procedure § 2024 at 364 (1994); *Otto v. Box U.S.A. Group,* 177 F.R.D. 698 (D.Ga.1997)(a party may create Rule 26(b)(3) material before securing the assistance of counsel); *Augenti v. Cappellini,* 84 F.R.D. 73 (M.D.Pa.1979)(a party's pre-litigation notes may be work product). Plaintiff's argument is contrary to the express language of Rule 26(b)(3) and therefore rejected.

Defendant has satisfied all three requirements of Rule 26(b)(3). After the party asserting Rule 26(b)(3) has made the necessary showing, the burden shifts to the party seeking discovery to show (1) a substantial need for the materials and (2) that the party is unable, without undue hardship, to obtain the substantial equivalent of the material by other means. Plaintiff has made no attempt to show either in its brief; thus, Broxterman's memorandum is protected from discovery by Rule 26(b)(3)....

IT IS THEREFORE ORDERED that plaintiff's motion to compel (Doc. 22) is DENIED.

Notes

1. *What is being protected?* The work-product doctrine protects documents and other tangible materials, not the underlying information contained therein. As the court said in *Raso v. CMC Equipment Rental, Inc.,* 154 F.R.D. 126 (E.D.Pa.1994), "Rule 26(b)(3) pertains to the production of documents and tangible things and not to the knowledge of the other party.... [T]he work product doctrine does not apply to facts within the knowledge of the person who is to be deposed...." This means that, very much like the attorney-client privilege, a party cannot use the work product rule as a shield against the discovery of facts that would be otherwise discoverable. In *Raso,* this meant that plaintiffs were allowed to depose an investigator who had conducted an investigation of an accident about "his observations made at the accident location, individuals he spoke with ... and the facts he learned during the investigation and from whom such facts were discovered," even though the documents he produced in that investigation might be work product.

2. *"Selection and compilation" exception.* Normally, the work product doctrine does not protect materials in a lawyer's possession that were not prepared by either the client, the lawyer or the agents of either. See, e.g., *In re Grand Jury Subpoenas (United States v. Doe)*, 959 F.2d 1158 (2d Cir. 1992) (telephone company records in lawyer's possession not entitled to work product protection). There is some authority for a narrow exception to this general rule, where the lawyer has selected and compiled third-party materials in anticipation of litigation, and discovery of the materials in that form would improperly intrude into the lawyer's strategic thinking. See *Sporck v. Peil*, 759 F.2d 312 (3d Cir. 1985); *Shelton v. American Motors Corp.*, 805 F.2d 1323 (8th Cir. 1986). A lawyer seeking to invoke this exception must demonstrate a real, rather than speculative, concern that discovery would reveal such strategic thinking. See, e.g., *In re Grand Jury Subpoenas Dated March 19, 2002 and August 2, 2002 (Mercator Corp. v. United States)*, 318 F.3d 379 (2d Cir. 2003).

3. *"In anticipation of litigation."* The work-product doctrine does not protect everything a party or a lawyer writes. Rather, its protection is limited in virtually all jurisdictions to material prepared in anticipation of litigation, or during ongoing litigation. See *In re Powerhouse Licensing, LLC*, 441 F.3d 467 (6th Cir. 2006) (documents in law firm's possession relevant to structuring of allegedly fraudulent transfers were not prepared in anticipation of litigation, and thus were discoverable by judgment creditor); *Lazar v. Riggs*, 79 P.3d 105 (Colo. 2003) (statements made by client to an insurance adjuster before litigation was initiated or imminent were not protected).

The contours of this limitation are not always clear on the facts of particular cases. This is especially so if a lawyer prepares material for possible litigation that never occurs. How does anyone really know what motivated the lawyer's work under such circumstances? In *United States v. Adlman*, 68 F.3d 1495 (2d Cir. 1995), two wholly-owned subsidiaries of a corporation were planning to merge. The lawyer for the corporate parent asked an accountant to prepare an analysis of the tax consequences of the proposed merger. The analysis as prepared focused on the Internal Revenue Service's possible challenges to the merger, as well as the corporation's possible claim of a tax refund. It included an analysis of an expected litigation between the corporation and the IRS. After the merger was completed, the IRS sought the report and the corporation claimed the work-product immunity. The trial court found the immunity inapplicable because litigation had in fact never occurred and, at the time the report was written, the merger had not happened, either. The Second Circuit reversed: "There is no rule," the court said, "that bars application of work product protection to documents created prior to the event giving rise to litigation." On remand the trial court again held the report was not work product, and the circuit court again reversed. *United States v. Adlman*, 134 F.3d 1194 (2d Cir. 1998). The court held that the view that the work-product rule protects only documents "prepared to assist in litigation" is far too narrow, and belied by the test of FRCP 26(b)(3). Documents prepared to assist in the making of a business decision, when litigation is reasonably anticipated, are protected. See also *In re: Sealed Case*, 146 F.3d 881 (D.C.Cir.1998) (holding that the fact that a "specific claim" had not yet arisen was "just one factor that courts should consider in determining whether the work-product privilege applies"; the ultimate question is whether the lawyer prepared the materials in anticipation of litigation).

4.   *Materials developed "in the ordinary course of business."* Most states afford work product protection only to materials prepared in anticipation of litigation, which means that documents prepared in the ordinary course of business are not protected. The rationale is that they would have been prepared anyway, and need no special protection. See *In re Grand Jury Subpoena*, 220 F.R.D. 130 (D. Mass. 2004) (lawyer's notes of meeting with FDA regarding client's product were not work product, since meeting was in the regular course of business and was not related to any planned or pending litigation). What if a document is prepared in anticipation of litigation but also serves a dual purpose, such as to assist with a purely business decision? Does it lose work-product protection? See *Caremark, Inc. v. Affiliated Computer Services, Inc.*, 195 F.R.D. 610 (N.D.Ill.2000) (no).

5.   *Broader formulations of the work-product doctrine.* In a few states the work-product doctrine has been extended to documents prepared by lawyers in connection with a *transaction*, such as memos written in connection with the negotiation of business deals, to the extent that those documents reflect the lawyers' legal opinions and conclusions. See, e.g., *State Comp. Ins. Fund v. Superior Court*, 91 Cal.App.4th 1080, 111 Cal.Rptr.2d 284 (2001); *County of Los Angeles v. Superior Court*, 82 Cal.App.4th 819, 98 Cal.Rptr.2d 564 (2000).

6.   *When is ordinary work product discoverable?* As the *Stewart* case makes clear, ordinary work product is discoverable if the party seeking discovery can prove two things: (1) a substantial need for the material; and (2) the inability, without undue hardship, to obtain the substantial equivalent by other means. The most common examples of material that becomes discoverable via such showings are accident reports prepared by a party or an investigator immediately afterwards. See, e.g., *Coogan v. Cornet Transp. Co.*, 199 F.R.D. 166 (D.Md.2001) (reasoning that a party usually has a need for such reports and cannot obtain another contemporaneous statement without undue hardship, if at all); *National Union Fire Ins. Co. v. Murray Sheet Metal Co.*, 967 F.2d 980 (4th Cir.1992) (same); *Jenkins v. Rainner*, 69 N.J. 50, 350 A.2d 473 (1976) (allowing discovery of motion picture films of a personal-injury plaintiff made by investigator during investigation of claim).

7.   *Discoverability of opinion work product: Putting-in-issue.* Most courts hold that the mental impressions of a lawyer as reflected in work-product material are not discoverable. However, one recognized exception is where a party raises an issue in the litigation that depends upon an evaluation of the legal theories, opinions and conclusions of counsel.

This might occur, for example, when a party sues a lawyer for malicious prosecution or bad faith litigation. See, e.g., *Morrow v. Brown, Todd & Heyburn*, 957 S.W.2d 722 (Ky.1997) (collecting cases from several jurisdictions).

Another aspect of this rule is that if material prepared in anticipation of litigation is reasonably expected or intended to be used as an exhibit or as evidence at trial, it is fully discoverable; only material that is used for "strategy and trial preparation purposes only" are protected by the work product doctrine. *Northup v. Acken*, 865 So.2d 1267 (Fla. 2004).

Notions of forensic fairness undergird the "putting-in-issue" exception: it is unfair to a party's adversary to allow the party to assert particular contentions and then "rely on its privileges to deprive its adversary of access to material that might disprove or undermine the party's contentions." *In re Grand Jury Proceedings (John Doe Co. v. United States)*, 350 F.3d 299 (2d Cir. 2003).

8. *Discoverability of opinion work product: Experts.* When work-product material is provided to a testifying expert witness, most federal courts hold that the immunity is waived under FRCP 26 even for opinion work product. The primary rationale for this holding is that the rule itself requires parties to submit reports for testifying experts, including any information the expert used in formulating his or her opinion. See, e.g, *Regional Airport Auth. of Louisville & Jefferson County v. LFG, LLC*, 460 F.3d 697 (6th Cir. 2006); *In re Pioneer Hi–Bred International Inc.*, 238 F.3d 1370 (Fed.Cir.2001); *contra, Haworth, Inc. v. Herman Miller, Inc.*, 162 F.R.D. 289 (W.D. Mich. 1995). State courts construing their own state's procedural and evidentiary rules do not necessarily agree with the majority federal approach, in part because their procedural rules may not be identical. *Compare Gall v. Jamison*, 44 P.3d 233 (Colo.2002) (work product protection is lost even where expert witness merely reviewed the material but did not rely on it in forming an opinion) *with Crowe Countryside Realty Assocs.*, 891 A.2d 838 (R.I. 2006) (ordinary work product becomes discoverable when shown to a testifying expert, but opinion work product does not).

Opinion work product generated by an expert is generally discoverable if the expert testifies, but remains privileged if the expert is a nontestifying consultant. See *In re Cendant Corp. Securities Lit.*, 343 F.3d 658 (3d Cir. 2003).

9. *Duration.* Does the work product doctrine cover materials prepared for anticipated litigation that is different from the case in which the material is sought? And does work product immunity last longer than the case for which the material was prepared? The usual answer to both questions is yes. In *In re Murphy*, 560 F.2d 326 (8th Cir. 1977), the court reasoned:

> Counsel should be allowed to amass data and commit his opinions and thought process to writing free of the concern that, at some later date, an opposing party may be entitled to secure

any relevant work product documents merely on request and use them against his client. The work product privilege would be attenuated if it were limited to documents that were prepared in the case for which discovery is sought. What is needed, if we are to remain faithful to the articulated policies of *Hickman*, is a perpetual protection for work product. . . .

Accord, e.g., *Shook v. City of Davenport*, 497 N.W.2d 883 (Iowa 1993) (giving identical scope to the Iowa state version of FRCP 26).

10. *Losing work-product protection through improper or "unprofessional" conduct.* Some courts have held that materials prepared in anticipation of litigation are not entitled to work-product protection because of the "unprofessional" or improper way they were prepared. For example, where a party secretly tapes a conversation with witnesses or other parties, the privilege may be held to have been vitiated. See, e.g., *Otto v. Box U.S.A. Group, Inc.*, 177 F.R.D. 698 (N.D.Ga.1997); *Ward v. Maritz Inc.*, 156 F.R.D. 592 (D.N.J.1994) (noting the "unprofessional behavior" of the lawyers in recommending the secret taping). Does this limitation make sense given the broad goals of the work-product doctrine itself?

---

2. The Attorney–Client Privilege

As one court aptly put it, "Although the attorney-client privilege may be the most venerable of the privileges for confidential communications, its accoutrements are not the most clearly delineated." *In re Keeper of the Records (XYZ Corp. v. United States)*, 348 F.3d 16 (1st Cir. 2003). That is to say that the attorney-client privilege is frequently litigated, and judicial decisions on the privilege are not always reconcilable with one another. Indeed, each of the requirements of the attorney client privilege has produced a great deal of case law and scholarly commentary. Some of the key issues are referenced below, keyed to the Restatement's list of the privilege's four basic requirements.

a. Communication

A communication includes any expression that is an attempt to convey information and any document or other record that reveals such an expression. Restatement § 69. A communication may be written or oral, or even demonstrative, such as a client's opening his jacket to show a blood stain on his shirt.

The privilege protects *communications*, but not necessarily the *information* conveyed in the communications. See *Upjohn*, supra. For example, suppose a client goes to a lawyer for advice about an automobile accident he was involved in. He shows the lawyer a complaint that has been filed in state court by the other driver. The client tells the lawyer all about how the accident occurred. Would this communication, even if conducted in the privacy of the lawyer's office, keep the opposing party from asking the client about how the accident occurred? Of course not. The attorney-client privilege does not allow a client to "immunize" facts simply by telling them to his lawyer in confidence. On the other hand, the attorney-client privilege would prevent the client from being compelled to answer the opponent's question, "What did you say to your lawyer about the accident?" *That* is a protected "communication."

In the *Upjohn* case, notice, while the questionnaires were held to be privileged, the court said that the IRS could interview Upjohn employees who had filled them out about the information contained in them. Thus filling out a questionnaire to be sent to a lawyer does not "immunize" from discovery the information itself that is contained in the questionnaire. Similarly, it is clear that if a document that was not privileged when originally generated does not become privileged simply by a client's sending it to an attorney. Why would that be the rule? What would occur if the rule were otherwise?

In general, the identity of a client and the mere fact of consultation are not privileged because they are not considered "communications," or more properly, because their revelation does not reveal any protected communications. See, e.g., *Chirac v. Reinicker*, 24 U.S. (11 Wheat.) 280, 6 L.Ed. 474 (1826). However, in those rare cases where the disclosure of the client's identity would also disclose a privileged communication, then the privilege may protect the client's identity. In *Baird v. Koerner*, 279 F.2d 623 (9th Cir. 1960), for example, lawyer Baird sent a cashier's check to the IRS on behalf of anonymous clients for additional taxes due. The IRS sought the identities of these clients and Baird refused. The Ninth Circuit held that the identities were in fact privileged, because disclosure of the anonymous clients' identities to the IRS would necessarily disclose their motive for consulting Baird, which itself was a privileged communication. See also *United States v. Under Seal*, 204 F.3d 516 (4th Cir. 2000)(client identity privileged where it would reveal confidential communication).

While retainer agreements and fee arrangements are generally not privileged, either, for the same reasons that client identity is not, the same caveat would appear to apply: if revelation of such agreements would reveal confidential communications, the privilege should attach to that extent. By statute, written fee agreements are confidential in California, thus subject to the attorney-client privilege. Cal. Bus. & Prof. Code § 6149.

b. Made Between Privileged Persons

To be protected by the privilege, the communication must occur between privileged persons. Obviously, the lawyer and the client qualify. Even a prospective client is a privileged person, so that an initial confidential communication between a lawyer and a person about a potential representation that does not occur may still be privileged. Further, if a client reasonably believes the person with whom she is speaking is a lawyer, the conversation may still be privileged even if the client is mistaken. See, e.g., Cal. Evid. Code § 950 (defining "lawyer" to include a person "reasonably believed by the client to be authorized to practice law in any state or nation"). Why would this be?

Can anyone else be in the room when the client and lawyer are communicating without destroying the privilege? Consider the next case.

STROH v. GENERAL MOTORS CORP.

New York Supreme Court, Appellate Division, First Department, 1995.
213 A.D.2d 267, 623 N.Y.S.2d 873.

Before ELLERIN, J.P., and WALLACH, ROSS and WILLIAMS, JJ.

Order, Supreme Court, New York County (William J. Davis, J.), entered June 14, 1994, which granted the motion of defendant General Motors Corporation ("GMC"), pursuant to CPLR 3124, to compel defendant Stella Maychick at her deposition to answer co-defendant GMC's questions, over objection by her counsel, on the ground of attorney-client privilege, unanimously reversed, on the law, and the motion denied, without costs.

This action arises out of a highly publicized accident which occurred at Washington Square Park in Manhattan on April 23, 1992. When Mrs. Maychick lost control of the Oldsmobile she was driving, the car jumped the sidewalk curb, hurtled into the park, and injured at least a dozen people. Twelve separate actions, now consolidated, were commenced, seeking damages against Mrs. Maychick as owner and operator of the vehicle, and against GMC as its manufacturer.

At two depositions conducted of the 76–year-old Mrs. Maychick by GMC, the latter's attorneys sought to elicit details of all of her discussions with her own lawyers. GMC contended, and the motion court agreed, that because Mrs. Maychick's daughter, Diana, was present during those conversations, the statutory attorney-client privilege which would normally protect those communications from compulsory disclosure (CPLR 4503[a]) did not attach. GMC argues that the daughter's presence negated the vital element of confidentiality necessary to invoke the privilege (see, People v. Harris, 57 N.Y.2d 335, 456 N.Y.S.2d 694, 442 N.E.2d 1205, cert. denied 460 U.S. 1047, 103 S.Ct. 1448, 75 L.Ed.2d 803). We disagree.

Generally, the circumstances of each case will determine whether a communication by a client to an attorney should be afforded the cloak of privilege. In our assessment of this record, the existing circumstances weigh heavily in favor of preservation of the privilege. We are here presented with an aged woman required to recall, and perhaps relive, what was probably the most traumatic experience of her life. Her daughter selected the law firm to represent her, transported her to the law office, and put her sufficiently at ease to communicate effectively with counsel. "[C]ommunications made to counsel through ... one serving as an agent of ... [the] client to facilitate communication, generally will be privileged" (*People v. Osorio,* 75 N.Y.2d 80, 84, 550 N.Y.S.2d 612, 549 N.E.2d 1183).

Furthermore, it appears that Diana had been a passenger who had alighted from the vehicle just before it proceeded to the accident site. Diana's role as a possible witness to aid the memory of her mother cannot be overlooked. The scope of the privilege is not to be defined by a third party's employment or function; it rather depends upon whether the client had "a reasonable expectation of confidentiality under the circumstances." We think it unreasonable to discern any other expectation by either Mrs. Maychick or her attorneys, because Diana was clearly acting as her mother's agent in this setting. . . .

Notes

1.   Suppose that the client in *Stroh* had been a 30-year-old, healthy, fully competent adult, accompanied by her 35-year-old adult sister who was present only for "moral support." Would the communication between the lawyer and the client have been privileged? What would you as a lawyer tell a client who wanted to bring along a family member to an otherwise-private meeting?

2.   What if a lawyer, alone with his client in the lawyer's office, telephones the person who later becomes the adversary in a lawsuit? In *Cooney v. Booth,* 198 F.R.D. 62 (E.D.Pa.2000), the Cooneys contacted attorney Fine for advice about a possible medical malpractice claim. With the Cooneys in his office, Fine telephoned Dr. Mantell, the doctor who performed one of the operations at issue. Later, Fine met alone with Mantell to gather more facts. Another lawyer subsequently took on the Cooneys' case and sued Dr. Mantell for medical malpractice. Mantell sought to depose Fine in order to learn what the Cooneys claimed that Mantell had told Fine about the medical procedure involved in the case. The Cooneys claimed that the conversations between Fine and Mantell were protected by the attorney-client privilege and/or the work-product doctrine. Held, the communications were not privileged. Indeed, nothing in the first meeting between the Cooneys and Fine was privileged because "a third party, Dr. Mantell, participated in the conversation. This is true even though Dr. Mantell was not in the room during the

conversation but on the telephone." The latter conversation between Fine and Mantell was not privileged "because conversations occurring between a client's attorney and a third party are not protected." Thus Mantell could depose Fine and ask him about those conversations.

3. What if the doctor in *Cooney* had not been an adversary of the clients', but rather an ally? Suppose, for example, that the lawyer, in the client's presence, had phoned the client's doctor to get the doctor's interpretation of what the client was telling him about injuries that occurred in a car accident. Would that communication be privileged? In *United States v. Kovel*, 296 F.2d 918 (2d Cir. 1961), the court held that an accountant's presence at a lawyer-client meeting did not destroy the privilege: "Accounting concepts are a foreign language to some lawyers in almost all cases, and to almost all lawyers in some cases. Hence the presence of an accountant, whether hired by the lawyer or by the client, while the client is relating a complicated tax story to the lawyer, ought not to destroy the privilege, any more than would that of the linguist." The accountant's participation in the meeting under such circumstances was "necessary, or at least highly useful, for the effective consultation between the client and the lawyer which the privilege is designed to permit."

4. *Public relations consultants.* In *Calvin Klein Trademark Trust v. Wachner*, 198 F.R.D. 53 (S.D.N.Y. 2000), the court held that documents exchanged between the plaintiffs' lawyer and a public relations firm allegedly hired to help the lawyers understand the possible public relations fallout of the lawsuit were not privileged. Even if such documents were privileged to begin with, such privilege was lost when they were disclosed to the PR firm; the PR firm was "at most, simply providing ordinary public relations advice," rather than serving as a "translator" like the accountant in *Kovel*, who helped the lawyer "to understand aspects of the client's own communications that could not otherwise be appreciated in the rendering of legal advice."

But in *In re Grand Jury Subpoenas Dated March 24, 2003*, 265 F.Supp.2d 321 (S.D.N.Y. 2003), the court held that confidential communications between lawyers and PR consultants hired by the lawyers to assist them in dealing with the media on the client's behalf were protected by the attorney-client privilege. The court factually distinguished *Calvin Klein* by noting that in that case, the PR firm had a relationship with the client that predated the litigation, rather than being hired by the lawyers after litigation had commenced. More fundamentally, however, the court expressed its disagreement with the *Calvin Klein* court's apparent assumption of a negative answer to a key question: "whether a lawyer's public advocacy on behalf of the client is a professional legal service that warrants extension of the privilege to confidential communications between and among the client, the lawyer, and any public relations consultant the lawyer may engage to advise on the performance of that function." Dealing with the media effectively, the court said, is part of a good lawyer's arsenal—and thus lawyers need to "engage in frank discussions of facts and strategies with the lawyers' public relations consultants" without fear of disclosure.

5. The law's lack of clarity about precisely whose presence will destroy the privilege has led some of the country's greatest legal minds to make errors. In *In re Grand Jury Subpoena Duces Tecum*, 112 F.3d 910 (8th Cir. 1997), then-First Lady (now Senator) Hillary Rodham Clinton was subpoenaed to appear before a grand jury investigating the Whitewater real estate matter. She arrived at the courthouse accompanied by her own counsel from Williams & Connolly as well as by an assistant White House counsel. Although the lawyers were not allowed in the grand jury room during her testimony, Clinton met with them during breaks. The White House lawyer took notes of these meetings. Special Counsel Kenneth Starr subpoenaed these notes. Clinton asserted the attorney-client privilege. But the court held that they were not privileged because the presence of the White House counsel—who was not Clinton's personal lawyer—destroyed the privilege.

6. *Common-interest doctrine and co-client rule.* The attorney-client privilege and work-product doctrine apply in a special way in multi-party situations. When two or more parties are represented by separate counsel in a "matter of common interest," each party has a privilege to refuse to disclose and to prevent the other parties from disclosing confidential information "made for the purpose of facilitating the rendition of professional services." Proposed Fed. R. Evid. 503(b). Accord, Restatement § 76(1); *OXY Resources California LLC v. Superior Court*, 115 Cal.App.4th 874, 9 Cal.Rptr.3d 621 (2004)(applying Cal. Evid. Code § 962). While such communications are privileged as against third persons, there is no privilege for such communications between the "common interest" parties if they wind up suing each other. Id. § 76(2). The same rules apply to co-clients being represented by a single lawyer. See Restatement § 75.

NOTE: ORGANIZATIONAL CLIENTS

As *Upjohn* clearly illustrates, the attorney-client privilege applies to corporations as well as to individual clients. Application of the privilege in the corporate setting, however, is not as simple as it is with individual clients. For example, when a corporate employee is communicating something to a lawyer working for the corporation, is that employee speaking on behalf of the corporate client? Is that employee herself a client? Prior to the *Upjohn* opinion, some lower federal courts had held that only those within the corporation's "control group" (those, generally in the upper ranks of the corporate ladder, who have the power to direct the corporate entity do something) were considered as speaking for the corporation and were thus "privileged persons." While *Upjohn* rejected that position, it did not clearly articulate an alternative, leaving federal law in something of an unsettled state. *Upjohn* applies only to federal court claims, so, state courts remain free to construe the privilege differently. Many states have continued to apply the "control group" test rejected by *Upjohn*. See, e.g., *Consolidation Coal Co. v. Bucyrus–Erie Co.*, 89 Ill.2d 103, 59 Ill.Dec. 666, 432 N.E.2d 250 (1982).

The Restatement provides that when the client is an organization—such as a corporation, unincorporated association, partnership, trust, estate, sole proprietorship—the organization can claim the attorney-client privilege only where the communication "concerns a legal matter of interest to the organization" and is disclosed only to privileged persons and "agents of the organization who reasonably need to know of the communication" in order to act on the organization's behalf. Restatement § 73.

Can a lawyer represent both the organization and one or more executives or employees of the company? Yes, although such dual representation must comply with the rules on conflicts of interest that we will see in detail in Chapter Six. A lawyer who represents an organization should make clear to any constituent of that organization that the lawyer represents the organization itself. A corporate employee who is not represented by the corporation's lawyer does not have the right to assert the attorney-client privilege with respect to communications between himself and the corporation's lawyer. See, e.g., *In re Grand Jury Subpoena: Under Seal*, 415 F.3d 333 (4th Cir. 2005); cf. *Lane v. Sharp Packaging Sys., Inc.*, 251 Wis.2d 68, 640 N.W.2d 788 (2002) (former director of corporation cannot waive corporation's attorney-client privilege in litigation arising out of his termination, since corporation is sole holder of the corporate privilege). Slim authority points in the opposite direction. See *Inter-Fluve v. Montana Eighteenth Judicial Dist. Ct.*, 327 Mont. 14, 112 P.3d 258 (2005) (former director could discover communications between corporate counsel and other directors, since directors and corporation were "joint clients" with respect to assertion of the attorney-client privilege).

The same general rules apply where the client is a governmental organization. Restatement § 74. The client of a lawyer employed by the government is the government itself, not any individual government official or employee. Where a government official has consulted a government lawyer, the attorney-client privilege may protect the communication from disclosure to third parties, but it cannot be used to keep information from the very same government itself. This situation has arisen in criminal matters, and courts have held that a government lawyer cannot refuse to divulge communications between the lawyer and a government official where the communication is relevant to a criminal matter being investigated by the same government. See, e.g., *In re: A Witness Before the Special Grand Jury*, 288 F.3d 289

(7th Cir. 2002) (state government official and state government lawyer); *In re Lindsey*, 148 F.3d 1100 (D.C.Cir. 1998) (federal government attorney could not refuse to divulge communications between himself and federal government official to a federal grand jury investigating criminal activity in White House; no attorney-client privilege applies). At least one court has held that a state governor's office can assert the attorney-client privilege to protect communications with state-government lawyers in an investigation being conducted by the federal government. *In re Grand Jury Investigation (United States v. Doe)*, 399 F.3d 527 (2d Cir. 2005).

c. In Confidence

For the attorney-client privilege to attach, the persons communicating must reasonably believe at the time that only privileged persons will learn the contents of the communication. Restatement § 71. That is, the privilege will not protect any communication that is not intended or reasonably expected to be and remain confidential.

This means that information that is publicly available will not become privileged by virtue of being contained in a communication between a lawyer and a client. Further, if the client tells the lawyer something but intends to convey the same information to other people, that communication is not made "in confidence." For example, if a client tells a lawyer some information unknown to anyone but the client, but at the same time tells the lawyer that she is going to give the information to the New York Times as soon as she leaves the lawyer's office, no attorney-client privilege attaches.

What if a lawyer and client meet for lunch in a busy restaurant and have a conversation in loud voices about the client's legal matters. Would that be "in confidence," do you think?

d. For the Purpose of Obtaining or Providing Legal Assistance

Are all confidential conversations between a lawyer and a client, where no one else is present, privileged? Do the purposes behind the privilege as recited by Justice Rehnquist in *Upjohn* suggest an answer to this? For example, what if a client asks a lawyer for investment advice that has nothing to do with the law? Would such a communication be privileged? See, e.g., *Miles v. Martin*, 147 N.C.App. 255, 555 S.E.2d 361 (2001) (where lawyer doubled as an investment broker, no privilege attaches to communications with investment clients). See also *In re Keeper of the Records (XYZ Corp. v. United States)*, 348 F.3d 16 (1st Cir. 2003)(corporation's outside lawyer's purely business advice was not privileged); *In re Grand Jury Subpoenas Dated March 9, 2001*, 179 F.Supp.2d 270 (S.D.N.Y.2001) (lawyers who helped fugitive financier Marc Rich gain an executive pardon from President

Clinton were acting as "lobbyists" rather than lawyers, rendering the documents memorializing their communications with Rich unprivileged); *United States v. Knoll*, 16 F.3d 1313 (2d Cir.1994) (documents given by client to lawyer relating solely to business transactions between the two of them were not privileged).

This requirement is of particular importance in the in-house corporate setting. It is not always clear whether an in-house lawyer employed by a corporation is giving legal advice or business advice. If the latter, there is no privilege for the communication. See, e.g., *Georgia-Pacific Corp. v. GAF Roofing Mfg. Corp.*, 1996 WL 29392 (S.D.N.Y.1996). What if the communication appears to have a dual purpose—in part to provide legal advice, in part to provide purely business advice? See *2,022 Ranch, L.L.C. v. Superior Court*, 113 Cal.App.4th 1377, 7 Cal.Rptr.3d 197 (2004) (court applies a "dominant purpose test," seeking to ascertain the dominant purpose for the communication and for the lawyer's work more generally).

The crime-fraud exception. What if the client seeks the lawyer's services in furtherance of the commission of an ongoing or future crime or fraud? Are communications relating to *that* covered by the attorney-client privilege? The clear answer is no— such a communication is subject to the "crime-fraud exception." Its basic thrust was explained succinctly in *United States v. Hodge and Zweig*, 548 F.2d 1347 (9th Cir.1977): "Because the attorney-client privilege is not to be used as a cloak for illegal or fraudulent behavior, it is well-established that the privilege does not apply where legal representation was secured in furtherance of intended, or present, continuing illegality."

Most courts hold that the crime-fraud exception applies only where the client's purpose in seeking the lawyer's advice was to use that advice to further a criminal or fraudulent scheme of some kind. See, e.g., *United States v. Bauer*, 132 F.3d 504 (9th Cir.1997) (stressing the need to "discern a causal connection or functional relationship" between the lawyer's advice and criminal actions taken by the client in order for the exception to apply). The exception applies "even when the attorney is completely unaware that his advice is sought in furtherance of such an improper purpose." *Hodge and Zweig*, 548 F.2d at 1354. Does the focus on the client's motives in communicating with the lawyer, as opposed to the lawyer's knowledge of the client's motives, make sense? Who is the holder of the privilege?

Most states have codified the crime-fraud exception. For example, Texas Rule of Criminal Evidence 503(d)(1) states: "There is no privilege under this rule ... [i]f the services of the lawyer were sought or obtained to enable or aid anyone to commit or plan to commit what the client knew or reasonably should have known to be a crime or fraud." Based on its plain language, this statute has been held to apply only where the client has sought or used the lawyer's services "to further the activity in question." It is not enough that the client threatens future crime or fraud during a conversation with the lawyer. *Henderson v. State*, 962 S.W.2d 544 (Tex.Crim.App.1997). Most states interpret the exception in just this way. Nor will the crime-fraud exception apply where the lawyer "stops the client's scheme dead in its tracks" by talking the client out of committing the crime or fraud he contemplates. *In re Public Defender Service*, 831 A.2d 890 (D.C. 2003).

Conceptually, isn't the crime-fraud exception really just part of a basic definition of what "legal advice" entails or does not entail? In *United States v. Zolin*, 491 U.S. 554, 109 S.Ct. 2619, 105 L.Ed.2d 469 (1989), the Court explained that while the privilege "requires that clients be free to 'make full disclosure to their attorneys' of past wrongdoings, in order that the client may obtain the 'aid of persons having knowledge of the law and skilled in its practice,'" these reasons cease to operate "where the desired advice refers *not to prior wrongdoing*, but to *future wrongdoing*" (emphasis in original). Does the privilege ever attach to such a communication? (Note that even if you accept this reasoning, a party seeking to obtain discovery of information on this ground has the burden of proving that the crime-fraud exception applies.)

What if a client blurts out a threat to commit a future crime during an otherwise privileged communication, but is neither seeking legal advice on that topic nor intending to use the lawyer's advice to further it? The crime-fraud exception does not apply, but is the communication still privileged? See *United States v. Alexander*, 287 F.3d 811 (9th Cir. 2002) (client's threats during a communication to kill the lawyer and others held to be "clearly not communications in order to obtain legal advice," thus unprivileged). Cf. Cal. Evid. Code § 956.5 ("There is no privilege ... if the lawyer reasonably believes that disclosure of any confidential communication ... is necessary to prevent the client from committing a criminal act that the lawyer believes is likely to result in death or serious bodily harm.")

If a client seeks a lawyer's advice intending to use that advice to commit a crime or fraud, does this serve to render unprivileged *all* communications between the lawyer and the client, or only those communications that were in furtherance of the criminal or fraudulent conduct? See *In re: Grand Jury Subpoena*, 419 F.3d 329 (5th Cir. 2005) (holding: the latter).

C. Duration of the Privilege

IN RE: INVESTIGATING GRAND JURY (STRETTON)

Superior Court of Pennsylvania, 2005.
887 A.2d 257.

OPINION BY KLEIN, J.:

Samuel C. Stretton, Esquire, was held in contempt of court for invoking the attorney-client privilege regarding statements made to him by a former client and for refusing to testify before a grand jury. . . .

Attorney Stretton was privately retained and represented "Mr. Y," who was convicted of first-degree murder, kidnapping, rape, and robbery and sentenced to death. "Mr. Y" was upset with the result and Attorney Stretton's representation. A direct appeal to the Pennsylvania Supreme Court was filed in February 1983, and on April 28, 1983, Attorney Stretton filed a motion to withdraw, which was granted on May 10, 1983. The Office of the Public Defender was appointed to represent "Mr. Y" on appeal.

In the course of the appeal, the matter was remanded for new counsel to pursue ineffectiveness claims against Attorney Stretton. In that 1984 hearing, for the purpose of defending against the ineffectiveness charge, the trial judge ruled that the attorney-client privilege did not apply.

In September 2003, because advanced DNA testing results were exculpatory, upon the parties' joint request, the sentence was vacated. Later, the case was *nol prossed,* and "Mr. Y" was released.

Suspecting that "Mr. Y" made inculpatory statements to Attorney Stretton in a telephone call from prison *after* Attorney Stretton was relieved as counsel, the Commonwealth re-investigated these charges before a grand jury. Attorney Stretton was subpoenaed to appear before the grand jury. There, he invoked the attorney-client privilege and refused to testify as to what he was told by "Mr. Y." There is no indication that "Mr. Y" ever waived the privilege. The trial court ultimately found him in contempt and fined him $100 per day to accrue from October 2004. It was understood that if it is ultimately determined through this litigation that Stretton must testify and in fact he does, then the fine will be remitted.

The Commonwealth notes, and we agree, that this appears to be a case of first impression in Pennsylvania. The Commonwealth takes the position that once the formal representation ends, any statement by a former client is not made in the course of seeking legal assistance and, therefore, is not privileged. In this particular case, "Mr. Y" was angry with Attorney Stretton, knew that

Attorney Stretton no longer represented him, and thus the conversation did not involve a client seeking legal advice from his lawyer.

The Commonwealth acknowledges that due to public policy considerations, all confidential communications and disclosures made by a client to his lawyer in the course of obtaining professional aid or advice is strictly privileged. The Commonwealth contends, however, that the privilege is limited to confidential communications made in connection with the provision of legal services, and that was not the purpose of the instant conversation. Therefore, the Commonwealth argues that the communication did not relate to a fact that would be of any assistance in a legal proceeding. . . .

RULE

Attorney Stretton argues that the privilege should be read broadly and notes that the burden of proof is on the Commonwealth to show an absence of privilege. Not only is there a common law privilege, but the privilege also has been adopted by statute, as follows:

> In a criminal proceeding counsel shall not be competent or permitted to testify to confidential communications made to him by his client, nor shall the client be compelled to disclose the same, unless in either case this privilege is waived upon the trial by the client.

STATUTE DQ

42 Pa.C.S.A. § 5916.

. . . Attorney Stretton asserts that while the conversation probably occurred after his representation formally ended, it is not clear whether "Mr. Y," who was incarcerated, had communicated yet with his new lawyer before calling Stretton. In any event, Attorney Stretton had been his counsel for some time and was relieved of representation, at most, a few months before the telephone call.

It is undisputed that the conversation was about the case. "Mr. Y" was upset with both the representation and the result. Although "Mr. Y" had called to express his anger toward Attorney Stretton, the conversation nonetheless revolved around the case. While Attorney Stretton never told "Mr. Y" that the conversation was privileged, he also did not tell him that the conversation was *not* privileged. Attorney Stretton maintains that the conversation was privileged and that, in his view, "Mr. Y" also believed it was confidential.

Not every lawyer-client conversation takes place in the context of formal representation. Often clients consult lawyers to see if the lawyer is willing to represent them and if they want to retain the lawyer. Those conversations are privileged.

A case does not automatically end simply because there is a change in lawyers. It is the obligation of a lawyer to continue to cooperate with new counsel. It would not advance public policy to provide that absent a formal contract of representation, legal matters discussed between an attorney and someone seeking legal advice are privileged unless it is clear that there is no lawyer-client relationship and it is just a casual conversation.

As Attorney Stretton aptly argued in his brief:

... Any attorney who represents clients on a regular basis recognizes that clients will call even after their cases have concluded and the file is in storage. A client will call and talk to the lawyer sometimes generally and sometimes about issues of the prior representation. [Mr. Y] did the same. Clients expect that these calls are confidential. Unless the lawyer indicates to the contrary, these conversations should and must be treated as confidential.

* * * * *

... The real world does not recognize a complete break of the privilege with the appointment of new counsel. There is no straight line in real world representation.... Further, the former client should be allowed to discuss and speak with his attorney about the representation even if it is to express displeasure[,] with the privilege remaining intact. If the attorney does not want the conversation to be privileged, then it is the attorney's obligation to advise the client. No such advice was ever given.

* * * * *

If a former client cannot call to discuss their previous case and/or cannot call an attorney and expect confidentiality on other matters, there would be a major problem. People often call the lawyer who previously represented them for advice. Because there has been a prior representation, the client assumes that the matter is still confidential. Without the lawyer indicating to the contrary, the confidentiality must be maintained.

In reaching our decision, we are mindful of *Commonwealth v. Hutchinson*, 290 Pa.Super. 254, 434 A.2d 740 (1981), which appears to be the only Pennsylvania case involving a similar issue. In that case, Hutchinson made a privileged statement to an investigator from the public defender's office while that office represented him. After the public defender's office withdrew, but before Hutchinson had the opportunity to confer with his newly appointed counsel, he repeated the statement to the public defender. The *Hutchinson* Court upheld the privilege under those circumstances. The Court noted that Hutchinson had reiterated a previous statement made during the representation. The Court also relied on the facts that Hutchinson had not yet spoken to his new counsel and the public defender never told him that the statement was not privileged. Thus, while *Hutchinson* is not exactly on point, its holding is consistent with our decision today.

Because of the strong public policy encouraging clients to talk freely with their attorneys, the fine line between when there is or is not representation is often not known to clients. Here, "Mr. Y" had paid Attorney Stretton to represent him and had worked with him for many months. He likely believed that as his case was continuing, he had the ability to hash things out with Attorney Stretton that could be used to his advantage in future representation with another lawyer. It was reasonable for "Mr. Y" to believe that because of their prior relationship, confidentiality remained between them.

Under these circumstances, we conclude that Attorney Stretton appropriately invoked the attorney-client privilege and should not be held in contempt.

Order reversed.

Notes

1. *Pre-representation protection*. The attorney-client privilege attaches when a client communicates with a lawyer for the purpose of hiring that lawyer, even if the lawyer is never retained. Perhaps this is an obvious corollary to the rule that the privilege protects communications made for the purpose of "obtaining" legal advice. See *Barton v. United States District Court*, 410 F.3d 1104 (9th Cir. 2005) (holding that questionnaires completed on-line by prospective clients in a planned class action case are protected by the privilege); Restatement § 70, comment *c*. Cf. Cal. State Bar Standing Comm. on Prof'l Resp., Formal Op. 2003-161 (responding to a person's questions even in a non-office setting may create a duty of confidentiality).

2. *Post-representation protection*. Does the court's holding in *Stretton* follow logically from the rule that the privilege belongs to the client rather than the lawyer? Should courts construe the privilege in such a way as to protect a client's reasonable but mistaken belief that a communication is confidential?

SWIDLER & BERLIN v. UNITED STATES

Supreme Court of the United States, 1998.
524 U.S. 399, 118 S.Ct. 2081, 141 L.Ed.2d 379.

Chief Justice REHNQUIST delivered the opinion of the Court.

... This dispute arises out of an investigation conducted by the Office of the Independent Counsel into whether various individuals made false statements, obstructed justice, or committed other crimes during investigations of the 1993 dismissal of employees from the White House Travel Office. Vincent W. Foster, Jr., was Deputy White House Counsel when the firings occurred. In July 1993, Foster met with petitioner [James] Hamilton, an attorney at petitioner Swidler & Berlin, to seek legal representation concerning possible congressional or other investigations of the firings. During a 2–hour meeting, Hamilton took three pages of handwritten notes. One of the first entries in the notes is the word "Privileged." Nine days later, Foster committed suicide.

In December 1995, a federal grand jury, at the request of the Independent Counsel, issued subpoenas to petitioners Hamilton and Swidler & Berlin for, *inter alia*, Hamilton's handwritten notes of his meeting with Foster. Petitioners filed a motion to quash, arguing that the notes were protected by the attorney-client privilege and by the work-product privilege. The District Court, after examining the notes *in camera*, concluded they were protected from disclosure by both doctrines and denied enforcement of the subpoenas. [The Court of Appeals reversed, holding that the work product privilege did not apply and that the attorney-client privilege in this setting was subject to a balancing test.] It thus held that there is a posthumous exception to the privilege for communications whose relative importance to particular criminal litigation is substantial. . . .

The issue presented here is the scope of [the attorney-client] privilege; more particularly, the extent to which the privilege survives the death of the client. . . . The Independent Counsel argues that the attorney-client privilege should not prevent disclosure of confidential communications where the client has died and the information is relevant to a criminal proceeding. [Very little authority supports this position, and longstanding common law doctrine holds that the privilege survives the client's death.]

[T]here are weighty reasons that counsel in favor of posthumous application. Knowing that communications will remain confidential even after death encourages the client to communicate fully and frankly with counsel. While the fear of disclosure, and the consequent withholding of information from counsel, may be reduced if disclosure is limited to posthumous disclosure in a criminal context, it seems unreasonable to assume that it vanishes altogether. Clients may be concerned about reputation, civil liability, or possible harm to friends or family. Posthumous disclosure of such communications may be as feared as disclosure during the client's lifetime.

The Independent Counsel suggests, however, that his proposed exception would have little to no effect on the client's willingness to confide in his attorney. He reasons that only clients intending to perjure themselves will be chilled by a rule of disclosure after death, as opposed to truthful clients or those asserting their Fifth Amendment privilege. This is because for the latter group, communications disclosed by the attorney after the client's death purportedly will reveal only information that the client himself would have revealed if alive.

The Independent Counsel assumes, incorrectly we believe, that the privilege is analogous to the Fifth Amendment's protection against self-incrimination. But as suggested above, the privilege serves much broader purposes. Clients consult attorneys for a wide variety of reasons, only one of which involves possible criminal liability. Many attorneys act as counselors on personal and family matters, where, in the course of obtaining the desired advice, confidences about family members or financial problems must be revealed in order to assure sound legal advice. The same is true of owners of small businesses who may regularly consult their attorneys about a variety of problems arising in the course of the business. These confidences may not come close to any sort of admission of criminal wrongdoing, but nonetheless be matters which the client would not wish divulged.

The contention that the attorney is being required to disclose only what the client could have been required to disclose is at odds with the basis for the privilege even during the client's lifetime. In related cases, we have said that the loss of evidence admittedly caused by the privilege is justified in part by the fact that without the privilege, the client may not have made such communications in the first place. This is true of disclosure before and after the client's death. Without assurance of the privilege's posthumous application, the client may very well not have made disclosures to his attorney at all, so the loss of evidence is more apparent than real. In the case at hand, it seems quite plausible that Foster, perhaps already contemplating suicide, may not have sought legal advice from Hamilton if he had not been assured the conversation was privileged.

The Independent Counsel additionally suggests that his proposed exception would have minimal impact if confined to criminal cases, or, as the Court of Appeals suggests, if it is limited to information of substantial importance to a particular criminal case. However, there is no case authority for the proposition that the privilege applies differently in criminal and civil cases. . . . In any event, a client may not know at the time he discloses information to his attorney whether it will later be relevant to a civil or a criminal matter, let alone whether it will be of substantial importance. Balancing *ex post* the importance of the information against client interests, even limited to criminal cases, introduces substantial uncertainty into the privilege's application. For just that reason, we have rejected use of a balancing test in defining the contours of the privilege. . . .

NO BALANCING TEST!

It has been generally, if not universally, accepted, for well over a century, that the attorney-client privilege survives the death of the client in a case such as this. While the arguments against the survival of the privilege are by no means frivolous, they are based in large part on speculation—thoughtful speculation, but speculation nonetheless—as to whether posthumous termination of the privilege would diminish a client's willingness to confide in an attorney. In an area where empirical information would be useful, it is scant and inconclusive. . . .

Reversed.

Justice O'CONNOR, with whom Justice SCALIA and Justice THOMAS join, dissenting.

Although the attorney-client privilege ordinarily will survive the death of the client, I do not agree with the Court that it inevitably precludes disclosure of a deceased client's communications in criminal proceedings. . . .

I agree that a deceased client may retain a personal, reputational, and economic interest in confidentiality. But, after death, the potential that disclosure will harm the client's interests has been greatly diminished, and the risk that the client will be held criminally liable has abated altogether. . . . This diminished risk is coupled with a heightened urgency for discovery of a deceased client's communications in the criminal context. The privilege does not "protect disclosure of the underlying facts by those who communicated with the attorney," *Upjohn, supra,* at 395, and were the client living, prosecutors could grant immunity and compel the relevant testimony. After a client's death, however, if the privilege precludes an attorney from testifying in the client's stead, a complete "loss of crucial information" will often result.

[T]he costs of recognizing an absolute posthumous privilege can be inordinately high. Extreme injustice may occur, for example, where a criminal defendant seeks disclosure of a deceased client's confession to the offense. See *State v. Macumber,* 112 Ariz. 569, 571, 544 P.2d 1084, 1086 (1976); cf. *In the Matter of John Doe Grand Jury Investigation,* 408 Mass. 480, 486, 562 N.E.2d 69, 72 (1990) (Nolan, J., dissenting). In my view, the paramount value that our criminal justice system places on protecting an innocent defendant should outweigh a deceased client's interest in preserving confidences. Indeed, even petitioners acknowledge that an exception may be appropriate where the constitutional rights of a criminal defendant are at stake. An exception may likewise be warranted in the face of a compelling law enforcement need for the information. . . . Given that the complete exclusion of relevant evidence from a criminal trial or investigation may distort the record, mislead the factfinder, and undermine the central truth-seeking function of the courts, I do not believe that the attorney-client privilege should act as an absolute bar to the disclosure of a deceased client's communications. When the privilege is asserted in the criminal context, and a showing is made that the communications at issue contain necessary factual information not otherwise available, courts should be permitted to assess whether interests in fairness and accuracy outweigh the justifications for the privilege. . . .

I would affirm the judgment of the Court of Appeals. . . .

Notes

1. Are you convinced that the purposes behind the attorney-client privilege are so strong that the privilege should survive the death of the client, even where assertion of the privilege might result in an innocent person going to jail? What if such testimony would prevent the State from putting an innocent person to death? Cf. *In re: Investigation of the Death of Miller*, 357 N.C. 316, 584 S.E.2d 772 (2003) (authorizing a court to order disclosure of privileged communications when "extraordinary circumstances" trump the interest in confidentiality).

2. If a deceased client retains an attorney-client privilege, then a survivor (such as a spouse) should be empowered to waive it. Many state statutes contain express provisions. See, e.g., *State v. Doe*, 101 Ohio St.3d 170, 803 N.E.2d 777 (2004) (construing Ohio R.C. § 2317.02(A)).

3. *Testamentary exception.* One situation in which the privilege does not survive the client's death is where there is a dispute about the deceased client's disposition of property. In such a context, many courts have held that previously-privileged communications may be disclosed to the client's heirs, on the rationale that the client's intent is furthered by such disclosure. About half the states provide by statute that the deceased client's personal representative can waive the privilege when heirs claim through the client. See Restatement § 81 (providing that the privilege simply "does not apply" to a communication from or to a deceased client, where it is relevant to a contested issue between parties who claim an interest through that client). Some courts have construed this exception more narrowly than others. See *Gould, Larson, Bennet, Wells and McDonnell, P.C. v. Panico*, 273 Conn. 315, 869 A.2d 653 (2005) (lawyer who met with client to discuss estate plans, but did not draft a will for the client, cannot be compelled to disclose substance of those discussions).

Some state statutes provide that a deceased client's attorney-client privilege terminates when the estate is distributed and the personal representative is discharged, since at that point there is no one authorized by law to assert the privilege. See *HLC Properties, Ltd. v. Superior Court*, 35 Cal.4th 54, 105 P.3d 560, 24 Cal.Rptr.3d 199 (2005) (construing Cal. Evid. Code § 954).

4. The majority in *Swidler & Berlin* did not reach the work product issue because of its ruling on attorney-client privilege. But do

you think the notes were work product? Does it matter that the notes at issue concern a client who cannot be a party to adversarial litigation because he is dead?

D. Waiver

The attorney-client and work-product privileges are subject to waiver. A client is fully empowered to waive either privilege voluntarily. For example, a client may intentionally disclose a privileged communication to others, thus repudiating the confidentiality of the communication and waiving the privilege. Waiver also occurs if a claim of privilege is not asserted in a proper and timely manner. See, e.g., *Kaye Scholer LLP v. Zalis*, 878 So.2d 447 (Fla. App. 2004) (failure to produce a privilege log in a timely manner waives the privilege). Remember that a client is usually bound by his lawyer's deeds, even if those deeds flow from incompetence. That rule applies here, too. Thus if a lawyer erroneously waives the privilege, even if instructed not to by the client—such as by himself disclosing the communication or by failing to assert an entitlement to a privilege during a proceeding—the privilege is usually lost and the client's remedy, if any, will lie against the lawyer for malpractice. See Chapter 2, §§ 1 & 2, *infra*. Three waiver situations are considered in more detail below.

1. *Inadvertent Disclosure*

SECURITIES AND EXCHANGE COMMISSION
v. CASSANO

United States District Court, S.D. New York, 1999.
189 F.R.D. 83.

KAPLAN, District Judge.

By letter dated September 21, 1999, the plaintiff informally applied for an order (i) requiring defense counsel to return an internal SEC staff memorandum that the Commission produced in discovery, and (ii) enjoining defense counsel from further disclosing its contents. The Court now has received responses to the SEC's request, a reply from the SEC, heard argument and, in the interests of expedition and with the consent of the parties, treats the informal application as a motion for the relief sought therein.

FACTS

The facts are set forth in the parties' correspondence and are not the subject of any material dispute. In briefest compass, the memorandum in question, a document of nearly 100 pages, is a draft of an action memo prepared by staff for presentation to the Commission. It reviews and weighs the Commission's evidence, provides legal analysis, and discusses the strengths and weaknesses of the Commission's case.... [I]t was not stamped "privileged" or "confidential," and it (or a copy of it) was included in a quantity of documents made available for inspection by defense counsel at the SEC offices.

It is not entirely clear how the document came to be among those produced to the defendants. According to the SEC, the investigation that led to this action was conducted out of the Boston Regional Office ("BRO"), and the documents were in that location. In preparation for production in this case, the privileged documents (in theory) were separated from those intended for production. Fifty to fifty-two cartons of material were identified as producible to the defendants. An experienced SEC staff attorney then reviewed that material over a period of days for the purpose of ensuring that no privileged documents were included. Following the completion of her review, those cartons were shipped to the SEC's New York Regional Office ("NYRO") for the purpose of making them available to defense counsel. The privileged documents that had been culled from the Commission's files were retained at the BRO.

The SEC and defense counsel reached an agreement that the documents produced would be available for inspection at the NYRO for a thirty day period. Defense counsel would identify those documents they wished to have copied for them during that period. The SEC then would send all the requested documents to a copying service, which would make the copies requested.

At the start of the appointed inspection period, a number of defense counsel appeared at the NYRO. Within a comparatively short period, one of them found the document in question, which was located in a file that contained documents produced by Russo Securities. This memorandum was located immediately behind a page containing only a handwritten notation, affixed by the SEC staff attorney in Boston, stating in substance that the documents behind the cover page had come from Russo Securities.

Defense counsel understandably were very much interested in this document. Those present read it and at least one took extensive notes. One of their number then took this memorandum—alone out of the 50 or 52 boxes of material made available for inspection—to the SEC paralegal supervising the defendants' document review and requested that she copy it for defense counsel immediately rather than put it aside for later copying with all other materials of interest to the defense. The paralegal telephoned plaintiff's lead counsel in Boston, told him that defense counsel had asked that she copy "one particular document" that day, instead of waiting until the end of the month in accordance with the prearrangement, and sought clearance to provide the requested copy. The SEC attorney acknowledged at oral argument that he asked for and received the Bates numbers stamped on the document. He did not retrieve the copy of the document retained in the BRO, either to ensure that the requested document was not privileged or to determine what particular document was perceived by defense counsel to be so important that they wanted it copied immediately. He simply told the paralegal that the document could be copied and turned over to the defense on the assumption that it had come from the nonprivileged production boxes. The paralegal promptly did so.

When defense counsel returned to his office, he checked the privilege log and found that this memorandum is not specifically listed there. He thereupon telephoned two of his colleagues and asked them to circulate the memorandum to three of his clients and a number of other attorneys and others. By this time, the memorandum has been distributed to and studied by five defense attorneys, at least four clients, at least four other persons, and one member of Congress and his staff.

The SEC attorney in charge of this case finally learned on September 14 that the action memorandum had been produced twelve days earlier. This application was submitted on the following day.

DISCUSSION

The law governing this issue in this circuit is straightforward. As the SEC contends, inadvertent production of a privileged document does not waive the privilege unless the producing party's conduct was "so careless as to suggest that it was not concerned with the protection of the asserted privilege."[4] In determining whether the production was inadvertent, courts consider (1) the reasonableness of the precautions taken to prevent inadvertent disclosure, (2) the time taken to rectify the error, (3) the scope of the discovery and extent of the disclosure, and (4) overarching issues of fairness.

As far as the BRO review is concerned, one of two things must be true. The document may have been in the materials intended for production, in which case the experienced staff attorney simply overlooked it. Alternatively, the document was not there when the review was made, the attorney missed nothing, but the document was inserted into the file after the review was completed. In the former case, the staff was careless. In the latter, it took insufficient precautions—none, so far as the record discloses—to ensure that the integrity of the boxes that had been reviewed for privileged materials was maintained. Moreover, it is

---

4. *Aramony v. United Way of Am.*, 969 F.Supp. 226, 235 (S.D.N.Y.1997). In truth, this formulation perhaps is not the most felicitous expression of what is intended. Counsel virtually always are "concerned" with protecting the confidentiality of privileged material. The same point might more accurately be put in terms of whether the party producing privileged material has been so careless as to surrender any claim that it has taken reasonable steps to ensure confidentiality.

difficult to understand why this document, given its sensitive nature, was not stamped "confidential" or "privileged."

But the review in the Boston office, in the Court's view, is not the proper or, at least, the principal focus. Here, defense counsel selected a single document and asked that it be copied immediately rather than treated as the parties had agreed. The specific document was brought to the attention of the attorney in charge of the case. The circumstances of the request clearly should have suggested to the SEC attorney that defense counsel had found what they regarded as gold at the end of the proverbial rainbow. Any attorney faced with such a request in comparable circumstances should have reviewed the document immediately, if only to find out what the other side thought so compelling. After all, these events should have suggested to SEC counsel that perhaps he had erred in assessing the case or previously failed to appreciate the significance of the document, even putting aside any question of inadvertent production of a privileged document. Yet the SEC attorney authorized production of this document, sight unseen. Any other precautions that were taken, and there certainly were some, fade into insignificance in the face of such carelessness.

Much the same considerations compel the conclusion that the scope of the discovery and the extent of the disclosure favor the defendants as well. These factors recognize that the inadvertent production of one or a few privileged documents in a massive disclosure is not necessarily inconsistent with the exercise of due care to avoid such occurrences, as it is virtually impossible to avoid any error whatsoever in dealing with large volumes. The Commission understandably points to the 50 plus boxes of documents, which would be appropriate if the defense had requested that all of the documents be copied and this one had been copied along with everything else. But it is not appropriate here. This specific document was called to counsel's attention. A deliberate decision was made to produce it without looking at it. . . .

Although the SEC acted promptly once it determined that the document had been produced, a factor cutting in its favor, the time taken to rectify the error, in all the circumstances, was excessive. There was no excuse for waiting 12 days to find out what the document was.

Finally, there are no overarching concerns of fairness dictating a contrary result. While the Commission, to be sure, is entitled to privacy for its deliberative communications with counsel, it has the same obligation to protect the confidentiality of its communications as any private party. There is no reason why its carelessness should be disregarded. Moreover, this document has been distributed to a number of others. Although distribution has not been [overly] wide, . . . this bell nevertheless would be very difficult to unring. Surely there would be little equity in some defendants going forward with the benefit of counsel who have read the memorandum while others do not. . . .

Accordingly, the plaintiff's motion is denied.[10]

SO ORDERED.

Notes

1. As the case indicates, the attorney-client and work product privileges may be waived accidentally. Courts today follow at least three distinct approaches to the issue of inadvertent disclosure of privileged documents. One group follows a kind of "strict liability," meaning that any disclosure, even if inadvertent, waives the privilege. See, e.g., *In re Sealed Case*, 877 F.2d 976 (D.C. Cir. 1989). Another group follows essentially the opposite approach, holding that any waiver must be deliberate. See, e.g., *Harold Sampson Children's Trust v. Linda Gale Sampson 1979 Trust*, 271 Wis.2d 610, 679 N.W.2d 794 (2004) (holding also that only the *client's* deliberate waiver is effective). Most courts appear to follow a third test, which balances a number of factors, including the reasonableness of the measures taken to protect the privilege; this is often called the "totality of the circumstances" test. See *United States ex rel. Bagley v. TRW, Inc.*, 204 F.R.D. 170 (C.D.Cal. 2001) (discussing all three approaches and adopting the third). Which test best furthers the purposes of the attorney-client privilege?

2. Many inadvertent disclosure cases arise in the context of large document productions. In *Amgen, Inc. v. Hoechst Marion Roussel, Inc.*, 190 F.R.D. 287 (D.Mass. 2000), attorneys at Boston's Choate, Hall & Stewart were representing two corporate clients in a complex patent case against Amgen. Five lawyers and two legal assistants from Choate spent weeks examining over 200,000 documents from the files of one of their clients, Hoechst, for the purpose of identifying privileged documents and producing documents responsive to an Amgen document request. The privileged documents were culled from this group (almost 4,000 pages, filling four small boxes) and segregated from the other documents. A Choate paralegal erroneously mixed the four small boxes with 70,000 other documents as they were being sent out for photocopying.

When Amgen's lawyer received the privileged documents, he called opposing counsel to find out whether they had been erroneously produced. The Choate lawyers told him yes, and asked for the documents back. Amgen refused, although Amgen's counsel agreed not to look at

---

10. Although the Court has concluded that the Commission has waived the privilege as to this document, it expresses no opinion as to whether those defense counsel who reviewed the document acted appropriately, particularly prior to the point at which SEC counsel approved copying the document for defense counsel. See, e.g., *American Express v. Accu–Weather, Inc.*, No. 91 Civ. 6485 (RWS), 1996 WL 346388, *2 (S.D.N.Y. June 25, 1996); Am. Bar Ass'n Standing Comm. on Ethics and Prof. Resp., Formal Op. 92–368 (1992).

the documents pending a court ruling. Hoechst then moved to compel the return of the privileged documents.

The court applied the "totality of circumstances" (or "middle") test, and held that the privilege had been waived. The Choate firm's precautions fell short, the court said; "easily-accomplished additional precautions were obviously still needed." For example, the firm should have had a "knowledgeable attorney or legal assistant" review the outside copier's performance to check whether the proper documents were copied. Further, the sheer magnitude of the error tended to show that the precautions were unreasonable. Thus the documents did not have to be returned.

3. *The receiving lawyer's obligations.* Did the defense lawyers in *Cassano* act properly, especially up to the point at which the SEC attorney approved copying the document for them? The court in *Cassano* expressly declined to reach that issue. Model Rule 4.4(b), adopted after *Cassano* was decided, says that a lawyer who receives a document and knows or reasonably should know that it was inadvertently produced "shall promptly notify the sender." Prior to this rule's adoption, the ABA and many state ethics opinion took the position that a lawyer who receives privileged documents in error should refrain from reading them, comply with any requests to return them unread, and refrain from using them until a court resolves the issue. See ABA Formal Op. 94–382 (1994); ABA Formal Op. 92–368 (1992); Md. State Bar Ass'n Comm. on Ethics, Op. 2000–04 (2000) (opining that a lawyer who fails to do this would be violating Rule 8.4(c)'s prohibition on engaging in dishonest conduct); New York County Lawyers' Ass'n Comm. on Prof. Ethics, Op. 730 (2002). The ABA has withdrawn both of its formal opinions cited above in light of the new Model Rule. ABA Formal Op. 05–437 (2005); ABA Formal Op. 06–440 (2006).

In April 2006, the U.S. Supreme Court forwarded to Congress a proposed amendment to FRCP 26(b)(5)(B), which became effective in December, 2006. The new provision states that in the event that privileged or work-product material is produced in discovery and the receiving lawyer is notified of that fact by the producing lawyer, "a party must promptly return, sequester, or destroy the specified information and any copies it has and may not use or disclose the information until the claim is resolved." The rule applies by its own terms only to discovery in a federal court action.

If you received a privileged document in error that clearly benefitted your own client, what do you think you would do, assuming that the new Federal Rule is inapplicable, and that your jurisdiction has not adopted MR 4.4(b) and has no authoritative rulings on this subject? What interests and duties would you consider in reaching your decision?

2. *Subsequent Disclosure in a Non–Privileged Setting*

If the lawyer, or client, or an authorized agent voluntarily discloses a privileged communication in a non-privileged setting, the privilege is waived. Restatement § 79. What if a lawyer discloses facts that were disclosed to her in confidence by the client, but does not disclose where those facts came from? See *id.*, comment *e.* Waiver?

Partial disclosure. For purely tactical reasons, a party might try to "selectively" waive the attorney-client privilege by putting into evidence only part of a communication between lawyer and client. Is there anything unfair about this? If the adversary seeks disclosure of the entire communication, should that be allowed? All courts agree that where the partial disclosure of privileged matter would be unfair, such as by giving the jury distorted view of the evidence, the partial disclosure should result in waiver of the privilege for all otherwise-privileged communications on the same subject matter. Most courts apply the same rule even outside the courtroom, such as in pretrial discovery. This prevents parties from using the privilege as a "sword" as well as a "shield."

Disclosure to government investigators. When a client is being investigated by the government, can the client submit to the government selected privileged materials without waiving the privilege with respect to all communications on the same subject, even against litigation opponents other than the government? This question has divided the federal circuits, although most have held that a client cannot selectively waive the privilege in this context, meaning that a disclosure of some privileged material to government investigators results in a potentially very broad waiver. See, e.g., *In re Columbia/HCA Healthcare Corp. Billing Practices Litig.*, 293 F.3d 289 (6th Cir. 2002) (holding that disclosure to the government waives the privilege, even if the government and the client have entered into an agreement stating otherwise). A proposed Federal Rule of Evidence, Rule 502, would protect clients in this setting: disclosure to a federal government agency exercising regulatory, investigative, or enforcement authority does not constitute a waiver at all as to non-governmental persons or entities, in state or federal court. The U.S. Judicial Conference Advisory Committee on Evidence Rules has set a February, 2007, deadline for comments on the proposed rule. See 75 U.S.L.W. 2007 (2006).

Disclosure to testifying experts. FRCP 26 provides that a testifying expert must prepare a written report containing "a complete statement of all opinions to be expressed and the basis and reasons therefor" as well as "the data or other information considered by the witness in forming the opinions." When a lawyer gives a testifying expert privileged materials for the expert's review, both the attorney-client and work-product privileges may be held to be waived by this act. In *In re Pioneer Hi–Bred International, Inc.*, 238 F.3d 1370 (Fed.Cir.2001), disclosure to an expert was held to waive the privilege even for "opinion" work product. "We are quite unable to perceive what interests would be served by permitting counsel to provide core work product to a testifying expert and then to deny discovery of such material to the opposing party.... [A]ny disclosure to a testifying expert in connection with his testimony assumes that privileged or protected material will be made public." Accord, *Karn v. Ingersoll–Rand*, 168 F.R.D. 633 (N.D.Ind.1996); contra, *Haworth Inc. v. Herman Miller Inc.*, 162 F.R.D. 289 (W.D.Mich.1995)(holding that FRCP 26(a)(2)(B) applies only to "factual information considered by the expert," not privileged matters).

3. *Waiver by Putting-in-Issue*

The attorney-client privilege may also be waived if the client makes the confidential communication itself an issue in litigation. This generally occurs in one of two ways: (a) the client may assert that he acted on the advice of a lawyer in engaging in the conduct at issue in the case; or (b) the client may assert that the lawyer's advice was negligent or wrongful, as in an action claiming ineffective assistance of counsel. See, e.g., *United States v. Bilzerian*, 926 F.2d 1285 (2d Cir.1991) (privilege waived by invocation of "advice of counsel" defense). This form of waiver is based on the same general notions of forensic fairness that undergird the "partial waiver" rules described above in subsection 2. If the opposing party could not delve into the complete truth of the communications being made an issue, the proceeding would be fundamentally unfair. Restatement § 80 (1). In two recent cases, courts held that when a client asserts in a complaint that the statute of limitations was tolled, this waived the attorney-client privilege because communications with counsel about the claim were brought into issue. *Lama v. Preskill*, 353 Ill.App.3d 300, 288 Ill.Dec. 755, 818 N.E.2d 443 (2004); *Jackson Medical Clinic for Women, P.A. v. Moore*, 836 So.2d 767 (Miss. 2003). If the client sues the lawyer (for legal malpractice or breach of fiduciary duty, for example), this too waives the privilege and allows the lawyer to speak freely about communications that relate to the plaintiff's allegations. Restatement § 83.

§ 2. THE ETHICAL DUTY OF CONFIDENTIALITY

A. Scope of the Duty

The ethical duty of confidentiality, embodied in each state's code of professional responsibility, is a variant of an important duty owed by all agents to their principals: an agent can neither disclose nor use information confidentially given to him by the principal or acquired by him during the relationship. Restatement (Third) of Agency § 8.05 (2006); Restatement (Second) of Agency § 395 (1958).

The duty of confidentiality is broader than the attorney-client and work product privileges in several respects. First, the attorney-client privilege pertains only to the admissibility of particular evidence in a judicial proceeding when the client or lawyer have been asked to divulge or produce that evidence. By contrast, the duty of confidentiality applies beyond that setting; it instructs a lawyer not to use or divulge protected information in any setting, unless an exception applies. Second, remember that the evidentiary privileges protect communications, not information. By contrast, the duty of confidentiality protects "information relating to representation of a client." MR 1.6(a); Restatement § 59. Third, the attorney-client privilege protects only communications between the client and the lawyer (and their agents). The duty of confidentiality applies to all information, whatever its source; even information obtained from a third party is protected.

The upshot of all of this is that even if the content of some communication is not protected by the attorney-client privilege—meaning that the client or lawyer could be compelled to divulge the information if asked about it and ordered to do so in a proceeding—that same information might well be protected by the ethical duty of confidentiality. That duty requires the lawyer to refrain from voluntarily divulging the information outside of any proceeding, and subjects the lawyer to discipline if he does so. (Note that if a court orders a lawyer to testify concerning client information, the lawyer must do so, and does not violate the ethics rules for obeying such an order. MR 1.6(b)(6).)

Almost all states have voluntarily adopted ABA Model Rule 1.6(a)'s basic confidentiality provision. It provides that a lawyer "shall not reveal information relating to the representation of a client" unless the client consents, or unless some listed exception applies.

A few states, most notably New York, retain a version of the older ABA Model Code's confidentiality provision. The Model Code, in DR 4–101, separates protected information into two categories: "confidences," which refers to communications protected by the attorney-client privilege, and "secrets," which refers to "other information gained in the professional relationship that the client has requested be held inviolate or the disclosure of which would be embarrassing or would be likely to be detrimental to the client." In New York, for example, a lawyer "shall not knowingly: (1) Reveal a confidence or secret of a client; (2) Use a confidence or secret of a client to the disadvantage of the client; [or] (3) Use a confidence or secret of a client for the advantage of the lawyer or of a third person," unless the client consents or a listed exception applies. 22 NYCRR 1200.19 (DR 4–101(b)). California's confidentiality rule also references "confidences" and "secrets," but is otherwise unique. As recited both in Business & Professions Code § 6068(e) and Rule 3–100 (effective July 1, 2004), California's rule provides: "It is the duty of an attorney [t]o maintain inviolate the confidence, and at every peril to himself to preserve the secrets, of his client.''

Why have all states adopted an ethics rule (or statute) that prohibits lawyers from revealing client information? What is the purpose of such a prohibition? Look back at the *Upjohn* case in Section 1 of this chapter. Why doesn't the attorney-client privilege provide adequate protection for these interests? Are the interests being served by the ethical duty somehow broader than those served by the evidentiary privilege?

All states agree that the scope of the duty of confidentiality is broad. Is the Model Rule broader than the Model Code, in terms of what is being protected? In what ways? Which is preferable?

The ethical rules' protection for client information is not contained completely in a single rule. Because of the fundamental nature of the duty of confidentiality, it is incorporated by reference in many other rules. In most of these instances, the "other rule" provides an exemption from its duty where the duty of confidentiality might be compromised. In other words, the duty of confidentiality is often a "trump card" that overcomes competing duties. For example, MR 8.3, requiring a lawyer to "inform the appropriate professional authority" about the serious misconduct of other lawyers, expressly "does not require disclosure of information otherwise protected by Rule 1.6." Obviously, the broader the protection of MR 1.6, the broader the exception to MR 8.3. There are many other examples in the Model Rules. See MR 1.8(b) & (f) (conflicts of interest); 1.9(b) and (c) (conflicts of interest); 1.10(b) (imputed disqualification); 2.3(b) (evaluation for use by third persons); 4.1(b) (truthfulness in statements to others); 8.1 (bar admission and disciplinary matters). Only with respect to a lawyer's duties of candor toward a tribunal does the confidentiality rule give way to a superior interest: Model Rule 3.3 provides that a lawyer's duties of candor "apply even if compliance requires disclosure of information otherwise protected by Rule 1.6." All of this means that the contours of a particular state's confidentiality rule will have a profound impact on the scope of several other ethics rules.

No provision of the ABA Models has produced more controversy, it seems, than the rule on confidentiality. But the primary debate has not been about the basic scope of protection; rather, it has been about the exceptions. That is our next topic.

B. Exceptions

Adopting a broad ethical duty of confidentiality means that lawyers may be subject to discipline for disclosing a broad class of information. Many exceptions exist, however. A few exceptions are relatively noncontroversial and may be described briefly here. First, a client may voluntarily consent to waive the confidentiality of particular information. Since the duty of confidentiality is for the client's benefit, the lawyer must abide by any such decision. Second, certain disclosures may be "impliedly authorized" by the client in order to carry out the representation effectively. See MR 1.6(a). For example, a lawyer negotiating a settlement may make disclosures in order to achieve a favorable result for the client. *Id.*, comment [5]. Of course, a lawyer cannot disclose a particular piece of information if the client forbids it. *Id.* Third, if some "other law" (outside the ethics rules) or a court order requires disclosure of otherwise-protected information, the ethics rule must give way. See MR 1.6(b)(6). ("Other law" always trumps the ethics rules, so this is hardly surprising.) Fourth, a lawyer is allowed to reveal confidences to secure legal advice about the lawyer's compliance with the ethics rules. MR 1.6(b)(4). Finally, in almost all states a lawyer has a mandatory duty to disclose information, even if protected by the ethical rule on confidentiality, to avoid defrauding or misleading the court. See MR 3.3; Restatement § 120(2); *In re Seelig*, 180 N.J. 234, 850 A.2d 477 (2004)(defense counsel violated Rule 3.3 by failing to inform the court that indictable charges were pending against his client, when the court was deciding whether to accept the client's guilty plea on less serious charges). We will see this duty in more detail in Chapter 7.

Other exceptions, or possible exceptions, are more controversial. Should a lawyer be allowed to disclose information to save someone's life? What if disclosure would prevent the client from committing some other kind of crime, like fraud, that could destroy some innocent person's financial well-being? What if a lawyer believes she has a need to divulge client information to avoid being prosecuted or sued by someone? What if a lawyer's client fails to pay a fee and the lawyer needs to reveal client information to prove a claim for compensation? These have proved to be matters about which some very good people have differed, either categorically or as applied to particular facts. These differences of opinion are reflected most notably in the variety of exceptions each state has recognized.

1. *Prevention of Death or Serious Bodily Harm*

SPAULDING v. ZIMMERMAN

Supreme Court of Minnesota, 1962.
263 Minn. 346, 116 N.W.2d 704.

THOMAS GALLAGHER, Justice.

[Defendants appeal from a trial court order vacating and setting aside a prior order which had approved a settlement made on behalf of David Spaulding, a minor.]

The prior action was brought against defendants by Theodore Spaulding, as father and natural guardian of David Spaulding, for injuries sustained by David in an automobile accident, arising out of a collision which occurred August 24, 1956, between an automobile driven by John Zimmerman, in which David was a passenger, and one owned by John Ledermann and driven by Florian Ledermann.

On appeal defendants contend that the court was without jurisdiction to vacate the settlement solely because their counsel then possessed information, unknown to plaintiff herein, that at the time he was suffering from an aorta aneurysm which may have resulted from the accident, because (1) no mutual mistake of fact was involved; (2) no duty rested upon them to disclose information to plaintiff which they could assume had been disclosed to him by his own physicians; (3) insurance limitations as well as physical injuries formed the basis for the settlement; and (4) plaintiff's motion to vacate the order for settlement and to set aside the releases was barred by the limitations provided in Rule 60.02 of Rules of Civil Procedure. [Note: Minn. Rule 60.02 is substantially similar to FRCP 60(b), referenced in the *Bailey* case in Chapter 2, § 1.]

After the accident, David's injuries were diagnosed by his family physician, Dr. James H. Cain, as a severe crushing injury of the chest with multiple rib fractures; a severe cerebral concussion, probably with petechial hemorrhages of the brain; and bilateral fractures of the clavicles. At Dr. Cain's suggestion, on January 3, 1957, David was examined by Dr. John F. Pohl, an orthopedic specialist, who made X-ray studies of his chest. Dr. Pohl's detailed report of this examination included the following:

'* * * The lung fields are clear. The heart and aorta are normal.'

Nothing in such report indicated the aorta aneurysm with which David was then suffering. On March 1, 1957, at the suggestion of Dr. Pohl, David was examined from a neurological viewpoint by Dr. Paul S. Blake, and in the report of this examination there was no finding of the aorta aneurysm.

In the meantime, on February 22, 1957, at defendants' request, David was examined by Dr. Hewitt Hannah, a neurologist. On February 26, 1957, the latter reported to Messrs. Field, Arveson, & Donoho, attorneys for defendant John Zimmerman, as follows:

The one feature of the case which bothers me more than any other part of the case is the fact that this boy of 20 years of age has an aneurysm, which means a dilatation of the aorta and the arch of the aorta. Whether this came out of this accident I cannot say with any degree of certainty and I have discussed it with the Roentgenologist and a couple of Internists. * * * Of course an aneurysm or dilatation of the aorta in a boy of this age is a serious matter as far as his life. This aneurysm may dilate further and it might rupture with further dilatation and this would cause his death.

'It would be interesting also to know whether the X-ray of his lungs, taken immediately following the accident, shows this dilatation or not. If it was not present immediately following the accident and is now present, then we could be sure that it came out of the accident.'

Prior to the negotiations for settlement, the contents of the above report were made known to counsel for defendants Florian and John Ledermann.

The case was called for trial on March 4, 1957, at which time the respective parties and their counsel possessed such information as to David's physical condition as was revealed to them by their respective medical examiners as above described. It is thus apparent that neither David nor his father, the nominal plaintiff in the prior action, was then aware that David was suffering the aorta aneurysm but on the contrary believed that he was recovering from the injuries sustained in the accident.

On the following day an agreement for settlement was reached wherein, in consideration of the payment of $6,500, David and his father agreed to settle in full for all claims arising out of the accident.

Richard S. Roberts, counsel for David, thereafter presented to the court a petition for approval of the settlement, wherein David's injuries were described as:

'* * * severe crushing of the chest, with multiple rib fractures, severe cerebral concussion, with petechial hemorrhages of the brain, bilateral fractures of the clavicles.'

Attached to the petition were affidavits of David's physicians, Drs. James H. Cain and Paul S. Blake, wherein they set forth the same diagnoses they had made upon completion of their respective examinations of David as above described. At no time was there information disclosed to the court that David was then suffering from an aorta aneurysm which may have been the result of the accident. Based upon the petition for settlement and such affidavits of Drs. Cain and Blake, the court on May 8, 1957, made its order approving the settlement.

Early in 1959, David was required by the army reserve, of which he was a member, to have a physical checkup. For this, he again engaged the services of Dr. Cain. In this checkup, the latter discovered the aorta aneurysm. He then reexamined the X rays which had been taken shortly after the accident and at this time discovered that they disclosed the beginning of the process which produced the aneurysm. He promptly sent David to Dr. Jerome

Grismer for an examination and opinion. The latter confirmed the finding of the aorta aneurysm and recommended immediate surgery therefor. This was performed by him at Mount Sinai Hospital in Minneapolis on March 10, 1959.

Shortly thereafter, David, having attained his majority, instituted the present action for additional damages due to the more serious injuries including the aorta aneurysm which he alleges proximately resulted from the accident. As indicated above, the prior order for settlement was vacated. In a memorandum made a part of the order vacating the settlement, the court stated:

> 'The facts material to a determination of the motion are without substantial dispute. The only disputed facts appear to be whether * * * Mr. Roberts, former counsel for plaintiff, discussed plaintiff's injuries with Mr. Arvesen, counsel for defendant Zimmerman, immediately before the settlement agreement, and, further, whether or not there is a causal relationship between the accident and the aneurysm.

> 'Contrary to the * * * suggestion in the affidavit of Mr. Roberts that he discussed the minor's injuries with Mr. Arvesen, the Court finds that no such discussion of the specific injuries claimed occurred prior to the settlement agreement on March 5, 1957.

> ' * * * the Court finds that although the aneurysm now existing is causally related to the accident, such finding is for the purpose of the motions only and is based solely upon the opinion expressed by Dr. Cain (Exhibit 'F'), which, so far as the Court can find from the numerous affidavits and statements of fact by counsel, stands without dispute.

> 'The mistake concerning the existence of the aneurysm was not mutual. For reasons which do not appear, plaintiff's doctor failed to ascertain its existence. By reason of the failure of plaintiff's counsel to use available rules of discovery, plaintiff's doctor and all his representatives did not learn that defendants and their agents knew of its existence and possible serious consequences. Except for the character of the concealment in the light of plaintiff's minority, the Court would, I believe, be justified in denying plaintiff's motion to vacate, leaving him to whatever questionable remedy he may have against his doctor and against his lawyer.

> 'That defendants' counsel concealed the knowledge they had is not disputed. The essence of the application of the above rule is the character of the concealment. Was it done under circumstances that defendants must be charged with knowledge that plaintiff did not know of the

injury? If so, an enriching advantage was gained for defendants at plaintiff's expense. There is no doubt of the good faith of both defendants' counsel. There is no doubt that during the course of the negotiations, when the parties were in an adversary relationship, no rule required or duty rested upon defendants or their representatives to disclose this knowledge. However, once the agreement to settle was reached, it is difficult to characterize the parties' relationship as adverse. At this point all parties were interested in securing Court approval. * * *

'But it is not possible to escape the inference that defendants' representatives knew, or must be here charged with knowing, that plaintiff under all the circumstances would not accept the sum of $6500.00 if he or his representatives knew of the aneurysm and its possible serious consequences. Moreover, there is no showing by defendants that would support an inference that plaintiff and his representatives knew of the existence of the aneurysm but concluded that it was not causally related to the accident.

'When the adversary nature of the negotiations concluded in a settlement, the procedure took on the posture of a joint application to the Court, at least so far as the facts upon which the Court could and must approve settlement is concerned. It is here that the true nature of the concealment appears, and defendants' failure to act affirmatively, after having been given a copy of the application for approval, can only be defendants' decision to take a calculated risk that the settlement would be final. * * *

'To hold that the concealment was not of such character as to result in an unconscionable advantage over plaintiff's ignorance or mistake, would be to penalize innocence and incompetence and reward less than full performance of an officer of the Court's duty to make full disclosure to the Court when applying for approval in minor settlement proceedings.'

The principles applicable to the court's authority to vacate settlements made on behalf of minors and approved by it appear well established. With reference thereto, we have held that the court in its discretion may vacate such a settlement, even though it is not induced by fraud or bad faith, where it is shown that in the accident the minor sustained separate and distinct injuries which were not known or considered by the court at the time settlement was approved....

From the foregoing it is clear that in the instant case the court did not abuse its discretion in setting aside the settlement which it had approved on plaintiff's behalf while he was still a minor. It is undisputed that neither he nor his counsel nor his medical attendants were aware that at the time settlement was made he was suffering from an aorta aneurysm which may have resulted from the accident. The seriousness of this disability is indicated by Dr. Hannah's report indicating the imminent danger of death therefrom. This was known by counsel for both defendants but was not disclosed to the court at the time it was petitioned to approve the settlement. While no canon of ethics or legal obligation may have required them to inform plaintiff or his counsel with respect thereto, or to advise the court therein, it did become obvious to them at the time, that the settlement then made did not contemplate or take into consideration the disability described. This fact opened the way for the court to later exercise its discretion in vacating the settlement and under the circumstances described we cannot say that there was any abuse of discretion on the part of the court in so doing....

Affirmed.

Notes

1. The court says that the lawyers were under no legal or ethical obligation to disclose to Spaulding their doctor's diagnosis of a life-threatening condition that he did not know about. Should they nonetheless have done so? Why?

2. If a rule actually *prohibited* the lawyers from telling Spaulding about the diagnosis, should they have done so anyway?

3. Should the rules of lawyer ethics parallel generally-held views of morality? Even if this is desirable, is it possible?

4. Might the lawyers have tried to convince their own clients to divulge the diagnosis to Spaulding? Would there have been anything improper about that?

5. How would you analyze the lawyers' duty of confidentiality if Model Rule 1.6(b)(1) had been in effect in Minnesota at the time *Spaulding* arose?

6. The ABA's current Model Rule 1.6(b)(1) was adopted in 2002, and parallels Restatement § 66, promulgated earlier by the ALI. Assume that State A has adopted that rule, and that all the following events occur in State A. Lawyer (admitted in State A) is representing a corporate client who is being sued by a landowner for polluting his lake and killing the fish in it. The defendant's lawyer, in the course of representation, learns from his client that the pollution is far worse than the plaintiff believes. Indeed, human life and health may be risked, and far more people might be exposed to the pollutants. The plaintiff's lawyers seem inept and appear unlikely to uncover this information; the

defendant does not want to divulge it. Under the new rule, would the lawyer have discretion to tell the plaintiff, or perhaps environmental authorities, about the true extent of the pollution? If you think the answer is yes, then what is the likelihood that the corporate client would ever tell the lawyer such information? In other words, might clients not give their lawyers all of the facts, if they believe the lawyer could make them public over the client's objections? Is this a problem?

7. Do the provisions of MR 1.6(b)(1) and Restatement § 66 go far enough? Should a lawyer have a *mandatory* duty to disclose client information, even over a client's objections, where the lawyer reasonably believes that such disclosure is necessary to save a life? See Tenn. Rule 1.6(c)(1). Does the scenario in Note 6 above influence your analysis?

8. For over a century, California's ethics code contained no confidentiality provision at all, and the legislatively-enacted Business and Professions Code § 6068(e) contained no exceptions. Both situations have now changed, although perhaps not dramatically enough for some. The lone listed exception to the duty of confidentiality is that "a member may, but is not required to, reveal confidential information relating to the representation of a client to the extent that the member reasonably believes the disclosure is necessary to prevent a criminal act that the member reasonably believes is likely to result in death of, or substantial bodily harm to, an individual." Cal. Rule 3–100(B); Cal. Bus. & Prof. Code 6068(e)(2). How would you analyze the lawyers' duties in *Spaulding* if this had been the governing rule?

9. What if the lawyer reasonably believes that his own client is going to commit suicide, but is also pretty sure that the client does not want that fact revealed. Can the lawyer divulge that fact? Under MR 1.6(a), a lawyer would be allowed to reveal the information in order to prevent the client's "reasonably certain death or substantial bodily harm." See also Rest. § 66(1). In a state that allows disclosure of information to prevent any client crime, or client crime that threatens serious bodily harm (see the section immediately below), disclosure would be an option if suicide is a crime. What about a state that allows disclosure of the client's intention to commit a crime that would result in serious bodily harm, but does not regard suicide as a crime? Is there another relevant rule? See Alaska Bar Ass'n Ethics Comm., Op. 2005–1 (2005) (disclosure would be authorized, but optional, under Rule 1.14(b), the rule on clients with diminished capacity). The Alaska Ethics Opinion notes that Rule 1.14(b) "overrides" any seeming prohibition in Rule 1.6; there must be an exception to confidentiality based on "the overriding value of life and physical integrity."

Do you think a lawyer should have a mandatory duty to disclose such information to save the client's life? In *People v. Fentress*, 103 Misc.2d 179, 425 N.Y.S.2d 485 (Cty.Ct.1980), the court said that "[t]o exalt the oath of silence, in the face of imminent death, would, under these circumstances, be not only morally reprehensible, but ethically unsound ... If the ethical duty exists primarily to protect the client's interests, what interest can there be superior to the client's life itself?"

10. Notice that the *Spaulding* court vacated the settlement only because of Spaulding's age. If he had been an adult, he would have been bound by the settlement, although he might have had a remedy against his own lawyer or doctor for malpractice. See Chapter 2, §§ 1 & 2.

2. Protection of Others From the Client's Criminal Acts

a. Crimes in General and Crimes of Violence

Can a lawyer reveal confidential information in order to prevent the client from committing a crime? This issue has divided the ABA House of Delegates, and state supreme courts, for years. The Model Code, DR 4–101(C)(3), which many states adopted, allowed a lawyer to reveal "the intention of his client to commit a crime and the information necessary to prevent the crime." But the ABA dropped this provision when the Model Rules were promulgated in 1983, replacing it with MR 1.6(b)(1), allowing disclosure only "to prevent the client from committing a criminal act that the lawyer believes is likely to result in imminent death or substantial bodily harm." Roughly two decades later, the ABA amended that rule to allow for disclosure "to prevent reasonably certain death or substantial bodily harm," the provision we saw above in the Notes after *Spaulding*. In 2003, the ABA again amended MR 1.6(b) by adding two additional exceptions for client crime; both provisions allow for disclosure to prevent client crime or fraud "that is reasonably certain to result in substantial injury to the financial interests or property of another," or to rectify the effects of such a crime or fraud, where the client has used the lawyer's services to facilitate the wrong. MR 1.6(b)(2) & (3).

The ABA's decision to change the Model Code's straightforward exception was never particularly popular with the states. Even today, a large number of states allow a lawyer to reveal a client's intention to commit any crime. Some states go even further, and *require* a lawyer to disclose a client's intention to commit a crime of any kind, See Fla. Rule 4–1.6(b)(1); Va. Rule 1.6(c)(1), or at least a crime involving serious bodily harm, see Ariz. Rule 1.6(b); Ill. Rule 1.6(b); Nev. Rule 156(2); N.J. Rule 1.6(b)(1); Tex. Rule 1.05(e); Vermont rule 1.6(b)(1); Wis. Rule 20:1.6(b). The remaining states diverge wildly; many statutory supplements now contain an all-but-indispensable chart of current state variations.

How does an ethical rule allowing (or even mandating) disclosure by a lawyer of a client's intention to commit a crime relate to the attorney-client privilege, and more specifically, to the crime-fraud exception? Consider the next case.

attorney for Tyree

PURCELL v. DISTRICT ATTORNEY

Supreme Judicial Court of Massachusetts, 1997.
424 Mass. 109, 676 N.E.2d 436.

WILKINS, Chief Justice.

Disclosed threat of crime

On June 21, 1994, Joseph Tyree, who had received a court order to vacate his apartment in the Allston section of Boston, consulted the plaintiff, Jeffrey W. Purcell, an attorney employed by Greater Boston Legal Services, which provides representation to low income individuals in civil matters. Tyree had recently been discharged as a maintenance man at the apartment building in which his apartment was located. On the day that Tyree consulted Purcell, Purcell decided, after extensive deliberation, that he should advise appropriate authorities that Tyree might engage in conduct harmful to others. He told a Boston police lieutenant that Tyree had made threats to burn the apartment building.

The next day, constables, accompanied by Boston police officers, went to evict Tyree. At the apartment building, they found incendiary materials, containers of gasoline, and several bottles with wicks attached. Smoke detectors had been disconnected, and gasoline had been poured on a hallway floor. Tyree was arrested and later indicted for attempted arson of a building.

Pf

In August, 1995, the district attorney for the Suffolk district subpoenaed Purcell to testify concerning the conversation Purcell had had with Tyree on June 21, 1994. A Superior Court judge granted Purcell's motion to quash the subpoena. The trial ended in a mistrial because the jury was unable to reach a verdict.

The Commonwealth decided to try Tyree again and once more sought Purcell's testimony. Another Superior Court judge concluded that Tyree's statements to Purcell were not protected by the attorney-client privilege, denied Purcell's motion to quash an anticipated subpoena, and ordered Purcell to testify. Purcell then commenced this action, pursuant to G.L. c. 211, § 3 (1994 ed.), in the single justice session of this court. The parties entered into a stipulation of facts, and a single justice reserved and reported the case to the full court.

Rule of mass

There is no question before this court, directly or indirectly, concerning the ethical propriety of Purcell's disclosure to the police that Tyree might engage in conduct that would be harmful to others. As bar counsel agreed in a memorandum submitted to the single justice, this court's disciplinary rules regulating the practice of law authorized Purcell to reveal to the police "[t]he intention of his client to commit a crime and the information necessary to prevent the crime." S.J.C. Rule 3:07, Canon 4, DR 4–

[handwritten margin note: Mandatory disclosure v. in admiss. in court]

101(C)(3), as appearing in 382 Mass. 778 (1981).[1] The fact that the disciplinary code permitted Purcell to make the disclosure tells us nothing about the admissibility of the information that Purcell disclosed. See *Kleinfeld v. State*, 568 So.2d 937, 939–940 (Fla.Dist. Ct.App.1990).

. . . The debate here is whether Tyree is entitled to the protection of the attorney-client privilege in the circumstances. The district attorney announces the issue in his brief to be whether a crime-fraud exception to the testimonial privilege applies in this case. He asserts that, even if Tyree's communication with Purcell was made as part of his consultation concerning the eviction proceeding, Tyree's communication concerning his contemplated criminal conduct is not protected by the privilege. We shall first consider the case on the assumption that Tyree's statements to Purcell are protected by the attorney-client privilege unless the crime-fraud exception applies.

"It is the purpose of the crime-fraud exception to the attorney-client privilege to assure that the 'seal of secrecy,' . . . between lawyer and client does not extend to communications 'made for the purpose of getting advice for the commission of a fraud' or crime" (citation omitted). *United States v. Zolin*, 491 U.S. 554, 563, 109 S.Ct. 2619, 2626, 105 L.Ed.2d 469 (1989), quoting *O'Rourke v. Darbishire*, [1920] App.Cas. 581, 604 (P.C.). There is no public interest in the preservation of the secrecy of that kind of communication.

[While the exception has not been defined with precision, cases indicate that it applies to "conferences in which the attorney's advice was sought in furtherance of a crime or to obtain advice or assistance with respect to criminal activity." No such showing was made in this case. Without] evidence tending to show that Tyree discussed a future crime with Purcell and that thereafter Tyree actively prepared to commit that crime . . . , the crime of arson would appear to have no apparent connection with Tyree's eviction proceeding and Purcell's representation of Tyree. . . . The evidence in this case . . . was not sufficient to warrant the judge's finding that Tyree consulted Purcell for the purpose of obtaining advice in furtherance of a crime. Therefore, the order

[handwritten margin note: DQ]

---

1. The same conclusion would be reached under Rule 1.6(b)(1) of the Proposed Massachusetts Rules of Professional Conduct, now pending before the Justices. Under rule 1.6(b)(1), as now proposed, a lawyer may reveal confidential information relating to a client "to prevent the commission of a criminal or fraudulent act that the lawyer reasonably believes is likely to result in death or substantial bodily harm, or in substantial injury to the financial interests or property of another." Unlike DR 4– 101(C)(3), which allows disclosure of a client's intention to commit any crime, disclosure of a client's intention to commit a crime is permissible under proposed rule 1.6(b)(1) only as to crimes threatening substantial consequences, and disclosure is permitted based on an attorney's reasonable belief of the likely existence of the threat rather than, as is the case under DR 4– 101(C)(3), a known intention of the client to commit a crime.

denying the motion to quash because the crime-fraud exception applied cannot be upheld.

There is a consideration in this case that does not appear in other cases that we have seen concerning the attorney-client privilege. The testimony that the prosecution seeks from Purcell is available only because Purcell reflectively made a disclosure, relying on this court's disciplinary rule which permitted him to do so. Purcell was under no ethical duty to disclose Tyree's intention to commit a crime. He did so to protect the lives and property of others, a purpose that underlies a lawyer's discretionary right stated in the disciplinary rule. The limited facts in the record strongly suggest that Purcell's disclosures to the police served the beneficial public purpose on which the disciplinary rule was based.

We must be cautious in permitting the use of client communications that a lawyer has revealed only because of a threat to others. Lawyers will be reluctant to come forward if they know that the information that they disclose may lead to adverse consequences to their clients. A practice of the use of such disclosures might prompt a lawyer to warn a client in advance that the disclosure of certain information may not be held confidential, thereby chilling free discourse between lawyer and client and reducing the prospect that the lawyer will learn of a serious threat to the well-being of others. To best promote the purposes of the attorney-client privilege, the crime-fraud exception should apply only if the communication seeks assistance in or furtherance of future criminal conduct. When the opponent of the privilege argues that the communication itself may show that the exception applies and seeks its disclosure in camera, the judge, in the exercise of discretion on the question whether to have an in camera proceeding, should consider if the public interest is served by disclosure, even in camera, of a communication whose existence is known only because the lawyer acted against his client's interests under the authority of a disciplinary rule. The facts of each situation must be considered. . . .

A statement of an intention to commit a crime made in the course of seeking legal advice is protected by the privilege, unless the crime-fraud exception applies. That exception applies only if the client or prospective client seeks advice or assistance in furtherance of criminal conduct. It is agreed that Tyree consulted Purcell concerning his impending eviction. Purcell is a member of the bar, and Tyree either was or sought to become Purcell's client. The serious question concerning the application of the privilege is whether Tyree informed Purcell of the fact of his intention to commit arson for the purpose of receiving legal advice or assistance in furtherance of criminal conduct. [On remand] Purcell's presentation of the circumstances in which Tyree's statements were made is likely to be the only evidence presented.

This is not a case in which our traditional view that testimonial privileges should be construed strictly should be applied. A strict construction of the privilege that would leave a gap between the circumstances in which the crime-fraud exception applies and the circumstances in which a communication is protected by the attorney-client privilege would make no sense. The attorney-client privilege "is founded upon the necessity, in the interest and administration of justice, of the aid of persons having knowledge of the law and skilled in its practice, which assistance can only be safely and readily availed of when free from the consequences or the apprehension of disclosure." *Matter of a John Doe Grand Jury Investigation,* 408 Mass. 480, 481–482, 562 N.E.2d 69 (1990), quoting *Hunt v. Blackburn,* 128 U.S. 464, 470, 9 S.Ct. 125, 127, 32 L.Ed. 488 (1888). Unless the crime-fraud exception applies, the attorney-client privilege should apply to communications concerning possible future, as well as past, criminal conduct, because an informed lawyer may be able to dissuade the client from improper future conduct and, if not, under the ethical rules may elect in the public interest to make a limited disclosure of the client's threatened conduct.

A judgment should be entered in the county court ordering that the order denying the motion to quash any subpoena issued to Purcell to testify at Tyree's trial is vacated and that the matter is remanded for further proceedings consistent with this opinion.

So ordered.

Notes

1. The court's decision demonstrates the interconnectedness of the evidentiary rules and the ethics rules on confidentiality. The court attempted to strike a balance between two. Did it do a good job, in your view?

2. Do you agree that if the intention to commit a future crime is not privileged under the evidentiary rule, then a lawyer in a state which allows lawyer disclosure of that intention should warn the client of that situation before beginning a consultation? What about a state that compels disclosure of that intention and does not make the communication privileged?

3. In *McClure v. Thompson,* 323 F.3d 1233 (9th Cir. 2003), a lawyer was retained to represent McClure, who had been arrested in connection with the murder of a woman and the disappearance of her children. Over the next few days, McClure told his lawyer, in often ambiguous and bizarre, rambling ways, where the children could be found, at one point drawing a map. It was not clear whether the children were alive or dead. McClure subsequently told his lawyer that "Satan killed Carol [the woman]" but that "Jesus saved the kids." The lawyer never asked his client directly whether the children were alive or dead.

The lawyer then had his secretary place an anonymous phone call to the sheriff's department to inform them of the suspected whereabouts of the children. Both children were found dead. McClure was found guilty of all three murders, and claimed on habeas appeal that his lawyer's revelations were improper and violated his right to effective assistance of counsel. The court affirmed his conviction, finding it a "close case" on whether the lawyer's actions were reasonable under the *Strickland* ineffectiveness standard. Taking as true the district court's findings that the lawyer believed the children were alive, and quoting the pre–2002 version of MR 1.6(b)(1), the appeals court concluded that the lawyer's disclosure was made upon the reasonable belief that it was necessary to prevent the client from committing a criminal act that was likely to result in imminent death or serious bodily harm—the lawyer was trying to prevent an apparent kidnapping from becoming a murder. The lawyer therefore "did not violate the duty of confidentiality in a manner that rendered his assistance constitutionally ineffective."

4.   Breach of the duty of confidentiality may subject a lawyer to discipline, civil claims of malpractice and breach of fiduciary duty, and could form the basis of an ineffective assistance claim. But could a lawyer be liable in tort to a third person harmed by the client, when the lawyer failed to prevent the client's criminal act by *not* revealing the client's intention to commit it? No court has clearly stated that such a duty exists on the part of lawyers, although psychologists have been held to owe a duty to disclose a patient's intention to kill a person. See *Tarasoff v. Regents of Univ. of California*, 17 Cal.3d 425, 131 Cal.Rptr. 14, 551 P.2d 334 (1976). Perhaps the closest any court has come to applying *Tarasoff* to lawyers is *Hawkins v. King County*, 24 Wn.App. 338, 602 P.2d 361 (1979). Lawyer Sanders was appointed to defend client Hawkins on a marijuana possession charge. Sanders was told by a lawyer whom Hawkins' mother had retained, and by a psychiatrist, that Hawkins was mentally ill and posed a danger to himself and others. At a bail hearing, Sanders said nothing about this information (nor was he asked), and Hawkins was released. About a week later, Hawkins attacked his mother and tried to kill himself by jumping off a bridge, resulting in the amputation of both legs. Hawkins and his mother then sued Sanders on a *Tarasoff*-type theory that he was negligent in failing to divulge the information about Hawkins' mental illness at the bail hearing. The court said: "The common law duty to volunteer information about a client to a court considering pretrial release must be limited to situations where information gained convinces counsel that his client intends to commit a crime or inflict injury upon unknowing third persons." On the facts, however, no duty was found. *Tarasoff* was distinguished on at least three grounds: Mrs. Hawkins already knew of the risk; Sanders had no knowledge that Hawkins was going to hurt anyone, just that he was mentally ill; and Sanders did not get any information from Hawkins himself. Should lawyers have a common-law tort duty to disclose client information to protect third persons from crimes?

b. Client Fraud and Crimes Involving Substantial Financial Loss to Another

In the wake of the financial scandals of the early 2000's (Enron being the most notable), the ABA adopted two additional exceptions to the confidentiality rule, both dealing with financial crimes or non-criminal fraud the client either intended to perpetrate, or had perpetrated with the lawyer's assistance (usually unwitting). Model Rule 1.6(b)(2) and (3), as amended in 2003, allows disclosures to prevent a client from committing a crime or fraud that is reasonably certain to result in "substantial injury to the financial interests or property of another" and to "prevent, mitigate or rectify" such injury, but only where the client has used the lawyer's services in furtherance of the crime or fraud. The Restatement provides such an exception in section 67, where the "client has employed or is employing the lawyer's services in the matter in which the crime or fraud is committed."

A growing number of states have adopted the ABA's new formulation, and we can expect many changes in the next few years with respect to what particular states decide to do on this subject. At this point in time, some states continue to distinguish between criminal and non-criminal fraud, such as by allowing (or even mandating) disclosure in the former situation but not in the latter.

Comments to the Restatement recognize that giving lawyers the discretion to divulge client information to prevent financial crime or fraud "may to an unknowable extent lessen some clients' willingness to consult freely with their lawyers." Restatement § 67, comment *b*. Do the benefits of granting this discretion outweigh this risk?

Should a lawyer for an organizational client have the ability to "blow the whistle" on wrongdoing within the organization that threatens to cause substantial injury to the organization? Remember that a lawyer for an organization (either working in-house or retained as outside counsel) represents the organization itself. See MR 1.13(a). Such a lawyer has a duty to keep the confidences of the entity client, and may also be placed in a position where confidences must be revealed in order to protect the entity. Model Rule 1.13, as amended in 2003, contains some explicit guidance for this situation. The rule sets forth guidelines for lawyers faced with the wrongdoing of officers or employees or associates of the organization "that is a violation of a legal obligation to the organization, or a violation of law which reasonably might be imputed to the organization, and is likely to result in substantial injury to the organization." MR 1.13(b).

The broad rule is that the lawyer must "proceed as is reasonably necessary in the best interests of the organization." *Id.* More particularly, the lawyer is instructed to refer the matter to "higher authority in the organization," even to the organization's "highest authority" (often meaning the Board of Directors). If the highest authority fails to address the problem, then the lawyer "may reveal information ... whether or not rule 1.6 permits such disclosure." MR 1.13(c). A comment explains that "Paragraph (c) of this rule supplements Rule 1.6(b) by providing an additional basis upon which the lawyer may reveal information relating to the representation." Notice that this discretionary revelation is for the protection of the client (the organization), not any third party. Further, MR 1.13(c)'s "additional basis" for disclosure does not apply if a lawyer is hired by an organization to investigate an alleged violation of law, or to defend the organization or its constituents against a claim arising out of an alleged violation of law. MR 1.13(d).

While MR 1.13(c) *adds* a ground for lawyer disclosure of information, it does not otherwise modify other provisions in the Rules. This means, for example, that if the lawyer's services are being used by the organization to commit a crime or non-criminal fraud, the lawyer may reveal information pursuant to MR 1.6(b)(2) and (3). And if the lawyer's services are being used by the organization to further a crime or fraud, the lawyer must resign pursuant to MR 1.2(d), which prohibits assisting a client in conduct the lawyer knows is criminal or fraudulent. See MR 1.13, comment [6]; MR 1.16, comment [2].See also MR 4.1(b), comment [3] (to avoid assisting a client's crime or fraud, "[s]ometimes it may be necessary for the lawyer to give notice of the fact of withdrawal and to disaffirm an opinion, document, affirmation or the like. In extreme cases, substantive law may require a lawyer to disclose information relating to the representation to avoid being deemed to have assisted the client's crime or fraud.").

In 2002, Congress enacted and President Bush signed the Sarbanes–Oxley Act of 2002, 116 Stat. 745, P.L. 107–204 (2002). Among its many provisions is Section 307, which requires attorneys who appear and practice before the Securities and Exchange Commission "to report evidence of a material violation of securities law or breach of fiduciary duty or similar violation by the company or any agent thereof, to the chief legal counsel or chief executive officer of the company"; and if that person does not "appropriately respond, ... to report the evidence to the audit committee of the board of directors" or to the board itself. The statute itself is silent on disclosing such evidence outside the organization, but makes mandatory the "up the ladder" conception that is merely suggested in Model Rule 1.13.

The rules adopted by the Securities and Exchange Commission pursuant to Sarbanes–Oxley go one step further, expressly allowing a lawyer to reveal to the SEC, even without the issuer's consent, "confidential information relating to the representation" to the extent the lawyer reasonably believes necessary (1) to prevent the issuer from committing a material violation of federal or state law "that is likely to cause substantial injury to the financial interest or property of the issuer or investors"; (2) to prevent the issuer from committing a fraud on the SEC; or (3) to rectify the consequences of a material violation of law "that caused, or may cause, substantial injury to the financial interest or property of the issuer or investors in the furtherance of which the attorney's services were used." 17 C.F.R. § 205.3(d)(2) (effective 2003).

Whether this provision, which "federalizes" an exception to the confidentiality rules for many lawyers, will influence states to revise the lawyer ethics rules of general applicability remains to be seen. *Compare* N.C. State Bar Ethics Comm'n, 2005 Formal Ethics Op. No. 9 (2006) (disclosure requirements in Sarbanes–Oxley Act and SEC regulations preempt state confidentiality requirements to the extent they differ), *with* Wash. Formal Ethics Op. Re Effect of SEC's Sarbanes–Oxley Regulations on Washington Attorneys' Obligations Under the RPC's (2003) (Washington-state lawyers must follow Washington ethics rules even if in contravention of Sarbanes–Oxley and SEC regulations). For a complete scholarly analysis, see Roger C. Cramton, George M. Cohen & Susan P. Koniak, *Legal and Ethical Duties of Lawyers After Sarbanes–Oxley*, 49 Vill.L.Rev. 725 (2004) (concluding, among other things, that the Act preempts contrary state disciplinary rules).

The Government client. Whistle-blowing within the government presents some special problems. While Model Rule 1.13 does apply by its own terms to governmental organizations, the comment recognizes that "a government lawyer may have authority under applicable law to question such conduct more extensively than that of a lawyer for a private organization in similar circumstances." MR 1.13, comment [9]. Specifically, the comment states that because "public business is involved," a "different balance" may be appropriate between protection of client information and "assuring that the wrongful act is prevented or rectified." State and federal statutes often apply to specific situations and settings.

3. Lawyer Self–Defense

A lawyer can disclose otherwise confidential information to defend himself or an associate against a charge or threatened charge by any person alleging that the lawyer or associate acted wrongfully in connection with representing a client. Restatement § 64; MR 1.6(b)(5). The discretion to divulge such information would arise if the lawyer is sued by the client (such as in a malpractice case), or by a third person where the lawyer's representation is part of the allegation of wrongful conduct. Such a rule leaves many questions unanswered, however, when it must be applied to actual facts.

MEYERHOFER v. EMPIRE FIRE & MARINE INSURANCE CO.

United States Court of Appeals, Second Circuit, 1974.
497 F.2d 1190.

Find new case!

MOORE, Circuit Judge:

[The trial court disqualified the plaintiffs' law firm, and plaintiffs and several defendants cross-appealed.]

Empire Fire and Marine Insurance Company on May 31, 1972, made a public offering of 500,000 shares of its stock, pursuant to a registration statement filed with the Securities and Exchange Commission (SEC) on March 28, 1972. The stock was offered at $16 a share. Empire's attorney on the issue was the firm of Sitomer, Sitomer & Porges. Stuart Charles Goldberg was an attorney in the firm and had done some work on the issue.

Plaintiff Meyerhofer, on or about January 11, 1973, purchased 100 shares of Empire stock at $17 a share. He alleges that as of June 5, 1973, the market price of his stock was only $7 a share—hence, he has sustained an unrealized loss of $1,000. Plaintiff Federman, on or about May 31, 1972, purchased 200 shares at $16 a share, 100 of which he sold for $1,363, sustaining a loss of some $237 on the stock sold and an unrealized loss of $900 on the stock retained.

On May 2, 1973, plaintiffs, represented by the firm of Bernson, Hoeniger, Freitag & Abbey (the Bernson firm), on behalf of themselves and all other purchasers of Empire common stock, brought this action alleging that the registration statement and the prospectus under which the Empire stock had been issued were materially false and misleading. Thereafter, an amended complaint, dated June 5, 1973, was served. The legal theories in both were identical, namely, violations of various sections of the Securities Act of 1933, the Securities Exchange Act of 1934, Rule 10b–5, and common law negligence, fraud and deceit. Damages for all members of the class or rescission were alternatively sought.

The lawsuit was apparently inspired by a Form 10–K which Empire filed with the SEC on or about April 12, 1973. This Form revealed that 'The Registration Statement under the Securities Act of 1933 with respect to the public offering of the 500,000 shares of Common Stock did not disclose the proposed $200,000 payment to the law firm as well as certain other features of the compensation arrangements between the Company (Empire) and such law firm (defendant Sitomer, Sitomer and Porges).' Later that month Empire disseminated to its shareholders a proxy statement and annual report making similar disclosures.

The defendants named were Empire, officers and directors of Empire, the Sitomer firm and its three partners, A. L. Sitomer, S.

J. Sitomer and R. E. Porges, Faulkner, Dawkins & Sullivan Securities Corp., the managing underwriter, Stuart Charles Goldberg, originally alleged to have been a partner of the Sitomer firm, and certain selling stockholders of Empire shares.

On May 2, 1973, the complaint was served on the Sitomer defendants and Faulkner. No service was made on Goldberg who was then no longer associated with the Sitomer firm. However, he was advised by telephone that he had been made a defendant. Goldberg inquired of the Bernson firm as to the nature of the charges against him and was informed generally as to the substance of the complaint and in particular the lack of disclosure of the finder's fee arrangement. Thus informed, Goldberg requested an opportunity to prove his non-involvement in any such arrangement and his lack of knowledge thereof. At this stage there was unfolded the series of events which ultimately resulted in the motion and order thereon now before us on appeal.

Goldberg, after his graduation from Law School in 1966, had rather specialized experience in the securities field and had published various books and treatises on related subjects. He became associated with the Sitomer firm in November 1971. While there Goldberg worked on phases of various registration statements including Empire, although another associate was responsible for the Empire registration statement and prospectus. However, Goldberg expressed concern over what he regarded as excessive fees, the nondisclosure or inadequate disclosure thereof, and the extent to which they might include a 'finder's fee,' both as to Empire and other issues.

The Empire registration became effective on May 31, 1972. The excessive fee question had not been put to rest in Goldberg's mind because in middle January 1973 it arose in connection with another registration (referred to as 'Glacier'). Goldberg had worked on Glacier. Little purpose will be served by detailing the events during the critical period January 18 to 22, 1973, in which Goldberg and the Sitomer partners were debating the fee disclosure problem. In summary Goldberg insisted on a full and complete disclosure of fees in the Empire and Glacier offerings. The Sitomer partners apparently disagreed and Goldberg resigned from the firm on January 22, 1973.

On January 22, 1973, Goldberg appeared before the SEC and placed before it information subsequently embodied in his affidavit dated January 26, 1973, which becomes crucial to the issues now to be considered.

Some three months later, upon being informed that he was to be included as a defendant in the impending action, Goldberg asked the Bernson firm for an opportunity to demonstrate that he had been unaware of the finder's fee arrangement which, he said, Empire and the Sitomer firm had concealed from him all along.

Goldberg met with members of the Bernson firm on at least two occasions. After consulting his own attorney, as well as William P. Sullivan, Special Counsel with the Securities and Exchange Commission, Division, of Enforcement, Goldberg gave plaintiffs' counsel a copy of the January 26th affidavit which he had authored more than three months earlier. He hoped that it would verify his nonparticipation in the finder's fee omission and convince the Bernson firm that he should not be a defendant. The Bernson firm was satisfied with Goldberg's explanations and, upon their motion, granted by the court, he was dropped as a defendant. After receiving Goldberg's affidavit, the Bernson firm amended plaintiffs' complaint. The amendments added more specific facts but did not change the theory or substance of the original complaint.

By motion dated June 7, 1973, the remaining defendants moved 'pursuant to Canons 4 and 9 of the Code of Professional Responsibility, the Disciplinary Rules and Ethical Considerations applicable thereto, and the supervisory power of this Court' for the order of disqualification now on appeal.

By memorandum decision and order, the District Court ordered that the Bernson firm and Goldberg be barred from acting as counsel or participating with counsel for plaintiffs in this or any future action against Empire involving the transactions placed in issue in this lawsuit and from disclosing confidential information to others.

The complaint was dismissed without prejudice. The basis for the Court's decision is the premise that Goldberg had obtained confidential information from his client Empire which, in breach of relevant ethical canons, he revealed to plaintiffs' attorneys in their suit against Empire. The Court said its decision was compelled by 'the broader obligations of Canons 4 and 9.'

There is no proof—not even a suggestion—that Goldberg had revealed any information, confidential or otherwise, that might have caused the instigation of the suit. To the contrary, it was not until after the suit was commenced that Goldberg learned that he was in jeopardy. The District Court recognized that the complaint had been based on Empire's—not Goldberg's—disclosures, but concluded because of this that Goldberg was under no further obligation 'to reveal the information or to discuss the matter with plaintiffs' counsel.'

Despite the breadth of paragraphs EC 4–4 and DR 4–101(B), DR 4–101(C) recognizes that a lawyer may reveal confidences or secrets necessary to defend himself against 'an accusation of wrongful conduct.' This is exactly what Goldberg had to face when, in their original complaint, plaintiffs named him as a defendant who wilfully violated the securities laws.

The charge, of knowing participation in the filing of a false and misleading registration statement, was a serious one. The complaint alleged violation of criminal statutes and civil liability computable at over four million dollars. The cost in money of simply defending such an action might be very substantial. The damage to his professional reputation which might be occasioned by the mere pendency of such a charge was an even greater cause for concern.

Under these circumstances Goldberg had the right to make an appropriate disclosure with respect to his role in the public offering. Concomitantly, he had the right to support his version of the facts with suitable evidence.

The problem arises from the fact that the method Goldberg used to accomplish this was to deliver to Mr. Abbey, a member of the Bernson firm, the thirty page affidavit, accompanied by sixteen exhibits, which he had submitted to the SEC. This document not only went into extensive detail concerning Goldberg's efforts to cause the Sitomer firm to rectify the nondisclosure with respect to Empire but even more extensive detail concerning how these efforts had been precipitated by counsel for the underwriters having come upon evidence showing that a similar nondisclosure was contemplated with respect to Glacier and their insistence that full corrective measures should be taken. Although Goldberg's description reflected seriously on his employer, the Sitomer firm and, also, in at least some degree, on Glacier, he was clearly in a situation of some urgency. Moreover, before he turned over the affidavit, he consulted both his own attorney and a distinguished practitioner of securities law, and he and Abbey made a joint telephone call to Mr. Sullivan of the SEC. Moreover, it is not clear that, in the context of this case, Canon 4 applies to anything except information gained from Empire. Finally, because of Goldberg's apparent intimacy with the offering, the most effective way for him to substantiate his story was for him to disclose the SEC affidavit. It was the fact that he had written such an affidavit at an earlier date which demonstrated that his story was not simply fabricated in response to plaintiffs' complaint.

The District Court held: 'All that need be shown . . . is that during the attorney-client relationship Goldberg had access to his client's information relevant to the issues here.' See Emle Industries, Inc. v. Patentex, Inc., 478 F.2d 562 (2d Cir. 1973). However, the irrebuttable presumption of Emle Industries has no application to the instant circumstances because Goldberg never sought to 'prosecute litigation,' either as a party, compare Richardson v. Hamilton International Corp., 62 F.R.D. 413 (E.D.Pa.1974), or as counsel for a plaintiff party. Compare T.C. Theatre Corporation v. Warner Brothers Pictures, 113 F.Supp. 265 (S.D.N.Y.1953). At most the record discloses that Goldberg might be called as a witness for the plaintiffs but that role does not invest him with the intimacy with the prosecution of the litigation which must exist for the Emle presumption to attach. . . .

Emle Industries, Inc. v. Patentex, Inc., supra, requires that a strict prophylactic rule be applied in these cases to ensure that a lawyer avoids representation of a party in a suit against a former client where there may be the appearance of a possible violation of confidence. To the extent that the District Court's order prohibits Goldberg from representing the interests of these or any other plaintiffs in this or similar actions, we affirm that order. We also affirm so much of the District Court's order as enjoins Goldberg from disclosing material information except on discovery or at trial.

The burden of the District Court's order did not fall most harshly on Goldberg; rather its greatest impact has been felt by Bernson, Hoeniger, Freitag & Abbey, plaintiffs' counsel, which was disqualified from participation in the case. The District Court based its holding, not on the fact that the Bernson firm showed bad faith when it received Goldberg's affidavit, but rather on the fact that it was involved in a tainted association with Goldberg because his disclosures to them inadvertently violated Canons 4 and 9 of the Code of Professional Responsibility. Because there are no violations of either of these Canons in this case, we can find no basis to hold that the relationship between Goldberg and the Bernson firm was tainted. The District Court was apparently unpersuaded by appellees' salvo of innuendo to the effect that Goldberg 'struck a deal' with the Bernson firm or tried to do more than prove his innocence to them. Since its relationship with Goldberg was not tainted by violations of the Code of Professional Responsibility, there appears to be no warrant for its disqualification from participation in either this or similar actions. A fortiori there was no sound basis for disqualifying plaintiffs or dismissing the complaint.

Order dismissing action without prejudice and enjoining Bernson, Hoeniger, Freitag & Abbey from acting as counsel for plaintiffs herein reversed. Upon cross-appeal by Empire, Gross, Kaplan, Phillips, Kratky, Lalich, Swick and Jennings, Jr., and cross-appeal by Sitomer, Sitomer and Porges, A. L. Sitomer, S. J. Sitomer and R. E. Porges insofar as said orders failed to enjoin plaintiffs from disclosing confidential information regarding Empire and to disqualify plaintiffs from representing themselves or a similar class of Empire stockholders, appeals dismissed. To the extent that the orders appealed from prohibit Goldberg from acting as a party or as an attorney for a party in any action arising out of the facts herein alleged, or from disclosing material information except on discovery or at trial, they are affirmed.

Notes

1. If Model Rule 1.13, discussed at the end of the previous section, had been in effect at the time this case arose, would Goldberg have acted properly in going to the SEC before discussing the matter with company officials at Empire Fire & Marine?

2. Did Goldberg act properly in going to the SEC before any formal charge was made against him by the SEC? What does Model Rule 1.6(b) allow?

3. The court says that there is no evidence that Goldberg's disclosure caused the instigation of the lawsuit. Why does this matter?

4. Was the scope of Goldberg's disclosure to the Bernson firm proper? What do the current rules say about that?

5. Should the Bernson firm have been allowed to remain in the case representing the plaintiffs? Didn't Goldberg's information give them an unfair advantage over the defendants, even if their receipt of the information was "untainted?"

4.   *Establishing a Claim Against a Client*

a.   **Wrongful Termination Suits by In-House Lawyers**

Under Model Rule 1.6(b)(5), a lawyer is given discretion to reveal confidential information "to establish a claim . . . on behalf of the lawyer in a controversy between lawyer and client." The ABA has taken the position that this provision allows an in-house lawyer alleging wrongful termination by his employer-client to use confidential information to establish the claim. ABA Formal Op. 01–424 (2001). Most courts have allowed lawyers to make such disclosures in wrongful termination suits, many of which involve claims that the termination was in violation of public policy. See, e.g., *Spratley v. State Farm Mut. Auto. Ins. Co.*, 78 P.3d 603 (Utah 2003); *Crews v. Buckman Labs. Int'l, Inc.*, 78 S.W.3d 852 (Tenn. 2002). Some have gone the other way. In *Balla v. Gambro, Inc.*, 145 Ill.2d 492, 164 Ill.Dec. 892, 584 N.E.2d 104 (1991), the court held that an in-house lawyer could not maintain a suit for retaliatory discharge, reasoning that allowing such a suit would have a "chilling effect on the communications between the employer/client and the in-house counsel." *Balla* was reaffirmed in *Ausman v. Arthur Andersen, LLP*, 348 Ill.App.3d 781, 284 Ill.Dec. 776, 810 N.E.2d 566, *appeal denied*, 221 Ill.2d 570, 291 Ill.Dec. 376, 823 N.E.2d 962 (2004).

Is it proper for a lawyer to use confidential information as a "sword" under these circumstances? One court, in explaining its holding that an in-house lawyer could use confidential information in his suit against his employer, in which he alleged that he was fired for blowing the whistle on corporate wrongdoing, reasoned that "a lawyer ... does not forfeit his rights simply because to prove them he must utilize confidential information. Nor does the client gain the right to cheat the lawyer by imparting confidences to him." *Willy v. Administrative Review Bd.*, 423 F.3d 483 (5th Cir. 2005).

b. Fee and Compensation Disputes

A lawyer is also allowed to reveal client information (even privileged information) if necessary to resolve a dispute with a client about a fee or other compensation. See Restatement § 65 (confidential client information); Restatement § 83(1) (privileged communications); MR 1.6(b)(5); DR 4–101(C)(4). Does this give the lawyer the right to threaten to disclose in order to force the client to pay?

STATE EX REL. COUNSEL FOR DISCIPLINE OF NEBRASKA SUPREME COURT v. LOPEZ WILSON

Supreme Court of Nebraska, 2001.
262 Neb. 653, 634 N.W.2d 467.

PER CURIAM.

This is an original proceeding seeking to discipline respondent, Joseph Lopez Wilson, for violating his oath of office as an attorney and Canon 1, DR 1–102(A)(1) and (6), of the Code of Professional Responsibility.... Respondent filed an answer admitting the essential factual allegations of the formal charges, but denying that his conduct violated the Code of Professional Responsibility....

BACKGROUND

Respondent was admitted to the practice of law in the State of Nebraska on September 17, 1986. At all times relevant hereto, the respondent engaged in the private practice of law in Douglas County, Nebraska. In 1995, respondent obtained an "H–1B1" professional visa for Carlos Moreno to work for U.S. Software, Inc. (USSI). Respondent was paid for his services. A few years later, the company that Moreno was working for subsequently underwent reorganization, and Moreno no longer worked for USSI.

In 1996, Moreno and his wife decided to obtain a divorce. Respondent represented Moreno in the divorce, and a decree was entered on June 13, 1997. Respondent was paid for his services. Over the years, respondent and Moreno became close friends, a friendship which in the words of respondent, was "as close as brothers." During these years, respondent provided legal services to Moreno in a number of other matters. Respondent did not charge Moreno for these services because of their friendship.

During this time period, respondent and his wife separated, and unbeknownst to respondent, his ex-wife and Moreno began an intimate relationship. When respondent eventually learned of the relationship between his ex-wife and Moreno, he threatened to report information to the Immigration and Naturalization Service (INS) that Moreno's job status had changed.

Respondent further threatened to reopen the Moreno divorce case and report to the court that Moreno had misstated his assets and thus committed a fraud upon the court and Moreno's ex-wife. Respondent conditioned his not carrying through with the threats by insisting that Moreno pay respondent $5,000 for the professional services respondent had previously provided to Moreno at no charge. Respondent subsequently lowered his demand to $3,000. Later, at the Committee on Inquiry hearing, respondent testified that he believed that certainly fraud was a ground to reopen the case.

In December 1999, Moreno eventually obtained a protection order against respondent. In the petition and affidavit to obtain the harassment protection order, Moreno wrote that respondent's

> [i]ntention [was] clear that [respondent] is trying to harrash [sic] me with the legal cases he have [sic] been representing me. This makes me think that he is trying to performe [sic] a personal vendeta [sic] against me because of a personal situation. [Respondent] has been trying to scare me with faxes, phone calls, and comming [sic] to my apartment.

In the petition and affidavit to obtain the harassment protection order, Moreno stated respondent came to his apartment on several occasions. Respondent came to Moreno's apartment on November 25, 1999, at approximately 10 p.m., at 10:30 p.m., and again at 11 p.m. Respondent was "kno[c]king [on] the door in a very hard way," but Moreno did not answer the door due to respondent's hostile behavior. Respondent also called Moreno at 10:45 p.m. on November 25. Respondent left a paper on Moreno's front door reading, "[Y]ou have been busted. You better seek a new attorney."

On November 26, 1999, at approximately 4:30 a.m., respondent went to Moreno's apartment and "knock[ed] strongly at the front door." Moreno opened the door, and respondent came in "acting in [a] way that made [Moreno think respondent] was out of control." Respondent wanted to know what was going on between Moreno and respondent's ex-wife. Respondent threatened to drop Moreno's INS case. Respondent also sent a fax to Moreno on November 26, which had attached to it a copy of a letter from respondent to the INS advising that he was withdrawing, effective immediately, as Moreno's attorney of record. The letter further stated:

I respectfully request that you review Mr. Moreno's status in the U.S. and revoke same because Mr. Moreno no longer is employed by USSI as it no longer exists. It is my understanding that Mr. Moreno now works for ACI worldwide at 330 South 108 in Omaha, NE. in a totally different capacity than approved under the original labor certification through the Iowa department of labor. I submit to you that his H–1 is also through USSI and should be revoked as well.

Moreno testified at the Committee on Inquiry hearing that respondent was threatening him with several faxes asking for money. If the money was not received, respondent threatened to destroy Moreno's INS case or reopen Moreno's divorce case.

One of these faxes, dated November 25, 1999, contains respondent's request for $5,000. If the $5,000 was not paid on that day, respondent wrote he would advise the INS that Moreno no longer worked for USSI. Respondent also stated, "I will be looking to reopen your divorce case and ask the court to grant your ex[-wife] 1/2 of your assetts [sic] since you failed to fully disclose your assetts [sic] during your divorce proceeding."

Moreno testified that respondent "didn't have authorization to disclose any information from any of the clients, which are myself and my company." Moreno felt that respondent was trying to "blackmail" him and felt threatened, so Moreno decided he should file a complaint with the proper disciplinary entity in the NSBA.

Respondent admitted that it "looks bad to have a restraining order against your lawyer." Respondent testified that he did not show up for the show cause hearing because he felt it was ridiculous and did not merit a response and that he also had a conflict on the morning of the hearing. . . .

ANALYSIS

Relator argues that the foregoing acts of respondent constitute a violation of his oath of office as an attorney licensed to practice law in the State of Nebraska, as provided by Neb.Rev. Stat. § 7–104 (Reissue 1997). Relator further argues that respondent's actions are in violation of DR 1–102(A)(1) and (6) of the Code of Professional Responsibility. DR 1–102 states in pertinent part: "Misconduct. (A) A lawyer shall not: (1) Violate a Disciplinary Rule. . . . (6) Engage in any other conduct that adversely reflects on his or her fitness to practice law." . . .

Disciplinary charges against an attorney must be established by clear and convincing evidence. . . . Based on [the] record, we find, in our de novo review, by clear and convincing evidence that respondent has violated DR 1–102(A)(1) and (6).

... Canon 4, EC 4–5, of the Code of Professional Responsibility states in pertinent part, "A lawyer should not use information acquired in the course of the representation of a client to the disadvantage of the client.... " The nature of the offense in this case encompasses respondent's coercive threats to force Moreno to pay him money. Respondent threatened disclosure of confidential information if this money was not paid. Respondent argues he performed valuable services for Moreno and "[i]t would be a gross imposition by the client to not pay for services rendered." Respondent further states that "[s]ometimes an attorney must take steps to collect the fee to prevent gross imposition by the client," citing Canon 2, EC 2–23, of the Code of Professional Responsibility.

Ethical code 2–23 states, "A lawyer *should be zealous in his or her efforts to avoid controversies over fees with clients and should attempt to resolve amicably any differences on the subject. The lawyer should not sue a client for a fee unless necessary to prevent fraud or gross imposition by the client.*" (Emphasis supplied.) Threatening telephone calls, faxes, and visits to a client's home are not efforts which should be used to comply with the letter or the spirit of EC 2–23.

Disciplinary rule 4–101(C) of the Code of Professional Responsibility states in pertinent part, "A lawyer may reveal: ... (4) Confidences or secrets necessary to establish or collect the lawyer's fee or to defend the lawyer or his or her employees or associates against an accusation of wrongful conduct." However, a disciplinary rule prohibiting disclosure of client confidences except in certain limited circumstances, including when attorney reasonably believes disclosure is necessary for resolution of a fee dispute, does not permit an attorney to threaten a former client with disclosure of client confidences in order to resolve a fee dispute.

An attorney such as respondent is expected to use legal means to enforce his rights, not violent threats. See *In re Rosenblatt,* 253 A.D.2d 106, 687 N.Y.S.2d 23 (1999).

Respondent's conduct has a chilling effect on the public's perception of attorneys and the NSBA in general. The maintenance of the reputation of the NSBA as a whole depends in part on the client's ability to be able to fully confide in his or her attorney. If clients do not believe they can do this, then attorneys will no longer be able to fully and zealously represent their clients....

Based on the above, we find in our de novo review that respondent should be suspended from the practice of law for a period of 2 years from the date of this opinion....

Notes

1. The court is quite critical of the lawyer's methods to try to collect a fee. Did the lawyer have a right to collect a fee at all, do you think?

2. Would the court's analysis have been any different under the Model Rules?

3. As we will see in Chapter 5, many states have set up alternative dispute resolution procedures for resolving fee disputes. Does a case like *Lopez Wilson* help explain why such procedures might be beneficial to clients?

Chapter 4

THE CLIENT–LAWYER RELATIONSHIP

The client-lawyer relationship is an expansive topic that extends well beyond this single chapter. Indeed, most issues of ethical lawyering relate in some significant way to the client-lawyer relationship. In this chapter, we explore some foundational but discrete issues, such as the rules and law on formation of the client-lawyer relationship; the rules forbidding interfering with another lawyer's clients; the duties owed by all lawyers to maintain the relationship, including the duty to counsel clients effectively; the formal division of labor between lawyer and client in both civil and criminal cases; the duty to safeguard client funds and property; and the law and rules on how a client-lawyer relationship may be terminated.

§ 1. MODELS OF THE RELATIONSHIP

Establishing and maintaining an efficacious and professional relationship with clients is a hallmark of all successful lawyers. Of course, no two clients or lawyers are exactly alike, which means that no two relationships are alike, either. All such relationships involve power, and the allocation of that power is almost always a subject of negotiation, however informal. See Austin Sarat & William L.F. Felstiner, Divorce Lawyers and Their Clients: Power and Meaning in the Legal Process (1995) (analyzing client-lawyer interactions in divorce cases).

For purposes of analysis, scholars have developed theoretical models of the client-lawyer relationship which may prove helpful as you think about what kind of lawyer you want to be, and as you look critically at the law and ethical rules that help define the client-lawyer relationship itself. Three models have emerged in the scholarly literature: (1) the traditional model; (2) the participatory model; and (3) the hired gun model.

The traditional model. The "traditional" lawyer-client relationship is one in which the lawyer is the dominant figure,

225

paternalistically making decisions for a passive client. (Indeed, one would never imagine a "traditional" relationship of this kind being labeled a "client-lawyer" relationship!) The lawyer's authority and autonomy to control the client's affairs is unchallenged. This is not to say that the lawyer is self-centered; indeed, the lawyer in the traditional model attempts to act in the client's best interests. But the client is wholly dependent on the lawyer to protect those interests, and is not an active participant in the decisions made in the course of representation.

The participatory model. In a "participatory" client-lawyer relationship, the parties share the responsibility for the success of the representation. Both the client and the lawyer play active roles. Of course, the client and lawyer often do not have expertise in the same relevant subjects. The lawyer is the legal expert, whose perspectives on the legal ramifications of the operative facts may well be entitled to significant deference by the client. But the client may know the facts more completely than the lawyer. And the client certainly knows better than the lawyer what the client wants out of the representation. On these matters the client's views may be entitled to deference. It is, in short, a relationship in which both lawyer and client have power to make decisions and neither party passively accepts the other's authority in a broad sense.

The "hired gun" model. At the polar extreme of the "traditional model" stands the "hired gun" model, a relationship in which the client is dominant and the lawyer passive. (This model may also be called "client-dominant.") In this relationship, it is the lawyer who often accepts the client's decisions unquestioningly. Power is not shared in any meaningful sense. Such a relationship might arise, for example, between a wealthy (or organizational) client and a lawyer who is financially dependent on that single client.

Which model is best? Categorically condemning any of the three theoretical models is probably not a meaningful exercise. A lawyer's relationship with Client A may tend towards one model, while that same lawyer's relationship with Client B may resemble another. Actual relationships are fluid and complex, and even a single client-lawyer relationship may go through stages that resemble each of the three models. That being said, however, it is clear that the participatory model—the "shared responsibility" model—has become for good reason the preferred one in both the ethics rules and in lawyering skills and legal ethics textbooks used in law schools. Indeed, both the traditional and "hired gun" models have drawn severe criticism from many scholars, on both moral and utilitarian grounds. Not only is a participatory relationship the only one that recognizes and preserves the autonomy and dignity of both lawyer and client, it is the kind of relationship that is more likely to lead to a successful conclusion of the legal matter that gave rise to the client-lawyer relationship in the first place. See Douglas Rosenthal, Lawyer and Client: Who's In Charge? (1974) (developing the models and applying them to actual client-lawyer interactions observed by the author).

The Model Rules themselves strongly reflect an image of the relationship between lawyer and client in which the client has a significant role to play in directing the representation. Further, the Rules instruct lawyers to establish and maintain the relationship in ways that nurture the client's participatory role. Perhaps the core "participatory" rule is Model Rule 1.2, which instructs lawyers to "abide by a client's decisions concerning the objectives of the representation" and to "consult with the client as to the means by which they are to be pursued." As the Comment to Model Rule 1.14 puts it, "The normal client-lawyer relationship is based on the assumption that the client, when properly advised and assisted, is capable of making decisions about important matters."

Model Rule 1.4 also represents a kind of codification of the participatory model. It places the lawyer under a mandatory duty "to explain a matter to the extent reasonably necessary to permit the client to make informed decisions regarding the representation." MR 1.4(b). Further, the lawyer must keep the client "reasonably informed" and must "promptly comply with reasonable [client] requests for information." MR 4.1(a). The lawyer must consult with the client about any need for consent, the means to be used in the representation, and the limits on the lawyer's conduct when the client is asking for impermissible assistance. Id. The comment to this rule, in line with those quoted above, explains that it springs from the notion that the client "should participate intelligently in decisions" about the representation "to the extent the client is willing and able to do so." MR 1.4, comment [5]. See also Cal. Rule 3–500 (echoing Rule 1.4).

This same shared responsibility conception of legal representation is found in numerous other rules (most of which we will encounter at other points in the course) that require the lawyer to disclose matters to clients and obtain the client's consent to particular matters. It is also found in rules (and in the law outside the ethics rules) that require the lawyer to abide by client decisions about many matters. For example, we saw in Chapter 3 that the client, not the lawyer, determines whether to assert the attorney-client privilege; even if the lawyer objects, the client's wishes govern.

A participatory relationship may not naturally arise without conscious effort. The reality is that the lawyer, by virtue of education and expertise, is often the dominant person in the client-lawyer relationship. Especially with clients who are unaccustomed to dealing with lawyers, there may be a tendency to lapse into a more traditional model. The client might even expect that, perhaps by analogy to other professionals the client has encountered in life, such as doctors. Of course, in some settings the natural tendency might be in the opposite direction, towards the adoption of a "hired gun" model. For example, if the lawyer is an inexperienced associate at a firm, working for a partner whose career is closely tied to retaining a particular corporate client, that young associate might well regard that client as the more powerful in the relationship. The lawyer in that situation may believe that doing whatever that client wants is what is in the lawyer's (and firm's) best interest.

Not all clients prefer a fully participatory relationship, for any number of reasons. A participatory arrangement involves the client more pervasively in the representation than does a traditional one, and the client may not want to (or be able to) spend the time to participate fully. Some clients are "avoiders" who would rather have the lawyer handle the matter as opposed to getting more involved in it themselves. While a lawyer should be certain that a client is freely choosing a relationship that is closer to the "traditional" model, the ethics rules themselves contemplate the possibility that a client will not want to participate in a legal representation to any significant degree. See MR 1.4, comment [5]. Where the client expresses such a preference, a lawyer should respect it.

Clients with diminished capacity. Particular challenges arise when the client is very young or very old, or has diminished mental capacity or a mental or emotional disability. Can such a client participate fully in the representation? Perhaps not. But the ethics rules instruct lawyers to "maintain a normal client-lawyer relationship" with such a client "as far as reasonably possible." MR 1.14(a). The comment to this rule recognizes that "a client with diminished capacity often has the ability to understand, deliberate upon, and reach conclusions about matters affecting the client's own well being.... The fact that a client suffers a disability does not diminish the lawyer's obligation to treat the client with attention and respect." _Id._, comment [1] & [2]. If the lawyer reasonably believes that the client is at risk of substantial harm (physical or financial, for example), and cannot act in his or her own interest, the rules authorize the lawyer to take "necessary protective action" such as consulting with others or even seeking the appointment of a guardian or conservator. MR 1.14(b). In taking any such protective action, the lawyer must act in the client's best interests, "maximizing client capabilities and respecting the client's family and social connections." _Id._, comment [5]. Restatement § 24 is in accord. See also _In re M.R._, 135

case update

N.J. 155, 638 A.2d 1274 (1994) (stating that the primary duty of counsel for the developmentally disabled is to protect that person's rights).

With any client, creating and maintaining a healthy and efficacious relationship should be a conscious, advertent enterprise. And it is the lawyer, not the client, who has the burden of clarifying what the relationship is and how it will continue. Most problems arise not because the lawyer consciously decided on a particular course of action, but because the lawyer failed to think of ways to avoid difficulties in the first place.

§ 2.   FORMING THE RELATIONSHIP

A.   How Is the Relationship Created?

The client-lawyer relationship is usually formed by an express contract called a retainer agreement or an engagement letter. (Some states require a lawyer to provide clients with a written retainer agreement, *see, e.g.*, N.Y. Comp. Codes R. & Regs. tit.22, § 1215.1–.2, although the Model Rules contain no such requirement.) This agreement generally specifies the scope of the representation (such as describing the matter or matters to be handled by the lawyer and any limitations on the lawyer's representation); the staffing of the matter (which lawyers or non-lawyer assistants will work on the case); any ethical issues that either exist or may arise in the future (such as conflicts of interest); and the arrangements on fees and other expenses. The length and amount of detail in a retainer agreement will vary, depending on a number of factors. See Jeffrey M. Smith & Ronald E. Mallen, Preventing Legal Malpractice § 2.9 (1989) (also providing examples of several kinds of retainer agreements).

NY rules any other states? did MR's adopt?

AC Source

However, a client-lawyer relationship may be formed inadvertently, usually to the lawyer's detriment, where no agreement of any kind has been drafted or signed and no money has changed hands. What factors are most important in judging whether a relationship between client and lawyer should be implied, any what are the ramifications of such a conclusion?

IN THE MATTER OF ANONYMOUS

Supreme Court of Indiana, 1995.
655 N.E.2d 67.

PER CURIAM.

[The Disciplinary Commission filed two complaints for disciplinary action against the respondent attorney in separate, unrelated cases alleging similar violations of the Indiana Rules of Professional Conduct. In the first of these cases, the Commission alleged that respondent violated the conflicts of interest rules

(Rules 1.7 and 1.9(a)) by representing more than one client in conflicting matters. The Court appointed a hearing officer who tendered her findings of fact and conclusions of law, concluding that respondent did violate these provisions. She recommended a private reprimand. Both the Commission and the respondent appealed.]

[I]n 1988, respondent was a member of a law firm. Late that year, a company (the "company") retained the respondent to defend it against certain grievances initiated by a labor union (the "union"). The union alleged that the company failed to properly contribute funds pursuant to a collective bargaining agreement. Specifically, the respondent was retained to represent the company regarding several issues between the two parties that were to be arbitrated. Both parties recognized that an individual holding the position of trustee and financial secretary of the union (the "trustee") was a key witness, since he negotiated the collective bargaining agreement between the company and the union. The respondent met with the trustee on December 22, 1988, as well as on several other occasions in late 1988, and discussed the pending grievances. At a deposition, the trustee testified that he informed the company it would not have to contribute funds pursuant to the agreement. He was effectively discharged as a trustee of the union in late 1988, apparently due to the union's perception that he provided certain information detrimental to its position in the grievance litigation. He formally resigned from his elected position of financial secretary in February, 1989.

At hearing of this matter, the trustee testified that, on December 22, 1988, he met with an attorney in the respondent's firm to inquire about representation in a wrongful discharge suit he intended to file against the union. The trustee was referred to the respondent because the respondent handled the bulk of the firm's labor matters. The respondent and the trustee met later that day, and, in addition to discussing the upcoming labor grievance proceedings, discussed the trustee's termination from his positions at the union and the possibility of filing a lawsuit against the union's president for wrongful termination. The respondent gave the trustee a document regarding RICO actions and assisted him in revising a statement the trustee planned to deliver to union members.

On December 27, 1988, the respondent's law firm opened a client file for the trustee. The file jacket indicated that the firm represented him. A code on the file reflected the respondent's having opened the file. The respondent and the trustee subsequently met two more times. The trustee testified that, at one such meeting, they discussed a possible contingency fee arrangement. The trustee testified that the respondent told him he thought his case may have been worth one million dollars. In addition, the trustee sent the respondent audio tapes of his recollection of the events surrounding his termination from the union, and wrote at least five letters to the respondent. These materials were placed in the trustee's file. On March 17, 1989, the respondent posted a billing slip to the file, memorializing a March 17, 1989 meeting between them. The respondent and the trustee never entered a formal employment agreement. The respondent never billed the trustee, nor did he ever expressly accept employment as the trustee's attorney.

The respondent ceased employment with the law firm in May, 1989, and began practicing law in another office nearby. Upon learning that the respondent no longer was associated with the firm, the trustee retrieved his case file from the firm's offices, believing that he was the respondent's client. However, the trustee never delivered his file to the respondent's new office, nor did he thereafter communicate directly with the respondent regarding his case. In 1990, the union settled its dispute with the company. Despite the meetings between the respondent and the trustee, the respondent did not use the trustee as a witness in the grievance proceedings.

On May 3, 1990, the respondent filed a fraud action on behalf of the company against the trustee and others, alleging that the trustee had fraudulently represented to the company that it would not have to contribute to the union's benefit plan. . . .

In his petition for review, the respondent contends that the hearing officer erroneously concluded that the trustee and the respondent formed an attorney-client relationship. He argues that no such relationship was ever formed between them, and thus that no conflict could have arisen. Specifically, the respondent asserts that he met with the trustee solely because the trustee was the "key witness" in the labor grievance. He claims that he met with the trustee in late 1988 only to go over his testimony for the grievance proceedings and not to discuss the trustee's employment problems. The respondent claims indicia of an attorney-client relationship are lacking and that the trustee did not even have a legal basis for a wrongful discharge suit.

Creation of an attorney-client relationship is not dependent upon the formal signing of an employment agreement or upon the payment of attorney fees. An attorney-client relationship need not be express, but may be implied by the conduct of the parties. Such a relationship exists "only after both attorney and client have consented to its formation."

Attorney-client relationships have been implied where a person seeks advice or assistance from an attorney, where the advice sought pertains to matters within the attorney's professional competence, and where the attorney gives the desired advice or assistance. *Bays v. Theran* (1994), 418 Mass. 685, 639 N.E.2d 720; *McVaney v. Baird, Holm, McEachen, Pedersen, Hamann &*

Strasheim *(1991), 237 Neb. 451, 466 N.W.2d 499;* Committee on Professional Ethics and Conduct of the Iowa State Bar Association v. Wunschel *(1990), Iowa, 461 N.W.2d 840.* See also People v. Morley *(1986), Colo., 725 P.2d 510 (the relationship may be established when it is shown that the client seeks and receives the advice of the attorney on the legal consequences of the client's past or contemplated actions). An important factor is the putative client's subjective belief that he is consulting a lawyer in his professional capacity and on his intent to seek professional advice.* Dalrymple v. National Bank & Trust Co. of Traverse City *(1985), D.C.Mich., 615 F.Supp. 979,* citing Westinghouse Electric Corp. v. Kerr–McGee Corp. *(1978), 7th Cir., 580 F.2d 1311,* cert. denied, *439 U.S. 955, 99 S.Ct. 353, 58 L.Ed.2d 346.* See also People v. Bennett *(1991), Colo., 810 P.2d 661 (the proper test is subjective; an important factor is whether the client believed the relationship existed);* State v. Hansen *(1993), 122 Wash.2d 712, 720, 862 P.2d 117 (client's belief will control where it is reasonably formed based on attending circumstances, including attorney's words and actions);* In re Johore Investment Co. (U.S.A.), Inc. *(1985), D.Hawaii, 157 B.R. 671 (in the preliminary consultation context, the existence of the relationship rests upon the client's belief that he is consulting the lawyer in a professional capacity and his manifested intention to seek legal advice).*

The hearing officer specifically found that an attorney-client relationship was implied from the parties' conduct. There is ample evidence in the record indicating that the respondent met with the trustee on several occasions and discussed a potential wrongful termination suit, a matter within the respondent's professional competence. The trustee testified that the respondent eventually concluded that the trustee had a strong wrongful termination case. The respondent testified that he did not consider the trustee to be his client.[3] There is, however, evidence tending to establish that both the respondent and the trustee consented to formation of an attorney-client relationship.[4] We are convinced that the

---

3. On cross examination by the Commission, the respondent stated:

[The trustee's case] was an evolving process ... [he] conveyed to me that he was anticipating all kinds of horrible things happening to him, employment wise. And in the event that [he] was wrongfully discharged, I anticipated that [he] and I might undertake litigation. [He] was a prospective client, but that's all he was.... I talked to him about the possibility of a case ...

4. Relevant portions of the trustee's testimony reveal that both the respondent and the trustee believed they had formed an attorney-client relationship at the December 22 meeting:

[Commission]: Okay. When you went in to meet with [the respondent], what was the topic of your conversation with him?

[Trustee]: Well, first I asked him about the representation because that's what I was there for, and, uh, he said uh, Yes, I certainly can. He said, I'll represent you. And I had a letter—we had a meeting, I believe, it was that night in Countryside, and I had a statement handwritten,—my wife had written some stuff—and I wanted to—if he was going to be my counsel, have him look it over and make sure that it—that there was nothing in there that could possibly get me in trouble or anything. And uh, so after he assured me he'd be my attorney, then I went ahead and gave him this.

respondent provided advice to the trustee regarding matters within his professional competence. It is clear that the trustee thought the respondent was acting as his attorney. Finally, we are also convinced that the respondent should have been aware that the trustee thought the respondent was representing him. The respondent did nothing to dispel this belief.

Contrary to the respondent's assertions, the existence of an attorney-client relationship is in no way dependent on the ultimate viability of potential causes of action discussed by the parties. Its existence is dependent only on the nature of the interaction between the parties and their consent, express or implied, to such a relationship.

The testimony of the trustee and of the respondent conflicts. The hearing officer heard this testimony at hearing, where she had the opportunity to "observe witnesses, absorb the nuances of unspoken communication, and by this process, attach credibility." *In re Cook* (1988), Ind., 526 N.E.2d 703, 706. She concluded that the parties formed an attorney-client relationship.... [O]ur review of the record reveals ample evidence upon which a finding that the parties formed an attorney-client relationship may be based. We now find, as did the hearing officer, that the respondent and the trustee formed an attorney-client relationship during their meetings in late 1988 and early 1989. [Respondent therefore violated the rules prohibiting representing more than one client in matters in which their interests were in material conflict, without consent.]

[W]e conclude that a private reprimand is the appropriate sanction for the misconduct in this case....

Notes

1. Whenever a formal retainer agreement has not been entered into, uncertainties can arise as to whether a client-lawyer relationship has been formed. As you can see in the case above, this is a fact question that can be quite complicated, with often-conflicting testimony coming from the lawyer and putative client. Notably, the Model Rules disclaim any attempt to define when a client-lawyer relationship arises. See MR, Scope, para. [17] ("[P]rinciples of law external to these rules determine whether a client-lawyer relationship exists."). The Restatement posits that such a relationship is created whenever a person manifests the intent to create such a relationship and the lawyer either consents or fails to manifest a lack of consent. See Restatement § 14.

2. The case law reflects that one important (and often overriding) factor is whether the client reasonably believed that such a relationship was being formed. See, e.g., *Cody v. Cody*, 889 A.2d 733 (Vt. 2005). What

could a lawyer do to minimize the risk of inadvertently forming a client-lawyer relationship after an encounter with a prospective client whom the lawyer does not want to represent? Does the *Togstad* case (Chapter 2, § 2) give you any ideas?

3.   Another important factor to many courts is whether the putative client has shared confidential information with the lawyer. As we will see in Chapter 6, this is particularly important when the issue is whether the attorney has a disqualifying conflict of interest. See *State v. Bedell*, 191 W.Va. 513, 446 S.E.2d 906 (1994) (one-hour preliminary consultation in which no confidences were divulged did not create client-lawyer relationship for conflicts purposes); Cf. *Westinghouse Electric Corp. v. Kerr–McGee Corp.*, 580 F.2d 1311 (7th Cir. 1978) (client-lawyer relationship for conflicts purposes found to exist between a lawyer—whose retainer agreement was with a trade association—and corporations who were members of that association, where they had shared confidential information with the lawyer). How does the client's sharing of confidences relate to the Restatement test described in Note 1 above?

4.   Can an attorney-client relationship be created by implication between a lawyer-husband and his non-lawyer wife, based on the husband's preparation of divorce papers for his wife's signature and his appearance in court alone at the divorce proceedings? See *Williams v. Waldman*, 108 Nev. 466, 836 P.2d 614 (1992) (yes; a client-lawyer relationship may be created even though no agreement was signed, no fees were charged, and the parties are related by blood or marriage).

5.   Whether or not a particular person or entity is a client is important for a number of different reasons. Many legal claims and disciplinary rules turn initially on whether such a relationship ever formed. In *Todd v. State*, 113 Nev. 18, 931 P.2d 721 (1997), a criminal defendant's sentence was overturned because five pages of handwritten notes that had been given to a lawyer who had come to the jail to visit another person were held to be privileged–the brief encounter in the jail was enough to create a client-lawyer relationship for purposes of the evidentiary privilege. In *In re Anonymous*, the fact that a client-lawyer relationship existed created an impermissible conflict of interest. This led to discipline and would also have led to the lawyer's disqualification from representing parties in cases where their interests conflicted. In *Togstad*, the creation of a client-lawyer relationship between Mrs. Togstad and lawyer Miller produced a situation in which Miller could be sued by Togstad for legal malpractice. In *Moen v. Thomas*, 628 N.W.2d 325 (N.D. 2001), lawyer Rathert had a retainer agreement with Jay Thomas. In connection with this representation, Rathert met several times with Jay's family members to discuss Jay's will and the formation of a trust. After Jay's death, several of these family members sued Rathert for legal malpractice. The trial court found no client-lawyer relationship as a matter of law, but the Supreme Court disagreed. Reversing a summary judgment for Rathert, the court said that "[a]n attorney who advises multiple parties in a complex string of transactions like this runs the risk of creating attorney-client relationships with all of

the parties unless there is a clear disclaimer advising them that the attorney is not representing them and that they should seek their own counsel.''

6. *Prospective clients.* We have seen that a client-lawyer relationship may be created rather casually with someone whom the lawyer regards only as a prospective client. But remember that the existence of such a relationship is a factual matter. Where the facts show that the lawyer made it clear he did not want to represent the prospective client and the client had no reasonable belief otherwise, no relationship should form. See, e.g., *Clark Capital Management Group, Inc. v. Annuity Investors Life Ins. Co.*, 149 F.Supp.2d 193 (E.D.Pa.2001) (brief telephone calls between a defendant's attorney and a lawyer at another firm, inquiring about the latter's interest in joining the matter as co-counsel did not create a client-lawyer relationship). Remember too, however, that certain duties arise even if a person remains only a prospective client and no client-lawyer relationship ever forms. See MR 1.18. A lawyer must protect a prospective client's confidences, use reasonable care to extent any services or advice are given, and protect any property given to the lawyer. Restatement § 15. Whether a consultation with a merely prospective client may produce a disqualifying conflict of interest is an issue we will see in Chapter 6.

7. *Scope of representation.* A lawyer is under no compulsion to accept a particular person as a client, unless ordered to do so by a court. Once a person is a client, must the lawyer provide "full service" on the particular matter that brought the client to the lawyer's office, or can the scope of representation be limited? Model Rule 1.2(c) provides that a lawyer may limit the scope of the representation, where such limitation is reasonable and the client gives informed consent. This is commonly called "unbundling" of legal services—performing only discrete tasks rather than handling an entire matter. This is permissible, as long as the conditions of the rule are met. See *Lerner v. Laufer*, 359 N.J.Super. 201, 819 A.2d 471 (2003). These conditions are not met if, for example, the client did not fully understand exactly what the lawyer was going to do or not do, and had thus not given valid consent to limited representation. See *Janik v. Rudy, Exelrod & Zieff*, 119 Cal.App.4th 930, 14 Cal.Rptr.3d 751 (2004) (class counsel owes duty to class members extending beyond prosecution of class claims as they are literally described in the class certification order). Just how limited can a representation be? For example, would it be reasonable for a lawyer to agree to give a "quick and dirty" legal opinion without doing any legal research at all? See MR 1.2, comment [7]. Do you think a client could give truly "informed consent" to such limited advice?

8. One form of limited representation that is gaining in popularity is "ghostwriting" for pro se litigants. In this arrangement, a litigant hires a lawyer to write particular pleadings or other documents, and to do nothing else—and the lawyer's role is never revealed to the court. Since individuals have the right to self-representation, such a practice does not violate the rule against assisting the unauthorized practice of

law. But is it proper otherwise? Authorities do not all agree, although the weight of authority is disapproving. Courts condemning the practice have pointed to the rule that papers submitted by pro se litigants are to be interpreted liberally, and ghostwriting is thus misleading to the court. See, e.g., *Duran v. Carris*, 238 F.3d 1268 (10th Cir. 2001). Federal courts often conclude that ghostwriting violates Rule 11, on the ground that a lawyer is drafting a pleading without signing it (and is thus not subject to the literal sweep of the Rule on frivolous claims and defenses). See, e.g., *Laremont-Lopez v. S.E. Tidewater Opportunity Center*, 968 F.Supp. 1075 (E.D.Va. 1997). Ethics opinions have also criticized ghostwriting, typically finding that it violates Model Rules 3.3(a) (making a false statement of fact or law to a tribunal) and 8.4(c) (engaging in conduct involving dishonesty, fraud, deceit or misrepresentation). See, e.g., ABA Informal Op. 1414 (1978); Conn. Bar Ass'n Comm. on Prof'l Ethics, Op. 98–5 (1998). Contra, State Bar of Ariz. Comm. On Rules of Prof'l Conduct, Op. 05–06 (2005); Cal. Rule of Court 5.70 (2003). For a thorough analysis of the ghostwriting phenomenon and the official responses to it, see Lauren A. Weeman, *Bending the Ethical Rules in Arizona: Ethics Opinion 05–06's Approval of Undisclosed Ghostwriting May Be a Sign of Things to Come*, 19 Geo. J. Legal Ethics 1041 (2006).

9. A lawyer could perhaps charge a much lower fee for services if he or she got the client to sign an agreement in advance promising not to sue for legal malpractice. Do you think such an agreement would be proper? See MR 1.8(h)(1); Cal. Rule 3–400.

10. Does a lawyer retained for some limited purpose have a good argument that the scope of representation is so limited that no client-lawyer relationship was created at all? Or that some different standard of care should apply to limited-representation situations? Consider the case below.

———

STREIT v. COVINGTON & CROWE, 82 Cal.App.4th 441, 98 Cal.Rptr.2d 193 (2000). The law firm representing a client in litigation retained lawyers from the firm of Covington & Crowe to enter a "special appearance" in court on the client's behalf on a hearing on a summary judgment motion. At the conclusion of the case the client sued the primary law firm and Covington & Crowe (and lawyers from both firms). All defendants moved for summary judgment. The trial court granted the motion by Covington & Crowe, finding that no one in the firm gave advice to the client, and that the "special appearance" at a single hearing was "solely an accommodation" to the primary law firm. Thus, there was no client-lawyer relationship at all between the client and Covington & Crowe. *Held*, reversed. The Court of Appeal explained that "[a]lthough the [client-lawyer] relationship usually arises from an express contract between the attorney and the client, it may also arise by implication.... The relationship may arise without any direct dealings between the client and the attorney. For instance, by retaining a single attorney, a client establishes an attorney-client relationship with any attorney who is a partner of or is employed by the retained attorney. The relationship also arises from a simple *association* for a particular case." Covington & Crowe's argument that a "specially-appearing" attorney owes a duty only to the client's primary law firm, not to the client, was flatly rejected. When a client's primary firm associates another firm for a limited purpose, both firms have a client-lawyer relationship with the client until that association is terminated. "By appearing at a hearing in a case in which the attorney has no personal interest, the attorney is obviously representing the interests of someone else, someone who is a party to that action. The client is such a person; the client's attorney of record is not.... An attorney owes a professional duty of care to every person with whom that attorney has an attorney-client relationship. Whether the attorney was selected directly by the client or associated by the attorney of record, that relationship exists.... Nor does it make any difference that the associated attorney is being compensated by the attorney of record rather than the client, or is not being compensated monetarily at all."

Notes

1. Covington & Crowe also argued in this case that the court should adopt a rule of "limited liability" for firms who enter special appearances as a courtesy to a client's primary lawyers, at least where the appearance was "perfunctory." The majority summarily rejected the idea. In a separate concurrence, Justice Ward addressed it more fully:

> Defendant attorneys speak of "perfunctory" appearances. What does that mean? On an extreme end of the spectrum, we can envision a court appearance which requires no particular knowledge of the case and requires only that some person attend, for example, to set a trial date. I feel constrained to point out that something must be seriously wrong with our system if we require attorneys, at substantial hourly rates, to actually appear in court, when any warm body would do just as well....
>
> On the other hand, the business under consideration may genuinely require the attorneys to be physically present, that is, when some meaningful exchange can be anticipated. If personal presence is imperative, then certainly it shortchanges the client to have an attorney appear who is not fully able to represent the client's interests. A major drawback of defendant attorneys' proposal for "limited liability" representation on "perfunctory" matters, is that we do not know when the "no-brainer" appear-

ance will suddenly transform into the crucial turning point of the case. Consider the situation where the accommodating attorney goes to court to arrange for a continuance of the trial, only to be told by the judge to call his or her first witness.

Defendant attorneys' proposed limited liability appearance not only diminishes the rights of clients, it also tramples on the court's right and duty to control the proceedings. Consider the judge who tries to solve some pressing problem in the case by seeking a stipulation from counsel, only to be told that an appearing attorney has only limited authority or inadequate knowledge of the matter. If we must choose between a process which encourages inadequate preparation or a process which demands competent performance, there is no real choice—our professional duty demands excellence. I am reminded of my father's constant repetition of the old saw, "if a job is worth doing, it is worth doing well." In the case of the sacred trust between attorney and client, we would do well to apply that admonition to every aspect of representation of the client's interest. . . .

Is Justice Ward suggesting that some advance limitations on the scope of a particular engagement simply might not turn out as the parties intended?

2.   Will the *Streit* decision increase the cost of legal services by making it impossible or more expensive to hire contract attorneys to make "special appearances" in distant locations? Why might it? Or does it call into question the need to have duly-admitted attorneys make "special appearances" in court on routine matters?

3.   Would it have made sense for the court to have held that a "specially appearing" attorney owes a duty only to the law firm that arranged for its retention, and not to the client? Why or why not?

NOTE: SPECIAL ISSUES OF CLIENT IDENTITY

Sometimes the existence of a client-lawyer relationship is contested because it is not clear who the client is. This issue arises in some contexts more frequently than others, and both the ethics rules and the case law (now largely reflected in the Restatement rules) attempt to clarify those commonly-encountered questions. While there are some hard-and-fast rules here, resolution in close cases turns on the kind of factual analysis we have seen in this Chapter. Many of these issues arise in the context of conflict of interest cases (which we will see in more detail in Chapter 6), but they are worth noting briefly here.

Representing insureds. Who is the client when a lawyer is retained by an insurance company to represent one of their insureds? Is it the insurance company? The insured person? Both? The rule in most states is that the insured is the sole client. See ABA Formal Opinion 282 (1950) (stating that a lawyer in such an arrangement "shall represent the insured as his client with undivided fidelity"). This is true even where the insurer is the one paying the fees, and perhaps even the one who chose the lawyer to represent the insured. However, even in those states that do not regard the insurer as a co-client, the lawyer owes duties to the insurer as well, primarily because of the legal relationship between the insurer and its insured. Most insurance policies contain a provision requiring insureds to cooperate with the insurer in settling third-party claims against the insured. Thus the lawyer, even though representing the insured, may well have a duty to share information with the insurer in order to assist the client (the insured) to comply with that contractual requirement. The Restatement provides that a lawyer owes a duty of care to a nonclient when the lawyer knows that the client "intends as one of the primary objectives of the representation that the lawyer's services benefit the nonclient." Restatement § 51(3). The comment to this section makes clear that lawyers owe a duty to insurers when they represent insureds, when both the client and the insurer have a reasonable expectation that the lawyer's work will benefit both of them. *Id.*, comment *g*. See *Paradigm Ins. Co. v. Langerman*, 200 Ariz. 146, 24 P.3d 593 (2001) (citing the Restatement, holding that a client-lawyer relationship might arise by implication between an insurer and an attorney for the insured, and in any event the lawyer owes a duty to the insurer). That being said, where the interests of the insured-client and the insurer are in conflict—as may occur in the event of a coverage dispute—the lawyer must protect the client's interests. See Restatement § 51(3)(b) & comment *g; Swiss Reinsurance America Corp. v. Roetzel & Andress*, 163 Ohio App.3d 336, 837 N.E.2d 1215 (2005).

Representing organizations. We have already seen that a lawyer retained to represent an organization represents the organizational entity itself, not any of that organization's officers, employees, shareholders or other constituents. This is true whether the organization is a corporation, a partnership, a joint venture, or any other form of entity. See Restatement § 96, comments *b* & *c*; MR 1.13(a). However, an entity cannot communicate with the lawyer except through people who work for that entity. Thus a lawyer's true "relationship" will be with live people who work for (and perhaps speak for) the client, but who are not themselves clients. Where the organizational client's interests appear to be adverse to those of the constituent with whom the lawyer is dealing, the lawyer must make clear that the organization itself is the client. MR 1.13(d).

Can a lawyer retained by an organization enter into a formal client-lawyer relationship with one or more of the organization's constituents? In other words, could a lawyer for a corporation also represent directors, officers, or employees? Model Rule 1.13(e) says yes, as long as the rules on conflicts of interest (which we will see in Chapter 6) are not violated by such a dual representation. These conflicts rules will usually require the organization's consent to that dual representation, and the consent must be given by some official within the entity other than the individual(s) to be represented.

Can a client-lawyer relationship nonetheless arise by implication between the lawyer and a constituent of an organizational client? The answer is yes. The same legal rules that we have seen in this section apply here. If a constituent of an organizational client treats the lawyer as such, and the lawyer fails to clarify that he or she represents the entity itself, not the constituent, the lawyer may be found to have created a client-lawyer relationship with that individual. See *Manion v. Nagin*, 394 F.3d 1062 (8th Cir. 2005) (executive director of corporation sought and received legal advice from lawyer for corporation; this sufficiently established a client-lawyer relationship between the two). This might form the predicate to a civil suit against the lawyer (by either client); disciplinary action; or disqualification. Further, when the lawyer represents a small entity, such as a partnership or a closely-held corporation with just a few shareholders, a few courts have held that the lawyer either represents the constituents as co-clients, or that the lawyer owes fiduciary duties to individual partners or shareholders because of the trust and confidence these constituents have placed in the lawyer. See, e.g., *In re Banks*, 283 Or. 459, 584 P.2d 284 (1978) (co-clients); *Fassihi v. Sommers, Schwartz, Silver, Schwartz & Tyler, P.C.*, 107 Mich.App. 509, 309 N.W.2d 645 (1981) (fiduciary duty).

Representing a class. A lawyer who represents a class of plaintiffs (in a class action litigation) represents the class itself. That being said, a class is not the same kind of entity as a formal organization. And a class is certainly not like an individual client. Indeed, a class is the lawyer's creation and the lawyer may make all decisions about the litigation, almost as if the lawyer himself was both the client and the lawyer. Many scholars have criticized this as ethically problematic. As one study puts it, "When one's client is unknowable or incoherent, one's duty will always be unclear.... With meaningless law and shapeless clients, the lawyer's self-interest is her only guide. The unchecked self-interest of lawyers drives class action practice today." Susan P. Koniak & George M. Cohen, *In Hell There Will Be Lawyers without Clients or Law*, 30 Hofstra L.Rev. 129 (2001).

B. Initiating the Relationship: Client Interviews

1. Purposes of Client Interviews

Most client-lawyer relationships begin with a client interview. Both the initial interview and subsequent follow-ups serve a number of purposes.

• First, the client interview initiates the formation of the relationship itself. The client decides whether to retain the lawyer and the lawyer decides whether to accept the job of representing the client. A retainer agreement may very well be one significant outcome of an initial consultation. This agreement embodies the client's choice to utilize this particular lawyer to handle this particular matter. Further, client interviews set the tone for the relationship. A lawyer (and client) who want to forge a more participatory relationship (see § 1) must build a relationship of mutual trust and respect.

• Second, the lawyer must explain some foundational matters to the client, such as the contemplated scope of the representation and the contours of the attorney-client privilege and confidentiality rules. The lawyer must check to see whether taking on the client's matter will create any conflicts of interest that might cause problems later, and must explain the law and rules on that topic as well. Lawyers and firms should always develop adequate "intake procedures" to pre-screen prospective clients for conflicts before any lawyer in the firm engages such a person in a lengthy discussion of the merits of a matter. (We will explore conflicts of interest in detail in Chapter 6.) The client's responsibility for attorneys' fees, costs and expenses should also be explained early in the representation. Most of this kind of information will ultimately be memorialized in the retainer agreement. The best agreements will resolve the kinds of ambiguities that often come back to haunt lawyers.

• Third, the lawyer must begin to gather the facts that will be relevant to the representation. In order to competently represent a client, the lawyer must learn facts from the client and diagnose the client's legal problem. See MR 1.1, comment [5] ("Competent handling of a particular matter includes inquiry into and analysis of the factual and legal elements of the problem"). As Justice Rehnquist said in *Upjohn*, reprinted in Chapter 3, § 1, "The first step in the resolution of any legal problem is ascertaining the factual background and sifting through the facts with an eye to the legally relevant." While the specific facts gathered will vary with the matter, a lawyer should always ascertain sufficient facts to spot whether the statute of limitations is an issue. See, e.g., *Togstad*, reprinted in Chapter 2, § 2. A lawyer should also ascertain whether there is a need for urgent action to protect the client's interests.

The law and ethics rules prohibit a lawyer from fabricating evidence or suborning perjury. See, e.g., MR 3.4(b). A lawyer must take care in client interviews not to imply that the client can "invent" good facts. Lawyers might bumble into this by asking narrow, leading questions that signal to the client that a particular answer would be legally preferable; the client might then give the answer the lawyer appears to want, as opposed to a more accurate response.

Good lawyers must have a broad view of relevance as they begin gathering facts from a client. Non-legal concerns may be of even greater importance to a client than legal ones, even if they are "irrelevant" in an evidentiary sense. The lawyer should cast a "wide net" in investigating the facts, especially at the beginning of the representation. Remember that ultimately, the client's problem will more likely be resolved by negotiation, not by a court. This means that a narrow focus on what a court could grant may leave better solutions unexplored.

• Fourth, the lawyer must learn the client's goals for the representation. Model Rule 1.2(a) provides that "a lawyer shall abide by a client's decisions concerning the objectives of representation, and as required by Rule 1.4, shall consult with the client as to the means by which they are to be pursued." Fulfilling these duties requires the lawyer to probe effectively for what it is the client wants the lawyer to achieve. In the ideal world, a client would enter the lawyer's office knowing precisely the goals of the representation. But of course, we don't live in an ideal world. In reality, the client is often unaware of what goals can be achieved through law and must be counseled about remedial possibilities and limitations. Thus the client's goals may well shift and become more refined as the representation progresses. The best lawyers know that client desires are fluid, not static, and constructs the relationship so that the client's changing desires are both heard and addressed promptly.

What if the client's goals for the representation are improper? Should the lawyer still work to achieve those goals? Should the lawyer try to talk the client out of pursuing such goals? Superficially these are easy questions; in the real, nuanced world they may not be. Model Rule 1.2(d) prohibits a lawyer from counseling to engage, or assisting a client, in conduct that the lawyer knows is criminal or fraudulent. The same provision, however, allows the lawyer to discuss with the client "the legal consequences of any proposed course of conduct." Model Rule 8.4 states that it is "professional misconduct" to knowingly assist another person in violating the rules or to "engage in conduct involving dishonesty, fraud, deceit or misrepresentation." MR 8.4(a) & (c). *What do you think the lawyer should say to a client whose goals appear to be illegal? Will such a communication be privileged?* Model Rule 1.16(a) provides that a lawyer "shall not represent a client" if (1) the representation will result in violation of the rules of professional conduct or other law. *Is a client's suggestion of an illegal or improper goal enough to mandate not taking on a matter?* See MR 1.16, comment [2].

What if the client's goals are neither illegal nor fraudulent, but merely offensive or even repugnant to the lawyer? Model Rule 1.2(b) states that a lawyer's representation of a client "does not constitute an endorsement of the client's political, economic, social or moral views or activities." If you, as a lawyer, profoundly disagree with a client's political or moral views, and those views are driving the client's goals for the representation, do you think you could represent the client competently? If not, should you take on such a matter in the first place? Cf. MR 1.16, comment [7].

2. *Lawyering Skills Involved in Client Interviews*

Lawyers are primarily problem-solvers, and—perhaps contrary to popular opinion—the best lawyers are creative. Lawyers interact with clients in order to help clients achieve particular goals. Doing this competently (or hopefully, better than competently) involves applying a bundle of skills. Some lawyers are innately better at some of these skills than others, but all lawyers can and should learn to get better at them. In 1992, an ABA task force published a Statement of Fundamental Lawyering Skills and Professional Values that detailed a number of fundamental skills with which lawyers should be familiar as they undertake client representation. Specifically, ten broad skill areas were examined: (1) problem solving; (2) legal analysis; (3) legal research; (4) factual investigation; (5) communication, both written and oral; (6) counseling; (7) negotiation; (8) litigation and alternative dispute resolution procedures; (9) organization and management of legal work; and (10) recognizing and resolving ethical dilemmas. ABA Task Force on Law Schools and the Profession, Statement of Fundamental Lawyering Skills and Professional Values (1992).

In initiating a relationship with a client, many of these skills come into play. For example, the lawyer must utilize good communication skills in order to build a meaningful relationship, gather facts efficiently and accurately, and answer a client's questions about a variety of perhaps unfamiliar and technical subjects. This means that the lawyer must be able not only to speak and write clearly, but also to *listen* well. A lawyer who is always in "output mode," pontificating about the law and more concerned with what questions he is asking than what answers he is or is not receiving is not an effective communicator. The client should be allowed to tell the story of what has happened, and what the client wants, without obtrusive interruptions. Additionally, a lawyer must be able to analyze the legal framework presented by the client's matter in order to know what facts to gather and clarify. Law students get used to seeing canned "fact patterns" in law school, presented either in reported cases or hypothetical problems. But in practice, facts are not "given." They are investigated, explored, and developed. And always, the client is a key source of such facts. Effective fact-gathering is an art, and like all arts, involves creativity. The lawyer who is inquisitive, knowledgeable about the law, and sensitive to the client's goals and needs is far more likely to uncover facts that will prove useful in the representation.

C. Non–Clients and the "No Contact" Rule

As discussed above, a lawyer cannot competently handle any client matter without gathering facts. A good percentage of the facts may be provided by the client, both orally and through documents. But often, facts must also be obtained from others. While the lawyer's primary motivation in these circumstances is to further the client's interests, the lawyer must also respect the rights of other persons with whom the lawyer interacts during the representation. See, e.g., MR 4.1(a) (prohibiting lawyers from making "a false statement of material fact or law to a third person" in the course of representing a client); MR 4.4(a) ("a lawyer shall not use means that have no other substantial purpose other than to embarrass, delay or burden a third person, or use methods of obtaining evidence that violate the legal rights of such a person"). Other rules restrict lawyers further in gathering information from non-clients, as we see in the materials that follow.

PATRIARCA v. CENTER FOR LIVING & WORKING, INC.

Supreme Judicial Court of Massachusetts, 2002.
438 Mass. 132, 778 N.E.2d 877.

SPINA, J.

A judge in the Superior Court issued a protective order on the basis of Mass. R. Prof. C. 4.2, 426 Mass. 1402 (1998),[3] barring counsel for the plaintiff, Ellen L. Patriarca, from any ex parte contact with former or future employees of the defendant, the Center for Living & Working, Inc. (center), on matters concerning their former employment or the pending litigation unless that contact were made with leave of court or of opposing counsel.... Because the former employees in question are neither actually represented by the center, nor the type of employee covered by

---

3. Rule 4.2 of Massachusetts Rules of Professional Conduct, 426 Mass. 1402 (1998), entitled, "Communication with person represented by counsel," states: "In representing a client, a lawyer shall not communicate about the subject of the representation with a person the lawyer knows to be represented by another lawyer in the matter, unless the lawyer has the consent of the other lawyer or is authorized by law to do so."

rule 4.2, as construed in *Messing, Rudavsky & Weliky, P.C. v. President and Fellows of Harvard College,* 436 Mass. 347, 764 N.E.2d 825 (2002) (*Messing*), the protective order must be vacated. . . .

Background. Patriarca filed suit against the center, its board of directors, and Robert Bailey, executive director of the center, alleging wrongful termination from her employment as a registered nurse supervising the center's personal care attendant program. In the course of discovery Patriarca stated in her answer to an interrogatory that she had contacted four former employees of the center and had "discussed events which had occurred while we were both employed at [the center]." The defendants filed a motion for a protective order seeking to bar Patriarca and her counsel from having ex parte contact with the center's former employees on matters concerning their employment and the pending litigation. A judge in the Superior Court, who did not have the benefit of our decision in the *Messing* case, concluded that rule 4.2 may prohibit ex parte contact with former employees. He found that, in this case, the statements of former employees could be potentially admissible against the center, or that the former employees' acts or omissions could be imputed to the center. He issued an order barring Patriarca's counsel from "contacting any former employees of the defendant corporation on matters concerning their former employment and this litigation unless defense counsel is present or permission is granted from this [c]ourt or from opposing counsel."

. . . A threshold question is whether a particular employee is actually represented by corporate counsel. An organization may not assert a preemptive and exclusive representation by the organization's lawyer of all current (or former) employees as a means to invoke rule 4.2 and insulate them all from ex parte communication with the lawyers of potential adversary parties.[6] See *Messing, supra* at 356–357, 764 N.E.2d 825. The American Bar Association Committee on Ethics and Professional Responsibility has stated that Model Rule 4.2, on which our rule 4.2 is based, "does not contemplate that a lawyer representing the entity can invoke the rule's prohibition to cover all employees of the entity, by asserting a blanket representation of all of them." ABA Formal Op. 95–396, § VI (1995). Thus, the center may not invoke rule 4.2 to claim that all current and former employees are represented, and therefore the protective order is overbroad. Any analysis must be employee specific. The center has made no

---

6. As set forth in comment [4] to rule 4.2, if the person is in fact represented by his or her own counsel, then it is that counsel's permission that must be obtained prior to ex parte contact. *DaRoza v. Arter,* 416 Mass. 377, 381–382, 622 N.E.2d 604 (1993) (setting out circumstances in which implied attorney-client relationship can arise).

factual showing that the former employees in question are actually represented by the center's (or their own personal) counsel.

We turn to the rule in the *Messing* case to determine whether the employees in question may be considered represented for purposes of rule 4.2. The purpose of rule 4.2 is to "protect the attorney-client relationship and prevent clients from making ill-advised statements without the counsel of their attorney." *Messing, supra* at 358, 764 N.E.2d 825. However, we recognized that prohibiting ex parte contact with all employees of a represented organization went beyond the purpose of the rule, which was not to "protect a corporate party from the revelation of prejudicial facts." *Id.,* quoting *Dent v. Kaufman,* 185 W.Va. 171, 175, 406 S.E.2d 68 (1991). We sought a balance between the need to discover relevant facts and the competing need to protect the attorney-client relationship. We construed rule 4.2 (and comment [4] thereto) to prohibit an attorney from having ex parte contact only with certain employees of an organization, namely, those "who exercise managerial responsibility in the matter, who are alleged to have committed the wrongful acts at issue in the litigation, or who have authority on behalf of the corporation to make decisions about the course of the litigation." As construed, the rule allows "ex parte interviews without prior counsel's permission when an employee clearly falls outside of the rule's scope." *Id.* at 359, 764 N.E.2d 825.

Patriarca was employed by the center as a registered nurse whose job responsibility was to manage the personal care attendant program, a program that provides persons who have permanent or chronic disabilities with assistance to allow them to live independently in their community instead of being institutionalized. See 130 Code Mass. Regs. §§ 422.416–422.423 (1999). Two of the former employees with whom she made contact had been occupational therapists. A third was an assistant community department manager-supervisor and skills trainer. These three had worked closely with Patriarca and Bailey at the center. The fourth had been a business manager at the center and had witnessed the events which led to Patriarca's separation from the center.

These four former employees of the center do not come within any category of employee covered by rule 4.2. See *Messing, supra* at 357, 764 N.E.2d 825. None of them is alleged to have committed the wrongful acts at issue in the litigation. There is no evidence, under their job descriptions or otherwise, that any of them had authority on behalf of the corporation to make decisions about the course of the litigation....

[N]one of the four former employees in this case came within a protected category of employee identified by the *Messing* case while she was employed by the center. Thus, none would have been protected from ex parte contact while an active employee of the center. A change in status from current to former employee does not change the fact that each falls "outside of the rule's scope." *Messing, supra* at 359, 764 N.E.2d 825. They are not protected by rule 4.2 from ex parte contact by Patriarca's counsel. In making any ex parte contact with these former employees, Patriarca's counsel must, of course, be assiduous in meeting other ethical and professional standards found outside rule 4.2.

   ... The protective order issued by the Superior Court is vacated. The case is remanded to the Superior Court for further proceedings consistent with this opinion.

   So ordered.

Notes

   1. *Contacts with non-clients.* As *Patriarca* explains, if a lawyer knows that a person is represented by another lawyer, the consent of that lawyer must be obtained before communicating with that person in connection with the representation. See MR 4.2; Cal. Rule 2–100; Restatement §§ 99–102. If the non-client is not represented by counsel at all, the lawyer must not state or imply that the lawyer is disinterested, must clarify any misunderstanding about the lawyer's role, and must not give that person legal advice except for the advice to secure counsel. See MR 4.3; Restatement § 103. Do the restrictions on contacts with these two kinds of people derive from the same concerns? Or do they address different potential abuses? What are the potential abuses and perceived problems that these rules address?

   2. *Organizations.* Special problems arise when organizations, rather than simply individuals, are involved in the matter being investigated. The Model Rules approach, adopted by Massachusetts, is applied in *Patriarca.* Mass. Rule 4.2, comment [4] provides: "In the case of an organization, this [r]ule prohibits communications by a lawyer for another person or entity concerning the matter in representation only with those agents or employees who exercise managerial responsibility in the matter, who are alleged to have committed the wrongful acts at issue in the litigation, or who have authority on behalf of the organization to make decisions about the course of the litigation.... " Restatement § 100(c) adds that contact with a particular employee is improper if the statement of that employee, under the rules of evidence, would "have the effect of binding the organization with respect to proof of the matter." A lawyer who violates the no-contact rule and makes ex parte contact with the opposing party's employees may be disqualified from the representation. See, e.g., *Weeks v. Independent School Dist. No. I–89,* 230 F.3d 1201 (10th Cir.2000) (applying Oklahoma law).

   3. *Former employees of an organization.* Most courts that have addressed the issue have concluded that a lawyer does not need to obtain the organization's consent to interview its *former* employees. See., e.g., *Clark v. Beverly Health & Rehab. Services, Inc.,* 440 Mass. 270, 797

N.E.2d 905 (2003); *Humco, Inc. v. Noble,* 31 S.W.3d 916, 920 (Ky.2000); *H.B.A. Mgt., Inc. v. Estate of Schwartz,* 693 So.2d 541, 542 (Fla.1997); *Niesig v. Team I,* 76 N.Y.2d 363, 559 N.Y.S.2d 493, 558 N.E.2d 1030 (1990). The Model Rules are in accord. See MR 4.2, comment [7] ("Consent of the organization's lawyer is not required for communication with a former constituent.") Of course, if any former employee is represented by another lawyer, then that lawyer's consent would have to be obtained first. If, on the other hand, the former employee was not represented at all, the rules on contact with unrepresented persons would have to be followed.

4.   *Use of non-lawyer assistants to gather facts.* Can a lawyer get around the restrictions applied in *Patriarca* by directing a non-lawyer to conduct the interviews? See MR 5.3.; *Midwest Motor Sports v. Arctic Cat Sales,* 347 F.3d 693 (8th Cir. 2003) (use of undercover investigator).

5.   *Communication initiated by the non-client.* Does it matter if the person who initiates the communication is not the lawyer but is rather the non-client who is represented by other counsel? After all, if the purpose of the rule is to prohibit overreaching and an interference with the client-lawyer relationship, aren't those interests impliedly waived by a non-client who initiates contact? See MR 4.2, comment [3].

6.   *When the lawyer is a party.* Should the no-contact rule apply to bar a lawyer from contacting represented non-lawyers who had sued him personally? See *In re Conduct of Knappenberger,* 338 Or. 341, 108 P.3d 1161 (2005).

§ 3.   MAINTAINING THE RELATIONSHIP

A.   Scope of Authority Between Lawyer and Client

1.   *Civil Cases*

MOORES v. GREENBERG

United States Court of Appeals, First Circuit, 1987.
834 F.2d 1105.

SELYA, Circuit Judge.

Ralph W. Moores, Jr., plaintiff, was injured while laboring as a longshoreman in Maine. After collecting compensation benefits from the stevedoring firm for which he worked—benefits actually paid by that firm's insurer, Liberty Mutual Insurance Company (LMIC)—he brought a third-party liability suit against the shipowners in Maine's federal district court. Nathan Greenberg was his attorney. They agreed that the lawyer's compensation would be contingent: the standard one-third of any judgment or settlement. But, the case was lost.

Moores wasted little time in turning upon his erstwhile champion. He sued for malpractice in a Massachusetts state court.

Greenberg removed the case to the United States District Court for the District of Massachusetts. Following a jury trial, Moores was awarded $12,000. Although both parties assign error, we find no reason to forsake the verdict. . . .

Greenberg contests the district court's denial of his motion for a directed verdict. He asserts that the evidence presented was insufficient as a matter of law to support liability. Given the operative facts of the case, however, this asseveration need not occupy us for long. . . . Greenberg has not come close to meeting [the] rigorous standard [for reversal of such a decision].

At a very minimum, there was evidence before the jury which, if believed, proved that while the third-party suit was in progress, the shipowners offered to settle first for $70,000 and later for $90,000. There was also evidence that Greenberg failed to relay either offer to plaintiff. In the subsequent malpractice suit, Moores claimed that he would have accepted the $90,000 offer had he been informed of it. Instead of a fat settlement, he received nothing but a rebuff from the jury.

This evidence was, we think, more than ample. In representing his client, an attorney has a duty to use that degree of skill, diligence, and judgment ordinarily to be expected of a member of the bar practicing in the same (or a similar) locale. As part and parcel of this duty, a lawyer must keep his client seasonably apprised of relevant developments, including opportunities for settlement.

Greenberg says that, even if this be true, the sums mentioned to him were too niggardly to be relayed. We need not decide today whether a lawyer has an obligation to transmit a patently unreasonable offer to his client. *See Smith v. Ganz*, 219 Neb. 432, 436, 363 N.W.2d 526, 530 (1985). The overtures which the defense made in the liability case were neither so totally divorced from a realistic appraisal of the merits nor so unresponsive to the upside and the downside of the litigation that they could blithely be ignored. The ongoing risk/reward calculus had many variables, some of an imponderable nature. These manifold uncertainties added up to at least one bit of certitude: the shipowners' $90,000 offer could not be said, as a matter of law, to be a patently ridiculous one. On this scumbled record, the district court did not err in permitting the jury to determine whether reasonably competent counsel would have informed Moores of the $90,000 offer and whether the client, had he been told, would have clasped it to his bosom. . . .

We conclude that this suit was properly assigned to the jury calendar; that the evidence of negligence was adequate to warrant jury submission; and that the liability finding in plaintiff's favor was supportable. . . . We therefore leave the parties as we found them.

Affirmed. No costs.

Notes

1. *Damages computation in* Moores. The plaintiff in *Moores* received only $12,000, rather than $90,000, because of a number of adjustments: (1) the lawyer and client had agreed on a one-third contingent fee. Thus $30,000 was subtracted from the judgment to reflect the fee that plaintiff would have paid had the $90,000 settlement offer been accepted; (2) the lawyer had advanced costs of $5,000 which were contractually subject to reimbursement; and (3) the plaintiff had accepted compensation benefits from an insurer pursuant to federal law, in the amount of $43,000. The insurer would have been able to attach a subrogation lien on the proceeds of any settlement. Thus the $12,000 net recovery represented $90,000 (the amount of the settlement offer never relayed), less these three sums totaling $78,000. Query whether the court was correct to reduce the recovery by the amount of the agreed-upon contingent fee, when the lawyer's conduct so clearly breached a duty to the client. See *Carbone v. Tierney*, 151 N.H. 521, 864 A.2d 308 (2004); Restatement § 37.

2. The decision to accept or reject a settlement in a civil case is the client's alone. *See* MR 1.2(a); Restatement § 22(1). This means not only that the lawyer must tell the client of settlement offers, but also that the lawyer must take action to accept a settlement if instructed to do so by the client. Further, it means that a lawyer cannot unilaterally cause a settlement to be entered in a case when the client has instructed the lawyer not to settle. See *In re Harshey*, 740 N.E.2d 851 (Ind. 2001)(lawyer for corporation negotiated a settlement and convinced a judge to approve it, despite corporate president's clear objection; public reprimand ordered for violation of Rule 1.2(a)).

3. If a lawyer is duty-bound to inform a client of all settlement offers, what is to prevent the client from accepting an unreasonably low settlement? Can the lawyer do nothing to prevent that?

4. The Restatement provides that the decision whether to appeal from an adverse judgment in a civil case is also the client's alone. Restatement § 22(1).

2. Criminal Cases

JONES v. BARNES

Supreme Court of the United States, 1983.
463 U.S. 745, 103 S.Ct. 3308 77 L.Ed.2d 987.

Chief Justice BURGER delivered the opinion of the Court.

We granted certiorari to consider whether defense counsel assigned to prosecute an appeal from a criminal conviction has a constitutional duty to raise every nonfrivolous issue requested by the defendant.

I

[Respondent David Barnes was convicted by a New York state jury of robbery and assault. Lawyer Michael Melinger was appointed by the court to represent Barnes on appeal. Barnes sent Melinger "a letter listing several claims that he felt should be raised." Barnes enclosed a copy of a *pro se* brief he had written. Melinger wrote Barnes back, rejecting most of Barnes's suggestions. Melinger explained that the claims he was rejecting could not be made on appeal because they were not based on evidence in the record. Melinger listed seven potential claims he was considering and sought Barnes's input. Apparently Barnes never responded to Melinger's letter.]

Melinger's brief to the Appellate Division concentrated on three of the seven points he had raised in his letter to respondent. . . . In addition, Melinger submitted respondent's own *pro se* brief. Thereafter, respondent filed two more *pro se* briefs, raising three more of the seven issues Melinger had identified.

At oral argument, Melinger argued the three points presented in his own brief, but not the arguments raised in the *pro se* briefs. [The appeals court affirmed Barnes's conviction, and the high court of New York denied appeal. Barnes filed a writ of habeas corpus in federal court. All levels of the federal court denied the petition. Barnes then began another round of state appeals. He now alleged for the first time that Melinger had provided ineffective assistance. After the state courts denied these appeals, Barnes petitioned for habeas relief on the ground that Melinger had provided ineffective assistance. The trial court denied this claim, but the Second Circuit Court of Appeals reversed, holding that when "the appellant requests that [his attorney] raise additional colorable points [on appeal], counsel must argue the additional points to the full extent of his professional ability."]

II

. . . [No] decision of this Court suggests . . . that [an] indigent defendant has a constitutional right to compel appointed counsel to press nonfrivolous points requested by the client, if counsel, as a matter of professional judgment, decides not to present those points. . . .

This Court [has] recognized the superior ability of trained counsel in the "examination into the record, research of the law, and marshalling of arguments on [the appellant's] behalf," Yet by promulgating a *per se* rule that the client, not the professional advocate, must be allowed to decide what issues are to be pressed, the Court of Appeals seriously undermines the ability of counsel to present the client's case in accord with counsel's professional evaluation.

Experienced advocates since time beyond memory have emphasized the importance of winnowing out weaker arguments on appeal and focusing on one central issue if possible, or at most on a few key issues. Justice Jackson, after observing appellate advocates for many years, stated:

> "One of the first tests of a discriminating advocate is to select the question, or questions, that he will present orally. Legal contentions, like the currency, depreciate through over-issue. The mind of an appellate judge is habitually receptive to the suggestion that a lower court committed an error. But receptiveness declines as the number of assigned errors increases. Multiplicity hints at lack of confidence in any one.... [E]xperience on the bench convinces me that multiplying assignments of error will dilute and weaken a good case and will not save a bad one." Jackson, *Advocacy Before the Supreme Court,* 25 Temple L.Q. 115, 119 (1951).

Justice Jackson's observation echoes the advice of countless advocates before him and since....

There can hardly be any question about the importance of having the appellate advocate examine the record with a view to selecting the most promising issues for review. This has assumed a greater importance in an era when oral argument is strictly limited in most courts—often to as little as 15 minutes—and when page limits on briefs are widely imposed. Even in a court that imposes no time or page limits, however, the new *per se* rule laid down by the Court of Appeals is contrary to all experience and logic. A brief that raises every colorable issue runs the risk of burying good arguments—those that, in the words of the great advocate John W. Davis, "go for the jugular," Davis, *The Argument of an Appeal,* 26 A.B.A.J. 895, 897 (1940)—in a verbal mound made up of strong and weak contentions.

... [T]he role of the advocate "requires that he support his client's appeal to the best of his ability." Here the appointed counsel did just that. For judges to second-guess reasonable professional judgments and impose on appointed counsel a duty to raise every "colorable" claim suggested by a client would disserve the very goal of vigorous and effective advocacy ...

The judgment of the Court of Appeals is accordingly *Reversed.*

Justice BRENNAN, with whom Justice MARSHALL joins, dissenting.

... I find myself in fundamental disagreement with the Court over what a right to "the assistance of counsel" means. The import of words like "assistance" and "counsel" seems inconsistent with a regime under which counsel appointed by the State to represent a criminal defendant can refuse to raise issues with arguable merit on appeal when his client, after hearing his assessment of the case and his advice, has directed him to raise them. . . .

. . . The Constitution does not on its face define the phrase "assistance of counsel," but surely those words are not empty of content. No one would doubt that counsel must be qualified to practice law in the courts of the State in question, or that the representation afforded must meet minimum standards of effectiveness. To satisfy the Constitution, counsel must function as an advocate for the defendant, as opposed to a friend of the court. Admittedly, the question in this case requires us to look beyond those clear guarantees. What is at issue here is the relationship between lawyer and client—who has ultimate authority to decide which nonfrivolous issues should be presented on appeal? I believe the right to "the assistance of counsel" carries with it a right, personal to the defendant, to make that decision, against the advice of counsel if he chooses.

If all the Sixth Amendment protected was the State's interest in substantial justice, it would not include such a right. However, in *Faretta v. California,* 422 U.S. 806, 95 S.Ct. 2525, 45 L.Ed.2d 562 (1975), we decisively rejected that view of the Constitution. . . . Holding that the Sixth Amendment requires that defendants be allowed to represent themselves, we observed:

> It is undeniable that in most criminal prosecutions defendants could better defend with counsel's guidance than by their own unskilled efforts. But where the defendant will not voluntarily accept representation by counsel, the potential advantage of a lawyer's training can be realized, if at all, only imperfectly. To force a lawyer on a defendant can only lead him to believe that the law contrives against him. . . . Personal liberties are not rooted in the law of averages. The right to defend is personal. The defendant, and not his lawyer or the State, will bear the personal consequences of a conviction. It is the defendant, therefore, who must be free personally to decide whether in his particular case counsel is to his advantage. And although he may conduct his own defense ultimately to his own detriment, his choice must be honored out of 'that respect for the individual which is the lifeblood of the law.'

Faretta establishes that the right to counsel is more than a right to have one's case presented competently and effectively. It is predicated on the view that the function of counsel under the Sixth Amendment is to protect the dignity and autonomy of a person on trial by *assisting* him in making choices that are his to make, not to make choices for him, although counsel may be better able to decide which tactics will be most effective for the defendant. *Anders v. California* also reflects that view. Even when appointed counsel believes an appeal has no merit, he must furnish his client a brief covering all arguable grounds for appeal so that the client may "raise any points that he chooses." 386 U.S., at 744, 87 S.Ct., at 1400.

The right to counsel . . . is not an all-or-nothing right, under which a defendant must choose between forgoing the assistance of counsel altogether or relinquishing control over every aspect of his case beyond its most basic structure (*i.e.,* how to plead, whether to present a defense, whether to appeal). A defendant's interest in his case clearly extends to other matters. Absent exceptional circumstances, he is bound by the tactics used by his counsel at trial and on appeal. He may want to press the argument that he is innocent, even if other stratagems are more likely to result in the dismissal of charges or in a reduction of punishment. He may want to insist on certain arguments for political reasons. He may want to protect third parties. This is just as true on appeal as at trial, and the proper role of counsel is to *assist* him in these efforts, insofar as that is possible consistent with the lawyer's conscience, the law, and his duties to the court. . . .

. . . [T]he Court argues that good appellate advocacy demands selectivity among arguments. That is certainly true—the Court's advice is good. It ought to be taken to heart by every lawyer called upon to argue an appeal in this or any other court, and by his client. It should take little or no persuasion to get a wise client to understand that, if staying out of prison is what he values most, he should encourage his lawyer to raise only his two or three best arguments on appeal, and he should defer to his lawyer's advice as to which are the best arguments. The Constitution, however, does not require clients to be wise, and other policies should be weighed in the balance as well.

It is no secret that indigent clients often mistrust the lawyers appointed to represent them. There are many reasons for this, some perhaps unavoidable even under perfect conditions—differences in education, disposition, and socio-economic class—and some that should (but may not always) be zealously avoided. A lawyer and his client do not always have the same interests. Even with paying clients, a lawyer may have a strong interest in having judges and prosecutors think well of him, and, if he is working for a flat fee—a common arrangement for criminal defense attorneys—or if his fees for court appointments are lower than he would receive for other work, he has an obvious financial incentive to conclude cases on his criminal docket swiftly. Good lawyers undoubtedly recognize these temptations and resist them, and they endeavor to convince their clients that they will. It would be naive, however, to suggest that they always succeed in either task. A constitutional rule that encourages lawyers to disregard their clients' wishes without compelling need can only exacerbate the clients' suspicion of their lawyers. As in *Faretta,* to force a lawyer's *decisions* on a defendant "can only lead him to believe that the law conspires against him." See 422 U.S., at 834, 95 S.Ct., at 2540. In the end, what the Court hopes to gain in effectiveness of appellate representation by the rule it imposes today may well be lost to decreased effectiveness in other areas of representation.

The Court's opinion also seems to overstate somewhat the lawyer's role in an appeal. While excellent presentation of issues, especially at the briefing stage, certainly serves the client's best interests, I do not share the Court's implicit pessimism about appellate judges' ability to recognize a meritorious argument, even if it is made less elegantly or in fewer pages than the lawyer would have liked, and even if less meritorious arguments accompany it. If the quality of justice in this country really depended on nice gradations in lawyers' rhetorical skills, we could no longer call it "justice." Especially at the appellate level, I believe that for the most part good claims will be vindicated and bad claims rejected, with truly skillful advocacy making a difference only in a handful of cases. In most of such cases—in most cases generally—clients ultimately will do the wise thing and take their lawyers' advice. I am not willing to risk deepening the mistrust between clients and lawyers in all cases to ensure optimal presentation for that fraction-of-a-handful in which presentation might really affect the result reached by the Court of Appeals.

. . . [T]oday's ruling denigrates the values of individual autonomy and dignity central to many constitutional rights, especially those Fifth and Sixth Amendment rights that come into play in the criminal process. Certainly a person's life changes when he is charged with a crime and brought to trial. He must, if he harbors any hope of success, defend himself on terms—often technical and hard to understand—that are the State's, not his own. As a practical matter, the assistance of counsel is necessary to that defense. Yet, until his conviction becomes final and he has had an opportunity to appeal, any restrictions on individual autonomy and dignity should be limited to the minimum necessary to vindicate the State's interest in a speedy, effective prosecution. The role of the defense lawyer should be above all to function as the instrument and defender of the client's autonomy and dignity in all phases of the criminal process. . . .

The Court subtly but unmistakably adopts a different conception of the defense lawyer's role—he need do nothing beyond what the State, not his client, considers most important. In many ways, having a lawyer becomes one of the many indignities visited upon someone who has the ill fortune to run afoul of the criminal justice system.

I cannot accept the notion that lawyers are one of the punishments a person receives merely for being accused of a crime. Clients, if they wish, are capable of making informed judgments about which issues to appeal, and when they exercise that prerogative their choices should be respected unless they would require lawyers to violate their consciences, the law, or their duties to the court. On the other hand, I would not presume lightly that, in a particular case, a defendant has disregarded his lawyer's obviously sound advice. Cf. *Faretta v. California,* 422 U.S., at 835–836, 95 S.Ct., at 2541 (standards for waiver of right to counsel). The Court of Appeals, in reversing the District Court, did not address the factual question whether respondent, having been advised by his lawyer that it would not be wise to appeal on all the issues respondent had suggested, actually insisted in a timely fashion that his lawyer brief the nonfrivolous issues identified by the Court of Appeals. Cf. *ante,* at 3312, n. 4. If he did not, or if he was content with filing his *pro se* brief, then there would be no deprivation of the right to the assistance of counsel. I would remand for a hearing on this question.

Notes

1. Model Rule 1.2(a) provides that in a criminal case, a number of decisions belong to the client: the plea to be entered, whether to waive jury trial, and whether the client will testify. The ABA's specialized ethics code for criminal defense lawyers is to the same effect, adding explicitly that the decision to appeal is the client's as well. ABA Defense Function Standard 4–5.2(a). That standard instructs that "strategic and tactical decisions should be made by defense counsel after consultation with the client where feasible and appropriate." Standard 4–5.2(b). Examples of such strategic decisions include what witnesses to call, whether and how to conduct a cross-examination, what jurors to accept in jury selection, what motions to bring, and what evidence to introduce. *Id.* Further, defense counsel is authorized to "engage in plea discussions with the prosecutor," but may not recommend acceptance of a plea "unless appropriate investigation and study of the case has been completed." Standard 4–6.1.

2. *"No merit" appeals in criminal cases.* A lawyer should normally not file a frivolous appeal in any kind of case, and should withdraw rather than doing that, as we will see in Chapter 7. What if an appeal simply looks like it has very little chance of success? A lawyer in a civil case would probably not to pursue it at all. Is a criminal defense lawyer under a different duty? In *Anders v. California,* 386 U.S. 738, 87 S.Ct. 1396, 18 L.Ed.2d 493 (1967), the Court held that an appointed counsel who sought permission to withdraw from representing a criminal defendant on appeal must discuss in an appellate brief "anything in the record that might arguably support the appeal." The Court cut back on *Anders* in *McCoy v. Court of Appeals of Wisconsin,* 486 U.S. 429, 108 S.Ct. 1895,

100 L.Ed.2d 440 (1988), which approved of the constitutionality of a Wisconsin rule that required counsel to include in any *Anders* brief a discussion of "why the issue lacks merit." In *Smith v. Robbins*, 528 U.S. 259, 120 S.Ct. 746, 145 L.Ed.2d 756 (2000), the Court largely abandoned this *Anders* brief requirement. In a 5–4 decision, the *Smith* Court held that the *Anders* procedure was "not obligatory" on the states, and was just "one method" to protect the right to counsel. The majority found constitutionally acceptable California's procedure for handling "no merit" criminal appeals, as laid out in *People v. Wende*, 25 Cal.3d 436, 600 P.2d 1071, 158 Cal.Rptr. 839 (1979), in which counsel files a brief summarizing the factual and procedural history of the case, with citations to the record, but makes no arguments at all.

States are still free to require an *Anders* brief, and several do. See, e.g., *People v. Stokes*, 95 N.Y.2d 633, 744 N.E.2d 1153, 722 N.Y.S.2d 217 (2001).

3. *Duty to consult about an appeal.* Is it ineffective assistance of counsel for a lawyer to fail to consult a convicted client about an appeal? Not necessarily, said the Court in *Roe v. Flores–Ortega*, 528 U.S. 470, 120 S.Ct. 1029, 145 L.Ed.2d 985 (2000). In the case, Lucio Flores–Ortega had pleaded guilty to murder and was sentenced to 15 years to life. After sentencing, Flores–Ortega claimed that he spoke to his trial counsel about filing an appeal. His lawyer did not remember promising to file an appeal, but did have a note in his file that said "bring appeal papers." Flores–Ortega brought a claim of ineffective assistance of counsel when no timely appeal was filed. A federal magistrate found that it was clear that the client had "little or no understanding" of the appeals process, but concluded that he had failed to prove by a preponderance of the evidence that his lawyer had actually promised to file an appeal. The Ninth Circuit reversed, holding that a failure of trial counsel to file a notice of appeal in the absence of the client's explicit instructions not to constituted deficient representation per se. The Supreme Court, 6–3, vacated and remanded. Applying *Strickland's* highly deferential standard to counsel's performance, the Court said that there is no per se rule that lawyers must always consult with their clients about filing an appeal. Justice O'Connor noted that in most cases, trial counsel will have a duty to consult about appeals. Here, however, the client did not prove that he wanted to file an appeal and it was reasonable for the lawyer to conclude that he would not want to.

4. *Client's right to waive appeal and choose death.* Is a convicted criminal allowed to waive appeals and demand that a death sentence be carried out forthwith? In *Gilmore v. Utah*, 429 U.S. 1012, 97 S.Ct. 436, 50 L.Ed.2d 632 (1976), convicted murderer Gary Gilmore (the subject of Norman Mailer's bestselling book *The Executioner's Song*) instructed his lawyers not to file any appeal and not to seek a stay of his execution. His mother, claiming to act as Gilmore's "next friend," filed an application for a stay of execution, and the Supreme Court granted a temporary stay the next day. Ten days later the court lifted the stay. The Court noted that "[t]his case may be unique in the annals of the Court," since

Gilmore's "only complaint against Utah or its judicial process ... has been with respect to the delay on the part of the State in carrying out the sentence." The Court concluded that Gilmore knowingly waived his right to appeal after being well advised by counsel that there was a chance that Utah's death penalty statute would be held to be unconstitutional. He had this right, the Court said, and no one else had standing to object to his execution. Justices White, Brennan and Marshall dissented, arguing that validating Gilmore's waiver deprived the state courts of Utah from resolving "the obvious serious doubts about the validity of the state statute." Under the circumstances, they said, Gilmore should not be allowed to agree to be executed under a statute that is arguably unconstitutional.

MARTINEZ v. COURT OF APPEAL OF CALIFORNIA

Supreme Court of the United States, 2000.
528 U.S. 152, 120 S.Ct. 684, 145 L.Ed.2d 597.

Justice STEVENS delivered the opinion of the Court.

The Sixth and Fourteenth Amendments of our Constitution guarantee that a person brought to trial in any state or federal court must be afforded the right to the assistance of counsel before he can be validly convicted and punished by imprisonment. In *Faretta v. California,* 422 U.S. 806, 95 S.Ct. 2525, 45 L.Ed.2d 562 (1975), we decided that the defendant also "has a constitutional right to proceed *without* counsel when he voluntarily and intelligently elects to do so." Although that statement arguably embraces the entire judicial proceeding, we also phrased the question as whether a State may "constitutionally hale a person into its criminal courts and there force a lawyer upon him, even when he insists that he wants to conduct his own defense." *Ibid.* Our conclusion in *Faretta* extended only to a defendant's "constitutional right to conduct his own defense." Accordingly, our specific holding was confined to the right to defend oneself at trial. We now address the different question whether the reasoning in support of that holding also applies when the defendant becomes an appellant and assumes the burden of persuading a reviewing court that the conviction should be reversed. We have concluded that it does not.

I

Martinez describes himself as a self-taught paralegal with 25 years' experience at 12 different law firms. While employed as an office assistant at a firm in Santa Ana, California, Martinez was accused of converting $6,000 of a client's money to his own use. He was charged in a two-count information with grand theft and the fraudulent appropriation of the property of another. He chose to represent himself at trial before a jury, because he claimed " 'there wasn't an attorney on earth who'd believe me once he saw my past [criminal record].' " The jury acquitted him on Count 1, grand theft, but convicted him on Count 2, embezzlement. The jury also found that he had three prior convictions; accordingly, under California's "three strikes" law, the court imposed a mandatory sentence of 25–years-to-life in prison. See Cal.Penal Code Ann. §§ 667(d) and (e)(2) (West 1999). Martinez filed a timely notice of appeal as well as a motion to represent himself and a waiver of counsel. The California Court of Appeal denied his motion, and the California Supreme Court denied his application for a writ of mandate. . . . We now affirm.

II

The *Faretta* majority based its conclusion on three interrelated arguments. First, it examined historical evidence identifying a right of self-representation that had been protected by federal and state law since the beginning of our Nation. Second, it interpreted the structure of the Sixth Amendment, in the light of its English and colonial background. Third, it concluded that even though it "is undeniable that in most criminal prosecutions defendants could better defend with counsel's guidance than by their own unskilled efforts," a knowing and intelligent waiver "must be honored out of 'that respect for the individual which is the lifeblood of the law.' Some of the Court's reasoning is applicable to appellate proceedings as well as to trials. There are, however, significant distinctions.

The historical evidence relied upon by *Faretta* as identifying a right of self-representation is not always useful because it pertained to times when lawyers were scarce, often mistrusted, and not readily available to the average person accused of crime.[3] For one who could not obtain a lawyer, self-representation was the only feasible alternative to asserting no defense at all. Thus, a government's recognition of an indigent defendant's right to represent himself was comparable to bestowing upon the homeless beggar a "right" to take shelter in the sewers of Paris. Not surprisingly, early precedent demonstrates that this "right" was not always used to the defendant's advantage as a shield, but

---

3. "The colonists brought with them an appreciation of the virtues of self-reliance and a traditional distrust of lawyers. When the Colonies were first settled, 'the lawyer was synonymous with the cringing Attorneys–General and Solicitors–General of the Crown and the arbitrary Justices of the King's Court, all bent on the conviction of those who opposed the King's prerogatives, and twisting the law to secure convictions.' This prejudice gained strength in the Colonies where 'distrust of lawyers became an institution.' Several Colonies prohibited pleading for hire in the 17th century. The prejudice persisted into the 18th century as 'the lower classes came to identify lawyers with the upper class.' The years of Revolution and Confederation saw an upsurge of antilawyer sentiment, a 'sudden revival, after the War of the Revolution, of the old dislike and distrust of lawyers as a class.' " *Faretta,* 422 U.S., at 826–827, 95 S.Ct. 2525 (footnotes omitted)

rather was often employed by the prosecution as a sword. The principal case cited in *Faretta* is illustrative. In *Adams v. United States ex rel. McCann,* 317 U.S. 269, 63 S.Ct. 236, 87 L.Ed. 268 (1942), the Court relied on the existence of the right of self-representation as the basis for finding that an unrepresented defendant had waived his right to a trial by jury.

It has since been recognized, however, that an indigent defendant in a criminal trial has a constitutional right to the assistance of appointed counsel, see *Gideon v. Wainwright,* 372 U.S. 335, 83 S.Ct. 792, 9 L.Ed.2d 799 (1963). Thus, an individual's decision to represent himself is no longer compelled by the necessity of choosing self-representation over incompetent or nonexistent representation; rather, it more likely reflects a genuine desire to " 'conduct his own cause in his own words.' " *Faretta,* 422 U.S., at 823, 95 S.Ct. 2525. Therefore, while *Faretta* is correct in concluding that there is abundant support for the proposition that a right to self-representation has been recognized for centuries, the original reasons for protecting that right do not have the same force when the availability of competent counsel for every indigent defendant has displaced the need—although not always the desire—for self-representation.

The scant historical evidence pertaining to the issue of self-representation on appeal is even less helpful. The Court in *Faretta* relied upon the description of the right in § 35 of the Judiciary Act of 1789, 1 Stat. 92, which states that "the parties may plead and manage their own causes personally or by the assistance of such counsel. . . . " It is arguable that this language encompasses appeals as well as trials. Assuming it does apply to appellate proceedings, however, the statutory right is expressly limited by the phrase "as by the rules of the said courts." 1 Stat. 92. Appellate courts have maintained the discretion to allow litigants to "manage their own causes"—and some such litigants have done so effectively. That opportunity, however, has been consistently subject to each court's own rules.

We are not aware of any historical consensus establishing a right of self-representation on appeal. We might, nonetheless, paraphrase *Faretta* and assert: No State or Colony ever forced counsel upon a convicted appellant, and no spokesman ever suggested that such a practice would be tolerable or advisable. Such negative historical evidence was meaningful to the *Faretta* Court, because the fact that the "[dog] had not barked"[6] arguably demonstrated that early lawmakers intended to preserve the "long-respected right of self-representation" at trial. *Ibid.* Historical silence, however, has no probative force in the appellate context because there simply was no long-respected right of self-represen-

---

6. A. Conan Doyle, Silver Blaze, in The Complete Sherlock Holmes 383, 400 (1938).

tation on appeal. In fact, the right of appeal itself is of relatively recent origin.

Appeals as of right in federal courts were nonexistent for the first century of our Nation, and appellate review of any sort was "rarely allowed." *Abney v. United States,* 431 U.S. 651, 656, n. 3, 97 S.Ct. 2034, 52 L.Ed.2d 651 (1977). The States, also, did not generally recognize an appeal as of right until Washington became the first to constitutionalize the right explicitly in 1889. There was similarly no right to appeal in criminal cases at common law, and appellate review of any sort was "limited" and "rarely used." Thus, unlike the inquiry in *Faretta,* the historical evidence does not provide any support for an affirmative constitutional right to appellate self-representation.

The *Faretta* majority's reliance on the structure of the Sixth Amendment is also not relevant. The Sixth Amendment identifies the basic rights that the accused shall enjoy in "all criminal prosecutions." They are presented strictly as rights that are available in preparation for trial and at the trial itself. The Sixth Amendment does not include any right to appeal. As we have recognized, "[t]he right of appeal, as we presently know it in criminal cases, is purely a creature of statute." *Abney,* 431 U.S., at 656, 97 S.Ct. 2034. It necessarily follows that the Amendment itself does not provide any basis for finding a right to self-representation on appeal.

The *Faretta* majority's nontextual interpretation of the Sixth Amendment also included an examination of British criminal jurisprudence and a reference to the opprobrious trial practices before the Star Chamber. These inquiries into historical English practices, however, again do not provide a basis for extending *Faretta* to the appellate process, because there was no appeal from a criminal conviction in England until 1907. Indeed, none of our many cases safeguarding the rights of an indigent appellant has placed any reliance on either the Sixth Amendment or on *Faretta.*

Finally, the *Faretta* majority found that the right to self-representation at trial was grounded in part in a respect for individual autonomy. This consideration is, of course, also applicable to an appellant seeking to manage his own case. As we explained in *Faretta,* at the trial level "[t]o force a lawyer on a defendant can only lead him to believe that the law contrives against him." *Ibid.* On appellate review, there is surely a similar risk that the appellant will be skeptical of whether a lawyer, who is employed by the same government that is prosecuting him, will serve his cause with undivided loyalty. Equally true on appeal is the related observation that it is the appellant personally who will bear the consequences of the appeal.

In light of our conclusion that the Sixth Amendment does not apply to appellate proceedings, any individual right to self-representation on appeal based on autonomy principles must be grounded in the Due Process Clause. Under the practices that prevail in the Nation today, however, we are entirely unpersuaded that the risk of either disloyalty or suspicion of disloyalty is a sufficient concern to conclude that a constitutional right of self-representation is a necessary component of a fair appellate proceeding. We have no doubt that instances of disloyal representation are rare. In both trials and appeals there are, without question, cases in which counsel's performance is ineffective. Even in those cases, however, it is reasonable to assume that counsel's performance is more effective than what the unskilled appellant could have provided for himself.

No one, including Martinez and the *Faretta* majority, attempts to argue that as a rule *pro se* representation is wise, desirable, or efficient. Although we found in *Faretta* that the right to defend oneself at trial is "fundamental" in nature, it is clear that it is representation by counsel that is the standard, not the exception. Our experience has taught us that "a pro se defense is usually a bad defense, particularly when compared to a defense provided by an experienced criminal defense attorney."

As the *Faretta* opinion recognized, the right to self-representation is not absolute. The defendant must " 'voluntarily and intelligently' " elect to conduct his own defense, and most courts require him to do so in a timely manner. He must first be "made aware of the dangers and disadvantages of self-representation." A trial judge may also terminate self-representation or appoint "standby counsel"—even over the defendant's objection—if necessary. We have further held that standby counsel may participate in the trial proceedings, even without the express consent of the defendant, as long as that participation does not "seriously undermin[e]" the "appearance before the jury" that the defendant is representing himself. *McKaskle v. Wiggins,* 465 U.S. 168, 187, 104 S.Ct. 944, 79 L.Ed.2d 122 (1984). Additionally, the trial judge is under no duty to provide personal instruction on courtroom procedure or to perform any legal "chores" for the defendant that counsel would normally carry out. Even at the trial level, therefore, the government's interest in ensuring the integrity and efficiency of the trial at times outweighs the defendant's interest in acting as his own lawyer.

In the appellate context, the balance between the two competing interests surely tips in favor of the State. The status of the accused defendant, who retains a presumption of innocence throughout the trial process, changes dramatically when a jury returns a guilty verdict. We have recognized this shifting focus and noted: ... "it is ordinarily the defendant, rather than the State, who initiates the appellate process, seeking not to fend off the efforts of the State's prosecutor but rather to overturn a finding of guilt made by a judge or a jury below." In the words of the *Faretta* majority, appellate proceedings are simply not a case of "hal[ing] a person into its criminal courts."

The requirement of representation by trained counsel implies no disrespect for the individual inasmuch as it tends to benefit the appellant as well as the court. Courts, of course, may still exercise their discretion to allow a lay person to proceed *pro se*. We already leave to the appellate courts' discretion, keeping "the best interests of both the prisoner and the government in mind," the decision whether to allow a *pro se* appellant to participate in, or even to be present at, oral argument. Considering the change in position from defendant to appellant, the autonomy interests that survive a felony conviction are less compelling than those motivating the decision in *Faretta*. Yet the overriding state interest in the fair and efficient administration of justice remains as strong as at the trial level. Thus, the States are clearly within their discretion to conclude that the government's interests outweigh an invasion of the appellant's interest in self-representation.

III

For the foregoing reasons, we conclude that neither the holding nor the reasoning in *Faretta* requires California to recognize a constitutional right to self-representation on direct appeal from a criminal conviction. Our holding is, of course, narrow. It does not preclude the States from recognizing such a right under their own constitutions. Its impact on the law will be minimal, because a lay appellant's rights to participate in appellate proceedings have long been limited by the well-established conclusions that he has no right to be present during appellate proceedings, or to present oral argument. Meanwhile the rules governing appeals in California, and presumably those in other States as well, seem to protect the ability of indigent litigants to make *pro se* filings. In requiring Martinez, under these circumstances, to accept against his will a state-appointed attorney, the California courts have not deprived him of a constitutional right. Accordingly, the judgment of the California Supreme Court is affirmed.

Notes

1. Why isn't the Sixth Amendment particularly helpful to the analysis of whether a criminal defendant has the right of self-representation on appeal? Isn't there a constitutional right to appeal a criminal case?

2. The court holds here only that the U.S. Constitution does not require a state to allow a criminal defendant to represent himself on appeal. So the issue as to whether a criminal defendant should have the right to represent himself on appeal could certainly arise at the state level. Should such self-representation be allowed? Why or why not?

3. Do you agree with the Court's balancing between the appellant's interest in autonomy and the state's interest in the "integrity and efficiency" of the appeals process? How is it that having a lawyer on appeal contributes to the integrity and efficiency of the process?

4. Does *Martinez* harmonize well with *Jones v. Barnes*? How do the two cases compare on the topic of court efficiency versus client autonomy?

5. Justices Brennan and Marshall were no longer on the Court at the time *Martinez* was decided. If they had been, do you think they would have dissented, based on the dissent in *Jones*?

B. The Duty to Counsel Effectively

1. The Consequences of Ineffective Counseling

As we have seen in this Chapter, the ethics rules contemplate a shared, participatory relationship between client and lawyer. The lawyer has an affirmative duty to abide by a client's decisions about the goals of the representation and to consult with the client about the means used to achieve those goals. What if it is not possible for a client to know what his goals are, because he does not know his legal rights? Does the lawyer have some affirmative duty to help the client set his goals?

NICHOLS v. KELLER

California Court of Appeal, Fifth District, 1993.
15 Cal.App.4th 1672, 19 Cal.Rptr.2d 601.

MARTIN, Acting Presiding Justice.

[Plaintiff Warren Nichols appeals from summary judgments in a legal malpractice action. Nichols was working for a subcontractor on a job site as a boilermaker when he was struck on the head by a piece of metal and had to have stitches in his scalp. About two months later, he and his wife met with defendant E. Paul Fulfer, a lawyer with the firm of Fulfer & Fulfer, to discuss the accident and his legal remedies. Fulfer had plaintiff sign a workers compensation application and filed it with the proper state department. Fulfer then associated defendant Edward Keller, another lawyer, to prosecute the workers' compensation claim. Keller and plaintiff met shortly thereafter. Keller told plaintiff he would be representing him in the workers' compensation action against plaintiff's employer.]

[Several months later, plaintiff and his wife were on a trip to the San Francisco Bay area. They spoke about plaintiff's injury to two union members at the Boilermakers Union Hall. The union members suggested the plaintiff meet with another lawyer, and scheduled an appointment with James Butler in San Francisco. When plaintiff and his wife met with Butler, he told them that a third-party claim should have been brought in connection with the accident.[1] Butler suggested that plaintiff may have a legal claim against Keller and Fulfer for failing to advise him of that claim. On March 21, 1990, plaintiff sued Keller, Fulfer and their law firms for legal malpractice.]

[Defendants' motions for summary judgment were granted in part on the ground that defendants owed no duty to counsel plaintiff about any claims beyond the workers' compensation action against plaintiff's employer, since that was the claim they were retained to bring. Plaintiff filed this appeal.]

The question of the existence of a legal duty of care in a given factual situation presents a question of law which is to be determined by the courts alone.... A significant area of exposure for the workers' compensation attorney concerns that attorney's responsibility for counseling regarding a potential third-party action. One of an attorney's basic functions is to advise. Liability can exist because the attorney failed to provide advice. Not only should an attorney furnish advice when requested, but he or she should also volunteer opinions when necessary to further the client's objectives. The attorney need not advise and caution of every possible alternative, but only of those that may result in adverse consequences if not considered. Generally speaking, a workers' compensation attorney should be able to limit the retention to the compensation claim if the client is cautioned (1) there may be other remedies which the attorney will not investigate and (2) other counsel should be consulted on such matters. However, even when a retention is expressly limited, the attorney may still have a duty to alert the client to legal problems which are reasonably apparent, even though they fall outside the scope of the retention. The rationale is that, as between the lay client and the attorney, the latter is more qualified to recognize and analyze the client's legal needs. The attorney need not represent the client on such matters. Nevertheless, the attorney should inform the client of the limitations of the attorney's representation and of the possible need for other counsel....

In their motions for summary judgment, defendant attorneys maintained they agreed to undertake only a limited employment. Attorney Fulfer asserted he agreed to represent plaintiff in the workers' compensation matter only and, even then, for two specific purposes: (1) to file a workers' compensation application on plaintiff's behalf and (2) to refer plaintiff to defendant Keller, so the latter could actually prosecute the workers' compensation claim on plaintiff's behalf. Attorney Keller argued the attorney-client relationship between the plaintiff and himself was solely for the purpose of representation in the workers' compensation claim.

---

1. (Workers' compensation is the exclusive remedy against an injured worker's employer; a third-party claim is a tort action against a party other than the employer. In this case, the third-party claim would have been a negligence suit against the general contractor on the job site.—*Ed.*)

Keller claimed he owed only a duty to prosecute that claim and not to prosecute any possible third-party claim or to advise plaintiff as to the prosecution of such a claim. Defendants reiterate these positions on appeal....

Thus, defendants maintained they undertook limited duties to plaintiff and, as a matter of law, they owed him no duty to advise about possible third-party claims, while plaintiff's expert, Yale Jones, [a certified specialist attorney in workers' compensation law] declared their duties were far more expansive and required both counsel to advise plaintiff about various workers' compensation and civil remedies, the applicable statute of limitations for a third-party action, the propriety of obtaining a "second opinion" as to available rights and remedies, and the precise scope of defendants' representation....

A determination that defendants owe plaintiff no duty of care would negate an essential element of plaintiff's cause of action for negligence.... Whether a duty of care exists is a question of law for the court and is reviewable de novo....

Foreseeability of harm, though not determinative, has become the chief factor in duty analysis.... It seems to us the foreseeability factor compels a finding of duty in cases of this type. A trained attorney is more qualified to recognize and analyze legal needs than a lay client, and, at least in part, this is the reason a party seeks out and retains an attorney to represent and advise him or her in legal matters. As Justice Brandeis observed a century ago:

> " 'The duty of a lawyer today is not that of a solver of legal conundrums: he is indeed a counsellor at law. Knowledge of the law is of course essential to his efficiency, but the law bears to his profession a relation very similar to that which medicine does to that of the physicians. The apothecary can prepare the dose, the more intelligent one even knows the specific for most common diseases. It requires but a mediocre physician to administer the proper drug for the patient who correctly and fully describes his ailment. The great physicians are those who in addition to that knowledge of therapeutics which is open to all, know not merely the human body but the human mind and emotions, so as to make themselves the proper diagnosis—to know the truth which their patients fail to disclose.... ' " (Mason, Brandeis: A Free Man's Life (1946) p. 80.)

What was true in 1893 is certainly true today in this increasingly complex and technologically advanced society in which we live. In the context of personal injury consultations between lawyer and layperson, it is reasonably foreseeable the latter will offer a selective or incomplete recitation of the facts underlying the claim; request legal assistance by employing such everyday terms as "workers' compensation," "disability," and "unemployment"; and rely upon the consulting lawyer to describe the array of legal remedies available, alert the layperson to any apparent legal problems, and, if appropriate, indicate limitations on the retention of counsel and the need for other counsel. In the event the lawyer fails to so advise the layperson, it is also reasonably foreseeable the layperson will fail to ask relevant questions regarding the existence of other remedies and be deprived of relief through a combination of ignorance and lack or failure of understanding. And, if counsel elects to limit or prescribe his representation of the client, i.e., to a workers' compensation claim only without reference or regard to any third party or collateral claims which the client might pursue if adequately advised, then counsel must make such limitations in representation very clear to his client. Thus, a lawyer who signs an application for adjudication of a workers' compensation claim and a lawyer who accepts a referral to prosecute the claim owe the claimant a duty of care to advise on available remedies, including third-party actions. . . .

The lower court erroneously granted summary judgment on the duty element of legal negligence and reversal is required. . . .

Notes

1. Counseling a client is seldom an end in itself. Rather, counseling is a means to some end, such as resolving a dispute satisfactorily or completing a transaction. Because of this, effective counseling involves, among other things, an ongoing exploration by the lawyer of what the client wants to accomplish with the lawyer's services. What errors do you think were made by the first two lawyers consulted by the plaintiff in *Nichols*? Do you think they did a good job of gathering facts?

2. As we saw earlier in this Chapter, lawyers may be retained only for a limited purpose, if such limitation is reasonable and the client gives informed consent. MR 1.2(c). What was wrong with the lawyers' argument in *Nichols* that they were retained only to prosecute a workers' comp claim? Competently representing a client, even if a limited-representation agreement has been entered into, may involve advising the client beyond the terms of the agreement. See *Janik v. Rudy, Exelrod & Zieff*, 119 Cal.App.4th 930, 14 Cal.Rptr.3d 751 (2004) ("An attorney who undertakes one matter on behalf of a client owes that client the duty to at least consider and advise the client if there are apparent related matters that the client is overlooking and that should be pursued to avoid prejudicing the client's interests.")

3. Competent counseling is unambiguously an affirmative duty of lawyers who represent clients. Restatement § 20(1) echoes Model Rule 1.4 on this point, saying that "A lawyer must keep a client reasonably informed about the matter and must consult with a client to a reasonable extent concerning decisions to be made" in the course of representation. Model Rule 1.3 requires a that a lawyer act "with reasonable

diligence and promptness in representing a client." Violation of these related rules, especially repeated violations, has led to serious disciplinary sanction. See, e.g., *In re Stanton*, 860 A.2d 369 (D.C. 2004) (indefinite suspension that has lasted over 20 years); *In re Gordon*, 258 Kan. 784, 908 P.2d 169 (1995) (indefinite suspension).

2. Counseling Skills and Purposes

As with interviewing, a number of skills are fundamental to effective counseling. There is, of course, much overlap. A good counselor, like a good interviewer, is an effective communicator who can listen with sensitivity and explain things well. But counseling is far more than fact-gathering, and far more than merely a meeting to cement the client-lawyer relationship. Counseling, in many ways, is at the heart of lawyering and involves most of the skills learned in three years of law school. It is what the client came to the lawyer for in the first place.

Counseling is the process in which the lawyer gives the client advice about legal options in the representation and helps the client reach a decision about what action to take. Doing this well requires that the lawyer be fully aware of the ethically-proper division of labor: the client determines the goals of the representation and must be consulted about the means used to achieve those goals. MR 1.2(a). Remember that the power relationship between client and lawyer is not static, and is itself something that will develop as the client-lawyer relationship moves along. The most effective lawyers see the client as a teammate, not as merely the generator of a "fact pattern."

The client expects the lawyer to give advice, and the lawyer should do so. The ethics rules require the lawyer to "exercise independent professional judgment and render candid advice." MR 2.1. Sometimes a client's options are limited or unpleasant. The lawyer "should not be deterred from giving candid advice by the prospect that the advice will be unpalatable to the client." MR 2.1, comment [1]. Of course, the lawyer can "put advice in as acceptable a form as honesty permits." *Id*. But a lawyer should never tell a client that everything will be all right when it probably will not be.

• *How does a lawyer prepare to counsel a client on options?* At least three core pieces of information are indispensable at the outset of this process: (1) the facts relevant to the matter at hand; (2) the law; and (3) the client's perspective, including the client's goals and concerns. Armed with this knowledge, a lawyer will be able to identify those options that appear to further or accomplish the client's goals; evaluate those options for suitability and feasibility; and even generate new and better options that arise as part of the creative analytical process.

The facts. The lawyer will have no way of knowing what options are appropriate without a clear understanding of the facts. The facts gained through interviewing the client, and perhaps others, and examining documents and other evidence, become crucial in the counseling phase of the representation. Before the lawyer presents options, he or she must make certain that the factual basis for those options exists. Verification of facts gathered earlier from the client, or from other sources, is an important step in effective counseling.

The law. A client generally expects a lawyer to give legal advice, and such an expectation is entirely reasonable. Quite obviously, an understanding of the applicable law is a precondition to competent counseling. See MR 1.1 ("Competent representation requires the legal knowledge, skill, thoroughness and preparation reasonably necessary for the representation."). That understanding will usually require legal research. When a lawyer presents the client with a particular option when the law says it is not available at all, the lawyer is not counseling competently. When a lawyer fails to present a particular option because he or she believes that the law forecloses it when it does not, the lawyer is not counseling competently. When a lawyer fails to present an option because the lawyer did incomplete research, but would have found the option with more complete research, the lawyer is not counseling competently.

The client's perspective. Remember that any client's goals may change in the course of representation. One reason, of course, is that people change their minds. Another is that the information known to the client may change. As a representation progresses, both the lawyer and the client learn facts that influence their views of possible satisfactory outcomes for the representation. It may be, for example, that the lawyer learns that the client's adversary in a dispute is perfectly willing to take some action that the client believed would not be taken. The client's perspective on that option may well do a complete reversal based on the lawyer's communication of that new information. What might have seemed the best course of conduct on Day One may not even be feasible, let alone preferable, on Day Ninety. The client may also have concerns about such things as the cost of getting or implementing particular solutions. As information becomes better known about those concerns, the client's assessment of acceptable options may well change. The lawyer who knows the facts and the law (and thus would probably score a high grade on a law school essay exam) but ignores the client's perspective will be an incompetent counselor.

     • *How does a lawyer discuss options with the client?* A lawyer who adopts a traditional model of the relationship might actually skip this step entirely, and instead tell the client which option is best for the client, and why. But such an approach would not comport with the participatory model that we see embodied in the ethics rules, and is not as efficacious as allowing the client to choose the best option.

Presenting the client with options. The lawyer must explain options in plain language rather than legalese, but must not oversimplify to an extent that would be misleading. The lawyer who knows the client well will better able to tailor the presentation to the client's particular level of understanding. For example, if the client is a lawyer, the lawyer can obviously be much more detailed in describing the theories underlying various options than if the client is uneducated and inexperienced in legal matters. Distinct options should be presented separately, in an organized way that facilitates understanding.

Helping the client evaluate the options. Remember that in the participatory client-lawyer relationship, the client is more likely to be an expert on what the client wants and the lawyer is more likely to be an expert on the client's legal rights. The client will therefore be unable to evaluate options adequately without counseling from the lawyer about the effect of each option on the client's legal rights. In other words, the lawyer must explain the legal framework in which the options sit. The lawyer might also be able to predict the likelihood of achieving various options, based on prior experience or legal research. The client will undoubtedly have questions about the law, and the lawyer should answer them completely and clearly, without overwhelming with detail or lapsing into jargon.

The counselor-lawyer must be more than a narrow legal technician. The client will likely need, and expect, the lawyer to help evaluate each option in terms of how well it fulfills the client's goals for the representation. The lawyer's ultimate job, remember, is to help the client achieve legitimate goals, *see* MR 1.2(a) & 1.4(b), not merely to explain the legal ramifications of various options and leave it at that. Of course, the lawyer must respect the fact that the client may in the course of a counseling session revise the goals for the representation, or state for the first time that one set of goals is more important than another. The good counselor is flexible and prepared for the unexpected.

Advising on non-legal concerns. Sometimes, non-legal concerns are the most important to a client. The client may, for example, not want to involve a particular person in a lawsuit or to harm some particular third-party's interests in a transaction. These concerns, when taken seriously, sometimes foreclose what otherwise appears to be the best option. A lawyer is not a psychiatrist or a member of the clergy (usually, that is), and legal counseling is not therapy. (Indeed, some lawyers routinely refer clients to therapists if they appear to need it.) But as the Model Rules recognize, "[a]dvice couched in narrow legal terms may be of little value to a client, especially where practical considerations, such as cost or effects on other people, are predominant." MR 2.1, comment [2]. The Rules expressly authorize a lawyer to "refer not only to law but to other considerations such as moral, economic, social or political factors, that may be relevant to the client's situation." MR 2.1. The law itself is not a narrow, technical body of rules; moral and ethical issues "impinge upon most legal questions and may decisively influence how the law will be applied." MR 2.1, comment [2]. What if a client asks for strictly "legal" counseling? Should a lawyer simply accept such a request at face value? See MR 2.1, comment [3].

Litigation: advising on ADR. When presenting options to a client seeking resolution of a dispute, a competent counselor will incorporate advice on the various processes of dispute resolution that may be available, including any appropriate alternatives to court adjudication. See MR 2.1, comment [5]. While a mandatory rule requiring such advice is not contained in the Model Rules and has found little favor in the states thus far, most litigated matters are terminated by processes other than a final ruling by a court. Especially if a client is inexperienced in legal processes, the lawyer should inform the client of those dispute resolution processes (1) that are mandatory in the particular jurisdiction, and (2) that may be agreed to by the parties and may satisfy some of the client's goals for the representation. For a thumbnail description of major ADR processes, see Chapter 7, § 6.

● *How does a lawyer implement the client's decision on which options to pursue?* When a client reaches a decision as to some particular option to pursue, the lawyer should clarify the steps to be taken next by both the client and the lawyer. The lawyer may need to obtain the client's consent in order to take certain steps, such as communicating otherwise confidential client information to another party. See MR 1.6.

Developing the skills needed for effective lawyering continues throughout a lawyer's career, beginning in law school. Practicing lawyers learn not only by doing and observing others doing, but also through in-house training and continuing legal education courses. Students should take every opportunity to hone these skills through course work and extracurricular activities while in law school.

C. Assisting the Client in Wrongful Conduct

COMMITTEE ON LEGAL ETHICS OF THE WEST VIRGINIA STATE BAR v. HART

Supreme Court of Appeals of West Virginia, 1991.
186 W.Va. 75, 410 S.E.2d 714.

PER CURIAM:

In this attorney disciplinary proceeding, the Committee on Legal Ethics of the West Virginia State Bar ("the Committee") recommends that this Court annul the license to practice law of the respondent, Henry Clay Hart, Jr. Mr. Hart plead guilty in United States District Court for the Southern District of California to aiding and assisting in the preparation and presentation of a false and fraudulent federal income tax return in violation of 26 U.S.C. § 7206(2) (1988).[1] ...

I

An information dated October 12, 1990, was filed against Mr. Hart in the United States District Court of the Southern District of California charging that he willfully aided and assisted in, and procured, counseled and advised, the preparation and presentation of an individual income tax return to the Internal Revenue Service which was false and fraudulent as to a material matter. The information charged that the income tax return of Robert G. Brown represented that Mr. Brown was entitled under the provisions of the Internal Revenue Laws to claim a partnership operation loss of $13,509.00 and a $25,732.00 tax credit resulting from investing in Whitewater River Electric Power Limited, a windmill partnership. The information further charged that Mr. Hart knew that Mr. Brown was not entitled to claim either the operating loss or the tax credit for 1984. On October 12, 1990, Mr. Hart signed a waiver of indictment in which he agreed that the proceedings in this case would be by information rather than by indictment.

On January 22, 1991, Mr. Hart pleaded guilty to aiding and assisting in the preparation and presentation of a false and fraudulent federal income tax return in violation of 26 U.S.C. § 7206(2) (1988). Mr. Hart was sentenced to a term of imprisonment for a period of eighteen months.

The Committee contends that Mr. Hart's license to practice law should be annulled because he was convicted of crimes involv-

---

1. 26 U.S.C § 7206(2) (1988) provides, in relevant part, that any person who

"[w]illfully aids or assists in, or procures, counsels, or advises the preparation or presentation under, ... , the internal revenue laws, of a return, ... , which is fraudulent or is false as to any material matter, ... shall be guilty of a felony and, upon conviction thereof, shall be fined not more than $100,000 ($500,000 in the case of a corporation), or imprisoned not more than three years, or both, together with the costs of prosecution.

ing moral turpitude and professional unfitness within the meaning of section 23 of article VI of the *By-Laws* of the West Virginia State Bar and crimes that reflect adversely on the lawyer's honesty, trustworthiness, and fitness as a lawyer in other respects within the meaning of 8.4(b) of the Rules of Professional Conduct. Mr. Hart maintains that he has a bona fide defense to the Committee's allegations and requests an evidentiary mitigation hearing.

II

The burden of proof is on the Committee to prove by full, preponderating and clear evidence the charges contained in the complaint filed on behalf of the Committee. However, we recognized in *Committee on Legal Ethics v. Folio,* 184 W.Va. 503, 401 S.E.2d 248 (1990), that proof of a final conviction satisfies the Committee's burden of proof.... The Committee in the case before us has satisfied its burden of proving Mr. Hart's conviction by providing this Court with a copy of the order of conviction.

Under section 23 of article VI of the State Bar *By-Laws,* an attorney's license shall be annulled upon proof that he has been convicted of any crime involving moral turpitude or professional unfitness.... However, as we pointed out in *Committee on Legal Ethics v. Boettner,* 183 W.Va. at 139, 394 S.E.2d at 738, under our new professional code, Rule 8.4 of the Rules of Professional Conduct, the focus has shifted from "illegal conduct involving moral turpitude" to "a criminal act that reflects adversely on the lawyer's honesty, trustworthiness or fitness in other respects." Rule 8.4 now concentrates on the lawyer's criminal act as it reflects on his or her fitness to practice law rather than on the concept of "moral turpitude." *Id.*

This Court recognized in earlier cases decided prior to the adoption of Rule 8.4 that the filing of a false and fraudulent income tax return in an attempt to defraud the government is a crime involving moral turpitude. Upon considering this same criminal act under Rule 8.4, we find that Mr. Hart's attempt to defraud the government by filing a false and fraudulent income tax return for his client was a flagrant violation of Rule 8.4 and clearly indicates that Mr. Hart is unfit to practice law.

Mr. Hart asks this Court to grant his request for an evidentiary hearing to allow him to introduce mitigating factors which may bear on the disciplinary punishment to be imposed. However, there is no absolute right to a mitigation hearing in every disciplinary proceeding. As we pointed out in syllabus point 3 of *Folio, supra:*

The cases in which a mitigation hearing will be appropriate are the exception rather than the rule. Whether a mitigation hearing is appropriate in a particular instance will depend upon a variety of factors, including but not limited to, the nature of the attorney's misconduct, surrounding facts and circumstances, previous ethical violations, the willfulness of the conduct, and the adequacy of the attorney's previous opportunity to present evidence sufficient for determination of appropriate sanctions.

In the case now before us, Mr. Hart plead guilty to the offense of aiding and assisting in the preparation and presentation of a false and fraudulent income tax return in violation of 26 *U.S.C.* 7206(2) (1988). Mr. Hart is currently serving his eighteen-month sentence. In his response to the Committee's petition to have his law license annulled, Mr. Hart did not identify any circumstances surrounding the case which would prompt this Court to grant him a mitigation hearing. We therefore deny Mr. Hart's request for an evidentiary mitigation hearing.

For the reasons stated above, we shall follow the recommendation of the Committee and order the annulment of Mr. Hart's license to practice law in the State of West Virginia. We shall also require Mr. Hart to reimburse the Committee for the costs it has incurred in connection with this proceeding.

License Annulled.

Notes

1. A lawyer is subject to the law, both civil and criminal, as is anyone else. But, as noted in Chapter 1 § 2.C, lawyers are often more exposed to liability because of their insider roles in client activity, if that activity is improper. Many cases in which lawyers are held liable involve bad clients—clients that an honest lawyer should probably have not gotten involved with at all.

2. Some reported cases read like Greek tragedies, the lawyer exhibiting a pure heart and all the best helping motives, but ultimately bending then breaking the rules in a misguided attempt to help the client. For example, in *In re McBride*, 642 A.2d 1270 (D.C. 1994), the lawyer was in his 70s, never before disciplined, with a 28–year record of good service in the Department of Justice as a tax crimes prosecutor. Upon his retirement, he became a sole practitioner, devoting most of this time to pro bono work. One of his pro bono clients, a Pakistani immigrant, pleaded with the lawyer to help her get a U.S. passport when she was faced with having to return to Pakistan to face an abusive husband. She persuaded him to obtain a passport using the identification of her neighbor, who was also one of the lawyer's pro bono clients. The lawyer went with his Pakistani client to the passport office, where she passed herself off as the other client (a U.S. citizen). Ultimately they were both arrested; the lawyer pleaded guilty of aiding and abetting his client's misdemeanor. Affirming his one-year suspension from practice, the court noted, "Respondent's conduct harmed no one and, although misguided, was intended to help a friend." See also *In re Young*, 49 Cal.3d 257, 776

P.2d 1021, 261 Cal.Rptr. 59 (1989) (lawyer was suspended for five years after being convicted of aiding a felony; lawyer helped his client, "an occasional employee, and friend" avoid arrest for robbery after trying to convince him to give himself up); *In re Siegel*, 118 A.D.2d 190, 504 N.Y.S.2d 117 (1986) (lawyer suspended after being convicted of willfully aiding and abetting his client in remaining a fugitive from justice for several years; the client was an old friend of almost 20 years about whom the lawyer had developed "great sympathy ... as he did for other such clients").

3.   Sometimes, a lawyer remains "willfully blind" to his bad client's shortcomings—and ultimately pays the price for it. In *United States v. Flores*, 454 F.3d 149 (3d Cir. 2006), the court affirmed a lawyer's 32–month sentence for conspiracy to commit money laundering, money laundering, and conspiracy to structure money transactions, in violation of federal statutes. The lawyer, a sole practitioner, was visited in his office by Altamirano, who said he was an Ecuadorian businessman eager to set up an import/export business in the U.S. Over the next several years, the lawyer formed several corporations for Altamirano, opening bank accounts for them, and obtaining taxpayer identifications for them using false Social Security numbers. The lawyer received a fee of $2,000 each week, in cash. The lawyer also became president of several of these corporations, and in that role was the only person authorized to sign checks and transfer money. Large amounts of money flowed through the corporations and into several bank accounts; none of the money had any connection to a legitimate import/export business. When a bank and an accountant became suspicious, the scheme fell apart and criminal charges were filed. Convicting the lawyer required the government to prove that he knew that the financial transactions represented the proceeds of some form of illegal activity. The lawyer argued that he was an innocent dupe. The court said: "In response to the substantial evidence that Altamirano was involved in some sort of illegal activity, Flores willfully blinded himself to the truth. He never requested any proof of the legitimacy of the transactions from Altamirano or even any further explanation addressing either the bank manager's or account-ant's concerns. That Flores did not ask the natural follow-up questions to determine the source of these funds could reasonably be considered by a jury to be evidence of willful blindness." This was enough to prove "knowledge" beyond a reasonable doubt.

4.   Lawyers are frequently the target of civil suits by third parties in connection with their legal work for clients. Claims of conspiracy, fraud, and civil RICO, for example, do not have the same duty limita-tions we saw with legal malpractice. See, e.g., *Banco Popular N.A. v. Gandi*, 184 N.J. 161, 876 A.2d 253 (2005) (civil conspiracy, for advising a client to transfer assets to avoid creditor claims); *Vega v. Jones, Day, Reavis & Pogue*, 121 Cal.App.4th 282, 17 Cal.Rptr.3d 26 (2004) (share-holder suit for fraudulent concealment of facts concerning pre-acquisi-tion financing of acquired corporation with "toxic" stock); *Morganroth & Morganroth v. Norris, McLaughlin & Marcus, P.C.*, 331 F.3d 406 (3d

Cir. 2003) (creditor suit alleging that law firm participated in client's fraudulent scheme to avoid execution on his property); *In re Enron Corp. Sec., Deriv. & ERISA Litig.*, 235 F.Supp.2d 549 (S.D. Tex. 2002) (shareholder suit for fraud and misrepresentation, for various legal work done by principal outside counsel on behalf of Enron); *Thomas v. Ross & Hardies*, 9 F.Supp.2d 547 (D. Md. 1998) (civil RICO, for diverting mortgage proceeds).

5. Discipline may be imposed even if the lawyer's assistance of the client is neither criminal nor civilly actionable. See, e.g., *Louisiana State Bar Ass'n v. Warner*, 576 So.2d 14 (La. 1991) (lawyer reprimanded for aiding an elaborate scheme to coerce a property owner to sell property by misrepresenting the identity of the buyers).

6. *The innocent client.* What if the client is completely innocent and it's the lawyer who is the miscreant? Can the client be vicariously liable for the lawyer's intentionally bad acts? See *Horwitz v. Holabird & Root*, 212 Ill.2d 1, 816 N.E.2d 272, 287 Ill.Dec. 510 (2004) (no; clients are not vicariously liable for lawyers' acts, and did not ratify them).

§ 4. SAFEGUARDING CLIENT FUNDS AND CLIENT PROPERTY

Lawyers owe a fiduciary duty to clients to safeguard any of their funds or property that have come into the lawyer's possession. A breach of that duty can give rise to civil liability. Additionally, all state ethics rules place stringent duties on lawyers to segregate client monies and property from the lawyer's, to keep accurate records, and to inform the client of any disbursements. Violating these rules is both stupid and costly.

Model Rule 1.15(a)—which codifies common law agency and trust rules—provides that funds belonging to the client or a third party "shall be kept in a separate account maintained in the state where the lawyer's office is situated, or elsewhere with the consent of the client or third person." See also Restatement § 44 (echoing the same requirements). This separate account is known as a trust account; some states call it a "lawyer's trust account," some a "client trust account." Generally speaking, a lawyer needs to have only one trust account for all clients' funds, but under some circumstances multiple accounts might be needed. See MR 1.15, comment [1]. Opening a trust account is not difficult. You simply go to a bank and open one. See, e.g., Cal. Rule 4–100 (specifying simply that the account be "labelled 'Trust Account,' 'Client's Funds Account' or words of similar import," in a California bank or, with the client's written consent, a bank in another state with a sufficient nexus to the client).

The purpose of this account is to keep client monies separate from lawyer monies. Thus lawyers are strictly prohibited from "commingling" their money with client money. (The lone exception is for funds needed to pay bank service charges, MR 1.15(b).)

What kinds of "client money" goes into the trust account? Any kind. For example, a lawyer might receive a check from an adversary in settlement of a client's case. That goes in the trust account. The lawyer might receive a check from an insurance company in payment of a client's medical expenses. That goes in the trust account, too. The lawyer might be given a check by the client to pay for fees and costs not yet earned or incurred. That also goes into the account until earned. For a fairly complete list, and a wealth of practical pointers, *see* Jay G Foonberg, ABA Guide to Lawyer Trust Accounts (1996).

Each state sets its own recordkeeping requirements for trust accounts. While a description of those various requirements will almost certainly fade from your memory quickly if recited here, remember that these recordkeeping requirements are usually intricate, and that as a lawyer, you must comply with them strictly or face serious sanction. See, e.g., *Inquiry Comm'n v. Lococo*, 18 S.W.3d 341 (Ky.2000) (inadequate recordkeeping and failure to maintain adequate accounting system warranted lawyer's suspension); *Office of Disciplinary Counsel v. France*, 93 Ohio St.3d 169, 753 N.E.2d 202 (2001) (mishandling jailed client's trust fund account and failing to keep adequate records warranted two-year suspension).

THE FLORIDA BAR v. BAILEY

Supreme Court of Florida, 2001.
803 So.2d 683.

PER CURIAM.

[In 1994, lawyer F. Lee Bailey represented Claude Duboc in a federal criminal case in which Duboc was accused of drug smuggling. The indictment also included forfeiture claims under Title 18 of the United States Code. Bailey worked out a deal with the prosecutors covering Duboc's plea, repatriation of assets, and payment of attorneys' fees.] Under the agreement, Duboc would plead guilty and forfeit all of his assets to the United States Government. All of Duboc's cash accounts from around the world would be transferred to an account identified by the U.S. Attorney's Office. To deal with the forfeiture of Duboc's real and personal property, 602,000 shares of Biochem Pharma ("Biochem") stock, valued at $5,891,352.00, would be transferred into Bailey's Swiss account. Bailey would use these funds to market, maintain and liquidate Duboc's French properties and all other assets.... The forfeiture of the real and personal properties held in foreign countries presented some nettlesome problems. Duboc owned two large estates in France and valuable car collections, boats, furnishings and art works. Most of these properties were physically located in France. The two estates required substantial infusions of cash for maintenance.

The idea proposed by [Bailey] was to segregate an asset, a particular asset, one that would appreciate in value over time, so that when it came time for Duboc to be sentenced following entry of a plea of guilty, the United States Government would not argue in opposition to a defense claim that part of the appreciation in value was not forfeitable to the United States. Ultimately, the object was to sequester a fund which would not be entirely subject to forfeiture.

The identified asset was 602,000 shares of Biochem Pharma Stock. This would serve as a fund from which [Bailey] could serve as trustee and guardian of Duboc's French properties. Duboc's primary interest was to maximize the amount of forfeitures that would be turned over to the United States. This stock would provide a sufficient fund from which to market, maintain and liquidate the French properties and all other assets. . . .

Money was transferred immediately into a covert account identified by the United States Attorney's Office. Duboc provided written instructions to the various financial institutions and the orders were then faxed. On April 26, 1994, the Biochem stock certificates were transferred to [Bailey's] Swiss account at his direction. . . .

On May 17, 1994, [the trial judge] held a pre-plea conference in his chambers. At the conference, the following arrangement as to attorneys' fees, including those for Bailey, was reached: "[T]he remainder value of the stock which was being segregated out would be returned to the court at the end of the day, and from that asset the Judge would be—a motion would be filed for a reasonable attorney's fee for Mr. Bailey." Later in the day on May 17, Duboc pled guilty to two counts in open court and professed his complete cooperation with the U.S. Attorney's Office.

[The Florida Bar filed a complaint against Bailey alleging seven counts of misconduct in violation of various Rules Regulating the Florida Bar.] Count I of the Bar's complaint charged Bailey with commingling. Bailey was entrusted with liquidating stock that belonged to Duboc, referred to as "the Japanese Stock." Upon liquidation, Bailey was then to transmit the proceeds to the United States. Bailey sold the Japanese stock and deposited approximately $730,000 into his Credit Suisse account on or about July 6, 1994. Bailey then transferred the money into his Barnett Bank Money Market Account. The money was paid to the United States Marshal on or about August 15, 1994. The referee found that Bailey admitted that his money market account was not a lawyer's trust account, nor did Bailey create or maintain it as a separate account for the sole purpose of maintaining the stock proceeds. In concluding that Bailey had engaged in commingling, the referee rejected Bailey's claims that there were no personal funds in the Barnett Bank account at the time Bailey transferred the funds from the Japanese Stock into this account, and that Bailey's deposit of the proceeds into a non-trust account was "inadvertent error." The referee concluded that Bailey violated Rule Regulating the Florida Bar 4–1.15(a) by failing to set up a separate account for these funds and also by commingling client funds with his personal funds.

Count II of the Bar's complaint charged Bailey with misappropriating trust funds and commingling. On or about May 9, 1994, the 602,000 shares of Biochem stock were transferred into Bailey's Credit Suisse Investment Account. Bailey sold shares of stock and borrowed against the stock, deriving over $4 million from these activities. Bailey then transferred $3,514,945 of Biochem proceeds from the Credit Suisse account into his Barnett Bank Money Market Account. Bailey had transferred all but $350,000 of these proceeds into his personal checking account by December 1995. From this account, Bailey wrote checks to his private business enterprises totaling $2,297,696 and another $1,277,433 for other personal expenses or purchases. Bailey further paid $138,946 out of his money market account toward the purchase of a residence.... The referee found Bailey guilty of violating Rules Regulating the Florida Bar 3–4.3 (lawyer shall not commit any act that is contrary to honesty and justice), 4–1.15(a) (commingling funds), 4–8.4(b) (lawyer shall not commit a criminal act that reflects adversely on the lawyer's honesty, trustworthiness, or fitness as a lawyer), 4–8.4(c) (lawyer shall not engage in conduct involving deceit, dishonesty, fraud or misrepresentation), and 5–1.1 (requiring money or other property entrusted to an attorney to be held in trust and applied only for a specific purpose).

[The referee also found Bailey guilty on Count III, which alleged that he continued to expend Biochem funds in contravention of two federal court orders; on Count IV, which alleged that Bailey testified falsely before the trial judge that he did not see the court's orders until some later date; on Count V, which charged Bailey with self-dealing and using information relating to his representation of Duboc to the Duboc's disadvantage; and on Count VII, which charged Bailey with ex parte communications, self-dealing, and disclosure of confidential information.]

Preliminarily, the referee noted that Bailey was 67 years old at the time of the report. He has been a member of The Florida Bar since 1989, and was admitted to the Massachusetts Bar in 1960. The referee further states "[a]ccording to the Respondent, he is a member of The Supreme Court of the United States, every circuit in the United States, the Tax Court, the Federal Court of Claims, and as of the time of the hearing was admitted in North Carolina and California pro hac vice on two cases."

... [T]he referee stated that "any of the violations of the rules regulating the Florida Bar which have been proven by the Bar as set forth above, would singularly warrant the recommended discipline [of disbarment]. Collectively, the numerous violations, all of which are serious and egregious, plainly warrant permanent disbarment." ... Bailey petitioned this Court for review, challenging multiple aspects of the referee's report.

ANALYSIS

... The most contested issue in this case is whether a trust was created with the transfer of the Biochem stock from Duboc to Bailey. The Bar argued that the plea agreement with the U.S. Government provided that Bailey was to hold the stock in trust for the benefit of the U.S. Government. Bailey would use the stock to maintain and liquidate Duboc's properties. After this was accomplished, the stock or its replacement assets would be forfeited to the United States in order to maximize any benefit to Bailey's client for his cooperation. However, Bailey argued that the stock was transferred to him in fee simple. He agreed that he was required to utilize the Biochem stock to derive the funds necessary to maintain and liquidate the French properties. However, Bailey asserted that after the properties were sold, he was only accountable to the United States for the value of the stock on the date that Duboc transferred it to Bailey's Swiss account (which was approximately $6 million), and not for any appreciation—which, as of January 1996, amounted to over $10 million. In other words, Bailey claims that he was entitled to all of the Biochem stock and proceeds from the sale of the stock, minus the approximate $6 million for which he was accountable to the U.S. Government. As he wrote Judge Paul in his letter of January 21, 1996:

> I viewed [the value of the stock of $5,891,352.00 on May 9, 1994] as an account in which the United States had an interest to this extent: after the payment of costs associated with the case and fees approved by Your Honor, any balance of the $5,891,352.00 remaining would revert to the United States. Because of this view, I did not declare the funds to be income to myself. (Emphasis omitted.)

We conclude that regardless of the manner in which he was to hold the stock, Bailey is guilty of the most serious and basic trust account violations. The stock, by his own admission, was given to Bailey by his client neither as a gift, nor as an earned fee. Rather, the stock was given to Bailey to be used for the benefit of Duboc, and ultimately the U.S. Government. Bailey was required to use the stock to maximize Duboc's forfeitures to the U.S. Government in the hope that Duboc would receive a reduction of sentence for his cooperation. In his January 21, 1996, letter to Judge Paul, even Bailey recognized that the U.S. Government had an interest in the transfer value of the Biochem stock. Nevertheless, from the day it was transferred to him, Bailey treated the money as his own.

FL Rule

... Rule 4–1.15 provides:

A lawyer shall hold in trust, separate from the lawyer's own property, funds and property of clients or third persons that are in a lawyer's possession in connection with a representation. All funds, including advances for costs and expenses, shall be kept in a separate account maintained in the state where the lawyer's office is situated or elsewhere with the consent of the client or third person, provided that funds may be separately held and maintained other than in a bank account if the lawyer receives written permission from the client to do so and provided that such written permission is received prior to maintaining the funds other than in a separate bank account. *In no event may the lawyer commingle the client's funds with those of the lawyer or those of the lawyer's law firm.* Other property shall be identified as such and appropriately safeguarded. (Emphasis added.)

Bailey admits that he was accountable to the United States for the approximate $6 million value of the Biochem stock on the day of transfer. Nevertheless, when the stock was transferred, Bailey made absolutely no effort to segregate or safeguard this money. Rather, he commingled the money with the funds in his Credit Suisse account, sold shares of the stock, and obtained a line of credit on the stock, deriving over $4,000,000 from these activities. As noted by the Bar at oral argument, if on January 1, 1996, the value of Biochem stock fell to zero, Bailey would have already taken $3.5 million out of the Biochem stock fund and transferred it to his personal money market account. Bailey transferred all but $350,000 of these proceeds into his personal checking account and used some or all of this money to pay for various business and personal expenses.

Further and importantly, Bailey admits that Judge Paul would approve the amount of Bailey's fee for representing Duboc, and that his fee would be taken from the approximate $6 million value of the Biochem proceeds. Therefore, even if some of the initial $6 million corpus was to be used for payment of an attorneys' fee, Bailey was not entitled to the fee until it was approved by Judge Paul—a fact that Bailey admits in his January 21 letter to Judge Paul, and that he admits in this case. Indeed, in a letter written to his own client, Duboc, before a falling out occurred, Bailey explained that:

You do not face the dilemma since I will be paid with Chief Judge Paul's approval—only that amount which is commensurate with the result achieved in your case, and the amount of work that went into it. Our interests are therefore in perfect alignment.

Rule 5–1.1(a) provides: "Money or other property entrusted to an attorney for a specific purpose, including advances for costs and expenses, is held in trust and must be applied only to that purpose." When the approximate $6 million transfer value of the Biochem stock was given to Bailey, it was given to him for specific purposes: to maintain the property of his client and then to return the remainder to the U.S. Government. Therefore, under Rule Regulating the Florida Bar 5–1.1, Bailey had a duty to safekeep this property and use it only for the aforementioned purposes. The transfer value of this stock or its proceeds could neither be commingled nor could it be withdrawn. The fact that a portion of this fund was to be used for payment of any attorneys' fees only serves to highlight this fact—that the monies were to be held in trust for a specific purpose.

If Bailey's fee had been earned, then it could have and should have been withdrawn from a trust account; the failure to do so would have been a violation of trust account rules. *See Florida Bar v. Tillman,* 682 So.2d 542 (1996) (holding that rule 4–1.15(c) requires fees to be withdrawn when they become due and the failure to do so constitutes a trust account violation). However, if money is given to a client to be applied to fees when they become earned, much like a retainer, these monies cannot be withdrawn from a trust account and spent until they are earned. *See In re Sather,* 3 P.3d 403, 410 (Colo.2000) ("[U]nearned portion[s] of ... advance fees must be kept in trust and cannot be treated as the attorney's property until earned."). In this case, by express agreement, Bailey was not entitled to any fees until determined and approved by Judge Paul. Thus, he was expressly prohibited from withdrawing and spending any portion of the stock for his own personal benefit until approved by Judge Paul. *See generally Spann,* 682 So.2d at 1070–71.

In light of the foregoing, we conclude that regardless of the manner in which the stock was transferred to Bailey and the exact words used, Bailey violated rule 4–1.15 and rule 5–1.1(a) as to approximately $6 million (i.e., the value of the stock at the time it was transferred to Bailey).

We further note that even if there was no precise agreement with the U.S. Government regarding the necessity to segregate and safeguard the stock and its proceeds, Bailey's obligations as to his client's property or the property of a third party flow from the Rules Regulating the Florida Bar, rules that are imposed as a condition of all attorneys' membership in The Florida Bar. Indeed, one of the most solemn obligations that separate lawyers from any other professionals relates to the safeguarding and segregation of a client's property. . . .

DISCIPLINE

... Disbarment is the presumed discipline for many of these acts of misconduct. For example, as to Bailey's mishandling of the Biochem stock, Standard 4.11 of the Florida Standards for Imposing Lawyer Sanctions provides: "Disbarment is appropriate when a lawyer intentionally or knowingly converts client property regardless of injury or potential injury." ...

Bailey has committed some of the most egregious rules violations possible, evidencing a complete disregard for the rules governing attorneys. "[M]isuse of client funds is one of the most serious offenses a lawyer can commit. Upon a finding of misuse or misappropriation, there is a presumption that disbarment is the appropriate punishment." ...

As we have repeatedly stated, discipline must serve three purposes:

First, the judgment must be fair to society, both in terms of protecting the public from unethical conduct and at the same time not denying the public the services of a qualified lawyer as a result of undue harshness in imposing penalty. Second, the judgment must be fair to the respondent, being sufficient to punish a breach of ethics and at the same time encourage reformation and rehabilitation. Third, the judgment must be severe enough to deter others who might be prone or tempted to become involved in like violations.

Florida Bar v. Brake, 767 So.2d 1163, 1169 (Fla.2000) (quoting *Florida Bar v. Cibula,* 725 So.2d 360, 363 (Fla.1998)).

In light of Bailey's egregious and cumulative misconduct, and the absence of any mitigating factors, we conclude that disbarment is not only appropriate in this case, but necessary to fulfill the threefold purpose of attorney discipline. By this disbarment, Bailey's status as a member of The Florida Bar shall be terminated and he may not reapply for readmission for a period of five years, and then he may "only be admitted again upon full compliance with the rules and regulations governing admission to the bar." R. Regulating Fla. Bar 3–5.1(f). This includes retaking the Florida bar examination, complying with the rigorous background and character examination, and demonstrating knowledge of the rules of professional conduct required of all new admittees.

Accordingly, F. Lee Bailey is hereby disbarred from the practice of law in the State of Florida. The disbarment will be effective thirty days from the filing of this opinion so that Bailey can close out his practice and protect the interests of existing clients. If Bailey notifies this Court in writing that he is no longer practicing and does not need the thirty days to protect existing clients, this Court will enter an order making the disbarment effective immediately. Bailey shall accept no new business from the date this opinion is filed until he is readmitted to the practice of law in Florida. Judgment is entered for The Florida Bar ... for recovery of costs from F. Lee Bailey in the amount of $24,418.60, for which sum let execution issue.

It is so ordered.

Notes

1. The rules on safeguarding client property may seem mundane, but as the *Bailey* case makes clear, failure to abide by them is one of the most serious professional offenses an attorney can commit, and lawyers must take them very seriously. Massachusetts subsequently disbarred Bailey as reciprocal discipline. *In re Bailey*, 439 Mass. 134, 786 N.E.2d 337 (2003). Disbarment is the presumed sanction for intentional violations of this sort in virtually all states. See, e.g., *People v. Coyne*, 913 P.2d 12 (Colo. 1996) (disbarment for knowing conversion of client funds); *In re Teichner*, 104 Ill.2d 150, 470 N.E.2d 972, 83 Ill.Dec. 552 (1984) (same). Even where a lawyer's mismanagement of client trust accounts is simply due to negligent bookkeeping, the sanction can be severe. See, e.g., *Florida Bar v. Smith*, 866 So.2d 41 (Fla. 2004) (one-year suspension).

2. Why is mixing client funds with the lawyer's personal funds (commingling) considered such a serious offense even where the lawyer can prove that the client funds have not been removed from the account and could be returned in toto? That is, where no harm is actually done to the client, why is this such a big deal?

3. *IOLTA.* In general, if a client's funds held by a lawyer would generate any significant interest, they must be placed in a separate interest-bearing trust account and the interest is the client's. But in many situations, the client funds are held for such a short amount of time that the interest on that particular account is de minimis to the client. In the aggregate, however, the interest generated in a multiple-client account may not be de minimis. Each state now has a program to administer and distribute interest generated from these client funds to benefit legal services to the poor or client protection funds. These are called "IOLTA" programs, an acronym for "Interest on Lawyer Trust Accounts." *See* Jay G Foonberg, ABA Guide to Lawyer Trust Accounts 14–17, 167–74 (1996) (describing the programs and providing directory of all state IOLTA programs).

The ABA has consistently supported IOLTA programs, which provide a crucial source of funding for legal services to the indigent. But they have been attacked by conservative groups as an unlawful taking of private property. In *Phillips v. Washington Legal Foundation*, 524 U.S. 156, 118 S.Ct. 1925, 141 L.Ed.2d 174 (1998), the Supreme Court held 5–4 that interest on a client's funds held in a trust account by a lawyer belongs to a client, even where bank charges would "eat up" that

interest. The Court did not decide whether the IOLTA scheme itself
constituted an unconstitutional taking of private property. In *Brown v.
Legal Foundation of Washington*, 538 U.S. 216, 123 S.Ct. 1406, 155
L.Ed.2d 376 (2003), the Court held—again by a 5–4 margin, that
Washington State's IOLTA program was not a regulatory taking, and
since the clients suffered no net loss, no compensation was due. The
majority stressed that under Washington's plan, lawyers are required to
deposit client funds in non-IOLTA accounts whenever those funds could
generate net earnings for the client. While a law that requires interest
on non-IOLTA accounts to be transferred to another owner for a
legitimate public use could be a per se taking, that was not the case here,
and here the plaintiffs suffered no loss. Therefore there was no constitutional violation shown. The dissenters (Scalia, Rehnquist, Kennedy and
Thomas) argued that the majority had undercut *Phillips* and created a
"novel exception" to the rule that just compensation must be paid to the
owners of confiscated property.

4. *Safeguarding client papers*. The rule on safeguarding property
covers all kinds of client property, including documents given to the
lawyer. The rule has been held to apply to prospective clients, meaning
that a lawyer can be disciplined for failing to safeguard papers given to
him by a person who did not ultimately become a client. *In re Conduct of
Spencer*, 335 Or. 71, 58 P.3d 228 (2002).

§ 5. TERMINATING THE RELATIONSHIP

A. Methods of Termination

The client-lawyer relationship should terminate as it was
begun: intentionally and formally. See Jeffrey M. Smith & Ronald
E. Mallen, Preventing Legal Malpractice § 2.12 (1989) (providing
a sample disengagement letter). Under normal circumstances, a
lawyer's representation of a client on a particular matter terminates upon completion of that matter. See MR 1.16, comment [1].
If there is any ambiguity that the relationship has been completed, however, the burden is on the lawyer to clarify that fact. The
comment to Model Rule 1.3 instructs:

> Unless the relationship is terminated as provided in Rule
> 1.16, a lawyer should carry through to conclusion all
> matters undertaken for a client. If a lawyer's employment
> is limited to a specific matter, the relationship terminates
> when the matter has been resolved. If a lawyer has
> served a client over a substantial period in a variety of
> matters, the client sometimes may assume that the law-
> yer will continue to service on a continuing basis unless
> the lawyer gives notice of withdrawal. Doubt about
> whether a client-lawyer relationship still exists should be
> clarified by the lawyer, preferably in writing, so that the
> client will not mistakenly suppose the lawyer is looking

after the client's affairs when the lawyer has ceased to do so.

MR 1.3, comment [4]. See also Restatement § 31(2).

check sources *1986 case*

HANLIN v. MITCHELSON

United States Court of Appeals, Second Circuit, 1986.
794 F.2d 834.

MESKILL, Circuit Judge:

[Hermine Hanlin, *pro se,* appeals from a judgment of the United States District Court for the Southern District of New York, denying her motion to amend her legal malpractice complaint and granting lawyer Marvin Mitchelson's motion for summary judgment dismissing Hanlin's complaint. Hanlin had entered into a written partnership agreement with four members of the singing group "The Manhattans," providing that she would be an equal business partner and the group's manager. In 1981, after the Manhattans had won a Grammy award, they had a falling out with Hanlin. Each side claimed the other owed money. Pursuant to a clause in the partnership agreement, the dispute went to arbitration. Hanlin retained Mitchelson, a California attorney, to represent her in the arbitration proceedings. Hanlin's verbal agreement with Mitchelson required her to pay a flat fee of $25,000 in advance, plus expenses, and (according to her) obligated him to handle the case "as far as it has to go." She paid the $25,000.]

. . . The arbitral award, issued on December 23, 1982, directed the Manhattans to pay Hanlin $20,620 and directed Hanlin to pay [the group's manager] $26,750. The award also declared that Hanlin had percentage interests in certain Manhattans contracts and directed the parties to execute assignments in connection with those interests. According to Hanlin, these assignments were never executed and the award to her was never confirmed.

Hanlin was unhappy with the arbitral award and urged Mitchelson to appeal it and to persuade the arbitral panel to correct alleged errors. Mitchelson did obtain a "Clarification of Award," issued by the panel on February 18, 1983, which explained an apparent discrepancy between the award and one of the assignments.

Hanlin, still dissatisfied, continued to urge Mitchelson by telephone, mail and telegraph to appeal. Not satisfied with his response, she wrote to him on March 28, 1983, asking that he return the $25,000 fee she had paid. A lawyer in Mitchelson's Los Angeles office responded by letter on March 30, 1983, refusing to make any refund, stating that the arbitration award was "final and . . . not appealable," and offering "to assist any counsel you may choose with a legal case history or any other service which I can reasonably provide" if Hanlin wished to sue any of the individual defendants in New York. Hanlin responded by letter on April 6, 1983, asking for further advice about obtaining performance of the arbitral award without mentioning her earlier request for a refund.

Mitchelson himself wrote to Hanlin on April 21, 1983, saying that he had been unable to answer her letters because he had been involved in an automobile accident and had just been released from the hospital. Mitchelson reiterated that the arbitration was "binding" and explained why the award to Kelley might have been within the scope of the arbitration. He then offered to seek to reopen the arbitration, but added "I cannot act for you if you are going to be hostile and keep asking me to return fees to you." Mitchelson stated that Hanlin was not entitled to a fee refund, noting also that Hanlin owed his office $6,500 in "costs" for the arbitration.

On May 24, 1983, New York attorney Neal Rosenberg wrote to Mitchelson stating that he had "been retained by Ms. Hanlin in reference to the enclosed correspondence." The "correspondence" was apparently the series of letters described above in which Hanlin had urged an appeal and Mitchelson had declined to pursue one. Rosenberg disagreed with Mitchelson's assessment that the arbitral award could not have been appealed. He stated, however, that the deadline had passed for seeking an order to vacate or modify the award and asked Mitchelson to "advise us as to how you intend to resolve this matter." On June 21, 1983, an attorney in Mitchelson's office responded to Rosenberg, defending Mitchelson's "good faith opinion" that no appeal to the arbitral panel had been warranted and asserting that "any other relief," presumably including an appeal to a court, was beyond the scope of Mitchelson's representation of Hanlin.

On April 6, 1984, Hanlin filed the instant diversity action against Mitchelson in the district court seeking compensatory and punitive damages for "intimidation," negligence, defamation and malpractice. Mitchelson counterclaimed for the $6,500 in costs and expenses allegedly owed to him by Hanlin. He then filed a single motion seeking either dismissal of the complaint under Fed.R.Civ.P. 12(b)(6) or summary judgment under Fed.R.Civ.P. 56.

[The trial court dismissed the claims for intimidation and defamation, and granted partial summary judgment on the negligence and malpractice claims, which were treated as one claim.] Hanlin then moved for leave to amend her complaint based on Mitchelson's alleged failure to confirm the arbitral award within the one year limitations period.... [The case was reassigned to a second district judge, who denied leave to amend and dismissed the complaint.]

... The decision to deny leave [to amend] was based on three premises: that Mitchelson's failure to confirm the award in time was known to Hanlin when she filed her original complaint; that Mitchelson would be prejudiced by an amendment after discovery and after the filing of his motion for summary judgment; and that the allegations in the proposed amended complaint were frivolous because Mitchelson's representation of Hanlin had terminated before the alleged failure to confirm the arbitral award occurred. We reject each of these premises and hold that the denial of leave to amend was an abuse of discretion....

[Regarding the court's first premise,] Hanlin's original complaint indicates that she had been unable to "collect on the award of the arbitrators," but does not indicate why that was so. She explained at oral argument that she thought she had a valid, enforceable award and that she did not understand what was going on when the various other parties to the award refused to honor it. She states that at the time of her complaint she was unaware of the one year statute of limitations for confirmation of the award, or indeed of the need for confirmation at all.... To prevent Hanlin from amending her complaint based on what she should have known would add insult to the injury she alleges she suffered at the hands of her attorney.... Hanlin alleges that she did not know about the deadline for confirmation because Mitchelson failed to tell her.

[Regarding the court's second premise, the allegations in Hanlin's original complaint were sufficient to put Mitchelson on notice that Hanlin was asserting a claim that Mitchelson was negligent and breached a contract when he failed to confirm the arbitral award. Mitchelson thus would not be unduly prejudiced by amendment.]

... The district court's third basis for denying leave to amend was that Hanlin's amended claims would be frivolous because the failure to confirm the award occurred after Hanlin had terminated Mitchelson's representation. We reject this notion for the following reasons.

It is not altogether clear that the attorney-client relationship between Hanlin and Mitchelson had terminated. The exchange of letters between Hanlin and Mitchelson's office certainly suggests that the relationship was strained. However, the letters, taken together, do not indicate conclusively that the relationship was at an end.

For example, when Hanlin demanded on March 28, 1983, that Mitchelson refund her fee, Mitchelson's office responded not be declaring the representation over but by justifying the fee and offering to assist New York counsel in preparing for suits against the individual Manhattans. Thereafter, on April 6, Hanlin wrote to Mitchelson again asking for legal advice, apparently still viewing him as her lawyer. Mitchelson responded on April 21, warning Hanlin about her "hostile" activity toward him but nevertheless offering to seek a reopening of the arbitration for her. The clear implication of the April 21 letter is that on that date Mitchelson, too, saw his attorney-client relationship with Hanlin as still intact. Even when Attorney Rosenberg wrote to Mitchelson stating that he had been retained by Hanlin at least as to the matter of the appeal, the response from Mitchelson's office, in addition to raising questions about the scope of Mitchelson's representation, not only defended past acts but also sought current information about Hanlin's arbitration-related activities, apparently recognizing some continued responsibility.

"As between attorney and client, no special formality is required to effect the discharge of the attorney. 'Any act of the client indicating an unmistakable purpose to sever relations is enough.'" A client's malpractice suit against an attorney is enough to indicate that the client has terminated the relationship. Short of instituting a malpractice suit, however, a client may question her attorney's tactics, suggest alternatives and even consult another attorney without automatically terminating the attorney-client relationship. We have refused to find a termination even when the plaintiff and her newly retained attorney directly asked the first attorney to withdraw from the case.

We conclude that the status and scope of the attorney-client relationship here prior to the commencement of the instant suit are unresolved questions of fact. The termination of the relationship was not so clear as to render Hanlin's proposed amendment frivolous and, therefore, no proper basis appears for denying leave to amend.

Furthermore, even if the letter from Attorney Rosenberg did terminate the attorney-client relationship between Hanlin and Mitchelson, the fact of termination would not end the malpractice inquiry. Questions would still remain about Mitchelson's handling of the termination.

Ordinarily, for example, a withdrawing attorney must give a client "clear and unambiguous" notice of the attorney's intent to withdraw from representation. There is no indication on the record that such notice was ever given to Hanlin. Beyond this notice requirement, the Code of Professional Responsibility imposes a broader duty. The Code plainly states that "a lawyer shall not withdraw from employment until he has taken reasonable steps to avoid foreseeable prejudice to the rights of the client." N.Y.Jud. Law (App.) Code of Prof.Resp. DR 2–110(A)(2) (McKinney Supp. 1986). See also id. at EC 2–32 ("Even when withdrawal is justifiable, a lawyer should protect the welfare of the client ... endeavoring to minimize the possibility of harm."). Whether Mitchelson fulfilled these duties is another open question on this record....

[Summary judgment reversed in part; denial of leave to amend reversed.] This case is remanded for further proceedings consistent with this opinion.

Notes

1. What should Mitchelson have done differently if he truly believed his representation of Hanlin was over?

2. Pursuant to both the Model Rules and the Restatement, a lawyer's representation terminates if the client discharges the lawyer. MR 1.16(a)(3); Restatement § 31(2)(a). Can a lawyer terminate a representation before it is completed? The answer is yes, but because the client's interests may be damaged by such an act, the lawyer's ability to do so is circumscribed by the ethics rules. Further, a lawyer who withdraws from a representation prior to its completion may be liable for malpractice if the withdrawal is unreasonable and causes legally-cognizable harm. See, e.g., *Gilles v. Wiley, Malehorn & Sirota*, 345 N.J.Super. 119, 783 A.2d 756 (2001); *Central Cab Co. v. Clarke*, 259 Md. 542, 270 A.2d 662 (1970).

3. The rules do provide that under some circumstances the lawyer either must or may withdraw from a matter. We consider below (1) mandatory withdrawal; (2) permissive withdrawal; and (3) the client's rights after the lawyer has withdrawn. We will see the lawyer's rights to fees after withdrawal or termination in Chapter 5.

B. Lawyer Duties and Client Rights

1. *Mandatory Withdrawal*

Model Rule 1.16(a) provides that a lawyer *must* withdraw from the representation of a client if (1) the representation will result in violation of the rules or other law; or (2) the lawyer's physical or mental condition materially impairs the lawyer's ability to competently conduct the representation; or (3) if the lawyer is discharged. The Model Code, as still in effect in New York, for example, also requires withdrawal where the lawyer knows that the client is taking action "merely for the purpose of harassing or maliciously injuring any person." N.Y. DR 2–110(b) [22 NYCRR 1200.15]. See also Cal. Rule 3–700 (substantially identical to the New York rule).

Even where withdrawal is mandatory, the lawyer engaged in a litigation matter may have to seek permission of the tribunal. See MR 1.16(c); N.Y. DR 2–110(a)(1) & (b) [22 NYCRR 1200.5]; Cal. Rule 3–700(A)(1) & (B). If the court orders the lawyer to remain on the case, the lawyer must do so. Restatement §§ 31(1) & 32(5). Any such order may be appealed by the lawyer. See, e.g., *Whiting v. Lacara*, 187 F.3d 317 (2d Cir.1999) (reversing a trial court's denial of counsel's motion to withdraw on the eve of a civil trial, finding that the client had placed the lawyer in an "impossible situation" by insisting on dictating trial strategies and threatening to sue for legal malpractice if the lawyer did not do as he was instructed).

2. *Permissive Withdrawal*

A lawyer may withdraw, even though not required to do so, under a number of circumstances. First, a lawyer may withdraw if the client consents to such withdrawal. Restatement § 32(3)(c). Pursuant to the Model Rules, the New York rules and the Restatement, the lawyer may also withdraw "if withdrawal can be accomplished without material adverse effect on the interests of the client." MR 1.16(b)(1); N.Y. DR 2–110(c) [22 NYCRR 1200.15]; Restatement § 32(3)(a). California's rules, however, do not allow a lawyer to withdraw simply where there would be no material adverse effects on the client's interests. Even permissive withdrawal in California requires good cause, in the form of one of eleven enumerated reasons. Cal. Rule 3–700(C).

The more specific grounds available for permissive withdrawal may be categorized as those involving client misconduct and those involving lawyer hardship. In the first category, for example, a lawyer is allowed to withdraw where the client insists on taking action involving the lawyer's services that the lawyer believes is criminal or fraudulent, MR 1.16(b)(2) or repugnant to the lawyer, or about which the lawyer has a "fundamental disagreement," MR 1.16(b)(4). In the second category, a lawyer may withdraw if the client has failed to pay for services and has been given adequate warning of withdrawal, MR 1.16(b)(5), or if continuing the representation will put an unreasonable financial burden on the lawyer, or would be "unreasonably difficult" for some other reason, MR 1.16(b)(6). The list of specific grounds is virtually identical in all states. See, e.g., Cal. Rule 3–700(C); N.Y. DR 2–110(c) [22 NYCRR 1200.15].

Of course, where the lawyer seeks to withdraw from a litigated matter pursuant to the permissive withdrawal provisions, the court's permission must be obtained if the court's rules require it. See MR 1.16(c); N.Y. DR 2–110(a)(1); Cal. Rule 3–700(A)(1) & (C). A trial court's denial of a motion to withdraw is reviewed for an abuse of discretion.

FIDELITY NATIONAL TITLE INS. CO. v. INTERCOUNTY NATIONAL TITLE INS. CO.

United States Court of Appeals, Seventh Circuit, 2002.
310 F.3d 537.

EASTERBROOK, Circuit Judge.

Fidelity National Title Insurance contends that $20 million vanished from real estate escrow accounts under the control of defendants and related entities. It seeks a judgment for that amount in this diversity litigation. Five of the defendants—Intercounty National Title Insurance Co., Intercounty Title Co., INTIC Holding Co., Terry Cornell, and Susan Peloza (collectively the INTIC parties)—retained Myron M. Cherry & Associates LLC to represent them in the suit. The three corporations are defunct but have made claims against co-defendants (and third parties) that may have value; the financial status of Cornell and Peloza, who controlled the three corporations, is unclear. The INTIC parties promised to pay Cherry an hourly fee for its services and to reimburse expenses. For some time they kept this promise. But about a year ago they began to fall behind, and by July 2002, when Cherry first moved to withdraw, they owed more than $430,000 in fees and out-of-pocket expenses. (The total now exceeds $470,000.) Cherry informed the district court that its clients had stopped paying and were making no efforts to engage new counsel. The district judge denied this motion to withdraw and a later one, making it clear that in her view Cherry must represent the INTIC parties to the bitter end, no matter how much this costs (and no matter how little the INTIC parties pay), unless a new lawyer files an appearance on their behalf. Substitution is unlikely, because the district court's order provides Cherry's clients with free legal assistance, while the INTIC parties would have to give any replacement a hefty retainer (for Cherry anticipates that the trial of the suit may require lawyers' time plus outlays for copying, transcripts, and other expenses that will bring the total tab to $1 million). Cherry, which does not fancy throwing good time after bad, asks us to reverse the district court's order and to permit its withdrawal. . . .

[T]he INTIC parties have made it clear that they do not have another lawyer. Nor do they promise to retain one or to pay Cherry. It is therefore difficult to see why Cherry should be obliged to provide them with future legal services. Litigants have no right to free legal aid in civil suits. The INTIC parties do not appear to be good candidates for *pro bono* representation—which is at any event voluntary rather than compulsory. See *Mallard v. United States District Court,* 490 U.S. 296, 109 S.Ct. 1814, 104 L.Ed.2d 318 (1989). Corporations don't qualify for even the slight benefit of proceeding *in forma pauperis.*

The ABA's *Model Rules of Professional Conduct* state that lawyers are entitled to stop working when clients stop paying. Rule 1.16(b) provides that a lawyer may withdraw if

> (5) the client fails substantially to fulfill an obligation to the lawyer regarding the lawyer's services and has been given reasonable warning that the lawyer will withdraw unless the obligation is fulfilled;

(6) the representation will result in an unreasonable financial burden on the lawyer or has been rendered unreasonably difficult by the client; or

(7) other good cause for withdrawal exists.

Failure to cover $470,000 in legal fees and expenses (despite undertaking via contract to do so) satisfies subsection (5), and the prospect of a further uncompensated outlay worth $500,000 satisfies subsection (6), especially because Cherry is a small law firm (it has four lawyers). See Geoffrey C. Hazard, Jr. & W. William Hodes, 1 *The Law of Lawyering: A Handbook on the Model Rules of Professional Conduct* § 1.16:303 (1990 & 1998 Supp.). The Northern District of Illinois has promulgated ethical rules that depart slightly from the *Model Rules,* but Local Rule PRC 1.16(b)(1)(F) permits a lawyer to withdraw if the client "substantially fails to fulfill an agreement or obligation to the lawyer as to expenses or fees." More than $470,000 in unpaid bills, with the meter still running and poor prospects of future payment, is substantial by any reckoning.

Surprisingly, the district judge did not mention either Local Rule PRC 1.16(b)(1)(F) or Model Rule 1.16(b) when denying Cherry's motion. A law firm might promise its client not to take advantage of options under these rules, but the contract between Cherry and its clients did not restrict its ability to withdraw; to the contrary, it expressly entitles the firm to do so if fees are not paid. Instead of discussing either the rules or the contract, the district judge denied the motion because, in her view, it had been filed too late.

A lawyer engaged in strategic conduct may forfeit any right to withdraw. One form of strategic behavior is waiting until the client is over a barrel and then springing a demand for payment (perhaps enhanced payment). This would be equivalent to the coercive tactics used by the seamen, and condemned by the court, in *Alaska Packers' Ass'n v. Domenico,* 117 F. 99 (9th Cir.1902), which held that a promise to pay double wages, extracted after the ship was at sea, was unenforceable. Avoiding such tactics is a point of the proviso in Model Rule 1.16(b)(5) that counsel must give "reasonable warning." The district judge did not doubt that warning had been given (a requirement at any event omitted from the Northern District's version of Rule 1.16); nor did she find that Cherry had its clients at its mercy. The firm did not seek to withdraw on the first day of trial, for example, but instead represented the INTIC parties through the end of discovery and sought to withdraw in a quiet period before trial. An effort to withdraw earlier—while discovery deadlines were looming—might have been thought opportunistic. Instead Cherry protected its clients' interests through discovery and sought to withdraw only when substitution of counsel would be relatively simple. It is hard to see why this forbearance, from which the clients received a substantial benefit, should compel Cherry to contribute unpaid services for the indefinite future.

Severe prejudice to third parties—who might have more to lose than the unpaid lawyer—is another potential ground for denying a motion to withdraw. This is not because Cherry owes any obligation to protect the interests of the INTIC parties' *adversaries;* it is again a matter of timing, and a judge may insist that counsel resolve differences with clients in a fashion that curtails strangers' avoidable losses. The district judge hinted that there was some potential for prejudice. Yet none of the other litigants perceived any. Asked in open court whether Cherry's withdrawal would cause prejudice, each of the other parties gave a negative answer. That pattern has been repeated on appeal.... Most likely, Cherry's withdrawal would leave the INTIC parties unrepresented, leading to default judgments against the three corporations (which can appear *only* by counsel). That would expedite rather than delay the conclusion of the case. It would injure the INTIC parties if they have good third-party claims, but in that event they should be able to secure a new lawyer, if necessary by offering a contingent fee to be paid out of third-party recoveries. At all events, we do not see how third parties stand to lose more if Cherry withdraws now than Cherry stands to lose if it must provide future services and bear out-of-pocket expenses that are unlikely to be compensated.

The district court's order denying Cherry's motion to withdraw was an abuse of discretion and is REVERSED.

Note

Judge Easterbrook suggests that a motion to withdraw because the client has not paid its fees might properly be denied where the lawyer is trying to take advantage of the client. Isn't a lawyer's threat to seek permission to withdraw if fees are not paid coercive in and of itself? Is the idea that it is not *improperly* coercive?

3. Lawyer's Duties After Withdrawal

a. Acting Reasonably to Protect Client Interests

Neither the ethics rules nor other law prohibits a lawyer from terminating the lawyer-client relationship before a matter is concluded. But the rules and law require the lawyer to take reasonable steps to minimize the negative impact of that action on the client's interests. See MR 1.16(d); N.Y. DR 2–110(a)(2); Cal. Rule 3–700(A)(2). Failure to take such steps could lead to discipline or civil liability, as the court suggested in *Hanlin v. Mitchelson* above. Should these duties apply when an entire law firm dissolves? That is, should partners of a dissolved law firm owe the firm's former clients a duty to protect their interests? See *RLS Assocs. v. United Bank of Kuwait PLC*, 417 F.Supp.2d 417 (S.D.N.Y. 2006).

b. Returning Client Papers and Property

After withdrawal, the lawyer must under most circumstances return client papers, and must return client property and refund any unearned fees. See MR 1.16(d); N.Y. DR 2–110(a)(2); Cal. Rule 3–700(D); Restatement §§ 33(1), 45 & 46. See also *Swift, Currie, McGhee & Hiers v. Henry*, 276 Ga. 571, 581 S.E.2d 37 (2003) (absent showing of good cause by the lawyer, client was entitled to get document prepared by lawyer during representation); *Sage Realty Corp. v. Proskauer Rose Goetz & Mendelsohn L.L.P.*, 91 N.Y.2d 30, 689 N.E.2d 879, 666 N.Y.S.2d 985 (1997) (former client must be allowed to inspect and copy any documents in the lawyer's possession which relate to the former representation, absent substantial grounds for refusing access, such as possible violation of confidentiality owed to other clients).

Can a lawyer withhold a client's papers when the client has failed to pay attorney's fees? Most states say yes; this is called a "retaining lien." The Restatement rejects this approach, finding "the use of the client's papers against the client" to be "in tension with the fiduciary responsibilities of lawyers." Restatement § 43, comment *b*.

In *Academy of California Optometrists, Inc. v. Superior Court*, 51 Cal.App.3d 999, 124 Cal.Rptr. 668 (1975), a lawyer in a litigated matter was discharged by the client organization, whose leaders had grown unhappy with his excessive charges. The lawyer refused to sign a substitution of attorneys or to turn over the case files until his $9,300 fee was paid. The files filled three large manila folders, and included pleadings, briefs, interrogatories, depositions, notes and correspondence accumulated over five years of representation. The client sought an order forcing the lawyer to deliver the files to it. *Held*, such an order must issue. The court found that the papers had no value to the lawyer, except as coercion, and were of substantial value to the client. The lawyer, said the court, "is in the untenable position of insisting upon his contractual right to damage his client's cause (the same cause which he hitherto espoused and which generated fees to him, both disputed and undisputed), unless the client pays him the disputed fees in full and foregoes his right to honestly litigate the dispute. The client's cause, sacred as it is to a member of the legal profession, may not be so abused."

The Restatement allows a lawyer to retain a document only "if the client has not paid all fees and disbursements due for the lawyer's work in preparing the document and nondelivery would not unreasonably harm the client or former client." Restatement § 43(1). The idea behind this provision is that the client who has failed to pay for the work on a particular document is generally not entitled to have it. However, the lawyer should not retain even unpaid-for documents where such action would damage the client's interests. *Id.*, comment c.

Are the approaches of the Restatement and California better than the majority's? Should a lawyer ever be allowed to retain documents in order to coerce the payment of fees? For one leading scholar's perspective, see John Leubsdorf, *Against Lawyer Retaining Liens*, 72 Fordham L. Rev. 849 (2004).

c. Fulfilling Continuing Duties

Even after a client-lawyer relationship has terminated, the lawyer continues to owe certain duties to the now-former client. For example, the duty of confidentiality continues indefinitely. Pursuant to agency principles, the lawyer must also refrain from taking any unfair advantage of a former client by abusing any knowledge or trust acquired through the client-lawyer relationship. See Restatement § 33(2).

C. Leaving a Law Firm
1. A Firm's Duties to the Departing Lawyer
a. Wrongful Termination and Related Claims

JACOBSON v. KNEPPER & MOGA, P.C.

Supreme Court of Illinois, 1998.
185 Ill.2d 372, 706 N.E.2d 491, 235 Ill.Dec. 936.

Justice NICKELS delivered the opinion of the court:

We are asked here to consider the issue of whether an attorney who has been discharged by his law firm employer should be allowed the remedy of an action for retaliatory discharge. We hold that an attorney may not maintain such an action.

BACKGROUND

Plaintiff, Alan P. Jacobson, filed a one-count complaint in the circuit court of Cook County against the law firm of Knepper & Moga, P.C. (hereinafter, the firm), alleging that he had been wrongfully discharged in retaliation for reporting the firm's illegal practices to a principal partner of the firm. In his complaint, plaintiff made the following factual allegations. In July 1994, plaintiff was hired as an associate attorney of the firm. Shortly thereafter, plaintiff discovered that the firm was filing consumer debt collection actions in violation of the venue provisions of the Fair Debt Collection Practices Act (15 U.S.C. § 1692i(a)(2)(B) (1988)) and the Illinois Collection Agency Act (225 ILCS 425/9(a)(20) (West 1994)). Plaintiff spoke with James Knepper, one of the firm's principal partners, regarding the filing practice and was advised that the matter would be remedied.

In April 1995, plaintiff was given the responsibility of reviewing and signing all complaints filed by the firm in consumer debt collection cases. In this role, plaintiff learned that the firm continued to file actions in violation of the venue provisions of the above-referenced acts. Plaintiff reiterated his complaint to Knepper, who again assured plaintiff that the practice would be corrected. Shortly thereafter, plaintiff was relieved of the responsibility to review and sign complaints in consumer debt collection cases. Less than three months later, plaintiff discovered that the firm had not ceased the practice of filing complaints in the improper venue. Plaintiff approached Knepper regarding the matter for a third time. Approximately two weeks later, plaintiff was terminated.

Plaintiff's complaint alleged that he had been discharged in retaliation for his insistence that the firm cease its practice of filing consumer debt collection actions in the wrong venue. The firm filed a motion to dismiss, [arguing] that Illinois courts have refused to extend the tort of retaliatory discharge to employees who are licensed attorneys. [The circuit (trial) court denied the motion.] The appellate court held that plaintiff was not precluded from maintaining an action for retaliatory discharge against his employing firm. We granted the firm's petition for leave to appeal.

ANALYSIS

Generally, an employer may fire an employee-at-will for any reason or no reason at all. Nevertheless, this court has recognized the limited and narrow tort of retaliatory discharge as an exception to the general rule of at-will employment. *Balla v. Gambro, Inc.,* 145 Ill.2d 492, 498–99, 164 Ill.Dec. 892, 584 N.E.2d 104 (1991), citing *Kelsay v. Motorola, Inc.,* 74 Ill.2d 172, 23 Ill.Dec. 559, 384 N.E.2d 353 (1978). To establish a cause of action for retaliatory discharge, a plaintiff must demonstrate that (1) he was discharged in retaliation for his activities; and (2) the discharge is in contravention of a clearly mandated public policy.

While there is no precise definition of what constitutes clearly mandated public policy, a review of Illinois case law reveals that retaliatory discharge actions are allowed in two settings. The first situation is when an employee is discharged for filing, or in anticipation of the filing of, a claim under the Workers' Compensation Act. The second situation is when an employee is discharged in retaliation for the reporting of illegal or improper conduct, otherwise known as "whistle blowing." See, *e.g., Palmateer v. International Harvester Co.,* 85 Ill.2d 124, 52 Ill.Dec. 13, 421 N.E.2d 876 (1981). Here, it is plaintiff's contention that the enactment of the provisions of the Fair Debt Collection Practice

Act and the Illinois Collection Agency Act, violations of which are alleged in the complaint, articulate a clearly mandated public policy. Plaintiff argues that, because he alleged that he was terminated in retaliation for his reporting of the firm's violations of these acts, his complaint states a cause of action.

The tort of retaliatory discharge is a limited cause of action which "seeks to achieve 'a proper balance * * * among the employer's interest in operating a business efficiently and profitably, the employee's interest in earning a livelihood, and society's interest in seeing its public policies carried out.' " *Balla,* 145 Ill.2d at 501, 164 Ill.Dec. 892, 584 N.E.2d 104. In this case, the public policy to be protected, that of protecting the debtor defendants' property and ensuring them due process, is adequately safeguarded without extending the tort of retaliatory discharge to employee attorneys.

Plaintiff was a licensed attorney at all times throughout this controversy and, as such, he was subject to the Illinois Rules of Professional Conduct (134 Ill.2d Rs. 1.1 through 8.5). The firm's conduct of intentionally filing collection actions against debtors in a county which it knows venue is improper clearly violates Rule 3.3 of the Rules of Professional Conduct. See 134 Ill.2d R. 3.3(a)(1) (lawyer shall not make a statement of material fact or law to a tribunal which the lawyer knows or reasonably should know is false). Further, the Rules of Professional Conduct prohibit a lawyer from engaging in conduct involving dishonesty, fraud, deceit, or misrepresentation. 155 Ill.2d R. 8.4(a)(4). Because plaintiff possessed unprivileged knowledge that the firm engaged in conduct involving dishonesty, fraud, deceit, or misrepresentation, he was required to report such knowledge to a tribunal or other authority empowered to investigate or act upon such violation. See 134 Ill.2d R. 8.3(a); *In re Himmel,* 125 Ill.2d 531, 541, 127 Ill.Dec. 708, 533 N.E.2d 790 (1988).

Therefore, the attorney's ethical obligations serve to adequately protect the public policy established by the collection statutes. Because sufficient safeguards exist in this situation, it is unnecessary to expand the limited and narrow tort of retaliatory discharge to the employee attorney. As this court has previously observed, "[a]n attorney's obligation to follow these Rules of Professional Conduct should not be the foundation for a claim of retaliatory discharge." *Balla,* 145 Ill.2d at 505. Although plaintiff attempts to limit the application of *Balla* to in-house counsel, the *Balla* court based its decision "as much on the nature and purpose of the tort of retaliatory discharge, as on the effect on the attorney-client relationship that extending the tort would have." *Balla,* 145 Ill.2d at 501. Attorneys employed by law firms have the same ethical obligations as those imposed upon in-house counsel.

Thus, we hold that plaintiff, as a licensed attorney employed as such by the defendant law firm, cannot maintain a cause of action for retaliatory discharge because the ethical obligations imposed by the Rules of Professional Conduct provide adequate safeguards to the public policy implicated in this case.... Accordingly, we reverse the judgments of the appellate and circuit courts and remand this cause with directions that defendant's motion to dismiss be granted.

Chief Justice FREEMAN, dissenting:

I respectfully dissent.

The majority concludes that an attorney's obligation to follow the Rules of Professional Responsibility should not be the foundation for a claim of retaliatory discharge. I note that, in resolving this issue, the majority relies primarily on our 1991 decision in *Balla v. Gambro, Inc.*, 145 Ill.2d 492, 164 Ill.Dec. 892, 584 N.E.2d 104 (1991), which involved an in-house attorney's attempt to sue his corporate employer for retaliatory discharge after the attorney advised his employer that it failed to comply with certain federal regulations promulgated by the Federal Food and Drug Administration. I dissented in *Balla*, arguing, *inter alia*, that the court's confidence in the Rules' existence as a shield from an employer's illegal acts was unwise and misplaced. I warned then that the court's decision did "nothing to encourage respect for the law by corporate employers nor [did it] encourage respect by attorneys for their ethical obligations." Seven years later, these concerns unfortunately still ring true, as the facts in this case sadly demonstrate. Nevertheless, my colleagues today now extend the *Balla* holding to law firms and their employee attorneys. Thus, one class of employees in this state, attorneys, has been stripped of a remedy which Illinois clearly affords to all other employees in such "whistle-blowing" situations. Today's opinion serves as yet another reminder to the attorneys in this state that, in certain circumstances, it is economically more advantageous to keep quiet than to follow the dictates of the Rules of Professional Conduct. For this reason, and the reasons expressed in my dissent in *Balla*, I would ... affirm the judgments of both the appellate and circuit courts.

Notes

1. Jurisdictions have split on the issue that divided the court in *Jacobson*. Compare, e.g., *Snow v. Ruden, McCloskey, Smith, Schuster & Russell, P.A.*, 896 So.2d 787 (Fla. App. 2005) (agreeing with *Jacobson* on similar facts), with *Crews v. Buckman Labs. Int'l, Inc.*, 78 S.W.3d 852 (Tenn. 2002) (in-house lawyer could sue for retaliatory discharge when she was fired for reporting that her employer's general counsel was

engaged in the unauthorized practice of law), and *General Dynamics Corp. v. Superior Court*, 7 Cal.4th 1164, 876 P.2d 487, 32 Cal.Rptr.2d 1 (1994) (in-house lawyer could sue for retaliatory discharge where lawyer's adherence to professional duty clashed with employer's illegitimate demands). Cf. *Wieder v. Skala*, 80 N.Y.2d 628, 609 N.E.2d 105, 593 N.Y.S.2d 752 (1992) (not allowing a fired associate's claim for "abusive discharge," but holding that the lawyer stated a claim for breach of contract based on the firm's firing him for insisting that the firm report another associate's professional misconduct).

2. Do you agree with the *Jacobson* majority's statement of the relevant "public policy" at stake? Does the dissenting justice state a more compelling one?

3. *Statutory claims*. State and federal statutes may give a fired lawyer a cause of action even where the common law does not. In the landmark case of *Hishon v. King & Spalding*, 467 U.S. 69, 104 S.Ct. 2229, 81 L.Ed.2d 59 (1984), the Court held that a former associate could sue under Title VII, 42 U.S.C. § 2000e, for sex-based discrimination in an adverse partnership decision. Statutory claims will often turn on the wording of the particular statute, of course. Title VII protects "employees" from discrimination. Is a law firm partner covered? See, e.g., *Solon v. Kaplan*, 398 F.3d 629 (7th Cir. 2005) (no, so the partner had no Title VII claim in his case alleging he was fired for his opposition to sexual harassment within the firm). The federal Age Discrimination in Employment Act, on the other hand, protects both partners and associates from adverse employment actions by their law firm based on age. See, e.g., *EEOC v. Sidley Austin LLP*, 437 F.3d 695 (7th Cir. 2006).

b. Restrictions on Practice

EISENSTEIN v. CONLIN

Supreme Judicial Court of Massachusetts, 2005.
444 Mass. 258, 827 N.E.2d 686.

MARSHALL, C.J.

In 1999, Ronald Eisenstein and David Resnick resigned from the law firm Dike, Bronstein, Roberts & Cushman LLP (DBRC) to become partners in another law firm. Several DBRC clients retained them in the new firm. Eisenstein and Resnick, their new firm, and DBRC became embroiled in litigation over those events, resulting in this appeal. At issue is the enforceability of provisions of the DBRC partnership agreement (agreement) that require departing partners to remit payment to DBRC a portion of the fees they generate at their new firm as a result of work performed for certain current and former DBRC clients. DBRC appeals from a Superior Court judge's grant of summary judgments in favor of Eisenstein, Resnick, and their new firm, concluding that the disputed provisions are unenforceable as against public policy. We transferred the case here on our own motion to determine whether a law firm may contractually bind former partners to share fees they earn from the firm's current and former clients after the partners leave the firm. We conclude that, in the circumstances of this case, the provisions in controversy impinge on the "strong public interest in allowing clients to retain counsel of their choice," *Meehan v. Shaughnessy*, 404 Mass. 419, 431, 535 N.E.2d 1255 (1989), and are therefore unenforceable. We affirm.

holding

YES

1. *Background.* Viewed most favorably to DBRC, the non-moving party, the facts are as follows. The predecessor of DBRC was established in 1971 as a law firm specializing in patent, trademark, and copyright law. During the relevant period, the firm was organized pursuant to the agreement, which had been drafted in 1978 and subsequently amended several times. The agreement provides that, for compensation purposes, partners receive different levels of credit for work performed for the firm's clients. A partner receives credit for 100% of billings for clients "credited" to that partner, that is, clients whom the partner brought to the firm, even if other partners later obtain new work from the clients. A partner is credited for 90% of billings for noncredited clients, that is, clients attributed to another DBRC partner, with the remaining 10% credit going to the originating partner.

Paragraph 5A of the agreement provides that when a partner retires "from the practice of patent, trademark and/or copyright law" or on the partner's death, the remaining partners "or any individual partner practicing alone or with another firm" must pay to the partner or the partner's estate 10.5% per cent of billings for the retired or deceased partner's credited clients. Paragraph 5B obligates any partner who withdraws from DBRC to pay to a remaining DBRC partner (or the partner's estate) 15% of billings for each noncredited client for whom the departing partner performed work after withdrawing from DBRC. The required payments were to be made for a period of four years after the former partner's withdrawal from DBRC.

Eisenstein became a partner at DBRC in 1989. Resnick became a partner at DBRC in 1995. Both men executed amendments to the agreement that ratified the terms and conditions of the agreement. In 1999, Eisenstein and Resnick left DBRC to accept positions as partners in the firm Peabody & Brown, a predecessor firm to Nixon Peabody, LLP. At Nixon Peabody they both performed legal work for certain present and former clients of DBRC.

In May, 2001, Eisenstein and Resnick filed their complaint in the Superior Court against the DBRC entities ... seeking an accounting and the payment of amounts allegedly due to them pursuant to the agreement for their share of profits, personal property, and a return of their capital contribution. [Defendants counterclaimed for breach of contract and breach of fiduciary duty, among other claims. Various other parties, including Nixon Peabody, joined the case. Plaintiffs moved for summary judgment, alleging that paragraphs 5A and 5B, on which the claims against them were grounded, were void and unenforceable. The trial court granted summary judgment, and DBRC appealed.]

2. *Discussion.* In their summary judgment motions, Eisenstein and Resnick and Nixon Peabody argued that the provisions of the agreement on which DBRC's counterclaims rely are unenforceable because they violate Mass. R. Prof. C. 5.6, 426 Mass. 1411 (1998).[13] We first discuss rule 5.6 and then turn to a discussion of the merits.

a. *Rule 5.6.* Rule 5.6 provides in pertinent part: "A lawyer shall not participate in offering or making . . . a partnership . . . agreement that restricts the right of a lawyer to practice after termination of the relationship, except an agreement concerning benefits upon retirement. . . . "

Rule 5.6 exists to protect the strong interests clients have in being able to choose freely the counsel they determine will best represent their interests. The rule furthers the client's right freely to select counsel by prohibiting attorneys from engaging in certain practices that effectively shrink the pool of qualified attorneys from which clients may choose. See *Pettingell v. Morrison, Mahoney & Miller,* 426 Mass. 253, 257, 687 N.E.2d 1237 (1997) (rule safeguards interests of clients by providing "the fullest possible freedom of choice to clients" in selecting counsel). See also *id.* at 255, 687 N.E.2d 1237 (rule designed primarily to protect "the interests of clients, not the interrelationship of the partners and former partners as such"). As we explained in *Meehan* and *Pettingell,* the "strong public interest in allowing clients to retain counsel of their choice outweighs any professional benefits derived from" provisions that restrict "the right of a lawyer to practice law after the termination of a relationship created by the agreement." Thus, in *Pettingell,* we voided provisions of a partnership agreement that required a partner to forfeit payments to which he otherwise would be entitled had he not withdrawn from, and then competed with, his former firm because an "enforceable forfeiture-for-competition clause would tend to discourage a lawyer who leaves a firm from competing with it," which "in turn would tend to restrict a client or potential client's choice of counsel."[14]

13. Rule 5.6 of the Massachusetts Rules of Professional Conduct, 426 Mass. 1411 (1998), is substantively identical to the predecessor rule it replaced, S.J.C. Rule 3:07, Canon 2, DR 2–108(A), 382 Mass. 773 (1981).

14. We recognize a limited exception to the general policy in favor of client choice where the actions of a former partner would jeopardize a firm's legitimate interest in survival, thus shrinking the available market of attorneys. See *Pettingell, supra* at 258, 687 N.E.2d 1237. Thus, we have declined to adopt "a per se rule against forfeiture provisions." We also reasoned, however, that a contractual limitation on a former partner's right to practice law after withdrawing from the partnership "would be more difficult to justify if it applied to a withdrawing partner who competes but not to all withdrawing partners."

The scope of rule 5.6 is not limited to agreements that directly penalize a withdrawing attorney for competing by denying that attorney compensation already earned while at the firm. See *id.* ("Courts generally view a substantial penalty for competing as a restriction on the right of the withdrawing partner to practice, even though the agreement does not explicitly bar the withdrawing lawyer from competing with the former firm"). The "broad prophylactic object" of rule 5.6, *id.* at 257, 687 N.E.2d 1237, requires close judicial scrutiny of any partnership provision that imposes financial disincentives on attorneys who leave a firm and then compete with it. We turn now to a review of the contractual provisions at issue.

b. *Partnership agreement.* Here, paragraphs 5A and 5B of the agreement are unenforceable because they erect obvious economic disincentives to competition that cannot reasonably be justified by any legitimate interest DBRC had in its own survival. See note 14, *supra.* Under these paragraphs, the economic disincentives imposed on withdrawing counsel and the attorneys with whom they subsequently affiliate are manifold. Both provisions exact a higher percentage of noncredited client billings from withdrawing partners than from remaining partners for the same work for the same clients. Both provisions reach all fees a withdrawing partner's new firm receives from DBRC clients, even if the new firm had a prior relationship with the client. Finally, the disputed provisions apply to fees for work performed by any partner or associate of the new firm, and regardless whether the client's choice of the new firm had any relation to the actions of the withdrawing partner.

In light of the fact that DBRC's practice concentrated solely on intellectual property matters and that their clients necessarily had to look elsewhere to meet other legal needs, paragraphs 5A and 5B are especially punitive and anticompetitive. Enforcing paragraphs 5A and 5B would provide a windfall to DBRC by channeling fees to the firm for work it would not have, and could not have, undertaken. More importantly, if enforced, these provisions would provide clear disincentives for former DBRC partners to provide legal services to current or former DBRC clients, even where those clients have determined that their own interests would best be served by such representation. A withdrawing partner who retains only 85% or 89.5% of the billings from Client A, because of the need to share fees with DBRC or one of its retired partners, versus 100% of the billings from Client B, likely would pursue Client B more aggressively than Client A, all else being equal, and notwithstanding Client A's preferences. In some circumstances the new firm with which a withdrawing partner becomes associated may not permit representation of a client if the firm is to retain only 85% or 89.5% of the billings, notwithstanding the client's preferences. Moreover, paragraph 5A discourages a departing partner from accepting the former clients of a retired partner, who by definition is no longer available to represent them, even though the clients are in need of new counsel.

While we agree with DBRC that paragraphs 5A and 5B of the agreement differ from the provisions we rejected in *Meehan* and *Pettingell*, the artificial limitations that these provisions place on the market of available attorneys are as evident here as in the earlier cases. If enforced, the disputed provisions "would tend to discourage a lawyer who leaves [DBRC] from competing with it. This in turn would tend to restrict a client or potential client's choice of counsel." Because the "law should provide the fullest possible freedom of choice to clients," we conclude that paragraphs 5A and 5B violate rule 5.6 and are unenforceable against Eisenstein and Resnick. . . . [19]

3. *Conclusion.* For the reasons stated above, we affirm the grant of summary judgments in favor of Eisenstein, Resnick, and Nixon Peabody. *So ordered.*

Notes

1. Model Rule 5.6(a)'s prohibition on agreements that restrict the right of a lawyer to practice after leaving a firm is also reflected in Cal. Rule 1–500 and N.Y. DR 2–108. Such agreements are often critiqued not in disciplinary cases, however, but rather in civil cases in which one party seeks to enforce such an agreement (or to have the court hold such an agreement unenforceable). Restatement § 13, comment *a*.

2. The comment to Model Rule 5.6 explains that an agreement restricting the right of a lawyer to practice after leaving a firm not only limits that lawyer's "professional autonomy but also limits the freedom of clients to choose a lawyer." MR 5.6, comment [1]. Is this really a rule protecting client choice, or is it about protecting the right of lawyers to earn a living? Can the two be separated?

3. Would enforcement of the kind of agreement at issue in *Eisenstein* make it harder for lawyers to move from one firm to another? What, if anything, would be wrong with that?

4. Most courts have no trouble striking down restrictive clauses such as those in *Eisenstein*. See, e.g., *Stevens v. Rooks Pitts and Poust,*

---

19. We reject DBRC's argument that paragraph 5A is permissible as "an agreement concerning benefits upon retirement." Mass. R. Prof. C. 5.6(a). The rule's exception allows an agreement restricting the right of a retiring attorney to practice in exchange for that attorney's receipt of retirement benefits. The exception does not permit an agreement that provides benefits to a retired attorney that also restricts the right of an attorney who has not retired to practice, which is what paragraph 5A does. Moreover, because paragraph 5A is unenforceable against Eisenstein and Resnick, it is immaterial whether Sewall P. Bronstein, P.C., qualifies as a retired partner for purposes of that paragraph, a status the parties dispute.

[handwritten: striking down these provisions cases]

[handwritten: 1997 case]

289 Ill.App.3d 991, 682 N.E.2d 1125, 225 Ill.Dec. 48 (1997) (partnership agreement required departing lawyer to give up compensation if he competed with the firm in particular geographical area, for a period of one year); *Jacob v. Norris, McLaughlin & Marcus*, 128 N.J. 10, 607 A.2d 142 (1992) (agreement barred compensation to departing partners who rendered services to clients of the firm within one year of their termination date). Might a more carefully-drafted agreement fare better? In *Anderson, McPharlin & Connors v. Yee*, 135 Cal.App.4th 129, 37 Cal. Rptr.3d 627 (2005), the court enforced a provision in a firm's partnership agreement in which the partner "acknowledged that the firm had invested a substantial amount of money in generating business and that the firm would lose money if he left and took clients with him, and agreed that if he did leave and take clients he would make payments to the firm" of 25 percent of revenues attributable to those clients over a two-year period after his departure. The court said that "there is nothing unreasonable or onerous" about such a clause. Rather inexplicably, neither party raised the rule prohibiting restrictions on practice and the court did not discuss it. Should the departing lawyer have raised that rule?

[handwritten: case where allowed careful wording]

5. Could a firm enforce an agreement in which the firm agrees to pay severance compensation to a departing associate in return for the associate's promise not to steal any of the firm's clients for two years? See R.I. Supreme Ct. Ethics Advisory Panel, Op. 2003–07 (2003) (no, it would violate Rule 5.6).

[handwritten: check source]

2. A Lawyer's Duties to the Firm

PRINCE, YEATES & GELDZAHLER v. YOUNG

Supreme Court of Utah, 2004.
94 P.3d 179.

WILKINS, Justice. . . .

In April 1995, Prince Yeates hired Young as an associate attorney. Previously, Young had spent the majority of his twelve-year legal career as general counsel for Rocky Mountain Helicopters, where he acquired considerable experience in helicopter crash litigation. Prior to joining Prince Yeates, Young met with John Ashton, the firm's then-president, to discuss compensation. Under the terms of his original employment agreement, which was never reduced to writing, Young accepted a starting salary of $70,000 per year. During their discussions, Ashton also indicated to Young that the firm would evaluate his performance after the first year and that, as a general rule, attorneys at Prince Yeates typically received increased compensation based on performance and positive results. In addition, with respect to becoming a shareholder, Ashton told Young that, depending upon his performance, the usual partnership track for a lateral hire with Young's experience ranged from two to three years.

In 1996, Young agreed to represent Charles Krause, who had sustained serious injuries in a helicopter crash, in a personal injury action in Texas. At approximately the same time, Young also undertook the representation of Mountain West Helicopters, the owner of the helicopter involved in Krause's accident, in a related lawsuit filed in federal court in Utah. As well as being the originating attorney, Young was the only lawyer at Prince Yeates who performed any work on either case.

For the next two years, Young spent considerable time on these two contingent fee cases, which resulted in lower collections and higher work-in-process figures compared to other Prince Yeates attorneys. As a result, some members of the firm began to question Young's overall profitability and readiness to become a shareholder. In September 1998, perhaps sensing this tension, Young inquired as to how the contingent fee in the Krause case (assuming a successful outcome) would be divided between himself and Prince Yeates. The firm's Board of Directors ("the Board") responded by assigning Ashton and John Chindlund, Prince Yeates' then-president, to explore the possibility of reaching an agreement with Young on the Krause fee.... Ultimately, the two parties reached a tentative verbal agreement under which Young would take one-third of the Krause fee, with the remaining two-thirds going to the firm. On May 5, 1999, Chindlund memorialized this proposal in writing and requested that Young sign it to acknowledge his acceptance. Young did not sign.

On June 14, 1999, Young learned that the Krause case had settled three days earlier at a mediation in Texas, which he did not attend, and that the contingent fee recovery would be nearly $650,000. The following day, June 15, without disclosing his knowledge of the settlement to his employer, Young made a counteroffer to the firm's May 5 proposal. In his counteroffer, Young agreed to divide the Krause fee one-third to himself and two-thirds to the firm, provided Prince Yeates made him a shareholder, allowed him a voice in that year's bonus distribution, and guaranteed an increased salary for the next two years. According to Young, over the course of their numerous meetings, Ashton and Chindlund promised him that the firm would fulfill these additional conditions upon the successful resolution of the Krause case. Ashton and Chindlund denied making such promises, and the firm did not respond to Young's proposal. Finally, on July 2, Young wrote a memo to the Board, informing them that he would leave Prince Yeates in two weeks if an agreement could not be reached on his counteroffer. The firm accepted Young's resignation on July 7.

After his departure, Prince Yeates learned that Young had represented certain clients during 1998 and 1999 without disclosing the representation to the firm, while simultaneously using firm resources and filing pleadings in the firm's name in connection with these matters. In addition, Young retained all fees derived from these cases for himself. Prince Yeates then filed suit against Young for breach of fiduciary duty, and Young counter-claimed alleging, among other causes of action, breach of oral contract. The firm twice moved for summary judgment on Young's counterclaim, and the district court denied both motions with respect to the contract claims. Prince Yeates and Young also each moved for partial summary judgment on the breach of fiduciary duty claim. The district court denied the firm's motion, granted Young's, and the case proceeded to trial.

[At trial, the jury found in Young's favor on the breach of contract counterclaim and awarded him $280,000. On appeal, Prince Yeates argues that the trial judge should have granted its summary judgment motions on Young's breach of contract coun-terclaim, and on its breach of fiduciary duty claim.] Because the case is fully resolved by our analysis of the district court's sum-mary judgment rulings, we do not address the other issues raised.

ANALYSIS

[First, as a matter of law, Prince Yeats was entitled to summary judgment on Young's breach of contract counterclaim, since no express contract was created under which Prince Yeats promised Young additional compensation based on his recovery of the Krause fee.]

Prince Yeates next argues that Young breached his fiduciary duty of loyalty—specifically, a duty of non-competition—when he represented clients in the firm's name without disclosing the representation to the firm, expended firm resources and filed pleadings in the firm's name in connection with these matters, and retained all fees derived from these cases for himself. The district court denied Prince Yeates' motion for partial summary judgment on the issue of liability and granted Young's cross-motion, reasoning that, as a mere employee, he owed no fiduciary duty of non-competition to the firm. Once more, we disagree.

As a general matter, the second Restatement of Agency pro-vides that "[u]nless otherwise agreed, an agent is subject to a duty not to compete with the principal concerning the subject matter of his agency." *Restatement (Second) of Agency* § 393 (1958). . . . Although this court has not directly addressed the issue of wheth-er "mere employees" owe their employers a fiduciary duty of non-competition, other jurisdictions have. In *Fryetech, Inc. v. Harris*, the defendants argued that the fiduciary duties of good faith and loyalty did not apply to "mere employees." 46 F.Supp.2d 1144, 1152 (D.Kan.1999). The court rejected this contention, emphasiz-ing that "[w]hile most of the cases which have addressed the fiduciary responsibilities of agents ... have involved corporate directors or officers, there is no basis for concluding these are the only types of agents subject to fiduciary duties." *Id.* Rather, "the cases speak of the duties of agents without respect to their exact status." *Id.; see also Bessman v. Bessman,* 214 Kan. 510, 520 P.2d 1210, 1217 (1974) ("An agent or employee of another is prohibited from acting in any manner inconsistent with his agency or trust and is at all times bound to exercise the utmost good faith and loyalty in the performance of his duties." (internal quotations omitted)); *Chernow v. Reyes,* 239 N.J.Super. 201, 570 A.2d 1282, 1283, 1284 (Ct.App.Div.1990) (holding that even though an employee's oral employment contract did not specifically prohibit competition, "[a]n employee owes a duty of loyalty to the employer and must not, while employed, act contrary to the employer's interest," which necessarily includes "a duty not to compete with the employer's business") . . . .

In the relationship of a lawyer and his or her employer, there does exist a duty of honest and ethical behavior. Because of the privilege granted to engage in the practice of law, we impose upon members of our bar a fiduciary duty that encompasses the obligation to not compete with their employer, which we define as any law firm or legal services provider who may employ them in a legal capacity, without the employer's prior knowledge and agreement.

We therefore hold, as a matter of law, that the district court erred in denying Prince Yeates' motion for partial summary judgment on its breach of fiduciary duty claim and in granting Young's cross-motion. To hold otherwise would imply that attorneys are free to join law firms, derive benefits from that association, and essentially operate as sole practitioners while simultaneously receiving a salary and using firm resources for their independent legal activities. If Young was unhappy at Prince Yeates, he was free, as an at-will employee, to leave at any time and presumably take those clients who wished to follow him. Merely because he was afraid that his interest in the Krause fee would be jeopardized does not justify his non-disclosure of representation and subsequent retention of fees. He had a higher duty to Prince Yeates than that. With that in mind, we now turn to the question of the firm's remedy.

REMEDY

Regarding an appropriate remedy, Prince Yeates urges us to require the forfeiture of both Young's share of the Krause fee (determined by the jury to be $280,000) and all compensation paid by the firm to Young from January 26, 1998 through July 7, 1999—the time period during which Young breached his fiduciary duty of non-competition. . . . Although we acknowledge that total forfeiture may be proper in certain circumstances, we decline to implement such a harsh remedy in this case. Given that the number of undisclosed clients and the amount of retained fees were comparatively small, Young's conduct, while unquestionably giving rise to liability, does not warrant so punitive a sanction. Moreover, with our reversal today of the summary judgment rulings already described, Young has no share of the Krause fee to forfeit, due in no small part to Young's own lack of honesty and candor with Prince Yeates when the Krause case was settled. However, we do hold that the appropriate remedy for Young's breach of fiduciary duty is the disgorgement of the fees charged and collected by Young while employed at the firm but not previously paid over to Prince Yeates. As such, we remand this issue to the district court, with instructions to determine the amount of those fees and order their payment to the firm forthwith. . . .

Notes

1.   As the case makes clear, it is not proper for a lawyer in a firm to compete with the firm while the lawyer is still employed, such as by working for clients "on the side." See also *Rogers v. Mississippi Bar*, 731 So.2d 1158 (Miss. 1999) (upholding sanctions against a partner for secretly representing clients and keeping fees for himself). We saw in the preceding subsection that a firm cannot restrict a departing lawyer from competing with the firm once he or she has left. But this leaves a middle ground: what duties does a lawyer owe to the firm with respect to how the lawyer leaves, or how the lawyer begins to compete upon departure?

A new ethics rule in Florida, Rule 4–5.8 (2005), forbids a lawyer who is leaving a firm from contacting clients about the departure, unless the lawyer has engaged in good faith negotiations with the firm to send a joint notice to those clients. If the departing lawyer and the firm have not agreed on a joint notice, the lawyer is allowed to contact clients, but any such notice must make clear that it is each client's choice whether to change firms, and must accurately inform them about any potential liability for legal fees and costs that have not been paid to their existing firm. Cf. ABA Formal Ethics Op. 99–414 (1999) (while joint notice of a lawyer's departure from a firm is preferable, a lawyer may unilaterally notify current clients of an impending departure, "as long as the lawyer also advises the client of the client's right to choose counsel and does not disparage her law firm or engage in conduct that involves dishonesty, fraud, deceit, or misrepresentation"). Should other states follow Florida's lead?

2.   In *Dowd and Dowd, Ltd. v. Gleason*, 352 Ill.App.3d 365, 816 N.E.2d 754, 287 Ill.Dec. 787 (2004), a law firm successfully sued departing lawyers for breach of fiduciary duty and interference with prospective economic advantage. The facts were extreme. The departing partners did not tell their firm that they were planning to leave, but let their clients know that they were going to form another firm and actively solicited them. The departing partners accepted large bonuses for themselves just before they left the firm, and after they had begun discussing

forming a new firm. They solicited other attorneys and employees of the firm to join their new firm. They used some confidential information of existing clients, including the firm's largest single client, in preparation for soliciting them to come over to the new firm. The court ordered the departing partners to forfeit their bonuses and their salary and compensation earned during the time they were in the process of starting their new firm. The court also awarded the law firm punitive damages of $200,000 since the departing partners' actions were both "secretive and malicious."

3. In *Reeves v. Hanlon*, 33 Cal.4th 1140, 95 P.3d 513, 17 Cal. Rptr.3d 289 (2004), the court held that a law firm could recover damages for intentional interference with contractual relations against former lawyers who lured away several of the firm's employees and clients. The court said that while it is ordinarily not tortious to hire someone else's employees for your business, it does become tortious when "unfair methods" are used; here, the court found, the lawyers had engaged in "unlawful and unethical conduct in mounting a campaign to deliberately disrupt the former firm's business."

4. Wrongful actions in leaving a firm may give rise to disciplinary sanction and even criminal liability. In *Attorney Grievance Com'n of Maryland v. Potter*, 380 Md. 128, 844 A.2d 367 (2004), a departing associate was found to have committed a criminal act that reflected adversely on the lawyer's honesty, trustworthiness or fitness as a lawyer, in violation of Rule 8.4(b), by willfully deleting client files from the law firm's computers prior to leaving the firm. He took the paper files with him in hopes of luring the clients away; this was found to violate Rules 8.4 (c) and (d).

Chapter 5

ATTORNEYS' FEES

§ 1. TYPES OF FEES AND BASIC RESTRICTIONS

Lawyers usually get paid for their services in one of four ways: (1) an hourly fee, computed by multiplying an hourly rate times the amount of time (often computed to the quarter-hour or tenth of an hour) actually expended to perform a particular job; (2) a flat fee (for example, charging $250 to prepare a will); (3) a contingent fee, meaning a fee that is earned at all only if a favorable outcome is obtained; or (4) a proportional fee, computed as a percentage of the value of a particular transaction, for example.

Both the type of fees and the amount of those fees are largely a matter of contract. Thus a lawyer and client may contract for fees that combine characteristics of more than one of the types listed above. Indeed, the classic "contingent fee" in plaintiffs' personal injury practice is actually a combination of a contingent and a proportional fee: the lawyer gets paid only if the case is successful, then the amount of fees is determined by multiplying the amount of recovery times a particular percentage, usually between 25 and 50 percent. Or the lawyer and client may agree on an entirely different kind of fee arrangement, such as payment in stock in a client's start-up company. See ABA Formal Op. 00–418 (2000) (authorizing such fee arrangements if done in compliance with ethics rules).

Fee arrangements are *largely* a matter of contract, but not *completely*. Ethics rules and other law place restrictions on both the amount of fees that may be collected, and, in certain contexts, the types of fees that can be sought or agreed upon. Model Rule 1.5 is the key rule, followed in most states. It provides that any fee must be "reasonable." In its latest iteration, the rule states that a lawyer shall not "make an agreement for, charge, or collect an unreasonable fee or an unreasonable amount for expenses." MR 1.5(a). Eight factors are then listed as relevant to a determination of reasonableness. See *id*. The Model Code is quite similar, al-

311

though it uses a different operative term. It provides that a lawyer
"shall not enter into an agreement for, charge, or collect an illegal
or clearly excessive fee." DR 2–106(A). That rule then lists eight
factors that are relevant to a finding that a fee is "clearly
excessive." DR 2–106(B). These factors are identical to those used
in the Model Rules. California's operative term is different still:
Cal. Rule 4–200(A) prohibits a lawyer from entering into an
agreement for, charging or collecting "an illegal or unconscionable
fee." That rule then lists eleven factors to be considered in
determining the "conscionability of a fee." Cal. Rule 4–200(B).
One important factor in California's list but not explicitly mentioned in either the Model Rules or the Model Code is "the
relative sophistication of the member and the client." Cal. Rule 4–
200(B)(2). Do you think that factor is irrelevant in any other
state?

The Restatement explains that the ethics rules' multiple
factors respond primarily to three questions: (1) at the time the
contract for fees was entered into, was the client given a "free and
informed choice" to accept or reject it?; (2) was the agreed-upon
fee "within the range commonly charged by other lawyers in
similar representations?"; and (3) was there some change in
circumstances that rendered the agreement unreasonable, even if
it was reasonable when entered into? Restatement § 34, comment
c. This final question perhaps deserves some explanation. While
the reasonableness of a fee agreement is usually judged by the
circumstances that existed at the time of contracting, there may
be later circumstances that render the actual fee unreasonable.
For example, if a lawyer and client agree to an hourly fee but the
lawyer charges an excessive number of hours, the actual fee will
not be reasonable. See, e.g., *In re Fordham*, reprinted in section 2
below.

Although discipline for charging an unreasonable fee is one
possible remedy, most fee disputes are not fought out in disciplinary proceedings. Rather, they arise in litigation between lawyer
and client, or in fee-arbitration proceedings. If a court determines
that a lawyer's fee is excessive, the lawyer will be unable to collect
that fee, even if an otherwise-valid contract exists for its payment.
As the Restatement explains, "Courts are concerned to protect
clients, particularly those who are unsophisticated in matters of
lawyers' compensation, when a lawyer has overreached." Restatement § 34, comment b. Because clients typically have little information about fees charged by lawyers and lack bargaining power,
they must place trust in lawyers not to overreach. Thus "lawyers
owe their clients greater duties than are owed under the general
law of contracts." *Id.*

Contingent fees. All types of fees must be "reasonable," or
"not excessive," or "not unconscionable," depending on what
state you are in. But contingent fees raise distinct issues and are

therefore subject to another distinct layer of rules. For example, most states prohibit a lawyer's entering into, charging or collecting contingent fees in most domestic relations and criminal defense cases. See MR 1.5(d). Many state statutes also restrict the percentage that can be charged in certain kinds of cases. We see contingent fees in more detail in section 3 below.

Fees and conflicts of interest: Literary rights. As we will see in detail in the next chapter, conflicts of interest between a lawyer's personal interests and a client's interests are to be avoided whenever possible, and minimized when avoidance is not possible. Some fee agreements create such conflicts. This means that at times, because of the fee agreement, a lawyer will be unable to recommend a particular course of action freely, because the lawyer has other interests that would be damaged if the client chose that course of action. To some degree, almost all fee agreements create such a conflict of interest. For example, a lawyer working on an hourly basis has a personal financial stake (at least a short-term stake) in billing as many hours as possible. This interest may conflict with the client's interest in a swift resolution of the matter. A lawyer who has a contingent fee agreement with a client in which he is paid a higher percentage of the recovery if the case goes to trial has a financial interest in taking the case to trial, whereas the client may have an interest in fast settlement.

These kinds of conflicts are inherent, and largely tolerated by the system. See, e.g., MR 1.8(j)(2). Other kinds of conflicts are both more pronounced and less tolerated. One such conflict occurs when a lawyer takes, in lieu of a fee (or in lieu of a higher fee) an interest in the literary rights to the client's story, before the lawyer's work for the client is over. The Restatement takes the position that a lawyer is prohibited, before the representation has terminated, from making "an agreement giving the lawyer literary or media rights to a portrayal or account based in substantial part on information relating to the representation." Restatement § 36(3). The Model Rules and Model Code also prohibit such agreements. MR 1.8(d); DR 5–104(B). What kind of conflict of interest is spawned by such a fee arrangement? Is an absolute prohibition warranted? See Restatement § 36, comment *d*.

Litigation: Who pays? Grasping this country's rules on attorneys' fees requires an understanding of our system of paying for litigation. In most nations, the loser of a litigated case must pay the attorneys' fees of the winner. This is usually called the "English rule," although that label is misleading since the rule can be traced back to Roman law and has never been limited to England—indeed, most countries follow it. In the United States, by contrast, pursuant to the so-called "American rule," each party bears its own attorney's fees, win or lose. Our system removes a good deal of the risk of filing suit that exists in other countries. A plaintiff who loses a case in the United States will not have to reimburse the defendant for its attorneys' fees, as he would in most other countries, unless some exception to the rule applies.

There are some common-law exceptions to the American rule. For example, the "common fund" exception allows a fee recovery where a lawyer's work on behalf of a prevailing party has benefit-ted many others. See Charles W. Wolfram, Modern Legal Ethics § 16.6.2 (1986); *Blum v. Stenson*, 465 U.S. 886, 104 S.Ct. 1541, 79 L.Ed.2d 891 (1984) ("Under the 'common fund' doctrine, . . . a reasonable fee is based on a percentage of the fund bestowed on the class."). A related exception, sometimes codified in the states, is often called the "private attorney general" exception, allowing for recovery of fees when a party's litigation success has resulted in the enforcement of an important right affecting the public interest. See, e.g., Cal. Code Civ. Proc. § 1021.5 (1993). Some states allow fee recoveries in third-party tort litigation based on breach of fiduciary duty; in legal malpractice cases; and in cases where an executor or trustee has been proven guilty of undue influence. See, e.g., *In re Trust Created March 31, 1992 (Niles)*, 176 N.J. 282, 823 A.2d 1 (2003). Fees may also be awarded to a party in litigation whose opponent has litigated in bad faith or has made frivolous claims, a rule fully explored in Chapter 7.

By far the most important exceptions to the American rule, however, are fee-shifting statutes. There are over 100 federal statutes that provide for fee-shifting, and close to 2,000 state statutes that do the same. Most of these statutes provide for "one-way" shifting. That means that a prevailing plaintiff in an action based on the particular statute is entitled to have its reasonable attorneys' fees paid by the losing defendant, but that a winning defendant has no such entitlement. The statute of greatest import (and the model for most others) is the Civil Rights Attorney's Fees Act of 1976, 42 U.S.C. § 1988. Fee-shifting statutes are examined in more detail in section 4 below.

Fee agreements. Model Rule 1.5 requires that a contingent fee agreement be embodied in writing, but does not place a writing requirement on other kinds of fees. MR 1.5(b) & (c). Clearly, however, the best practice is to put all fee agreements in writing so that there is no misunderstanding between lawyer and client. Failing to communicate clearly a fee agreement may make the fee unenforceable, and even result in discipline. See, e.g., *In re Disciplinary Proceedings Against Grover*, 196 Wis.2d 678, 539 N.W.2d 448 (1995). Under normal circumstances the fee agree-ment will be part of a more general engagement letter or reten-tion agreement, which explicitly explains not only fees but also the scope of representation, staffing (who will do what), and any ethical issues that are relevant, such as waivers of conflicts of interest. See Jeffrey M. Smith and Ronald E. Mallen, Preventing Legal Malpractice § 2.9 (1989). The Model Rules require that the scope of representation, the basis of the fee, and the expenses for which the client will be responsible "shall be communicated to the client, preferably in writing, before or within a reasonable time after commencing the representation," unless the lawyer has represented the client before and the fee agreement is unchanged. MR 1.5(b). (The ABA's Ethics 2000 Commission recommended the adoption of a requirement that all fee agreements be in writing, but the House of Delegates rejected that proposal.)

Engagement retainer fees and other "non-refundable" fees. A kind of fee that sometimes comes under particular scrutiny is the "engagement retainer fee," that is, a non-refundable payment by a client to a lawyer simply to guarantee that the lawyer will be available to perform services if asked. Such a fee is separate from any payment for actual work done. The reasonableness of such a fee is judged primarily by whether the amount "bears a reasonable relationship to the income the lawyer sacrifices or expense the lawyer incurs by accepting it, including such costs as turning away other clients, ... hiring new associates, ... and the like." Restatement § 34, comment *e*. Where the client is sophisticated and experienced in paying such retainers, they will almost always be upheld as reasonable. For example, in *Raymark Industries, Inc. v. Butera, Beausang, Cohen & Brennan*, 193 F.3d 210 (3d Cir. 1999), the corporate client retained a number of firms by paying them $1 million each. Ten weeks into the representation, the Butera firm and the client became embroiled in a heated dispute about the need to conduct further investigation before filing a lawsuit (the firm wanted more time to investigate). The client demanded its $1 million back. The court held that the money did not have to be returned, pointing to the client's sophistication and the lack of any wrongdoing on the firm's part.

Lawyers may be seen to have overreached, however, when they charge inexperienced and unsophisticated clients any kind of purportedly non-refundable fee before legal work is done. See, e.g., *In re Cooperman*, 83 N.Y.2d 465, 611 N.Y.S.2d 465, 633 N.E.2d 1069 (1994) (imposing two-year suspension on a lawyer who told his client that no part of a retainer paid in advance would be returned once he entered an appearance in the case). Courts have also held that a fee that represents an advance on future fees (as opposed to a true engagement retainer) can never be "non-refundable." See, e.g., *In re Kendall*, 804 N.E.2d 1152 (Ind. 2004); see also MR 1.5, comment [4] ("A lawyer may require advance payment of a fee, but is obliged to return any unused portion."). How would a lawyer's demand for a large non-refundable fee to be paid "up front" possibly impinge on a client's rights? See MR 1.16(a)(3); DR 1–110(B)(4).

Enforcing fee agreements. Most states allow a lawyer to enforce liens to collect unpaid fees. State statutes frequently provide for two kinds of liens: (1) the charging lien, which allows a lawyer to claim against the proceeds of a settlement or judgment in the amount of unpaid fees; and (2) the retaining lien, which allows a lawyer to retain client documents prepared by the lawyer until fees are paid. The Restatement takes the position that a lawyer and client may enter into a contract granting the lawyer a lien on the proceeds of the representation to secure payment of fees and other expenses, unless prohibited by other law. Restatement § 43(2). Typically, charging liens must meet the requirements of the rules on business transactions with clients. See, e.g., *Fletcher v. Davis*, 33 Cal.4th 61, 90 P.3d 1216, 14 Cal.Rptr.3d 58 (2004) (holding that a lawyer who failed to comply with such rules could not enforce a charging lien); ABA Formal Op. 02–427 (2002) (allowing such liens as long as they comply with MR 1.8 on entering into business transactions with clients).

Lawyers who abuse the charging lien process do so at their peril. See, e.g., *In re Adkins*, 277 Ga. 757, 596 S.E.2d 1 (2004) (lawyer disbarred for, among other things, filing numerous liens for amounts that exceeded what the lawyer was owed). And a lawyer who has engaged in serious misconduct in representing a client may not be able to enforce a lien to get fees in that matter. See *Kourouvacilis v. American Fed'n of State, County & Mun. Employees*, 65 Mass.App.Ct. 521, 841 N.E.2d 1273 (2006).

No rule or law prohibits a lawyer from suing a client for an unpaid fee, although suing for fees is a good way to invite a counter-suit for legal malpractice. The fee agreement between lawyer and client may provide for arbitration of any fee disputes, and such provisions are generally enforceable. See ABA Formal Op. 02–425 (2002) (approving such contracts, but stressing that lawyers must give clients sufficient information under MR 1.4(b) to advise the client of the pros and cons of such a provision). Further, a growing number of states have set up alternative dispute resolution processes for clients to utilize to resolve fee disputes, even where the contract itself is silent on such procedures. According to the ABA's Standing Committee on Client Protection, twelve states had mandatory fee arbitration rules as of April, 2006. New York and California's fee arbitration plans are quite similar to one another. See N.Y. Comp. Codes R. & Regs., tit. 22 § 137; Cal. Bus. & Prof. Code §§ 6200–6203. Both states provide that arbitration of fee disputes, unless otherwise agreed to by contract, is voluntary for the client and mandatory for the lawyer, at the client's request. *Id.* This means that the client can elect an ADR process, but will not be forced into it involuntarily.

Fees and the criminal defense bar. The federal Money Laundering Act of 1986 bars monetary transactions involving "criminally derived property." A "safe harbor" provision of that law, 18 U.S.C. § 1957, appears to allow criminal defendants to pay their attorneys' fees, as necessary to preserve the right to counsel. But in *United States v. Monsanto*, 491 U.S. 600, 109 S.Ct. 2657, 105 L.Ed.2d 512 (1989) and *Caplin & Drysdale v. United States*,

491 U.S. 617, 109 S.Ct. 2667, 105 L.Ed.2d 528 (1989), the Supreme Court held that criminal defendants had no right to pay their lawyers with "tainted money." This means that criminal defense lawyers who accept money (often cash) from their clients may be targeted for prosecution for money laundering. In 2001, a Florida lawyer pleaded guilty to such charges relating to fees he accepted from a client accused of drug offenses. *See* David E. Rovella, *Going from Bad to Worse: Defense Bar Fears Jail Over Tainted Fees*, Nat'l L.J., Mar. 11, 2002, at A1, A9. While lawyers who have no reason to know the money is tainted should not be at risk, prosecutors are reportedly arguing that a lawyer's "deliberate ignorance" of the source of fees is sufficient for a conviction. *Id.* Do you think a criminal defense lawyer who receives $50,000 in cash as payment of fees should know that the money is criminally derived? Should such a payment subject the lawyer to criminal prosecution?

The United States Treasury Department's Office of Foreign Assets Control prohibits lawyers from accepting fees from persons or entities suspected of aiding terrorists or being drug traffickers, without first obtaining a license from the Office. 31 C.F.R. Ch. 5. The Office maintains a list of such persons and entities. Failure to comply with these regulations can subject a lawyer to fines of up to $1 million for unintentional violations, and fines of up to $10 million and imprisonment from 10 to 30 years for willful violations. The list, by all accounts, is growing.

§ 2. HOURLY FEES

IN THE MATTER OF FORDHAM

Supreme Judicial Court of Massachusetts, 1996.
423 Mass. 481, 668 N.E.2d 816.

O'CONNOR, Justice.

This is an appeal from the Board of Bar Overseers' (board's) dismissal of a petition for discipline filed by bar counsel against attorney Laurence S. Fordham. On March 11, 1992, bar counsel served Fordham with a petition for discipline alleging that Fordham had charged a clearly excessive fee in violation of S.J.C. Rule 3:07, DR 2–106, as appearing in 382 Mass. 772 (1981), for defending Timothy Clark (Timothy) in the District Court against a charge that he operated a motor vehicle while under the influence of intoxicating liquor (OUI) and against other related charges. [The full board, reviewing the findings of the board's hearing committee, voted to dismiss the petition for discipline, and bar counsel appealed to county court. That court denied Fordham's motion to dismiss. This appeal followed.]

We summarize the hearing committee's findings. On March 4, 1989, the Acton police department arrested Timothy, then twenty-one years old, and charged him with OUI, operating a motor vehicle after suspension, speeding, and operating an unregistered motor vehicle. At the time of the arrest, the police discovered a partially full quart of vodka in the vehicle. After failing a field sobriety test, Timothy was taken to the Acton police station where he submitted to two breathalyzer tests which registered .10 and .12 respectively.

Subsequent to Timothy's arraignment, he and his father, Laurence Clark (Clark) consulted with three lawyers, who offered to represent Timothy for fees between $3,000 and $10,000. Shortly after the arrest, Clark went to Fordham's home to service an alarm system which he had installed several years before. While there, Clark discussed Timothy's arrest with Fordham's wife who invited Clark to discuss the case with Fordham. Fordham then met with Clark and Timothy.

At this meeting, Timothy described the incidents leading to his arrest and the charges against him. Fordham, whom the hearing committee described as a "very experienced senior trial attorney with impressive credentials," told Clark and Timothy that he had never represented a client in a driving while under the influence case or in any criminal matter, and he had never tried a case in the District Court. The hearing committee found that "Fordham explained that although he lacked experience in this area, he was a knowledgeable and hard-working attorney and that he believed he could competently represent Timothy. Fordham described himself as 'efficient and economic in the use of [his] time.' . . .

"Towards the end of the meeting, Fordham told the Clarks that he worked on [a] time charge basis and that he billed monthly. . . . In other words, Fordham would calculate the amount of hours he and others in the firm worked on a matter each month and multiply it by the respective hourly rates. He also told the Clarks that he would engage others in his firm to prepare the case. Clark had indicated that he would pay Timothy's legal fees." After the meeting, Clark hired Fordham to represent Timothy.

According to the hearing committee's findings, Fordham filed four pretrial motions on Timothy's behalf, two of which were allowed. One motion, entitled "Motion in Limine to Suppress Results of Breathalyzer Tests," was based on the theory that, although two breathalyzer tests were exactly .02 apart, they were not "within" .02 of one another as the regulations require. The hearing committee characterized the motion and its rationale as "a creative, if not novel, approach to suppression of breathalyzer results." Although the original trial date was June 20, 1989, the trial, which was before a judge without jury, was held on October

10 and October 19, 1989. The judge found Timothy not guilty of driving while under the influence. . . .

[Fordham sent bills to Clark in April through July, and in October and November, 1989.] The bills totaled $50,022.25, reflecting 227 hours of billed time, 153 hours of which were expended by Fordham and seventy-four of which were his associates' time. Clark did not pay the first two bills when they became due and expressed to Fordham his concern about their amount. Clark paid Fordham $10,000 on June 20, 1989. At that time, Fordham assured Clark that most of the work had been completed "other than taking [the case] to trial." Clark did not make any subsequent payments. . . .

Bar counsel and Fordham have stipulated that all the work billed by Fordham was actually done and that Fordham and his associates spent the time they claim to have spent. They also have stipulated that Fordham acted conscientiously, diligently, and in good faith in representing Timothy and in his billing in this case. . . .

The board dismissed bar counsel's petition for discipline against Fordham because it determined, relying in large part on the findings and recommendations of the hearing committee, that Fordham's fee was not clearly excessive. Pursuant to S.J.C. Rule 3:07, DR 2–106(B), "a fee is clearly excessive when, after a review of the facts, a lawyer of ordinary prudence, experienced in the area of the law involved, would be left with a definite and firm conviction that the fee is substantially in excess of a reasonable fee." The rule proceeds to list eight factors to be considered in ascertaining the reasonableness of the fee:

"(1) The time and labor required, the novelty and difficulty of the questions involved, and the skill requisite to perform the legal service properly.

"(2) The likelihood, if apparent to the client, that the acceptance of the particular employment will preclude other employment by the lawyer.

"(3) The fee customarily charged in the locality for similar legal services.

"(4) The amount involved and the results obtained.

"(5) The time limitations imposed by the client or by the circumstances.

"(6) The nature and length of the professional relationship with the client.

"(7) The experience, reputation, and ability of the lawyer or lawyers performing the services.

"(8) Whether the fee is fixed or contingent."

. . . [Upon] reviewing the hearing committee's and the board's analysis of the various factors, as appearing in DR 2–106(B), which are to be considered for a determination as to whether a fee is clearly excessive, . . . we are persuaded that the hearing committee's and the board's determinations that a clearly excessive fee was not charged are not warranted.

The first factor listed in DR 2–106(B) requires examining "[t]he time and labor required, the novelty and difficulty of the questions involved, and the skill requisite to perform the legal service properly." Although the hearing committee determined that Fordham "spent a large number of hours on [the] matter, in essence learning from scratch what others . . . already know," it "[did] not credit Bar Counsel's argument that Fordham violated DR 2–106 by spending too many hours." The hearing committee reasoned that even if the number of hours Fordham "spent [were] wholly out of proportion" to the number of hours that a lawyer with experience in the trying of OUI cases would require, the committee was not required to conclude that the fee based on time spent was "clearly excessive." It was enough, the hearing committee concluded, that Clark instructed Fordham to pursue the case to trial, Fordham did so zealously and, as stipulated, Fordham spent the hours he billed in good faith and diligence. We disagree.

Four witnesses testified before the hearing committee as experts on OUI cases. One of the experts, testifying on behalf of bar counsel, opined that "the amount of time spent in this case is clearly excessive." He testified that there were no unusual circumstances in the OUI charge against Timothy and that it was a "standard operating under the influence case." . . . The witness estimated that it would have been necessary, for thorough preparation of the case including the novel breathalyzer suppression argument, to have billed twenty to thirty hours for preparation, not including trial time.

A second expert, testifying on behalf of bar counsel, expressed his belief that the issues presented in this case were not particularly difficult, nor novel, and that "[t]he degree of skill required to defend a case such as this . . . was not that high." He did recognize, however, that the theory that Fordham utilized to suppress the breathalyzer tests was impressive and one of which he had previously never heard. Nonetheless, the witness concluded that "clearly there is no way that [he] could justify these kind of hours to do this kind of work." He estimated that an OUI case involving these types of issues would require sixteen hours of trial preparation and approximately fifteen hours of trial time. . . .

An expert called by Fordham testified that the facts of Timothy's case presented a challenge and that without the suppression of the breathalyzer test results it would have been "an almost impossible situation in terms of prevailing on the trier of fact."

He further stated that, based on the particulars in Timothy's case, he believed that Fordham's hours were not excessive and, in fact, he, the witness, would have spent a comparable amount of time. The witness later admitted, however, that within the past five years, the OUI cases which he had brought to trial required no more than a total of forty billed hours, which encompassed all preparation and court appearances. . . .

The fourth expert witness, called by Fordham, testified that she believed the case was "extremely tough" and that the breathalyzer suppression theory was novel. She testified that, although the time and labor consumed on the case was more than usual in defending an OUI charge, the hours were not excessive. They were not excessive, she explained, because the case was particularly difficult due to the "stakes [and] the evidence." She conceded, however, that legal issues in defending OUI charges are "pretty standard" and that the issues presented in this case were not unusual. . . . Finally, she stated that she thought she may have known of one person who might have spent close to one hundred hours on a difficult OUI case; she was not sure; but she had never heard of a fee in excess of $10,000 for a bench trial.

In considering whether a fee is "clearly excessive" within the meaning of S.J.C. Rule 3:07, DR 2–106(B), the first factor to be considered pursuant to that rule is "the novelty and difficulty of the questions involved, and the skill requisite to perform the legal service properly." DR 2–106(B)(1). . . . Based on the testimony of the four experts, the number of hours devoted to Timothy's OUI case by Fordham and his associates was substantially in excess of the hours that a prudent experienced lawyer would have spent. According to the evidence, the number of hours spent was several times the amount of time any of the witnesses had ever spent on a similar case. We are not unmindful of the novel and successful motion to suppress the breathalyzer test results, but that effort cannot justify a $50,000 fee in a type of case in which the usual fee is less than one-third of that amount.

The board determined that "[b]ecause [Fordham] had never tried an OUI case or appeared in the district court, [Fordham] spent over 200 hours preparing the case, in part to educate himself in the relevant substantive law and court procedures." Fordham's inexperience in criminal defense work and OUI cases in particular cannot justify the extraordinarily high fee. It cannot be that an inexperienced lawyer is entitled to charge three or four times as much as an experienced lawyer for the same service. A client "should not be expected to pay for the education of a lawyer when he spends excessive amounts of time on tasks which, with reasonable experience, become matters of routine." *Matter of the Estate of Larson*, 103 Wash.2d 517, 531, 694 P.2d 1051 (1985). . . .

DR 2–106(B) provides that the third factor to be considered in ascertaining the reasonableness of a fee is its comparability to "[t]he fee customarily charged in the locality for similar legal services." The hearing committee made no finding as to the comparability of Fordham's fee with the fees customarily charged in the locality for similar services. However, one of bar counsel's expert witnesses testified that he had never heard of a fee in excess of $15,000 to defend a first OUI charge, and the customary flat fee in an OUI case, including trial, "runs from $1,000 to $7,500." Bar counsel's other expert testified that he had never heard of a fee in excess of $10,000 for a bench trial. In his view, the customary charge for a case similar to Timothy's would vary between $1,500 and $5,000. One of Fordham's experts testified that she considered a $40,000 or $50,000 fee for defending an OUI charge "unusual and certainly higher by far than any I've ever seen before." The witness had never charged a fee of more than $3,500 for representing a client at a bench trial to defend a first offense OUI charge. She further testified that she believed an "average OUI in the bench session is two thousand [dollars] and sometimes less." ... The other expert witness called by Fordham testified that he had heard of a $35,000 fee for defending OUI charges, but he had never charged more than $12,000 (less than twenty-five per cent of Fordham's fee).

Although finding that Fordham's fee was "much higher than the fee charged by many attorneys with more experience litigating driving under the influence cases," the hearing committee nevertheless determined that the fee charged by Fordham was not clearly excessive because Clark "went into the relationship with Fordham with open eyes." ... [This conclusion] was based on the finding that Clark hired Fordham after being fully apprised that he lacked any type of experience in defending an OUI charge and after interviewing other lawyers who were experts in defending OUI charges. Furthermore, the hearing committee and the board relied on testimony which revealed that the fee arrangement had been fully disclosed to Clark including the fact that Fordham "would have to become familiar with the law in that area." It is also significant, however, that the hearing committee found that "[d]espite Fordham's disclaimers concerning his experience, Clark did not appear to have understood in any real sense the implications of choosing Fordham to represent Timothy. Fordham did not give Clark any estimate of the total expected fee or the number of $200 hours that would be required." The express finding of the hearing committee that Clark "did not appear to have understood in any real sense the implications of choosing Fordham to represent Timothy" directly militates against the finding that Clark entered into the agreement "with open eyes." ...

Finally, bar counsel challenges the hearing committee's finding that "if Clark objected to the numbers of hours being spent by

Fordham, he could have spoken up with some force when he began receiving bills.'' Bar counsel notes, and we agree, that "[t]he test as stated in the DR 2–106(A) is whether the fee 'charged' is clearly excessive, not whether the fee is accepted as valid or acquiesced in by the client." Therefore, we conclude that the hearing committee and the board erred in not concluding that Fordham's fee was clearly excessive. . . .

In charging a clearly excessive fee, Fordham departed substantially from the obligation of professional responsibility that he owed to his client. . . . Accordingly, a judgment is to be entered in the county court imposing a public censure. . . .

Notes

1. *Billing for "learning time."* Fordham told the client that he had never worked on this kind of case before, and to do a competent job he undoubtedly had to educate himself about the law. What was wrong with billing for that time? The Model Code instructs: "While the licensing of a lawyer is evidence that he has met the standards then prevailing for admission to the bar, a lawyer generally should not accept employment in any area of the law in which he is not qualified. However, he may accept such employment if in good faith he expects to become qualified through study and investigation, as long as such preparation would not result in unreasonable delay or expense to his client." EC 6–3.

2. *History of the hourly fee.* Billing by the hour is the most common form of attorneys' fee. But it is actually of recent vintage. Hourly billing did not become common until the 1960s. Not until the late 1960s did most large and mid-sized law firms shift to this form of billing. *See* ABA Commission on Billable Hours Report 2001–02, at 3. In the years before this, most lawyers' billing arrangements were guided by minimum fee schedules—a system in which state and local bar associations set fixed fees for certain kinds of legal matters and prohibited lawyers from charging less than that. When the Supreme Court declared minimum fee schedules a violation of antitrust laws in *Goldfarb v. Virginia State Bar*, 421 U.S. 773, 95 S.Ct. 2004, 44 L.Ed.2d 572 (1975), the stage was set for the hourly fee to "reign supreme," as it has now done for decades. ABA Billable Hours Report, *supra* at *ix*, 11.

3. Imagine yourself an associate in a law firm, required to bill 2,100 hours per year. Does such a situation place your own interests in conflict with those of the clients on whose matters you are working? In what way might that be true?

4. *Model Rule variations.* Florida's Rule 4–1.5 explicitly says that a fee is "clearly excessive when: . . . (2) the fee is sought or secured by the attorney by means of intentional misrepresentation or fraud upon the client." Does such a rule cover the situation in which the efficient lawyer who completes a brief in ten hours bills the client for fifteen?

5. *Double-billing.* Is it ethically proper to bill two clients for the same time period? For example, what if a lawyer has to wait for an hour in a courtroom for Client A's hearing to begin, and while there works on a document for Client B's matter. Can the lawyer bill one hour to Client A and one hour to Client B? Or suppose a lawyer flies from Los Angeles to New York for a meeting with Client A, and while on the seven-hour flight reads material in a matter involving Client B. Can he bill seven hours to Client A and seven hours to Client B? In *In re Berg*, 1997 WL 469003 (Cal. Bar. Ct.), a lawyer was found to have billed the insurance companies for his personal-injury clients in excess of 24 hours a day, on some days exceeding 100 hours in a day. He called this "bulk billing." He was disbarred.

6. *Changing billing rates.* Model Rule 1.5(b) says that "[a]ny changes in the basis or rate of the fee or expenses shall be communicated to the client." Lawyers who change rates without advance notice to clients will generally be stuck with the earlier-quoted rates, at best. See, e.g., *Severson & Werson v. Bolinger*, 235 Cal.App.3d 1569, 1 Cal.Rptr.2d 531 (1991).

7. *Time increments.* Can a lawyer safely round up time spent on a matter? If so, by how much? The answers to these questions depend on what is considered reasonable, and on whether the lawyer is lying about time spent to such a degree that it is considered dishonest or fraudulent. Note that courts have opined that billing by the quarter-hour is generally not reasonable. See, e.g., *Swisher v. United States*, 262 F.Supp.2d 1203 (D. Kan. 2003). Most lawyers who bill by the hour use tenths. Might that be improper under certain circumstances?

NOTE: THE CURRENT DEBATE OVER HOURLY FEES

Average hourly rates have continued to skyrocket in recent years. A survey of law firms in 2000 showed that over half of law firm partners bill their time at a rate of $300 or higher. A 2001 National Law Journal survey of the 250 largest law firms showed that at 14 of them, the top partner billing rate was $600 or more per hour. By 2005, the same survey showed that at many firms, the average partner bills in the $400–600 range. The most expensive partner per hour: $1,000, according to the 2005 survey.

The number of hours that firms expect lawyers to bill has also increased in recent years, although it has perhaps hit a plateau that cannot be topped. Associates are required to bill 2,000 or more hours in many big-city firms, much more than that at some. A now-infamous 2002 inter-office memorandum from one large firm's associates to the partners complained about the firm's requirement that each associate bill 2,420 hours per year. This is all the more extraordinary in light of a 1958 ABA study that concluded that there are about 1,300 legitimate fee-earning hours in a year, assuming that lawyers both need some time off, and must work about three hours in order to generate two billable hours.

In 2001, ABA President Robert Hirshon made the hourly fee a central priority of his term and appointed a commission to study its consequences and to propose some alternatives. The commission's report, published in August, 2002 (and available on the ABA's website), is a scathing indictment of the negative impact of hourly fees on the profession. In its Foreword, U.S. Supreme Court Justice Stephen Breyer criticizes the "continuous push to increase billable hours" on the ground that it makes pro bono work difficult if not impossible. "How can a practitioner undertake pro bono work, engage in law reform efforts, even attend bar association meetings," he asks, "if that lawyer must also produce 2100 or more billable hours each year, say sixty-five or seventy hours in the office each week. The answer is that most cannot...." ABA Billable Hours Report, *supra* at *vii*. In the Preface, President Hirshon states that "It has become increasingly clear that many of the legal profession's contemporary woes intersect at the billable hour." *Id.* at *ix*. He decries the "unintended consequences" of hourly billing, noting among other things the "negative effect . . . on family and personal relationships." *Id.*

No punches are pulled in the body of the report, either. In a section titled "The Corrosive Impact of Emphasis on Billable Hours," the report lists no fewer than fifteen severe problems with hourly billing. *Id.* at 5. Overreliance on billable hours "penalizes the efficient and productive lawyer, . . . discourages communication between lawyer and client, . . . fails to discourage excessive layering and duplication of effort, . . . [and] puts the client's interests in conflict with [the] lawyer's interests," among other things. *Id.*

The report recognizes that despite these problems, hourly billing will likely remain entrenched for the foreseeable future. "[L]aw firms understandably cling to a system that minimizes responsibility for efficiency and maximizes ability to earn money." *Id.* at 8. Because of this reality, the report contains a Model Law Firm Policy Regarding Billable Hours that law firms can use to lessen some of the negative impacts of hourly billing. Among its recommendations are that associates not be required to bill more than 1,900 hours on billable client work. *Id.* at 49–51.

Do firms have incentives to move away from hourly billing? Clearly, yes—especially if clients object. Yet monetary incentives to continue billing by the hour clearly pull in the opposite direction. As most firms are now structured, equity partners make more money the more hours the associates bill (assuming the clients pay). The profit per partner at firms has grown astronomically with the rise of hourly billing and hourly billing rates. In a

Check for new survey of partner profits

2005 survey of the nation's 100 largest law firms, 37 reported average profits per partner of $1 million or more. Eight firms reported average profits per partner of $2 million or more.

§ 3. CONTINGENT FEES

A. Entitlement to a Contingent Fee

CULPEPPER & CARROLL, PLLC v. COLE

Supreme Court of Louisiana, 2006.
929 So.2d 1224.

PER CURIAM.

Connie Daniel Cole seeks review of a judgment of the court of appeal affirming an award of attorney's fees to his former counsel. For the reasons that follow, we reverse the judgment of the court of appeal.

FACTS AND PROCEDURAL HISTORY

Connie Daniel Cole retained attorney Bobby Culpepper of the law firm of Culpepper & Carroll, PLLC to represent him in a contest of his mother's will. Mr. Cole requested that the firm handle the matter on a one-third contingent fee basis, and Mr. Culpepper agreed to do so. On September 20, 2000, Mr. Culpepper sent Mr. Cole a letter in which he confirmed that he would accept the representation on a contingent fee basis of one-third "of whatever additional property or money we can get for you."

After negotiation between Mr. Culpepper and counsel for the estate of Mr. Cole's mother, Mr. Cole was offered property worth $21,600.03 over and above what he would have received under the terms of the decedent's will. Mr. Culpepper thought the compromise was reasonable and recommended to Mr. Cole that he accept the offer. However, Mr. Cole refused to settle his claim for that amount, believing he was entitled to a larger share of his mother's succession as a forced heir. When Mr. Culpepper refused to file suit in the matter, Mr. Cole terminated his representation. Mr. Cole then proceeded in proper person to challenge his mother's will, but he was unsuccessful and recovered nothing.

On April 12, 2004, Mr. Culpepper filed a "Petition on Open Account" on behalf of the Culpepper law firm. The suit was filed in Ruston City Court against Mr. Cole, seeking the sum of $6,950.01,[2] [plus some additional sums]. Attached to the petition were Mr. Culpepper's invoice for attorney's fees and a demand

---

2. This sum represents one-third of the $21,600.03 in property Mr. Cole would have received had he accepted Mr. Culpepper's settlement recommendation, less a credit of $250 for costs paid by Mr. Cole in advance.

letter to Mr. Cole seeking the payment of "the entire balance of $6,950.01 that you owe Culpepper & Carroll, PLLC."

Mr. Cole, appearing in proper person, answered the law firm's petition and denied that he owed any money. Mr. Cole explained in his answer that "Mr. Culpepper did this on a contingency fee basis," that Mr. Culpepper "quit the case," and that Mr. Cole paid court costs but Mr. Culpepper "would not go to court."

Following a trial on the merits, at which both parties testified, the city court rendered judgment in favor of the law firm, awarding the sum of $6,950.01, plus [the additional sums requested]. In oral reasons for judgment, the city court judge stated that a "contingency fee was present" based on the record, including the testimony in open court and the written admission in Mr. Cole's answer that there was a contingent fee arrangement. The court noted that "work was accomplished" by Mr. Culpepper and further noted that, according to the testimony, the settlement would have produced a better result than if the case had gone to trial on the issue of forced heirship. Thus, the court was satisfied that the law firm met its burden of proof.

Mr. Cole appealed the city court's judgment, and in a 2–1 ruling, the court of appeal amended the judgment and affirmed. The majority agreed that a valid contingent fee contract existed between Mr. Cole and Mr. Culpepper, and found that by refusing to sign the "favorable settlement" negotiated by Mr. Culpepper before he was discharged, Mr. Cole was in effect depriving Mr. Culpepper of the contingent fee he had already earned. Accordingly, the court of appeal affirmed the award to Mr. Culpepper of $6,950.01 in attorney's fees, plus legal interest. . . .

Judge Caraway dissented. He recognized that a contingent fee contract existed in this case, but found that because there was ultimately no recovery in the case, no fee was due to Mr. Culpepper. Judge Caraway further observed that to allow an attorney to collect a fee when the client rejects a settlement offer and later recovers nothing "ignores multiple and serious concerns embodied in the rules of professional conduct."

Upon Mr. Cole's application, we granted certiorari to review the correctness of the court of appeal's ruling.

DISCUSSION

As a threshold matter, we note the trial court made a finding of fact that a contingent fee contract existed between Mr. Cole and Mr. Culpepper. Based on our review of the record, we find no manifest error in this determination.

Having found a contingent fee contract exists, we now turn to the question of whether Mr. Culpepper is entitled to recover any attorney's fees under this contract. Pursuant to the parties' agreement, Mr. Culpepper is entitled to one-third "of whatever additional property or money" he obtained on behalf of Mr. Cole. It is undisputed that Mr. Cole recovered no additional property or money as a result of the litigation against his mother's estate. Because Mr. Cole obtained no recovery, it follows that Mr. Culpepper is not entitled to any contingent fee.[3]

Nonetheless, Mr. Culpepper urges us to find that his contingency should attach to the settlement offer he obtained on behalf of his client, even though his client refused to accept that offer. According to Mr. Culpepper, he did the work for which Mr. Cole retained him, and he is therefore entitled to one-third of the amount offered in settlement, notwithstanding Mr. Cole's rejection of the settlement offer.

With the benefit of hindsight, it would have been in Mr. Cole's best interest to accept the settlement offer obtained by Mr. Culpepper. However, it is clear that the decision to accept a settlement belongs to the client alone. *See* Rule 1.2(a) of the Rules of Professional Conduct ("A lawyer shall abide by a client's decision whether to settle a matter."). Therefore, regardless of the wisdom of Mr. Cole's decision, his refusal to accept the settlement was binding on Mr. Culpepper.

To allow Mr. Culpepper to recover a contingent fee under these circumstances would penalize Mr. Cole for exercising his right to reject the settlement. We find no statutory or jurisprudential support for such a proposition....

In summary, we find that Mr. Culpepper did not obtain any recovery on behalf of Mr. Cole. In the absence of a recovery, it follows that Mr. Culpepper cannot collect a contingent fee for his services.[4] Accordingly, we must reverse the judgment of the court of appeal awarding a contingent fee to Mr. Culpepper.

DECREE

For the reasons assigned, the judgment of the court of appeal is hereby reversed. All costs in this court are assessed against plaintiff.

Notes

1. Could a lawyer avoid the problem in *Culpepper* by including in the retainer agreement a provision requiring the lawyer's approval

---

3. As Judge Caraway aptly observed, "One-third times zero equals no contingency fee." His mathematic acumen is impeccable in this instance.

4. As an alternative to his claims under the contingent fee contract, Mr. Culpepper also seeks attorney's fees under the theory of quantum meruit. Because there was no recovery by the client, it follows there is no basis for quantum meruit recovery.

before a settlement could be either rejected or accepted? See MR 1.2(a); *Hall v. Orloff*, 49 Cal.App. 745, 194 P. 296 (1920). See also Annot., 121 A.L.R. 1122 (1939) (collecting cases).

2. What if a client acts in bad faith in discharging a lawyer, in a blatant effort to avoid paying an agreed-upon contingent fee? Might the lawyer have a claim for breach of the covenant of good faith and fair dealing? Or does the client's right to fire a lawyer bar any such claim? See *Dweck Law Firm, L.L.P. v. Mann*, 340 F.Supp.2d 353 (S.D.N.Y. 2004). More cases on lawyers' rights to fees after termination are found in section 3.D.

3. *History of the contingent fee.* Until the late 19th Century, contingent fees were either frowned upon or disallowed in most states. This was because such fees were thought to represent a "champertous practice" in which lawyers stirred up litigation in order to make money for themselves. See Charles W. Wolfram, Modern Legal Ethics § 9.4, at 526–27 (1986). The ancient common law crimes of maintenance (stirring up litigation without just cause), champerty (investing in litigation upon the promise of a percentage of recovery) and barratry (urging others to litigate), while of limited importance today, stood as a barrier to the use of contingent fees. See *id*. § 8.13, at 489–90. In the 1908 Canons, contingent fees were grudgingly accepted as proper, with one caveat: such fees "should always be subject to the supervision of a court, as to its reasonableness." Canon 13. By the time of the Model Code's adoption, contingent fees were well accepted, and both the Code and the Rules expressly authorize them. See also Restatement § 35.

4. *Rationale.* Lawyers are generally prohibited, even today, from acquiring an interest in a litigated matter that the lawyer is conducting for a client. See Restatement § 36. Why is a contingent fee exempted from this rule? What purposes are served by allowing such a fee? See Restatement § 35, comment *b*.

B. The Reasonableness Requirement

GAGNON v. SHOBLOM

Supreme Judicial Court of Massachusetts, 1991.
409 Mass. 63, 565 N.E.2d 775.

NOLAN, Justice.

On June 9, 1988, at 1 P.M., a truck operated by Donald Shoblom crashed into a parked trailer, killing Susan J. Thompson and severely injuring Donald Gagnon. Gagnon retained Attorney Alan R. Goodman in pursuit of his claim against Shoblom and Shoblom's employer, and for his workers' compensation claim. Gagnon and Mr. Goodman signed a contingent fee agreement in which Gagnon agreed that Mr. Goodman's compensation would amount to 33 1/3% of the recovery in his personal injury claim....

Mr. Goodman commenced an action and, after extensive discovery and investigation, a structured settlement of $2,925,000 (present cash value) was reached. . . .

A Superior Court judge conducted a hearing and indicated his approval of the terms of the settlement agreement except the provision for recovery of 33 1/3% of the settlement which amounted to $975,000. The judge called this fee unconscionable. There was an evidentiary hearing on the reasonableness of the settlement agreement. Gagnon testified that he voluntarily signed the contingent fee agreement and that he was satisfied that Mr. Goodman had earned his agreed fee. Additionally, a leading member of the bar who specializes in prosecuting personal injury claims for plaintiffs testified as to the reasonableness of the fee. The attorney who defended the action in the case testified as to the impressive work performed by Mr. Goodman. There was no evidence tending to prove that the fee was anything but reasonable.

However, the judge filed a carefully crafted memorandum and order in which he ordered payment of legal fees to Mr. Goodman as follows: "Mr. Goodman handled the case expeditiously and well. He obtained what I consider to be a very fine result. As stated above, he is entitled to handsome compensation.

"Taking those factors into account, as well as Mr. Goodman's ability and reputation (both of which are good) the demand for his services by others, the time reasonably spent, the expenses reasonably incurred by him and the charges usually made for similar services by others in Western Massachusetts, I am satisfied that the 33 1/3% maximum rate provided for in his contingent fee agreement should only be applied to the first $300,000.00 of the recovery. A rate of 25% of the next $1,200,000.00, plus a rate of 20% of all amounts in excess of $1,500,000 would be reasonable. At those rates Mr. Goodman is entitled to an attorney's fee of $695,000.00, which I consider to be 'handsome' compensation. Anything in excess of that amount would be unreasonable and excessive."

We allowed Mr. Goodman's request for direct appellate review of the correctness of the judge's order regarding the fee. We hold that it was error for the judge to disapprove the agreed fee. . . .

We need not dwell on the validity of the contingent fee agreement per se. It is not an issue; only the amount of the fee is before us and more especially, the authority of the judge in the circumstances of this case to nullify the amount of the fee. [There was no need to seek the judge's approval of the settlement in this case, and the judge had no statutory authority to act as he did.] [N]o one is challenging the contingent fee agreement. Gagnon, the client, has intelligently and freely testified that he was satisfied with the amount of the fee.

The courts are not powerless to act in disapproving a fee which exceeds the percentage in the agreement, *Matter of Kerlinsky,* 406 Mass. 67, 73–74, 546 N.E.2d 150 (1989), a fee to which the client never agreed, see *DeSautels, petitioner,* 1 Mass.App. 787, 793–795, 307 N.E.2d 576 (1974), or a fee which is plainly unreasonable. On objection by a party entitled to challenge the lawfulness or reasonableness of a fee, a judge has inherent power to act. However, we need not discuss the court's inherent power in this case because no one is challenging the fee.

Accordingly, an order shall enter approving the entire settlement, including the amount of compensation due to Mr. Goodman under the contingent fee agreement.

So ordered.

GREANEY, Justice (concurring).

I do not agree with the court's conclusion that the judge lacked authority (apart from the Superior Court's inherent power) to examine the attorney's fees ..., [although] I agree with the court that the attorney's fee in this case should not have been reduced....

The judge, however, has touched upon a larger issue. His memorandum frames that issue in this manner:

> "Contingent fee agreements ... are no longer regarded as champertous, and they have become an important part of the administration of justice. They serve a very beneficial public purpose. They have been said to be the 'poor man's key to the courthouse' because they do provide a method whereby civil claims can be filed and litigated by persons who would otherwise be unable to afford the assistance of counsel. They are, nevertheless, a matter of special judicial concern and subject to strict supervision by the court....

> "I am satisfied (both on the basis of my own experience as a practicing attorney and as a trial judge as well as by the evidence presented at the hearings) that in the case of a civil tort action in which damages are sought for personal injuries a contingent fee of 33 1/3% of the amount recovered is reasonable to a point, depending (among other factors of course) upon the size of the recovery ultimately obtained. I am also satisfied, however, that as the size of the recovery (and hence the size of the fee) increases, the spread between the attorney's fee and the fair value of the time, effort and skill that he devoted to earning that fee widens—and at some point the fee becomes unreasonable and even (if the spread becomes wide enough) outrageous or unconscionable.

"One should not lose sight of the fact that under our law a recovery for a personal injury is limited, at least in theory, to the fair and reasonable value of the pain and suffering, mental anguish, reasonable medical expenses, disfigurement, disability and lost earning capacity, both past and future, *sustained by the client.* However, attorney's fees incurred by the client are not recoverable in such a case, either as part of or in addition to his damages. Any fee that the attorney exacts from the client under a contingent fee agreement must therefore reduce the client's compensation for his injury below what is fair and reasonable. When, as in this case, the injury sustained by the client is catastrophic, the amount of the reduction can become enormous unless some rule of reason is applied to the application of the contingent fee. It is, after all, Mr. Gagnon and not Mr. Goodman who must spend the remainder of his life confined to a wheelchair with no bowel or bladder control and with constant dependence upon others to assist him in the normal tasks of day-to-day living. . . . " (Emphasis in original; citation omitted.)

As the judge noted, the Legislature has dealt with this problem in the area of medical malpractice. That statute provides, in pertinent part, that an attorney may not contract for, or collect, a contingent fee in a medical malpractice action in excess of the following limits: (1) 40% of the first $150,000 recovered; (2) 33 1/3% of the next $150,000 recovered; (3) 30% of the next $200,000 recovered; and (4) 25% of any amount by which the recovery exceeds $500,000. The statute goes on to provide that nothing therein shall preclude a court from assessing reasonable attorney's fees at any amount below these specified limits, or from determining that attorney's fees below such limits are unreasonably high in a particular case.

At a time when the gap between the service and the fee in tort cases appears to be becoming more and more pronounced, there may be a need to establish a better sense of proportion. This case is illustrative of the problem.[1] The question raised by the judge deserves honest debate.

1. The judge noted the existence of facts which tended to question the reasonableness of the fee agreement. At the time of the accident, Gagnon was lawfully parked in the breakdown lane of the Massachusetts Turnpike near a disabled tractor-trailer truck. The disabled tractor-trailer was being driven by a young woman who had pulled off the travel lane because she had noticed that the mud flaps on her truck were rubbing against her rear trailer wheels. To help the woman, Gagnon went underneath the rear of the trailer to attempt to correct the problem. While he was in that position a loaded garbage truck operated by Shoblom veered off the highway into the breakdown lane and crashed into the tractor-trailer. The woman was killed as the result of the collision, and Gagnon sustained massive injuries which left him a paraplegic. Thus, when the contingent fee agreement was signed Goodman knew that the liability aspect of Gagnon's case was very strong, that his injuries were cata-

Notes

1. *Reasonableness.* Contingent fees, like all kinds of fees, must be "reasonable," or not unconscionable, or not excessive. How is that to be judged when the fee is a percentage of the recovery? For example, is it reasonable for an attorney to charge a client a one-third contingency fee in a case involving enormous damages that is an almost certain winner on liability? See Restatement § 35, comment c. Cf. *In re Teichner*, 104 Ill.2d 150, 470 N.E.2d 972, 83 Ill.Dec. 552 (1984) (charging client a percentage of an insurance payment that was not contested is unconscionable). Does the lawyer have the duty to explain to the client in such a case that the amount of the fee might be much greater than an hourly fee would be? If that is done, and the client chooses the contingent fee, can the client later fault the lawyer for charging an unreasonable fee? See *State ex rel. Okla. Bar Ass'n v. Flaniken*, 85 P.3d 824 (Okla. 2004).

2. In *Holmes v. Loveless*, 122 Wash.App. 470, 94 P.3d 338 (2004), two retired lawyers sued former clients seeking to enforce a contingent fee agreement that had been ongoing for 30 years, under which the lawyers received five percent of all cash distributions from a successful shopping center, in exchange for having provided discounted legal services. The now-30-year-old fee discount had been worth $8,000; the fee over the years totaled more than $380,000. The court concluded that the fee was excessive and that "[f]urther enforcement of this agreement cannot be justified on any principled basis."

3. Do you agree with Justice Greaney's view (concurring in *Gagnon*) that a judge should be able to review a contingent fee for reasonableness even where the client does not complain? Or does the client's satisfaction with the fee make it reasonable *per se*?

4. The limits on contingent fees in medical malpractice cases (also mentioned in the concurrence in *Gagnon*) are found in a number of states. See, e.g., Cal. Bus. & Prof. Code § 6146 (maximum limits of 40% of first $50,000; 33 1/3% of the next $50,000; 25% of the next $500,000; and 15% of any amount exceeding $600,000). Are such limitations wise? Do you think they make it more difficult for plaintiffs in these lawsuits to obtain counsel?

5. Should specific percentage limitations be extended to contingent fees generally, even outside the med-mal context? Florida Rule 4–1.5 sets maximum percentages on contingent fees in all personal injury cases, absent prior court approval, tied to the stage the case is in at the time of resolution. If a case settles prior to the filing of an answer or a demand for arbitration, the fee cannot exceed one-third of any recovery up to $1 million, plus 30% of the recovery between $1 million and $2 million, plus 20% of the recovery exceeding $2 million. If a case settles after an answer is filed, percentages go up slightly. Any fee charged in excess of

strophic, and that it was apparent that Gagnon would receive a very substantial judgment or settlement from Shoblom's corporate employer....

these percentages is presumptively "clearly excessive," although the presumption is rebuttable. Fla. Rule 4–1.5(4)(B). While percentage limitations of this type have been routinely upheld by courts, they are subject to attack if the legislation unduly restricts judicial review over fee determinations. See, e.g., *Irwin v. Surdyk's Liquor*, 599 N.W.2d 132 (Minn.1999) (holding unconstitutional a state statute setting percentage limits on contingent fees in workers compensation cases on that ground, saying that it violates the separation of powers doctrine).

6. *Writing requirement.* Contingent fees are used widely in plaintiffs' personal injury cases. Plaintiffs in such cases are not "repeat litigators," of course, as are many defendants in such cases. Virtually all states require that contingent fee agreements be in writing, and that the agreement contain certain specific information. See MR 1.5(c); N.Y. DR 2–106(d) [22 NYCRR 1200.11]; Cal. Bus. & Prof. Code § 6147. Does the nature of the typical client help explain why the Model Rules require that contingent fee agreements be in writing but not hourly fee agreements?

7. *Computation: Basis or rate.* One thing a lawyer must clarify with a client is the basis or rate of the fee. See Restatement § 38(1). In the context of a contingent fee, this would include the base on which the percentage will be applied. Ambiguities will be construed against the lawyer. In *Levine v. Bayne, Snell & Krause, Ltd.*, 40 S.W.3d 92 (Tex. 2001), a law firm entered into a written contingent fee contract with the Levines pursuant to which the lawyers would receive one third of "any amount received by settlement or recovery." The Levines won a jury verdict of $243 thousand. But the defendants were awarded $162 thousand on a counterclaim. The lawyers claimed that the fee agreement entitled them to one-third of the higher amount. The Levines disagreed and refused to pay the entire bill. The lawyers sued to collect. The court, citing Restatement § 35, held that the phrase "any amount received" meant net recovery—that is, the amount received by the Levines, less the amount of the counterclaim against the Levines. The court stressed that the lawyers had the duty to clarify the contract if they meant the fee to be based on anything other than the net amount of recovery. "To place this burden upon attorneys is justified not only by the attorney's sophistication," said the court, "but also by the relationship of trust between attorney and client." See also *Wampold v. E. Eric Guirard & Assocs.*, 442 F.3d 269 (5th Cir. 2006) (holding that the phrase "gross proceeds of recovery" did not include recovery of future, post-judgment disability benefits, construing any ambiguity against the lawyer).

Of course, where a contract unambiguously states the base on which the percentage will be applied (even if different from the "net recovery") it is likely to be upheld, especially where the client is sophisticated. See, e.g., *Cambridge Trust Co. v. Hanify & King, P.C.*, 430 Mass. 472, 721 N.E.2d 1 (1999) (enforcing contingent fee agreement which allowed the lawyers to recover a percentage of an arbitrator's award of damages *and* statutory attorney fees, stressing the client's sophistication and the precision of the fee agreement). In most states, a court has little power to revise a freely-negotiated contingent fee contract between lawyer and client based on its own idea of what is "fair." See, e.g., *Revere Transducers, Inc. v. Deere & Co.*, 637 N.W.2d 189 (Iowa 2001) (reversing trial court's determination that a law firm was entitled to 38% of compensatory award and 50% of punitive damages award, where the parties had agreed to a 38% contingent fee on the amount of recovery).

C. Categorical Restrictions on Contingent Fees

1. Criminal Law

FOGARTY v. STATE

Supreme Court of Georgia, 1999.
270 Ga. 609, 513 S.E.2d 493.

CARLEY, Justice.

Mark Joseph Fogarty was arrested and charged with kidnapping, aggravated assault, simple battery and nine counts of stalking. Acting without Fogarty's knowledge, his wife entered into an agreement to pay defense counsel's $25,000 fee in advance, but it was further agreed that, if the charges were dismissed and a new suspect identified, then the fee would be reduced to $10,000. The charges against Fogarty were not dismissed, and the case proceeded to trial. A jury acquitted Fogarty of six of the stalking counts, but found him guilty of the six other counts. Fogarty urged on appeal that the fee agreement created a conflict of interest which adversely affected his attorney's performance. The Court of Appeals found that the agreement was an improper contingency fee contract which "created an actual conflict of interest for his trial counsel in that it made it more lucrative for trial counsel not to pursue avenues that might lead to dismissal of the charges against [Fogarty] and the identification of a new suspect." However, the Court of Appeals affirmed Fogarty's convictions, concluding that he had failed to show that the fee arrangement had any adverse effect upon defense counsel's performance.... We conclude that, although the Court of Appeals proceeded upon an erroneous premise, Fogarty's convictions must be affirmed when the proper legal analysis is applied.

To prevail on an ineffective assistance of counsel claim, the defendant must show that his trial counsel's performance was deficient and that the deficient performance prejudiced the defense. *Strickland v. Washington*, 466 U.S. 668, 104 S.Ct. 2052, 80 L.Ed.2d 674 (1984). [Supreme Court precedents establish that where a lawyer has an actual conflict of interest,] the defendant "need not show that the result of the trial would have been different without the conflict of interest, only that the conflict had some adverse effect on counsel's performance." *McConico v. Alabama*, 919 F.2d 1543, 1548 (11th Cir.1990).

"But until a defendant shows that his counsel actively represented conflicting interests, he has not established the constitutional predicate for his claim of ineffective assistance." *Cuyler v. Sullivan,* 100 S.Ct. 1708. According to the Court of Appeals, Fogarty met this threshold requirement by showing that his trial counsel contracted for an improper contingency fee. The "critical element" in a contingency fee contract "is that there be some chance that the lawyer will not receive the fee because the representation ends with an unwanted result for the lawyer's client." Wolfram, Modern Legal Ethics, § 9.4.1, p. 526 (1986). "Public policy properly condemns contingent fee arrangements in criminal cases, largely on the ground that legal services in criminal cases do not produce a res with which to pay the fee." Georgia State Bar Rule 3–102, Ethical Consideration 2–20. Here, counsel agreed to provide Fogarty a complete defense for a fee of $25,000, and this fee was in no way contingent upon a successful final outcome of the criminal proceedings. Counsel was entitled to that fee even if the case went to trial and the trier of fact ultimately found Fogarty guilty. The only contingency contemplated by the agreement was the possible termination of the criminal proceedings short of disposition by trial. Should the case against Fogarty be dismissed rather than tried, counsel would be entitled to retain only $10,000 of the contemplated $25,000 fee. However, the fact that the agreement specified both a greater and a lesser fee, dependent upon the extent to which counsel's services would be required to provide Fogarty with a complete defense, does not make it an improper contingency fee contract. "[A]n agreement for payment of one amount if the case is disposed of without trial and a larger amount if it proceeds to trial is not a contingent fee but merely an attempt to relate the fee to the time and service involved." Standards for Criminal Justice, Standard 4–3.3, commentary at 4–37 (2d ed., 1980).

Thus, there was no improper "all-or-nothing" contingency fee agreement providing that the lawyer would get paid *only* in the event that Fogarty prevailed. The contractual contingency simply related to the *amount* of the fee that the attorney would receive, not to his right to receive any fee at all. It is completely irrelevant that the agreement specified that the lesser fee would be earned in the event that the case against Fogarty was dismissed, since any termination of a criminal prosecution against a defendant short of trial is necessarily a favorable result for him. What is controlling is that the agreement did not provide that counsel would be paid only in the event that the case against Fogarty was dismissed or he was acquitted. Instead, the contract evidenced an unconditional agreement to pay one of two set and determined amounts as attorney's fees at one of two possible end stages of the criminal prosecution. Where, as here, compensation is ultimately dependent upon the amount of time actually invested in a case, it is always more lucrative for the attorney to pursue avenues which might result in a larger fee. However, that fact alone does not compel the conclusion that counsel has an actual conflict of interest with his or her client. Indeed, under the concept of an improper contingency fee agreement which was adopted by the Court of Appeals, a criminal defense attorney who agrees to accept an hourly fee would have an actual conflict of interest with the client, simply because it would be more lucrative to allow the case to go to trial than to seek to resolve it favorably for the client beforehand. As a professional, Fogarty's attorney is entitled to the strong presumption that he "rendered adequate assistance and made all significant decisions in the exercise of reasonable professional judgment." *Strickland v. Washington,* 104 S.Ct. 2052. Thus, the applicable presumption in this case is that he faithfully represented Fogarty, and that he did not intentionally overlook avenues of defense because it may have been to his financial benefit to do so. . . .

Therefore, the Court of Appeals erred in its characterization of the contract with Fogarty's counsel as an improper contingency fee arrangement. The agreement resulted in a perfectly valid retention of counsel's services for the purpose of defending Fogarty against the criminal charges pending against him. Because there is no improper fee arrangement giving rise to any actual conflict of interest, there arises no presumption of any prejudice resulting from counsel's representation of Fogarty. Accordingly, in order to prevail on a claim of ineffective assistance of counsel, Fogarty must satisfy the traditional test by showing that his trial attorney's performance was defective and that the defective performance prejudiced the defense. *Strickland v. Washington,* supra. Fogarty has not made such a showing. To the contrary, the record demonstrates defense counsel's effectiveness in that he successfully obtained an acquittal on six of the twelve counts against Fogarty. Thus, the Court of Appeals correctly affirmed Fogarty's convictions on the remaining six counts.

Judgment affirmed.

SEARS, Justice, concurring specially.

Contingent: Possible, but not assured; doubtful or uncertain; conditioned upon the occurrence of some future event which is itself uncertain, or questionable. Synonymous with provisional. This term . . . implies that no present interest exists, and that whether such interest or right ever will exist depends upon a future uncertain event. Black's Law Dictionary, p. 290 (5th Ed. 1979).

As made clear by this definition, it would strain credulity to urge that the fee arrangement between Fogarty and his trial counsel—which provided for a fee of $25,000, payable in advance, to be reduced to $10,000 if the charges against Fogarty were dismissed and a new suspect identified—was not contingent. Counsel's $25,000 fee in this case was contingent upon Fogarty's prosecution proceeding to trial. If that contingency was not satisfied, then counsel would have been compelled to refund $15,000 already paid to him, reducing his fee by three-fifths. The majority opinion, therefore, should not be misunderstood for the proposition that the fee arrangement in this case was not contingent. Rather, the majority opinion must be read more narrowly—the fee arrangement in this case, although contingent, has not been shown to be improper.

The relevant ethical canons and commentaries based thereon establish two principles regarding contingency fee agreements in criminal cases: (1) It is absolutely prohibited to make an additional fee payment contingent upon the acquittal of an accused;[2] and (2) "An agreement for payment of one amount if the case is disposed of without trial and a larger amount if it proceeds to trial is not a contingent fee but merely an attempt to relate the fee to the time and services involved."[3] The absolute prohibition against making additional fees contingent upon acquittal is premised upon the fact that (as pointed out by the majority) in criminal cases, there is no *res* from which a contingent fee can be deducted,[4] and also upon concerns that such agreements may be detrimental to both the administration of justice and the best interests of criminal defendants.

As noted, though, a criminal defense lawyer is permitted to structure his fees to provide for one amount if a case is resolved without going to trial, and another, larger amount if the case does go to trial. For this reason, criminal defense lawyers are allowed to set "escalating" fee scales, which typically specify one fee to shepherd a case though its preliminary stages, and another fee which must be paid if the case actually proceeds to trial. In these permissible "escalating" fee arrangements, whether a criminal defense lawyer is paid his or her highest fee is contingent upon the case going to trial. This same contingency also provided the basis for Fogarty's fee arrangement with his counsel. It is true that, unlike an "escalating" fee scale, Fogarty's fee arrangement required full payment in advance. However, I do not believe that distinction, standing alone, is sufficient to place the fee arrangement in this case within the scope of prohibited contingency agreements, and therefore I must conclude that Fogarty's fee arrangement with counsel fell within the limited scope of permissible contingency agreements in criminal cases.

2. ABA Standards for Criminal Justice, Defense Function Standard 4–3.3; Rules and Regulations for the Government of the State Bar of Georgia ("Georgia Bar Rules"), Directory Rule 2–106(c).

3. Id.

4. See Georgia Bar Rules, Ethical Consideration 2–20.

Notes

1. The prohibition on contingent fees in criminal defense work is well-established. See Restatement § 35; MR 1.5(d)(2); DR 2–106(C). Why not allow a criminal defense lawyer to be hired under an agreement that he would be paid only if the defendant is acquitted? How about only if the defendant receives a particular sentence, or less? What's the concern in such a situation? Aren't the interests of the lawyer (in getting paid) and of the client (in being acquitted or getting a minimal sentence) perfectly aligned?

2. Do you think the fee agreement in *Fogarty* should have been upheld? Do you agree with the concurring opinion that it is, in fact, a kind of "contingent" fee? What kinds of incentives did the fee arrangement give defense counsel?

3. *Prosecutors*. In a number of states, private lawyers may be hired to prosecute particular criminal cases under certain circumstances. The prohibition on contingent fees applicable to criminal defense lawyers has generally extended to such part-time prosecutors as well; that is, a governmental unit is not allowed to hire a private attorney on a contingency basis to prosecute a case. See, e.g., *People ex rel. Clancy v. Superior Court*, 39 Cal.3d 740, 705 P.2d 347, 218 Cal.Rptr. 24 (1985); Restatement § 35(1)(a). What would be wrong with a city or county hiring a lawyer to prosecute a criminal case and agreeing to pay him only if he achieved a conviction? Aren't the lawyer's interests and those of the state perfectly aligned?

2. Family Law

BARNGROVER v. PETTIGREW

Supreme Court of Iowa, 1905.
128 Iowa 533, 104 N.W. 904.

[Syllabus by the court]:

Suit at law to recover for services rendered in divorce proceedings between the defendant and his wife. The plaintiff Barngrover is an attorney and the plaintiff Hughes is a detective. They learned that Mrs. Pettigrew was about to commence an action for a divorce from the defendant, and so informed him, and before notice of suit was served entered into a written agreement with him, which is as follows: "The first party has employed second party to prepare evidence in, and try in the district court of Union county, Iowa, for first party, the suit entitled Jessie Pettigrew v. J. S. Pettigrew, in which said first party is defendant; and said second party undertakes to furnish proof, in the trial of said cause, of the plaintiff's infidelity to first party, and to secure him a divorce from his wife on his cross-petition to be filed in said suit; and as compensation for said services, first party agrees to pay second party as follows: Twenty-five dollars cash, the receipt of which is hereby acknowledged, and then, when second party is successful in securing him a divorce from his wife on his cross-petition, or in case first party shall compromise said suit, or do any other act or thing to prevent second party from accomplishing said end, the further sum of $1,000. Said sums to be in full compensation for their services; and in case of the failure of said Barngrover and Hughes to obtain said divorce, except by reason of some act or thing done hereafter by the said Pettigrew, then the said second party will be entitled to receive only the said sum of $25 in hand paid; and it is further agreed that, in case the $1,000 is paid by first party to second party, then said second party will pay defendant's witness fees in said case, or depositions taken by him." The petition set out this contract and asked a recovery thereon, and also asked a recovery on a quantum meruit, alleging, further, that the suit between the defendant and his wife had been compromised, and that she had been permitted to secure a divorce without opposition. The answer put in issue the legality of the agreement, and on the trial there was a directed verdict for the defendant after the close of the plaintiffs' evidence. The plaintiffs appeal. Affirmed.

SHERWIN, C. J.

The clearly expressed object of the agreement was to bring about a dissolution of the marriage contract and to put an end to the various duties and obligations resulting from it. It is therefore against sound public policy and void. The marriage relation is sacred, and one which the law will encourage and maintain when formed. Its dissolution will not be left to the caprice of the parties themselves, nor will it be permitted to rest on the interference of strangers. Hence any agreement conditioned on the obtainment of divorce, or intended or calculated to facilitate its obtainment, is void. Such is the settled policy of the law as expressed in the universal rule adopted by the courts. 9 Cyc. 519, and cases cited; 15 Am. & Eng. Enc. Law, 956, and cases cited; Stokes v. Anderson (Ind.) 21 N. E. 331, 4 L. R. A. 313; McCurdy v. Dillon (Mich.) 98 N. W. 746. . . .

The appellants contend that, if the agreement be held to be invalid, they are still entitled to recover the reasonable value of their services on a quantum meruit. But the law will not imply a promise to pay for services which are in derogation of public policy, any more than it will enforce a specific contract having that object in view; and when a plaintiff cannot establish his cause of action without relying on an illegal contract, or on services which by their very nature contravene public policy, he cannot recover. Pangborn v. Westlake, 36 Iowa, 546; Reynolds v. Nichols & Co., 12 Iowa, 398; Miller v. Ammon, 145 U. S. 421, 12 Sup. Ct.

884, 36 L. Ed. 759; Pollock's Principles of Contracts, 253–260. In the light of this well-settled rule, it is manifest that there can be no recovery here on a quantum meruit; for the services rendered, as shown by the record, were along the line specified in the written agreement. The appellants cite many cases wherein recovery on a quantum meruit was allowed where the contract was found to be illegal. In many of the cases champertous contracts were involved, and in all the services actually rendered were not in themselves illegal; while in the case at bar, as we have seen, the services rendered were in themselves illegal, because their object was to procure a divorce for the defendant.

The judgment of the district court was clearly right, and it is affirmed.

Notes

1. The case is old, and so is the principle: contingent fees are improper in divorce and child custody matters, at least where a fee is contingent on obtaining a divorce, or achieving a particular result with respect to child custody or a property settlement. See Restatement § 35(1)(b); MR 1.5(d)(1); EC 2 20 ("contingent fee arrangements in domestic relation cases are rarely justified"). Do the rationales for the rule, as articulated in *Barngrover*, seem valid today? See *McCrary v. McCrary*, 764 P.2d 522 (Okla. 1988).

2. What if a client cannot afford a lawyer to obtain a divorce, and the state does not provide for any fee-shifting or legal aid assistance in such matters? Is a prohibition on contingent fees justified under such circumstances? See Restatement § 35, comment *g*; *Gross v. Lamb*, 1 Ohio App.3d 1, 437 N.E.2d 309 (1980).

3. Was the *Barngrover* court correct to deny *all* fees? Should fees have been awarded on a *quantum meruit* basis, based on the fair market value of the lawyer's services? Isn't the client "unjustly enriched" unless the lawyer gets something for his work? Restatement § 37 now provides that a lawyer who engaged in "clear and serious violation of duty to a client may be required to forfeit some or all of the lawyer's compensation for the matter." Was that the principle at work in *Barngrover*?

KING v. YOUNG, BERKMAN, BERMAN & KARPF

District Court of Appeal of Florida, 1998.
709 So.2d 572.

PER CURIAM.

Appellant Richard King appeals a final judgment awarding his prior counsel, Young, Berkman, Berman & Karpf, P.A., a money judgment for $525,000, plus costs and attorney's fees. The judgment, in effect, grants the appellee firm additional fees for the work it performed in representing King in the dissolution of his marriage. . . .

King retained the firm to represent him in his dissolution of marriage action. The firm prepared the fee agreement, which provided for a $25,000 non-refundable retainer and set the hourly rates at $325 per hour for Burton Young, $185 to $250 per hour for other partners, and $165 to $185 per hour for associate lawyers. The fee agreement also included the following clause:

> In the event this matter is settled, or the matter is concluded by the entry of a Final Judgment of Dissolution of Marriage (at the trial level), an *additional and final fee* will be determined as due us from you, taking into consideration the *results achieved* and the complexity of the matter. This 'bonus' fee shall be fair and reasonable. . . . (emphasis added).

Throughout the proceedings, King made full and timely payment of all legal fees demanded by the firm. Ultimately, King paid $342,989, the amount due under the fee agreement exclusive of the bonus provision. After the matter concluded, the firm made a demand for a $750,000 bonus which King did not pay. Unable to resolve the claim, the firm filed an action, in which it sought a bonus of $1,150,000. After a three-day trial, the trial court awarded the firm $525,000 as additional fees. . . .

King appeals arguing that the bonus provision is unenforceable because it improperly seeks a contingency fee based on results obtained in a dissolution action. We agree.

Rule 4–1.5(f)(3) of the Rules Regulating the Florida Bar provides that "[a] lawyer shall not enter into an arrangement for, charge or collect ... any fee in a domestic relations matter, the payment or amount of which is contingent upon the securing of a divorce or upon the amount of alimony or support, or a property settlement in lieu thereof. . . . " R. Regulating Fla. Bar 4–1.5(f)(3). The fee agreement between the firm and King expressly made a portion of the fee to be charged by the firm contingent upon the results obtained. Thus, the provision is void and unenforceable.

An attorney's fee agreement that includes an unenforceable contingency provision is void in its entirety. *See Chandris, S.A. v. Yanakakis,* 668 So.2d 180, 186 (Fla.1995) ("[A] contract that fails to adhere the [Florida Bar rule governing contingent fees] is against public policy and is not enforceable by the member of the Florida Bar who has violated the rule."); *see also Singleton v. Foreman,* 435 F.2d 962, 969 (5th Cir.1970) (holding that an invalid contingent fee in an attorney's fee agreement "made the entire contract void and unenforceable.")

When a fee agreement between attorney and client fails to comply with the Rules Regulating the Florida Bar, the attorney is entitled to recover on the basis of quantum meruit. In this case, the firm agreed to undertake the representation of King at high hourly rates. The firm has now been paid for all of its time, at those rates, for a total of $342,989. We conclude that the firm has already received fair compensation for the work performed, and limit the firm's quantum meruit award to $342,989.

We therefore reverse the award of a "bonus" fee, reverse the award of attorney's fees to the firm, deny the firm's motion for appellate attorney's fees, and grant an award of appellate fees in these proceedings to King.

GREEN, Judge, concurring in part and dissenting in part.

I fully concur with the majority's conclusion that the firm's retainer agreement with King has been rendered entirely unenforceable as a result of the contingency bonus fee provision. However, I must respectfully part company with the majority's remedy which is simply to find the firm's hourly rate in the now unenforceable contract to be reasonable as a matter of law. In my view, such a resolution is seemingly in direct conflict with an earlier pronouncement of this court that the rate billed by an attorney for legal services does not establish its reasonableness. *See Wackenhut Corp. v. Aetna Cas. & Sur. Co.,* 423 So.2d 410, 411 (Fla. 3d DCA 1982). In *Wackenhut,* where the client agreed to pay the attorney a reasonable fee for services, we said that "[t]he mere fact that the attorney had already billed and been paid by Wackenhut fees ... based on an hourly billing rate did not, contrary to the reasoning of the trial court, establish either an agreement to be limited to that amount or the outer limits of reasonableness,...." *Id.* (footnote omitted). Accordingly, we remanded *Wackenhut* to the trial court for its determination of a reasonable fee.

Similarly, in a case such as this, where a contract for attorney's fees has been found unenforceable and the attorney is entitled to a reasonable fee under a quantum meruit theory, we must remand this case back to the trial court for its determination of a reasonable fee. I am unaware of any decision which provides an appellate court with authority to assess a reasonable attorney's fee under a quantum meruit theory in the first instance, where that theory had not yet been pled or litigated by the parties at the trial level....

In light of what we said in *Wackenhut,* I believe that we are compelled to now wipe the slate clean and remand this cause back to the trial court for its determination of a reasonable attorney's fee under a quantum meruit theory and without any consideration of the provisions of the unenforceable contract. This necessarily means that both sides would be allowed to introduce evidence as to what an appropriate hourly rate should be for the firm in this cause. This also would mean that firm must either return all money previously paid by King or hold such funds in an escrow account or the court's registry pending the outcome of the evidentiary hearing.

Notes

1.   Should the firm in this case have been denied all fees, as in *Barngrover*? Is merely disallowing the "bonus" in this case sufficient sanction for the lawyers' attempt to get the client to pay an additional fee contingent on obtaining a divorce?

2.   Is Judge Green right that the fair value of the law firm's services cannot be proved simply by looking at what the client had already paid? Should the case have been remanded for more factfinding on the fair value of the lawyers' services?

3.   Should the prohibition on contingent fees apply in cases where a divorce has already been obtained and the only dispute is over the division of property? The states' ethics rules differ on this point. Compare, e.g., Ill. Rule 1.5(d) (allowing contingent fees) with Fla. Rule 4–1.5(f)(3)(A) (not allowing). Do the rationales for the prohibition support it when the marriage has already ended?

D.   Post–Termination Right to Fees

GALANIS v. LYONS & TRUITT

Supreme Court of Indiana, 1999.
715 N.E.2d 858.

BOEHM, Justice.

We hold that in the absence of express written fee agreements providing otherwise (1) a lawyer retained under a contingent fee contract but discharged prior to the contingency is entitled to recover the value of services rendered if there is a subsequent settlement or award; (2) the fee is to be measured by the proportion of the total fee equal to the contribution of the discharged lawyer's efforts to the ultimate result; and (3) a subsequent lawyer under a contingent fee agreement who knew of the previous lawyer's representation is responsible for paying the predecessor's fee out of the subsequent lawyer's fee. These are default settings the law supplies in the absence of fee agreements providing otherwise and parties and lawyers are not prevented from making other reasonable fee arrangements.

FACTUAL AND PROCEDURAL BACKGROUND

Suzanne Brown was injured in an automobile accident on September 7, 1988. Her first lawyer withdrew because of a conflict of interest and she discharged a second for failure to return phone calls. Brown then retained Robert Truitt of Lyons & Truitt to represent her. Truitt and an associate took several depositions and prepared for trial over the next two and one-half years. When Truitt was appointed to the Porter Superior Court in July of 1993, Brown discharged his firm and retained Michael Galanis. Brown signed a written contingent fee agreement providing that Galanis would receive 40% of the gross amount recovered if the case settled or went to trial plus an additional 10% if the case was appealed. The agreement made no reference to compensating Lyons for its apparently significant role in the case. When Galanis met with Truitt to obtain Brown's file, Truitt explained to Galanis that his firm had taken the case under the 1/3 contingent fee arrangement provided in the written agreement between Brown and her first lawyer.

Approximately four months after Galanis assumed the case, Brown was successful at trial and a jury awarded her $250,000. The case was then settled for $200,000. Shortly after settlement, Lyons sent Galanis an itemized list of its hours worked and expenses incurred on Brown's case, but requested no specific fee. Galanis communicated with Brown and Lyons on several occasions. Ultimately, Brown (through Galanis) offered Lyons $4,000 to settle the fee dispute and Lyons requested 1/3 of 1/3 of the recovery or $22,200. The parties could not reach an agreement.

Nearly two years after its first demand for payment, Lyons filed a complaint for declaratory judgment against Brown requesting that the trial court determine Brown's obligations under the two contingent fee agreements. Brown filed a cross-claim against Galanis asserting that Galanis, not Brown, was responsible for any fee owing to Lyons. Galanis filed a motion for summary judgment as to his exposure for Lyons's fees. The trial court held that Lyons was entitled to a reasonable fee, which was determined to be "commensurate with the hourly rate charged by an attorney in a similar case," and that Galanis was responsible for paying that fee. [Both parties appealed, and the Court of Appeals affirmed.]

I. A Discharged Lawyer is Entitled to the Reasonable Value of Services Rendered

"A client has a right to discharge a lawyer at any time, with or without cause, subject to liability for payment for the lawyer's services." Indiana Professional Conduct Rule 1.16 comment; *see Matter of Lansky*, 678 N.E.2d 1114, 1116 (Ind.1997). We assume that an agreement calling for a reasonable method of compensating a discharged lawyer may be enforceable according to its terms. Here, however, Lyons and Brown had reached no explicit agreement as to whether or how much Lyons was to be compensated if the firm was discharged before a result was known. The conventional rule is that "[a]n attorney who is employed under a contingent fee contract and discharged prior to the occurrence of the contingency is limited to quantum meruit recovery for the reasonable value of the services rendered to the client, and may not recover the full amount of the agreed contingent fee." As the Court of Appeals observed, "this rule strikes the proper balance by providing clients freedom in substituting counsel, prohibiting clients from being held responsible for attorney's fees not previously agreed to, and protecting an attorney's right to be compensated for services rendered."

A corollary of the client's right to discharge a lawyer is that a contract between the client and the lawyer that unduly impairs that right is invalid. 1 Geoffrey C. Hazard, Jr. & W. William Hodes, The Law of Lawyering § 1.16:201–1 (1990 & Supp.1998). Accordingly, even if an agreement calls for a full contingent fee in the event of discharge, it is likely to be unenforceable. If a client is required to pay the discharged lawyer the fee for the completed project, especially if this is a percentage contingent fee, and then pay a second fee for its completion, the client's right to discharge the lawyer may be too costly to assert. *Id.* at § 1.16:602 n. 2.1 (a client's right to discharge is not much of a right if it would be too costly to assert); *AFLAC, Inc. v. Williams,* 264 Ga. 351, 444 S.E.2d 314, 317 (1994) ("A client should not be deterred from exercising his or her legal right because of economic coercion."). Otherwise stated, holding a client responsible for the entire amount of a contract would chill a client's exercise of the right to discharge a lawyer. The requirement of Professional Conduct Rule 1.5 that a lawyer's fee be reasonable is also relevant. A full contingency for partial completion overcompensates the discharged lawyer by giving a full contingent fee for less than a full work load.

Similarly, however, allowing a full contingency to a successor may be unreasonable. If the former lawyer has contributed significantly to the result but the successor receives a full contingent fee, either the first lawyer remains uncompensated for that contribution or the client pays more than a full contingent fee. In either case, the successor gets a windfall in the form of being relieved of the effort contributed by the first lawyer but nonetheless receives a full contingent fee. None of these results is the desired default setting the law should provide in the absence of a contract spelling out exactly who pays how much under these circumstances.

II. Determining the Reasonable Value
of the First Lawyer's Services

Quantum meruit is an equitable doctrine that prevents unjust enrichment by permitting one to recover the "value of work performed or material furnished if used" by another and if valuable. Where there is a successor lawyer, the benefit the client received from the predecessor's work is either retained by the client in the form of obtaining a more favorable fee agreement, or it is transferred to the successor in the form of relieving the successor of the need to expend the same effort. As applied to this case, if Lyons is not compensated for the useful work it performed on Brown's case, either Brown or Galanis is unjustly enriched. The dollar value to offset the unjust enrichment is based on the value conferred on the client, not the effort expended by the lawyer, although the two may be the same in many instances.

Arriving at the proper number to place on the predecessor's services is ultimately a factual determination for the trial court. The trial court in this case held that the "reasonable value" of Lyons's work should be determined "commensurate with the hourly rate of a community attorney charging for similar services." Judge Staton, dissenting in the Court of Appeals in this case, read this as requiring a fee "equal [to] 'the hourly rate of a community attorney. . . .' " The parties apparently make the same assumption. Lyons challenges this method of calculating the reasonable value of the firm's work. If a fee agreement provides for an hourly rate in the event of a pre-contingency termination, it is presumptively enforceable, subject to the ordinary requirement of reasonableness. We agree with Lyons that, in the absence of such an agreement, the value of a discharged lawyer's work on a case is not always equal to a standard rate multiplied by the number of hours of work on the case. Where the lawyers have agreed to work on contingent fees and there is no contractual provision governing payment in the event of discharge, compensating the predecessor lawyer on a standard hourly fee could produce either too little or too much, depending on how the total hourly efforts of all lawyers compare to the contingent fee.

To illustrate the point, consider the lawyer who is terminated (or dies) while the jury is deliberating before returning a verdict that produces a contingent fee that is twice the hourly rate for the work expended. Where the successor is needed only to defend an appeal, it would be quite unreasonable to measure the discharged lawyer's contribution solely by the number of hours multiplied by a standard rate. The first lawyer accepted the risk of a loss and the second boarded the train when victory was in sight and when at least some recovery by a negotiated settlement was a high probability. At the other end of the spectrum, one can easily imagine scenarios where the predecessor has generated a vast amount of hourly charges but accomplished little or nothing, leaving the entire case development to the successor.

In the context of valuing a terminated predecessor's services, as is generally true, "[i]n determining the reasonable value of the legal services rendered, the time expended by the attorney alone is not a controlling factor. Among other things, consideration may be given to the general quality of the effort expended by the attorney." In this context, because both lawyers in this scenario accepted the risk of failure, in addition to the quality of work, each is entitled to consideration of that risk in determining the fair value of his services. Prof. Cond. R. 1.5(a)(8). And, because the underlying theory of payment is quantum meruit, if there is no fault to be attributed to either the client or the lawyer, as seems to be the case here, the measure of the benefit conferred is what is received by the client, not what is expended by the lawyer. That amount is the portion of contingent fee equal to the total effort expended to achieve the contingency that is attributable to the predecessor's work. Nonetheless, we agree that the relative amount of hourly time charges incurred by the predecessor and successor, adjusted for any unproductive or unnecessary efforts by either, is a likely candidate as a presumptive measure of the relative contribution of the two lawyers. If both lawyers agree that the time spent by each was productive, that will provide an easy resolution of the issue.

We are uncertain whether the trial court intended to award Lyons a fee equal to the hourly charges for the work performed or whether it was merely recognizing, as we do, that the relative hourly charges of the lawyers are relevant to apportioning the contingent fee. If the fee was to be equal to the time charges, it is unclear whether the trial court thought this was a required formula, or whether the same amount was determined to be a fair evaluation of Lyons's contribution in light of all relevant factors. Adherence to time charges is not required, but the latter determination by the trial court would be within its discretion in arriving at a reasonable fee. Remand to the trial court is required for a determination of the value of Lyons's contribution to Brown's case if the lawyers are unable to reach an agreement in light of this opinion.

III. Who Pays the First Lawyer's Fee

The next inquiry is who is responsible for paying Lyons's fee—Galanis or Brown—in the absence of any agreement on that point. Galanis argues that Lyons may recover its fee from Brown but not from him because in Indiana "parties pay their own fees." This may be true as a general matter in cases where the dispute is between two opposing parties. However, in this case, all agree that Brown has incurred a fee for her case in the form of at least a 40% contingent fee to Galanis. We agree with and adopt for Indiana the Louisiana Supreme Court's approach to fees for successive lawyers employed under contingent fee contracts.

> [O]nly one contingency fee should be paid by the client, the amount of the fee to be determined according to the highest ethical contingency percentage to which the client contractually agreed [and] ... that fee should in turn be allocated between or among the various attorneys involved in handling the claim in question....

Saucier v. Hayes Dairy Products, Inc., 373 So.2d 102, 118 (La. 1978). The fee should be apportioned according to the respective services and contributions of the lawyers based on the work each performed. *Id.*

In a system of professional responsibility that stresses clients' rights, it is incumbent upon the lawyer who enters a contingent fee contract with knowledge of a previous lawyer's work to explain fully any obligation of the client to pay a previous lawyer and explicitly contract away liability for those fees. If this is not done the successor assumes the obligation to pay the first lawyer's fee out of his or her contingent fee. Galanis was in the best position to evaluate and to reach an agreement as to a reasonable fee for the value of the work already done in Brown's case. "Lawyers almost always possess the more sophisticated understanding of fee arrangements. It is therefore appropriate to place the balance of the burden of fair dealing and the allotment of risk in the hands of the lawyer in regard to fee arrangements with clients." *In the Matter of Myers,* 663 N.E.2d 771, 774–75 (Ind.1996). Galanis also had the option to discuss with Brown the need for someone to pay Lyons's fee and to refuse to accept the case if Brown could not resolve any open issues with Lyons. He neither advised her of the need to pay the fee nor contracted away that responsibility for himself. Under these circumstances, Galanis, not Brown, should bear the burden of his silence. Accordingly, Lyons is entitled to recover the compensation due it from Galanis' contingent fee.

For the same reasons we reject the approach taken by some states that would require the client to pay fees to both lawyers and then attempt to recover the amount paid to the first from the second. *See* 1 Geoffrey C. Hazard, Jr. & W. William Hodes, The Law of Lawyering § 1.16:602 n. 7 (1990 & Supp.1998) (discussing *Plunkett & Cooney P.C. v. Capitol Bancorp Ltd.,* 212 Mich.App. 325, 536 N.W.2d 886 (1995)). Lawyers, as professionals, should be able to resolve these issues by agreement. If they cannot, they, not the client, should bear the cost of resolving a dispute over their relative contributions.

CONCLUSION

There are a number of factors that are relevant to a fair resolution of these issues, including whether the predecessor's compensation is contingent on the ultimate result, whether the predecessor's efforts served to reduce the work necessary to bring the case to conclusion, whether the efforts of each lawyer were reasonably efficient, and presumably many others. We assume that the vast majority of these fee arrangements are and should be resolved by agreement between the affected lawyers with appropriate deference to the assumption that each lawyer handled the case efficiently and productively. If not, finding the proper allocation of these contributions is the sort of fact issue trial courts resolve on a daily basis. To the extent an agreement cannot be reached, lawyers, like any other litigants, may take their factual dispute to a trial court. And, like any other litigant, if they do not spell out the arrangement in a written agreement, they take their chances on the deal the trial court will cut for them. Here, for the reasons given, the subsequent lawyer's fee, not the client, should be the source of payment of the predecessor.

The decision of the trial court is affirmed in part. This case is remanded for proceedings not inconsistent with this opinion.

Notes

1. A lawyer who withdraws voluntarily from a contingent fee case before it is resolved is generally not entitled to any fees at all, unless the withdrawal was for "good cause." See, e.g., *Rus, Miliband & Smith v. Conkle & Olesten*, 113 Cal.App.4th 656, 6 Cal.Rptr.3d 612 (2003) (law firm's withdrawal because of a "break-down in communications" was not sufficiently justifiable to warrant recovery of any fees); *Bell & Marra v. Sullivan*, 300 Mont. 530, 6 P.3d 965 (2000) (law firm failed to prove that financial burden of continuing representation was "good cause" for withdrawal, so not entitled to any fees).

2. A lawyer will forfeit some or all fees where there has been "clear and serious violation of duty to a client." Restatement § 37. If a lawyer breaches a fiduciary duty to the client, fees may be forfeited even in the absence of actual damages to the client. See, e.g., *Burrow v. Arce*, 997 S.W.2d 229 (Tex.1999).

3. Where the client fires a contingent-fee lawyer without good cause, most states hold that the lawyer is entitled to a fee based on the fair value of the services provided, in the absence of a contractual provision to the contrary. See *Malonis v. Harrington*, 442 Mass. 692, 816 N.E.2d 115 (2004).

4. A few states disagree, and instead require that the fee contract spell out explicitly any quantum meruit entitlement. For example, in *Dudding v. Norton Frickey & Assoc.*, 11 P.3d 441 (Colo.2000), a lawyer agreed to handle a wrongful termination case on a contingent-fee basis. The client dismissed the suit and accepted his old job back in lieu of damages. The lawyer argued that he was entitled to quantum meruit fees under these circumstances. But the court held that because the fee agreement did not explicitly notify the client of the lawyer's right to quantum meruit recovery, the lawyer was not entitled to fees at all. See also *Elliott v. Joyce*, 889 P.2d 43 (Colo.1994). Is this approach preferable to the majority rule we saw applied in *Galanis*?

5. Even in the absence of a contract, a lawyer is usually entitled to the fair value of the services provided. Restatement § 39. The comment to this section explains that in such a case, "[d]enying all compensation would be unfair to the lawyer and a windfall to the client," especially

given that "both usually expect that some payment will be due." *Id.*, comment *b*.

§ 4. FEE–SHIFTING STATUTES

FARRAR v. HOBBY

Supreme Court of the United States, 1992.
506 U.S. 103, 113 S.Ct. 566, 121 L.Ed.2d 494.

Justice THOMAS delivered the opinion of the Court.

We decide today whether a civil rights plaintiff who receives a nominal damages award is a "prevailing party" eligible to receive attorney's fees under 42 U.S.C. § 1988. The Court of Appeals for the Fifth Circuit reversed an award of attorney's fees on the ground that a plaintiff receiving only nominal damages is not a prevailing party. Although we hold that such a plaintiff is a prevailing party, we affirm the denial of fees in this case.

I

Joseph Davis Farrar and Dale Lawson Farrar owned and operated Artesia Hall, a school in Liberty County, Texas, for delinquent, disabled, and disturbed teens. After an Artesia Hall student died in 1973, a Liberty County grand jury returned a murder indictment charging Joseph Farrar with willful failure to administer proper medical treatment and failure to provide timely hospitalization. The State of Texas also obtained a temporary injunction that closed Artesia Hall.

Respondent William P. Hobby, Jr., then Lieutenant Governor of Texas, participated in the events leading to the closing of Artesia Hall. After Joseph Farrar was indicted, Hobby issued a press release criticizing the Texas Department of Public Welfare and its licensing procedures. He urged the department's director to investigate Artesia Hall and accompanied Governor Dolph Briscoe on an inspection of the school. Finally, he attended the temporary injunction hearing with Briscoe and spoke to reporters after the hearing.

Joseph Farrar sued Hobby, Judge Clarence D. Cain, County Attorney Arthur J. Hartell III, and the director and two employees of the Department of Public Welfare for monetary and injunctive relief under 42 U.S.C. §§ 1983 and 1985. The complaint alleged deprivation of liberty and property without due process by means of conspiracy and malicious prosecution aimed at closing Artesia Hall. Later amendments to the complaint added Dale Farrar as a plaintiff, dropped the claim for injunctive relief, and increased the request for damages to $17 million. After Joseph Farrar died on February 20, 1983, petitioners Dale Farrar and Pat

Smith, coadministrators of his estate, were substituted as plaintiffs.

The case was tried before a jury in the Southern District of Texas on August 15, 1983. Through special interrogatories, the jury found that all of the defendants except Hobby had conspired against the plaintiffs but that this conspiracy was not a proximate cause of any injury suffered by the plaintiffs. The jury also found that Hobby had "committed an act or acts under color of state law that deprived Plaintiff Joseph Davis Farrar of a civil right," but it found that Hobby's conduct was not "a proximate cause of any damages" suffered by Joseph Farrar. The jury made no findings in favor of Dale Farrar. In accordance with the jury's answers to the special interrogatories, the District Court ordered that "Plaintiffs take nothing, that the action be dismissed on the merits, and that the parties bear their own costs."

The Court of Appeals for the Fifth Circuit affirmed in part and reversed in part. The court affirmed the failure to award compensatory or nominal damages against the conspirators because the plaintiffs had not proved an actual deprivation of a constitutional right. Because the jury found that Hobby had deprived Joseph Farrar of a civil right, however, the Fifth Circuit remanded for entry of judgment against Hobby for nominal damages.

The plaintiffs then sought attorney's fees under 42 U.S.C. § 1988. On January 30, 1987, the District Court entered an order awarding the plaintiffs $280,000 in fees, $27,932 in expenses, and $9,730 in prejudgment interest against Hobby.... A divided Fifth Circuit panel reversed the fee award.... [T]he majority held that the plaintiffs were not prevailing parties and were therefore ineligible for fees under § 1988:

> "The Farrars sued for $17 million in money damages; the jury gave them nothing. No money damages. No declaratory relief. No injunctive relief. Nothing.... [T]he Farrars did succeed in securing a jury-finding that Hobby violated their civil rights and a nominal award of one dollar. However, this finding did not in any meaningful sense 'change the legal relationship' between the Farrars and Hobby. Nor was the result a success for the Farrars on a 'significant issue that achieve[d] some of the benefit the [Farrars] sought in bringing suit.' When the sole relief sought is money damages, we fail to see how a party 'prevails' by winning one dollar out of the $17 million requested."

The majority reasoned that even if an award of nominal damages represented some sort of victory, "surely [the Farrars'] was 'a technical victory ... so insignificant ... as to be insufficient to support prevailing party status.' " ...

II

The Civil Rights Attorney's Fees Awards Act of 1976, 90 Stat. 2641, as amended, 42 U.S.C. § 1988, provides in relevant part:

> "In any action or proceeding to enforce a provision of sections 1981, 1982, 1983, 1985, and 1986 of this title, title IX of Public Law 92–318 . . . , or title VI of the Civil Rights Act of 1964 . . . , the court, in its discretion, may allow the prevailing party, other than the United States, a reasonable attorney's fee as part of the costs."

"Congress intended to permit the . . . award of counsel fees only when a party has prevailed on the merits." *Hanrahan v. Hampton,* 446 U.S. 754, 758, 100 S.Ct. 1987, 1989, 64 L.Ed.2d 670 (1980) (*per curiam*). Therefore, in order to qualify for attorney's fees under § 1988, a plaintiff must be a "prevailing party." Under our "generous formulation" of the term, " 'plaintiffs may be considered "prevailing parties" for attorney's fees purposes if they succeed on any significant issue in litigation which achieves some of the benefit the parties sought in bringing suit.' " *Hensley v. Eckerhart,* 461 U.S. 424, 433, 103 S.Ct. 1933, 1939, 76 L.Ed.2d 40 (1983) (quoting *Nadeau v. Helgemoe,* 581 F.2d 275, 278–279 (C.A.1 1978)). "[L]iability on the merits and responsibility for fees go hand in hand; where a defendant has not been prevailed against, either because of legal immunity or on the merits, § 1988 does not authorize a fee award against that defendant." *Kentucky v. Graham,* 473 U.S. 159, 165, 105 S.Ct. 3099, 3104, 87 L.Ed.2d 114 (1985).

We have elaborated on the definition of prevailing party in three recent cases. In *Hewitt v. Helms,* 482 U.S. 755, 107 S.Ct. 2672, 96 L.Ed.2d 654 (1987), we addressed "the peculiar-sounding question whether a party who litigates to judgment and loses on all of his claims can nonetheless be a 'prevailing party.' "In his § 1983 action against state prison officials for alleged due process violations, respondent Helms obtained no relief. "The most that he obtained was an interlocutory ruling that his complaint should not have been dismissed for failure to state a constitutional claim." Observing that "[r]espect for ordinary language requires that a plaintiff receive at least some relief on the merits of his claim before he can be said to prevail," we held that Helms was not a prevailing party. We required the plaintiff to prove "the settling of some dispute which affects the behavior of the defendant towards the plaintiff."

In *Rhodes v. Stewart,* 488 U.S. 1, 109 S.Ct. 202, 102 L.Ed.2d 1 (1988) (*per curiam*), we reversed an award of attorney's fees premised solely on a declaratory judgment that prison officials had violated the plaintiffs' First and Fourteenth Amendment rights. By the time the District Court entered judgment, "one of the plaintiffs had died and the other was no longer in custody." Under these circumstances, we held, neither plaintiff was a prevailing party. We explained that "nothing in [*Hewitt*] suggested that the entry of [a declaratory] judgment in a party's favor automatically renders that party prevailing under § 1988." We reaffirmed that a judgment—declaratory or otherwise—"will constitute relief, for purposes of § 1988, if, and only if, it affects the behavior of the defendant toward the plaintiff." Whatever "modification of prison policies" the declaratory judgment might have effected "could not in any way have benefitted either plaintiff, one of whom was dead and the other released."

Finally, in *Texas State Teachers Assn. v. Garland Independent School Dist.*, 489 U.S. 782, 109 S.Ct. 1486, 103 L.Ed.2d 866 (1989), we synthesized the teachings of *Hewitt* and *Rhodes*. "[T]o be considered a prevailing party within the meaning of § 1988," we held, "the plaintiff must be able to point to a resolution of the dispute which changes the legal relationship between itself and the defendant." We reemphasized that "[t]he touchstone of the prevailing party inquiry must be the material alteration of the legal relationship of the parties." Under this test, the plaintiffs in *Garland* were prevailing parties because they "obtained a judgment vindicating [their] First Amendment rights [as] public employees" and "materially altered the [defendant] school district's policy limiting the rights of teachers to communicate with each other concerning employee organizations and union activities."

Therefore, to qualify as a prevailing party, a civil rights plaintiff must obtain at least some relief on the merits of his claim. The plaintiff must obtain an enforceable judgment against the defendant from whom fees are sought, or comparable relief through a consent decree or settlement. Whatever relief the plaintiff secures must directly benefit him at the time of the judgment or settlement. Otherwise the judgment or settlement cannot be said to "affec[t] the behavior of the defendant toward the plaintiff." *Rhodes, supra*, 488 U.S., at 4. Only under these circumstances can civil rights litigation effect "the material alteration of the legal relationship of the parties" and thereby transform the plaintiff into a prevailing party. *Garland, supra*, 489 U.S., at 792–793. In short, a plaintiff "prevails" when actual relief on the merits of his claim materially alters the legal relationship between the parties by modifying the defendant's behavior in a way that directly benefits the plaintiff.

III

A

Doubtless "the basic purpose of a § 1983 damages award should be to compensate persons for injuries caused by the deprivation of constitutional rights." *Carey v. Piphus*, 435 U.S. 247, 254, 98 S.Ct. 1042, 1047, 55 L.Ed.2d 252 (1978). For this reason, no compensatory damages may be awarded in a § 1983 suit absent proof of actual injury. We have also held, however, that "the denial of procedural due process should be actionable for nominal damages without proof of actual injury." *Carey, supra,* 435 U.S., at 266. The awarding of nominal damages for the "absolute" right to procedural due process "recognizes the importance to organized society that [this] righ[t] be scrupulously observed" while "remain[ing] true to the principle that substantial damages should be awarded only to compensate actual injury." [*Id.*] Thus, *Carey* obligates a court to award nominal damages when a plaintiff establishes the violation of his right to procedural due process but cannot prove actual injury.

We therefore hold that a plaintiff who wins nominal damages is a prevailing party under § 1988. When a court awards nominal damages, it neither enters judgment for defendant on the merits nor declares the defendant's legal immunity to suit. To be sure, a judicial pronouncement that the defendant has violated the Constitution, unaccompanied by an enforceable judgment on the merits, does not render the plaintiff a prevailing party. Of itself, "the moral satisfaction [that] results from any favorable statement of law" cannot bestow prevailing party status. No material alteration of the legal relationship between the parties occurs until the plaintiff becomes entitled to enforce a judgment, consent decree, or settlement against the defendant. A plaintiff may demand payment for nominal damages no less than he may demand payment for millions of dollars in compensatory damages. A judgment for damages in any amount, whether compensatory or nominal, modifies the defendant's behavior for the plaintiff's benefit by forcing the defendant to pay an amount of money he otherwise would not pay. As a result, the Court of Appeals for the Fifth Circuit erred in holding that petitioners' nominal damages award failed to render them prevailing parties.

We have previously stated that "a technical victory may be so insignificant . . . as to be insufficient to support prevailing party status." *Garland,* 489 U.S., at 792. The example chosen in *Garland* to illustrate this sort of "technical" victory, however, would fail to support prevailing party status under the test we adopt today. In that case, the District Court declared unconstitutionally vague a regulation requiring that "nonschool hour meetings be conducted only with prior approval from the local school principal." We suggested that this finding alone would not sustain prevailing party status if there were " 'no evidence that the plaintiffs were ever refused permission to use school premises during non-school hours.' " . . . Now that we are confronted with the question whether a nominal damages award is the sort of "technical," "insignificant" victory that cannot confer prevailing party status, we hold that the prevailing party inquiry does not turn on the magnitude of the relief obtained. We recognized as much in *Garland* when we noted that "the *degree* of the plaintiff's success" does not affect "eligibility for a fee award."

B

Although the "technical" nature of a nominal damages award or any other judgment does not affect the prevailing party inquiry, it does bear on the propriety of fees awarded under § 1988. Once civil rights litigation materially alters the legal relationship between the parties, "the degree of the plaintiff's overall success goes to the reasonableness" of a fee award under *Hensley v. Eckerhart,* 461 U.S. 424, 103 S.Ct. 1933, 76 L.Ed.2d 40 (1983). Indeed, "the most critical factor" in determining the reasonableness of a fee award "is the degree of success obtained." *Hensley, supra,* 461 U.S., at 436. In this case, petitioners received nominal damages instead of the $17 million in compensatory damages that they sought. This litigation accomplished little beyond giving petitioners "the moral satisfaction of knowing that a federal court concluded that [their] rights had been violated" in some unspecified way. *Hewitt, supra,* 482 U.S., at 762. We have already observed that if "a plaintiff has achieved only partial or limited success, the product of hours reasonably expended on the litigation as a whole times a reasonable hourly rate may be an excessive amount." *Hensley, supra,* 461 U.S., at 436. Yet the District Court calculated petitioners' fee award in precisely this fashion, without engaging in any measured exercise of discretion. "Where recovery of private damages is the purpose of . . . civil rights litigation, a district court, in fixing fees, is obligated to give primary consideration to the amount of damages awarded as compared to the amount sought." Such a comparison promotes the court's "central" responsibility to "make the assessment of what is a reasonable fee under the circumstances of the case." *Blanchard v. Bergeron,* 489 U.S. 87, 96, 109 S.Ct. 939, 946, 103 L.Ed.2d 67 (1989). Having considered the amount and nature of damages awarded, the court may lawfully award low fees or no fees without reciting the 12 factors bearing on reasonableness, or multiplying "the number of hours reasonably expended . . . by a reasonable hourly rate."

In some circumstances, even a plaintiff who formally "prevails" under § 1988 should receive no attorney's fees at all. A plaintiff who seeks compensatory damages but receives no more than nominal damages is often such a prevailing party. As we have held, a nominal damages award does render a plaintiff a prevailing party by allowing him to vindicate his "absolute" right to procedural due process through enforcement of a judgment against the defendant. *Carey,* 435 U.S., at 266. In a civil rights suit for damages, however, the awarding of nominal damages also highlights the plaintiff's failure to prove actual, compensable injury. . . . When a plaintiff recovers only nominal damages because of his failure to prove an essential element of his claim for monetary relief, the only reasonable fee is usually no fee at all. . . .

Although the Court of Appeals erred in failing to recognize that petitioners were prevailing parties, it correctly reversed the District Court's fee award. We accordingly affirm the judgment of the Court of Appeals.

So ordered.

[Concurring opinion of Justice O'CONNOR omitted.]

Justice WHITE, with whom Justice BLACKMUN, Justice STEVENS, and Justice SOUTER join, concurring in part and dissenting in part.

. . . [I agree with the majority that because] Farrar won an enforceable judgment against respondent, he has achieved a "material alteration" of their legal relationship, and thus he is a "prevailing party" under the statute.

However, I see no reason for the Court to reach out and decide what amount of attorney's fees constitutes a reasonable amount in this instance. That issue was neither presented in the petition for certiorari nor briefed by petitioners. The opinion of the Court of Appeals was grounded exclusively in its determination that Farrar had not met the threshold requirement under § 1988. At no point did it purport to decide what a reasonable award should be if Farrar was a prevailing party.

It may be that the District Court abused its discretion and misapplied our precedents by belittling the significance of the amount of damages awarded in ascertaining petitioners' fees. But it is one thing to say that the court erred as a matter of law in awarding $280,000; quite another to decree, especially without the benefit of petitioners' views or consideration by the Court of Appeals, that the only fair fee was no fee whatsoever.

Litigation in this case lasted for more than a decade, has entailed a 6–week trial and given rise to two appeals. Civil rights cases often are complex, and we therefore have committed the task of calculating attorney's fees to the trial court's discretion for good reason. Estimating what specific amount would be reasonable in this particular situation is not a matter of general importance on which our guidance is needed. Short of holding that recovery of nominal damages *never* can support the award of attorney's fees—which, clearly, the majority does not—the Court should follow its sensible practice and remand the case for reconsideration of the fee amount. Indeed, respondent's counsel all but conceded at oral argument that, assuming the Court found Farrar to be a prevailing party, the question of reasonableness should be addressed on remand.

I would vacate the judgment of the Court of Appeals and remand the case for further proceedings. Accordingly, I dissent.

Notes

1. Are one-way fee shifting statutes a good idea? What values do they serve? Would "both way" fee shifting statutes be an even better idea?

2. *Measurement.* As referenced in *Farrar*, when a plaintiff demonstrates that he or she is a "prevailing party" entitled to fees pursuant to a fee-shifting statute, the court must then determine what fee should be awarded. In federal court, a "lodestar" method is most often used. See *Burlington v. Dague*, 505 U.S. 557, 112 S.Ct. 2638, 120 L.Ed.2d 449 (1992). This means that a basic number, or "lodestar" is first determined by multiplying the number of hours reasonably spent by the prevailing party's lawyer, multiplied by a reasonable hourly rate. The court can then adjust this "lodestar" figure up or down to reflect other relevant considerations, such the quality of the lawyer's work or the risk involved in taking the case. See, e.g., *McDonald v. Pension Plan*, 450 F.3d 91 (2d Cir. 2006).

3. *Reduction for poor writing.* In *Devore v. City of Philadelphia*, 2004 WL 414085 (E.D.Pa.), a Title VII/ § 1983 plaintiff won a verdict of $430,000, and the plaintiff's lawyer sought to recover fees. After determining a "lodestar," Judge Jason Hart reduced the lawyer's fees by $150 per hour for written work that was "careless, to the point of disrespectful." Pages were missing from the Complaint, which was "nearly unintelligible" in parts. Judge Hart said the lawyer's "lack of care caused the court, and I am sure, defense counsel, to expend an inordinate amount of time deciphering the arguments and responding, accordingly." The filings "are replete with typographical errors," such as the consistent identification of the court as the "Easter District of Pennslyvania"; the judge wrote that "considering the religious persuasion of the presiding officer, the 'Passover' district would have been more appropriate. However, we took no personal offense at the reference." Even in response to the defendant's argument to reduce fees for poor writing, the lawyer filled his response with typos and odd sentence constructions. "If these mistakes were purposeful," said the judge, "they would be brilliant. However, based on the history of the case and [the lawyer's] filings, we know otherwise. Finally, in the most recent letter to the court ... [the lawyer] identified the undersigned as 'Honorable Jacon [sic] Hart.' I appreciate the elevation to what sounds like a character in *Lord of the Rings*, but alas, I am but a judge."

4. The factors listed in Model Rule 1.5 and DR 2–106 are still followed by many state courts in setting the amount of a fee pursuant to state fee-shifting statutes. What if a lawyer's request for fees is so outrageous that it shocks the conscience of the court? In *Fair Housing Council of Greater Washington v. Landow*, 999 F.2d 92 (4th Cir. 1993),

the court affirmed a trial judge's denial of the fee application in its entirety on that ground.

5. Was the majority right in holding that no fee should be awarded in *Farrar*? If the case had been remanded, as the dissenters wanted, do you think the trial judge would have been justified in awarding a fee using the "lodestar" method discussed above?

6. *Pro se litigants.* In *Kay v. Ehrler*, 499 U.S. 432, 111 S.Ct. 1435, 113 L.Ed.2d 486 (1991), the Court held that a pro se lawyer (a lawyer representing himself) was not entitled to fees under the civil rights fee-shifting statute, 42 U.S.C. § 1988. The court reasoned that the term "attorney" in the statute "assumes an agency relationship." What if a lawyer is representing himself and another lawyer in a civil rights case and wins for both of them. Should *Kay* bar his application for fees under § 1988? See *Schneider v. Colegio de Abogados de Puerto Rico*, 187 F.3d 30 (1st Cir.1999) (no, since the lawyer was both plaintiff and counsel, and the fees would have been the same even if he had not represented himself as well).

What if a lawyer represents his own child in a case seeking relief under the Individual with Disabilities Education Act, 20 U.S.C. § 1400, a statute that allows the court "to award reasonable attorneys' fees as part of the costs to the parents or guardian of a child or youth who is a prevailing party." Can that lawyer recover fees? In *Doe v. Board of Education of Baltimore County*, 165 F.3d 260 (4th Cir.1998), the defendant argued that Mr. Doe was acting pro se, in essence, and that *Kay* therefore barred his claim for fees. While disagreeing with that argument, the Fourth Circuit nonetheless held that no fees should be awarded on public policy grounds. Fee shifting statutes are intended to encourage litigants to retain independent counsel. "Like attorneys appearing pro se, attorney-parents are generally incapable of exercising sufficient independent judgment on behalf of their children to ensure that 'reason, rather than emotion' will dictate the conduct of the litigation." While it did not occur here, the court also noted that there was a risk that an "irrationally emotional" attorney-parent would "bungle" a meritorious claim. Awarding fees here, said the court, would encourage inexperienced attorney-parents to represent their own children in proceedings in which they should not do so. If no rule prohibits an attorney-parent from undertaking such representation, is a court justified in withholding fees to discourage it?

7. *Non-lawyer advocates.* State and federal regulations allow non-lawyers to represent parties before many administrative agencies. If such a non-lawyer helps a client prevail in a proceeding, can the non-lawyer get fees? See *Z.A. v. San Bruno Park Sch. Dist.*, 165 F.3d 1273 (9th Cir. 1999) (lawyer not admitted in California cannot get fees for representing a client in California administrative agency proceeding, even if the representation itself was authorized by agency regulations).

8. Can a court-awarded fee exceed the amount of damages won by the plaintiff? Yes. See, e.g., *City of Riverside v. Rivera*, 477 U.S. 561, 106

S.Ct. 2686, 91 L.Ed.2d 466 (1986) (upholding fee of $279,000 when jury had awarded civil rights plaintiff $33,350). As *Farrar* indicates, fees may also be awarded in cases in which the plaintiff wins only nominal damages; obviously in such cases the fee will exceed the one-dollar monetary recovery. See, e.g., *Mercer v. Duke Univ.*, 401 F.3d 199 (4th Cir. 2005) (affirming award of $350,000 in fees where Title IX plaintiff received only nominal damages); *Brandau v. State of Kansas*, 168 F.3d 1179 (10th Cir.1999) (affirming award of over $41,000 in fees where Title VII plaintiff received only nominal damages).

9. *Buckhannon.* Much litigation in fee-shifting cases centers on whether a plaintiff has in fact "prevailed." The Court has become more restrictive in its definition of that term in recent years. In *Buckhannon Board and Care Home, Inc. v. West Virginia Dept. of Health and Human Resources*, 532 U.S. 598, 121 S.Ct. 1835, 149 L.Ed.2d 855 (2001), the Court declared that in order to "prevail" under federal statutes using that term, a plaintiff must secure a judgment on the merits or a court-ordered consent decree. The Court thus rejected the so-called "catalyst theory," used by most Circuit courts at the time. Under the catalyst theory, a plaintiff could be a "prevailing party" even in the absence of a judgment or consent decree where he "has nonetheless achieved the desired result because the lawsuit brought about a voluntary change in the defendant's conduct." The majority said "enforceable judgments on the merits and court-ordered consent decrees create the 'material altera- tion of the legal relationship of the parties' necessary to permit an award of attorney's fees. . . . A defendant's voluntary change in conduct, al- though perhaps accomplishing what the plaintiff sought to achieve by the lawsuit, lacks the necessary judicial *imprimatur* on the change." Doesn't this ruling provide a strong incentive for a defendant in a civil rights lawsuit to change its challenged behavior before an adverse court ruling, thereby avoiding liability for fees? Is this good or bad? Justice Ginsburg, dissenting along with three others, argued that the case would "impede access to the court for the less well-heeled." What did she mean by that?

10. *Interpreting Buckhannon.* After *Buckhannon*, lower federal courts have struggled to interpret it. Did the court mean to say that a plaintiff was the "prevailing party" only where he won an enforceable judgment on the merits or a court-ordered consent decree? Or were those simply examples of "prevailing"? The majority of courts believe it is the latter; a judicial action other than a judgment or a consent decree can support an award of fees, "so long as such action carries with it sufficient judicial imprimatur." *Roberson v. Giuliani*, 346 F.3d 75 (2d Cir. 2003) (citing other Circuits as well).

11. *Other federal fee-shifting statutes.* The sweep of *Buckhannon* is not entirely clear, but on its face it extends to all federal fee-shifting statutes that award fees to a "prevailing party," period. See, e.g., *T.D. v. LaGrange Sch. Dist. No. 102*, 349 F.3d 469 (7th Cir. 2003). Some federal statutes are drafted more broadly. For example, the Endangered Species Act, 16 U.S.C. § 1540(g), authorizes courts to award fees "to any party,

whenever the court determines such award is appropriate." Courts have held that the catalyst theory remains viable for such statutes, even after *Buckhannon*. See, e.g., *Loggerhead Turtle v. County Council of Volusia County, Florida*, 307 F.3d 1318 (11th Cir.2002). Other statutes allow for fee shifting in exceptional cases, such as the losing party's having engaged in vexatious litigation conduct. See *TE–TA–MA Truth Foundation–Family of URI, Inc. v. The World Church of the Creator*, 392 F.3d 248 (7th Cir. 2004) (trademark infringement case under the Lanham Act); *Read Corp. v. Portec, Inc.*, 970 F.2d 816 (Fed. Cir. 1992) (Patent Act case).

12. *Contingent fees in fee-shifting situations.* If a lawyer represents a client in a case in which fees will be awarded by statute if the client prevails, can the lawyer also charge an additional percentage contingency fee? In *Venegas v. Mitchell*, 495 U.S. 82, 110 S.Ct. 1679, 109 L.Ed.2d 74 (1990), the Court said yes.

13. *State fee-shifting statutes.* State courts interpreting state statutes are, of course, not bound by U.S. Supreme Court interpretations of federal fee-shifting statutes. Still, some have followed the Court's holdings voluntarily when interpreting similar language. See, e.g., *McGrath v. Toys "R" Us*, 3 N.Y.3d 421, 821 N.E.2d 519, 788 N.Y.S.2d 281 (2004) (applying *Farrar* definition of "prevailing party" to New York City human rights law); *Tibbetts v. Sight 'N Sound Appliance Centers, Inc.*, 77 P.3d 1042 (Okla. 2003) (applying *Farrar* to state Consumer Protection Act case). Others have departed company with the Court on various issues in this context. See, e.g., *Tipton-Whittingham v. City of Los Angeles*, 34 Cal.4th 604, 101 P.3d 174, 21 Cal.Rptr.3d 371 (2004) (applying catalyst theory to claim under state Fair Employment and Housing Act); *Flannery v. Prentice*, 26 Cal.4th 572, 28 P.3d 860, 110 Cal.Rptr.2d 809 (2001) (holding that fees awarded under the FEHA belong to the lawyer, not the client, rejecting case law under federal civil rights statutes).

§ 5. FEE SHARING AND FEE SPLITTING

A. Between Lawyers in Different Firms

FORD v. ALBANY MEDICAL CENTER

New York Supreme Court, Appellate Division, 2001.
283 A.D.2d 843, 724 N.Y.S.2d 795.

LAHTINEN, J.

... In February 1998, plaintiff consulted with attorney Eugene R. Spada regarding a possible medical malpractice action pertaining to the treatment received by her daughter at defendant hospital. Using documents provided by plaintiff, Spada obtained an expert medical opinion that a viable medical malpractice case existed.

By letter dated April 8, 1998, attorney Charles R. Harding informed Spada that plaintiff had retained his office to proceed with the medical malpractice action and requested that Spada sign a consent to change attorney form. The letter acknowledged that plaintiff had originally retained Spada and agreed to split the counsel fees in "an equitable manner". On April 9, 1998, Spada had a telephone conversation with Harding wherein the attorneys agreed that Spada would receive 33.33% of any counsel fee. Spada, on the same day, wrote to Harding asking for confirmation of the agreement in writing. On May 7, 1998, Harding sent Spada a check to reimburse Spada's disbursements but made no mention of any agreement to split counsel fees. On May 12, 1998, Spada wrote Harding requesting that Harding forward the counsel fee agreement as soon as possible. Spada thereafter received a letter on Harding's legal letterhead, dated May 19, 1998, which stated that "[i]n response to your May 12, 1998 letter regarding legal fees, I agree to the split of 66.66% to myself and 33.33 to your firm. Thank you."

The medical malpractice case was eventually settled resulting in a fee which Supreme Court determined to be $99,701.48. Spada petitioned Supreme Court for an order directing payment of 33.33% of the fee to him in accordance with the parties' agreement and Harding cross-petitioned for an order extinguishing Spada's claim for counsel fees.

Supreme Court determined that Spada had a lawyer-client relationship with plaintiff entitling him to a legal fee based on quantum meruit to be determined at a hearing,[1] but that the May 19, 1998 letter was sent from Harding's law office without Harding's authorization and, therefore, did not create a binding agreement regarding the split of counsel fees. Spada appeals from that part of Supreme Court's order which rejected his claim that he and Harding entered into an enforceable fee split agreement....

Spada argues that Harding's May 19, 1998 letter legally bound Harding to pay him 33.33% of the earned legal fee and that Supreme Court erred by denying him a contractual lien....

Initially, we agree with Supreme Court that Spada and plaintiff had an attorney-client relationship. Despite plaintiff's affidavit insisting that no such relationship existed, the record shows that she visited his office on more than one occasion in connection with her possible medical malpractice case, left documents pertaining to that case at his office to enable him to pursue a course of action and signed a consent to change attorney form to substitute Harding as her new attorney. Harding, in turn, acknowledged in writing Spada's representation of plaintiff. Clearly, plaintiff met with Spada regarding a specific case which Spada undertook to

---

1. Spada has not appealed from Supreme Court's subsequent determination after a hearing (for which no order appears in the record) that he performed 3% of the work on the case and was entitled to counsel fees of $2,991.

prepare, an indicia of an attorney-client relationship. In addition, the actions of plaintiff, Spada and Harding subsequent to her initial consultation with Spada fully support Supreme Court's determination that Spada and plaintiff had an attorney-client relationship. Finally, the absence of a written retainer agreement does not require a different conclusion, especially since plaintiff had not yet been authorized to act as the personal representative of her daughter's estate when Spada was discharged.

Spada next claims that he had an enforceable agreement with Harding whereby he was to receive 33.33% of the total counsel fee ultimately recovered. Upon the facts presented here, even though we disagree with Supreme Court's conclusion that the attorneys did not reach an agreement as to a fee split, we find that such an agreement is unenforceable because it violates Code of Professional Responsibility DR 2–107(A)(2) (22 NYCRR 1200.12[a][2]), which provides:

> A.   A lawyer shall not divide a fee for legal services with another lawyer who is not a partner in or associates of the lawyer's law firm, unless:
>
>   * * *
>
> 2.   The division is in proportion to the services performed by each lawyer or, by a writing given to the client, each lawyer assumes joint responsibility for the representation.

The plain language of that portion of the Disciplinary Rule directs that where each lawyer does not assume joint responsibility for a client's representation in writing, the division of any fee must be in proportion to the services performed by each lawyer. Here there is absolutely no question that Spada did not assume joint responsibility for plaintiff's representation in writing or otherwise. As a consequence, Spada's claim for 33.33% of the counsel fee to be paid in this action based solely upon his purported agreement with Harding cannot be upheld. Accordingly, we agree that Supreme Court, after a hearing, properly computed Spada's fee on a contingent fee percentage based on quantum meruit and appropriately awarded Spada 3% of the total fee.

ORDERED that the order is affirmed, without costs.

Notes

1.   Model Rule 1.5(e) provides that lawyers not in the same firm may divide a fee only if (1) the division is made "in proportion to the services performed by each lawyer," or if both lawyers "assume joint responsibility" for the matter; (2) the client agrees to the arrangement in writing; and (3) the total fee is reasonable. The comment explains that fee division is most often used when the fee is contingent and a matter

has been referred by the original lawyer to a trial specialist. MR 1.5, comment [7]. Such referrals should be made only when the referring lawyer reasonably believes the second lawyer is competent to handle the case. Id.

2. Why is obtaining client consent so important? In *Margolin v. Shemaria*, 85 Cal.App.4th 891, 102 Cal.Rptr.2d 502 (2000), the court held that a referral agreement between two lawyers was unenforceable where the second lawyer failed to provide written disclosure to the client or obtain the client's written consent as required by Cal. Rule 2–200. In *Chambers v. Kay*, 29 Cal.4th 142, 56 P.3d 645, 126 Cal.Rptr.2d 536 (2002), the court ruled the same way in a fee-sharing agreement between two lawyers who both worked on a case for a single client, denying even quantum meruit recovery. In *Huskinson & Brown, LLP v. Wolf*, 32 Cal.4th 453, 84 P.3d 379, 9 Cal.Rptr.3d 693 (2004), the court allowed quantum meruit recovery by a law firm that had been retained via an oral agreement by another law firm. The court reasoned that Rule 2–200 did not apply since the plaintiff firm's services were retained by the defendant firm, not by the client.

3. What if a fee-sharing agreement between two lawyers is oral, and not disclosed to the client at the time, but then is ratified by the client after the matter is concluded? In *Saggese v. Kelley*, 445 Mass. 434, 837 N.E.2d 699 (2005), the court affirmed a judgment for the referring attorney against the lawyers retained by the referred client on these facts. The court reasoned that the rules requiring disclosure to the client and obtaining the client's consent are for the client's protection, not the lawyer's.

4. What if anything is wrong with one lawyer paying another a referral fee simply to "pass the case along?" Might not such fees encourage less experienced lawyers who are good at attracting clients to pass those clients along to more experienced attorneys who are not so good at attracting clients?

5. Some states have set up arbitration processes to resolve fee disputes between lawyers. See, e.g., *Shimko v. Lobe*, 103 Ohio St.3d 59, 813 N.E.2d 669 (2004) (upholding Ohio's process against constitutional attack).

B. Between Lawyers and Non–Lawyers

GORMAN v. GRODENSKY

New York Supreme Court, New York County, 1985.
130 Misc.2d 837, 498 N.Y.S.2d 249.

HERMAN CAHN, Justice:

[This case is before the court on cross-motions for summary judgment.] In the original complaint, plaintiff, Herman Gorman ("Gorman") alleges that since 1967 defendant Maurice A. Grodensky ("Grodensky") and one David B. LeSchack ("LeSchack") were the sole partners in the partnership of LeSchack & Grodensky. Both Grodensky and LeSchack were attorneys, practicing law, and the partnership was a law firm.... The partnership allegedly "maintained and operated a business, known as the 'Collection Division', engaged in the collection of debts". It is claimed that in 1967, the parties entered into an agreement which provided that Gorman would be employed as Office Manager of the Collection Division for as long as the firm existed, in return for which he would receive a salary of $350 per week plus one third of the net profits of the Collection Division. In 1970, when LeSchack died, the parties allegedly "amended their agreement to provide for a division of the net profit of the Collection Division with 50% to be paid to plaintiff and 50% to be paid to defendant Grodensky". In 1972, Grodensky formed a professional corporation known as LeSchack & Grodensky, P.C. Gorman alleges that he performed all of his duties under the agreement for the partnership and later, for the professional corporation, but that defendants breached the agreement by wrongfully terminating his employment and failing to pay the money due him....

Assuming, for the purposes of this decision only, that [the agreement] is authentic, an examination of some of its relevant provisions is important in analyzing the legal issues presented. First, the agreement provides that Gorman's employment was as Office Manager of the Collection Division and was to continue for as long as the firm of LeSchack and Grodensky continued in existence, or, in any event, for a period of five years. Next, Gorman was to receive a weekly salary of $350.00 plus, from time to time, a sum equal to one-third of the net profit of the Collection Division.

Defendant contends that it is entitled to dismissal of the complaint because, even if the purported contract is genuine, it is essentially an agreement to split attorney's fees and is therefore against public policy and unenforceable. By the terms of the purported agreement, Gorman, who is not an attorney was to receive a percentage of the net profits from the "Collection Division". Defendants argue that even if such a division did exist, the profit sharing arrangement is in violation of the Code of Professional Responsibility's disciplinary rule prohibiting the splitting of legal fees between attorneys and non-attorneys. [Code of Professional Responsibility DR3–102 (A) provides in relevant part: "(A) A lawyer or law firm shall not share legal fees with a non-lawyer, except that: (3) A lawyer or law firm may include non-lawyer employees in a retirement plan, even though the plan is based in whole or in part on a profit-sharing arrangement."]

The court must first determine whether the subject agreement (assuming its authenticity) is violative of that fee splitting provision: pursuant to the agreement, did the firm "share legal fees with a non-lawyer"? From an examination of the exceptions incorporated into DR3–102 the nature of the prohibition becomes more clear. The third exception permits the inclusion of non-lawyers in a retirement plan "even though the plan is based in whole or in part on a profit sharing arrangement". It would appear, and this court holds, that the essence of "fee-splitting" is the sharing of profits on a percentage basis, rather than payment of a fixed compensation or salary. The splitting of fees is prohibit-ed and disfavored by professions other than the legal one as well. It is against the public policy of this State for a licensed profes-sional to "split fees" with an unlicensed person. "[T]here is one course of conduct which in each and every profession is known as a matter of common knowledge to be improper and unprofession-al, that is conduct by which, after a professional man has been licensed by the State, he enters into a partnership in his profes-sional work with a layman, by the terms of which he divides with the latter, *on a percentage basis,* payments made by client or patient for professional services rendered." (emphasis added) *Mat-ter of Bell v. Board of Regents,* 295 N.Y. 101, 111, 65 N.E.2d 184.

The subject agreement clearly provides for a percentage of profits to be paid to plaintiff. That such payments were only to be from profits made by the collection division, does not circumvent the fee splitting prohibition. Although the collection activity and management of the collection division may not, strictly speaking, be the practice of law, division of the profits from the division does constitute sharing of legal fees. . . .

It is apparent . . . that although the agreement here called for Gorman to do work basically of a business nature, rather than of a legal nature, the compensation arrangement was violative of the fee splitting prohibition of DR3–102.

Because the contract is essentially one to split attorneys fees, it violates public policy and, is thereby rendered unenforceable. Even assuming the contract's authenticity, then, the cross motion to dismiss the complaint is granted.

Although the provisions of the Code of Professional Responsi-bility do not enjoy the status of decisional or statutory law, they are an explicit expression of the public policy of the State. An agreement made in violation of a code provision, ought not be sanctioned by the court, as would be the case if the court were to permit plaintiff to sue on the contract. The court will refuse to aid either party to enforce this alleged contract.

That the defendants may benefit from the court's refusal to enforce a contract is irrelevant, if enforcement would further a purpose in violation of public policy. In such a case, the law will not aid either party but will leave them as their acts have placed them. . . .

[Plaintiff's] motion for summary judgment is denied. The [defendant's] cross motion to dismiss the complaint is granted to the extent of dismissing the contract cause of action.

Notes

1. Why is fee-splitting with non-professionals thought to be so bad? Does such an arrangement threaten to break down the supposed wall between "professionals" and others? What interests are protected by the prohibition on fee splitting?

2. Model Rule 5.4(a) prohibits sharing legal fees with a non-lawyer, with a few narrow exceptions. A fee-sharing agreement between a lawyer and a non-lawyer is simply unenforceable, as against public policy. See, e.g., *McIntosh v. Mills*, 121 Cal.App.4th 333, 17 Cal.Rptr.3d 66 (2004). What if a lawyer agrees to pay a referral fee to a law professor who is a member of the state bar on inactive status? Is that agreement enforceable? See *Morris & Doherty, P.C. v. Lockwood*, 259 Mich.App. 38, 672 N.W.2d 884 (2003).

3. Model Rule 5.4 also prohibits a lawyer from forming a partnership with a non-lawyer "if any of the activities of the partnership consist of the practice of law," MR 5.4(b), and from practicing law within any organization in which a non-lawyer threatens to interfere with the lawyer's professional judgment, *see* MR 5.4(c).

4. *Lawyer referral services.* Model Rule 7.2(b)(2) allows lawyers to pay the "usual charges" of a "qualified lawyer referral service." Lawyer referral services are organizations that refer lay people to lawyers; a "qualified" service under the Rules is one "that is approved by an appropriate regulatory authority as affording adequate protections for prospective clients." MR 7.2, comment [6]. Is it unethical fee-splitting for a lawyer to agree to pay a referral service a percentage of any fees received from a referred client? In *Richards v. SSM Health Care, Inc.*, 311 Ill.App.3d 560, 244 Ill.Dec. 87, 724 N.E.2d 975 (2000), the court said it was not. Thus a lawyer could agree to pay 25% of any fees earned to a nonprofit referral service. Such a contract does not offend public policy since nonprofit referral services serve the public interest. The ABA has long approved of the practice, which has now become common among state and local bar association-sponsored referral services. See ABA Formal Op. 291 (1956): Va. State Bar Standing Comm. on Legal Ethics, Op. 1751 (2001).

NOTE: MULTI–DISCIPLINARY PRACTICE

The prohibition on splitting fees with non-lawyers is one of the most significant barriers to the development of what is called "multi-disciplinary practice," or "MDP." Some lawyers have for years urged the bar to ease ethics rules that deter or prohibit lawyers from affiliating with non-lawyers to offer clients integrated or "one-stop" services. For example, some lawyers would like to offer financial planning services as part of a unified law-and-planning business. Such arrangements are quite common in Western Europe.

Informal referrals between lawyers and other professionals has gone on for decades, but formal connections tend to run afoul of rules on fee-splitting (see MR 5.4(a)), assisting the unauthorized practice of law (see MR 5.5), non-lawyer interference with lawyers' independent judgment (see MR 5.4(d)), conflicts of interest (see MR 1.7, 1.8, 1.9, and 1.10), and advertising and solicitation (see MR 7.1 through 7.5). Lawyers are deeply divided over whether MDP is a good idea, and it is not clear how much client demand there would be for such blended services. The states differ over whether MDP should be prohibited entirely, or allowed with safeguards. See, e.g., D.C. Rule 5.4 (allowing lawyers to practice law in a partnership or other form of organization in which a financial interest or managerial authority is exercised by a non-lawyer, and authorizing fee-splitting under some circumstances); Pa. Rule 5.7 (allowing lawyers to provide both legal and non-legal services if the lawyer complies with all ethics rules applicable to lawyers). Many states and the ABA have studied MDP extensively in the last few years.

SEC rules promulgated in 2003 pursuant to the 2002 Sarbanes–Oxley Act, section 201, prohibit accounting firms from doing legal work for auditing clients, effectively ending a trend in that direction. This provision was enacted in the wake of the Enron scandal to prevent auditing firms from acting as advocates as well as watchdogs.

The ABA formed a Commission on Multidisciplinary Practice in 1998. Its 1999 report, recommending specific revisions in the Model Rules to allow MDP with certain restrictions, was met with a firestorm of disapproval within the ABA. The Commission recommended significant revisions to Model Rule 5.4 and the adoption of a new Rule 5.8, to be titled "Responsibilities of a lawyer in a multidisciplinary firm." The ABA's House of Delegates, in August 1999, adopted a resolution to make no change to the Rules "which permits a lawyer to offer legal services through a multidisciplinary practice unless and until additional study demonstrates that such changes will further the public interest without sacrificing or compromising lawyer independence and the legal profession's tradition of loyalty to clients." In July, 2000, the House adopted a recommendation to the states that urges preservation of the "core values of the legal profession" and "the lawyer's duty to help maintain a single professional of law."

In 2001, the New York Code of Professional Responsibility was amended to deal with MDP more directly. DR 1–106 and DR

1–107 now lay out in detail various safeguards that must be observed by lawyers providing "non-legal services" in conjunction with practicing law. DR 1–106(b) prohibits a lawyer from allowing any non-lawyer "to direct or regulate the professional judgement of the lawyer or law firm in rendering legal services to any person," or to cause the lawyer or firm to "compromise its duty" to preserve confidences and secrets of its clients. DR 1–107(a) takes the position that MDP "between lawyers and nonlawyers is incompatible with the core values of the legal profession and therefore, a strict division between services provided by lawyers and those provided by nonlawyers is essential to protect those values." Nonetheless, a lawyer may enter into a contractual arrangement with a non-lawyer to provide both legal and non-legal services, as long as a number of specific conditions are met. The prohibition on splitting fees remains in the New York rule. See DR 1–107(a)(2).

The dust seems to have settled for now on this issue. Time will tell whether the organized bar in various states will move toward continued acceptance of MDP, or whether the "separateness" of law practice will continue to exert its strong gravitational pull in opposition to MDP.

Chapter 6

CONFLICTS OF INTEREST

§ 1. INTRODUCTION

A. What's Wrong With Conflicts of Interest?

As we have seen already, lawyers owe a number of core duties to clients, including duties of competence, loyalty and confidentiality. When a lawyer labors under a conflict of interest, all of these duties may be compromised. A conflict of interest exists when a lawyer cannot, in the exercise of independent judgment, freely recommend a course of action to a client because of conflicting duties owed to someone else. This "someone else" might be another client, a third party, or the lawyer himself or herself.

In law as in life, conflicts of interest are impossible to avoid entirely. Thus neither the ethics rules nor the law reflects an absolute prohibition. Instead, conflicts are regulated and restricted, and remedies for conflicts are flexible and varied. Conflicts that are especially serious, implicating core functions of a lawyer and core duties owed to clients, are to be avoided entirely. Conflicts that are only potential, developing only in the realm of distant possibility, probably raise no issue at all. In between, of course, where most issues lurk, is where our attention here largely lies.

Lawyer conflicts of interest were regulated as early as the Thirteenth century in England. Today, conflicts of interest are the most commonly-litigated category of lawyer misconduct. A lawyer whose representation of a client is found to be tainted by an impermissible conflict is subject to a number of sanctions: First, because the ethics rules in all states regulate conflicts, a lawyer can be disciplined by the bar. Second, because a conflict of interest may constitute a breach of duty to the client (because the duties of competence, loyalty and confidentiality may be implicated), a lawyer may be sued by an aggrieved client for legal malpractice or breach of fiduciary duty, or for rescission of a conflict-tainted transaction. Third, for the same reasons, a lawyer might be ordered to give up fees earned, or might be told by a court that no fee can be charged for a conflicted representation. Fourth, and most commonly, a lawyer might be disqualified from representing a particular client because of a conflict of interest.

B. Types of Conflicts

Conflicts of interest occur in many different forms and settings. Conflicts may involve: (1) the interests of two or more of the lawyer's current clients (often called a "concurrent conflict"); (2) the interests of a current client and a former client (often called a "successive conflict"); (3) the interests of a current client and those of the lawyer, including both personal interests and financial interests; and (4) the interests of a current client and those of a non-client third party to whom the lawyer or client (or both) owe duties. In this chapter, we look at each of these kinds of conflicts in that order. Each presents its own distinct set of issues and concerns, and each is covered by different ethics rules.

C. Curing Conflicts

1. The Basic Requirements

Can a lawyer sometimes represent a client despite a conflict of interest? Yes. Perhaps the strongest case for allowing a conflicted representation is where the client freely consents to waive the conflict of interest. When former client conflicts are present, informed consent does indeed generally cure the problem. In most states, however, client consent to conflicts is necessary but not sufficient for a conflicted representation involving either the lawyer's own interests or current clients to continue.

Model Rule 1.7 deals primarily with current client conflicts. The only flat prohibitions on representing two or more clients with conflicting interests are where the representation is "prohibited by law," or where the representation involves "the assertion of a claim by one client against another client . . . in the same litigation." MR 1.7(b)(2) & (3). Otherwise, a lawyer may represent a client despite a concurrent conflict with another client if two conditions are met: (1) each client gives informed written consent *and* (2) the lawyer reasonably believes that he will be able to provide competent and diligent representation to each client. MR 1.7(b). Note that second condition means that some conflicts are "nonconsentable." If the lawyer does not reasonably believe that competent and diligent representation can be afforded to each client, a lawyer cannot properly even ask for client consent, and even where it is volunteered it would not be not sufficient to allow the conflicted representation. See MR 1.7, comment [5].

California's concurrent conflict rules, most notably Rule 3–310, allows a lawyer to undertake such representation as long as all affected clients give informed written consent; there is no "extra" requirement in California that parallels MR 1.7(b)(1). But because of California's strict confidentiality provisions (*see* Chapter 3), California lawyers may find it more difficult to provide one client sufficient information about the representation of another client in order to obtain informed consent. *Query:* Even if the ethics rules allow it, *should* a lawyer seek client consent to a current conflict if the lawyer believes that the representation of one or both cannot be undertaken competently and diligently? If the lawyer winds up representing one client incompetently, do you think the client will be happy? Do you think the client might have remedies against the lawyer even if the client signed a consent form?

Model Rule 1.9 deals with conflicts between a current client and a former client. A conflict exists at all in that setting only if the interests of the two clients are "materially adverse," and the two matters are "the same or substantially related." Even when both conditions are present, the representation may be undertaken if the former client gives informed written consent. There is no "additional requirement" *a la* Rule 1.7(b)(1). Why are current and former client conflicts treated differently in this respect? Are the interests of former clients not the same as those of current clients?

These conflicts rules are relaxed when a lawyer represents a client through a program operated by a nonprofit group, or by a court, which offers short-term limited legal services such as an *ad hoc* legal clinic, specific counseling or a legal advice "hotline." In that setting, where neither the lawyer nor the client expects the relationship to continue beyond that single consultation, a lawyer is subject to Rules 1.7 or 1.9 only if the lawyer knows at the time that the representation involves a conflict of interest. MR 6.5(a).

Model Rule 1.8 deals most directly with conflicts between a lawyer's own interests and those of the client. Mainly, as we will see, the rule covers financial interests. In that context, client consent coupled with other conditions will often cure the conflict. For example, Rule 1.8(a) on business transactions forbids lawyer-client transactions unless the "transaction and terms on which the lawyer acquires the interest" are fair to the client and transmitted in writing; the client is advised in writing of his opportunity to seek independent legal advice; and the client gives written informed consent to the terms of the deal and the lawyer's role in it. Rule 1.7 also covers conflicts between a lawyer's personal (non-financial) interests and those of a current client.

Conflicts may also be created between a current client and a third party, most commonly when a third party (i.e., someone not a client at all) is paying the lawyer's fees on behalf of the client. Model Rule 1.8(f) forbids a lawyer from accepting payment from a third party unless the client gives informed consent, protects the client's confidences from the third party, and there is no interference with the lawyer's independent professional judgment and the lawyer's relationship with the client. Rule 5.4(c) underscores these conditions.

2. *Obtaining Informed Consent*
a. The Information a Lawyer Must Convey

Obtaining client consent is a serious matter. In order for consent to be valid, the client must be given enough information to make a reasoned decision about the risks and ramifications of waiving the right to an unconflicted representation. The lawyer, then, must be able to provide each affected client with "adequate information and explanation about the material risks of and reasonably available alternatives to" the conflicted representation. MR 1.0(e)(defining "informed consent"). California's rule requires a lawyer to inform each affected client of "the relevant circumstances and ... the actual and reasonably foreseeable adverse consequences" of agreeing to a conflicted representation. Cal. Rule 3–310(A)(1). Under certain conditions, this may simply be impossible, rendering a conflict unwaivable. See, e.g., *State ex rel. Union Planters Bank v. Kendrick*, 142 S.W.3d 729 (Mo. 2004) ("[I]n a class action, consultation and consent concerning any serious conflict is extremely difficult, if not impossible, to obtain" because each individual class member would have to give consent after full disclosure by counsel).

The Restatement provides a helpful summary of the kind of information that a lawyer must generally give a client in order for that client's consent—which itself must be clearly and unambiguously manifested—to be valid:

> In a multiple-client situation, the information normally should address the interests of the lawyer and other client giving rise to the conflict; contingent, optional and tactical considerations and alternative courses of action that would be foreclosed or made less readily available by the conflict; the effect of the representation or the process of obtaining other clients' informed consent upon confidential information of the client; any material reservations that a disinterested lawyer might reasonably harbor about the arrangement if such a lawyer were representing only the client being advised; and the consequences and effects of a future withdrawal of consent by any client.... Where the conflict arises solely because a proposed representation will be adverse to an existing client in an unrelated matter, knowledge of the general nature and scope of the work being performed for each client normally suffices....
>
> When the consent relates to a former-client conflict, it is necessary that the former client be aware that the

consent will allow the former lawyer to proceed adversely to the former client. Beyond that, the former client must have adequate information about the implications (if not readily apparent) of the adverse representation, the fact that the lawyer possesses the former client's confidential information, the measures that the former lawyer might undertake to protect against unwarranted disclosures, and the right of the former client to refuse consent. The former client will often be independently represented by counsel. If so, communication with the former client ordinarily must be through successor counsel. . . .

Restatement § 122, comment *c(i)*. As must be apparent from this description, consent to waive a conflict of interest is anything but a *pro forma* matter. Notably, if a lawyer is prohibited by the state's confidentiality rules from disclosing enough information about Client A's interests (or the nature of the lawyer's representation of Client A) to obtain Client B's informed consent, then the consent simply cannot be obtained and the representation cannot go forward. The Restatement echoes this caution: "Disclosing information about one client or prospective client to another is precluded if information necessary to be conveyed is confidential. . . . If means of adequate disclosure are unavailable, consent to the conflict may not be obtained." *Id.* A comment to Model Rule 1.7 explains that "[u]nder some circumstances it may be impossible to make the disclosure necessary to obtain consent. For example, when the lawyer represents different clients in related matters and one of the clients refuses to consent to the disclosure necessary to permit the other client to make an informed decision, the lawyer cannot properly ask the latter to consent." MR 1.7, comment [19].

b. The Timing of Consent

Consent to waive a conflict of interest should (and often *must*) be obtained at the outset of a representation. See MR 1.7, comment [2]. Certainly it is not sufficient to seek client consent near the end of a representation, when the conflict was apparent at an earlier point. In *Office of Disciplinary Counsel v. Wittmaack*, 513 Pa. 609, 522 A.2d 522 (1987), a lawyer represented both the buyer and the seller in a real estate transaction, but neglected to inform the buyer of this fact until the close of the transaction. The court held that handing the client a multiple-representation agreement at that point, without prior notice or an explanation of what it meant, did not satisfy the requirement of informed client consent to the conflict and rendered the consent invalid. (The lawyer also forged client signatures on a conflict-waiver document in another conflicted transactional representation, leading to the sanction of disbarment.)

Advance waiver of conflicts. Many law firms now routinely place advance waiver clauses in their retainer agreements, seeking to obtain client consent to waive a conflict before one even arises. The Model Rules (and the Restatement) do not frown on this practice, but provide that any advance waiver is subject to the same rules of validity as any other putative consent to conflict would be. Thus, for example, to be valid the advance waiver must represent the client's "informed consent" under Rule 1.7(b)(4). The most important question raised by this type of waiver is whether the client reasonably understands the material risks the waiver presents. MR 1.7, comment [22]. Does the client's sophistication and experience in legal matters seem relevant to whether any advance consent is truly "informed?" *See Id.*; Restatement § 122, comment *d*; *Visa U.S.A., Inc. v. First Data Corp.*, 241 F.Supp.2d 1100 (N.D. Cal. 2003) (upholding waiver of prospective conflicts).

ABA Formal Op. 05–436 (2005) opines that "the more comprehensive the explanation of the types of future representations that might arise and the actual and reasonably foreseeable adverse consequences of those representations," the more likely the client will be found to have reasonably understood the risks entailed by the waiver. General or open-ended waivers, says the ABA, "ordinarily will be ineffective," unless the client is experienced and represented by other, independent counsel in giving consent. *Id.*

Would a clause purporting to waive all future conflicts be enforceable years after the fact? What do you see as the key issues in such a situation? See *Worldspan, L.P. v. Sabre Group Holdings, Inc.*, 5 F.Supp.2d 1356 (N.D.Ga.1998).

D.   Imputed Conflicts

One more rule of general applicability is worth our attention here. The restrictions imposed by conflicts of interest on one lawyer are extended, with only a few exceptions, to all lawyers with whom that lawyer is affiliated. The Restatement provides that this imputation of conflicts extends to any lawyers who (1) are associated with the conflicted lawyer through a law partnership, professional corporation, sole proprietorship or similar association; (2) are employed with the conflicted lawyer by an organization that renders legal services either to itself or to others; or (3) share office space and do not have adequate measures to protect confidential information. Restatement § 123. Model Rule 1.10(a) contains a similar rule. While California lacks a rule on imputation of conflicts, case law in that state recognizes it. See, e.g., *People v. SpeeDee Oil Change Systems, Inc.*, 20 Cal.4th 1135, 86 Cal.Rptr.2d 816, 980 P.2d 371 (1999)("When a conflict of interest requires an attorney's disqualification from a matter, the disqualification normally extends vicariously to the attorney's entire law firm.'').

The imputed conflicts rule rests on the presumption that confidences shared by the client with his lawyer will in turn be shared by that lawyer with all affiliated lawyers. This presumption of ''shared confidences'' might be said to derive from the fiction that all lawyers practicing together are considered to be one lawyer for conflicts purposes. This rule gives the other conflicts rules real teeth. See, e.g., *Westinghouse Electric Corp. v. Kerr–McGee Corp.*, 580 F.2d 1311 (7th Cir.1978) (conflicts on the part of lawyers in Washington office causes all lawyers in Chicago office of large firm to be disqualified from a matter). Cf. *Hempstead Video Inc. v. Incorporated Village of Valley Stream*, 409 F.3d 127 (2d Cir. 2005) (lawyer who was ''of counsel'' to a firm had a relationship that was ''too attenuated and too remote'' from other lawyers in the firm to warrant an irrebuttable presumption of shared confidences). Under some circumstances, the presumption of shared confidences can be rebutted. We will see this issue in more detail in section 3 of this chapter.

§ 2. CONFLICTS BETWEEN CURRENT CLIENTS

A. Civil Cases

IN RE DRESSER INDUSTRIES, INC.

United States Court of Appeals, Fifth Circuit, 1992.
972 F.2d 540.

E. GRADY JOLLY, Circuit Judge:

In this petition for a writ of mandamus, we determine whether a law firm may sue its own client, which it concurrently represents in other matters. In a word, no; and most certainly not here, where the motivation appears only to be the law firm's self-interest.[1] We therefore grant the writ, directing the district judge to disqualify counsel.

I

The material facts are undisputed. This petition arises from a consolidated class action antitrust suit brought against manufacturers of oil well drill bits. *Red Eagle Resources et al. v. Baker Hughes, et al.*, No. H–91–0627, 1992 WL 170614 (S.D.Tex.) (''*Drill Bits*'').

Dresser Industries, Inc., (''Dresser'') is now a defendant in *Drill Bits,* charged—by its own lawyers—with conspiring to fix the

---

1. Drill Bits was going to be a case that was going to be active, big, protracted, the first price fixing case that's come along in Houston in a long time. I had made some-what of a reputation in that area, and I guess it's kind of painful not to be able to play in the game anymore, ...
Deposition of Stephen D. Susman.

prices of drill bits and with fraudulently concealing its conduct. Stephen D. Susman, with his firm, Susman Godfrey, is lead counsel for the plaintiff's committee. As lead counsel, Susman signed the amended complaint that levied these charges against Dresser, his firm's own client.

Susman Godfrey concurrently represents Dresser in two pending lawsuits. *CPS International, Inc. v. Dresser Industries, Inc.,* No. H–85–653 (S.D.Tex.) ("*CPS*"), is the third suit brought by CPS International, a company that claims Dresser forced it out of the compressor market in Saudi Arabia. CPS International initially sued Dresser for antitrust violations and tortious interference with a contract. The antitrust claim has been dismissed, but the tort claim is scheduled for trial. Susman Godfrey has represented Dresser throughout these actions, which commenced in 1985. During its defense of Dresser, Susman Godfrey lawyers have had relatively unfettered access to data concerning Dresser's management, organization, finances, and accounting practices. Susman Godfrey's lawyers have engaged in privileged communications with Dresser's in-house counsel and officers in choosing antitrust defenses and other litigation strategies. Susman Godfrey has also, since 1990, represented Dresser in *Cullen Center, Inc., et al. v. W.R. Gray Co., et al.,* a case involving asbestos in a Dresser building, which is now set for trial in Texas state court.

On October 24 and November 24, 1991, Susman Godfrey lawyers wrote Dresser informing it that Stephen Susman chaired the plaintiffs' committee in *Drill Bits*, that Dresser might be made a *Drill Bits* defendant, and that, if Dresser replaced Susman Godfrey, the firm would assist in the transition to new counsel. Dresser chose not to dismiss Susman Godfrey in *CPS* and *Cullen Center*.

Dresser was joined as a defendant in *Drill Bits* on December 2, 1991. Dresser moved to disqualify Susman as plaintiffs' counsel on December 13. Both Dresser and Susman Godfrey submitted affidavits and depositions to the district court, which, after a hearing, issued a detailed opinion denying the motion.

The district court noted that Southern District local rule 4B provides that the code of professional responsibility for lawyers practicing in that district is the Code of Responsibility of the State Bar of Texas. Although the court further noted that other district courts look to other codes in deciding motions to disqualify, nevertheless, it concluded that "Dresser's motion to disqualify Susman Godfrey is governed wholly by the Texas Disciplinary Rules of Professional Conduct." The court then focused on Texas Disciplinary Rule 1.06, which provides:

> (b) ... [E]xcept to the extent permitted in paragraph (c), a lawyer shall not represent a person if the representation of that person:

(1) involves a substantially related matter in which that person's interests are materially and directly adverse to the interests of another client of the lawyer or the lawyer's firm; or

(2) reasonably appears to be or become adversely limited by the lawyer's or law firm's responsibilities to another client or to a third person or by the lawyer's or law firm's own interests.

(c) A lawyer may represent a client in the circumstances described in (b) if:

(1) the lawyer reasonably believes the representation of each client will not be materially affected; and

(2) each affected or potentially affected client consents to such representation after full disclosure. . . .

The district court described the *Drill Bits* complaint as a civil antitrust case, thus somewhat softening Dresser's description of it as an action for fraud or criminal conduct. The court held, "as a matter of law, that there exists no relationship, legal or factual, between the *Cullen Center* case and the *Drill Bits* litigation," and that no similarity between *Drill Bits* and the *CPS* suits was material. The court concluded that "Godfrey's representation of the plaintiffs in the *Drill Bits* litigation does not reasonably appear to be or become adversely limited by Susman Godfrey's responsibilities to Dresser in the *CPS* and *Cullen Center* cases," and accordingly denied the motion to disqualify. . . .

II

. . . In evaluating a motion to disqualify, we interpret the controlling ethical norms governing professional conduct as we would any other source of law. When the facts are undisputed, district courts enjoy no particular advantage over appellate courts in formulating ethical rules to govern motions to disqualify. Thus, in the event an appropriate standard for disqualification is based on a state's disciplinary rules, a court of appeals should consider the district court's interpretation of the state disciplinary rules as an interpretation of law, subject essentially to *de novo* consideration.

III

The district court clearly erred in holding that its local rules, and thus the Texas rules, which it adopted, are the "sole" authority governing a motion to disqualify. Motions to disqualify are substantive motions affecting the rights of the parties and are determined by applying standards developed under federal law. . . .

IV

We apply specific tests to motions to disqualify counsel in circumstances governed by statute or the Constitution. When presented with a motion to disqualify counsel in a more generic civil case, however, we consider the motion governed by the ethical rules announced by the national profession in the light of the public interest and the litigants' rights. Our source for the standards of the profession has been the canons of ethics developed by the American Bar Association. . . .

Our most far-reaching application of the national standards of attorney conduct to an attorney's obligation to avoid conflicts of interest is *Woods v. Covington County Bank,* 537 F.2d 804 (5th Cir.1976) (attorney in army reserve not barred from privately representing clients in securities matters he had investigated while on active duty). We held in *Woods* that standards such as the ABA canons are useful guides but are not controlling in adjudicating such motions. *Id.* The considerations we relied upon in *Woods* were whether a conflict has (1) the appearance of impropriety in general, or (2) a possibility that a specific impropriety will occur, and (3) the likelihood of public suspicion from the impropriety outweighs any social interests which will be served by the lawyer's continued participation in the case.

We applied the *Woods* standard to a conflict that arose when an attorney brought a suit against a former client in *Brennan's Inc. v. Brennan's Restaurants, Inc.,* 590 F.2d 168 (5th Cir.1979). In *Brennan's,* the plaintiffs moved to have the court disqualify the attorney for the defendants because, prior to the litigation, the attorney had jointly represented both parties. We affirmed the disqualification of the attorney, holding that an attorney could not sue a former client in a matter substantially related to the representation of a former client. Similarly, in *Wilson P. Abraham Construction Corp. v. Armco Steel Corp.,* 559 F.2d 250, 253 (5th Cir.1977), we held that the court should bar an attorney from suing the co-defendant of a former client if the co-defendants and their attorneys exchanged information.

In *Woods, Wilson Abraham,* and *Brennan's,* we applied national norms of attorney conduct to a conflict arising after the attorney's prior representation had been concluded. Now, however, we are confronted with our first case arising out of concurrent representation, in which the attorney sues a client whom he represents on another pending matter. We thus consider the problem of concurrent representation under our framework in *Woods* as tailored to apply to the facts arising from concurrent representation.

We turn, then, to the current national standards of legal ethics to first consider whether this dual representation amounts to impropriety. Neither the ABA Model Rules of Professional

Conduct [MR 1.7] nor the Code of Professional Responsibility [EC 5–2 & 5–19] allows an attorney to bring a suit against a client without its consent.[9] This position is also taken by the American Law Institute in its drafts of the *Restatement of the Law Governing Lawyers.*

Unquestionably, the national standards of attorney conduct forbid a lawyer from bringing a suit against a current client without the consent of both clients. Susman's conduct violates all of these standards—unless excused or justified under exceptional circumstances not present here.

Exceptional circumstances may sometimes mean that what is ordinarily a clear impropriety will not, always and inevitably, determine a conflicts case. Within the framework we announced in *Woods,* Susman, for example, might have been able to continue his dual representation if he could have shown some social interest to be served by his representation that would outweigh the public perception of his impropriety. Susman, however, can present no such reason. There is no suggestion that other lawyers could not ably perform his offices for the plaintiffs, nor is there any basis for a suggestion of any societal or professional interest to be served. This fact suggests a rule of thumb for use in future motions for disqualification based on concurrent representation: However a lawyer's motives may be clothed, if the sole reason for suing his own client is the lawyer's self-interest, disqualification should be granted.

V

We find, therefore, that Dresser's right to the grant of its motion to disqualify counsel is clear and indisputable. We further find that the district court clearly and indisputably abused its discretion in failing to grant the motion. We have thus granted the petition and have issued the writ of mandamus, directing the United States District Court for the Southern District of Texas to enter an order disqualifying Stephen D. Susman and Susman Godfrey from continuing as counsel to the plaintiffs in *Red Eagle Resources et al. v. Baker Hughes, et al.,* No. H–91–0627, 1992 WL 170614.

WRIT GRANTED.

9. The agreement between the Code and Rules on this point is made obvious in the practice guide of the *ABA/BNA Lawyer's Manual On Professional Conduct,* which discusses the obligations of a lawyer under both the ABA rules and code. The practice guide describes a bar to a nonconsensual representation adverse to the client: A lawyer may not represent one client whose interests are adverse to those of another current client of the lawyer's even if the two representations are unrelated, unless the clients consent and the lawyer believes he or she is able to represent each client without adversely affecting the other. Courts and ethics panels generally take a broad view of this restriction, and a specific adverse effect probably will not have to be shown. All that need be present is that one lawyer is or firm is representing two clients, even in unrelated matters, with potentially conflicting interests.

Notes

1. *Dresser Industries* presents a clear example of one kind of concurrent conflict of interest: a lawyer suing Client B on behalf of Client A, where the lawyer presently represents Client B on some unrelated matter. Why is this prohibited? What interests might be harmed if such representation was allowed? See Restatement § 121, comment *b* & § 128, comment *e*; MR 1.7, comment [6].

2. Concurrent conflicts are a real issue in large-firm practice, where firms represent many large corporations and their subsidiaries. Unless effective conflicts-checking procedures are followed diligently, a firm may find itself representing a client against, say, a subsidiary of another of the firm's clients. See, e.g., *J.P. Morgan Chase Bank ex rel. Mahonia Ltd. v. Liberty Mut. Ins. Co.*, 189 F.Supp.2d 20 (S.D.N.Y. 2002) (Davis Polk & Wardwell disqualified from representing J.P. Morgan Chase against a defendant which was a subsidiary of Chubb, another of the firm's clients).

3. *The "hot potato" doctrine.* What if a lawyer represents Client A on a small matter, and a prospective Client B comes along who wants to sue Client A in a very big matter. Can the lawyer drop Client A, thereby removing the current conflict, and take up Client B's case against the now-former Client A? The answer is no. A leading case (and the source of the rule's name) is *Picker International, Inc. v. Varian Assocs., Inc.*, 670 F.Supp. 1363 (N.D.Ohio 1987), *aff'd*, 869 F.2d 578 (Fed.Cir.1989). In *Picker*, a large law firm merged with a smaller one, producing a concurrent conflict of interest: Client A, a long-time client of the larger half, was suing Client B, who was being represented in a number of matters by the smaller half. The newly-formed firm sought to withdraw from representing Client B and continue the *A vs. B* lawsuit. The trial court held that "A firm may not drop a client like a hot potato, especially if it is in order to keep a far more lucrative client." Both A and B had to consent to the conflict, the court said, or the firm had to withdraw from representing either of them. Most courts follow this rule, which is now contained in a Restatement comment. See § 132, comment *c* ("The present-client conflict may not be transformed into a former-client conflict by the lawyer's withdrawal from the representation of the existing client.") Why not? What interests are being protected by the "hot potato" doctrine? See *id.*

4. *Disqualification.* The remedy in *Dresser Industries*—disqualification from the representation—is probably the most common remedy in conflicts cases involving litigation. When ruling on disqualification motions, courts look at the law beyond simply the applicable ethics rules. As the court notes in *Dresser*, a federal case, "Motions to disqualify are substantive motions affecting the rights of the parties and are determined by applying standards developed under federal law." As you can see, the court draws on "national standards of attorney conduct." Even in a state court, the court will look beyond its own ethics rules for

guiding principles in deciding disqualification motions. Why would this be? Why don't the ethics rules of the particular jurisdiction provide a complete answer to disqualification motions based on conflicts of interest? What interests are involved in such a motion? Cf. *Prudential Ins. Co. v. Anodyne, Inc.*, 365 F.Supp.2d 1232 (S.D. Fla. 2005) (denying firm's motion to withdraw as counsel despite finding a conflict of interest that violated Florida ethics rules).

5. *Civil liability.* If a lawyer's conflicted representation causes legally-cognizable harm, the client can sue for legal malpractice. See, e.g., *Woodruff v. Tomlin*, 616 F.2d 924 (6th Cir.1980) (lawyer represented multiple parties in automobile crash case). Representing adverse parties in transactions often leads to civil liability where the rules have not been complied with. See, e.g., *Hill v. Okay Construction Co.*, 312 Minn. 324, 252 N.W.2d 107 (1977) (lawyer represented buyer and seller in the transfer of a business; after litigation arose between them, lawyer was made to indemnify buyer for litigation costs and reimburse lawyer's fees of both).

6. *Discipline.* Discipline for representing conflicting interests is also a common remedy, since ethics rules in all states regulate such representation. See MR 1.7; DR 5–105; Cal. Rule 3–310. In *In re Cohen*, 316 Or. 657, 853 P.2d 286 (1993), Wife telephoned Lawyer and asked for legal assistance with a juvenile case and a possible criminal case, both arising from an incident in which Husband had beaten and injured Wife's nine-year-old daughter from a previous marriage. A petition had been filed in juvenile court with respect to the daughter, and criminal charges were expected to be filed against Husband. Husband and Wife came to see Lawyer together. Wife said that she feared that all three of her children would be taken away from her. Husband was contrite. Lawyer decided that he could represent both Husband and Wife, since they were in "complete agreement about what they wanted," namely, keeping Husband out of jail and the family together. After Husband's indictment and release on his own recognizance, things began to fall apart. Lawyer continued to represent both of them (Wife in the juvenile proceedings and Husband in the criminal case) despite receiving a pre-sentence report in Husband's case in which Wife accused Husband of beating their son and not attending anger management classes. The Oregon State Bar reprimanded Lawyer, concluding that he "violated the duty to his clients to avoid conflicts of interest" as embodied in DR 5–105(E). A more severe sanction was not warranted, said the court, because no actual harm to the clients actually occurred.

7. *"Accidental" conflicted representation.* A lawyer, acting on behalf of Client B, sues Client A, represented by his firm currently on other matters. Lawyer does not realize that Client A is a client of his firm. Is ignorance an excuse? See *Nebraska ex rel. State Bar Ass'n v. Frank*, 262 Neb. 299, 631 N.W.2d 485 (2001). See also MR 1.7, comment [3]. How could a law firm avoid these problems? See *id.*; N.Y. DR 5–105(e).

BOTTOMS v. STAPLETON

Supreme Court of Iowa, 2005.
706 N.W.2d 411.

TERNUS, Justice.

A minority shareholder brought this action against a limited liability company and its majority shareholder seeking damages for breach of fiduciary duty and conversion, judicial dissolution of the company, an accounting, and appointment of a receiver.... Upon the minority shareholder's motion to disqualify the defendants' counsel, the district court held that counsel could not represent the company, but could continue to represent the majority shareholder. We granted the defendants' application for interlocutory appeal [and now] reverse the district court's order and remand this case for further proceedings.

I. Background Facts and Proceedings.

The appellant, Paducah Gear & Machine Co., L.C., is an Iowa limited liability company that provides industrial machine shop repairs and service from a facility located in Paducah, Kentucky. Paducah Gear was formed in 1998 and has two shareholders. The appellant, Jack Stapleton, owns fifty-one percent of the company, and the appellee, Russell Bottoms, owns the remaining forty-nine percent.

Pursuant to the parties' agreement, Stapleton handled the financial, recordkeeping, and corporate aspects of the company from Iowa, where Stapleton lived, while Bottoms worked on site at the Paducah, Kentucky shop, supplying the machinist services and managing the machinist crew. After several years, the relationship between the co-owners began to deteriorate. In March 2002, Bottoms and Stapleton ceased doing business together. That same month Bottoms incorporated Global Gear & Machine Co. in competition with Paducah Gear.

On July 17, 2003, Bottoms filed this lawsuit against Stapleton and Paducah Gear. The plaintiff alleged "Stapleton converted certain assets of Paducah Gear to his own use, made certain distributions to himself at the expense of Plaintiff and Paducah Gear, and has refused to fulfill his contractual and fiduciary duties." Based on this conduct, the plaintiff pursued various remedies in six counts. In Count I Bottoms sought compensatory and punitive damages due to Stapleton's alleged breach of fiduciary duty to the plaintiff. In Count II Bottoms requested a judicial dissolution of Paducah Gear or, alternatively, an order requiring Paducah Gear to pay to Bottoms his "fair share of the assets" of the company. In Count III the plaintiff asserted Stapleton "intentionally misappropriated and took dominion and control over [the plaintiff's] ownership interests." As in Count I, the plaintiff sought a money judgment against Stapleton. In Count IV Bottoms demanded an accounting, and in Count V he asked for the immediate appointment of a receiver to control the assets of Paducah Gear. In Count VI Bottoms requested a temporary injunction as an alternative to the appointment of a receiver and sought an order preserving the assets of Paducah Gear.

The defendants, represented by Richard R. Chabot of Sullivan & Ward P.C., filed an answer denying the plaintiff's accusations of wrongdoing and entitlement to equitable relief. The defendants also filed counterclaims alleging Bottoms had misappropriated proprietary information and other assets of Paducah Gear and had improperly interfered with Paducah Gear's business relationships.

Subsequently, the plaintiff filed a motion to disqualify the law firm of Sullivan & Ward, P.C. from representing both defendants. This motion precipitated the appearance of Mark Weinhardt of the law firm of Belin Lamson McCormick Zumbach Flynn, A Professional Corporation, on behalf of the defendants and Sullivan & Ward. Bottoms then filed a motion to disqualify the Belin law firm as well from simultaneously representing Stapleton and Paducah Gear.

The district court granted the plaintiff's motions to disqualify and held that neither Sullivan & Ward nor the Belin law firm could represent Paducah Gear. It observed, "Assuming that the allegations of wrongdoing against Stapleton can be proven, there is a significant potential for divergence of the interests of Paducah and Stapleton." ... This court granted the defendants' application for interlocutory appeal. The sole issue on appeal is whether the district court abused its discretion in ruling the potential for a conflict of interest between Paducah Gear and its majority shareholder was sufficient to preclude joint representation of the company and Stapleton. A court abuses its discretion when its ruling is based on clearly untenable grounds, such as reliance upon an improper legal standard or error in the application of the law....

II. Discussion.

A. *General principles regarding attorney disqualification.* The right of a party to choose his or her own attorney is important, but it must be balanced against the need to maintain "the highest ethical standards" that will preserve the public's trust in the bar and in the integrity of the court system. In balancing these interests, a court must also be vigilant to thwart any misuse of a motion to disqualify for strategic reasons. *See* 1 Geoffrey C. Hazard, Jr. and W. William Hodes, *The Law of Lawyering* § 10.2, at 10–10 (3d ed. 2004 Supp.) (stating "policymaking with respect to conflicts of interest regulation must take account of the opportunities for manipulation and tactical infighting") [hereinafter *"The Law of Lawyering"*].

Thus, our starting point in evaluating a claim that an attorney should be disqualified from representing a party is the ethical principles outlined in the Iowa Rules of Professional Conduct. (We focus on the Iowa Rules of Professional Conduct, which became effective on July 1, 2005, since the future conduct of the attorneys in this litigation will be governed by these rules rather than the old Iowa Code of Professional Responsibility.) The rule governing the conflict at issue here is rule 32:1.7, which addresses the problem of concurrent conflicts of interest.[The court here quoted Iowa rule 32:1.7, identical in pertinent part to MR 1.7.]

Bottoms does not argue that the defendants' interests are "directly adverse," but rather that these parties have potentially differing interests. Therefore, we focus our discussion on rule 32:1.7(a)(2). *See* Iowa R. of Prof'l Conduct 32:1.7 cmt. [23] (stating "simultaneous representation of parties whose interests in litigation may conflict, such as coplaintiffs or codefendants, is governed by paragraph (a)(2)").

B. *Existence of disqualifying conflict.* The question to be answered under rule 32:1.7(a)(2) is whether there is "a significant risk" that counsel's representation of one client "will be materially limited by [his or her] responsibilities to another client." . . . A comment to rule 32:1.7 sheds light on when a conflict of interest will materially limit an attorney in the performance of the attorney's responsibilities:

> [A] conflict of interest exists if there is a significant risk that a lawyer's ability to consider, recommend, or carry out an appropriate course of action for the client will be materially limited as a result of the lawyer's other responsibilities. . . . The mere possibility of subsequent harm does not itself require disclosure and consent. The critical questions are the likelihood that a difference in interests will eventuate and, if it does, whether it will materially interfere with the lawyer's independent professional judgment in considering alternatives or foreclose courses of action that reasonably should be pursued on behalf of the client.

Iowa R. of Prof'l Conduct 32:1.7 cmt. [8]; *see also id.* r. 32:1.7 cmt. [29] ("[R]epresentation of multiple clients is improper when it is unlikely that impartiality can be maintained."). The representation of codefendants will give rise to a conflict in situations involving a "substantial discrepancy in the [represented] parties' testimony, incompatibility in positions in relation to an opposing party or the fact that there are substantially different possibilities of settlement of the claims or liabilities in question." *Id.* r. 32:1.7 cmt. [23].

Our examination of the plaintiff's brief shows a marked absence of any specification of the precise conflict in the present case. Nonetheless, since the plaintiff asks that we affirm the district court, we will examine the district court's ruling for an elucidation of the plaintiff's claim. As summarized by the district court, "[t]he gist of Bottoms' argument is that Stapleton has breached duties to the company by 'converting or embezzling funds' and that the interests of Stapleton and Paducah are therefore adverse to each other." The court's ruling was succinct:

> Assuming that the allegations of wrongdoing against Stapleton can be proven, there is a significant potential for divergence of the interests of Paducah and Stapleton. A potential conflict of interest is sufficient to require that steps be taken to assure that all parties are adequately represented.

In considering this ruling, we first note that the concept of a *potential* conflict of interest is foreign to the new ethical rule. That is because rule 32:1.7(a)(2) states that a conflict of interest "*exists* if . . . there is a significant risk that the representation of one or more clients will be materially limited by the lawyer's responsibilities to another client." Iowa R. of Prof'l Conduct 32:1.7(a)(2) (emphasis added). In other words, if there is a significant risk that representation of one client will materially limit the representation of another client, a conflict of interest actually exists; it is not merely potential. *See* 1 *The Law of Lawyering* § 10.4, at 10–13. Thus, only an actual conflict of interest, as defined in rule 32:1.7(a), will justify disqualification.

Our review, then, will focus on the district court's conclusion that "there is a significant potential for divergence of the interests of Paducah and Stapleton." Translated to the terminology of rule 32:1.7, the court, in essence, found there was a significant likelihood that the defendants would have differing interests in this lawsuit. *See* Iowa R. of Prof'l Conduct 32:1.7 cmt. [8] (stating one of the critical questions under rule 32:1.7 is "the likelihood that a difference in interests will eventuate"). We must decide whether there is substantial evidence to support this finding.

As the litigation is presently postured, the interests of Stapleton and Paducah Gear are not directly adverse. Bottoms' claims against Stapleton are brought in his individual capacity and not on behalf of the company. He seeks only amounts to which he is personally entitled as an owner of the company, including sums he claims were tortiously converted by Stapleton. Moreover, the equitable claims asserted by Bottoms against Paducah Gear are merely ancillary to his damage claims against Stapleton. Bottoms seeks to identify company assets and preserve them so he can receive his "fair share" of the company. Importantly, the plaintiff has not articulated why a defense of the claims against Stapleton would be inconsistent with Paducah Gear's defense of the claims alleged against it. . . .

Bottoms, as the moving party, bore the burden of proving facts that established the necessary factual prerequisite for disqualification. Our review of the record does not reveal substantial *evidence* that the defendants' interests will likely become adverse, particularly given the fact that one defendant is a limited liability company and the other defendant holds the controlling interest in the company. *Cf. Philips Med. Sys. Int'l B.V. v. Bruetman,* 8 F.3d 600, 606 (7th Cir.1993) (refusing to disqualify counsel jointly representing individual defendant and several corporations that he controlled, noting it appeared "the corporations have no interests separate from [the individual defendant]" and "[n]o determination of an actual conflict of interest was ever made"); *Field v. Freedman,* 527 F.Supp. 935, 940 (D.Kan.1981) (refusing to disqualify attorneys representing defunct corporation and majority shareholders in suit filed by minority shareholder). Counsel will not be disqualified simply because the opposing party *alleges* the *possibility* of differing interests.

Although we hold disqualification of the defendants' attorneys from dual representation is not mandated at this time, we make no determination that a divergence of interest may not in the future become sufficiently likely so as to warrant disqualification. Thus, the plaintiff is not precluded from reasserting its motion to disqualify if it has proof that the test set forth in rule 32:1.7(a) has been met. *See generally* Iowa R. of Prof'l Conduct 32:3.1 (stating "[a] lawyer shall not . . . assert . . . an issue . . . unless there is a basis in law and fact for doing so that is not frivolous"). Without prejudging what lies ahead, we simply observe that the defendants' attorneys should be mindful of their ethical obligations under rules 32:1.13 and 32:1.7 and their clients' interest in having consistent and continuing representation in this lawsuit. *See generally* Iowa R. of Prof'l Conduct 32:1.7 cmt. [29] (stating "a lawyer should be mindful that if the common representation fails because the potentially adverse interests cannot be reconciled, the result can be additional cost, embarrassment, and recrimination" and that "[o]rdinarily, the lawyer will be forced to withdraw from representing all of the clients if the common representation fails").

III. *Conclusion and Disposition.*

The plaintiff failed to produce evidence showing it is likely that a difference in interests will develop between the defendants. Therefore, the trial court's finding of a significant potential for a divergence of interests is not supported by substantial evidence. Accordingly, the court's disqualification of the defendants' attorneys was an abuse of discretion. Although the potential for divergent interests exists, we will not deprive the defendants of their counsel of choice based solely on the plaintiff's allegations that the company may have a claim against the majority shareholder, particularly when this lawsuit is based solely on wrongdoing that has purportedly harmed the *plaintiff's* ownership interests. We reverse the district court's ruling disqualifying Sullivan & Ward and the Belin law firm from representing Paducah Gear, and we remand this case for further proceedings.

REVERSED AND REMANDED.

Notes

1. In *Bottoms*, the two clients with allegedly conflicting interests were not "directly adverse" to each other under Rule 1.7(a). The trial judge nonetheless thought that there was an impermissible conflict of interest under Rule 1.7(b), because there was "a significant risk that the representation of one or more clients would be materially limited by the lawyer's responsibilities to another client."

2. Is the *Bottoms* court's rejection of a "potential" conflict as sufficient for disqualification justified on policy grounds? What policies are implicated when a lawyer is disqualified from representing a client?

3. *Aggregate settlement of multiple-client claims.* When a lawyer represents multiple clients on the same side in a single matter, it often appears at the outset that there is no conflict of interest at all—there is, instead, a common interest. But conflicts may emerge later, as the *Bottoms* court recognizes. One example of such a later conflict is when the adverse party makes an offer to settle all claims in the case at one time; some clients may want to accept their portion of the aggregate settlement, while others do not. Indeed, this is a risk of multiple representation that should ordinarily be discussed when getting each client's informed consent under MR 1.7 to the multiple representation in the first place. See MR 1.8, comment [13]. MR 1.8(g) speaks more pointedly to this kind of situation. It provides that a lawyer who represents more than one client party on one side of a case "shall not participate in making an aggregate settlement of the claims of or against the clients" unless each client gives informed written consent, after being informed by the lawyer of the "existence and nature of all the claims" and "the participation of each person in the settlement." See ABA Formal Op. 06–438 (2006). By its terms MR 1.8(g) applies to all cases, criminal or civil. See also Restatement § 128, comments *d-d(iii)*. The potential for lawyer abuse of aggregate settlements is particularly great, in the absence of compliance with this rule. See, e.g., *State ex rel. Oklahoma Bar Ass'n v. Watson*, 897 P.2d 246 (Okla. 1994) (lawyer settled claims of numerous personal-injury plaintiffs without giving them any breakdown of particular amounts, underpaying all and keeping over half the settlement money for himself; one-year suspension and restitution ordered).

FIANDACA v. CUNNINGHAM

United States Court of Appeals, First Circuit, 1987.
827 F.2d 825.

COFFIN, Circuit Judge.

This opinion discusses two consolidated appeals related to a class action brought by twenty-three female prison inmates sentenced to the custody of the warden of the New Hampshire State Prison. The suit challenges the state of New Hampshire's failure to establish a facility for the incarceration of female inmates with programs and services equivalent to those provided to male inmates at the state prison. After a bench trial on the merits, the district court held that the state had violated plaintiffs' right to equal protection of the laws and ordered the construction of a permanent in-state facility for plaintiffs no later than July 1, 1989. It also required the state to provide a temporary facility for plaintiffs on or before November 1, 1987, but prohibited the state from establishing this facility on the grounds of the Laconia State School and Training Center ("Laconia State School" or "LSS"), New Hampshire's lone institution for the care and treatment of mentally retarded citizens.

One set of appellants consists of Michael Cunningham, warden of the New Hampshire State Prison, and various executive branch officials responsible for the operation of the New Hampshire Department of Corrections ("state"). They challenge the district court's refusal to disqualify plaintiffs' class counsel, New Hampshire Legal Assistance ("NHLA"), due to an unresolvable conflict of interest. *See* N.H. Rules of Professional Conduct, Rule 1.7(b). They also seek to overturn that portion of the district court's decision barring the establishment of an interim facility for female inmates at LSS. . . .

The other group of appellants is comprised of the plaintiffs in a separate class action challenging the conditions and practices at the Laconia State School, *Garrity v. Sununu*, No. 78–116–D (D.N.H. filed April 12, 1978), including the New Hampshire Association for Retarded Citizens ("NHARC") and the mentally retarded citizens who currently reside at LSS (the "*Garrity* class"). This group sought unsuccessfully to intervene in the relief phase of the instant litigation after the conclusion of the trial, but prior to the issuance of the court's final memorandum order. On appeal, these prospective intervenors argue that the district court abused its discretion in denying their motion. . . .

This case began in June, 1983, when plaintiffs' appellate counsel, Bertram Astles, filed a complaint on behalf of several female inmates sentenced to the custody of the state prison warden and incarcerated at the Rockingham County House of Corrections. NHLA subsequently became co-counsel for plaintiffs and filed an amended complaint expanding the plaintiff class to include all female inmates who are or will be incarcerated in the custody of the warden. In the years that followed, NHLA assumed the role of lead counsel for the class, engaging in extensive discovery and performing all other legal tasks through the completion of the trial before the district court. Among other things, NHLA attorneys and their trial expert, Dr. Edyth Flynn, twice toured and examined potential facilities at which to house plaintiffs, including buildings at the Laconia State School, the New Hampshire Hospital in Concord, and the Youth Development Center in Manchester.

[The state offered to settle the litigation in August, 1986, in exchange for the establishment of a facility for female inmates at the current Hillsborough County House of Corrections in Goffstown. Plaintiffs rejected this offer because the Hillsborough facility would not be ready for three years.] The state extended a second offer of judgment to plaintiffs on October 21, 1986. This offer proposed to establish an in-state facility for the incarceration of female inmates at an existing state building by June 1, 1987. Although the formal offer of judgment did not specify a particular location for this facility, the state informed NHLA that it planned to use the Speare Cottage at the Laconia State School. NHLA, which also represented the plaintiff class in the ongoing *Garrity* litigation, rejected the offer on November 10, stating in part that "plaintiffs do not want to agree to an offer which is against the stated interests of the plaintiffs in the *Garrity* class." The state countered by moving immediately for the disqualification of NHLA as class counsel in the case at bar due to the unresolvable conflict of interest inherent in NHLA's representation of two classes with directly adverse interests. The court, despite recognizing that a conflict of interest probably existed, denied the state's motion on November 20 because NHLA's disqualification would further delay the trial of an important matter that had been pending for over three years. It began to try the case four days later.

The *Garrity* class filed its motion to intervene on December 11, ten days after the conclusion of the trial on the merits. The group alleged that it had only recently learned of the state's proposal to develop a correctional facility for women at the Laconia State School. The members of the class were concerned that the establishment of this facility at the school's Speare Cottage, which they understood to be the primary building under consideration, would displace 28 residents of the school and violate the remedial orders issued by Chief Judge Devine in *Garrity*, 522 F.Supp. at 239–44, as well as N.H.Rev.Stat.Ann. ch. 171–A. The district court denied the motion to intervene on December 23, assuring the applicant-intervenors that it would "never approve a settlement which in any way disenfranchises patients of LSS or contravenes the letter or intent of [Chief Judge] Devine's order in *Garrity.*"

[The court agreed to delay its decision on the merits pending completion of ongoing settlement negotiations.] Within approximately one week after the conclusion of the trial, the parties reached an understanding with regard to a settlement agreement which called for the establishment of a "fully operational facility at the present site of the Laconia State School for the incarceration of female inmates by November 1, 1987." The agreement also provided that all affected residents of LSS would receive appropriate placements at least two months prior to the opening of the correctional facility. After negotiating this agreement, NHLA moved to withdraw as class co-counsel on December 11 and attorney Astles signed the settlement agreement on plaintiffs' behalf. The state, however, refused to sign the agreement.

[The judge in this case, and the judge in the *Garrity* case, convened a joint settlement conference eleven days later. Both parties agreed to continue settlement negotiations.] Judge Loughlin, apparently believing that NIILA's conflict of interest prevented its effective performance as plaintiffs' class counsel, granted NHLA's pending motion to withdraw the day after the joint settlement conference. NHLA, however, had reconsidered its withdrawal from the case in light of the state's failure to sign the settlement agreement and it immediately petitioned the court to be reinstated as class counsel. The court denied the motion. . . .

[The court issued its decision on the merits in January, 1987, holding that the inferior treatment of female inmates in New Hampshire violates the Equal Protection clause of the Fourteenth Amendment.] As a primary remedy, it ordered the state to establish "a permanent facility comparable to all of the facilities encompassed at the [male-only] New Hampshire State Prison . . . to be inhabited no later than July 1, 1989." In crafting a temporary remedy, it reiterated that "there shall not be a scintilla of infringement upon the rights and privileges of the *Garrity* class," and proceeded to rule that the state had to provide plaintiffs with "a building comparable to the Speare Building," but that such facility "shall not be located at the Laconia State School or its environs." This appeal resulted. . . .

A. REFUSAL TO DISQUALIFY FOR CONFLICT OF INTEREST.

The state's first argument is that the district court erred in permitting NHLA to represent the plaintiff class at trial after its conflict of interest had become apparent. . . . We must determine, therefore, whether the court's denial of the state's disqualification motion amounts to an abuse of discretion in this instance.

The state's theory is that NHLA faced an unresolvable conflict because the interests of two of its clients were directly adverse after the state extended its second offer of judgment on October 21, 1986. The relevant portion of New Hampshire's Rules of Professional Conduct states:

> A lawyer shall not represent a client if the representation of that client may be materially limited by the lawyer's responsibilities to another client ... unless:
>
> > (1) the lawyer reasonably believes the representation will not be adversely affected; and
> >
> > (2) the client consents after consultation and with knowledge of the consequences.

* * *

N.H. Rules of Professional Conduct, Rule 1.7(b). The comment to Rule 1.7 prepared by the ABA goes on to state:

> Loyalty to a client is also impaired when a lawyer cannot consider, recommend or carry out an appropriate course of action for the client because of the lawyer's other responsibilities or interests. The conflict in effect forecloses alternatives that would otherwise be available to the client.

In this case, it is the state's contention that the court should have disqualified NHLA as class counsel pursuant to Rule 1.7 because, at least with respect to the state's second offer of judgment, NHLA's representation of the plaintiff class in this litigation was materially limited by its responsibilities to the *Garrity* class.

We find considerable merit in this argument. The state's offer to establish a facility for the incarceration of female inmates at the Laconia State School, and to use its "best efforts" to make such a facility available for occupancy by June 1, 1987, presented plaintiffs with a legitimate opportunity to settle a protracted legal dispute on highly favorable terms. As class counsel, NHLA owed plaintiffs a duty of undivided loyalty: it was obligated to present the offer to plaintiffs, to explain its costs and benefits, and to ensure that the offer received full and fair consideration by the members of the class. Beyond all else, NHLA had an ethical duty to prevent its loyalties to other clients from coloring its representation of the plaintiffs in this action and from infringing upon the exercise of its professional judgment and responsibilities.[4]

---

4. The fact that the conflict arose due to the nature of the state's settlement offer, rather than due to the subject matter of the litigation or the parties involved, does not render the ethical implications of NHLA's multiple representation any less troublesome. Among other things, courts have a duty to "ensur[e] that at all stages of litigation ... counsel are as a general rule available to advise each client as to the particular, individualized benefits or costs of a proposed settlement." *Smith v. City of New York,* 611 F.Supp. 1080, 1090 (S.D.N.Y. 1985).

NHLA, however, also represents the residents of the Laconia State School who are members of the plaintiff class in *Garrity*. Quite understandably, this group vehemently opposes the idea of establishing a correctional facility for female inmates anywhere on the grounds of LSS. As counsel for the *Garrity* class, NHLA had an ethical duty to advance the interests of the class to the fullest possible extent and to oppose any settlement of the instant case that would compromise those interests. In short, the combination of clients and circumstances placed NHLA in the untenable position of being simultaneously obligated to represent vigorously the interests of two conflicting clients. It is inconceivable that NHLA, or any other counsel, could have properly performed the role of "advocate" for both plaintiffs and the *Garrity* class, regardless of its good faith or high intentions. Indeed, this is precisely the sort of situation that Rule 1.7 is designed to prevent.

Plaintiffs argue on appeal that there really was no conflict of interest for NHLA because the state's second offer of judgment was unlikely to lead to a completed settlement for reasons other than NHLA's loyalties to the *Garrity* class. We acknowledge that the record contains strong indications that settlement would not have occurred even if plaintiffs had been represented by another counsel. For instance, in ruling on the intervention motion, the district court stated that, pursuant to its duties under Fed. R.Civ.P. 23(e), it would not approve a settlement that infringed in any way on the rights of the LSS residents. Furthermore, as plaintiffs contend, the second offer of judgment was unattractive because it was phrased in "best efforts" language and did not set a firm date for establishment of the facility. The question, however, is not whether the state's second offer of judgment would have resulted in a settlement had plaintiffs' counsel not been encumbered by a conflict of interest. Rather, the inquiry we must make is whether plaintiffs' counsel was able to represent the plaintiff class unaffected by divided loyalties, or as stated in Rule 1.7(b), whether NHLA could have reasonably believed that its representation would not be adversely affected by the conflict. Our review of the record and the history of this litigation—especially NHLA's response to the state's second offer, in which it stated that "plaintiffs do not want to agree to an offer which is against the stated interests of plaintiffs in the *Garrity* case"—persuade us that NHLA's representation of plaintiffs could not escape the adverse effects of NHLA's loyalties to the *Garrity* class.

Both the district court and plaintiffs on appeal have also advanced the belief that "necessity" outweighed the adverse effects of NHLA's conflict of interest in this instance and justified the denial of the state's pre-trial disqualification motion . . . . [W]e fail to see how the doctrine of *necessity* is implicated in a case such as this. As plaintiffs' counsel admitted at oral argument, there was no particular emergency at the time of the court's decision to ignore the conflict of interest and proceed to trial. Plaintiffs simply continued to suffer the effects of the same inequitable treatment that had persisted for many years. While it would have been desirable to avoid delaying the trial for up to a year or more, it certainly was not "necessary" in the sense of limiting the court to but one potential course of action....

Absent some evidence of *true* necessity, we will not permit a meritorious disqualification motion to be denied in the interest of expediency unless it can be shown that the movant strategically sought disqualification in an effort to advance some improper purpose. Thus, the state's motivation in bringing the motion is not irrelevant; as we recognized in *Kevlik,* "disqualification motions can be tactical in nature, designed to harass opposing counsel." However, the mere fact that the state moved for NHLA's disqualification just prior to the commencement of the trial is not, without more, cause for denying its motion. There is simply no evidence to support plaintiffs' suggestion that the state "created" the conflict by intentionally offering plaintiffs a building at LSS in an effort "to dodge the bullet again" with regard to its "failure to provide instate housing for the plaintiff class." We do not believe, therefore, that the state's second offer of judgment and subsequent disqualification motion were intended to harass plaintiffs. Rather, our reading of the record indicates that a more benign scenario is more probable: the state made a good faith attempt to accommodate plaintiffs by offering to establish a correctional facility in an existing building at the Laconia State School and, once NHLA's conflict of interest with regard to this offer became apparent, the state moved for NHLA's disqualification to preserve this settlement option.

As we are unable to identify a reasoned basis for the district court's denial of the state's pre-trial motion to disqualify NHLA from serving as plaintiffs' class counsel, we hold that its order amounts to an abuse of discretion and must be reversed.

B.   Proper Remedy

In light of the district court's error in ignoring NHLA's conflict of interest, we believe it necessary to remand the case for further proceedings. We must consider a further question, however: must the district court now start from scratch in resolving this dispute? ...

We do not doubt that NHLA's conflict of interest potentially influenced the course of the proceedings in at least one regard: NHLA could not fairly advocate the remedial option—namely, the alternative of settling for a site at the Laconia State School—offered by the state prior to trial. The conflict, therefore, had the potential to ensure that the case would go to trial, a route the state likely wished to avoid by achieving an acceptable settlement.

Nevertheless, we do not see how a trial on the merits could have been avoided given the manner in which the case developed below. . . .

The situation is different, however, with respect to the remedy designed by the district court. We believe that it would be inappropriate to permit the court's remedial order—which includes a specific prohibition on the use of LSS—to stand in light of the court's refusal to disqualify NHLA. The ban on the use of buildings located on the grounds of LSS is exactly the sort of remedy preferred by NHLA's *other* clients, the members of the *Garrity* class, and therefore has at least the appearance of having been tainted by NHLA's conflict of interest. Consequently, we hold that the district court's remedial order must be vacated and the case remanded for a new trial on the issue of the proper remedy for this constitutional deprivation. . . .

[C. DENIAL OF MOTION TO INTERVENE]

[Members of the *Garrity* class should have been allowed to intervene in this case.] We . . . believe that all concerned would have benefitted from the participation of the *Garrity* class in proceedings before the district court. . . . [T]he district court abused its discretion in denying the post-trial motion of the *Garrity* class members to intervene in the relief phase of the instant litigation. On remand, these parties shall be permitted to intervene and participate in the proceedings to the fullest extent.

The judgment of the district court with regard to the violation of plaintiffs' right to equal protection of the laws is affirmed. The remedial order of the district court is vacated and remanded for proceedings consistent with this opinion. The order of the district court denying appellants' motion to intervene is reversed. Each of the parties shall bear its own costs.

Notes

1. *Fiandaca* represents yet another form of concurrent conflict of interest: where the lawyer represents Client A in one matter in which Client A's interests come in conflict with the interests of current Client B, who is represented in a separate but related matter. Not all such arrangements will present a conflict, of course. See MR 1.7, comment [8]. Exactly what was the conflict in *Fiandaca*? What client interests were implicated?

2. The court says that the State did not create the conflict in bad faith. But didn't the State create the conflict by making the settlement offer that it did? Should an adversary be able to create a conflict and then move for disqualification based on that same conflict? Or should this be a problem only if the adversary's motive is impure?

3. What do you think of the court's remedy? Should an entirely new trial have been ordered? What interests were being balanced in the court's ruling on the scope of the remand?

NOTE: POSITIONAL CONFLICTS

Model Rule 1.7 identifies a conflict between current clients as involving either "direct adversity" or a situation in which there is a real risk that the lawyer's representation of one client will be "materially limited" by responsibilities to another client. California Rule 3–310(C)(3) speaks of a conflict when a lawyer represents a client in a matter and at the same time, in a separate matter, accepts a client "whose interest in the first matter is adverse to the client in the first matter." What if a lawyer is representing two clients in two different litigated matters, and is taking inconsistent positions on the law in those two cases? For example, what if the lawyer is arguing to enforce a particular statute for Client A in one case, while arguing that the same statute is unconstitutional in Client B's separate case. Client A is not suing Client B, and they are not parties in a single lawsuit. But is this a conflict of interest nonetheless?

Most lawyers will argue inconsistent legal positions for different clients at different times. That cannot, and should not, be prohibited, should it? What if it were? If you factor in the imputed conflicts rules, this kind of situation is certainly not uncommon in large multi-office law firms with sophisticated litigation practices. Indeed, in that setting it is probably not uncommon for one lawyer in the firm to take a position on some legal matter while at the same time another lawyer in the firm is taking a contrary position on the same issue.

Restatement § 128, comment *f*, explains that lawyers "may ordinarily take inconsistent legal positions in different courts at different times." But the rules are violated if the lawyer's argument in one case will adversely affect a client in the another case. *Id.* A comment to Model Rule 1.7 says that it is ordinarily proper for a lawyer to assert inconsistent legal positions "in different tribunals at different times on behalf of different clients." MR 1.7, comment [24]. A conflict would arise, however, "when a decision favoring one client will create a precedent likely to seriously weaken the position taken on behalf of the other client." *Id.* When might this occur? Could lawyers from one law firm argue for the constitutionality of a statute on behalf of Client A, while other lawyers from the same firm argue in a separate case for Client B that the same statute is unconstitutional, as long as the two cases are in different courts? What if the two cases are pending in the same appellate court? Both the Restatement and the Model Rules suggest a number of factors that might be relevant in determining whether such a conflict is problematic. If it is, then client consent must be obtained for either representation to continue. See Restatement § 128, comment *f*; MR 1.7, comment [24]. For a full discussion of these thorny issues, *see* John S. Dzienkowski, *Positional Conflicts of Interest*, 71 Tex. L. Rev. 457 (1993).

What about the simultaneous representation of two clients, in two separate matters, where the two clients are economic competitors? Is that a conflict of interest at all? See *Simpson Performance Prods. v. Horn*, 92 P.3d 283 (Wyo. 2004)(no disqualification necessary where a law firm represented two clients with differing economic interests; one client was suing NASCAR, another client was a supplier of products to NASCAR); *In re Caldor*, 193 B.R. 165 (Bankr. S.D.N.Y. 1996)(no conflict of interest where firm represented two national retailers emerging from insolvency).

B. Criminal Cases

HOLLOWAY v. ARKANSAS

Supreme Court of the United States, 1978.
435 U.S. 475, 98 S.Ct. 1173, 55 L.Ed.2d 426.

Mr. Chief Justice BURGER delivered the opinion of the Court.

Petitioners, codefendants at trial, made timely motions for appointment of separate counsel, based on the representations of their appointed counsel that, because of confidential information received from the codefendants, he was confronted with the risk of representing conflicting interests and could not, therefore, provide effective assistance for each client. We granted certiorari to decide whether petitioners were deprived of the effective assistance of counsel by the denial of those motions.

I

Early in the morning of June 1, 1975, three men entered a Little Rock, Ark., restaurant and robbed and terrorized the five employees of the restaurant. During the course of the robbery, one of the two female employees was raped once; the other, twice. The ensuing police investigation led to the arrests of the petitioners.

On July 29, 1975, the three defendants were each charged with one count of robbery and two counts of rape. On August 5, the trial court appointed Harold Hall, a public defender, to represent all three defendants. Petitioners were then arraigned and pleaded not guilty. Two days later, their cases were set for a consolidated trial to commence September 4.

On August 13 Hall moved the court to appoint separate counsel for each petitioner because "the defendants ha[d] stated to him that there is a possibility of a conflict of interest in each of their cases. . . . " After conducting a hearing on this motion, and on petitioners' motions for a severance, the court declined to appoint separate counsel.[1]

Before trial, the same judge who later presided at petitioners' trial conducted a ... hearing to determine the admissibility of a confession purportedly made by petitioner Campbell to two police officers at the time of his arrest. The essence of the confession was that Campbell had entered the restaurant with his codefendants and had remained, armed with a rifle, one flight of stairs above the site of the robbery and rapes (apparently serving as a lookout), but had not taken part in the rapes. The trial judge ruled the confession admissible, but ordered deletion of the references to Campbell's codefendants. At trial one of the arresting officers testified to Campbell's confession.

On September 4, before the jury was empaneled, Hall renewed the motion for appointment of separate counsel "on the grounds that one or two of the defendants may testify and if they do, then I will not be able to cross-examine them because I have received confidential information from them." The court responded, "I don't know why you wouldn't," and again denied the motion.

The prosecution then proceeded to present its case. The manager of the restaurant identified petitioners Holloway and Campbell as two of the robbers. Another male employee identified Holloway and petitioner Welch. A third identified only Holloway. The victim of the single rape identified Holloway and Welch as two of the robbers but was unable to identify the man who raped her. The victim of the double rape identified Holloway as the first rapist. She was unable to identify the second rapist but identified Campbell as one of the robbers.

On the second day of trial, after the prosecution had rested its case, Hall advised the court that, against his recommendation, all three defendants had decided to testify. He then stated:

> "Now, since I have been appointed, I had previously filed a motion asking the Court to appoint a separate attorney for each defendant because of a possible conflict of interest. This conflict will probably be now coming up since each one of them wants to testify.
>
> "THE COURT: That's all right; let them testify. There is no conflict of interest. Every time I try more than one person in this court each one blames it on the other one.
>
> "MR. HALL: I have talked to each one of these defendants, and I have talked to them individually, not collectively.
>
> "THE COURT: Now talk to them collectively."

---

1. No transcript of this hearing is included in the record, and we are not informed whether the hearing was transcribed.

The court then indicated satisfaction that each petitioner under-stood the nature and consequences of his right to testify on his own behalf, whereupon Hall observed:

"I am in a position now where I am more or less muzzled as to any cross-examination.

"THE COURT: You have no right to cross-examine your own witness.

"MR. HALL: Or to examine them.

"THE COURT: You have a right to examine them, but have no right to cross-examine them. The prosecuting attorney does that.

"MR. HALL: If one [defendant] takes the stand, some-body needs to protect the other two's interest while that one is testifying, and I can't do that since I have talked to each one individually.

"THE COURT: Well, you have talked to them, I assume, individually and collectively, too. They all say they want to testify. I think it's perfectly alright [*sic*] for them to testify if they want to, or not. It's their business.

* * *

"Each defendant said he wants to testify, and there will be no cross-examination of these witnesses, just a direct examination by you.

"MR. HALL: Your Honor, I can't even put them on direct examination because if I ask them—

"THE COURT: (Interposing) You can just put them on the stand and tell the Court that you have advised them of their rights and they want to testify; then you tell the man to go ahead and relate what he wants to. That's all you need to do."[4]

Holloway then took the stand on his own behalf, testifying that during the time described as the time of the robbery he was at his brother's home. His brother had previously given similar testimony. When Welch took the witness stand, the record shows Hall advised him, as he had Holloway, that "I cannot ask you any questions that might tend to incriminate any one of the three of you.... Now, the only thing I can say is tell these ladies and gentlemen of the jury what you know about this case.... " Welch responded that he did not "have any kind of speech ready for the jury or anything. I thought I was going to be questioned." When

---

4. The record reveals that both the trial court and defense counsel were alert to defense counsel's obligation to avoid assist-ing in the presentation of what counsel had reason to believe was false testimony, or, at least, testimony contrary to the version of facts given to him earlier and in confidence. Cf. ABA Project on Standards Relating to the Administration of Criminal Justice, The Defense Function § 7.7(c) p. 133 (1974).

Welch denied, from the witness stand, that he was at the restaurant the night of the robbery, Holloway interrupted, asking:

"Your Honor, are we allowed to make an objection?

"THE COURT: No, sir. Your counsel will take care of any objections.

"MR. HALL: Your Honor, that is what I am trying to say. I can't cross-examine them.

"THE COURT: You proceed like I tell you to, Mr. Hall. You have no right to cross-examine your own witnesses anyhow."

Welch proceeded with his unguided direct testimony, denying any involvement in the crime and stating that he was at his home at the time it occurred. Campbell gave similar testimony when he took the stand. He also denied making any confession to the arresting officers.

The jury rejected the versions of events presented by the three defendants and the alibi witness, and returned guilty verdicts on all counts. On appeal to the Arkansas Supreme Court, petitioners raised the claim that their representation by a single appointed attorney, over their objection, violated federal constitutional guarantees of effective assistance of counsel. In resolving this issue, the court relied on what it characterized as the majority rule:

"[T]he record must show some material basis for an alleged conflict of interest, before reversible error occurs in single representation of co-defendants." 260 Ark. 250, 256, 539 S.W.2d 435, 439 (1976).

Turning to the record in the case, the court observed that Hall had failed to outline to the trial court both the nature of the confidential information received from his clients and the manner in which knowledge of that information created conflicting loyalties. Because none of the petitioners had incriminated codefendants while testifying, the court concluded that the record demonstrated no actual conflict of interests or prejudice to the petitioners, and therefore affirmed.

II

More than 35 years ago, in *Glasser v. United States*, 315 U.S. 60, 62 S.Ct. 457, 86 L.Ed. 680 (1942), this Court held that by requiring an attorney to represent two codefendants whose interests were in conflict the District Court had denied one of the defendants his Sixth Amendment right to the effective assistance of counsel. In that case the Government tried five codefendants in a joint trial for conspiracy to defraud the United States. Two of the defendants, Glasser and Kretske, were represented initially by separate counsel. On the second day of trial, however, Kretske became dissatisfied with his attorney and dismissed him. The District Judge thereupon asked Glasser's attorney, Stewart, if he would also represent Kretske. Stewart responded by noting a possible conflict of interests: His representation of both Glasser and Kretske might lead the jury to link the two men together. Glasser also made known that he objected to the proposal. The District Court nevertheless appointed Stewart, who continued as Glasser's retained counsel, to represent Kretske. Both men were convicted.

Glasser contended in this Court that Stewart's representation at trial was ineffective because of a conflict between the interests of his two clients. This Court held that "the 'Assistance of Counsel' guaranteed by the Sixth Amendment contemplates that such assistance be untrammeled and unimpaired by a court order requiring that one lawyer should simultaneously represent conflicting interests." The record disclosed that Stewart failed to cross-examine a Government witness whose testimony linked Glasser with the conspiracy and failed to object to the admission of arguably inadmissible evidence. This failure was viewed by the Court as a result of Stewart's desire to protect Kretske's interests, and was thus "indicative of Stewart's struggle to serve two masters. . . . " After identifying this conflict of interests, the Court declined to inquire whether the prejudice flowing from it was harmless and instead ordered Glasser's conviction reversed. Kretske's conviction, however, was affirmed.

One principle applicable here emerges from *Glasser* without ambiguity. Requiring or permitting a single attorney to represent codefendants, often referred to as joint representation, is not *per se* violative of constitutional guarantees of effective assistance of counsel. This principle recognizes that in some cases multiple defendants can appropriately be represented by one attorney; indeed, in some cases, certain advantages might accrue from joint representation. In Mr. Justice Frankfurter's view: "Joint representation is a means of insuring against reciprocal recrimination. A common defense often gives strength against a common attack." *Glasser v. United States, supra,* at 92, 62 S.Ct., at 475 (dissenting opinion).

Since *Glasser* was decided, however, the courts have taken divergent approaches to two issues commonly raised in challenges to joint representation where—unlike this case—trial counsel did nothing to advise the trial court of the actuality or possibility of a conflict between his several clients' interests. First, appellate courts have differed on how strong a showing of conflict must be made, or how certain the reviewing court must be that the asserted conflict existed, before it will conclude that the defendants were deprived of their right to the effective assistance of counsel. Second, courts have differed with respect to the scope and nature of the affirmative duty of the trial judge to assure that criminal defendants are not deprived of their right to the effective assistance of counsel by joint representation of conflicting interests.

We need not resolve these two issues in this case, however. Here trial counsel, by the pretrial motions of August 13 and September 4 and by his accompanying representations, made as an officer of the court, focused explicitly on the probable risk of a conflict of interests. The judge then failed either to appoint separate counsel or to take adequate steps to ascertain whether the risk was too remote to warrant separate counsel. We hold that the failure, in the face of the representations made by counsel weeks before trial and again before the jury was empaneled, deprived petitioners of the guarantee of "assistance of counsel." . . .

This . . . has direct applicability in this case where the "possibility of [petitioners'] inconsistent interests" was "brought home to the court" by formal objections, motions, and defense counsel's representations. It is arguable, perhaps, that defense counsel might have presented the requests for appointment of separate counsel more vigorously and in greater detail. As to the former, however, the trial court's responses hardly encouraged pursuit of the separate-counsel claim; and as to presenting the basis for that claim in more detail, defense counsel was confronted with a risk of violating, by more disclosure, his duty of confidentiality to his clients.

Additionally, since the decision in *Glasser*, most courts have held that an attorney's request for the appointment of separate counsel, based on his representations as an officer of the court regarding a conflict of interests, should be granted. In so holding, the courts have acknowledged and given effect to several interrelated considerations. An "attorney representing two defendants in a criminal matter is in the best position professionally and ethically to determine when a conflict of interest exists or will probably develop in the course of a trial." Second, defense attorneys have the obligation, upon discovering a conflict of interests, to advise the court at once of the problem. Finally, attorneys are officers of the court, and " 'when they address the judge solemnly upon a matter before the court, their declarations are virtually made under oath.' " We find these considerations persuasive.

The State argues, however, that to credit Hall's representations to the trial court would be tantamount to transferring to defense counsel the authority of the trial judge to rule on the existence or risk of a conflict and to appoint separate counsel. In the State's view, the ultimate decision on those matters must remain with the trial judge; otherwise unscrupulous defense attorneys might abuse their "authority," presumably for purposes of delay or obstruction of the orderly conduct of the trial.[10]

The State has an obvious interest in avoiding such abuses. But our holding does not undermine that interest. When an untimely motion for separate counsel is made for dilatory purposes, our holding does not impair the trial court's ability to deal with counsel who resort to such tactics. Nor does our holding preclude a trial court from exploring the adequacy of the basis of defense counsel's representations regarding a conflict of interests without improperly requiring disclosure of the confidential communications of the client. In this case the trial court simply failed to take adequate steps in response to the repeated motions, objections, and representations made to it, and no prospect of dilatory practices was present to justify that failure.

III

The issue remains whether the error committed at petitioners' trial requires reversal of their convictions. It has generally been assumed that *Glasser* requires reversal, even in the absence of a showing of specific prejudice to the complaining codefendant, whenever a trial court improperly permits or requires joint representation. Some courts and commentators have argued, however, that appellate courts should not reverse automatically in such cases but rather should affirm unless the defendant can demonstrate prejudice. This argument rests on two aspects of the Court's decision in *Glasser*. First, although it had concluded that Stewart was forced to represent conflicting interests, the Court did *not* reverse the conviction of Kretske, Stewart's other client, because Kretske failed to "show that the denial of Glasser's constitutional rights *prejudiced* [him] in some manner." Second, the Court justified the reversal of Glasser's conviction, in part, by emphasizing the weakness of the Government's evidence against him; with guilt a close question, "error, which under some circumstances *would not be ground for reversal*, cannot be brushed aside as immaterial, since there is a real chance that it might have provided the slight impetus which swung the scales toward guilt." Assessing the strength of the prosecution's evidence against the defendant is, of course, one step in applying a harmless-error standard.

We read the Court's opinion in *Glasser*, however, as holding that whenever a trial court improperly requires joint representation over timely objection reversal is automatic. The *Glasser* Court stated:

> To determine the precise degree of prejudice sustained by
> Glasser as a result of the [district] court's appointment of

---

10. Such risks are undoubtedly present; they are inherent in the adversary system. But courts have abundant power to deal with attorneys who misrepresent facts.

Stewart as counsel for Kretske is at once difficult and unnecessary. The right to have the assistance of counsel is too fundamental and absolute to allow courts to indulge in nice calculations as to the amount of prejudice arising from its denial.

This language presupposes that the joint representation, over his express objections, prejudiced the accused in some degree. But from the cases cited it is clear that the prejudice is presumed regardless of whether it was independently shown. *Tumey v. Ohio,* 273 U.S. 510, 47 S.Ct. 437, 71 L.Ed. 749 (1927), for example, stands for the principle that "[a] conviction must be reversed if [the asserted trial error occurred], even if no particular prejudice is shown and even if the defendant was clearly guilty." The Court's refusal to reverse Kretske's conviction is not contrary to this interpretation of *Glasser.* Kretske did *not* raise his own Sixth Amendment challenge to the joint representation. As the Court's opinion indicates, some of the codefendants argued that the denial of Glasser's right to the effective assistance of counsel prejudiced them as alleged co-conspirators. In that context, the Court required a showing of prejudice; finding none, it affirmed the convictions of the codefendants, including Kretske.

Moreover, this Court has concluded that the assistance of counsel is among those "constitutional rights so basic to a fair trial that their infraction can never be treated as harmless error." Accordingly, when a defendant is deprived of the presence and assistance of his attorney, either throughout the prosecution or during a critical stage in, at least, the prosecution of a capital offense, reversal is automatic.

That an attorney representing multiple defendants with conflicting interests is physically present at pretrial proceedings, during trial, and at sentencing does not warrant departure from this general rule. Joint representation of conflicting interests is suspect because of what it tends to prevent the attorney from doing. For example, in this case it may well have precluded defense counsel for Campbell from exploring possible plea negotiations and the possibility of an agreement to testify for the prosecution, provided a lesser charge or a favorable sentencing recommendation would be acceptable. Generally speaking, a conflict may also prevent an attorney from challenging the admission of evidence prejudicial to one client but perhaps favorable to another, or from arguing at the sentencing hearing the relative involvement and culpability of his clients in order to minimize the culpability of one by emphasizing that of another. Examples can be readily multiplied. The mere physical presence of an attorney does not fulfill the Sixth Amendment guarantee when the advocate's conflicting obligations have effectively sealed his lips on crucial matters.

Finally, a rule requiring a defendant to show that a conflict of interests—which he and his counsel tried to avoid by timely objections to the joint representation—prejudiced him in some specific fashion would not be susceptible of intelligent, evenhanded application. In the normal case where a harmless-error rule is applied, the error occurs at trial and its scope is readily identifiable. Accordingly, the reviewing court can undertake with some confidence its relatively narrow task of assessing the likelihood that the error materially affected the deliberations of the jury. But in a case of joint representation of conflicting interests the evil—it bears repeating—is in what the advocate finds himself compelled to *refrain* from doing, not only at trial but also as to possible pretrial plea negotiations and in the sentencing process. It may be possible in some cases to identify from the record the prejudice resulting from an attorney's failure to undertake certain trial tasks, but even with a record of the sentencing hearing available it would be difficult to judge intelligently the impact of a conflict on the attorney's representation of a client. And to assess the impact of a conflict of interests on the attorney's options, tactics, and decisions in plea negotiations would be virtually impossible. Thus, an inquiry into a claim of harmless error here would require, unlike most cases, unguided speculation.

Accordingly, we reverse and remand for further proceedings not inconsistent with this opinion.

It is so ordered.

[Dissenting Opinion of Justice Powell, joined by Justice Blackmun and Justice Rehnquist, omitted.]

Notes

1. The rule in *Holloway*—that a criminal conviction must be reversed where the trial judge forces defense counsel to represent more than one defendant even after counsel has objected to the conflict of interest—remains good law even after *Strickland v. Washington*, 466 U.S. 668, 104 S.Ct. 2052, 80 L.Ed.2d 674 (1984), reprinted in Chapter 2. In that situation, prejudice is presumed. Is such a presumption warranted? What was the lawyer in *Holloway* prevented from doing for one client because of duties owed to another?

2. Later decisions of the Supreme Court have addressed questions that *Holloway* specifically left open. In *Cuyler v. Sullivan*, 446 U.S. 335, 100 S.Ct. 1708, 64 L.Ed.2d 333 (1980), defense counsel represented multiple defendants with conflicting interests. But in contrast to the *Holloway* case, no one objected to the multiple representation. The court held that *Holloway* did not compel reversal on those facts, concluding that where there is no objection, the trial court may normally conclude either that there is no conflict or that the clients have given consent. However, if the trial court knows or should know of a conflict, it must

ask about it. At bottom, under *Cuyler*, a defendant whose lawyer has not objected to a multiple-defendant conflict must prove that an actual conflict of interest adversely affected his lawyer's performance. If such a showing is made, then prejudice is presumed. See also *Wood v. Georgia*, 450 U.S. 261, 101 S.Ct. 1097, 67 L.Ed.2d 220 (1981)(duty to inquire and automatic reversal rule should apply when the trial court knows or reasonably should know of the conflict with multiple representation); *Burger v. Kemp*, 483 U.S. 776, 107 S.Ct. 3114, 97 L.Ed.2d 638 (1987) (stressing that *Holloway* rejected a per se approach, holding that prejudice is presumed only where counsel "actively represented conflicting interests" in a manner that "adversely affected [the] lawyer's performance").

3. In *Wheat v. United States*, 486 U.S. 153, 108 S.Ct. 1692, 100 L.Ed.2d 140 (1988), a defendant, just two days before trial, asked the court to allow him to be represented by the same lawyer who was representing other defendants being charged in the same grand drug conspiracy. The government objected, arguing that some of these other defendants would be witnesses. The trial court denied the defendant's request to substitute counsel. The Supreme Court affirmed, 5–4, saying that the "institutional interest in the rendition of just verdicts in criminal cases may be jeopardized by unregulated multiple representation." Was the Court right to approve the trial court's refusal to allow the defendant to waive his right to unconflicted counsel? Does this remind you of any other case we have read?

4. *Joint defense agreements.* When one client is being prosecuted along with others for the same offenses, it is common for all to be separately represented (for obvious reasons). But it is also common for all such defendants to agree to cooperate with each other pursuant to a "joint defense agreement," since their interests are generally aligned. In *United States v. Henke*, 222 F.3d 633 (9th Cir.2000), several defendants were party to such a joint defense agreement. One of the defendants was called as a witness against another. The lawyers for the other defendants objected that they would not be able to cross-examine this witness because they had received confidential information from him in connection with the joint defense agreement. The trial court denied their motions to withdraw, and all defendants were convicted. The court of appeals reversed, holding that the conflict of interest in this situation compelled a reversal of the convictions.

§ 3. CONFLICTS BETWEEN FORMER CLIENTS AND CURRENT CLIENTS

A. Civil Cases

EXTERIOR SYSTEMS, INC. v. NOBLE COMPOSITES, INC.

United States District Court, N.D. Indiana, 2001.
175 F.Supp.2d 1112.

NUECHTERLEIN, United States Magistrate Judge.

Plaintiff Exterior Systems, Inc. d/b/a Fabwel, Inc. ("ESI") seeks to disqualify counsel for Defendant Edward Welter. After reviewing all of the evidence (both in-camera and non-in-camera), the Court concludes that Attorney Cynthia Gillard's current representation of Welter conflicts with her past representation of Fabwel. Consequently, ESI's motion to disqualify counsel is GRANTED.

I. Factual Background

Defendant Welter's present counsel, Cynthia Gillard, is a member of a firm, Warrick & Boyn, that has represented Welter since 1972. In that year, Welter founded Fabwel, Inc. ("Fabwel") as an Indiana corporation that made fiberglass panels used in recreational vehicles. Welter served as Fabwel's majority shareholder, president and chief executive officer until he sold the company to ABF Investors, Inc. ("ABF") in 1987. Welter continued as president and chief executive officer of Fabwel under ABF's ownership. Warrick & Boyn continued to serve as counsel for Fabwel. As part of this representation, Attorney Gillard represented Fabwel in the purchase of Master Fab, Inc., a company owned and controlled by Defendant Larry Farver. Gillard prepared numerous contracts and other acquisition documents on behalf of Fabwel, including a February 10, 1988 non-competition/non-disclosure agreement between Fabwel and Larry Farver.

In 1985, Welter established the Executive Benefit Plan for executives of Fabwel. The initial plan used life insurance policies and forms supplied by a local Elkhart insurance agent. Fabwel supplemented the life insurance policies with its own funds held in trust. The Plan consisted of a series of separate agreements with individual Fabwel executives, including Welter. On June 11, 1990, Gillard drafted an amended Plan agreement between Fabwel and Welter. The 1990 amendment completely terminated and replaced the initial 1985 agreement.

In July 1992, Welter and twenty other minority investors bought Fabwel back from ABF. Among the twenty minority employee investors were Raymond Stout, ESI's current President;

Larry Farver, a Defendant and current investor in Defendant Noble Composites; and John Gardner, Fabwel's Chief Financial Officer until 1999 when he left and became a shareholder of Noble Composites. Welter continued as chairman of the board of directors and chief executive officer of Fabwel. Welter's counsel, including Ms. Gillard, continued as counsel for Fabwel.

In 1994, Attorney Gillard represented Fabwel in its initial public offering. In 1994 and 1995, she assisted Fabwel with its purchase of ITI Tuco, Inc. She prepared non-competition/non-disclosure agreements on behalf of Fabwel in conjunction with the ITI acquisition.

Welter and the other shareholders sold Fabwel to Fibreboard Corporation on May 5, 1997. On that day, Welter signed a consulting and non-competition/non-disclosure agreement with Fabwel. Welter and Fabwel also signed a May 5, 1997 amendment to the Executive Benefit Agreement. Gillard represented Welter and some of the other shareholders during these transactions, including Stout, Gardner, and Larry Farver. On May 22, 1997, Fabwel and Welter signed a second non-competition agreement. The second agreement enabled Welter to receive early retirement benefits as described by the Executive Benefit Agreement. Gillard represented Welter during this transaction.

In June 1997, Owens Corning bought Fibreboard and thus Fabwel. In December 1999, Owens Corning merged Fabwel into ESI, which is a subsidiary of Fibreboard, which is a subsidiary of Owens Corning. Fabwel, Inc., the Indiana corporation, ceased to exist. Fabwel is now operated as a division of ESI. . . .

In April 2000, Larry Farver, ESI's general manager, resigned and formed Noble Composites, Inc. with several other investors including, allegedly, Welter. ESI alleges that Noble Composites manufactures the same product as ESI and competes directly against it. Further, ESI alleges that Larry Farver and Welter breached their non-competition/non-disclosure agreements and raided ESI's workforce. In October 2000, ESI terminated the Executive Benefit Plan and allegedly stopped paying Welter early retirement benefits.

ESI filed suit in March 2001 claiming breach of the non-competition/non-disclosure agreements, misappropriation of trade secrets, intentional interference with employment relationships, and other claims. Defendants filed a motion to dismiss for lack of subject matter jurisdiction, which delayed matters for several months before the Court denied the motion. Defendants filed their answers in June 2001. . . .

II.   DISQUALIFICATION IS WARRANTED IF AN ATTORNEY'S REPRESENTATION
          FAILS THE SUBSTANTIAL RELATIONSHIP TEST

The critical importance of two considerations, the sacrosanct privacy of the attorney-client relationship and the prerogative of a party to proceed with counsel of its choice, requires a court to proceed with careful and thoughtful analysis when deciding motions to disqualify counsel. . . .

The Local Rules of the United States District Court for the Northern District of Indiana adopt Indiana's version of the Model Rules of Professional Conduct. Indiana Rule of Professional Conduct 1.9 states as follows:

> A lawyer who has formerly represented a client in a matter shall not thereafter:
>
> (a) represent another person in the same or a substantially related matter in which that person's interests are materially adverse to the interests of the former client unless the former client consents after consultation; or
>
> (b) use information relating to the representation to the disadvantage of the former client except as Rule 1.6 or Rule 3.3 would permit or require with respect to a client or when the information has become generally known.

Subsection (a) addresses the problem of attorney loyalty; subsection (b) deals with client confidences. Subsection (a)'s loyalty requirement extends beyond situations where client confidences are actually learned and used, but the duty of loyalty does not extend to the point of never allowing an attorney to take a position adverse to a former client. Subsection (a) extends the duty of loyalty to situations where it reasonably can be inferred that the attorney learned related confidences during the prior representation on a "substantially related matter."

In addition to the Indiana rule, the Seventh Circuit has adopted a federal common law standard for attorney disqualification. That standard, derived from the venerable *T.C. Theatre Corp. v. Warner Bros. Pictures,* 113 F.Supp. 265 (S.D.N.Y.1953), and followed by every jurisdiction in the United States, is known as the "substantial relationship" test:

> [T]he former client need show no more than that the matters embraced within the pending suit wherein his former attorney appears on behalf of his adversary are *substantially related* to the matters or cause of action wherein the attorney previously represented him, the former client. The Court will assume that during the course of the former representation confidences were disclosed to the attorney bearing on the subject matter of the representation. It will not inquire into their nature and extent. Only in this manner can the lawyer's duty of absolute fidelity be enforced and the spirit of the rule relating to privileged communication be maintained.

Id. at 268–69. Like Rule 1.9, the rule in *T.C. Theatre* sought to enforce (1) "the lawyer's duty of absolute fidelity" and (2) protection of "privileged communications" with former clients. Rule 1.9 is merely a codification of the *T.C. Theatre* test.

The Seventh Circuit's inquiry under the "substantial relationship" test is as follows:

> First, the trial judge must make a factual reconstruction of the scope of the prior legal representation. Second, it must be determined whether it is reasonable to infer that the confidential information allegedly given would have been given to a lawyer representing a client in those matters. Third, it must be determined whether that information is relevant to the issues raised in the litigation pending against the former client.

LaSalle Nat'l Bank v. County of Lake, 703 F.2d 252, 255–56 (7th Cir.1983) (citing *Westinghouse Elec. Corp. v. Gulf Oil Corp.,* 588 F.2d 221, 225 (7th Cir.1978)).

Once a substantial relationship has been found, it is irrebuttably presumed that counsel had access to confidential information. "[W]here a law firm which received confidences from one client now represents a second client in a substantially related matter and those clients now oppose each other, the presumption that the confidences were shared becomes irrebuttable and the law firm must be disqualified."

The Seventh Circuit has discussed three purposes behind the substantial relationship test: (1) to prevent disclosure of client confidences, *Analytica, Inc. v. NPD Research, Inc.,* 708 F.2d 1263, 1266 (7th Cir.1983) (noting that "a lawyer is prohibited from using confidential information that he has obtained from a client against that client on behalf of another one"); (2) to protect a client's interest in the loyalty of counsel, *id.* at 1269 (stating that a client has "a right not to see [its lawyer] reappear ... on the opposite side of a litigation"); and (3) to prevent the "unsavory appearance of conflict of interest that is difficult to dispel in the eyes of the lay public—or for that matter the bench and bar," *id.*

III. ATTORNEY GILLARD IS DISQUALIFIED BECAUSE HER PAST REPRESENTATION OF FABWEL IS SUBSTANTIALLY RELATED TO HER CURRENT REPRESENTATION OF WELTER AGAINST FABWEL ...

As explained in the factual background, Attorney Gillard and her firm have provided extensive legal counsel for both Mr. Welter and Fabwel. That past representation included Attorney Gillard's preparation of non-competition/non-disclosure agreements on behalf of Fabwel, including Defendant Larry Farver's agreement. She also prepared a replacement Executive Benefit Agreement between Fabwel and Welter in 1990.

In 1997, though, Attorney Gillard represented the shareholders of Fabwel in their sale of the company to Fibreboard. As part of the sale, she negotiated an amendment to the Executive Benefit Plan on behalf of Welter and the other shareholders. She also represented Welter when he signed two non-competition/non-disclosure agreements in 1997.

It is reasonable to infer that Fabwel provided Attorney Gillard with confidential information when she prepared the non-competition/non-disclosure agreements and the 1990 Executive Benefit Agreement on its behalf. By preparing both agreements, Attorney Gillard must have known Fabwel's reasons for wanting such agreements, Fabwel's concerns with entering into such agreements, and the interests of Fabwel at stake under each agreement. Good attorneys, such as Ms. Gillard, learn as much as they can about their client's motives, concerns, and interests before drafting documents that will legally bind the client. Good attorneys raise legal issues with their clients and discuss ways to address those issues. When preparing the agreements in this case, Attorney Gillard chose words and phrases designed to protect Fabwel's interests as she understood them. Confidential, attorney-client-protected information must have been exchanged.

The present suit involves matters related to Attorney Gillard's past representation of Fabwel. The starkest example of this relationship is the 1990 Executive Benefit Agreement. Welter's counterclaim alleges that ESI breached the Executive Benefit Agreement (the 1990 plan plus the 1997 amendment). The counterclaim attaches a copy of the 1990 agreement, the one prepared by Gillard on behalf of ESI's predecessor, Fabwel. In simple terms, Attorney Gillard's current client is suing the successor to her former client on a contract she created on behalf of her former client. This conflict, separate from any other potential conflicts, is sufficient to warrant disqualification of Gillard. . . .

Attorney Gillard's second conflict is not as direct. She represented Fabwel when she drafted Larry Farver's non-competition/non-disclosure agreement. ESI is now suing Farver based on that agreement. ESI alleges that Welter and Larry Farver are working together in violation of their non-competition/non-disclosure duties to ESI. While this fact is disputed, it would not be unreasonable in this case to assume that Gillard is cooperating with Farver's counsel in the defense of this case. But whether or not that is occurring is not essential to the resolution of this motion.

Also, ESI alleges that Welter breached his non-competition/non-disclosure agreement. The interests that ESI sought to protect with this agreement are similar to the interests Fabwel sought to protect when it hired Gillard to prepare non-competition/non-disclosure agreements on behalf of Fabwel. Gillard's exposure to Fabwel's confidential interests and concerns when drafting these agreements is likely to inform her defense of Welter against ESI's claims.

In sum, Gillard's current representation of Welter is directly related to the 1990 Executive Benefit Agreement, which she drafted on behalf of Fabwel. Standing alone, this is sufficient to warrant disqualification. The Court also has strong concerns about Gillard's past representation of Fabwel with respect to non-competition/non-disclosure agreements. This second area of conflict bolsters the Court's conclusion that Gillard's current representation of Welter fails the substantial relationship test....

IV. CONCLUSION

The Court ... is very reluctant to sever the longstanding relationship between Warrick & Boyn and Welter and to deny Welter his counsel of choice in this case. Nonetheless, the Court is convinced that under the unique facts of this case, the Indiana Rules of Professional Conduct 1.9 and the application of the "substantial relationship" test require the disqualification of Ms. Gillard and Warrick & Boyn as counsel for Defendant Welter.... All matters in this case are stayed until January 4, 2002, so that Defendant Welter may obtain new counsel and his counsel may become familiar with the case.

Notes

1. In most states, a conflict of interest between a current client and a former client exists only where two key factors are present: (1) the matter being handled for the current client and a matter formerly handled for the former client are "substantially related"; and (2) the interests of the current client are "materially adverse" to those of the former client. See MR 1.9(a). Both conditions must be met or there is simply not a conflict at all. Can you see why this has been said to be a rule against "switching sides?" Under the Model Rules, written informed consent by the former client cures any such conflict. Do you think most former clients would give such consent?

2. *Degree of lawyer's involvement in the two matters.* Comment [2] to Model Rule 1.9 says that "When a lawyer has been directly involved in a specific transaction, subsequent representation of other clients with materially adverse interests clearly is prohibited. On the other hand, a lawyer who recurrently handled a type of problem for a former client is not precluded from later representing another client in a wholly distinct problem of that type even though the subsequent representation involves a position adverse to the prior client.... The underlying question is whether the lawyer was so involved in the matter that the subsequent representation can be justly regarded as changing sides in the matter in question." Why is this the rule? Why should the rules not prohibit a lawyer from filing a lawsuit or taking a position in a transaction in

opposition to a former client, regardless of how related the new matter is to a previous matter, and regardless of the degree of the lawyer's involvement in the previous matter?

NOTE: FORMER PROSPECTIVE CLIENTS

We have already seen that lawyers owe certain duties of reasonable care to prospective clients, that is, persons or entities who have discussed retaining the lawyer's services but have not become clients. See *Togstad*, reprinted in Chapter 2, § 2, and accompanying Notes. Conflicts of interest may also arise between current clients and former prospective clients. See MR 1.18. Unless an exception applies, a lawyer or his firm cannot represent a client whose interests are materially adverse to those of the former prospective client if the lawyer "received information from the prospective client that could be significantly harmful to that person in the matter." MR 1.18(c). The exceptions, allowing a law firm to take on a matter adverse to the new client even after learning such material confidences, are: (1) if both the new client and the prospective client give informed written consent, or (2) the lawyer "took reasonable measures to avoid exposure to more disqualifying information than was reasonably necessary to determine whether to represent the prospective client," and that lawyer is screened from any participation in the new case. MR 1.18(d); see also Restatement § 15(2).

A comment to Model Rule 1.18 explains that the upshot of these rules is that "a lawyer considering whether or not to undertake a new matter should limit the initial interview to only such information as reasonably appears necessary for that purpose." MR 1.18, comment [4]. There is no prohibition on a lawyer's conditioning communications with a prospective client on that person's consent that nothing disclosed in the communications will prohibit the lawyer from subsequently representing an adverse party in the same matter. *Id.*, comment [5]. Such waivers are now widely sought and obtained by many firms. See Ass'n of the Bar of the City of N.Y. Comm'n on Prof'l & Judicial Ethics, Formal Op. 2006–2 (2006) (adopting and applying the approach of MR 1.18 and Restatement § 15 to "beauty contests" in which a company interviews several law firms before choosing one to represent it in a particular matter).

NOTE: "SUBSTANTIALLY RELATED"

Model Rule 1.9, comment [3], says that matters are substantially related "if they involve the same subject matter or if there otherwise is a substantial risk that confidential information as would normally have been obtained in the prior representation would materially advance the client's position in the subsequent matter." But courts have not agreed precisely on what "substantially related" means. In *In re Carey*, 89 S.W.3d 477 (Mo.2002), the court said that " 'Gallons of ink' have been consumed by those trying to articulate or explain the test for deciding whether a substantial relationship exists between two representations." The court identified three distinct tests used by courts to decide this question: (1) a comparison of the facts of the former and current representations; (2) comparing the legal issues in the two matters; and (3) a "blended" approach, looking at both the facts and the legal issues in the two matters. (*Exterior Systems*, reprinted above, applies this third approach.) Does it matter how much time has elapsed between the former and current representations? See *Healthnet, Inc. v. Health Net, Inc.*, 289 F.Supp.2d 755 (S.D. W.Va. 2003) (lawyer's work on validity of former client's trademark was substantially related to trademark litigation that was occurring 17 years later).

The Missouri Court in *Carey* also quoted the Kansas Supreme Court opinion in *Chrispens v. Coastal Ref. & Mktg., Inc.*, 257 Kan. 745, 897 P.2d 104 (1995), which developed a list of six non-exclusive factors that courts have used to determine whether a substantial relationship exists between two matters:

(1) the case involved the same client and the matters or transactions in question are relatively interconnected or reveal the client's pattern of conduct; (2) the lawyer had interviewed a witness who was key in both cases; (3) the lawyer's knowledge of a former client's negotiation strategies was relevant; (4) the commonality of witnesses, legal theories, business practices of the client, and location of the client were significant; (5) a common subject matter, issues and causes of action existed; and (6) information existed on the former client's ability to satisfy debts and its possible defense and negotiation strategies.

These are merely factors, not elements, and "[i]n some cases, one factor, if significant enough, can establish that the subsequent case is substantially related." *Id.*

California's former client conflict ethics rule does not use the term "substantially related" at all. Rather, it provides that a lawyer cannot, without the former client's informed written consent, accept employment in a matter adverse to the former client if "by reason of the representation of the ... former client," the lawyer "has obtained confidential information material to the employment." Cal. Rule 3–310. Case law in California, however, uses the "substantial relationship" test in the context of disqualification motions, to decide whether material confidential information was obtained. See, e.g., *People v. SpeeDee Oil Change Systems, Inc.*, 20 Cal.4th 1135, 86 Cal.Rptr.2d 816, 980 P.2d 371

(1999). Intermediate courts in California have more recently developed a two-part test to determine whether a former-client conflict should be disqualifying. First, the court asks whether the lawyer had a "direct" relationship with the former client, defined as "where the lawyer was personally involved in providing legal advice and services to the former client." *Jessen v. Hartford Cas. Ins. Co.*, 111 Cal.App.4th 698, 3 Cal.Rptr.3d 877 (2003). If the answer to that question is yes, then the court asks whether the matters are substantially related, meaning that "information material to the evaluation, prosecution, settlement or accomplishment of the former representation is also material to the evaluation, prosecution, settlement or accomplishment of the current representation given its factual and legal issues." *Id.* See also *Farris v. Fireman's Fund Ins. Co.*, 119 Cal.App.4th 671, 14 Cal.Rptr.3d 618 (2004) (disqualifying lawyer and firm in part because lawyer had obtained and had helped create his former-client insurance company's "strategies and philosophies" on dealing with coverage questions and disputes; the current action was a bad faith and breach of insurance contract case against the former client, thus "substantially related").

Given all of this, what do you see as the main purpose behind the "substantial relationship" test? What interests does the test protect?

KALA v. ALUMINUM SMELTING & REFINING CO.

Supreme Court of Ohio, 1998.
81 Ohio St.3d 1, 688 N.E.2d 258.

LUNDBERG STRATTON, Justice.

The issue before the court is whether a law firm should be automatically disqualified from representing a party when an attorney leaves his or her former employment with a firm representing a party and joins the law firm representing the opposing party, or whether that law firm may overcome any presumption of shared confidences by instituting effective screening mechanisms. Although this issue has been dealt with in many other jurisdictions, this is a case of first impression for Ohio....

II. Ethical Principles

... A fundamental principle in the attorney-client relationship is that the attorney shall maintain the confidentiality of any information learned during the attorney-client relationship. A client must have the utmost confidence in his or her attorney if the client is to feel free to divulge all matters related to the case to his or her attorney. [The Court quoted DR 4–101, Ohio's confidentiality rule.]

The obligation of an attorney to preserve the confidences and secrets of the client continues even after the termination of the attorney's employment. EC 4–6. In addition, DR 5–105 establishes when an attorney must refuse to accept or continue employment if the interests of another client may impair the independent professional judgment of the attorney and also speaks to imputed disqualification. [The court here quoted DR 5–105(A) and (D), and cited MR 1.10.]

In addition, an attorney should avoid even the appearance of impropriety. Canon 9 of the Code of Professional Responsibility; see, also, DR 9–101. Because of the importance of these ethical principles, it is the court's duty to safeguard the preservation of the attorney-client relationship. . . .

When an attorney leaves his or her former employment and becomes employed by a firm representing an opposing party, a presumption arises that the attorney takes with him or her any confidences gained in the former relationship and shares those confidences with the new firm. This is known as the presumption of shared confidences. Some courts have held that such a change of employment results in an *irrebuttable* presumption of shared confidences that necessitates the disqualification of the attorney (primary disqualification) and the entire new firm (imputed disqualification). *Cardona v. Gen. Motors Corp.* (D.N.J.1996), 942 F.Supp. 968, 969; *G.F. Industries, Inc. v. Am. Brands, Inc.* (1990), 245 N.J.Super. 8, 583 A.2d 765.

III.   CLIENT'S RIGHT TO CHOOSE COUNSEL

Balanced against the former client's interest in preventing a breach of confidence is the public policy interest in permitting the opposing party's continued representation by counsel of his or her choice. Disqualification interferes with a client's right to choose counsel. *Manning v. Waring, Cox, James, Sklar & Allen* (C.A.6, 1988), 849 F.2d 222, 224. . . . This issue has become increasingly important as the practice of law has changed. A review of the historical development of disqualification issues reveals the early conflicts created by the clash of the above principles.

IV.   HISTORY OF MOTIONS TO DISQUALIFY

Many of the early disqualification cases arose out of charges of conflict of interest where government attorneys left the public service and went into private practice. Early courts struggled with the need to fashion a rule that would preserve the confidences of the government client yet not discourage able attorneys from entering public service through fear of being locked forever into government service, unable to change positions. As the Court of Appeals for the Seventh Circuit noted:

"If past employment in government results in the disqualification of future employers from representing some of their long-term clients, it seems clearly possible that government attorneys will be regarded as 'Typhoid Marys.' Many talented lawyers, in turn, may be unwilling to spend a period in government service, if that service makes them unattractive or risky for large law firms to hire." *LaSalle Natl. Bank v. Lake Cty.* (C.A.7, 1983), 703 F.2d 252, 258.

As more and more private attorneys also began changing firms, motions to disqualify under the irrebuttable presumption of shared confidences increased, and inequities and abuses also began to surface. While some of these motions to disqualify were legitimate and necessary, such motions were also often misused to harass an opponent, disrupt the opponent's case, or to gain a tactical advantage, and therefore were viewed with increasing caution.

As a result, several federal cases began fashioning a way to deal with the competing interests caused by increased mobility of attorneys and the rise of motions to disqualify.... In *Analytica, Inc. v. NPD Research, Inc.* (C.A.7, 1983), 708 F.2d 1263, a strong dissent recognized the devastating effect even a *charge* of disqualification could have and foretold the trend of future case law in urging the abandonment of the irrebuttable presumption of shared confidences and automatic disqualification....

As a result of the changing legal profession, federal courts and the ABA Model Rules of Professional Conduct began allowing the use of various mechanisms to isolate an attorney who had transferred employment. Although originally applied only to government attorneys, these mechanisms have now been extended to situations involving transfers of private counsel as well.

V. Development of Standards for Disqualification

Several federal courts in addressing both primary and imputed disqualification have devised a three-part test to determine whether disqualification is proper when one attorney leaves a firm and joins another firm representing an opposing party. We believe this test adequately covers many different scenarios and will give the courts of Ohio guidance on disqualification issues.

First, a court must determine whether a substantial relationship exists between prior and present representations. If there is no substantial relationship, then no ethical problem exists. See *Uniweld Products, Inc. v. Union Carbide Corp.* (C.A.5, 1967), 385 F.2d 992. For example, when an attorney had represented a client in a trademark infringement case, the Court of Appeals for the Sixth Circuit denied disqualification in a later unrelated civil RICO case. *Dana Corp. v. Blue Cross & Blue Shield Mut. of N.*

Ohio (C.A.6, 1990), 900 F.2d 882. See, also, *Cleveland,* 440 F.Supp. 193, in which the court held that where a one-hundred-eighty-person law firm was clearly divided into separate, unrelated divisions, there was no presumption of shared confidences and actual proof of a substantial relationship was required.

Second, if a substantial relationship is found between the current matter and the prior matter, the court must examine whether the attorney shared in the confidences and representation of the prior matter. There is a presumption that such confidences would also be shared among members of the prior firm, but that presumption may be rebutted. *Novo Terapeutisk Laboratorium A/S v. Baxter Travenol Lab.* (C.A.7, 1979), 607 F.2d 186, 197; *Westinghouse Elec. Corp. v. Kerr–McGee Corp.* (C.A.7, 1978), 580 F.2d 1311, 1321; *Schiessle v. Stephens* (C.A.7, 1983), 717 F.2d 417 (attorney denied contact with case and prior client; challenging firm established by affidavit that attorney did have contact with the case and clients; presumption not rebutted).

In *Freeman,* the Court of Appeals for the Seventh Circuit, in setting the rules on primary disqualification, instructed the trial court that it could "rely on any of a number of factors, among them being the size of the law firm, the area of specialization of the attorney, the attorney's position in the firm, and the demeanor and credibility of witnesses at the evidentiary hearing."

If the presumption of shared confidences within the prior firm is rebutted by such evidence, then there is again no need for primary disqualification, as there are no confidences to be shared. However, if that presumption is not rebutted, and the attorney does or is presumed to possess client confidences, primary disqualification results, and a presumption of shared confidences arises between the attorney and the members of the attorney's *new* firm. The issue then is whether a presumption of shared confidences will also disqualify the entire new firm (imputed disqualification). Kala implies that this presumption should be *irrebuttable* and that once an attorney, particularly one as involved in the case as Pearson was, moves to opposing counsel's firm, no steps can be taken to restore confidence so as to overcome the appearance of impropriety; the entire firm must be disqualified.

Some courts have taken this approach. New Jersey has refused to adopt the rebuttable-presumption approach, finding that there is no way to overcome the appearance of impropriety in a "side-switching attorney" case. *Cardona,* 942 F.Supp. at 976–977. The New Jersey courts cite the impossibility of proving when a breach has been made, as those lawyers within the new firm are least likely to divulge such information. Judge Orlofsky in *Cardona* explained:

> "At the heart of every 'side-switching attorney' case is the suspicion that by changing sides, the attorney has

breached a duty of fidelity and loyalty to a former client, a client who had freely shared with the attorney secrets and confidences with the expectation that they would be disclosed to no one else. It is for this reason that the 'appearance of impropriety doctrine' was adopted to protect the public, our profession, and those it serves. In short, this much maligned doctrine exists to engender, protect and preserve the trust and confidence of clients.''

On the other hand, with the realities of modern-day practice, as discussed in the *Manning* case, such a hard-and-fast rule works an unfair hardship also. Ultimately, one must have faith in the integrity of members of the legal profession to honor their professional oath to uphold the Code of Professional Responsibility, safeguarded by the precautions required to rebut the presumption of shared confidences. If used properly, the process of screening attorneys who possess client confidences from other members of a firm can preserve those confidences while avoiding the use of the motion to disqualify as a device to gain a tactical advantage. Therefore, we believe that the fairer rule in balancing the interests of the parties and the public is to allow the presumption of shared confidences with members of the new firm to be rebutted.

Thus, the third part of the test on disqualification is whether the presumption of shared confidences with the new firm has been rebutted by evidence that a "Chinese wall" has been erected so as to preserve the confidences of the client.[6] The Chinese wall is the specific institutional screening mechanisms that will prevent the flow of confidential information from the quarantined attorney to other members of the law firm.

Factors to be considered in deciding whether an effective screen has been created are whether the law firm is sufficiently large and whether the structural divisions of the firm are sufficiently separate so as to minimize contact between the quarantined attorney and the others, the likelihood of contact between the quarantined attorney and the specific attorneys responsible for the current representation, the existence of safeguards or procedures which prevent the quarantined attorney from access to relevant files or other information relevant to the present litigation, prohibited access to files and other information on the case, locked case files with keys distributed to a select few, secret codes

---

6. "Chinese wall" has become the legal term to describe a "procedure which permits an attorney involved in an earlier adverse role to be screened from other attorneys in the firm so as to prevent disqualification of the entire law firm simply because one member of firm previously represented a client who is now an adversary of the client currently represented by the firm." Black's Law Dictionary (6 Ed.

Rev.1990) 240. This term refers historically to the Great Wall of China, which served ancient Chinese emperors as a barrier to invasion. Wolfram, Modern Legal Ethics (1986), Section 7.64. Ironically, however, the Great Wall of China was of limited military value. The concept is also referred to in cases and commentary as "screening devices," "ethical screens," or "institutional mechanisms for screening."

necessary to access pertinent information on electronic hardware, instructions given to all members of a new firm regarding the ban on exchange of information, and the prohibition of the sharing of fees derived from such litigation.

A very strict standard of proof must be applied to the rebuttal of this presumption of shared confidences, however, and any doubts as to the existence of an asserted conflict of interest must be resolved in favor of disqualification in order to dispel any appearance of impropriety.

Some courts have held that unrebutted affidavits attesting to a Chinese wall are sufficient to prevent disqualification. However, we reject such a bright-line test, as the court should maintain discretion to weigh issues of credibility. The court should be free to assess the reputation of an attorney and law firm for integrity and honesty. The court should also be free to balance the appearance of impropriety against the protections of a Chinese wall. For example, suppose a sole practitioner representing a plaintiff switches sides to a five-person defense firm representing the opposing party, leaving his former client to seek new counsel. The appearance of impropriety in such a fact pattern may be impossible to overcome.

If applied properly, screening mechanisms to insulate a quarantined attorney from the rest of the firm can protect client confidences while allowing for attorney mobility and the right of a client to choose counsel.

VI. ADDITIONAL FACTORS TO CONSIDER IN MOTIONS TO DISQUALIFY

In addition to the screening devices, there are other important factors to be considered by the trial court. First, the screening devices must be employed as soon as the disqualifying event occurs.... Instituting screens after a motion to disqualify is too late. Accordingly, a court must weigh the timeliness of the screening devices.

A second factor to consider is the hardship that a client would incur in obtaining new counsel if a motion to disqualify is granted. Hardship may be more of an issue if a conflict arose after a transfer. However, hardship may not carry much weight in a "side-switching" case. Ironically, where an attorney switches sides and joins an opposing counsel's firm, the attorney has de facto deprived his or her first client of the attorney of that client's choice, namely himself or herself. If the attorney has been lead counsel, other counsel in the firm must spend time and effort to take over the lead. If no one remaining in the prior firm is able to handle the matter, or if the attorney was a sole practitioner, the former client must seek out new counsel and incur the burden and expense created by the switch. In this scenario, the departing attorney has created a competing hardship for his or her former client, and the claim by the new firm of hardship created by its own doing in accepting the new attorney into the firm may no longer be persuasive. These are matters that should be left to the trier of fact to weigh.

In addition, a law firm contemplating hiring counsel who had been directly involved on the opposing side also has a duty to disclose to its own client that such a hiring may place the firm in conflict and could result in disqualification. [The court cited MR 1.9.] The law firm may have to subordinate its desire to augment its staff against its duties to its client and avoid placing the firm's interests above the client's interests.

Finally, the court should hold an evidentiary hearing on a motion to disqualify and must issue findings of fact if requested based on the evidence presented. Because a request for disqualification implies a charge of unethical conduct, the challenged firm must be given an opportunity to defend not only its relationship with the client, but also its good name, reputation and ethical standards. . . .

VII. THE REBUTTABLE-PRESUMPTION TEST FOR MOTIONS TO DISQUALIFY

In conclusion, we hold that in ruling on a motion for disqualification of either an individual (primary disqualification) or the entire firm (imputed disqualification) when an attorney has left a law firm and joined a firm representing the opposing party, a court must hold an evidentiary hearing and issue findings of fact using a three-part analysis:

(1) Is there a substantial relationship between the matter at issue and the matter of the former firm's prior representation;

(2) If there is a substantial relationship between these matters, is the presumption of shared confidences within the former firm rebutted by evidence that the attorney had no personal contact with or knowledge of the related matter; and

(3) If the attorney did have personal contact with or knowledge of the related matter, did the new law firm erect adequate and timely screens to rebut a presumption of shared confidences with the new firm so as to avoid imputed disqualification?

VIII. APPLICATION OF TEST TO THIS CASE

Under the facts of this case, Pearson clearly met the substantial-relationship test and possessed client confidences, as he was the lead attorney on Kala's lawsuit. Thus, the first two parts of the test require disqualification of Pearson and raise a presumption in favor of disqualification of [the entire] Duvin [law firm]. No one disputes that Pearson, himself, cannot work further on the case.

Therefore, we must determine whether the entire firm should be disqualified under the third part of the analysis, imputed disqualification.... Kala retained Pearson and the Spangenberg firm in 1993 as his attorneys. From 1993 through 1995, Kala trusted Pearson, relied upon him as his attorney, and disclosed all matters pertaining to his case involving his former employer, Aluminum Smelting. Pearson proceeded to file an appeal after the directed verdict and apparently even participated in a settlement conference with the Eighth District Court of Appeals on November 13, 1995. On January 8, 1996, Pearson obtained a continuance to file Kala's appellate brief. On January 22, 1996, Pearson left the Spangenberg firm and joined the Duvin firm, which was representing Aluminum Smelting and had been throughout the prior proceedings with Kala. The only conclusion that can be reached from the record is that Pearson was negotiating with Duvin while still actively representing Kala without disclosing to Kala his negotiations.

The appearance of impropriety is so strong that nothing that the Duvin firm could have done would have had any effect on Kala's perception that his personal attorney had abandoned him with all of his shared confidences and joined the firm representing his adversary while the case was still pending. No steps of any kind could possibly replace the trust and confidence that Kala had in his attorney or in the legal system if such representation is permitted. This is the classic "side-switching attorney" case.

We find that under this set of egregious facts, the appearance of impropriety was so great that the attempts made by Duvin to erect a Chinese wall were insufficient to overcome the appearance of impropriety. Accordingly, we affirm the disqualification ruling of the court of appeals.

Judgment affirmed.

Notes

1.   This case illustrates the conflicts of interest problems created by lawyers in private practice moving between firms. The ethics rules attempt to balance various competing concerns. How would you characterize these concerns?

2.   In *Kala*, lawyer Pearson had been the lead counsel in Kala's lawsuit against Aluminum Smelting. The court has no trouble finding that he personally cannot serve as a lawyer for Aluminum Smelting in the same case. Why is the entire Duvin firm disqualified? What rules does the court look to in making its decision that it must be?

3.   What if the facts of *Kala* were slightly different? In either of the three situations below, should Pearson be disqualified? Should the Duvin firm?

(a) Pearson had not worked at all on the *Kala v. Aluminum Smelting* case in his old firm, and did not know anything at all about it.

(b) Pearson had not worked on the *Kala* case in his old firm, but had discussed it at some length in the firm's lunchroom with lawyers who were working on it.

(c) Pearson was a low-level associate in his old firm who worked on the *Kala* case, but only on one task: he wrote a research memorandum for a partner. The research memo was based on a hypothetical fact pattern (based on the case) the partner gave him. Pearson never saw any documents in the case and never discussed the facts of the case, although he discussed his memo with the partner. He billed a total of 20 hours on the matter.

4. Change the facts of *Kala* again, slightly. Imagine that when Pearson left the Spangenberg firm, he took Kala as a client, and the *Kala v. Aluminum Smelting* case, with him to his new firm, Duvin. Imagine further that Duvin had never represented Aluminum Smelting on any matters. Nothing on those facts would prevent Pearson and Duvin from representing Kala. But could the Spangenberg firm now accept Aluminum Smelting as a client in *Kala v. Aluminum Smelting*? See MR 1.10(b).

5. *Negotiating a job with an adversary's law firm.* The *Kala* court points out that the facts indicate that Pearson "was negotiating with Duvin while still actively representing Kala without disclosing to Kala his negotiations." Was this ethically proper? Specifically, did Pearson violate duties to Kala by engaging in such talks with Duvin? Did Duvin violate any rules by engaging in such talks with Pearson?

6. *The appearance of impropriety.* The court cites Canon 9 of the Model Code, which says "a lawyer should avoid even the appearance of professional impropriety." The Model Rules dropped this rule, at least as a basis for discipline, primarily on the ground that it is too vague. See Restatement § 5, comment *c* (explaining the drafters' rationale in "purposefully" omitting the "appearance of impropriety" rule). But some courts continue to use the appearance of impropriety concept in non-disciplinary private-lawyer contexts, as the *Kala* court does here. Is that appropriate, or is the concept too vague even as used in *Kala*? Should lawyers *strive* to avoid even the appearance of impropriety, even if they cannot in most states be *disciplined* for failing to do so?

7. The court speaks of the disqualification remedy being increasingly abused by counsel, used as a tactical weapon in litigation. Is anything wrong with that? If so, does such abuse call for a revision of the conflicts rules, or could special litigation rules (such as those prohibiting bad faith filings and frivolous motions) cover the situation adequately?

NOTE: SCREENING TO CURE IMPUTED CONFLICTS

The court in *Kala* accepts in principle the idea that a law firm can avoid vicarious or imputed disqualification by adopting adequate screening measures (what it calls a "Chinese wall," although that term is not often used today). Screening is defined in the Model Rules as "the isolation of a lawyer from any participation in a matter through the timely imposition of procedures within a firm that are reasonably adequate ... to protect information that the isolated lawyer is obligated to protect." MR 1.0(k).

Screening to avoid firm-wide disqualification has been allowed for some years when a government lawyer goes into private practice, *see* MR 1.11(b), but with migratory private lawyers its use remains somewhat controversial. The Model Rules do not approve of a screening mechanism as a cure for imputed conflicts, other than for government lawyers or non-legal personnel. See MR 1.10, comment [4]. But a growing number of states have adopted ethics rules that allow a firm's screening of a lawyer coming from another private firm to cure an imputed conflict. Case law in other states has either expressly or tacitly approved of what is now a widespread practice in law firms throughout the nation. The Restatement permits screening as a cure, but only when information possessed by the screened lawyer "is not likely to be significant." Restatement § 124, comment *d(i)*.

The *Kala* court, and all states that allow for screening, require that screening measures be "timely," typically meaning that such protective measures must be in place before the new lawyer joins the firm. Why this requirement?

What if the screen is set up in a timely way, but proves to be ineffective? In *Spur Products Corp. v. Stoel Rives LLP*, 142 Idaho 41, 122 P.3d 300 (2005), the firm of Stoel Rives represented Spur Products in a dispute with Ikon Office Solutions. A lawyer for Stoel Rives had previously represented a subsidiary of Ikon. When he came to Stoel Rives he agreed in an affidavit to be screened from the Spur Products matter. But he received a memorandum about the Spur Products case in violation of that screening agreement. After the Spur–Ikon matter had settled, but knowing nothing about the improper leak to the conflicted lawyer, Spur Products sued Stoel Rives for legal malpractice. Upon learning of the breach of confidentiality, Spur sought to amend its complaint to add the breach, and the firm's failure to disclose it to Spur, as a separate count of malpractice. The trial court denied the motion to amend, but the Idaho Supreme Court held that this was an abuse of discretion. Stoel Rives' disclosure to the conflicted lawyer and its failure to inform Spur about it constituted "a viable claim for legal malpractice."

Should more states allow for screening of non-government lawyers? Or should the presumption that the new lawyer will share confidences with his new colleagues be irrebuttable? One trial judge has connected the trend towards allowing screening to an erosion of professional values:

> [T]he Court is troubled by the trend to dispose of centuries-old confidentiality rules solely for the convenience of modern lawyers who "move from one association to another several times in their careers." W. Va. R. Prof. Conduct 1.10 cmt. Lawyers and law firms are more than mere business entities. According to the preamble of the W. Va. R. Prof. Conduct, "[a] lawyer is a representative of clients, an officer of the legal system and a public citizen having special responsibility for the quality of justice." In an age of sagging public confidence in our legal system, maintaining confidence in that system and in the legal profession is of the utmost importance. In this regard, courts should be reluctant to sacrifice the interests of clients and former clients for the perceived business interests of lawyers, especially when the state supreme court, in promulgating the Rules of Professional Conduct, has failed to adopt contrary rules. While these considerations may dampen law firm mergers, such is the price that lawyers must pay for their special status in our society.

Roberts & Schaefer Co. v. San–Con, Inc., 898 F.Supp. 356, 363 (S.D. W.Va.1995), quoted by the same judge in *Healthnet, Inc. v. Health Net, Inc.,* 289 F.Supp.2d 755 (S.D. W.Va. 2003) (in response to both parties' agreement that screens should be allowed in general).

Do you tend to agree with the above criticisms, or are you convinced by the *Kala* court's reasoning that screening is good policy? See, e.g., *Adams v. Aerojet–General Corp.,* 86 Cal.App.4th 1324, 104 Cal.Rptr.2d 116 (2001).

NOTE: MOBILE NON–LEGAL PERSONNEL

Courts are increasingly facing disqualification motions based not only on lawyers who have moved from one firm to another, but also on non-lawyers who have moved from one firm to another. Many courts apply similar tests to non-legal personnel as those used for mobile lawyers, while recognizing that the issues raised are not completely identical. For example, in *Green v. Toledo Hospital,* 94 Ohio St.3d 480 764 N.E.2d 979 (2002), the court affirmed the denial of plaintiff's motion to disqualify defendant's lawyer, where a legal secretary employed by defense firm was previously the plaintiff's lawyer's secretary. The court found its decision in *Kala* (reprinted above) "instructive but distinguishable." Specifically, the court held that "the presumption of shared confidences that is at the core of *Kala* is inappropriate for nonattorneys. Many, if not most, nonattorneys at a law firm are not regularly exposed to confidential information about clients and their cases. Further, to expose nonattorneys to the same presumption as attorneys would unfairly taint them and make it more difficult for them to change employment." Thus a party moving for disqualification must present evidence that the former employee "has been exposed to confidential information in the relevant case." If such a showing is made, then a rebuttable presumption arises that the information has been shared with the new firm. The presumption is rebutted by a showing that the employee was screened from involvement in the case. In the case, the presumption was rebutted.

In *Leibowitz v. Eighth Judicial District Court*, 119 Nev. 523, 78 P.3d 515 (2003), a legal assistant once worked for a law firm representing the husband in a divorce, then moved to the law firm that represented the wife in the same case. Overruling an earlier opinion to the contrary, the court said that the imputed lawyer disqualification standards did not apply to non-legal personnel simply because they had exposure or access to the files of an adversary of the new firm's client. Only if the employee had actually acquired privileged, confidential information would the imputed disqualification rule apply at all, and even if it did a firm may avoid disqualification by the use of effective and timely screening. In the case, the firm had screened the new hire, so disqualification was not ordered.

With these two cases, compare *Zimmerman v. Mahaska Bottling Co.*, 270 Kan. 810, 19 P.3d 784 (2001). A legal secretary previously worked for the plaintiff's firm in a personal injury case, then nine months after the case had begun accepted a job with the firm representing the defendant. She testified that during her time at the plaintiff's firm she had been present when there were conversations about the case. The court disqualified the new firm, saying "paralegals and other nonattorney staff members are regularly exposed to confidential client information as part of their everyday work.... To allow such employees to change firms at random and without concern for the information they have acquired would be to undercut the rules applicable to attorneys.... [T]he policy of protecting the attorney-client privilege must be preserved through imputed disqualification when a nonlawyer employee, in possession of privileged information, accepts employment with a firm who represents a client with materially adverse interests." Was the real problem in the case the lack of an effective screen? See Maine Bd. of Bar Overseers Prof'l Ethics Comm'n, Op. 186 (2004) (approving screening of mobile non-legal personnel).

B. Criminal Cases

MICKENS v. TAYLOR

Supreme Court of the United States, 2002.
535 U.S. 162, 122 S.Ct. 1237, 152 L.Ed.2d 291.

Justice SCALIA delivered the opinion of the Court.

The question presented in this case is what a defendant must show in order to demonstrate a Sixth Amendment violation where the trial court fails to inquire into a potential conflict of interest about which it knew or reasonably should have known.

I

In 1993, a Virginia jury convicted petitioner Mickens of the premeditated murder of Timothy Hall during or following the commission of an attempted forcible sodomy. Finding the murder outrageously and wantonly vile, it sentenced petitioner to death. In June 1998, Mickens filed a petition for writ of habeas corpus in the United States District Court for the Eastern District of Virginia, alleging, *inter alia,* that he was denied effective assistance of counsel because one of his court-appointed attorneys had a conflict of interest at trial. Federal habeas counsel had discovered that petitioner's lead trial attorney, Bryan Saunders, was representing Hall (the victim) on assault and concealed-weapons charges at the time of the murder. Saunders had been appointed to represent Hall, a juvenile, on March 20, 1992, and had met with him once for 15 to 30 minutes some time the following week. Hall's body was discovered on March 30, 1992, and four days later a juvenile court judge dismissed the charges against him, noting on the docket sheet that Hall was deceased. The one-page docket sheet also listed Saunders as Hall's counsel. On April 6, 1992, the same judge appointed Saunders to represent petitioner. Saunders did not disclose to the court, his co-counsel, or petitioner that he had previously represented Hall. Under Virginia law, juvenile case files are confidential and may not generally be disclosed without a court order, see Va.Code Ann. § 16.1–305 (1999), but petitioner learned about Saunders' prior representation when a clerk mistakenly produced Hall's file to federal habeas counsel.

The District Court held an evidentiary hearing and denied petitioner's habeas petition. A divided panel of the Court of Appeals for the Fourth Circuit reversed, 227 F.3d 203 (2000), and the Court of Appeals granted rehearing en banc, 240 F.3d 348 (2001).... On the merits, the Court of Appeals assumed that the juvenile court judge had neglected a duty to inquire into a potential conflict, but rejected petitioner's argument that this failure either mandated automatic reversal of his conviction or relieved him of the burden of showing that a conflict of interest adversely affected his representation. Relying on *Cuyler v. Sullivan,* 446

U.S. 335, 100 S.Ct. 1708, 64 L.Ed.2d 333 (1980), the court held that a defendant must show "both an actual conflict of interest and an adverse effect even if the trial court failed to inquire into a potential conflict about which it reasonably should have known." Concluding that petitioner had not demonstrated adverse effect, it affirmed the District Court's denial of habeas relief. We granted a stay of execution of petitioner's sentence and granted certiorari.

II

The Sixth Amendment provides that a criminal defendant shall have the right to "the assistance of counsel for his defence." This right has been accorded, we have said, "not for its own sake, but because of the effect it has on the ability of the accused to receive a fair trial." *United States v. Cronic,* 466 U.S. 648, 658, 104 S.Ct. 2039, 80 L.Ed.2d 657 (1984). It follows from this that assistance which is ineffective in preserving fairness does not meet the constitutional mandate, see *Strickland v. Washington,* 466 U.S. 668, 685–686, 104 S.Ct. 2052, 80 L.Ed.2d 674 (1984); and it also follows that defects in assistance that have no probable effect upon the trial's outcome do not establish a constitutional violation. As a general matter, a defendant alleging a Sixth Amendment violation must demonstrate "a reasonable probability that, but for counsel's unprofessional errors, the result of the proceeding would have been different." *Id.,* at 694, 104 S.Ct. 2052.

There is an exception to this general rule. We have spared the defendant the need of showing probable effect upon the outcome, and have simply presumed such effect, where assistance of counsel has been denied entirely or during a critical stage of the proceeding. When that has occurred, the likelihood that the verdict is unreliable is so high that a case-by-case inquiry is unnecessary. But only in "circumstances of that magnitude" do we forgo individual inquiry into whether counsel's inadequate performance undermined the reliability of the verdict. *Cronic, supra,* at 659, n. 26, 104 S.Ct. 2039.

We have held in several cases that "circumstances of that magnitude" may also arise when the defendant's attorney actively represented conflicting interests. The nub of the question before us is whether the principle established by these cases provides an exception to the general rule of *Strickland* under the circumstances of the present case. To answer that question, we must examine those cases in some detail.

In *Holloway v. Arkansas,* 435 U.S. 475, 98 S.Ct. 1173, 55 L.Ed.2d 426 (1978), defense counsel had objected that he could not adequately represent the divergent interests of three codefendants. Without inquiry, the trial court had denied counsel's motions for the appointment of separate counsel and had refused to allow counsel to cross-examine any of the defendants on behalf of the other two. The *Holloway* Court deferred to the judgment of counsel regarding the existence of a disabling conflict, recognizing that a defense attorney is in the best position to determine when a conflict exists, that he has an ethical obligation to advise the court of any problem, and that his declarations to the court are "virtually made under oath." *Holloway* presumed, moreover, that the conflict, "which [the defendant] and his counsel tried to avoid by timely objections to the joint representation," undermined the adversarial process. The presumption was justified because joint representation of conflicting interests is inherently suspect, and because counsel's conflicting obligations to multiple defendants "effectively sea[l] his lips on crucial matters" and make it difficult to measure the precise harm arising from counsel's errors. *Holloway* thus creates an automatic reversal rule only where defense counsel is forced to represent codefendants over his timely objection, unless the trial court has determined that there is no conflict. *Id.,* at 488, 98 S.Ct. 1173 ("[W]henever a trial court improperly requires joint representation over timely objection reversal is automatic").

In *Cuyler v. Sullivan,* 446 U.S. 335, 100 S.Ct. 1708, 64 L.Ed.2d 333 (1980), the respondent was one of three defendants accused of murder who were tried separately, represented by the same counsel. Neither counsel nor anyone else objected to the multiple representation, and counsel's opening argument at Sullivan's trial suggested that the interests of the defendants were aligned. We declined to extend *Holloway*'s automatic reversal rule to this situation and held that, absent objection, a defendant must demonstrate that "a conflict of interest actually affected the adequacy of his representation." In addition to describing the defendant's burden of proof, *Sullivan* addressed separately a trial court's duty to inquire into the propriety of a multiple representation, construing *Holloway* to require inquiry only when "the trial court knows or reasonably should know that a particular conflict exists"—which is not to be confused with when the trial court is aware of a vague, unspecified possibility of conflict, such as that which "inheres in almost every instance of multiple representation." In *Sullivan,* no "special circumstances" triggered the trial court's duty to inquire.

Finally, in *Wood v. Georgia,* 450 U.S. 261, 101 S.Ct. 1097, 67 L.Ed.2d 220 (1981), three indigent defendants convicted of distributing obscene materials had their probation revoked for failure to make the requisite $500 monthly payments on their $5,000 fines. We granted certiorari to consider whether this violated the Equal Protection Clause, but during the course of our consideration certain disturbing circumstances came to our attention: At the probation-revocation hearing (as at all times since their arrest) the defendants had been represented by the lawyer for their employer (the owner of the business that purveyed the obscenity), and their employer paid the attorney's fees. The employer had promised his employees he would pay their fines, and had generally kept that promise but had not done so in these defendants' case. This record suggested that the employer's interest in establishing a favorable equal-protection precedent (reducing the fines he would have to pay for his indigent employees in the future) diverged from the defendants' interest in obtaining leniency or paying lesser fines to avoid imprisonment. Moreover, the possibility that counsel was actively representing the conflicting interests of employer and defendants "was sufficiently apparent at the time of the revocation hearing to impose upon the court a duty to inquire further." Because "[o]n the record before us, we [could not] be sure whether counsel was influenced in his basic strategic decisions by the interests of the employer who hired him," we remanded for the trial court "to determine whether the conflict of interest that this record strongly suggests actually existed."

Petitioner argues that the remand instruction in *Wood* established an "unambiguous rule" that where the trial judge neglects a duty to inquire into a potential conflict, the defendant, to obtain reversal of the judgment, need only show that his lawyer was subject to a conflict of interest, and need not show that the conflict adversely affected counsel's performance. He relies upon the language in the remand instruction directing the trial court to grant a new revocation hearing if it determines that "an actual conflict of interest existed," without requiring a further determination that the conflict adversely affected counsel's performance. As used in the remand instruction, however, we think "an actual conflict of interest" meant precisely a conflict *that affected counsel's performance*—as opposed to a mere theoretical division of loyalties. It was shorthand for the statement in *Sullivan* that "a defendant who shows that a conflict of interest *actually affected the adequacy of his representation* need not demonstrate prejudice in order to obtain relief." This is the only interpretation consistent with the *Wood* Court's earlier description of why it could not decide the case without a remand: "On the record before us, we cannot be sure whether counsel *was influenced in his basic strategic decisions* by the interests of the employer who hired him. *If this was the case,* the due process rights of petitioners were not respected. . . . " 450 U.S., at 272, 101 S.Ct. 1097 (emphasis added). The notion that *Wood* created a new rule *sub silentio*—and in a case where certiorari had been granted on an entirely different question, and the parties had neither briefed nor argued the conflict-of-interest issue—is implausible.[5]

---

5. We have used "actual conflict of interest" elsewhere to mean what was required to be shown in *Sullivan.* And we have used "conflict of interest" to mean a division of loyalties *that affected counsel's performance.* . . . Thus, the *Sullivan* stan- dard is not properly read as requiring inquiry into actual conflict as something separate and apart from adverse effect. An "actual conflict," for Sixth Amendment purposes, is a conflict of interest that adversely affects counsel's performance.

Petitioner's proposed rule of automatic reversal when there existed a conflict that did not affect counsel's performance, but the trial judge failed to make the *Sullivan*-mandated inquiry, makes little policy sense. As discussed, the rule applied when the trial judge is not aware of the conflict (and thus not obligated to inquire) is that prejudice will be presumed only if the conflict has significantly affected counsel's performance—thereby rendering the verdict unreliable, even though *Strickland* prejudice cannot be shown. See *Sullivan, supra,* at 348–349, 100 S.Ct. 1708. The trial court's awareness of a potential conflict neither renders it more likely that counsel's performance was significantly affected nor in any other way renders the verdict unreliable. Nor does the trial judge's failure to make the *Sullivan*-mandated inquiry often make it harder for reviewing courts to determine conflict and effect, particularly since those courts may rely on evidence and testimony whose importance only becomes established at the trial....

Since this was not a case in which (as in *Holloway*) counsel protested his inability simultaneously to represent multiple defendants; and since the trial court's failure to make the *Sullivan*-mandated inquiry does not reduce the petitioner's burden of proof; it was at least necessary, to void the conviction, for petitioner to establish that the conflict of interest adversely affected his counsel's performance. The Court of Appeals having found no such effect, the denial of habeas relief must be affirmed....

For the reasons stated, the judgment of the Court of Appeals is *Affirmed*.

[Concurring Opinions omitted]

Justice STEVENS, dissenting.

This case raises three uniquely important questions about a fundamental component of our criminal justice system—the constitutional right of a person accused of a capital offense to have the effective assistance of counsel for his defense. The first is whether a capital defendant's attorney has a duty to disclose that he was representing the defendant's alleged victim at the time of the murder. Second, is whether, assuming disclosure of the prior representation, the capital defendant has a right to refuse the appointment of the conflicted attorney. Third, is whether the trial judge, who knows or should know of such prior representation, has a duty to obtain the defendant's consent before appointing that lawyer to represent him. Ultimately, the question presented by this case is whether, if these duties exist and if all of them are violated, there exist "circumstances that are so likely to prejudice the accused that the cost of litigating their effect in a particular case is unjustified." *United States v. Cronic,* 466 U.S. 648, 658, 104 S.Ct. 2039, 80 L.Ed.2d 657 (1984).

I

The first critical stage in the defense of a capital case is the series of pretrial meetings between the accused and his counsel when they decide how the case should be defended. A lawyer cannot possibly determine how best to represent a new client unless that client is willing to provide the lawyer with a truthful account of the relevant facts. When an indigent defendant first meets his newly appointed counsel, he will often falsely maintain his complete innocence. Truthful disclosures of embarrassing or incriminating facts are contingent on the development of the client's confidence in the undivided loyalty of the lawyer. Quite obviously, knowledge that the lawyer represented the victim would be a substantial obstacle to the development of such confidence.

It is equally true that a lawyer's decision to conceal such an important fact from his new client would have comparable ramifications. The suppression of communication and truncated investigation that would unavoidably follow from such a decision would also make it difficult, if not altogether impossible, to establish the necessary level of trust that should characterize the "delicacy of relation" between attorney and client.

In this very case, it is likely that Mickens misled his counsel, Bryan Saunders, given the fact that Mickens gave false testimony at his trial denying any involvement in the crime despite the overwhelming evidence that he had killed Timothy Hall after a sexual encounter. In retrospect, it seems obvious that the death penalty might have been avoided by acknowledging Mickens' involvement, but emphasizing the evidence suggesting that their sexual encounter was consensual. Mickens' habeas counsel garnered evidence suggesting that Hall was a male prostitute; that the area where Hall was killed was known for prostitution; and that there was no evidence that Hall was forced to the secluded area where he was ultimately murdered. An unconflicted attorney could have put forward a defense tending to show that Mickens killed Hall only after the two engaged in consensual sex, but Saunders offered no such defense. This was a crucial omission—a finding of forcible sodomy was an absolute prerequisite to Mickens' eligibility for the death penalty. Of course, since that strategy would have led to conviction of a noncapital offense, counsel would have been unable to persuade the defendant to divulge the information necessary to support such a defense and then ultimately to endorse the strategy unless he had earned the complete confidence of his client.

Saunders' concealment of essential information about his prior representation of the victim was a severe lapse in his professional duty. The lawyer's duty to disclose his representation of a client related to the instant charge is not only intuitively obvious, it is as old as the profession. . . . Mickens' lawyer's violation of this fundamental obligation of disclosure is indefensible. The relevance of Saunders' prior representation of Hall to the new appointment was far too important to be concealed.

II

If the defendant is found guilty of a capital offense, the ensuing proceedings that determine whether he will be put to death are critical in every sense of the word. At those proceedings, testimony about the impact of the crime on the victim, including testimony about the character of the victim, may have a critical effect on the jury's decision. Because a lawyer's fiduciary relationship with his deceased client survives the client's death, *Swidler & Berlin v. United States,* 524 U.S. 399, 118 S.Ct. 2081, 141 L.Ed.2d 379 (1998), Saunders necessarily labored under conflicting obligations that were irreconcilable. He had a duty to protect the reputation and confidences of his deceased client, and a duty to impeach the impact evidence presented by the prosecutor.

Saunders' conflicting obligations to his deceased client, on the one hand, and to his living client, on the other, were unquestionably sufficient to give Mickens the right to insist on different representation. For the "right to counsel guaranteed by the Constitution contemplates the services of an attorney devoted solely to the interests of his client," *Von Moltke v. Gillies,* 332 U.S. 708, 725, 68 S.Ct. 316, 92 L.Ed. 309 (1948). Moreover, in my judgment, the right to conflict-free counsel is just as firmly protected by the Constitution as the defendant's right of self-representation recognized in *Faretta v. California,* 422 U.S. 806, 95 S.Ct. 2525, 45 L.Ed.2d 562 (1975).

III

When an indigent defendant is unable to retain his own lawyer, the trial judge's appointment of counsel is itself a critical stage of a criminal trial. At that point in the proceeding, by definition, the defendant has no lawyer to protect his interests and must rely entirely on the judge. For that reason it is "the solemn duty of a . . . judge before whom a defendant appears without counsel to make a thorough inquiry and to take all steps necessary to insure the fullest protection of this constitutional right at every stage of the proceedings."

This duty with respect to indigent defendants is far more imperative than the judge's duty to investigate the possibility of a conflict that arises when retained counsel represents either multiple or successive defendants. It is true that in a situation of retained counsel, "[u]nless the trial court knows or reasonably should know that a particular conflict exists, the court need not initiate an inquiry." *Cuyler v. Sullivan,* 446 U.S. 335, 347, 100 S.Ct. 1708, 64 L.Ed.2d 333 (1980). But when, as was true in this case, the judge is not merely reviewing the permissibility of the defendants' choice of counsel, but is responsible for making the choice herself, and when she knows or should know that a conflict does exist, the duty to make a thorough inquiry is manifest and unqualified.[9] Indeed, under far less compelling circumstances, we squarely held that when a record discloses the "possibility of a conflict" between the interests of the defendants and the interests of the party paying their counsel's fees, the Constitution imposes a duty of inquiry on the state court judge even when no objection was made. *Wood v. Georgia,* 450 U.S. 261, 267, 272, 101 S.Ct. 1097, 67 L.Ed.2d 220 (1981).

IV

Mickens had a constitutional right to the services of an attorney devoted solely to his interests. That right was violated. The lawyer who did represent him had a duty to disclose his prior representation of the victim to Mickens and to the trial judge. That duty was violated. When Mickens had no counsel, the trial judge had a duty to "make a thorough inquiry and to take all steps necessary to insure the fullest protection of" his right to counsel. *Von Moltke,* 332 U.S., at 722, 68 S.Ct. 316. Despite knowledge of the lawyer's prior representation, she violated that duty.

We will never know whether Mickens would have received the death penalty if those violations had not occurred nor precisely what effect they had on Saunders' representation of Mickens. We do know that he did not receive the kind of representation that the Constitution guarantees. If Mickens had been represented by an attorney-impostor who never passed a bar examination, we might also be unable to determine whether the impostor's educational shortcomings " 'actually affected the adequacy of his representation.' " We would, however, surely set aside his conviction if the person who had represented him was not a real lawyer. . . .

I respectfully dissent.

[Dissenting Opinions of Justice Souter and Justice Breyer (joined by Justice Ginsburg) omitted.]

---

9. There is no dispute before us as to the appointing judge's knowledge. The court below assumed, *arguendo,* that the judge who, upon Hall's death, dismissed Saunders from his representation of Hall and who then three days later appointed Saunders to represent Mickens in the kill-ing of Hall "reasonably should have known that Saunders labored under a potential conflict of interest arising from his previous representation of Hall." 240 F.3d 348, 357 (C.A.4 2001). This assumption has not been challenged.

Notes

1. Did Mickens' lawyer labor under an actual conflict of interest? Does the dissent convince you that he probably did? Did it affect his trial strategy to his client's detriment? Should this have led to a reversal of his conviction?

2. Does the Court's continuing interpretation of *Holloway*—that automatic reversal is required only when defense counsel objects to a conflict—adequately protect defendants whose lawyers actively conceal a conflict?

3. Should the Court distinguish between capital cases and non-capital cases? Justice Breyer, in dissent in *Mickens*, argued that in a death penalty case, "a categorical approach is warranted and automatic reversal is required."

4. Justice Breyer also argued in his dissent that carrying out a death sentence after such a tainted trial would "diminish that public confidence in the criminal justice system upon which the successful functioning of that system continues to depend." Does the majority place adequate emphasis on such institutional concerns? Could it draw on earlier cases we have read to find such an emphasis?

5. Does it, and should it, matter in a criminal case who is objecting to the conflict of interest? Compare *People v. Frisco*, 119 P.3d 1093 (Colo. 2005) (reversing the trial court's disqualification of criminal defendant's lawyer where the disqualification motion was made by the prosecutor and opposed by the defendant; a former client of the lawyer was an alleged co-conspirator and a potential prosecution witness) with *Lewis v. Mayle*, 391 F.3d 989 (9th Cir. 2004) (reversing a conviction on Sixth Amendment grounds where defendant had waived the conflict at trial, but then appealed claiming the waiver was not informed and that the conflict deprived him of effective assistance of counsel; a former client of the lawyer was the state's key witness).

C. Mobile Government Lawyers: The "Revolving Door"

Distinct conflict-of-interest issues arise when lawyers move from government service to private practice. Can a lawyer work on a case against the government after she has left the government? If the private matter is "substantially related" to matters handled for the former client (the government), then isn't that a disqualifying conflict of interest? If the former government lawyer were to be disqualified from representing private clients against the government, then wouldn't this conflict be imputed to all of the lawyers in the lawyer's new private firm? On the other hand, what if lawyers could with complete impunity move from government service into the private sector and use their knowledge of the inner workings of government to advantage private clients wealthy enough to pay for that knowledge?

IN RE SOFAER

District of Columbia Court of Appeals, 1999.
728 A.2d 625.

FARRELL, Associate Judge:

This case is before us on exceptions to the report and order of the Board on Professional Responsibility (the "Board") directing Bar Counsel to issue an informal admonition to respondent for having violated Rule 1.11(a) of the District of Columbia Rules of Professional Conduct. The rule states in relevant part:

A lawyer shall not accept other employment in connection with a matter which is the same as, or substantially related to, a matter in which the lawyer participated personally and substantially as a public officer or employee.

A hearing committee and the Board both concluded that respondent had violated this rule by undertaking to represent the government of Libya in connection with criminal and civil disputes and litigation arising from the 1988 bombing of Pan American Flight 103 over Lockerbie, Scotland, after respondent, while serving as Legal Advisor in the United States Department of State, took part personally and substantially in the government's investigation of the bombing and in related diplomatic and legal activities. We sustain the Board's order . . .

[The following facts are taken from the Board's report, which the court attached as an appendix.] On December 21, 1988, Pan American Flight 103 was blown up over Lockerbie, Scotland, killing everyone on board and 11 people in the town below. The United States undertook an intensive investigation to identify the perpetrators of this terrorist act, and the families of the victims sued Pan Am for damages arising from the bombing. At the time of the bombing and the beginning of the investigation, Respondent was the Legal Adviser in the United States Department of State. In June 1990, Respondent left the State Department to join the Washington office of the law firm of Hughes Hubbard & Reed (HH & R). In November 1991, two Libyans were indicted by a federal grand jury for the bombing. In July 1993, Respondent and HH & R were retained to represent Libya in connection with criminal and civil disputes and litigation arising from the Pan Am 103 bombing. Respondent intended to seek consensual monetary settlements with the families of the victims and negotiate arrangements by which Libya would surrender the two indicted Libyans for trial by the United States and the United Kingdom in a mutually agreeable venue. In mid-July 1993, soon after Respondent's retention by Libya became public, he and HH & R withdrew from the representation, stating that the adverse public and governmental reaction made it impossible to accomplish the purposes for which they were retained. Shortly thereafter, Bar Counsel initiated an investigation into Respondent's possible violation of District of Columbia Rule of Professional Conduct 1.11(a).... On July 25, 1995, Bar Counsel charged Respondent with violating this rule. Hearing Committee Number One conducted an evidentiary hearing on December 5 and 6, 1995. The Hearing Committee concluded ... that Respondent's representation of Libya constituted a violation of Rule 1.11(a), [and] recommended that Respondent receive an informal admonition for his misconduct....

Respondent argues that in defining the "matter" in which he took part while Legal Advisor as "the legal activities flowing from the government's efforts to address [the Pan Am 103 bombing]," the Board bundled together activities so diverse in nature as to give him no fair warning of a potential overlap when he accepted the private representation of Libya. We are not persuaded. The activities in question, including diplomatic intervention with an unnamed country, attendance at confidential briefings on the criminal investigation, and overseeing the State Department's response to civil third-party subpoenas, all centered about a distinct historical event involving specific parties,[2] whether or not all had been identified. As the Board recognized, "The 'matter' is not terrorism, or even Libyan terrorism"; rather, "[t]he core of fact at the heart of each piece of legal activity is ... why and how Pan Am 103 blew up over Lockerbie." The contours of the bombing and the government's investigation and related responses to it were defined sharply enough to constitute a "matter" under the Rule.

Respondent contends that his work as Legal Advisor concerned the Pan Am 103 bombing in ways that were too marginal, infrequent, or passive to amount to "personal and substantial" participation in the matter. The main feature of the government's response, he asserts, was the criminal investigation conducted by the Department of Justice, not the Department of State; State's role (hence respondent's) consisted largely of a routine response to a third-party subpoena issued by Pan Am in furtherance of its theory that the U.S. government had advance warning of the bombing but failed to act.

Respondent's discounting of the subpoena as routine depends partly on hindsight: the district court eventually quashed the subpoena. Until then, however, the subpoena had the potential of embroiling the government in the tort litigation, and so respondent's role in reviewing and approving the memorandum recom-

2. *See* Rule 1.11(a), comment [3] ("'Matter' ... encompass[es] only matters that are particular to a specific party or parties.").

mending the State Department's response to the subpoena cannot be considered perfunctory. But his participation went further. After Pan Am voiced its theory of government foreknowledge at a meeting with the Secretary of State which respondent either attended or knew of, respondent's judgment was sought on whether, or how fully, to inform the Department's designated witness in the subpoena matter of the meeting, in preparation for his testimony. That action, as Bar Counsel points out, did not become "insubstantial" because the legal judgment was easily arrived at or because the government subsequently concluded that Pan Am's theory of government complicity was unsupported.

Moreover, respondent's actions take on added significance when viewed in the context of his participation, as one of a small number of senior State Department officials, in confidential oral and written briefings which periodically included information about the progress of the criminal investigation and related diplomatic actions. The fact that respondent played no role in the investigation itself and was not shown to have recommended or taken action based on the briefings[4] is not critical. As the Board explained, "Respondent was much more than the passive recipient of general agency information. As chief legal officer of the State Department, [he] was kept abreast of the progress of the investigation and the diplomatic efforts in response to the bombing precisely so that he could provide legal advice and perform legal duties concerning the bombing when called upon to do so."

All told, respondent's active participation in the Pan Am 103 matter bears no resemblance to the merely peripheral or formal involvement in a matter which the Rule does not encompass. *See* Opinion No. 84, D.C. Bar Legal Ethics Committee (1980) (interpreting former DR 9–101).

Respondent's assertion that by emphasizing his receipt of confidential information from the briefings the Board confused Rule 1.11(a) with Rule 1.6 (restricting use of client confidences or secrets) is mistaken. While he is correct that "no one has ever suggested any improper disclosure of confidences by Respondent," Rule 1.11(a) bars participation in overlapping government and private matters where "it is reasonable to infer counsel may have received information during the first representation that might be useful to the second"; "the 'actual receipt of . . . information,'" and hence disclosure of it, is immaterial. *Brown v. District of Columbia Bd. of Zoning Adjustment,* 486 A.2d 37, 50 (D.C.1984) (en banc) (citations omitted).

Rule 1.11(a) prohibits a lawyer from accepting employment in connection with a matter "the same as, or substantially related

---

4. An apparent exception was respondent's participation, occasioned by the Pan Am 103 bombing, in a diplomatic exchange with an unnamed country intended to persuade the country to abate terrorist activity.

to," a matter in which he or she took part as a public officer or employee. The inquiry is a practical one asking whether the two matters substantially overlap.[5] Respondent insists that he stayed clear of that overlap by restricting the terms of his agreement to represent Libya so as to "assum[e] Libya's culpability for the [Pan Am 103] bombing." A lawyer may, of course, limit the objectives of a representation with client consent. Rule 1.2(c). But respondent's retainer agreement exemplifies why, in our view, limiting the private representation rarely will succeed in avoiding the convergence addressed by Rule 1.11(a). While stating that "[the firm's] efforts will not include substantial activities as litigators but rather would be limited to activities associated with agreed upon measures, including consensual dispositions," the agreement emphasized that "[m]easures will be taken only with your [*i.e.,* Libya's] prior consent, and *without admission of liability*" (emphasis added). The proposed activities included "investigating the facts and legal proceedings, preparing legal analyses, providing legal advice and proposing legal steps to deal with" the "ongoing civil and criminal disputes and litigation" stemming from the destruction of Pan Am 103—all clearly features of a comprehensive attorney-client relationship.

We do not question the sincerity of respondent's belief that the representation could be insulated, factually and ethically, from the investigation and diplomatic efforts of which he had been part. The "substantially related" test by its terms, however, is meant to induce a former government lawyer considering a representation to err well on the side of caution. Respondent did not do so.[6] ...

Joined by *amici curiae* who are former government officials, respondent urges that finding an ethical violation in this case will deter District of Columbia lawyers from entering the government or serving for long once there, lest Rule 1.11(a) trip them up after they enter private practice. We are sensitive to the concern, already voiced in *Brown, supra,* that over-zealous application of

---

5. As the Board explained, Rule 1.11(a) carries forward the test and methodology for determining whether matters are "substantially related" set forth in *Brown, supra. See* Rule 1.11(a), comment [4]. *Brown* "broadened the scope of the 'substantially related' test" over that applicable to side-switching in the private sphere. 486 A.2d at 50. At the same time, the Board recognized that we deal in this case with attorney discipline and not (as in *Brown*) a conflict of interest issue arising from a civil dispute. Thus, the Board was careful to view respondent's conduct, including the "substantial" overlap of the two matters, from the perspective of Bar Counsel's obligation to prove an ethical violation by clear and convincing evidence.

6. Our holding in *Brown, supra,* that the several transactions at issue in that case were not substantially related, hence were not the same "matter," comports with our conclusion here. That holding, although ultimately a "legal conclusion ... for this court to make," 486 A.2d at 54, rested critically upon findings of fact by the administrative agency negating any overlap between the earlier zoning matters and the later one. *Id.* at 52–58. Here, in contrast, the hearing committee made factual findings fully supporting our conclusion that respondent's representation of Libya was substantially related to his involvement as Legal Advisor in the post-bombing governmental actions.

the revolving-door rule would be "at the cost of creating an insular, permanent legal bureaucracy." 486 A.2d at 47. But that concern is misplaced here. Our finding that respondent violated Rule 1.11(a) is well within the heartland of Rule 1.11(a)'s application. Further, Bar Counsel aptly states why no lawyer need find himself inadvertently in the position of risk that respondent and amicus hypothesize:

> A former government lawyer in the Respondent's position is free to solicit the views of his or her former agency concerning the proposed private legal undertaking (which the Respondent deliberately elected not to do in this case), or to consult with ethics advisers in his or her law firm (which, again, the Respondent seems not to have done concerning Rule 1.11) or with the Legal Ethics Committee of the Bar (which the Respondent never suggested he did). If, while in government service or while contemplating entry into such service, the attorney deliberates the prospect that Rule 1.11 will narrow somewhat the career choices and client selections available to the attorney following departure from the government, then the Rule will have served one of its salutary objectives.

We affirm the Board's conclusion that respondent violated Rule 1.11(a) and the Board's order directing Bar Counsel to issue an informal admonition.

So ordered.

Notes

1. Model Rule 1.11 is specifically directed to government lawyers. Part (a), applied in *Sofaer*, sets forth the basic "revolving door" conflicts rule. Under that rule, a former government lawyer is disqualified from particular matters only where the lawyer has "participated personally and substantially" in the matter while employed in the government. See, e.g., *United States v. Philip Morris Inc.*, 312 F.Supp.2d 27 (D.D.C. 2004) (disqualifying former government attorney who had spent 382 hours working on a matter which was substantially related to the matter he was working on as a private attorney for a client against the government). The rule's comment explains that the rule "represents a balancing of interests." MR 1.11, comment [4]. What interests are those? Is the balance well struck?

2. *Imputed conflicts and screening.* Model Rule 1.11(b) is a special rule on imputed conflicts applicable to law firms for which a former government lawyer works. (The provisions of Model Rule 1.10 explicitly do not apply to imputed conflicts involving present or former government lawyers. See MR 1.10(d); MR 1.11, comment [2].) Rule 1.11(b) allows for screening, coupled with notice to the appropriate government agency, to remove any imputed conflicts from the other lawyers in the

former government lawyer's new firm. Why is screening thought to be appropriate in this context, where it might not be when a private lawyer moves between law firms?

3.   What if a lawyer, while in government service, gains confidential information about a private person, then joins a private firm that is suing that same private person in a matter in which that confidential information is material. Can the lawyer work on the case and use that confidential government information against the private person? See MR 1.11(c). If not, is the lawyer's new firm disqualified from the case? See *id.*

4.   Government lawyers are regulated not only by rules of ethics, but also a number of statutory proscriptions. See, e.g., 18 U.S.C. §§ 202– 09 (bribery, graft and conflicts of interest rules for current and former federal employees).

5.   *Former judges, neutrals and law clerks.* What if a former judge, now back in private practice, once acted as a judge in a case involving Smith Company. Can that former judge represent Smith Company in any matter? How about the same matter in which the former judge once participated? See MR 1.12(a) & (c). The rules apply equally to lawyers who were once arbitrators, mediators, or even law clerks to judges. MR 1.12(a). For a case disqualifying a former judge's entire law firm, where the judge had in his official capacity received ex parte confidences during settlement conferences in the same case, see *Cho v. Superior Court*, 39 Cal.App.4th 113, 45 Cal.Rptr.2d 863 (1996) (analogizing judge's official role to that of a mediator). Cf. *Comparato v. Schait*, 180 N.J. 90, 848 A.2d 770 (2004) (refusing to disqualify law firm representing his former wife in a divorce case where an associate in the firm had once clerked for the presiding judge, since former law clerk did not have "personal and substantial" participation in the case under Rule 1.12(a)).

6.   *Moving from private practice into government.* When a lawyer moves from private practice into government, the usual rules on former-client conflicts apply. See, e.g., *City and County of San Francisco v. Cobra Solutions, Inc.*, 43 Cal.4th 839, 135 P.3d 20, 43 Cal.Rptr.3d 771 (2006)(ordering disqualification of entire city attorney's office from prosecution of a case against a former client of city attorney; two cases were closely related and screening was insufficient given the city attorney's supervisory role in the office). This may be an area where courts are more likely to allow screening to cure conflicts, however. See *City of Santa Barbara v. Superior Court*, 122 Cal.App.4th 17, 18 Cal.Rptr.3d 403 (2004)(in a case of first impression, holding that assistant city attorney who had represented homeowners in a case against the city could be screened from the matter, thus avoiding disqualification of the entire office; court distinguished situation where lawyers moved between private firms).

§ 4. CONFLICTS WITH A LAWYER'S OWN INTERESTS

The Restatement provides that absent a client's informed consent, a lawyer is prohibited from representing a client "if there is a substantial risk that the lawyer's representation ... would be materially and adversely affected by the lawyer's financial or other personal interests." Restatement § 125. This directive is embodied in state ethics rules as well, as we will see.

A. Lawyer's Financial Interests

COMMITTEE ON PROFESSIONAL ETHICS AND CONDUCT OF IOWA STATE BAR ASS'N v. MERSHON

Supreme Court of Iowa, 1982.
316 N.W.2d 895.

McCORMICK, Justice.

This case involves review of a Grievance Commission report recommending that respondent be reprimanded for alleged ethical violations arising from a business transaction with a client. Because we find respondent's conduct violated the principle in DR5–104(A), we adopt the recommendation.

From our de novo review of the record, we find the facts as follows. Respondent is a Cedar Falls attorney. He began to do tax and property work for Leonard O. Miller, a farmer, in 1951. Miller owned 100 acres of farmland adjacent to a country club near the city. In 1969, when he was 68, Miller became interested in developing the land for residential purposes. He employed a landscape architect and R. O. Schenk, of Schenk Engineering Company, to prepare a preliminary plat and market study.

When the preliminary work was completed, Miller brought Schenk to meet with respondent to discuss the project. Miller wished to proceed with the development but did not have sufficient funds to pay engineering costs. Schenk suggested that the three men form a corporation to which Miller would contribute the land, Schenk would contribute engineering services, and respondent would contribute legal services. They agreed the land was worth approximately $400 an acre. Schenk estimated engineering costs at $400 an acre, and he said legal costs were usually one half that amount.

After several conferences in early 1970, the three men formed a corporation, Union Township Development, Inc. Subsequently Miller conveyed the farmland to the corporation at a capitalized value of $12,500 and received 400 shares of stock. Schenk gave the corporation a $12,500 promissory note and also received 400 shares of stock. Respondent gave the corporation a $6,250 promissory note and received 200 shares of stock. The promissory notes were interest free and due at the discretion of the corporation. They were to represent the services to be rendered by Schenk and respondent.

Development plans were premised on the corporation's ability to obtain financing on the security of the farmland. As it turned out, the corporation was unable to borrow money unless the three individuals would guarantee the obligation personally. They refused to do so, and financing was never obtained.

The trio met at least annually to discuss the development, but when Miller died on December 31, 1978, at the age of 77, the project was still at a stalemate. Respondent believed the parties had an oral agreement that if development did not occur he and Schenk would relinquish their interests in the corporation to Miller. Three days after Miller's death, he transferred his stock to the corporation. He asked Schenk to do the same thing, but Schenk refused, denying any obligation to do so.

Respondent was nominated in Miller's will as executor of his estate. He served in that capacity until Miller's two daughters expressed dissatisfaction with his role in Miller's conveyance of the farmland to the corporation. He then resigned as executor. Consistent with his view, he showed Miller as owner of all corporate stock in the preliminary probate inventory. The farmland was appraised at $4,000 an acre.

Although respondent had expended $900 in out-of-pocket expenses for the corporation and performed legal services worth more than $6,000, he did not intend to seek payment. Schenk, however, maintained at the time of the grievance hearing that he still owned one half of the outstanding stock of the corporation.

The determinative question in our review is whether this evidence establishes a violation of the principle in DR5–104(A), which provides:

> A lawyer shall not enter into a business transaction with a client if they have differing interests therein and if the client expects the lawyer to exercise his professional judgment therein for the protection of the client, unless the client has consented after full disclosure.

This provision was in the Iowa Code of Professional Responsibility for Lawyers when it was adopted on October 4, 1971. Because at least some of the material events in this case occurred before that date, we must first determine whether the principle was then in effect. We find that it was.

This court has recognized and applied the principle expressed in DR5–104(A) for many years. In *Healy v. Gray*, 184 Iowa 111, 118, 168 N.W. 222, 225 (1918), the court quoted the general rule under which all business transactions between an attorney and client are regarded with suspicion and disfavor:

> Transactions between attorney and client, as in all other cases where fiduciary relations exist between parties, one of whom possesses superior knowledge and ability and the other is subject to his influence, are regarded with a scrutinizing and jealous eye by courts of equity, and will be set aside and the clients protected, whenever advantage has been taken of them through the influence or knowledge of the attorneys, possessed by reason of their peculiar relations.

Before making a contract with a client, an attorney must fully disclose every relevant fact and circumstance which the client should know to make an intelligent decision concerning the wisdom of entering the agreement. *Ryan Bros. v. Ashton*, 42 Iowa 365, 369 (1876). "To prevent abuse of such confidential relationship by removing temptation the law presumes such contracts to be fraudulent." *Reeder v. Lund*, 213 Iowa 300, 310, 236 N.W. 40, 44 (1931). "The burden is on the attorney to show that in any contract or settlement with his client or dealing with his client's property he has acted in fairness and good faith with a disclosure of all the facts." *Donaldson v. Eaton & Estes*, 136 Iowa 650, 656, 114 N.W. 19, 21 (1907)....

In order to establish a violation of DR5–104(A) it is necessary to show that the lawyer and client had differing interests in the transaction, that the client expected the lawyer to exercise his professional judgment for the protection of the client, and that the client consented to the transaction without full disclosure.

The definitions section of the code of professional responsibility defines "differing interests":

> "Differing interests" include every interest that will adversely affect either the judgment or loyalty of a lawyer to a client, whether it be a conflicting, inconsistent, diverse, or other interest.

Miller and Mershon plainly had differing interests in at least two aspects of the transaction. One was the issue of giving respondent a present interest in the corporation in anticipation of future legal services. The fee agreement was made during the existence of the attorney-client relationship and thus was subject to the general principles governing attorney-client transactions. Because respondent's fee was tied to the amount of his stock in the corporation, he and Miller had differing interests concerning the extent of respondent's stock ownership. Another differing interest involved making respondent a debtor of the corporation to assure that the services would be performed. Because Miller's interest was aligned wholly with the corporation, he and respondent had differing interests with respect to respondent's promissory note. *See People v. Cameron*, 197 Colo. 330, 333, 595 P.2d 677, 679 (1979); *Attorney Grievance Commission v. Baker*, 285 Md. 45, 48–49, 399 A.2d 1347, 1349–50 (1979).

No dispute exists that Miller relied on respondent to exercise his professional judgment to protect him. One respect in which respondent did so was in preparing a written agreement to assure that Miller was reimbursed from the first profits of the corporation for the preincorporation expenses of preliminary studies. This, however, was the only agreement of the parties that was reduced to writing.

The fighting issue before the Commission was whether respondent made full disclosure to Miller within the meaning of the Canon before Miller entered the transaction. If full disclosure means only that respondent made Miller fully aware of the nature and terms of the transaction, this requirement was satisfied. Nothing was hidden from Miller, and he was an active participant in the transaction. Full disclosure, however, means more than this.

Because of the fiduciary relationship which exists, the attorney

> has the burden of showing that the transaction "was in all respects fairly and equitably conducted; that he fully and faithfully discharged all his duties to his client, not only by refraining from any misrepresentation or concealment of any material fact, but by active diligence to see that his client was fully informed of the nature and effect of the transaction proposed and of his own rights and interests in the subject matter involved, and by seeing to it that his client either has independent advice in the matter or else receives from the attorney such advice as the latter would have been expected to give had the transaction been one between his client and a stranger."

Goldman v. Kane, 3 Mass.App. 336, 341, 329 N.E.2d 770, 773 (1975) (citations omitted). *See Matter of Sedor*, 73 Wis.2d 629, 639, 245 N.W.2d 895, 900 (1976) ("An informed consent requires disclosure which details not only the attorney's adverse interest, but also the effect it will have on the exercise of his professional judgment.").

Respondent acknowledges he did not suggest to Miller that he obtain independent advice. The record does not show he otherwise gave Miller the kind of advice Miller should have had if the transaction were with a stranger. Respondent let Schenk estimate the value of his legal services and thus the extent of respondent's stock ownership without any investigation to determine whether the estimate was accurate. Nor did he suggest to Miller that he make such investigation. If Schenk's estimate was generous, the effect may have been to chill respondent's scrutiny of the benchmark for the valuation, which was Schenk's valuation of his own services. Furthermore there was no discussion or investigation concerning the reasonableness or wisdom of tying respondent's fee for future services to a present twenty percent interest in the corporation. Respondent acknowledges that the arrangement was at least a technical violation of section 496A.18, The Code.

Nothing was done to assure that Miller would get his farm back if either Schenk or respondent did not perform or if the development should not be undertaken. Nothing was done to protect Miller or his estate in the event of the death of any of the parties. The promissory notes could hardly have been on more favorable terms to the debtors. The record does not show whether Miller was informed of the difficulty the corporation might have in enforcing respondent's obligation. So far as the record shows, Miller was not told of any possible effect of respondent's differing interests on the exercise of his professional judgment.

The Commission found respondent is forthright and honest and gained no profit from the transaction. The record confirms this finding. As the Commission also found, however, a violation of DR5–104(A) was nevertheless established. Respondent had three alternatives when the Schenk proposal was first made. The safest and perhaps best course would have been to refuse to participate personally in the transaction. Alternatively, he could have recommended that Miller obtain independent advice. Finally, if Miller refused to seek independent advice or respondent did not recommend he do so, he could have made the least desirable choice. He could have attempted to meet the high standard of disclosure outlined in this opinion.

Having chosen to enter the transaction without recommending that Miller obtain independent advice, respondent was obliged to make full disclosure. Because the record does not show full disclosure was made before Miller consented to the transaction, a violation of DR5–104(A) has been established. This is true even though respondent did not act dishonestly or make a profit on the transaction.

In accordance with the Commission recommendation, we reprimand him for the violation.

Notes

1. *Mershon* is a leading case on doing business with clients. As you can see, a lawyer is not prohibited from entering into a business relationship with a client, even in a matter in which the lawyer is also serving as counsel. Such transactions can take a wide variety of forms: loans to or from the lawyer; investment by the lawyer in the client's business; purchase by the lawyer of the client's property; or acquisition of an interest in the subject matter of the representation, for example.

No matter the form, however, the law regards such transactions "with suspicion and disfavor," as the *Mershon* court puts it. Why is that so? Aren't the lawyer's interests and the client's interests completely aligned when both stand to make money if a transaction is successful? See Restatement § 126, comment *b*.

2. *Source of the rules*. The ethics rules on doing business with clients derive from well-established common law rules concerning fiduciary duties. Even if no disciplinary rules existed on this issue, the law would impose significant restrictions on lawyers who get involved with clients in business deals, other than in standard commercial transactions in which the lawyer is being treated as any other member of the public. See Restatement § 126, comment *c*. Should the ethics rules go further and prohibit business transactions (other than standard commercial transactions) between clients and lawyers? Is doing business with clients damaging to "professionalism" interests? How might that be so?

3. *Attorneys' fees*. The law and rules on doing business with clients do not apply to ordinary fee agreements such as those we saw in Chapter 5. However, when a lawyer takes an interest in the client's business as part or all of a fee, these rules do apply. See the notes after *Passante*, *infra*, this section.

4. *ABA ethics rules*. The Model Code's provision, DR 5–104(A), quoted in *Mershon*, was the ABA's first effort at a detailed rule on the topic of doing business with clients. The 1906 Canons, in Canon 11, simply said that the "lawyer should refrain from any action whereby for his personal benefit or gain he abuses or takes advantage of the confidence reposed in him by his client." Model Rule 1.8 is even more specific than the Model Code's rule. Part (a) sets forth particular conditions that must be complied with if a lawyer seeks to enter into a business transaction with a client, or obtain a pecuniary interest adverse to a client. Compare DR 1–104(A) and MR 1.8(a). How do they differ? Does one rule apply to a broader class of transactions than the other? Which is preferable?

5. *Burden of proof and remedies*. If a client challenges a transaction between himself and his lawyer in a civil action, the lawyer is given the burden of proving that the transaction was fair and reasonable to the client, and that any other legal requirements (such as written disclosures and independent legal advice, for example) have been met. See Restatement § 126, comment *a*. This allocation of the burden of proof is the norm in cases involving fiduciaries. If the lawyer fails to meet this burden, the client may have the transaction voided and is entitled to rescission or damages or both. See, e.g., *BGJ Assocs., LLC v. Wilson*, 113 Cal.App.4th 1217, 7 Cal.Rptr.3d 140 (2004) (joint venture agreement voided). Since state ethics rules also govern this area, a lawyer may be disciplined for any rule violations. In a disciplinary proceeding, once the bar prosecutor has proved that the lawyer entered into a business transaction with a client, the lawyer must prove that the transaction was fair to the client and that the client was given adequate information

about the terms and risks, as required by the applicable state ethics rules. See Restatement § 126, comment *a*. If the lawyer does not prove such facts, severe discipline may follow. See, e.g., *In re Timpone*, 208 Ill.2d 371, 804 N.E.2d 560, 281 Ill.Dec. 595 (2004) (42–month suspension for accepting loan from client without complying with rules); *Medina Cty. Bar Ass'n v. Carlson*, 100 Ohio St.3d 134, 797 N.E.2d 55 (2003) (two-year suspension for arranging to buy property from his mentally ill client at far below market rate).

6. *The independent advice requirement.* Case law has for centuries required that a lawyer engaged in a business transaction with a client must give the equivalent of independent legal advice against himself— that is, the kind of advice the lawyer would have given to any client, and the kind of advice the client would have received from an independent lawyer. See, e.g., *Gibson v. Jeyes*, 6 Vesey 266 (H.L.1801) (opinion of Lord Eldon); *Merryman v. Euler*, 59 Md. 588, 43 Am.Rep. 564 (1883) (citing old English and American cases). The difficulty of actually doing this helps explain the ethics rules' insistence that the client be advised of the desirability of seeking independent counsel for the transaction. See MR 1.8(a)(2) (requiring that such advice be placed in writing); Cal. Rule 3–300(B) (same); N.Y. DR 5–104(a) (same advice required, but not in writing). Do you think an unsophisticated client who does not seek independent legal advice—even if advised to do so—will have a good argument for later rescinding a transaction? Should a lawyer ever enter into a transaction with a client in which the client is not represented separately?

7. *Attorney liens.* Most states allow lawyers to obtain liens to enforce a client's payment of fees. See Chapter 5, § 2. In obtaining and enforcing such liens, however, lawyers must comply fully with the ethics rules on doing business with clients. See ABA Formal Op. 02–427 (2002); *Fletcher v. Davis*, 33 Cal.4th 61, 90 P.3d 1216, 14 Cal.Rptr.3d 58 (2004) (holding a charging lien unenforceable because of lawyer's failure to comply with rules).

8. *Literary rights.* Model Rule 1.8(d) flatly prohibits lawyers, prior to the conclusion of representation, from making or negotiating "an agreement giving the lawyer literary or media rights to a portrayal or account based in substantial part on information relating to the representation." Why? What kind of conflicts of interest does such an agreement raise? See MR 1.8, comment [9]; *People v. Corona*, 80 Cal.App.3d 684, 145 Cal.Rptr. 894 (1978). Should the client be able to consent to being represented by lawyers with whom he has negotiated a contract giving them literary rights to his story? See *Maxwell v. Superior Court*, 30 Cal.3d 606, 639 P.2d 248, 180 Cal.Rptr. 177 (1982). The rules do not forbid lawyers from negotiating a literary-rights agreement after the representation has ended. Should they? See, e.g., *In re von Bulow*, 828 F.2d 94 (2d Cir.1987) (involving the book *Reversal of Fortune*).

9. *Ancillary businesses.* Can a lawyer, who is also a licensed insurance agent, sell annuities for a fixed commission through his law firm to

his estate-planning clients? Does that involve the kind of conflict of interest targeted by DR 5–104(A) and MR 1.8(a)? See MR 5.7. If so, do you think a client could give informed consent to such a transaction? See Ohio S. Ct. Bd. of Comm'rs on Grievances and Discipline, Op. 2001–04.

10. *Competing with clients.* The law of fiduciaries also prohibits lawyers from using the client's opportunities to turn a personal profit. For example, a lawyer representing a client in a real estate transaction could not himself secretly purchase the property with the hopes of reconveying it to the client for a profit. Nor could a lawyer purchase a client's property at a foreclosure sale. Such actions, which are often fraudulently concealed from the client, represent a basic violation of the duties of loyalty and confidentiality. These transactions are voidable at the client's request, with any ill-derived profits being held in constructive trust for the client. See 2 Mallen & Smith, Legal Malpractice § 14.25 (4th ed. 1996). Model Rule 1.8(b) prohibits a lawyer, absent the client's informed consent, from using "information relating to representation of a client to the disadvantage of a client." Rule 1.8(a) regulates not only business transactions with clients but also the acquisition of "ownership, possessory, security or other pecuniary interest adverse to a client." See also Cal. Rule 3–300 (same).

11. *Soliciting client's investment in lawyer's business.* The doing-business-with-client rules apply in full force to a lawyer's solicitation of the client's investment in some business in which the lawyer has an interest. Obviously, then, a lawyer who engages in such a solicitation without telling the client that the lawyer has a personal interest in the investment is on thin ice indeed. See *Beery v. State Bar of California*, 43 Cal.3d 802, 739 P.2d 1289, 239 Cal.Rptr. 121 (1987) (lawyer convinced client to invest $35,000 of the settlement proceeds from a personal injury case in a business venture in which lawyer was a principal, while concealing the lawyer's interest; court ordered a two-year suspension and full restitution, among other things).

12. *Lawyers and class actions.* Can a lawyer serve both as the named class representative and counsel for a putative class? Most courts say no, pointing to a conflict of interest between the lawyer's interest in receiving a large fee and the interests of the putative class in receiving a greater settlement. See *Apple Computer, Inc. v. Superior Court (Cagney)*, 126 Cal.App.4th 1253, 24 Cal.Rptr.3d 818 (2005)(holding that trial court abused its discretion in not ordering disqualification of lawyer and his firm where lawyer was named plaintiff in class action).

PASSANTE v. McWILLIAM

California Court of Appeal, Fourth District, 1997.
53 Cal.App.4th 1240, 62 Cal.Rptr.2d 298.

SILLS, Presiding Justice.

As someone once said, if you build it they will come. And by the same token, if you make a baseball card that can't be counterfeited, they will buy it. Which brings us to the case at hand.

In 1988 the Upper Deck Company was a rookie baseball card company with an idea for a better baseball card: one that had a hologram on it. Holograms protect credit cards from counterfeiting, and the promoters of the company thought they could protect baseball cards as well. By the 1990's the Upper Deck would become a major corporation whose value was at least a quarter of a billion dollars. Collecting baseball cards, like baseball itself, is big business.

But the outlook wasn't brilliant for the Upper Deck back in the summer of 1988. It lacked the funds for a $100,000 deposit it needed to buy some special paper by August 1, and without that deposit its contract with the major league baseball players association would have been jeopardized.

The Upper Deck's corporate attorney, Anthony Passante, then came through in the clutch. Passante found the money from the brother of his law partner, and, on the morning of July 29, had it wired to a company controlled by one of the directors. That evening, the directors of the company accepted the loan and, in gratitude, agreed among themselves that the corporate attorney should have three percent of the firm's stock. The rest is history. Instead of striking out, the Upper Deck struck it rich.

At this point, if we may be forgiven the mixed metaphor, we must change gears. No good deed goes unpunished. Anthony Passante never sought to collect the inchoate gift of stock, and later, the company just outright reneged on its promise. Passante sued for breach of oral contract, and the jury awarded him close to $33 million—the value of three percent of the Upper Deck at the time of trial in 1993.

The trial judge, however, granted a judgment notwithstanding the verdict, largely because he concluded that Passante had violated his ethical duty as a lawyer to his client. There was no dispute that Passante did not tell the board that it might want to consult with another lawyer before it made its promise. Nor did Passante advise the board of the complications which might arise from his being given three percent of the stock.

The board had a clear moral obligation to honor its promise to Passante. He had, as the baseball cliche goes, stepped up to the plate and homered on the Upper Deck's behalf. And if this court could enforce such moral obligations, we would advise the company even yet to pay something in honor of its promise.

But the trial judge was right. If the promise was *bargained for,* it was obtained in violation of Passante's ethical obligations as an attorney. If, on the other hand, it was not bargained for—as the record here clearly shows—it was gratuitous. It was therefore legally unenforceable, even though it might have moral force. We must therefore, with perhaps a degree of reluctance, affirm the judgment of the trial court. . . .

As a matter of law, any claim by Passante for breach of contract necessarily founders on the rule that consideration must result from a bargain. . . . [I]f the stock promise was truly bargained for, then he had an obligation to the Upper Deck, as its counsel, to give the firm the opportunity to have separate counsel represent it in the course of that bargaining. The legal profession has certain rules regarding business transactions with clients. Rule 3–300 of the California Rules of Professional Conduct (formerly rule 5–101) forbids members from entering "a business transaction with a client" without first advising the client "in writing that the client may seek the advice of an independent lawyer of the client's choice."

Here it is undisputed that Passante did not advise the Upper Deck of the need for independent counsel in connection with its promise, either in writing or even orally. Had he done so *before* the Upper Deck made its promise, the board of directors might or might not have been so enthusiastic about his finding the money as to give away three percent of the stock. In a business transaction with a client, notes our Supreme Court, a lawyer is obligated to give "his client 'all that reasonable advice against himself that he would have given him against a third person.'" (*Beery v. State Bar* (1987) 43 Cal.3d 802, 813, 239 Cal.Rptr. 121, 739 P.2d 1289, quoting *Felton v. Le Breton* (1891) 92 Cal. 457, 469, 28 P. 490.) *Bargaining* between the parties might have resulted in Passante settling for just a reasonable finder's fee. Independent counsel would likely have at least reminded the board members of the obvious—that a grant of stock to Passante might complicate future capital acquisition.

For better or worse, there is an inherent conflict of interest created by any situation in which the corporate attorney for a fledgling company in need of capital accepts stock as a reward for past service. As events in this case proved out, had the gift of 3 percent of the company's stock been completed, it would have made the subsequent capital acquisition much more difficult.

Passante's rejoinder to the ethics issue is, as we have noted, to point to the evidence that the stock was virtually thrust at him in return for what he had done. The terms were totally dictated by the Upper Deck board. And that is it, precisely. There was no bargaining. . . .

The judgments in favor of McWilliam, the Upper Deck, and Korbel are affirmed.

Notes

1. *Gifts.* The *Passante* court rested its holding on a narrow basis: the promise of 3 percent of the company's stock was simply an inchoate gift. If the gift had been given and the company wanted it returned, would it have had grounds to do so? Restatement § 127(2) provides that a lawyer may not accept a gift from a client unless (1) the lawyer is a relative "or other natural object of the client's generosity"; (2) the value of the gift is "insubstantial"; or (3) the client, prior to making the gift, has obtained independent advice or has been encouraged to do so. Under that formulation, do you think Passante could have kept the $33 million gift? Model Rule 1.8(c) simply restricts a lawyer's solicitation of gifts and the lawyer's preparation of an instrument giving the lawyer a gift. In a comment, the ABA instructs that a lawyer may accept an unsolicited gift from a client, subject to standards of fairness and the rule of "undue influence, which treats client gifts as presumptively fraudulent." MR 1.8, comment [6]. See *In re Smith*, 572 N.E.2d 1280 (Ind. 1991) (suspending lawyers for accepting "gifts" from elderly, mentally incompetent client whose money they were managing). Might Passante have tried to negotiate a smaller gift? See Cal. Rule 4–400; MR 1.8, comment [6].

2. *Fees.* If Passante had been offered the stock as payment for his services, then the deal would have been subject to the law and rules on both fees and business transactions with clients. See ABA Formal Op. 00–418 (2000); N.Y. Formal Op. 2000–3; Restatement § 126, comment *a*. As the *Passante* court explains, Passante's failure to comply with the California rules on business transactions would have made any such deal voidable at the client's request. If the stock had been part of a fee agreement, would the amount have been an additional problem under California's rules on fees? See Cal. Rule 4–200; see also MR 1.5(a).

IN RE BLACKWELDER

Supreme Court of Indiana, 1993.
615 N.E.2d 106.

PER CURIAM.

... The respondent is a member of the Bar of this state, having been admitted on June 1, 1978. In October of 1988, Randall and Dianna Gosnell retained the respondent to pursue an appeal of a default judgment entered against the Gosnells. The clients had already filed a *pro se* Motion to Correct Error, and the trial court had denied it. Respondent filed a timely praecipe for the record, obtained and reviewed the record, but he miscalculated the deadline for filing the record, and, thus, missed the filing date.

Upon discovering his error, the respondent arranged a meeting with the clients and, on January 5, 1989, met with them for approximately two hours. They met again at respondent's office on February 2, 1989, at which time the respondent presented and read to the clients a "Retainer Agreement an (sic) Release of Claims and Covenant Not To Sue."

Therein, the respondent agreed to reimburse the Gosnells for their out-of-pocket expenses in connection with the appeal and to file a joint bankruptcy petition in return for a release. The clients agreed to " ... release, acquit and forever discharge Attorney from any and all claims, grievances, suits and causes of action, arising from Attorneys (sic) failure to perfect the appeal ... ", and, in a subsequent paragraph, agreed to " ... not file any complaint or grievance against Attorney with the Indiana Supreme Court Disciplinary Commission or any bar association." The document also stated that "Attorney also recommended that the Clients take sufficient time to thoroughly consider the offer and to seek the advice of another attorney(s) before making a final decision; and Whereas, Clients have considered the offer and have consulted with another attorney.... "

After the execution of the "Retainer Agreement and Release", the respondent refunded to the Gosnells $2,096.00 for expenses incurred by the appeal. Respondent filed the bankruptcy petition and paid the filing fees. The Gosnells obtained a discharge of the default judgment which the respondent had failed to appeal and of approximately $300,000 in unrelated debt.

The Gosnells filed a grievance with the Disciplinary Commission on March 7, 1990. By a letter dated March 5, 1990, to the respondent, Mr. Gosnell expressed his displeasure with respondent and advised that he deemed the "Mal (sic) Practice Agreement" breached by the respondent. In this letter, Gosnell also indicated that he was upset that the respondent had not paid some $450 to the U.S. Trustee's Office, which he felt should have been paid by the respondent pursuant to their agreement.... On December 21, 1990, the Gosnells filed a civil action for damages against him.

[At the Disciplinary Commission hearing,] the Gosnells testified that the respondent did not advise them to seek advice from other attorneys, that they did not consult other attorneys before signing the release, that they specifically told respondent that they had not sought independent advice, but signed the release notwithstanding the provision because the respondent advised that he needed the clause for his own protection.

Respondent, on the other hand, testified that he advised the Gosnells to consult independent counsel and that they informed him that they had contacted attorney Henry Price. Mr. Price testified that he had talked with the Gosnells. He had no notes or diary entries that identified the Gosnells by name and had no way to specifically fix the time, but there were two entries on an office log in January indicating he had talked with a potential client. His recollection was that the Gosnells wanted to discuss a potential employment involving a legal malpractice claim against the respondent. He did not discuss the wisdom of signing a release nor the proposed bankruptcy proceeding.

We find that the Gosnells spoke with Henry Price, at an undetermined time, about a possible malpractice suit against the respondent. This, however, in no way indicates that the respondent met his duty as set out in Prof.Cond.R. 1.8(h) or that the Gosnells in fact sought advice concerning the document they were to execute. To the contrary, Price testified that the release agreement was not discussed.

Prof.Cond.R. 1.8(h) provides that a lawyer shall not settle a claim of liability with an unrepresented client or former client without *first* advising that person *in writing* (emphasis added) that independent representation is appropriate in connection therewith. We note that the corresponding Disciplinary Rule 6–102 under the superseded *Code of Professional Responsibility* categorically prohibited all attempts to limit attorney's liability for malpractice. Such practices are still subject to close scrutiny but may not be subject to discipline under certain specific circumstances, where the client has been adequately advised in writing well in advance of final execution of any release or settlement. Providing to the client a copy of the proposed document so that it can be reviewed by independent counsel would further assure compliance with the intent of this rule.

Respondent failed to comply with the express requirement of this rule. The only written reference to the necessary advice was contained in the release prepared by Respondent and presented to the Gosnells at the time of execution. Such after-the-fact advice clearly fails to meet the letter and the spirit of the rule.

In light of the findings and the foregoing considerations, we conclude that, by limiting his liability for malpractice without adequate prior advice to seek independent counsel, the respondent violated Rule 1.8(h). We also conclude that respondent's conduct in preparing the release for his client's signature violates Rule 1.7(b). By procuring a promise not to file a disciplinary grievance, the respondent attempted to obstruct the disciplinary process and engaged in conduct prejudicial to the administration of justice, in violation of Prof.Cond.R. 8.4(d)....

The respondent had a duty of undivided loyalty to his clients and a duty to the public and the legal system to safeguard the orderly administration of justice, both of which he breached. We are convinced, however, that respondent's misconduct was more the result of negligent disregard of ethical requirements than of intentional design. Under these circumstances, a public reprimand appropriately censures respondent's acts. It is, therefore, ordered that Charles B. Blackwelder is reprimanded and admonished for his misconduct.

Note

Attempts to settle client claims against the lawyer. All states severely restrict a lawyer's ability to get the client to agree to limit prospectively the lawyer's malpractice liability. For example, a lawyer cannot freely ask the client to sign a retainer agreement at the outset of a representation in which the client waives the right to sue the lawyer for malpractice if the lawyer messes up. See MR 1.8(h) (allowing such agreements only if the client is "independently represented in making the agreement"); Cal. Rule 3–400 (absolute prohibition). With respect to the settlement of a client's potential malpractice claim against the lawyer after the lawyer has messed up, *Blackwelder* tells us that the rules are equally stringent. Why would that be so? Wasn't attorney Blackwelder trying in good faith to resolve the client's problem, albeit one he had created? See Restatement § 54, comment *c*. Is this essentially a "business transaction" with the client, requiring the lawyer to meet all of the conditions of those rules? See MR 1.8; Cal. Rule 3–400(B).

B. Lawyer's Personal Interests

1. *Sexual Relationships with Clients*

IN RE RINELLA

Supreme Court of Illinois, 1997.
175 Ill.2d 504, 677 N.E.2d 909, 222 Ill.Dec. 375.

Chief Justice HEIPLE delivered the opinion of the court:

The Administrator of the Attorney Registration and Disciplinary Commission filed a complaint with the Hearing Board charging respondent, Richard Anthony Rinella, with four counts of professional misconduct for engaging in sexual relations with clients and testifying falsely before the Commission. The Hearing Board found that respondent had committed the misconduct charged in each of the counts and recommended that respondent be suspended from the practice of law for a period of three years and until further order of this court.... [We] approve the recommendation of the Hearing Board. Respondent is suspended from the practice of law for three years and until further order of this court.

[Count I of the Administrator's complaint alleged that in July, 1983, Jane Doe (who asked that her real name not be revealed) retained respondent to represent her in a divorce and paid him a fee of $7,500. During Doe's second visit to respondent's office, he made sexual advances to her. At the hearing, Doe testified that she "did not want to engage in sexual activity with respondent but felt she had to because she had just changed lawyers and paid respondent a large retainer." Count II alleged that respondent lied about his sexual relationship with Doe when he testified under oath before the Commission.]

[Count III alleged that in November, 1983, Jeanne Metzger retained respondent to represent her in a divorce case. The following month, when Metzger visited respondent's office, he barred the door and initiated sexual contact with her. "Metzger submitted to respondent's sexual advances because she believed the quality of respondent's representation of her would be adversely affected if she refused." At the hearing, Metzger testified that while she did not want to have sex with respondent, "she felt she had to for the welfare of her children, whose custody was contested." Respondent had sex with Metzger on two other occasions, and asked her to give him nude pictures of herself. When she failed to bring an instant camera to a court appearance as respondent asked, he became angry and refused to discuss her case with her. Metzger then hired another attorney to represent her.]

[Count IV alleged that Sandra Demos retained Metzger's law firm to represent her in a divorce case in 1980. Although respondent did not work on Demos's case, he called her several times over a period of four months and asked her to meet with him socially. During these calls he remarked on personal matters that he could only have gleaned from her case file, including "her sexual history with her husband." In 1982, respondent made sexual advances to Demos. Demos "submitted to respondent's sexual advances because she believed that refusing to do so would adversely affect his firm's representation of her."]

[Respondent initially denied the allegations of having sexual relations with Doe, Metzger, or Demos. At the hearing he testified that he did have sex with Doe, but only after his representation of her had terminated. He said his false testimony before the commission was excusable because the matters alleged were "not a proper subject of the Commission's inquiry." He also argued that "no disciplinary rule specifically forbids sexual relations between an attorney and his client."]

The Hearing Board found that respondent engaged in sexual relations with each of the three women while he or his firm represented them. The Board found that this conduct by respondent constituted overreaching because he used his position of influence over the clients to pressure them to engage in sexual relations. The Board noted that all of the women testified that they did not want to engage in sexual relations with respondent but felt that they had to in order to ensure that they were effectively represented and because they could not afford to hire another lawyer.

The Hearing Board also found that respondent violated the following rules of the Code of Professional Responsibility: Rule 1–102(a)(5), by engaging in conduct prejudicial to the administration of justice; Rule 4–101(b)(3), by using client confidences for his own advantage in his dealings with Sandra Demos; Rule 5–101(a), by failing to withdraw from the women's cases when his professional judgment may have been affected by his own personal interest; and Rule 5–107(a), by failing to represent his clients with undivided fidelity. As to count II, the Board found that respondent violated Rules 8.1(a)(1), 8.4(a)(3), 8.4(a)(4), and 8.4(a)(5) of the Rules of Professional Conduct by giving false testimony before the Commission. Finally, the Board found that respondent violated Supreme Court Rule 771 by engaging in conduct which tends to defeat the administration of justice or bring the courts or the legal profession into disrepute. . . .

ANALYSIS

I. Respondent's Sexual Relations with Clients

Respondent takes exception to the Hearing Board's finding that he committed sanctionable misconduct. He contends that he cannot be sanctioned for engaging in sexual relations with his clients because no disciplinary rule specifically proscribes such conduct, and that imposing a sanction under these circumstances would violate due process because he did not have adequate notice that his conduct was prohibited. He also asserts that his conduct did not violate the specific rules cited by the Board and did not constitute overreaching.

Initially, we reject respondent's contention that attorney misconduct is sanctionable only when it is specifically proscribed by a disciplinary rule. On the contrary, the standards of professional conduct enunciated by this court are not a manual designed to instruct attorneys what to do in every conceivable situation. *In re Gerard,* 132 Ill.2d 507, 538, 139 Ill.Dec. 495, 548 N.E.2d 1051 (1989). As stated in the preamble to the Illinois Rules of Professional Conduct:

> "Violation of these rules is grounds for discipline. No set of prohibitions, however, can adequately articulate the positive values or goals sought to be advanced by those prohibitions. This preamble therefore seeks to articulate those values * * *. Lawyers seeking to conform their conduct to the requirements of these rules should look to the values described in this preamble for guidance in interpreting the difficult issues which may arise under the rules."

The preamble then likens the practice of law to a public trust, and charges lawyers with maintaining public confidence in the system of justice by acting competently and with loyalty to the best interests of their clients.

In support of his contention that only specifically proscribed conduct is sanctionable, respondent relies on *In re Corboy,* 124 Ill.2d 29, 124 Ill.Dec. 6, 528 N.E.2d 694 (1988). In that case, this court refused to impose sanctions on certain attorneys who made gifts to a judge because the attorneys could not reasonably have been on notice that their conduct was prohibited and because there was considerable belief among members of the bar that the attorneys had acted properly. In contrast, we do not believe that respondent, or any other member of the bar, could reasonably have considered the conduct involved here to be acceptable behavior under the rules governing the legal profession.

The Hearing Board found that respondent failed to withdraw from representation when the exercise of his professional judgment on behalf of his clients reasonably could have been affected by his own personal interests, thereby violating Rule 5–101(a) of the Code of Professional Responsibility. The Hearing Board also found that respondent failed to represent his clients with undivided fidelity, thereby violating Rule 5–107(a). We believe the record amply supports these findings. The Hearing Board was justified in concluding that respondent took advantage of his superior position as the women's legal representative to gain sexual favors from them during times when they were most dependent upon him. Each of the women testified that she did not want to engage in sexual relations with respondent, but felt she needed to submit to his advances in order to ensure the vigorous representation of her interests. By placing his clients in such situations of duress, respondent compromised the exercise of his professional judgment on their behalf and failed to represent them with undivided fidelity. Furthermore, with regard to Sandra Demos, the record supports the Hearing Board's finding that respondent used a confidence or secret of a client for his own advantage in violation of Rule 4–101(b)(3).

We also believe the record supports the Hearing Board's finding that respondent engaged in conduct prejudicial to the administration of justice, thereby violating Rule 1–102(a)(5). Two of the women described incidents in which respondent, during appointments he had scheduled with them in his office to discuss their cases, made completely unsolicited sexual advances which included undressing himself. Respondent's sexual relations with all three clients originated solely from the provision of legal services, since he did not know the women prior to their retaining him or his firm. These abuses of respondent's professional relationship with clients were clearly prejudicial to the administration of justice.

Respondent's conduct is also sanctionable as overreaching. An attorney commits overreaching when he takes undue advantage of the position of influence he holds *vis-a-vis* a client. *In re Stillo,* 68 Ill.2d 49, 53, 11 Ill.Dec. 289, 368 N.E.2d 897 (1977). By making lewd and unsolicited sexual advances to his clients during appointments purportedly scheduled to discuss their cases, and by causing the clients to believe that their interests would be harmed if they refused his advances, respondent took undue advantage of his position and thereby committed overreaching.

We further believe the Hearing Board was justified in finding that respondent's misconduct violated Supreme Court Rule 771 by tending to defeat the administration of justice or to bring the courts or the legal profession into disrepute.

Respondent contends that his alleged sexual misconduct should not be subject to sanction because there is no evidence that it adversely affected his or his firm's representation of the women. In this regard, we note that Jeanne Metzger testified that respondent refused to consult with her after a court appearance because he was angry that she had not brought a camera with her to take nude pictures. Even absent such evidence of actual harm, however, respondent's sexual conduct would still be sanctionable because it posed a significant risk of damaging the clients' interests. . . .

II. *Respondent's Prior Testimony Before the Commission*

Respondent contends that his admittedly false testimony before the Commission is not sanctionable because the questions posed to him were ambiguous, because information concerning his private sexual relations was protected by the right of privacy, and because he later recanted his false testimony. We find no merit in any of these contentions. Respondent was clearly asked if he had ever had sexual relations with Jane Doe, to which he falsely responded "no." Furthermore, to the extent that respondent's sexual conduct constituted an abuse of his professional position, that conduct took on a public concern. Finally, we observe that respondent did not voluntarily recant his false testimony, but rather recanted only when confronted with undeniable pictorial evidence that he had lied to the Commission. Under these circumstances, his false testimony is entirely inexcusable. . . .

III. *Propriety of Recommended Sanction*

. . . We do not believe that the recommended three-year suspension is an excessive sanction. Respondent violated numerous ethical standards in his dealings with three separate clients. He then compounded this misconduct by concealing and denying it while it was under investigation. Moreover, we believe that the seriousness of the violations in this case warrants imposition of the suspension until further order of this court, as recommended by the Hearing Board.

Accordingly, we approve . . . the recommendation of the Hearing Board. Respondent is suspended from the practice of law for three years and until further order of this court.

Respondent suspended.

Notes

1. Model Rule 1.8(j) prohibits a lawyer from having "sexual relations with a client unless a consensual sexual relationship existed between them when the client-lawyer relationship commenced."

2. California passed the first sex-with-clients rule in 1991. Rule 3–120 provides that a lawyer shall not require or demand sex "incident to or as a condition of" representation; use "coercion, intimidation or undue influence in entering into" a sexual relationship, or continue representing a client with whom the lawyer has had sex if that relationship causes the lawyer "to perform legal service incompetently in violation of rule 3–110." See also Cal. Bus. & Prof. Code §§ 6106.9, and 6106.8 (legislative findings). Florida's Rule 4–8.4, adopted in 2004, prohibits a lawyer from engaging in sexual conduct with a client or a client's representative "that exploits or adversely affects the interests of the client or the lawyer-client relationship," including, *inter alia*, "employing coercion, intimidation, or undue influence in entering into [such] sexual relations." Would Rinella have been subject to discipline under either of these rules? Are they preferable to the Model Rule?

3. *Ongoing sexual relationships.* Model Rule 1.8(j), quoted above in Note 1, does not prohibit a lawyer from representing a client with whom he or she has an ongoing intimate relationship, as long as it began before the representation did. California's rule, as noted in Note 2, prohibits such representation only if the relationship causes incompetence. See Cal. Rule 3–120(C)(stating that "ongoing consensual sexual relationships which predate the initiation of the lawyer-client relationship" are not prohibited). Why these limitations on the rules?

4. Should states adopt any rule on this topic at all? Or are existing rules of more general application, such as those applied in *Rinella*, adequate to address the problem of sexual exploitation of clients by lawyers?

5. Model Rule 1.7(b), prior to the ABA's 2002 revision (and prior to the adoption of Rule 1.8(j)), said that a lawyer shall not represent a client if the representation "may be materially limited . . . by the lawyer's own interests, unless: (1) the lawyer reasonably believes the representation will not be adversely affected; and (2) the client consents after consultation." Did that rule adequately address the sex-with-clients problem?

6. *Prior sexual relationship with client.* A lawyer had a prior sexual relationship (not a continuing one) with a woman whom he now represents in a lawsuit against her former employer. In her case, she alleges that she was fired from her job in retaliation for reporting her supervisors' sexual advances. The defendants moved to disqualify the lawyer because of his prior relationship. In *Horaist v. Doctor's Hospital of Opelousas,* 255 F.3d 261 (5th Cir.2001), the court held that disqualification should not be ordered. The court reasoned that while a current relationship would create a conflict and would interfere with the lawyer's professional judgment, prior relationships "do not give rise to the type of ethical violation requiring disqualification under the rules." The court looked primarily to Model Rule 1.7(b), quoted in Note 5 above. Can you imagine a situation under which a prior sexual relationship between lawyer and client would create a conflict of interest justifying disqualification?

2. Lawyer's Other Personal Interests

IN RE SWIHART

Supreme Court of Indiana, 1988.
517 N.E.2d 792.

PER CURIAM.

This proceeding was initiated by a Verified Complaint charging the Respondent in one count with various acts of misconduct under the *Code of Professional Responsibility.* The alleged misconduct stems from Respondent's representation of a young pregnant and unwed woman in an adoption matter. Respondent is charged with engaging in misconduct by continuing representation of this young woman after Respondent and his wife decided to adopt the child, by obtaining a consent form under improper circumstances, by prosecuting an adoption proceeding contrary to the wishes of his former client, by failing to seek the lawful objectives of his client and by damaging his client during the course of the professional relationship. . . .

[I]n October, 1984, the Respondent was retained to represent an unwed, pregnant, eighteen year old woman in the placement of her expected child with adoptive parents. The mother informed Respondent that she would rely upon his judgment for placement, but did not want to know the identity of the adoptive parents and did not want the child placed within the local area. The child was born on December 21, 1984, and on that evening the Respondent met with the mother and biological father. Respondent left a form of "Release and Power of Attorney" which the mother signed giving Respondent temporary custody of the child. Respondent informed the mother and father that he would take custody of the child for a few days until the child was placed with the adoptive parents.

On December 23, 1984, Respondent and his wife returned to the hospital, obtained the executed "Release and Power of Attorney" and left with the child. On the next day Respondent went to the mother's residence and obtained the executed "Consent for Adoption." Between December 24, 1984, and March, 1985, Respondent and his wife decided to themselves adopt this child who remained in their home.

On or about March 4, 1985, Respondent called the mother and natural father and stated that he was coming to see them with a Notary Public to have them sign new consent forms. The Notary was Joe Williams (Williams), an attorney and personal friend of Respondent. Upon arrival, Respondent introduced Williams, gave Williams a file and then left the residence and waited outside in his automobile. On at least two occasions the parties went outside to confer with Respondent. During his discussion with the mother and father, Williams commented on how well he knew the Respondent and how nice the Respondent's family was. Williams did not directly inform the mother and father that Respondent intended to adopt the child, although he was aware of the fact. When directly confronted by the mother as to whether Respondent intended to adopt the child, Williams replied, in substance, "Yes, didn't you know?"

Williams requested the mother and father to sign the consent forms. The couple was confused and the mother believed that she could change her mind before a court hearing. The mother and father signed the consent forms prepared by Respondent which erroneously recited that the consent "was voluntarily executed without disclosure of the name(s) or other identification of the adopting parent(s)." The forms further erroneously stated that the natural parents consented to adoption "by person(s) whose name(s) (is, are) not known to me."

After Respondent and Williams left the residence, the infant's mother and father decided that they did not want Respondent and his family to adopt the child in that they did not wish to know who the adoptive parents were or to have the child live in the local area. At no time prior to the meeting or March 4, 1985, had Respondent informed the mother and father that he intended to adopt the child or that he could no longer represent them because of his personal interest in the matter.

Shortly after the March 4, 1985 meeting, Respondent forwarded to the mother and father a proposed affidavit which recited, in part, that each "will not be appearing" for the hearing on waiver of prior written approval. Respondent also called the mother and father and inquired as to whether or not they were going to sign and return the affidavits. Consistent with their prior decision, the mother and father declined to sign the affidavits. Thereafter, another attorney was employed, written objections to the adoption were filed and the natural parents filed motions to withdraw their consents and revoked their "Release and Power of Attorney." Eventually, by court degree, the child was ordered to be returned to the mother and the consents for adoption were found to be invalid and ordered withdrawn. . . .

In examining these findings, it is clear to this Court that Respondent abandoned his professional relationship for the sake of a personal interest. This type of conduct is prohibited under Disciplinary Rule 5–101(A). It is also obvious that the Respondent used personal insights gained through confidential information disclosed during the course of his professional representation of his client to form the basis of his acts. The use of this confidential information by Respondent to his personal advantage violates Disciplinary Rule 4–101(B)(3). Additionally, by abandoning the legitimate objectives of his client, Respondent damaged the interests of his client and, accordingly, violated Disciplinary Rules 7–101(A)(1) and (3). And lastly, in toto, Respondent's acts demonstrate conduct prejudicial to the administration of justice which adversely reflects on his fitness to practice law in violation of Disciplinary Rules 1–102(A)(5) and (6). . . .

It is therefore Ordered that the Respondent be, and hereby is, suspended from the practice of law for a period of thirty (30) days beginning February 7, 1988. Upon completion of this period of suspension, the Respondent shall automatically be reinstated as a member of the Bar of this State.

Notes

1.   Model Rule 1.7(a)(2) identifies as one type of concurrent conflict of interest the situation in which there is a significant risk that the representation of a client will be "materially limited by . . . a personal interest of the lawyer." The *Swihart* case, decided before Indiana adopted the Model Rules, is an example of a lawyer's personal interest (having nothing to do with a financial interest) interfering with the client's best interests.

2.   The Comment to Restatement section 125 states the rationale for this personal-conflict rule: "Personal interests of a lawyer that are inconsistent with those of a client might significantly limit the lawyer's ability to pursue the client's interest. . . . Client interests include all those that a reasonable lawyer, unaffected by a conflicting personal interest, would protect or advance." Is the problem, then, one of incompetent lawyering caused by the conflict, or are there other core duties with which such a conflict interferes?

3.   In *In re Kern*, 555 N.E.2d 479 (Ind. 1990), a lawyer representing a criminal defendant became a primary focus of the prosecutor's investigation. The prosecutor offered the client immunity from prosecution if she would provide information that would implicate her lawyer. Does

this present a conflict of interest for the lawyer? Should client consent remove the conflict, if one exists? See MR 1.7(b); Restatement § 125, comment *c*.

4. Is a lawyer's personal-interest conflict imputed to all lawyers in the conflicted lawyer's firm? Given the rationales for imputing conflicts that we saw at the beginning of this chapter, what should the answer be? See MR 1.10(a).

C. Lawyer's Personal Beliefs

What if a lawyer's personal beliefs—political, religious, or moral, for example—are opposed to the client's interests in a matter in which the lawyer works? Is that a conflict of interest at all? Is it a conflict calling for some remedy?

Model Rule 1.2(b) states that a lawyer's representation of a client "does not constitute an endorsement of the client's political, economic, social or moral views or activities." On its face, this seems to say that a lawyer can provide competent representation even if the lawyer disagrees with the client's views or disapproves of the client's activities. But if a lawyer's disapproval is severe, is that still true? Model Rule 1.16(b)(4) allows a lawyer to withdraw from representing a client where "the client insists upon taking action that the lawyer considers repugnant or with which the lawyer has a fundamental disagreement." Comment [1] to this rule explains that a lawyer "should not accept representation in a matter unless it can be performed competently, promptly, without improper conflict of interest and to completion."

Imagine yourself an associate in a law firm that represents a client with whose interests you fundamentally disagree. For example, you are assigned to work on a case in which your firm's client, an oil company, seeks to overturn regulations on offshore oil drilling. You have long been a committed environmentalist and deeply oppose offshore oil drilling. Should you accept this assignment? Can you ethically do so?

The Model Rules on conflicts do not speak directly to this situation, beyond the provisions quoted above and in the preceding subsection. Model Rule 1.8 focuses on the lawyer's financial interests, with the exception of section (j)'s prohibition on sex with clients. Model Rule 1.7 lists "a personal interest of the lawyer" as a conflict creator, but is otherwise silent on personal-belief conflicts. A comment to 1.7 says simply that "[t]he lawyer's own interests should not be permitted to have an adverse effect on representation of a client." MR 1.7, comment [10]. So what do you do about representing the oil company?

Such conflicts raise particular problems in the criminal defense setting. What if a lawyer representing a criminal defendant becomes convinced of his guilt and subconsciously wants to see him convicted, even though the client has pleaded not guilty and has elected to go to trial. Can the lawyer ethically continue the representation? What rules would you look at to decide?

Law reform activities. What if a lawyer joins a group involved in law reform activities, but the reforms being advocated by that group conflict with the interests of the lawyer's clients? For example, what if a lawyer's clientele includes a number of landlords, and the lawyer is a member of a bar group that is proposing legislation that would make it more difficult for landlords to evict poor tenants. Can the lawyer continue her work for the law reform group under those circumstances? Would the lawyer need to get client consent to do so? See MR 6.4 and Restatement § 125, comment *e*. Do other rules suggest an answer to this question as well?

D.   The Special Case of Criminal Prosecutors

PEOPLE v. CONNER

Supreme Court of California, 1983.
34 Cal.3d 141, 666 P.2d 5, 193 Cal.Rptr. 148.

RICHARDSON, J.

The People challenge the trial court's recusal of the entire Santa Clara County District Attorney's office (hereinafter DA). The recusal was ordered because of an appearance of conflict created by the fact that a deputy district attorney who was employed in that office was both a witness to, and arguably a victim of, the criminal conduct giving rise to the offenses for which defendant is being prosecuted. We affirm the trial court's ruling that section 1424 of the Penal Code (further statutory references are to this code) requires such a recusal whenever there exists a conflict of interest so grave in nature as to render it unlikely that defendant otherwise will receive a fair trial.

In 1980, defendant James Edmund Conner was charged with armed robbery, burglaries, possession of stolen property and forgery. These charges were prepared and prosecuted by Deputy District Attorney Braughton, director of a three-attorney career criminal unit in the DA's office.

On February 17, 1981, while awaiting the commencement of defendant's trial on the foregoing charges, Braughton was in a courtroom speaking with a judge. At that time, defendant was in the custody of a deputy sheriff in a nearby jury room. Braughton then heard loud noises emanating from the room where defendant was being held. These were followed by the sound of a bullet hitting the wall. Braughton ran to the jury room and saw defendant holding a revolver and the deputy sheriff bent over in front of him. (It was later established that the deputy had been stabbed and shot.) Defendant turned around, and, after establishing eye contact with Braughton, swung his arm with the revolver toward Braughton, who immediately turned and ran from the room. As he did so, he heard the sound of a gunshot and saw a bullet hole in the wall approximately two feet from where he had been standing. Braughton was uncertain whether that hole was caused by the impact of a previous bullet or by that which had just been fired. Defendant then escaped but was promptly apprehended.

Braughton reported the incident to his immediate supervisor, made a written report to the district attorney, and subsequently discussed his experience directly with approximately 10 of the 25 deputy felony prosecutors in his office. Some of these conversations occurred in the course of routine office procedures relative to this case. Shortly thereafter, Braughton was interviewed by the news media, during which, in addition to describing the event, Braughton characterized defendant both as a dangerous felon and as an escape risk.

After the incident, all of the People's cases against defendant were reassigned from Braughton to Deputy District Attorney Nudelman, who although one of the 25 felony prosecutors in the office, was not a member of Braughton's unit. While not described as close friends, Braughton and Nudelman attended the weekly felony deputies' meetings. At no time, however, did Braughton discuss the case with Nudelman.

Following the February 17 incident, defendant was charged additionally with [a number of crimes, but] was not charged with any crime for his actions against Braughton.

Defendant moved for a change of venue and for recusal of the judge and of the entire DA's office from all of the pending prosecutions. At the hearing concerning the recusal of the DA's office, Braughton was the sole witness. He testified that he considered himself a witness, not a victim (although he had been in momentary fear), that he did not believe that defendant had intended to lure him into a dangerous position, that he had not discussed the event or the case with Nudelman, and that the February 17 incident had not resulted in any change in the dispositional offer previously made to defendant in connection with his prior charges.

Defendant contended that the court should recuse the entire DA's office if it could be demonstrated that there was at least an "appearance of conflict." If, on the other hand, the standard for recusal required an "actual conflict," defendant acknowledged that he had not presented any "hard evidence that there is prejudice within the [DA's] office [toward defendant] or pressure exerted upon Mr. Nudelman."

The trial court denied the motions for change of venue, recusal of the judge and recusal of the DA's office with respect to the original burglary and forgery charges, finding neither a conflict of interest nor prejudice to defendant. In regard to the escape charges, however, the court granted the motion to recuse the entire DA's office based upon the fact that Braughton was a witness to the event and a potential victim.

The People's position is that recusal should not be granted unless an "actual conflict" appears. It is contended that such evidence is lacking and that, in fact, the record tended to demonstrate the absence of such conflict.

Historically, courts have recognized their power to recuse in order both to assure fairness to the accused and to sustain public confidence in the integrity and impartiality of the criminal justice system.... Recently, in *People v. Superior Court (Greer)* (1977) 19 Cal.3d 255 [137 Cal.Rptr. 476, 561 P.2d 1164], we explored the rationale underlying a recusal noting:

> "A fair and impartial trial is a fundamental aspect of the right of accused persons not to be deprived of liberty without due process of law.... A district attorney may thus prosecute vigorously, but both the accused and the public have a legitimate expectation that his zeal, as reflected in his tactics at trial, will be born of objective and impartial consideration of each individual case.... [Thus] we conclude that a trial judge may exercise his power to disqualify a district attorney from participating in the prosecution of a criminal charge when the judge determines that the attorney suffers from a conflict of interest which might prejudice him against the accused and thereby affect, or appear to affect, his ability to impartially perform the discretionary function of his office."

Under our *Greer* standard, a conflict of interest disqualifies a DA from prosecuting a case if the conflict either affects or appears to affect his ability faithfully to perform the discretionary function of his office. Since 1977, *Greer* has been consistently applied. (See *Chadwick v. Superior Court, supra,* 106 Cal.App.3d 108 [recusal denied when DA currently assigned to represent juvenile had previously represented defendant while attorney in public defender's office]; *People v. Municipal Court (Henry)* (1979) 98 Cal. App.3d 690 [159 Cal.Rptr. 639] [DA alleged to be victim of similar crime; recusal denied for lack of DA's personal involvement in crime]; *Younger v. Superior Court* (1978) 77 Cal.App.3d 892 [144 Cal.Rptr. 34] [recusal ordered when defendant's previous private attorney appointed to high position in DA's office]; *People v. Battin* (1978) 77 Cal.App.3d 635 [143 Cal.Rptr. 731, 95 A.L.R.3d 248] [recusal denied despite DA's alleged personal animosity, involvement in previous civil suit, and service as witness].)

In 1980 the Legislature enacted section 1424, which provides, in relevant part, "The motion [to recuse] shall not be granted unless it is shown by the evidence that a conflict of interest exists such as would render it unlikely that the defendant would receive a fair trial." This standard differs from that enunciated by us in *Greer*. While section 1424 does not specify whether the disqualifying conflict must be "actual" or need only generate the "appearance of conflict," in either event, the conflict must be of such gravity as to render it unlikely that defendant will receive a fair trial unless recusal is ordered. . . .

In our view a "conflict," within the meaning of section 1424, exists whenever the circumstances of a case evidence a reasonable possibility that the DA's office may not exercise its discretionary function in an evenhanded manner. Thus, there is no need to determine whether a conflict is "actual," or only gives an "appearance" of conflict.

The DA's office is obligated not only to prosecute with vigor, but also to seek justice. This theme was stressed almost half a century ago by the United States Supreme Court in *Berger* v. *United States* (1935) 295 U.S. 78, 88 [79 L.Ed. 1314, 1321, 55 S.Ct. 629], "[The prosecutor] is the representative not of an ordinary party to a controversy, but of a sovereignty whose obligation to govern impartially is as compelling as its obligation to govern at all; and whose interest, therefore, in a criminal prosecution is not that it shall win a case, but that justice shall be done."

It seems clear that Braughton's status as a witness to, and a potential victim of, defendant's alleged criminal conduct would affect his relationship with the criminal proceedings. We neither doubt nor question Braughton's complete honesty and integrity in describing his responses to the incident. However, his harrowing experience and understandable emotional involvement in this case were communicated to his fellow workers via his own conversations with a substantial number of the DA's personnel and also through the media coverage and interviews concerning the incident. Because of the dramatic and gripping nature of the circumstances, the pervasiveness of the communications regarding Braughton's relationship to the incident, and the difficulty in gauging their cumulative effect, we conclude that substantial evidence supported the trial court's determination that there was a conflict of interest in this case.

Was this conflict so grave as to render it unlikely that defendant will receive fair treatment during all portions of the criminal proceedings? In answering this question, we examine the relevant factors of the size of the office, the communication of the threat by Braughton to his coworkers, the seriousness of the apparent threat to Braughton's safety and the impact of Braughton witnessing the serious injuries actually inflicted on the peace officer.

Braughton is inextricably involved in this case. He disclosed that involvement to a substantial number of his fellow workers. Because the felony division of the DA's office is composed of about 25 attorneys, we have no difficulty in assuming that there is a commendable camaraderie which exists among these officials. It is reasonable to conclude that an apparent threat to one deputy coupled with his witnessing the serious injury actually inflicted on the deputy sheriff during the same course of events may well prejudice the coworkers of Braughton and the deputy sheriff. While it may be difficult, if not impossible, to prove that a bias of the DA's office will *definitely* affect the fairness of a trial, the trial court is in a better position than are we to assess the likely effect of the shooting incident. We will not disturb the court's conclusion that the DA's discretionary powers exercised either before or after trial (e.g., plea bargaining or sentencing recommendations), consciously or unconsciously, could be adversely affected to a degree rendering it unlikely that defendant would receive a fair trial.

We review, of course, the trial court's decision only to determine whether there was substantial evidence presented to support its holding. "Substantial evidence" means that evidence which, when viewed in light of the entire record, is of solid probative value, maintains its credibility and inspires confidence that the ultimate fact it addresses has been justly determined.

While, singly, in this case the circumstances upon which the court relied in reaching its determination may be insufficient to render a fair trial unlikely, in combination, the aggregate effect of these factors is sufficient to sustain the trial court's ruling.

We affirm the trial court's order recusing the DA's office from the further prosecution of this case.

Notes

1. Prosecutors are subject to the regular ethics rules of any state in which they are admitted. Prosecutors are subject to another layer of ethical considerations, however. The ABA's Standards Relating to the Administration of Criminal Justice, as approved in 1992, make clear that a prosecutor fills a special role in the justice system. The prosecutor is more than an advocate; he or she is also an "administrator of justice" and an "officer of the court" whose duty "is to seek justice, not merely to convict." ABA Crim. Justice Standard 3–1.2(b) & (c). The Standards' conflict of interest provisions state that a "prosecutor should not permit his or her professional judgment or obligations to be affected by his or her own political, financial, business, property, or personal interests." Standard 3–1.3(f). California's statute, discussed in *Conner*, is but a more specific rule applying this general principle.

2. In *In re LaPinska*, 72 Ill.2d 461, 21 Ill.Dec. 373, 381 N.E.2d 700 (1978), lawyer LaPinska was the city attorney for the City of Princeton,

Illinois, and in that capacity was responsible for prosecuting quasi-criminal matters such as zoning violations. He also maintained a private practice. In his capacity as city attorney, LaPinska prosecuted a zoning violation case against Mr. Bird after a complaint by Mr. and Mrs. Kutella, a couple who had purchased property from Mr. Bird. Days after the hearing in which Mr. Bird was fined $15 by the city, Mr. and Mrs. Kutella came to LaPinska's office and complained about the leniency that had been shown Mr. Bird. LaPinska agreed to represent the Kutellas in a civil case for breach of contract and fraud against Mr. Bird arising from the sale of the property. While he was representing the Kutellas (without informing the city of this fact), he used his position as city attorney to file numerous continuing-violation zoning complaints against Bird. LaPinska met with Bird and his attorney and offered to drop the city's complaints if Bird would settle the Kutella's civil claim for $63,500—which would have netted LaPinska a $5,000 contingent fee pursuant to his retainer agreement with the Kutellas. Bird's lawyer shortly thereafter reported LaPinska to the state bar. The Illinois Supreme Court found LaPinska guilty of the "serious impropriety . . . of accepting private employment with respect to matters in which he has a substantial responsibility as a public official." The court rejected LaPinska's argument that the interests of the city and of the Kutellas were congruent rather than conflicting, saying:

> A congruence of purpose in the representation of multiple parties may not avert conflicts of interest. A conflict of interest arises whenever an attorney's independent judgment on behalf of a client may be affected by a loyalty to another party. Moreover, an attorney who represents the public must be particularly wary of potential conflicts because he is measured not only by the honesty of his intentions and motives, but by the suspicion with which his acts may be viewed by the public.

At bottom, the court said, LaPinska "intentionally used the leverage and power of his position as city attorney to secure personal gain and a favorable settlement in behalf of a private client." He was suspended from the practice of law for one year. One concurring judge said the suspension should have been "not less than three years."

3. Do you agree with the court-ordered recusal of the entire office in *Conner*? Deputy DA Braughton was removed from the case and did not speak to anyone else in the office about it. The Deputy DA assigned to the case was not a close friend of Braughton's. What, then, was the problem? Would the result have been the same if the office had 250 lawyers in it, instead of only 25?

4. In *People v. Superior Court (Greer)*, 19 Cal.3d 255, 137 Cal.Rptr. 476, 561 P.2d 1164 (1977), discussed briefly in *Conner*, the murder victim's mother was an employee in the prosecutor's office. Furthermore, one of the defendants in the murder trial was the victim's ex-wife (that is, the employee's former daughter-in-law). The prosecutors knew that the employee was going to be a witness at the trial, and also that

she was probably going to be awarded custody of her grandchild if her former daughter-in-law was convicted. In fact, the employee was embroiled in a custody battle with that defendant at the time of her arrest. The court, affirming the trial court's order of recusal of the county district attorney, said that "both the accused and the public have a legitimate expectation that [a prosecutor's] zeal, as reflected in his trial tactics, will be born of objective and impartial consideration of each individual case." Since the victim's mother worked in the very office in which the prosecution was being prepared, the prosecutor's impartiality could be questioned.

5. Should a court disqualify a prosecutor from a case involving a juvenile defendant accused of vandalizing the prosecutor's church? The court in *People v. C.V.*, 64 P.3d 272 (Colo. 2003), said no. It said that the case was no different from one in which a district attorney prosecuted a case involving the robbery of a store where he shopped, and that requiring disqualification on such facts "would greatly impair the independence of the district attorney and could serve to prejudice the constitutional duties he or she performs." Do you tend to agree?

6. *The flip side.* What if a prosecutor becomes convinced that the death penalty should never be sought, because of the chance of executing an innocent person? Can that prosecutor ethically keep her private views to herself as she is assigned to capital cases? Is this situation any different from the one in which a prosecutor wants badly to convict a particular person because of a personal interest in the case? Do the ABA Standards quoted in Note 1 above apply?

7. Can a prosecutor properly negotiate a plea agreement pursuant to which the defendant would make monetary donations to various charities chosen by the prosecutor? Does this create a conflict, or at least the appearance of one? See, e.g., *Morrissey v. Virginia State Bar*, 248 Va. 334, 448 S.E.2d 615 (1994).

§ 5. CONFLICTS CREATED BY THIRD PARTIES

A. Fees Paid by a Third Party

A conflict of interest may be created when a third party pays the lawyer's fees. Why would this be? How could the interests of the client and the payor diverge?

The Model Rules stress the lawyer's central role as provider of independent advice to a client. A number of rules are implicated when something or someone interferes with a lawyer's independent professional judgment and ability to render candid advice to the client. Most pointedly, Model Rule 2.1 provides that "a lawyer shall exercise independent professional judgment and render candid advice." Two rules specifically address the third-party fee payor situation. Rule 1.8(f) prohibits a lawyer from accepting a fee from a third party, unless the client consents, the client's confidences are protected, and "there is no interference with the lawyer's independence of professional judgment or with the client-lawyer relationship." Rule 5.4(c) similarly prohibits a lawyer from permitting a person who pays the lawyer "to direct or regulate the lawyer's professional judgment in rendering such legal services." As the comment to that rule puts it, "Where someone other than the client pays the lawyer's fee or salary, or recommends employment of the lawyer, that arrangement does not modify the lawyer's obligation to the client." MR 5.4, comment [1]. See also DR 5–107(A)(1) & (B); Cal. Rule 3–310(F) (substantially similar to MR 1.8(f)).

B.   Representing Insured Persons

ETHICAL OBLIGATIONS OF A LAWYER WORKING UNDER INSURANCE COMPANY GUIDELINES AND OTHER RESTRICTIONS

American Bar Association Formal Ethics Opinion 01–421, 2001.

A lawyer must not permit compliance with "guidelines" and other directives of an insurer relating to the lawyer's services to impair materially the lawyer's independent professional judgment in representing an insured. A lawyer may disclose the insured's confidential information, including detailed work descriptions and legal bills, to the insurer if the lawyer reasonably believes that doing so will advance the interests of the insured. A lawyer may not, however, disclose the insured's confidential information to a third-party auditor hired by the insurer without the informed consent of the insured. Moreover, if the lawyer reasonably believes that disclosure of the insured's confidential information to the insurer will affect a material interest of the insured adversely, the lawyer must not disclose such information without the informed consent of the insured.

The Committee addresses the ethical issues that arise under the Model Rules of Professional Conduct when a lawyer retained by an insurance company to defend an insured is required to work under litigation management guidelines or other restrictions imposed by the insurer. The Committee also addresses the ethical issues associated with insurance companies requiring a lawyer to submit detailed billing information to the insurer or an independent auditor so that the insurer can determine whether the lawyer's charges conform to the insurer's general requirements and guidelines.

. . . [W]e conclude that lawyers representing insured clients must not permit the client's insurance company to require compliance with litigation management guidelines the lawyer reasonably believes will compromise materially the lawyer's professional judgment or result in her inability to provide competent representation to the insured. A lawyer may not disclose the insured's confidential information to a third-party auditor hired by the insurer without the informed consent of the insured, but a lawyer may submit a client's detailed bills that contain confidential information to the client's insurer if the lawyer reasonably believes that disclosure: (1) impliedly is authorized and will advance the interests of the insured in the representation, and (2) will not affect a material interest of the insured adversely. If the lawyer believes that disclosure of billing statements or other confidential information to the insurer adversely will affect a material interest of the insured, the lawyer must not disclose such information without informing the client about the nature and potential consequences of both making and not making the requested disclosure and obtaining the client's informed consent to the release of the information. . . .

Notes

1. Ethics opinions in most states have agreed with the ABA and opine that a lawyer hired by an insurer must not allow the insurer to interfere with the exercise of independent judgment in the insured's interest. Maryland State Bar Ass'n Comm. on Ethics Op. 99–7 (1999) (discussing other states' opinions). More pointedly, most states that have addressed the issue have agreed that lawyers should not agree to follow insurance company guidelines that require the prior approval of the insurer before doing substantive work for the insured client. W. Va. State Bar Lawyer Disciplinary Bd., Op. 2005–01 (2005)(discussing other states' opinions).

2. When a client is sued, and it appears that the client is insured for the claim, the insurance company usually has a contractual duty to defend the case, although it may do so under a "reservation of rights" to argue ultimately that not everything is covered. The insurer often chooses a lawyer for its insured, at the insurer's expense. (Some states, including California, allow the insured to choose counsel at the insurer's expense.) In any event, the insured is one client, and in most states the insured is the sole client. But the insurer, because it is paying the bills and to an extent directing the lawyer's work (in part because it is paying for it), necessarily exerts a good deal of influence over the lawyer. The lawyer may, for example, be required to report directly to the insurer any developments in the case. In the nature of things, conflicts can arise between the interests of the insured and the insurer. For example, if the insured were sued for both negligent and intentional torts, only the former would be covered by insurance. It might be in the insurer's interests for the lawyer to recommend a quick settlement of the negligence claims, but such advice might disserve the insured, who would be left in a poor strategic position on the non-covered claims.

As one observer notes, even if the lawyer's primary duties are owed to the insured, in practice "the temptations for the lawyer are very great. The insurance company has direct control over her livelihood. It not only is paying for the existing litigation but also will decide whether the lawyer will be hired again in the future. It is only human nature for the lawyer to wonder what her chances may be of being retained in other cases if she fails to consider the insurer's goal of getting the covered claims resolved. The results can range from subtle influence on decision making to outright betrayal of the insured's interests." Robert E. Shapiro, Advance Sheet, 28:3 *Litigation* 65 (Spring 2002).

3.   The Florida Supreme Court in 2003 adopted a new ethics rule, 4–1.7(e), which provides:

> Upon undertaking the representation of an insured client at the expense of the insurer, a lawyer has a duty to ascertain whether the lawyer will be representing both the insurer and the insured as clients, or only the insured, and to inform both the insured and the insurer regarding the scope of the representation. All other Rules Regulating The Florida Bar related to conflicts of interest apply to the representation as they would in any other situation.

What if the lawyer is uncertain about who the client is? What does this new rule ask the lawyer to do? Is the new rule helpful to insured persons? How?

4.   In a state in which the insured is unambiguously the sole client, *see, e.g., State Farm Mutual Auto. Ins. Co. v. Traver*, 980 S.W.2d 625 (Tex.1998), do existing conflicts rules adequately address the conflicts created by an insurance company's attempts to control litigation costs and strategies? See *In re Rules of Professional Conduct and Insurer Imposed Billing Rules and Procedures*, 299 Mont. 321, 2 P.3d 806 (2000) (holding that "defense counsel in Montana who submit to the requirement of prior approval [of billings and the scope of representation] violate their duties under the Rules of Professional Conduct to exercise their independent judgment and to give their undivided loyalty to insureds," citing Rules 1.7(b), 1.8(f), 2.1, and 5.4).

5.   *In-house counsel.* In just two states, an insurance company cannot use in-house counsel to appear in court for insureds. See, e.g., *Gardner v. N.C. State Bar*, 316 N.C. 285, 341 S.E.2d 517 (1986); *American Ins. Ass'n v. Ky. Bar Ass'n*, 917 S.W.2d 568 (Ky.1996). Most states that have addressed the question, however, have held that in-house insurance counsel or "captive" law firms (i.e., firms that are staffed by insurance company employees and work solely on insurance cases) can represent insureds, as long as the general conflicts rules are obeyed. See ABA Formal Op. 03–340 (2003); see also *Cincinnati Ins. Co. v. Wills*, 717 N.E.2d 151 (Ind.1999). Maryland State Bar Ass'n Comm. on Ethics, Op. 00–23 (2000), opines that insurance company staff lawyers who represent insureds do not necessarily violate ethics rules by agreeing to obey the company's rules, which among other things empower the insurer to supervise and monitor the conduct of each case. The panel noted that under Maryland law, *Brohawn v. Transamerica Ins. Co.*, 276

Md. 396, 347 A.2d 842 (1975), a staff lawyer for an insurer represents and owes duties to both the insurer and the insured.

C. Other Third–Party Conflicts

Can other non-clients interfere with a lawyer's competence or diligence in representing a client? How about a lawyer's relationship with a party or a witness, or with some other person whose interests might be harmed by a particular outcome of the matter on which the lawyer is working? Neither the Model Rules nor the Model Code deal with such conflicts directly, although more general provisions appear to cover it. See MR 1.7(a)(2) ("A concurrent conflict of interest exists if: ... there is a significant risk that the representation ... will be materially limited by the lawyer's responsibilities to ... a third person or by a personal interest of the lawyer."); DR 5–101(A)(speaking of conflicts created by lawyer's "personal interests"). California's Rule 3–310 does contain a specific provision on such conflicts, however. A lawyer must provide "written disclosure" to the client—notice, this is not a requirement to obtain client consent—if the lawyer has a "legal, business, financial, professional, or personal relationship with a party or witness in the same matter," or if the lawyer knows or reasonably knows of a previous relationship of the same kind where that previous relationship "would substantially affect the member's representation." Cal. Rule 3–310(B)(1) & (2). Further, a lawyer must disclose in writing any current or past relationship (whether "legal, business, financial, professional or personal") with "another person or entity" that the lawyer knows or should know "would be affected substantially by resolution of the matter." Cal. Rule 3–310(B)(3). Even though client consent is not required by these California rules, if a client does not approve of the lawyer's relationships as disclosed in writing, can the client take any action?

What if a lawyer is related to another lawyer involved in the same matter, by blood or marriage? Does that create a conflict of interest? California Rule 3–320 requires a lawyer to inform the client in writing if "another party's lawyer is a spouse, parent, child or sibling" of the lawyer, is a client of the lawyer, or "has an intimate personal relationship" with the lawyer. As with Rule 3–310(B), disclosure, not consent, is required for compliance. The Model Code never contained such a provision. The pre–2002 version of the Model Rules requires client consent if the lawyer is "related as parent, child, sibling or spouse" to another lawyer representing an adverse party. MR 1.8(i) (pre–2002). That provision was deleted in the 2002 revision process, and its essential thrust moved to a comment to Rule 1.7. That comment now says that a client "is entitled to know" of such a relationship, and that ordinarily a lawyer should not undertake a representation absent informed consent. MR 1.7, comment [11]. Was the ABA right to "demote" this form of conflict from the rule to the comment level? Or do the more general provisions of Rule 1.7(a) adequately address it in any event? Should a lawyer always disclose such a close relationship with the opposing attorney? What if the lawyer did not disclose it to the client, and the client learned of it later? What do you think the client's reaction would be?

What if a lawyer is a director, officer or member of a legal services organization, in addition to being a member of a private law firm? Can the lawyer continue in such a role in the legal services group if the organization represents parties whose interests are adverse to those of some of the lawyer's private-firm clients? See MR 6.3. What policy concerns might influence the answer? See *id.*, comment [1].

Chapter 7

LITIGATION ETHICS

---

§ 1. THE ADVERSARY SYSTEM

The lawyer's legal and professional duties as an advocate cannot be understood without a grasp of the context in which those duties reside. What role does the adversary system contemplate for the lawyer? Is the lawyer supposed to zealously press the client's interests above all others? Is the lawyer supposed to aid in the decisionmaker's quest for truth, even if the truth does not benefit the lawyer's client? Does the lawyer owe duties to the adversary in litigation? If so, what are they? These are difficult questions with nuanced answers, and about which there is substantial disagreement. Consider the three excerpts that follow.

LON L. FULLER & JOHN D. RANDALL,
Professional Responsibility: Report of the Joint Conference
44 ABA Journal 1159 (1958).

. . . The lawyer appearing as an advocate before a tribunal presents, as persuasively as he can, the facts and the law of the case as seen from the standpoint of his client's interest. It is essential that both the lawyer and the public understand clearly the nature of the role thus discharged. Such an understanding is required not only to appreciate the need for an adversary presentation of issues, but also in order to perceive truly the limits partisan advocacy must impose on itself if it is to remain wholesome and useful.

In a very real sense it may be said that the integrity of the adjudicative process itself depends upon the participation of the advocate. . . . An adversary presentation seems the only effective means for combatting [the] natural human tendency to judge too swiftly in terms of the familiar that which is not yet fully known. The arguments of counsel hold the case, as it were, in suspension between two opposing interpretations of it. While the proper classification of the case is thus kept unresolved, there is time to explore all of its peculiarities and nuances. . . .

Without the participation of someone who can act responsibly for each of the parties, [an] essential narrowing of the issues becomes impossible. But here again the true significance of partisan advocacy lies deeper, touching once more the integrity of the adjudicative process itself. It is only through the advocate's participation that the hearing may remain in fact what it purports to be in theory: a public trial of the facts and issues. Each advocate comes to the hearing prepared to present his proofs and argument, knowing at the same time that his arguments may fail to persuade and that his proofs may be rejected as inadequate. It is a part of his role to absorb these possible disappointments. . . .

[P]artisan advocacy plays a vital and essential role in one of the most fundamental procedures of a democratic society. . . . [I]n whatever form adjudication may appear, the experienced judge or arbitrator desires and actively seeks to obtain an adversary presentation of the issues. Only when he has had the benefit of intelligent and vigorous advocacy on both sides can he feel fully confident of his decision.

Viewed in this light, the role of the lawyer as a partisan advocate appears not as a regrettable necessity, but as an indispensable part of a larger ordering of affairs. The institution of advocacy is not a concession to the frailties of human nature but an expression of human insight in the design of a social framework within which man's capacity for impartial judgment can attain its fullest realization.

When advocacy is thus viewed, it becomes clear by what principle limits must be set to partisanship. The advocate plays his role well when zeal for his client's cause promotes a wise and informed decision of the case. He plays his role badly, and trespasses against the obligations of professional responsibility, when his desire to win leads him to muddy the headwaters of decision, when, instead of lending a needed perspective to the controversy, he distorts and obscures its true nature. . . .

MARVIN FRANKEL,
The Search for Truth: An Umpireal View

123 Univ. of Pennsylvania Law Review 1031 (1975).

. . . We proclaim to each other and to the world that the clash of adversaries is a powerful means for hammering out the truth. Sometimes, less guardedly, we say it is "best calculated to getting out all the facts. . . ." That the adversary technique is useful within limits none will doubt. That it is "best" we should all doubt if we were able to be objective about the question. Despite our untested statements of self-congratulation, we know that others searching after facts—in history, geography, medicine, whatever—do not emulate our adversary system. We know that most countries in the world seek justice by different routes. What is much more to the point, we know that many of the rules and devices of adversary litigation as we conduct it are not geared for, but are often aptly suited to defeat, the development of the truth.

We are unlikely ever to know how effectively the adversary technique would work toward truth if that were the objective of the contestants. Employed by interested parties, the process often achieves truth only as a convenience, a by-product, or an accidental approximation. The business of the advocate, simply stated, is to win if possible without violating the law. (The phrase "if possible" is meant to modify what precedes it, but the danger of slippage is well known.) His is not the search for truth as such. To put that more exactly, truth and victory are mutually incompatible for some considerable percentage of the attorneys trying cases at any given time.

Certainly, if one may speak the unspeakable, most defendants who go to trial in criminal cases are not desirous that the whole truth about the matters in controversy be exposed to scrutiny. This is not to question the presumption of innocence or the prosecution's burden of proof beyond a reasonable doubt. In any particular case, because we are unwilling to incur more than a minimal risk of convicting the innocent, these bedrock principles must prevail. The statistical fact remains that the preponderant majority of those brought to trial did substantially what they are charged with. While we undoubtedly convict some innocent people, a truth horrifying to confront, we also acquit a far larger number who are guilty, a fact we bear with much more equanimity.

One reason we bear it so well is our awareness that in the last analysis truth is not the only goal. . . .

WILLIAM H. SIMON,
The Belated Decline of Literalism in Professional Responsibility Doctrine: Soft Deception and the Rule of Law

70 Fordham L. Rev. 1881 (2002).

. . . Some use the adversary system as a trump that favors any position that puts client loyalty above nonclient interests. But if we look for connotations that are both well-established in our system and distinguish it from other systems (notably those of the civil law countries), we find that the adversary system stands primarily for the principle of party autonomy. Under this principle, basic responsibility for defining issues and presenting evidence belongs to the parties and their counsel, rather than to public officials. One virtue claimed for this approach is that it increases the chance that the adjudicator will give fair consideration to all relevant points of view. The presence of competing advocates asserting their perspectives throughout the proceeding prevents the adjudicator from allowing preconceptions developed early on from dulling her sensitivity to inconsistent evidence. Another virtue is that parties are more likely to regard as legitimate a decision that follows consideration of the arguments and evidence they have chosen to present.

So viewed, the virtues of the adversary system depend on shared party control over the presentation of evidence to the trier. They do not depend at all on a party's unilateral control over the other's access to evidence. Quite the contrary. Meaningful control over presentation requires that each counsel have full access to the evidence that she might find relevant. Neither full consideration of points of view nor legitimacy can be achieved unless each party has had and believes that she has had full access. This suggests both that discovery rights should be broad and that such rights should be interpreted in the perspective of the asker. The responder is not in a position to make an objective judgment about materiality, but even if she were, such a judgment is beside the point. The key thing is that each party have an opportunity to present the evidence that she regards as probative. No doubt safeguards against unreasonable and bad faith demands are needed. . . .

[T]he adversary system encourages [lawyers in discovery to take the opposing party's point of view] by prescribing that each party have access to the evidence he believes is relevant. But clearly it also contemplates that the lawyer take his own client's point of view in preparing and presenting the case at trial. Thus, it requires the lawyer to shift back and forth between opposing points of view. [Justice] Scalia suggests that lawyers would have difficulty doing this and that the adversary system implies that client loyalty prevails.

This argument, however, misunderstands lawyering as it is practiced even under an ethic of strong client loyalty. As Anthony Kronman recently emphasized, the traditional self-image of the profession has emphasized, not just identification with, but also detachment from clients. Not client loyalty alone, but this simultaneous sympathy and detachment constitutes the distinctive trait of effective lawyering. The lawyer seeks to benefit the client by inducing trust and reliance in others. The lawyer could not perform this role if she were not able to understand the perspective of public officials and adverse parties. The "cardinal rule" in John W. Davis's famous article on advocacy is, not, Identify with the Client!, but, "Change places (in your imagination of course) with the Court." Roger Fisher and William Ury insist, "the ability to see the situation as the other side sees it . . . is one of the most important skills a negotiator can possess.'' . . .

The last refuge of arguments for overly-aggressive lawyering is the claim that lawyering is a game and that deception and concealment are part of the rules. Deceptive lawyering is, like bluffing in poker, permissible because everyone expects and accepts it. It is fair because the opportunities to deceive and conceal are available to everyone. And both historically and semantically, the adversary system has always connoted a role for strategic cleverness, even at the cost of obfuscation.

It is undeniable that game rhetoric and attitudes have always appealed to some lawyers. It is easy to see why. The game perspective puts the lawyers' technical skills at the center of the picture and makes them an end in themselves. It is natural for lawyers to take satisfaction in the products of their own cleverness. This view, however, has had little appeal to laypeople. Moreover, it is indefensible as an ethical basis for practical decision-making.

The game perspective is hard to criticize because it is rarely articulated reflectively, but we can note two important features of games that make them an inappropriate analogy to the legal process.

First, people usually play games voluntarily and for fun. By contrast, people have to enter the legal process to pursue and preserve basic social and economic goods. The fact that the rules are known and equally applied may be a sufficient guarantee of fairness where the costs of not playing are trivial, but where the stakes and pressures to play are high, more is required.

Second, the only measure of fairness in a game is procedural. But the legal process exists in substantial measure to vindicate the substantive law, and substantive legal norms provide an independent measure of the fairness of its results. A lawyering practice that impedes decision on the substantive merits cannot be just simply because everyone knows about it or has an opportunity to engage in it. . . .

Notes

1. Do you find any of these authors overly idealistic? Overly cynical? Can their views be harmonized, or do they diverge in some significant ways?

2. The Restatement explains that ''The adversary system is characterized by independent and contentious presentation of evidence and legal argument to establish a version of the events and a characterization of law that is favorable to the advocate's client.'' 2 Restatement, Chapter 7, Introductory Note, at 133. Is that brief explanation inconsis-

tent with a vision of a trial as a search for truth? Do you think a trial *is* a search for truth? If not, what is it?

3. *"Zealous" advocacy.* Both the Model Code and the Model Rules make reference to zealous advocacy: "The duty of a lawyer, both to his client and to the legal system, is to represent his client zealously within the bounds of the law. . . . " EC 7–1. "As an advocate, a lawyer zealously asserts the client's position under the rules of the adversary system." MR, Preamble, para. [2]. As we see in this section, the law and rules set some limits on this zeal, and "overzealous" advocacy is more often condemned than praised. As a comment in the Model Rules puts it, "The advocate has a duty to use legal procedure for the fullest benefit of the client's cause, but also a duty not to abuse legal procedure." MR 3.1, comment [1].

4. *Criminal law.* Most of the rules of litigation ethics apply to all lawyers, regardless of the particular adjudicative setting. But some litigation restrictions depend on the particular role of the advocate, most notably in criminal practice. For example, a lawyer defending one accused of crime may be given more tactical leeway than lawyers in other roles. See, e.g., MR 3.3, comments [6], [7], [8] & [12] (discussing distinctions between criminal defense lawyers and other lawyers with respect to client perjury). The defense lawyer's primary role "is to serve as the accused's counselor and advocate with courage and devotion." ABA Standards Relating to the Administration of Criminal Justice: The Defense Function, Standard 4–1.2(b). In death penalty cases, the ABA Standards say that defense counsel should make "extraordinary efforts on behalf of the accused." *Id.*, Defense Standard 4–1.2(c).

On the other side of the aisle, a criminal prosecutor is not just a zealous advocate against a person who has been arrested and charged with a crime; rather, the prosecutor is also "an administrator of justice" and "an officer of the court," who owes a duty "to seek justice, not merely to convict." ABA Standards Relating to the Administration of Criminal Justice: The Prosecution Function, Standard 3–1.2(b) & (c); see MR 3.8, comment [1]. As the Supreme Court said in *Berger v. United States,* 295 U.S. 78, 55 S.Ct. 629, 79 L.Ed. 1314 (1935), a prosecutor "is the representative not of an ordinary party to a controversy, but of a sovereignty whose obligation to govern impartially is as compelling as its obligation to govern at all; and whose interest, therefore, in a criminal prosecution is not that it shall win a case, but that justice shall be done." With that function in mind, a prosecutor must not institute or continue a prosecution "in the absence of sufficient admissible evidence to support a conviction." Prosecution Standard 3–3.9(a); see also MR 3.8(a); Cal. Rule 5–110. A prosecutor who has a "reasonable doubt about the guilt of the accused" is not supposed to be "compelled by his or her supervisor to prosecute" the case. Prosecution Standard 3–3.9(c). Prosecutors must not fail to disclose to the defense the existence of any evidence that might assist the defense. Prosecution Standard 3–3.11(a); MR 3.8(d); DR 7–103(B); see also *Brady v. Maryland,* 373 U.S. 83, 83 S.Ct. 1194, 10 L.Ed.2d 215 (1963); *United States v. Bagley,* 473 U.S. 667,

105 S.Ct. 3375, 87 L.Ed.2d 481 (1985) (constitutional restrictions on prosecutors' suppression of exculpatory evidence); *Kyles v. Whitley*, 514 U.S. 419, 115 S.Ct. 1555, 131 L.Ed.2d 490 (1995) (*Brady* duty extends to evidence known to anyone acting on government's behalf, including police). Prosecutors cannot use peremptory challenges in a purposefully discriminatory way so as to skew the racial makeup of the jury. *Batson v. Kentucky*, 476 U.S. 79, 106 S.Ct. 1712, 90 L.Ed.2d 69 (1986); *Johnson v. California*, 545 U.S. 162, 125 S.Ct. 2410, 162 L.Ed.2d 129 (2005); *Miller-El v. Dretke*, 545 U.S. 231, 125 S.Ct. 2317, 162 L.Ed.2d 196 (2005).

Why do we need such special rules for lawyers in criminal practice? See Bruce A. Green, *Prosecutorial Ethics As Usual*, 2003 U. Ill. L.Rev. 1573 (2003) (a sustained analysis of why "prosecutors' work is different from that of other lawyers," arguing that new ethics rules are needed).

5. Partisan advocacy is an important function of many lawyers, and honing advocacy skills is crucial for litigators. Part of becoming an effective advocate involves learning to adapt to and work within the many restrictions on that role, as contained in codes of ethics, rules of procedure, rules of evidence, and other law, both statutory and judge-made. As you read the materials in this chapter, think about whether the particular limitations under consideration seem to derive from or reflect an identifiable vision of the adversary system itself, and whether you share that vision.

§ 2.   SANCTIONS FOR IMPROPER ADVOCACY

A.   Trial Misconduct

1.   *Frivolous Claims and Arguments*

HUNTER v. EARTHGRAINS COMPANY BAKERY

United States Court of Appeals, Fourth Circuit, 2002.
281 F.3d 144.

KING, Circuit Judge.

By Order of October 23, 2000, appellant Pamela A. Hunter, a practicing attorney in Charlotte, North Carolina, and an active member of the North Carolina State Bar, was suspended from practice in the Western District of North Carolina for five years. Ms. Hunter appeals this suspension, imposed upon her pursuant to Rule 11 of the Federal Rules of Civil Procedure. As explained below, we conclude that her appeal has merit, and we vacate her suspension from practice by the district court.

I.

[Hunter, along with two co-counsel, represented a group of workers at a Charlotte, North Carolina bakery owned by Earthgrains. In 1997, after Earthgrains had closed the bakery, the lawyers filed a class action against Earthgrains, alleging violations of Title VII (race discrimination), among other things. Earthgrains denied all allegations and moved for summary judgment, arguing (1) that pursuant to their collective bargaining agreement, the employees were obligated to arbitrate their Title VII claims; (2) that plaintiffs had failed to establish a prima facie case of race discrimination; and (3) even if a prima facie case were shown, that plaintiffs had failed to rebut Earthgrains' legitimate nondiscriminatory reasons for closing the bakery. Plaintiffs argued in opposition, among other things, that the collective bargaining agreement did not apply to their Title VII claims. The district court granted summary judgment for Earthgrains, agreeing with all three of the defendant's arguments.]

[In the same order, on its own motion, the court ordered the plaintiffs' lawyers to show cause why Rule 11 sanctions should not be imposed on them. The lawyers asked for a stay of the show cause order, which was granted. They then filed two more lawsuits against Earthgrains on the same facts. (In the meantime, the Fourth Circuit affirmed the district court's grant of summary judgment in the first lawsuit.) Between 1998 and June of 2000, no action was taken with respect to the show cause order. In June, 2000, however, Earthgrains filed a motion in district court seeking Rule 11 sanctions. In October, the court entered the sanctions order now on appeal. The court found the lawyers' conduct sanctionable and barred Hunter from practicing law in the Western District of North Carolina for five years. The court based its order "first and foremost" on the lawyers' "assertion of a legal position contrary to the holding of our 1996 decision in *Austin v. Owens–Brockway Glass Container, Inc.*, 78 F.3d 875 (4th Cir. 1996)," an assertion which the court characterized as a "frivolous legal contention."]

II.

A.

We review for abuse of discretion a district court's imposition of Rule 11 sanctions on a practicing lawyer.[6] Advisory Committee

---

6. Rule 11 of the Federal Rules of Civil Procedure was first promulgated in 1937, and it was substantially amended in 1983 to increase its effectiveness and clarify the circumstances in which it applied. Rule 11 was further revamped in 1993, primarily to curb the collateral litigation resulting from the 1983 amendments and to introduce the notion of a "safe harbor" from Rule 11 sanctions. Rule 11(b), which contains most of the provisions relevant to this appeal, currently provides in relevant part as follows:

(b) Representations to Court. By presenting to the court (whether by signing, filing, submitting, or later advocating) a pleading, written motion, or other paper,

an attorney ... is certifying that to the best of [her] knowledge, information, and belief, formed after an inquiry reasonable under the circumstances—

(1) it is not being presented for any improper purpose, ... ;

(2) the claims, defenses, and other legal contentions therein are warranted by existing law or by a nonfrivolous argument for the extension, modification, or reversal of existing law or the establishment of new law;

(3) the allegations and other factual contentions have evidentiary support ... ; and

Notes to the 1993 Amendments, Fed.R.Civ.P. 11 ("Note, FRCP 11"); *Cooter & Gell v. Hartmarx Corp.*, 496 U.S. 384, 110 S.Ct. 2447, 110 L.Ed.2d 359 (1990). Of course, an error of law by a district court is by definition an abuse of discretion. As the Supreme Court has observed in the Rule 11 context, if a district court "rel [ied] on a materially incorrect view of the relevant law in determining that a pleading was not 'warranted by existing law or a good faith argument' for changing the law," we are justified in concluding that the district court abused its discretion. *Hartmarx*, 496 U.S. at 402, 110 S.Ct. 2447.

B.

Although Rule 11 does not specify the sanction to be imposed for any particular violation of its provisions, the Advisory Committee Note to the Rule's 1993 amendments provides guidance with an illustrative list. A court may, for example, strike a document, admonish a lawyer, require the lawyer to undergo education, or refer an allegation to appropriate disciplinary authorities.... While a reviewing court owes "substantial deference" to a district court's decision to suspend or disbar, *In re Evans,* 801 F.2d 703, 706 (4th Cir.1986), it is axiomatic that asserting a *losing* legal position, even one that fails to survive summary judgment, is not of itself sanctionable conduct. *Christiansburg Garment Co. v. EEOC,* 434 U.S. 412, 421–22, 98 S.Ct. 694, 54 L.Ed.2d 648 (1978); *In re Sargent,* 136 F.3d 349, 352 (4th Cir.1998) (noting that losing argument "well within the bounds of fair adversarial argument" was not sanctionable).

Under Rule 11, the primary purpose of sanctions against counsel is not to compensate the prevailing party, but to deter future litigation abuse. Importantly, a sua sponte show cause order deprives a lawyer against whom it is directed of the mandatory twenty-one day "safe harbor" provision provided by the 1993 amendments to Rule 11.[8] In such circumstances, a court is obliged to use extra care in imposing sanctions on offending lawyers. *United Nat'l Ins. Co. v. R & D Latex Corp.,* 242 F.3d 1102, 1115–16 (9th Cir.2001) (noting that sua sponte Rule 11 sanctions for allegedly baseless legal claims are to be examined closely as there is no "safe harbor" available). The Advisory Committee contemplated that a sua sponte show cause order would only be used "in situations that are akin to a contempt of court," and thus it was unnecessary for Rule 11's "safe harbor" to apply to sua sponte sanctions. Furthermore, when imposing sanctions under Rule 11,

(4) the denials of factual contentions are warranted.... Fed.R.Civ.P. 11(b).

8. The "safe harbor" of Rule 11 forbids filing or presenting a motion for sanctions to the court "unless, within 21 days after service of the motion ... , the challenged paper ... is not withdrawn or appropriately corrected." Fed.R.Civ.P. 11(c)(1)(A).

a court must limit the penalty to "what is sufficient to deter repetition of such conduct," and "shall describe the conduct determined to constitute a violation of this rule and explain the basis for the sanction imposed." Fed.R.Civ.P. 11(c).[9]

III.

A.

[The court expressed "serious concern" about the delay between the issuance of the show cause order in April 1998 and the entry of the sanctions order in October 2000. If the sanction was imposed pursuant to Earthgrains' motion, then it appears to have been untimely since the case had concluded. But the court accepted *arguendo* Earthgrains' argument that the suspension was imposed sua sponte by the court.]

B.

The primary basis for the suspension of Ms. Hunter is that she advanced a frivolous legal position in the First Lawsuit. By presentation of a pleading to a court, an attorney is certifying, under Rule 11(b)(2), that the claims and legal contentions made therein "are warranted by existing law or by a nonfrivolous argument for the extension, modification, or reversal of existing law or the establishment of new law." In its Sanctions Order, the district court found the legal assertions of Ms. Hunter to be "utter nonsense" that were "paradigmatic of a frivolous legal contention."

We have recognized that maintaining a legal position to a court is only sanctionable when, in "applying a standard of objective reasonableness, it can be said that a reasonable attorney in like circumstances could not have believed his actions to be legally justified." *In re Sargent*, 136 F.3d 349, 352 (4th Cir.1998). That is to say, as Judge Wilkins recently explained, the legal argument must have "absolutely no chance of success under the existing precedent." *Id.* Although a legal claim may be so inartfully pled that it cannot survive a motion to dismiss, such a flaw will not in itself support Rule 11 sanctions—only the lack of any legal or factual basis is sanctionable. We have aptly observed that "[t]he Rule does not seek to stifle the exuberant spirit of skilled advocacy or to require that a claim be proven before a complaint can be filed. The Rule attempts to discourage the needless filing of groundless lawsuits." *Cleveland Demolition Co. v. Azcon Scrap*

---

9. An order levying sanctions should spell out with specificity both the legal authority under which the sanctions are imposed and the particular behavior being sanctioned. Fed.R.Civ.P. 11; *Nuwesra v. Merrill Lynch, Fenner & Smith, Inc.*, 174 F.3d 87, 92–94 (2d Cir.1999). Although there are multiple sources of authority for the imposition of sanctions, not all sanctions upon lawyers are appropriate under each source; thus, a court must ensure that the authority relied upon supports the sanctions imposed. *See Sakon v. Andreo*, 119 F.3d 109, 113 (2d Cir.1997).

Corp., 827 F.2d 984, 988 (4th Cir.1987). And we have recognized that "[c]reative claims, coupled even with ambiguous or inconsequential facts, may merit dismissal, but not punishment." *Brubaker v. City of Richmond,* 943 F.2d 1363, 1373 (4th Cir.1991) (quoting *Davis v. Carl,* 906 F.2d 533, 536 (11th Cir.1990)).

In its Sanctions Order, the court maintained, with respect to Ms. Hunter, that "[p]laintiffs' standing to file suit was challenged based on a binding arbitration clause in the [Earthgrains] CBA. Plaintiffs' response to this gateway issue rested on a tenuous, if not preposterous, reading of the CBA and applicable law." The court was correct that the legal position it found frivolous—that a collective bargaining agreement ("CBA") arbitration clause must contain specific language to mandate arbitration of a federal discrimination claim—had been rejected by us four years earlier in *Austin v. Owens–Brockway Glass Container, Inc.,* 78 F.3d 875 (4th Cir.1996). However, our reasoning in *Austin,* as of April 22, 1998 (when the Show Cause Order issued), stood alone on one side of a circuit split. Six of our sister circuits (the Second, Sixth, Seventh, Eighth, Tenth, and Eleventh) had taken the legal position contrary to *Austin* on whether a CBA could waive an individual employee's statutory cause of action.[15] In point of fact, and consistent with the foregoing, none of our sister circuits, as of April 1998, had agreed with the position we took in *Austin.*

The circuit split evidenced by these decisions concerned whether collective bargaining agreements containing general language required arbitration of individuals' statutory claims, such as those arising under the ADEA and Title VII. The disagreement of the circuits on this issue resulted from varying interpretations of the Court's decisions in *Alexander v. Gardner–Denver Company,* 415 U.S. 36, 94 S.Ct. 1011, 39 L.Ed.2d 147 (1974), and *Gilmer v. Interstate/Johnson Lane Corp.,* 500 U.S. 20, 111 S.Ct. 1647, 114 L.Ed.2d 26 (1991).[16] This Court, in *Austin,* had deemed *Gilmer* to be the controlling authority, while the other circuits chose the alternate route, finding the Court's decision in *Alexander* to control.

In opposition to Earthgrains' summary judgment motion, Ms. Hunter repeatedly relied upon the Supreme Court's decision in *Alexander* (failing, however, to rely on the decisions of the six

---

15. On May 8, 1998 (shortly after issuance of the Show Cause Order), the Ninth Circuit rejected *Austin* in its decision in *Duffield v. Robertson Stephens & Co.,* 144 F.3d 1182 (9th Cir.1998).

16. In its 1974 decision in *Alexander,* the Court determined that an employee who had filed a grievance in accordance with a CBA did not forfeit a Title VII discriminatory discharge lawsuit, and it distinguished between contractual and statutory rights. In 1991, the Court concluded in *Gil-* *mer* that there was a presumption of arbitrability, and that an age discrimination claim could be subject to compulsory arbitration. Ms. Hunter, in response to the Show Cause Order, explained her basis for the First Lawsuit by making the pertinent observation that *Gilmer* involved an individual employment contract, while *Alexander* concerned arbitration under a CBA. She accordingly asserted that the *Alexander* decision controlled in the First Lawsuit.

circuits that had followed *Alexander*). She further sought to align her case against Earthgrains with *Alexander* by discussing the generality of the applicable clause of the Earthgrains CBA, which included the agreement not to "illegally discriminate." She contended that this provision was not sufficiently specific to require her clients to arbitrate.

The district court was particularly concerned with Ms. Hunter's attempt to distinguish her case from our decision in *Brown v. Trans World Airlines,* 127 F.3d 337 (4th Cir.1997). She maintained to the court that *Brown* had distanced itself from *Austin* on essentially the same facts, and she inferred from this the reluctance of our *Brown* panel to follow *Austin*. Ms. Hunter argued that, as in *Brown,* "the provisions of the collective bargaining agreement which allegedly proscribe racial discrimination, do not mention Title VII, 42 U.S.C. § 1981 or common law fraud," and that "the language of the collective bargaining agreement between plaintiffs and defendant is not sufficient to require plaintiffs to first arbitrate their claim." Earthgrains contended, on the other hand, that the agreement "not to *illegally* discriminate" in the Earthgrains CBA compelled arbitration of Title VII claims under *Austin*. The district court agreed with Earthgrains and based its suspension of Ms. Hunter largely on this legal contention. As we have pointed out, however, there was a good-faith basis for Ms. Hunter to assert the position she propounded. We would be reaching to conclude that, as of 1998, Ms. Hunter's position had "no chance of success" under existing law. *Sargent,* 136 F.3d at 352. And subsequent legal developments render Ms. Hunter's position on the *Austin* issue not only tenable, but most likely correct.

On November 16, 1998—nearly two years before the Sanctions Order of October 23, 2000—the Supreme Court decided that, in order for a CBA to waive individuals' statutory claims, it must at least "contain a clear and unmistakable waiver of the covered employees' rights to a judicial forum for federal claims of employment discrimination." *Wright v. Universal Mar. Serv. Corp.,* 525 U.S. 70, 82, 119 S.Ct. 391, 142 L.Ed.2d 361 (1998). The Court declined to address whether even a clear and unmistakable waiver of the right to take one's statutory discrimination claim to court would be enforceable. It also observed that "the right to a federal judicial forum is of sufficient importance to be protected against less-than-explicit union waiver in a CBA," and that a clause requiring arbitration of "matters under dispute" was not sufficiently explicit to meet the standard. The Court distinguished its earlier decision in *Gilmer* on the basis that *Gilmer* involved "an individual's waiver of his own rights, rather than a union's waiver of the rights of represented employees," and thus it was not subject to the "clear and unmistakable standard." When the district court suspended Ms. Hunter for advancing a legal position that was "not the law of this circuit," it was itself propounding a legal proposition in conflict with the Supreme Court's *Wright* decision.[17]

In *Blue v. United States Dept. of Army,* 914 F.2d 525 (4th Cir.1990), we had occasion to address a Rule 11 sanctions issue in a similar, but distinguishable, context. We there affirmed an award of sanctions where the attorneys had pursued a claim after it became clear that it was factually without merit. Of significance, the plaintiffs' counsel had espoused a legal position contrary to circuit precedent (regarding the necessary showing for a prima facie case of discrimination), but arguably more consistent with Supreme Court authority. In *Blue,* the district court recognized that the question of law at issue was "in a state of flux," and it declined to impose Rule 11 sanctions based on the legal contention being asserted. In this appeal, the suspension of Ms. Hunter was in large part premised on her legal contention on the arbitrability of discrimination claims under the Earthgrains CBA, a legal position being asserted in connection with a body of law that was "in a state of flux." Indeed, the district court sanctioned Ms. Hunter for advocating a legal proposition supported by a majority of our sister circuits, which was later substantially adopted by the Supreme Court.

In pursuing the First Lawsuit, Ms. Hunter, under Rule 11(b)(2), was plainly entitled (and probably obligated),[18] to maintain that *Austin* was incorrectly decided. While she could expect the district court to adhere to *Austin,* she was also entitled to contemplate seeking to have this court, en banc, correct the error (perceived by her) of its earlier *Austin* decision. If unsuccessful, she might then have sought relief in the Supreme Court on the basis of the circuit split. Indeed, our good Chief Judge, in his *Blue* decision, observed that if it were forbidden to argue a position contrary to precedent,

> the parties and counsel who in the early 1950s brought the case of *Brown v. Board of Ed.,* 347 U.S. 483, 74 S.Ct. 686, 98 L.Ed. 873 (1954), might have been thought by some district court to have engaged in sanctionable con-

---

17. After *Wright* was decided in 1998, and prior to the Sanctions Order of October 2000, our Court examined CBA provisions similar to the one at issue in this case and found that they did not compel plaintiffs to arbitrate. *See Carson v. Giant Food,* 175 F.3d 325, 331–32 (4th Cir.1999); *see also Brown v. ABF Freight Sys.,* 183 F.3d 319, 322 (4th Cir.1999) (finding "legally dispositive" difference "between an agreement not to commit discriminatory acts that are prohibited by law and an agreement to incorporate, in toto, the antidiscrimination statutes that prohibit those acts").

18. *See* North Carolina Rule of Professional Conduct 1.3 cmt. (2001) ("A lawyer should act with commitment and dedication to the interests of the client and with zeal in advocacy upon the client's behalf."); *McCoy v. Court of Appeals of Wisconsin,* 486 U.S. 429, 444, 108 S.Ct. 1895, 100 L.Ed.2d 440 (1988) ("In searching for the strongest arguments available, the attorney must be zealous and must resolve all doubts and ambiguous legal questions in favor of his or her client.") (discussing criminal defense attorneys).

duct for pursuing their claims in the face of the contrary precedent of *Plessy v. Ferguson,* 163 U.S. 537, 16 S.Ct. 1138, 41 L.Ed. 256 (1896). The civil rights movement might have died aborning.

Blue, 914 F.2d at 534.

This astute observation of Judge Wilkinson is especially pertinent in the context of this case. The district court's erroneous view of the law in its suspension of Ms. Hunter necessarily constitutes an abuse of discretion. Although Ms. Hunter and the other lawyers (i.e., her co-counsel and the lawyers for Earthgrains) failed to provide the court with a thorough exposition on the circuit split and the Supreme Court's decision in *Wright,* their lack of thoroughness does not render her position frivolous. Because Ms. Hunter's legal contentions in the First Lawsuit on the issue of arbitrability were not frivolous, her suspension from practice in the Western District of North Carolina on this basis does not withstand scrutiny....

IV.

Pursuant to the foregoing, we vacate the suspension of Ms. Hunter from practice in the Western District of North Carolina....

Notes

1.   Rule 11 of the Federal Rules of Civil Procedure is an important provision judges can use to combat abuse of the litigation process. The *Hunter* court provides a brief history of the rule in footnote 6; the 1993 version is the one in place today. One of the major changes of the 1993 amendments was the "safe harbor" provision quoted in footnote 8 in *Hunter*: a Rule 11 motion for sanctions cannot be filed unless the challenged paper is not withdrawn or corrected within 21 days after service of the motion. See, e.g., *Brickwood Contractors, Inc. v. Datanet Engineering, Inc.,* 369 F.3d 385 (4th Cir. 2004) (en banc). Is this "safe harbor" provision a good idea? Does your judgment on this question turn on what you see as the main purpose of Rule 11?

2.   *Scope of Rule 11.* Rule 11 covers only a paper filed in civil litigation in federal court, other than certain discovery documents covered by more specific rules. Sanctions under the rule may be ordered against a lawyer or a party, or both, depending on who has signed the offending pleading, motion or other paper filed with the district court. If a court finds a Rule 11 violation, it may impose "an appropriate sanction." As the *Hunter* court explains, a number of sanctions are possible, ranging from discipline of the lawyer to striking an offending document, to making the offender pay some or all of the attorneys' fees expended by the adversary as a direct result of the violation. The purpose of Rule 11 sanctions is to deter future litigation abuse. FRCP

11(c)(2). While Rule 11 applies only in federal court, many states have similar provisions. See Restatement § 110, comment *c*.

3. *Improper purpose.* Each obligation of Rule 11(b) must be satisfied, which means that violation of any one of the four listed grounds can lead to sanction. Even if a paper does not contain frivolous contentions, then, a lawyer may be sanctioned if the paper is "presented for any improper purpose." This provision was the basis of Rule 11 sanctions against a creditor's attorney in *Whitehead v. Food Max of Mississippi, Inc.*, 332 F.3d 796 (5th Cir. 2003), where the attorney's purpose in obtaining a writ of execution was to embarrass the debtor and to promote himself. This bad motive was proved by evidence that the lawyer accompanied federal marshals and media representatives to the judgment debtor's retail store for the execution of the writ; the lawyer also made various gratuitous comments to the media, including an allegation that there was not enough cash in the store to pay the judgment and that the writ of execution really wasn't needed because the judgment was a lien on the debtor's property. The court further noted that the lawyer's misconduct in obtaining the writ of execution followed several instances of improper conduct during the underlying trial.

4. *The "reasonable inquiry" standard.* Rule 11(b), quoted in *Hunter*, requires that a lawyer certify to the court that to the best of his or her knowledge, "formed after an inquiry reasonable under the circumstances," that legal contentions are warranted by existing law or a non-frivolous argument for change in the law, and that factual contentions have or will have evidentiary support. This means that a lawyer's failure to investigate an allegation, especially a factual allegation, can give rise to Rule 11 sanctions. See, e.g., *Balthazar v. Atlantic City Med. Ctr.*, 279 F.Supp.2d 574 (D.N.J. 2003) (lawyer sanctioned for filing a RICO claim against defendants in federal court after state appeals court had ruled that there was no evidence to support the claim).

5. *Legal contentions.* Can a lawyer make a legal argument at odds with controlling precedent without being subject to sanction under Rule 11? If a lawyer could not do so, what would happen to legal doctrine? What do you think a "non-frivolous" argument for change in the law looks like?

6. *Factual contentions.* Rule 11(b)(3) and (4) identify sanctionable factual contentions. A lawyer must certify that factual contentions either have "evidentiary support" now, or, "if specifically so identified, are likely to have evidentiary support after a reasonable opportunity for further investigation or discovery." FRCP 11(b)(3). Courts have said that factual contentions are sanctionable only if they are "utterly lacking in support." *Storey v. Cello Holdings, L.L.C.*, 347 F.3d 370 (2d Cir. 2003). Denials of factual assertions must either have evidentiary support or, "if specifically so identified, are reasonably based on a lack of information or belief." FRCP 11(b)(4).

7. *The "bad faith" exception to the American Rule.* Recall that the general rule in the United States (called the American Rule) is that each party bears its own attorneys' fees. One common-law exception to this rule is where a party opponent is found to have acted "in bad faith, vexatiously, wantonly, or for oppressive reasons." *United States v. McCall*, 235 F.3d 1211 (10th Cir. 2000). For this exception to apply, the offending party must have made an assertion or claim that is both entirely groundless *and* asserted for some improper purpose; that is, the offending party must have acted subjectively in bad faith. See *FTC v. Kuykendall*, 466 F.3d 1149 (10th Cir. 2006) (upholding trial court's denial of fees).

8. *Other federal rules.* A wide panoply of federal rules and statutes also provide for sanctions for frivolous or abusive advocacy. Some of these apply generally to all kinds of proceedings; we will see the most important of these in this section. Others cover particular kinds of cases. See, e.g., 18 U.S.C. § 3006A (the Hyde Amendment, authorizing the recovery of attorneys' fees against the United States when it is shown that the government initiated criminal proceeding in a "vexatious" manner); 15 U.S.C. §§ 77aa(c)(1–3), 78u(c)(1)-(3) & 77z–1(c)(1)-(3)(Private Securities Litigation Reform Act, mandating Rule 11 sanctions for frivolous papers in federal securities fraud class action cases).

9. *Ethics rules on frivolous advocacy.* A lawyer may be disciplined for making a frivolous claim or argument or asserting a frivolous defense. Model Rule 3.1 largely tracks the language of Rule 11. See also DR 7–102(A)(2); Cal. Rule 3–200 (similar). Discipline may be severe. See, e.g., *In re Hawkley*, 140 Idaho 322, 92 P.3d 1069 (2002) (3–year suspension for filing two frivolous § 1983 lawsuits alleging extensive conspiracies by defendants). A lawyer can be disciplined for bringing a frivolous case on his own behalf. See, e.g., *In re Spikes*, 881 A.2d 1118 (D.C. 2005) (lawyer suspended for filing an unfounded defamation suit against a person who made a complaint against him with the state bar).

10. *Federal rules on frivolous appeals.* Rule 11 applies only to papers filed in federal district court. **Rule 38** of the Federal Rules of Appellate Procedure provides: "If a court of appeals shall determine that an appeal is frivolous, it may, after a separately filed motion or notice from the court and reasonable opportunity to respond, award just damages and single or double costs to the appellee." What constitutes a "frivolous appeal?" Could a lawyer argue a position on appeal that had been rejected by every federal court of appeals? See *McKnight v. General Motors Corp.*, 511 U.S. 659, 114 S.Ct. 1826, 128 L.Ed.2d 655 (1994) (despite uniform adverse holdings at the court of appeals level, no sanction allowed where the issue had divided district courts and had not yet been ruled on by the Supreme Court). Title **28 U.S.C. § 1912** also allows for sanctions for a frivolous appeal, providing in its entirety: "Where a judgment is affirmed by the Supreme Court or a court of appeals, the court in its discretion may adjudge to the prevailing party just damages for his delay, and single or double costs." Courts have interpreted section 1912 as authorizing an award of attorneys' fees

against a violator. Appeals courts also possess the inherent power to sanction parties in various ways. See, e.g., *Custom Vehicles, Inc. v. Forest River, Inc.*, 464 F.3d 725 (7th Cir. 2006) (Easterbrook, J.) (characterizing appellant's motion to strike portions of appellee's brief "absurd," deducting twice the length of the motion from the permissible length of the offending party's reply brief; court says this sort of motion "does nothing but squander time").

11. *State rules on frivolous appeals.* Most states have analogous rules to those recited in Note 10 above. State appeals courts also possess the inherent power to sanction lawyers for filing frivolous appeals, although such powers are used sparingly. See, e.g., *People ex rel. Lockyer v. Brar*, 115 Cal.App.4th 1315, 9 Cal.Rptr.3d 844 (2004) (noting that "[t]his is about as patently frivolous an appeal taken for purposes of delay as is imaginable," and that the offending lawyer's "one substantive argument is a loser, at a mere glance").

2. *Overzealous Advocacy*

LEE v. AMERICAN EAGLE AIRLINES, INC.

United States District Court, S.D. Florida, 2000.
93 F.Supp.2d 1322.

MIDDLEBROOKS, District Judge.

This Cause came before the Court upon Plaintiff's Amended Verified Motion for Attorney's Fees and Costs, filed November 4, 1999. . . .

I.   INTRODUCTION

"Let's kick some ass," Marvin Kurzban said loudly to his client, Anthony Lee, and his co-counsel, Ira Kurzban. I had taken the bench, and Court was in session. Opposing counsel and their client representatives were seated across the aisle. The jury was waiting to be called into the courtroom. Mr. Kurzban's comment was suited more to a locker room than a courtroom of the United States, and the conduct of Plaintiff's counsel that followed disrupted the adversary system and interfered with the resolution of a civil dispute.

The trial of this case lasted approximately fourteen days. The jury found that American Eagle Airlines had subjected Mr. Lee to a racially hostile work environment in violation of Title VII of the Civil Rights Act of 1964, 42 U.S.C. § 2000e, *et seq.*, and 42 U.S.C. § 1981. As compensation, the jury awarded Mr. Lee $300,000. In addition, the jury awarded Mr. Lee $650,000 in punitive damages. The jury denied Mr. Lee's other claim, also premised on Title VII and § 1981, finding that Mr. Lee had not been terminated because of his race. This motion seeking attorney's fees and costs pursuant to 42 U.S.C. § 1988 followed.

As the prevailing party in a Title VII action, the Plaintiff now seeks $1,611,910.50 in attorney's fees. This request presents the question of whether unprofessional and disruptive conduct of counsel which prolongs the proceedings and creates animosity which interferes with the resolution of a cause can be considered in determining an award of attorney's fees.

In their post-trial motions, counsel for the parties filed opposing affidavits concerning additional misconduct that was not directly observed by the Court. Since these affidavits presented vastly different versions of events, an evidentiary hearing was held; counsel and other witnesses testified.

These issues have been distasteful and time consuming. There is a great temptation to simply move on and ignore the issue. It is unpleasant to hear lawyers accusing each other of lies and misrepresentations. Unprofessionalism on the part of lawyers is a distraction and takes time away from other pending cases; it also embroils the Court in charges and counter charges. However, the functioning of our adversary system depends upon being able to rely upon what a lawyer says. So, confronted by affidavits of counsel that were directly contradictory, I decided to hear testimony and make credibility findings. These findings are based upon direct observations by the Court, the transcript of the trial, and the evidentiary hearing.

In addition, we contacted the Florida Bar to determine whether counsel had been the subject of complaints regarding unprofessional conduct. The Florida Bar forwarded a record of a previous complaint by a state court judge concerning the conduct of Marvin Kurzban. In response to that complaint, and immediately before the trial in this cause, the Florida Bar had directed Mr. Kurzban to attend an ethics class and pay a fine.

II. Findings of Fact Pertaining to Misconduct by Counsel

Discovery in this case was rancorous from the beginning. As is often the case, counsel for both sides contributed to the lack of civility. The tone of depositions was harsh, witnesses were treated with discourtesy, and discovery disputes were abundant. The transcripts of the depositions in this case are weighted down with bitter exchanges between the lawyers.

Testimony at the evidentiary hearing reflected that this uncivil conduct also continued during conversations between counsel. The testimony of a young lawyer formerly with the Defendant's counsel's law firm was particularly poignant. This lawyer testified that during telephone conversations with Ira Kurzban, she was hung up on, told that she had only been assigned to work on the case because she was African–American, and wrongly accused of misrepresentations. She testified that her experience with opposing counsel in this case was a factor in her decision to leave her litigation practice.

This testimony was not only powerful and credible, but it also reflects the corrosive impact this type of unprofessional behavior can have upon the bar itself. A litigation practice is stressful and often exhausting. Unprofessional litigation tactics affect everyone exposed to such behavior and the ripple effect of incivility is spread throughout the bar.

The trial began. Testimony at the evidentiary hearing reveals that Mr. Kurzban's "Let's kick some ass" comment was not an aberration. A client representative of the Defendant, a lawyer for American Airlines, testified that she and others were subjected to a barrage of comments out of the hearing of the Court and jury which she likened to trash talk at a sporting event. Local counsel for the Defendant was called a "Second Rate Loser" by Marvin Kurzban. She testified that each day as court began, Marvin Kurzban would say, "Let the pounding begin." In front of defense counsel's client, Mr. Kurzban would ask, "How are you going to feel when I take all of your client's money?" When walking out of the courtroom, Marvin Kurzban would exclaim, "Yuppies out of the way."

Other than Mr. Kurzban's opening comment, I was unaware of this conduct towards opposing counsel and their client's representatives, although counsel for the Defendants alluded to it during the trial. However, I observed continuing misconduct during the trial itself.

[The court first recited an instance of the Kurzban's improper contact with a witness during a break in the trial.] Shortly afterward, Marvin Kurzban objected to a question, and I overruled his objection. He continued to argue his point, then he visibly expressed his dismay with the ruling. I asked counsel to approach for a sidebar conference, wherein I advised him that for the third time he had made visible displays of disagreement with rulings by nodding his head or looking upward at the ceiling. I told him to stop that conduct and to cease making speaking objections. . . . Ira Kurzban responded that he was way beyond acrimony with opposing counsel. . . .

Despite repeated warnings, Plaintiff's counsel continued to address comments to opposing counsel rather than to the Court and interject inappropriate comments before the jury.

The belligerence of Plaintiff's counsel, particularly Marvin Kurzban, spread like a contagion through the courtroom. On September 22, 1999, I returned to the bench after a luncheon break. Marvin Kurzban wanted to raise a matter prior to the jury's return. [Kurzban complained about a verbal altercation he had with the court reporter.] At the next recess, I asked the Court Reporter what had happened. He indicated that at the break, which was a brief break for him inasmuch as we had a calendar call scheduled during that luncheon break, Marvin Kurzban asked him for a portion of transcript. The reporter responded that he could not produce those pages over the break (because he had to report the calendar call). Marvin Kurzban responded, "What are you here for, just to look pretty?" The Court Reporter responded with an epithet, at which point Marvin Kurzban remarked, "We're not talking about your family." Then Mr. Kurzban said, "I guess money talks," suggesting that since the Defendant was ordering daily copy, the reporter was biased in their favor. At that point, the Court Security Officer intervened.

I required the Court Reporter to apologize for his behavior. Because of the accusation of bias, I arranged for other Court Reporters to cover the remainder of the trial....

[The court cited numerous instances in which the Kurzbans accused the court of bias in response to adverse rulings.] Disturbing behavior by both Marvin Kurzban and Ira Kurzban occurred repeatedly during the trial. When confronted about their conduct, they would deny that which I had just observed and then lash out in a personal attack. For instance, after I overruled an objection made by Ira Kurzban, Marvin Kurzban laughed. Other examples of their conduct following rulings include Marvin Kurzban tossing a pen; Ira Kurzban exclaiming, "This is outrageous"; the rolling of eyes; exasperated looks at the ceiling; and flailing of arms. I warned counsel about this behavior.

After the episode of Marvin Kurzban laughing at my ruling, I asked counsel to approach the bench. Marvin Kurzban responded: "I didn't laugh. What I started doing was writing a note, saying to my brother ... I didn't realize I was saying it out loud—we're not trying his case. That's what the objection was, because he's telling about his problems." Ira Kurzban then interjected: "I'd like to add, Your Honor, there's a continuing pattern of conduct we believe shows enormous bias and has turned this trial into a circus-like atmosphere." ...

At the end of the trial, defense counsel Connor approached Ira Kurzban and offered his hand in congratulations. Mr. Kurzban refused to shake his hand. The trial ended much like it had begun.

At the evidentiary hearing, Plaintiff's counsel were unrepentent, attacking opposing counsel and accepting no responsibility for their own actions. They argued that the perceived misconduct was only a matter of style and the exercise of first amendment rights. In keeping with that "style," Marvin Kurzban ended the hearing with the proclamation that he had called his opponent a loser, but not a second-rate loser because, "I don't rate losers." Mr. Kurzban's testimony reflects that he has no clue about what it means to be a lawyer.

III. ANALYSIS

Courts presiding over civil rights actions may, in their discretion, award the prevailing party a "reasonable attorney's fee (including expert fees)" as part of its costs. *See* 42 U.S.C. § 1988; 42 U.S.C. § 2000e–5(k). Although the presiding court has discretion, a prevailing plaintiff is to be awarded attorney's fees "in all but special circumstances." . . .

Courts determining attorney's fee awards begin by determining the "lodestar": the product of the number of hours reasonably expended on the litigation and a reasonable hourly rate for the attorney's services. This lodestar may then be adjusted for the results obtained.

1. *The reasonable hourly rate*

"A reasonable hourly rate is the prevailing market rate in the relevant legal community for similar services by lawyers of reasonably comparable skills, experience, and reputation." . . .

Prior to adoption of the lodestar formula, the so-called "*Johnson* factors" governed fee awards. *See Johnson v. Georgia Highway Express, Inc.*, 488 F.2d 714, 717–19 (5th Cir.1974). Although the lodestar formula has since displaced the "*Johnson* factors," the Eleventh Circuit has permitted district courts to consider the factors in establishing a reasonable hourly rate. Among those factors is the experience, reputation, and ability of the attorneys and the skill requisite to perform the legal service properly. . . . [T]he conduct of Ira Kurzban and Marvin Kurzban both during and prior to trial was very troubling. In my estimation, the manner in which a lawyer interacts with opposing counsel and conducts himself before the Court is as indicative of the lawyer's ability and skill as is mastery of the rules of evidence. Upon review of the trial transcripts and the evidence presented during the evidentiary hearing on attorney conduct and based on observations at trial, I find that the conduct of Ira Kurzban and Marvin Kurzban in the litigation of this case fell far below acceptable standards, especially in light of the $300 hourly rate the attorneys claim. Accordingly, I find "special circumstances" justifying a departure from counsels' requested rates: Ira Kurzban shall be awarded $150 per hour for his pretrial work and $0 for his trial work; Marvin Kurzban's rate for this action is $0.

For further support of the above rate reductions, we rely upon our "inherent power" to sanction attorney misconduct. "It is well-established that '[c]ertain implied powers must necessarily result to our Courts of justice from the nature of their institution,' powers 'which cannot be dispensed with in a Court, because they are necessary to the exercise of all others.' For this reason, 'Courts of justice are universally acknowledged to be vested, by their very creation, with power to impose silence, respect, and decorum, in their presence, and submission to their lawful mandates.' These powers are 'governed not by rule or statute but by the control necessarily vested in courts to manage their own affairs so as to achieve the orderly and expeditious disposition of cases.'" *Chambers v. NASCO, Inc.*, 501 U.S. 32, 43, 111 S.Ct. 2123, 115 L.Ed.2d 27 (1991)....

2. *The number of hours reasonably expended*

Defendant argues that not all of the 3,269.54 hours claimed by Plaintiff were "reasonably expended." Specifically, Defendant contends that Plaintiff claims hours from another case, which are not compensable in this matter, and that Plaintiff did not exercise proper billing judgment.... [The court analyzed the number of hours expended on the case, based on billing records.] To account for the excessive number of hours claimed in this case, we reduce Plaintiff's counsels' hours by 40% across-the-board....

V. Conclusion

As I considered this issue, I reflected upon a letter recently received from a trial lawyer following a discussion on civility and professionalism with the Miami Chapter of the American Board of Trial Advocates. This lawyer stated:

> It seems to me that the courts are basically facing this issue as one of education. Hence we have seminars, guidelines and articles from both that state and federal bench explaining what lawyers should do to be civil and professional to each other. However, I do not think that problem is that lawyers do not know how to act in a civil manner. Rather, I think some lawyers will simply do that with which they can get away.

> Special masters, grievance committees and educational seminars are not as effective as a sanction for uncivil behavior.

> I know our federal court is quite busy and that the time it takes to consider uncivil behavior may have to be taken from some other pending case. However, I would submit that eliminating uncivil behavior not only helps that case, but every other case in which that lawyer is involved. Moreover, as the word spreads as to the price to be paid for unprofessionalism, other lawyers and other cases will be implicated.

I believe that this reduction in attorney fees is an appropriate response to the conduct by Plaintiff's counsel in this case, but I am not convinced it will deter future misconduct. I frankly considered denying fees altogether but while I have reviewed many of the depositions, I did not observe everything that happened during the pretrial phase of the case. The reduction in attorneys' fees based upon misconduct of counsel is therefore approximately $358,423.20.

For the foregoing reasons, it is hereby ORDERED AND ADJUDGED that Plaintiff's Amended Verified Motion for Attorney's Fees and Costs is GRANTED. Based on the foregoing we award Plaintiff $312,324.63 in fees and costs.

Furthermore, because of the misconduct of counsel which occurred in this case, a copy of this order shall be sent to the Florida Bar and the Peer Review Committee for the Southern District of Florida for any action deemed appropriate.

Notes

1. *Inherent power: Chambers v. NASCO.* The broadest ground for sanctioning a party for litigation abuse is the inherent power of the court, utilized in *Chambers v. NASCO, Inc.*, 501 U.S. 32, 111 S.Ct. 2123, 115 L.Ed.2d 27 (1991), to sanction a party for almost a million dollars. This power, recognized by both federal and state courts, is simply a by-product of the courts' need to "manage their own affairs," and does not derive from any particular rule or statute. *Link v. Wabash R.R.*, 370 U.S. 626, 82 S.Ct. 1386, 8 L.Ed.2d 734 (1962). A court can use its inherent power to sanction conduct even if the same conduct could also be sanctioned under more specific statutes or rules. *Chambers, supra.* Reliance on inherent powers may also allow a court to award sanctions where there is some barrier to awarding those sanctions under a more specific rule. See, e.g., *Methode Electronics, Inc. v. Adam Technologies, Inc.*, 371 F.3d 923 (7th Cir. 2004) (upholding trial court's inherent power to award attorneys' fees as a sanction, where court's stated Rule 11 ground could not be upheld); *In re DeVille*, 361 F.3d 539 (9th Cir. 2004) (bankruptcy court could use its inherent powers to sanction counsel where other rules and statutes were inadequate). In short, a court may use its inherent power to sanction anyone, from litigant to lawyer, for abusive, vexatious or bad faith conduct, and such sanctions can be quite large. See, e.g., *Lubrizol Corp. v. Exxon Corp.*, 957 F.2d 1302 (5th Cir.1992) (awarding $2.4 million in attorneys' fees pursuant to inherent power). How did the court utilize its inherent power in *Lee*? Was its sanction appropriate?

2. *Contempt.* Judges have the inherent power to punish lawyers for contempt of the court's authority. Procedural safeguards must be adhered to, but a lawyer can be held in contempt of court either for courtroom behavior or for disobeying a court order. See, e.g., *In re Hampton*, 919 So.2d 949 (Miss. 2006) (criminal contempt sanction for willfully failing to appear at a hearing); *Papa v. 24 Caryl Avenue Realty Co.*, 14 A.D.3d 600, 788 N.Y.S.2d 611 (2005) (criminal contempt sanction for violating a court order). A lawyer may even be held in contempt for giving a client the advice to disobey a court order. See, e.g., *Chicago Truck Drivers, Helpers & Warehouse Workers Union Pension Fund v. Brotherhood Labor Leasing*, 406 F.3d 955 (8th Cir. 2005). In many

jurisdictions the contempt power has been codified. See, e.g., 18 U.S.C. §§ 401–02.

3. *Vexatious multiplication of proceedings: section 1927.* Title 28 U.S.C. § 1927, first enacted in 1813, now provides that any lawyer "who so multiplies the proceedings in any case unreasonably and vexatiously may be required by the court to satisfy personally the excess costs, expenses and attorneys' fees reasonably incurred because of such conduct." Section 1927 covers all federal litigation conduct, whether in a criminal or civil case and whether at the trial or appellate level. It thus serves—as does the "inherent power" discussed in Note 1—to fill any gaps in Rule 11 when a lawyer acts improperly in litigation. See, e.g., *Riddle & Assocs., P.C. v. Kelly*, 414 F.3d 832 (7th Cir. 2005). Could the lawyers in *Lee* have been sanctioned under section 1927?

4. *Duty to respect others in litigation.* A lawyer representing a client in litigation may not use means that have no other purpose than to embarrass, delay or burden a third person. Restatement § 106. A lawyer is subject to discipline by state bar authorities for such conduct, and other forms of overzealousness. See, e.g., *In re Winkler*, 834 N.E.2d 85 (Ind. 2005) (lawyer suspended for surreptitiously pilfering defendant's deposition notes, then feigning ignorance when challenged); see MR 3.5, comment [4] ("Refraining from abusive or obstreperous conduct is a corollary of the advocate's right to speak on behalf of litigants."); MR 4.4(a) (using means that have no purpose other than to embarrass, delay or burden a third person).

5. *Duty not to falsely impugn judges.* Ethics rules also prohibit falsely impugning the integrity of a judge, MR 8.2(a), or engaging in conduct that is "prejudicial to the administration of justice," MR 8.4(d). Lawyer criticism of judges (who, after all, represent the government) has First Amendment protection, but when a lawyer falsely impugns a judge's integrity, with no reasonable basis for making such statements, constitutional protection is lost and the disciplinary authorities may appear. See, e.g., *In re Cobb*, 445 Mass. 452, 838 N.E.2d 1197 (2005) (noting also that such statements about a judge in a pending case in which the attorney is engaged are "especially disfavored"); *Board of Prof'l Responsibility v. Slavin*, 145 S.W.3d 538 (Tenn. 2004) (two-year suspension for making false and degrading references to judges in motions and argument). Disciplinary authorities may even order that a lawyer abstain from engaging in such activities, since they are constitutionally unprotected. See *Anthony v. Virginia State Bar*, 270 Va. 601, 621 S.E.2d 121 (2005) (letters to the justices of the Supreme Court, alleging a conspiracy between them and the lawyer's adversaries, violated ethics rules; lawyer reprimanded and ordered not to write any more letters). What if a lawyer who angrily berates a judge claims to have been provoked? Is that a good excuse? See *Office of Disciplinary Counsel v. Mills*, 93 Ohio St.3d 407, 755 N.E.2d 336 (2001).

6. *Trial tactics unsupported by admissible evidence.* Model Rule 3.4(e) prohibits a lawyer from alluding at trial to any matter that the

lawyer does not reasonably believe is relevant, or that will not be supported by admissible evidence. Relatedly, remember, Model Rule 3.1 forbids a lawyer from asserting or controverting an issue in a proceeding "unless there is a basis in law and fact for doing so that is not frivolous." Violations of those rules are likely to implicate Model 8.4(d) as well—the rule on misconduct prejudicial to the administration of justice. In *In re Zawada*, 208 Ariz. 232, 92 P.3d 862 (2004), a prosecutor was found to have violated those rules (among others) in his over-zealous prosecution of a first-degree murder case. Six mental health professionals had examined the defendant, and all had found him to be mentally ill. The defendant pled insanity. At the trial, while cross-examining one of the defense psychiatric experts, Zawada "baselessly" suggested that the expert fabricated his diagnosis. In closing argument Zawada suggested that the defense lawyer paid the expert to lie, and also "improperly invoked personal fear in the jury to create unfair prejudice." In an earlier decision, the Arizona Supreme Court reversed the defendant's conviction based on this misconduct, *State v. Hughes*, 193 Ariz. 72, 969 P.2d 1184 (1998). In this case, the Court suspended Zawada for six months and a day.

7. *Other prohibited tactics.* A lawyer may not, in the presence of the trier of fact, express a personal opinion about the justness of a cause, the credibility of witnesses, the culpability of a civil litigant, or the guilt or innocence of a person accused of a crime. Restatement § 107(1); MR 3.4(c) (stating personal opinion about the case or about witnesses); see also Cal. Rule 5–200(E) (asserting personal knowledge of the facts at issue). Why would any of these things be prohibited? Don't juries understand the role of lawyers?

8. *Prohibited prosecutorial statements.* Because of the constitutional rights afforded persons accused of crime, prosecutors are more restricted than are others in terms of what they can say at trial. See, e.g., *Griffin v. California*, 380 U.S. 609, 85 S.Ct. 1229, 14 L.Ed.2d 106 (1965) (prosecutor may not comment in closing argument that the defendant has exercised Fifth Amendment right not to testify); *Pennsylvania v. DeJesus*, 580 Pa. 303, 860 A.2d 102 (2004) (death penalty vacated because of prosecutor's comments that jury should "send a message"); *Payton v. State*, 785 So.2d 267 (Miss.1999) (murder conviction reversed because of prosecutor's closing argument stating that jury should "send a message to these older, more mature criminals"). Even where prosecutors make improper remarks, the defendant will gain some remedy only if those remarks had some prejudicial effect, such as denying due process. See, e.g., *State v. Ceballos*, 266 Conn. 364, 832 A.2d 14 (2003) (prosecutor's summation, which invoked various religious characters including God and Satan, and implied divine punishment for worldly transgressions, deprived defendant of due process rights when seen in context of the entire trial); *Portuondo v. Agard*, 529 U.S. 61, 120 S.Ct. 1119, 146 L.Ed.2d 47 (2000) (prosecutor's comments in closing argument that the defendant had had an opportunity to tailor his own testimony since he had heard the other witnesses, did not to violate his constitu-

tional rights). Many of these issues arise in the context of *Strickland* claims that allege the failure of defense counsel to object (*see* Chapter 2, § 3), and such claims require a showing of lawyer error and prejudice. See, e.g., *People v. Johnson*, 218 Ill.2d 125, 842 N.E.2d 714, 299 Ill.Dec. 677 (2005) (prosecutor improperly suggested that criminal defendant in DUI case had failed to clear himself by taking a breath test, but defendant failed to prove prejudice); *People v. Slaughter*, 27 Cal.4th 1187, 120 Cal.Rptr.2d 477, 47 P.3d 262 (2002) (prosecutor improperly made Biblical references in closing argument during penalty phase of death penalty case; no prejudice shown).

9. *"Civility codes."* A number of groups, including some courts, have promulgated codes of civility or courtesy in litigation. Such codes are typically aspirational only and do not provide a basis for discipline. See, e.g., *Dondi Properties Corp. v. Commerce Sav. and Loan Ass'n*, 121 F.R.D. 284, 288 (N.D.Tex.1988)(en banc) (listing eleven specific standards of practice and noting that "[t]hose litigators who persist in viewing themselves solely as combatants, or who perceive that they are retained to win at all costs ... will find that their conduct does not square with the practices we expect of them" and may instead find themselves sanctioned). Are such codes a good idea? Do you think that lawyers who are inclined to act discourteously will read and heed such codes?

10. In *Thomas v. Tenneco Packaging Co.*, 293 F.3d 1306 (11th Cir.2002), the lawyer for a race discrimination plaintiff filed five documents with the court which contained numerous instances of personal invective against the defendant's lawyer, making fun of his appearance and demeanor (likening it to the Grand Wizard of the KKK) and accusing him of racism. Even though many of the documents were affidavits written by others, the court held that the lawyer could be sanctioned pursuant to the trial court's inherent power. The court stressed that while clients are often angry at each other, lawyers should not allow that to influence their own behavior. "A lawyer should not make unfair or derogatory personal reference to opposing counsel. Haranguing and offensive tactics by lawyers interfere with the orderly administration of justice and have no proper place in our legal system." The court also noted that while the district court did not cite any ethics rules, the filing of the five offending documents violated several ethics rules, including DR 7–102, MR 3.1, and MR 4.4.

11. *In re Vincenti*, 92 N.J. 591, 458 A.2d 1268 (1983), was a disciplinary action against a lawyer who engaged in repeated offensive conduct both inside and outside the courtroom. During trial, the lawyer made accusations that the judge was "conducting a sham hearing" and in his "own little dream world"; accused opposing counsel of being "a thief, a liar and a cheat"; and said that an expert witness was an extortionist. Outside the courtroom, he called opposing counsel various obscene names, including "fuckface," and told opposing counsel to "fuck off" and "shove it up your ass." The court specifically found these instances of misconduct (and others) a "reprehensible" attempt to

intimate participants in his client's case. There is a requirement, said the court, "that lawyers display a courteous and respectful attitude not only towards the court but towards opposing counsel, parties in the case, witnesses, court officers, clerks—in short, towards everyone and anyone who has anything to do with the legal process. Bullying and insults are no part of a lawyer's arsenal." Civility and decorum "are essential to an atmosphere in which justice can be done." A one-year suspension was upheld.

12. In *Hagen v. Faherty*, 133 N.M. 605, 66 P.3d 974 (App. 2003), the court issued its rather routine ruling on equitable estoppel in a medical malpractice case, and then added the following, under the heading "A Comment on Professionalism":

> Finally, we wish to call attention to our disappointment with an aspect of the way this case was briefed. Without wishing to sanction or single out any of the counsel, the problem appears to have begun with one attorney characterizing one of the other attorney's arguments as disingenuous, a characterization which is on the borderline of acceptable briefing. This characterization precipitated a number of unacceptable characterizations in return—vacuous, grand mischaracterization, long-winded, motivated by hopes that nuisance value would create a settlement, last-ditch, etc.

>> Advocacy is supposed to be helpful, to make it easier for judges to understand the facts and legal issues of the case. Yet too much advocacy today is the opposite of helpful. It favors exaggeration over accuracy, attack over debate, and indiscriminate barrage over efficiency and cooperation. A culture of belligerence has taken root in our legal system, and it is an affliction on the day-to-day business of judging.

> Elliot L. Bien, *Viewpoint: A new way for courts to promote professionalism*, 86 Judicature No. 3, 132 (2002). We think the parties' arguments in this case could have been made more effectively if they were less strident and more tailored as a logical refutation of the other side's arguments.

Should more judges write paragraphs like this one? Would that deter some litigation excesses?

3. Lack of Candor

JORGENSON v. COUNTY OF VOLUSIA

United States Court of Appeals, Eleventh Circuit, 1988.
846 F.2d 1350.

PER CURIAM:

The appellants, attorneys Eric Latinsky and Fred Fendt, were sanctioned by the district court pursuant to Fed.R.Civ.P. 11 for failing to cite adverse, controlling precedent in a memorandum filed in support of an application for a temporary restraining order and a preliminary injunction. In the appellants' initial appeal to this court, the case was remanded to the district court because the court had failed to notify the attorneys in advance that it was considering sanctions, and did not give them an opportunity to respond. On remand, the district court reaffirmed the imposition of sanctions, and the attorneys appeal. We affirm.

Appellants filed an application in the district court for a temporary restraining order and a preliminary injunction on behalf of their clients, who own and operate a lounge known as "Porky's." In support of the application, appellants filed a memorandum of law which challenged the validity of a Volusia County ordinance prohibiting nude or semi-nude entertainment in commercial establishments at which alcoholic beverages are offered for sale or consumption. The memorandum failed to discuss or cite two clearly relevant cases: *City of Daytona Beach v. Del Percio,* 476 So.2d 197 (Fla.1985) and *New York State Liquor Authority v. Bellanca,* 452 U.S. 714, 101 S.Ct. 2599, 69 L.Ed.2d 357 (1981). We find that this failure supports the imposition of Rule 11 sanctions in the circumstances of this case.

The field of law concerning the regulation of the sale and consumption of alcohol in connection with nude entertainment is a narrow and somewhat specialized field. Prior to the opinion of the Supreme Court of Florida in *Del Percio,* the critical question of whether the state of Florida had delegated its powers under the Twenty–First Amendment to counties and municipalities had gone unanswered. In some circles, that decision was long-awaited. If the state had delegated the authority, local ordinances regulating the sale or consumption of alcohol would be entitled to a presumption in favor of their validity which is conferred by the Twenty–First Amendment. *See Bellanca,* 452 U.S. at 718, 101 S.Ct. at 2601. If the state had not delegated the authority, the ordinances would be subject to the stricter review applicable to exercises of the general police power. *See Krueger v. City of Pensacola,* 759 F.2d 851, 852 (11th Cir.1985).

The question regarding Florida's delegation of its powers under the Twenty–First Amendment was answered by the Supreme court of Florida in *Del Percio,* a case in which one of the appellants, Latinsky, participated. The court held that the powers had been delegated. Less than one year later, on or about January 13, 1986, Latinsky and an associate brought the instant suit seeking a declaration that a similar ordinance was unconstitutional and requesting a temporary restraining order and a preliminary injunction. In their presentation to the court, the appellants cited a number of cases describing the limits on the exercise of the general police power. However, they did not advise the court in any way that *Del Percio* had been decided, despite the fact that

Del Percio required that the validity of the ordinance be judged in light of powers retained under the Twenty–First Amendment rather than the general police power.

The appellants purported to describe the law to the district court in the hope that the description would guide and inform the court's decision. With apparently studied care, however, they withheld the fact that the long-awaited decision by the Supreme Court of Florida had been handed down. This will not do. The appellants are not redeemed by the fact that opposing counsel *subsequently* cited the controlling precedent. The appellants had a duty to refrain from affirmatively misleading the court as to the state of the law. They were not relieved of this duty by the possibility that opposing counsel might find and cite the controlling precedent, particularly where, as here, a temporary restraining order might have been issued *ex parte*.

In this court, appellants argue that the cases were not cited because they are not controlling. We certainly acknowledge that attorneys are legitimately entitled to press their own interpretations of precedent, including interpretations which render particular cases inapplicable. It is clear, however, that appellants' attempts to show that *Del Percio* and *Bellanca* are not controlling are simply post hoc efforts to evade the imposition of sanctions. Neither the original complaint nor the memorandum of law filed by appellants in the district court reflect or support the arguments they now raise. Indeed, it is likely that the arguments were not raised previously because they are completely without merit. In the circumstances of this case, the imposition of Rule 11 sanctions by the district court was warranted. The judgment of the district court is AFFIRMED.

Notes

1. *Failure to cite adverse authority.* Why should lawyers have a duty to cite controlling authority adverse to their position? Isn't that the adversary's job? See MR 3.3, comments [2] & [4]. What should an advocate do upon uncovering directly adverse authority that the adversary has not cited? Must the advocate simply concede? See *In re Thonert*, 733 N.E.2d 932 (Ind.2000) (also noting that failing to tell the client that there was directly adverse authority was a violation of the duty embodied in Rule 1.4(b)).

2. In the *Jorgenson* case above, why did the court say that the adversary's *subsequent* citation of the authority did not cure the problem? Is a lawyer who fails to cite controlling adverse authority making a "false statement of law" to the court? See Restatement § 111, comment *c*; see also MR 3.3(a)(1); N.Y. DR 7–102(a)(5) [22 NYCRR 1200.33]; Cal. Rule 5–200. Or perhaps just not practicing competently?

3. *Misquoting law.* What if a lawyer cites to controlling authority, but misquotes it by removing some language and replacing it with

ellipses? By providing the citation, doesn't the lawyer place the burden on the adversary or the court to see what the case actually says? See *Precision Specialty Metals, Inc. v. United States*, 315 F.3d 1346 (Fed.Cir. 2003).

4. *Misstating facts.* Obviously, a lawyer cannot knowingly misstate facts to the court. See MR 3.3(a); N.Y. DR 7–102(a)(5) [22 NYCRR 1200.33]; Cal. Rule 5–200; Restatement § 120(1)(b); see also, e.g., *In re Kalal*, 252 Wis.2d 261, 643 N.W.2d 466 (2002) (publicly reprimanding lawyer for making factual misstatements in response to Wisconsin Supreme Court members' questions during oral argument). Does a violation of Model Rule 3.3(a) require bad faith on the part of the lawyer? See *State ex rel. Okla. Bar Ass'n v. Johnston*, 863 P.2d 1136 (Okla. 1993)(no). A lawyer appearing pro se may be disciplined for making false statements to the court while representing himself. *O'Meara's Case*, 150 N.H. 157, 834 A.2d 235 (2003).

5. *Concealing facts.* It is equally improper to fail to disclose facts which should be disclosed. See, e.g., *In re Forrest*, 158 N.J. 428, 730 A.2d 340 (1999) (lawyer suspended for six months for failing to tell the court that opposing counsel's motion to compel the client to appear for an examination was moot because the client had died).

6. *Using false testimony or evidence.* Model Rule 3.3 prohibits lawyers from knowingly offering false evidence; the same rule allows a lawyer to refuse to offer any evidence, other than the testimony of a defendant in a criminal matter, that the lawyer "reasonably believes" is false. (The problem of perjury by a criminal defendant is explored more deeply in section 3 of this chapter.) Intentionally presenting false testimony is a very serious infraction. See, e.g., *In re Peasley*, 208 Ariz. 27, 90 P.3d 764 (2004) (prosecutor disbarred for knowingly presenting the false testimony of a police detective in capital murder trials). If evidence or testimony has been offered earlier, and the lawyer subsequently learns of its falsity, the same rule mandates that the lawyer take "reasonable remedial measures, including, if necessary, disclosure to the tribunal." MR 3.3(a)(3).

7. *Prosecution use of inconsistent factual theories.* Cases have held that a prosecutor cannot use inconsistent factual theories to convict co-defendants in separate trials. See *In re Sakarias*, 35 Cal.4th 140, 106 P.3d 931, 25 Cal.Rptr.3d 265 (2005) (prosecutor's inaccurate and inconsistent portrayal of the two defendants' roles in a murder at their separate trials violated both men's due process rights, and was prejudicial as to one of them); *Smith v. Groose*, 205 F.3d 1045 (8th Cir. 2000) (prosecutor violated defendant's due process rights when it used one of co-defendant's factually contradictory version of events of murders to convict defendant, then used other version of events to convict another person later of the same murders). Cf. *Bradshaw v. Stumpf*, 545 U.S. 175, 125 S.Ct. 2398, 162 L.Ed.2d 143 (2005) (prosecutor's use of two conflicting theories to convict defendant and his accomplice of murder did not render defendant's guilty plea unknowing, involuntary or unin-

telligent; defendant failed to prove how use of inconsistent facts against his accomplice affected his prior guilty plea).

8. *Plagiarism*. Is it proper for a lawyer to file a brief that plagiarizes another source? Nothing in the brief is false, is it? Is it a problem if the lawyer seeks court-awarded fees for work on the brief? See *Iowa Supreme Court Bd. of Prof. Ethics and Conduct v. Lane*, 642 N.W.2d 296 (Iowa 2002).

9. *Ex parte proceedings*. Misstatements of fact or law are especially serious in ex parte proceedings, which by definition are held in the absence of the adversary. See MR 3.3(d) (placing lawyers in such a proceeding under a duty to "inform the tribunal of all material facts ... whether or not the facts are adverse"); Restatement § 112 (same). In *Daniels v. Alander*, 268 Conn. 320, 844 A.2d 182 (2004), the court held that an associate had a duty under Rule 3.3(d) to correct factual misrepresentations made by a partner in the associate's presence to a judge during an ex parte proceeding. The court said that "separate and apart from the obligations imposed independently by rule 3.3(d), the very fact that this action began as an ex parte proceeding was a unique circumstance that created an enhanced duty of candor toward the trial court."

10. *Misrepresentations during investigations*. Can a lawyer make misrepresentations during the investigation of a case? Authorities are not in complete agreement. Most, but not all, accept the propriety of a government lawyer taking part in lawful covert investigations of criminal or terrorist activities. See, e.g., Ore. Rev. Stat. § 9.528 (allowing lawyers employed by state or federal law enforcement agencies to take part in such investigations even if they involve dishonesty); Utah State Bar Ethics Advisory Op. 02–05 (2002) (same). There is a more pronounced split in authorities with respect to lawyers investigating civil matters. Compare, e.g., *In re Ositis*, 333 Or. 366, 40 P.3d 500 (2002) (private lawyer who hired an investigator to pose as a journalist to interview an adverse party violated ethics rules, including DR 1–102(A)(3)), with Arizona State Bar Comm. on Rules of Prof. Conduct, Op. 99–11 (1999) (permissible for lawyer to employ private investigators to pose as someone else to investigate a client's discrimination claim); *Apple Corps Ltd. v. International Collectors Soc'y*, 15 F.Supp.2d 456 (D.N.J.1998) (permissible for private lawyers to make misrepresentations about identity or purpose to gather evidence for client's case).

11. *Advocacy in non-adjudicative settings*. Model Rule 3.9 provides that a lawyer serving as an advocate before a legislative group or administrative agency must abide by Rules 3.3, 3.4 and 3.5. Thus, for example, a lawyer would not be allowed to make misrepresentations to a governmental body engaged in a rulemaking process any more than the lawyer could make misrepresentations in court.

4. Improper Influence

A lawyer may not attempt to exert improper influence over the decisionmakers in a proceeding. A lawyer may not communicate with or seek to influence a person known to be in the jury pool, or on a jury. Restatement § 115. Nor may a lawyer attempt to influence a judge, either by communicating ex parte about the proceeding, or by making a gift or loan prohibited by law. *Id.*, § 113. A lawyer is also prohibited from attempting to exert improper influence over witnesses. While a lawyer is allowed to interview prospective witnesses (*see* § 116, comment *b*) the lawyer may not counsel a witness to testify falsely (*see* § 120(1)(a)) or offer the witness an improper fee for testifying (*see* § 117). Note that expert witnesses are entitled to fees for their testimony, but non-experts may not generally be paid any more than their reasonably-incurred expenses. *Id.* No witness, including an expert, may be paid a fee contingent on the outcome of the matter. *Id.*; see *Florida Bar v. Wohl*, 842 So.2d 811 (Fla. 2003) (lawyer suspended for agreeing to pay fact witness up to $1 million, depending on her "usefulness").

These restrictions derive primarily from the criminal law. See, e.g., Restatement § 118, comment *a*. That is, it is a crime to tamper with evidence or to improperly influence or attempt to influence jurors, judges or witnesses. See, e.g., 18 U.S.C. § 1503 (influencing or intimidating juror or court officer by threats or force); 18 U.S.C. § 1504 (attempting to influence a juror by means of a written communication); 18 U.S.C. § 1512 (tampering with witnesses or victims).

Not surprisingly, these prohibitions are further echoed in the ethics rules. See MR 3.5(a) (lawyer shall not "seek to influence a judge, juror, prospective juror, or other official" by prohibited means); MR 3.5(b) (prohibiting unauthorized ex parte contacts with the judge during a proceeding); DR 7–108 (communications with jurors); DR 7–109 (contact with witnesses); DR 7–110 (contacts with and attempts to influence judges); Cal. Rule 5–300 (attempts to influence a judge); Cal. 5–310 (prohibited contact with witnesses); Cal. 5–320 (prohibited contact with jurors). Is it equally improper for a lawyer to tell a client that the judge could be bribed if the client comes up with the money? See MR 8.4(e); *Dayton Bar Ass'n v. O'Brien*, 103 Ohio St.3d 1, 812 N.E.2d 1263 (2004) (ordering indefinite suspension for violation of Ohio DR 9–101(C)).

B. Discovery Abuses

POULIS v. STATE FARM FIRE AND CASUALTY CO.

United States Court of Appeals, Third Circuit, 1984.
747 F.2d 863.

SLOVITER, Circuit Judge.

This appeal ... is brought from a final order dismissing the complaint with prejudice due to counsel's failure to meet court-imposed deadlines and other procedural requisites.

I.

BACKGROUND

[Lefteri and Athena Poulis sued State Farm in November, 1981, to recover money under an insurance policy after a fire at their home. State Farm denied liability, contending that plaintiffs had intentionally caused the fire, had concealed and misrepresented information, and had not filed their action in time. In March, 1982, the district court set a discovery schedule and a date for the pre-trial conference. Plaintiffs apparently sought no discovery.]

On April 15, State Farm filed notice of service of interrogatories on plaintiffs. No answers to these interrogatories were or have ever been filed, and plaintiffs did not file their pre-trial statement by July 5 as required. Therefore defendant filed its pre-trial statement first, on July 28, together with a motion to compel answers to interrogatories. A member of the district judge's staff advised plaintiffs' counsel, George Retos, Jr., that the statement was overdue and Retos promised to submit a statement by the next day. He neither did so nor requested any extension. On August 5 the district court, *sua sponte,* dismissed the case with prejudice for plaintiffs' failure to comply with the orders to file the pre-trial statement.

Retos filed a pre-trial statement on August 9, together with a motion under Rule 60(b) to reconsider and set aside the dismissal, alleging that an illness prevented him from working between July 6 through July 17; that other attorneys could not have taken over because only Retos spoke Greek and could communicate with plaintiff Lefteri Poulis; that Retos' pregnant wife went into false labor on July 29 and 30, and that he had "inadvertently set aside the required work for the instant case on July 29, 1982, due to his concern for his wife" and was "render[ed] unable to prepare the necessary Pre–Trial Statement;" that on his return to work other tasks had backlogged; and that although he had dictated a statement on August 4, it had been mailed on August 6 when it was typed and ready.

The district court denied reconsideration. On appeal, this court vacated the order of dismissal. We noted there was "no allegation that plaintiffs, as distinguished from their counsel, were in any way responsible for the failure to comply with the court's order." We recognized that in *National Hockey League v. Metropolitan Hockey Club, Inc.,* 427 U.S. 639, 96 S.Ct. 2778, 49 L.Ed.2d 747 (1976), a dismissal was upheld where plaintiffs had acted in "flagrant bad faith" and counsel "had behaved with 'callous disregard' of [his] responsibilities," but observed that "[t]he case at hand is not as extreme." ... However, because Retos' excuses failed to account for many days on which a pre-trial statement could have been filed, we observed that some sanction was "amply justified." Accordingly, we vacated the dismissal and remanded to permit the district court to consider alternatives to dismissal, stating, "Alternatives are particularly appropriate when the plaintiff has not personally contributed to the delinquency."

[On remand, the trial court ordered briefing on appropriate alternative sanctions. Retos filed his brief four days late. State Farm urged the court to reopen discovery to give it "the opportunity to examine plaintiffs' Answers to Interrogatories, conduct further investigation if necessary, and depose the plaintiffs or other witnesses known to plaintiffs if such action is deemed necessary and appropriate." State Farm itself suggested that the remedy of "limiting or restricting plaintiffs' witnesses at trial" would be "somewhat harsh." State Farm also asked for an award of $750 in attorneys' fees it incurred because of the dismissal and appeal.]

Notwithstanding the defendant's submission, the district court reinstated its *sua sponte* sanction of dismissal, stating that there was no appropriate alternative. . . .

Although sanctions are a necessary part of any court system, we are concerned that the recent preoccupation with sanctions and the use of dismissal as a necessary "weapon" in the trial court's "arsenal" may be contributing to or effecting an atmosphere in which the meritorious claims or defenses of innocent parties are no longer the central issue. It does not further the goal of a court system, that of delivering evenhanded justice to litigants, to suggest, as did the district court here, that the plaintiffs would have a remedy by suing their counsel for malpractice, since this would only multiply rather than dispose of litigation.

We reiterate what we have said on numerous occasions: that dismissals with prejudice or defaults are drastic sanctions, termed "extreme" by the Supreme Court, *National Hockey League,* 427 U.S. at 643, 96 S.Ct. at 2781, and are to be reserved for comparable cases.

II.

ANALYSIS

In exercising our appellate function to determine whether the trial court has abused its discretion in dismissing, or refusing to lift a default, we will be guided by the manner in which the trial court balanced the following factors, which have been enumerated in the earlier cases, and whether the record supports its findings: (1) the extent of the *party*'s personal *responsibility;* (2) the *prejudice* to the adversary caused by the failure to meet scheduling orders and respond to discovery; (3) a *history* of dilatoriness; (4) whether the conduct of the party or the attorney was *willful* or in *bad faith;* (5) the effectiveness of sanctions other than dismissal, which entails an analysis of *alternative sanctions;* and (6) the *meritoriousness* of the claim or defense.

We turn to apply these factors in the circumstances of this case.

1. *The extent of the party's personal responsibility.*

There has been no suggestion by any party or by the district court that the Poulis plaintiffs are personally responsible for the late pretrial statement, which was the basis for the dismissal. Indeed, Retos has acknowledged the delays were his responsibility and assigned as the reason his illness from July 6 through 17 and the subsequent false labor of his wife on July 29 and 30.

This is therefore unlike the *National Hockey League* case where the Supreme Court upheld the "extreme sanction of dismissal" after noting that there had been "flagrant bad faith" on the part of the plaintiffs as well as "callous disregard" by their counsel of their responsibilities. However, the Poulis' lack of responsibility for their counsel's dilatory conduct is not dispositive, because a client cannot always avoid the consequences of the acts or omissions of its counsel.

2. *Prejudice to the adversary.*

As the district court stated, there has been prejudice to the defendant by the plaintiffs' counsel's conduct. The interrogatories were never answered nor were objections filed; defense counsel was obliged to file a motion to compel answers, and was obliged to file its pretrial statement without the opportunity to review plaintiffs' pretrial statement which was due to be filed first. The court's finding that "defendant encountered lack of cooperation from the plaintiff in areas where the plaintiff should cooperate under the spirit of the federal procedural rules" is supported by the record.

3. *A history of dilatoriness.*

As noted above, this litigation has been characterized by a consistent delay by plaintiffs' counsel.... Time limits imposed by the rules and the court serve an important purpose for the expeditious processing of litigation. If compliance is not feasible, a timely request for an extension should be made to the court. A history by counsel of ignoring these time limits is intolerable.

4. *Whether the attorney's conduct was willful or in bad faith.*

Although the district court concluded that "plaintiffs' counsel's conduct [was] of such a dilatory and contumacious nature to require dismissal," there is nothing in the record to support [the finding that counsel's conduct was "contumacious"]. Nothing in the court's discussion preceding this conclusion is directed toward the willfulness issue but only toward dilatoriness. There has been no suggestion or indication that counsel's illness during July 1982 and his wife's late pregnancy and false labor at the end of that month did not occur as he represented....

5. *Alternative sanctions.*

The district court concluded that it had "no alternative but dismissal" because no other sanctions were appropriate. The district court stated that there was no authority for levying a fine against plaintiffs' counsel as a penalty. However, the court also stated that "there are no costs which can be charged to plaintiffs' counsel at this point." This finding was erroneous. Defendant's counsel had asked the court to impose as a sanction the $750 attorney fee which it had incurred in defending the appeal [from the dismissal].... The district court also could have imposed on plaintiffs' counsel the costs, including attorney's fees, of preparing the motion to compel answers to interrogatories and the brief on alternative sanctions, all of which were incurred because of the dilatoriness of plaintiffs' counsel.

Under the Federal Rules of Civil Procedure and the 1983 amendments, the district court is specifically authorized to impose on an attorney those expenses, including attorneys' fees, caused by unjustified failure to comply with discovery orders or pretrial orders. *See* Fed.R.Civ.P. 16(f), 37(a)(4), 37(b), 37(d) and 37(g). *See also* 28 U.S.C. § 1927. The most direct and therefore preferable sanction for the pattern of attorney delay such as that which the district court encountered in this case would be to impose the excess costs caused by such conduct directly upon the attorney, with an order that such costs are not to be passed on to the client, directly or indirectly. This would avoid compelling an innocent party to bear the brunt of its counsel's dereliction. Dismissal must be a sanction of last, not first, resort.

6. *Meritoriousness of the claim.*

In considering whether a claim or defense appears to be meritorious for this inquiry, we do not purport to use summary judgment standards. A claim, or defense, will be deemed meritorious when the allegations of the pleadings, if established at trial, would support recovery by plaintiff or would constitute a complete defense....

Certainly, the defense that the plaintiffs' claim must fail because it has not been brought within the one year limitation provision of the policy is, on its face, compelling. In their complaint plaintiffs made no allegation that would avoid this facial untimeliness by invoking Pennsylvania's law of waiver of the time limit set forth in an insurance policy. Moreover, plaintiffs filed no answer to the motion to dismiss. For the purpose of evaluating the facial validity of the claim or defense, we cannot rely on the vague and nonspecific statements in plaintiffs' pretrial memorandum that they would produce witnesses to show that defendant led them to believe they would not be barred from filing an action on the claim more than 12 months from the date of the fire. While we express no opinion on whether summary judgment or dismissal would have been warranted on this ground, the existence of a prima facie defense is a factor to be weighed along with the foregoing factors.

III.

CONCLUSION

The above factors should be weighed by the district courts in order to assure that the "extreme" sanction of dismissal or default is reserved for the instances in which it is justly merited. In this case, although there was no contumacious behavior, the pattern of dilatory behavior is compounded by the plaintiffs' failure to file any answers to interrogatories, defendant was compelled to file its pretrial statement without such answers and without seeing plaintiffs' pretrial statement, and there is a prima facie defense to the claim. Under these circumstances, although we might not have reached the same result as did this district court judge, we cannot say that the district court abused its discretion in ordering the dismissal. Therefore, we will affirm the judgment of the district court.

Notes

1.   Were you at all surprised by the court's ultimate conclusion? Do you think lesser alternative sanctions were more appropriate in this case? What did the standard of review have to do with the result?

2.   *Federal rules on discovery abuse.* The 1993 amendments to Rule 11 make it inapplicable to discovery abuses. FRCP 11(d). But most agree that Rule 11 is not needed for this purpose, since many other federal rules provide for sanctions for discovery misconduct in civil cases brought in federal court. **Rule 16(f)** empowers a judge to order a party or a party's attorney to pay sanctions, including the reasonable expenses incurred because of a violation, if a party or a party's attorney "fails to obey a scheduling or pretrial order," or "fails to participate [in a pretrial conference] in good faith." If a violation is found, sanctions are mandatory under Rule 16(f). **Rule 26(g)** is similar in format to Rule 11, requiring a lawyer (or an unrepresented party) to sign all disclosures, discovery requests, responses and objections, and to certify that any such papers are warranted in fact and law and not improper. FRCP 26(g)(2). If a violation is found, sanctions are mandatory. FRCP 26(g)(3). **Rule 30(d)** sets forth rules for depositions, including the following: that all objections "must be stated concisely and in a non-argumentative and non-suggestive manner"; that the court may award costs and attorneys' fees incurred by any party because of "any impediment, delay, or other conduct [that] has frustrated the fair examination of the deponent"; and that the court is empowered to stop or limit a deposition that is "being conducted in bad faith or in such manner as unreasonably to annoy, embarrass, or oppress the deponent or party." **Rule 37** allows for

sanctions for failure to comply with discovery orders, such as deposition notices, interrogatories and requests for admission.

3. *Ethics rules.* Ethics rules specifically relevant to discovery abuses include MR 3.2 (duty to expedite litigation "consistent with the interests of the client"); MR 3.3 (candor toward the tribunal); and MR 3.4 (a) (prohibiting concealing, altering or destroying evidence, or obstructing a party's access to it); 3.4(b) (prohibiting falsifying evidence or counseling a witness to testify falsely); 3.4(d) (prohibiting making a "frivolous discovery request" or failing to make a reasonably diligent effort to comply with an opponent's discovery request); and 3.4(f) (prohibiting asking a person other than a client from refraining from voluntarily giving relevant information to another party, with narrow exceptions). Thus a lawyer who counseled and assisted in his client's formulation of inaccurate and incomplete sworn responses to interrogatories, knowing they were inaccurate, is subject to sanction. See *Feld's Case*, 149 N.H. 19, 815 A.2d 383 (2002) (one-year suspension). See also *Cincinnati Bar Ass'n v. Statzer*, 101 Ohio St.3d 14, 800 N.E.2d 1117 (2003) (one-year suspension for using deception during deposition).

4. Rules against abusive conduct apply in the discovery process, also. In *Paramount Communications Inc. v. QVC Network Inc.*, 637 A.2d 34 (Del.1994), the court labeled as "unprofessional" and "unacceptable" the conduct of Texas lawyer Joseph Jamail, who while defending a deposition in the case called the opposing counsel "asshole," said counsel "could gag a maggot off a meat wagon," and accused counsel of "hav[ing] no concept of what you're doing." Jamail's conduct, the court said, in addition to being "extraordinarily rude, uncivil and vulgar," improperly obstructed the questioner from eliciting relevant testimony. But the court said it could not discipline Jamail since he was not admitted in Delaware. Jamail's vulgarity was not nearly as succinct as that of lawyer Leonard Jacques, in *Carroll v. The Jacques Admiralty Law Firm*, 110 F.3d 290 (5th Cir.1997), who at the end of his own videotaped deposition in a fraud suit by a former client commented simply, "Fuck you, you son of a bitch." For this and similar comments during the deposition, he was sanctioned $7,000.

5. Courts also have the power to hold lawyers in contempt for some discovery abuses. See, e.g., *Dietz v. Kautzman*, 686 N.W.2d 110 (N.D. 2004) (failure to pay sanction awarded in prior discovery-abuse order).

C. Extrajudicial Statements by Litigators

IOWA SUPREME COURT BOARD OF PROFESSIONAL ETHICS AND CONDUCT v. VISSER

Supreme Court of Iowa, 2001.
629 N.W.2d 376.

LARSON, Justice.

This respondent, Kevin J. Visser, is an attorney practicing in Cedar Rapids.... One of his business clients became involved in a dispute with a former employee that ended up in litigation. The respondent was contacted by a newspaper reporter who obtained a statement from him resulting in these disciplinary charges. The Grievance Commission found this statement violated DR 7–107(G)(1), (2), and (4) (prohibiting extrajudicial statements by lawyer involved in civil litigation). Although the Board of Professional Ethics and Conduct had also charged a violation of DR 1–102(A)(1), (4), and (5) (prohibiting misleading statements), the commission made no findings as to that charge. The commission recommended a public reprimand. On our review, we conclude the board did not establish a violation of DR 7–107 but did establish a violation of DR 1–102(A). We admonish the respondent for that violation.

I.   FACTS AND PRIOR PROCEEDINGS

[Visser's client, an insurance agency located in Cedar Rapids, was contemplating a business venture with a business located in Waterloo, Iowa. An employee of the insurance agency objected to the proposed venture and was fired. He filed two lawsuits against the agency. A reporter from the *Waterloo Courier* newspaper, Pat Kinney, called Visser about the litigation. Visser was in a deposition when Kinney called; Kinney left a message to call him. Visser ultimately faxed Kinney a letter that same day. The letter discussed the litigation. Kinney's story about the matter appeared in the Courier the next day. The story quoted Visser's letter at length.]

II.   THE CHARGES

The board's complaint alleged violations of DR 7–107(G)(1), (2), and (4) and DR 1–102(A)(1), (4), (5), and (6) of the Iowa Code of Professional Responsibility for Lawyers. DR 7–107(G), dealing with trial publicity, states:

A lawyer or law firm associated with a civil action shall not during its investigation or litigation make or participate in making an extrajudicial statement, other than a quotation from or reference to public records, that a reasonable person would expect to be disseminated by means of public communication and that relates to:

(1) Evidence regarding the occurrence or transaction involved.

(2) The character, credibility, or criminal record of a party, witness, or prospective witness. . . .

(4) An opinion as to the merits of the claims or defenses of a party, except as required by law or administrative rule.

(5) Any other matter reasonably likely to interfere with a fair trial of the action.

The commission found Visser violated DR 7–107 but made no finding as to DR 1–102(A).

III. RESOLUTION

... A. *The charge under DR 7–107(G).* The board contends the statements made by the respondent to the *Waterloo Courier* violated DR 7–107(G) under subparts 1 (commenting on evidence), 2 (commenting on the character or credibility of a party), and 4 (expressing an opinion on the merits of the claim). The respondent counters that DR 7–107(G) is unconstitutional on its face and as applied to him. According to him, the rule is so broad it impinges on lawyers' First Amendment rights because the rule is susceptible of application to protected expression, *i.e.,* out-of-court statements that do not create any real threat to the fairness of the proceedings. *See Gentile v. State Bar of Nevada,* 501 U.S. 1030, 1077, 111 S.Ct. 2720, 2746, 115 L.Ed.2d 888, 925 (1991) (Rehnquist, C.J., dissenting):

> [E]ven those lawyers involved in pending cases can [under a state disciplinary rule and the First Amendment] make extrajudicial statements as long as such statements do not present a substantial risk of material prejudice to an adjudicative proceeding.

... Disciplinary rules restricting communications by lawyers are "necessarily constrained by the First Amendment." *Peel v. Attorney Disciplinary Comm'n,* 496 U.S. 91, 108, 110 S.Ct. 2281, 2292, 110 L.Ed.2d 83, 99 (1990) (lawyer advertising); *Iowa Supreme Ct. Bd. of Prof'l Ethics & Conduct v. Wherry,* 569 N.W.2d 822, 825 (Iowa 1997) (same). Similarly, lawyers' out-of-court statements regarding matters in litigation are entitled to First Amendment protection.

The Nevada disciplinary rule in *Gentile* was substantially different from our rule. Also, *Gentile* involved a lawyer's comments at a press conference about a pending criminal, not a civil, case. Nevertheless, the Court made it clear that, to avoid running afoul of the First Amendment, a rule must be restricted to speech that creates a "substantial likelihood of material prejudice." *Gentile,* 501 U.S. at 1075, 111 S.Ct. at 2745, 115 L.Ed.2d at 923. Four members of the Court also stated:

> While it is true that [the rule's] standard for controlling pretrial publicity must be judged at the time a statement is made, *ex post* evidence can have probative value in some cases.

Id. at 1047, 111 S.Ct. at 2730, 115 L.Ed.2d at 905 (plurality opinion). In view of this principle, these four justices concluded that later events bore on the question of the publicity's effect on the right to a fair trial. This included the fact that no request had been made for a change of venue, the jury was impaneled without apparent difficulty, members of the jury panel had only vague recollections of news reports, and "not a single juror indicated any recollection of [the lawyer] or his press conference." These four justices would have held there was not a "likelihood of material prejudice."

The Restatement of the Law Governing Lawyers adopts the view that, to be sanctionable, a statement must be one reasonably likely to affect the outcome. Section 109 of the Restatement provides:

> An Advocate's Public Comment on Pending Litigation.
>
> (1) In representing a client in a matter before a tribunal, a lawyer may not make a statement outside the proceeding that a reasonable person would expect to be disseminated by means of public communication *when the lawyer knows or reasonably should know that the statement will have a substantial likelihood of materially prejudicing a juror or influencing or intimidating a prospective witness in the proceeding.* However, a lawyer may in any event make a statement that is reasonably necessary to mitigate the impact on the lawyer's client of substantial, undue, and prejudicial publicity recently initiated by one other than the lawyer or the lawyer's client.

2 Restatement (Third) of the Law Governing Lawyers § 109, at 160–61 (1998) (emphasis added).

If we were to apply rule 7–107(G)(1), (2), and (4) without any limitation as to the potential effect of the lawyer's comments, this would clearly make the rules violative of a lawyer's First Amendment rights because they would proscribe statements that do not pose "a substantial risk of material prejudice" to the judicial proceeding in question. *See Gentile,* 501 U.S. at 1075, 111 S.Ct. at 2745, 115 L.Ed.2d at 923.

Pennsylvania's commonwealth court interpreted their rule similar to our rule 7–107 to incorporate a requirement that the statement be "reasonably likely to interfere with a fair hearing." *Widoff v. Disciplinary Bd.,* 54 Pa.Cmwlth. 124, 420 A.2d 41 (1980). . . . [In *Widoff,* the relevant disciplinary rule forbade extra-judicial statements of four specific types as well as "any other matter reasonably likely to interfere with a fair hearing." The "reasonably likely to interfere" language did not appear in the paragraphs listing the four specific kinds of forbidden statements. The *Widoff* court held that the "reasonable likelihood" standard "supplements and modifies each of paragraphs (1) through (4)," and that as so modified, the restrictions "passed First Amendment scrutiny."]

We agree with this analysis. In order for DR 7–107(G) to pass constitutional muster, the statements made here must have been reasonably likely to affect the fairness of the proceedings.

In applying the rule as so interpreted, we look to the facts surrounding the statements at the time they were made, but we also look to the *ex post* evidence that relates to the likelihood of prejudice. The newspaper article spawned by the respondent's letter was published in Waterloo, which is over fifty miles from Cedar Rapids, where the trial was held. This article, which was the only one published in connection with the case, was published on November 6, 1998—almost two years before the trial. None of the jurors had even heard of the parties. Patrick Roby, an attorney testifying for Visser before the commission, said he did not believe the *Courier* article had any impact on the trial, stating "I don't know where you'd find a *Waterloo Courier* in Cedar Rapids."

On our review of the record, we believe a reasonable fact finder would not conclude that the statement in question was reasonably likely to affect the fairness of the proceeding. We therefore find no violation of DR 7–107(G).

B. *The charge under DR 1–102(A).* . . . [T]he respondent said in his letter to the *Courier* reporter that "one judge has already determined that [the plaintiff] is unlikely to succeed on the merits of his far-fetched claims." As the respondent concedes, this is only partially true. This comment by the judge was only in connection with the plaintiff's first suit requesting an injunction. The judge expressed no opinion on the merits of the second suit, under which the claims were different.

The board charged this statement by the respondent violated DR 1–102(A) [which states in subsection (4) that a lawyer shall not engage in "conduct involving dishonesty, fraud, deceit or misrepresentation."] . . . Although we realize the statement was made under the pressure of the situation, the fact is it was only partially true and was therefore a misrepresentation under DR 1–102(A)(4). We admonish the respondent, and the bar generally, that we do not condone such conduct.

We do not agree with the commission that the board established a violation of DR 7–107(G). However, we admonish the respondent for his violation of DR 1–102(A).

Notes

1. *Gentile*, quoted in the *Visser* case, is the leading authority on the proper level of restriction on litigators' extrajudicial statements. Does that case, with its focus on the likelihood that the statements would affect the fairness of the proceeding, strike a good balance? It is now embodied in Model Rule 3.6(a), as well as California's Rule 5–120(A). A comment to the Model Rule admits that "[i]t is difficult to strike a

balance between protecting the right to a fair trial and safeguarding the right of free expression." MR 3.6, comment [1]. Rules patterned on *Gentile* have been upheld against constitutional challenge. See, e.g., *Grievance Administrator v. Fieger*, 476 Mich. 231, 719 N.W.2d 123 (2006); *Commission for Lawyer Discipline v. Benton*, 980 S.W.2d 425 (Tex.1998); *In re Morrissey*, 168 F.3d 134 (4th Cir.1999); *United States v. Cutler*, 58 F.3d 825 (2d Cir.1995).

2. *Special duties of prosecutors*. A prosecutor's extrajudicial statements not only risk prejudicing a proceeding, but also risk raising public resentment against a person accused of crime. See MR 3.8, comment [5]. Prosecutors are thus covered by two special rules on extrajudicial statements, embodied in MR 3.6(a)(7) and 3.8(f). Not all extrajudicial statements are prohibited, but lawyers in this role are more restricted than others with respect to what can be said publicly about active cases. See Restatement § 109, comment *e*. Could a prosecutor's extrajudicial statements be actionable under § 1983? Proving such a claim would require that the prosecutor act under color of state law, and deprive the plaintiff of a constitutionally-protected right. In *Mezibov v. Allen*, 411 F.3d 712 (6th Cir. 2005), a criminal defense lawyer made such an allegation, asserting that the county prosecutor's statements to the media were an attempt to retaliate against him and deter him from engaging in activities protected by the First Amendment, namely, filing motions and advocating for his client in court. The court held as a matter of first impression that the plaintiff's claim faltered on the second element: a lawyer retains no personal First Amendment rights when he represents his client in courtroom proceedings.

3. *Misleading extrajudicial statements*. Was the *Visser* court right to discipline the lawyer for making a misleading statement to the press, even where the statement did not risk prejudice to a fair trial? Should that have been considered protected speech?

4. *Gag orders*. Can a court issue an order forbidding lawyers from making public statements about a case? The answer is yes, but because of "prior restraint" problems, such orders must be narrowly tailored. See, e.g., *Twohig v. Blackmer*, 121 N.M. 746, 918 P.2d 332 (1996)(striking down overbroad gag order on free speech grounds); *United States v. Brown*, 218 F.3d 415 (5th Cir.2000) (upholding narrowly-drawn gag order).

5. *Extrajudicial statements by former counsel*. Can a gag order apply to a lawyer who no longer represents a party before the court? In *United States v. Scarfo*, 263 F.3d 80 (3d Cir.2001), the trial court had issued a gag order against lawyer Manno after he had been disqualified as Scarfo's lawyer in a criminal case. Manno appealed the gag order, and the Third Circuit reversed, holding that there were no credible findings of any risk of prejudice, let alone a substantial likelihood of material prejudice under the *Gentile* standard. The court did recognize that Manno, even after his disqualification, remained an insider with close

ties to Scarfo, and thus could not be treated as just a member of the public.

6. *Extrajudicial criticism of judges.* The Restatement provides that a lawyer may not "knowingly or recklessly" publicly utter a "false statement of fact" about the qualifications or integrity of a judge or a candidate for a judicial office. Restatement § 114; see also MR 8.2(a) (same). Such conduct is often found to be conduct prejudicial to the administration of justice. See, e.g., *Mississippi Bar v. Lumumba*, 912 So.2d 871 (Miss. 2005) (six-month suspension for comments to newspaper). As noted elsewhere, lawyers do have First Amendment rights to criticize judges, but First Amendment rights are never absolute Why isn't such speech protected by the First Amendment? Compare, e.g., *The Florida Bar v. Ray*, 797 So.2d 556 (Fla.2001) (upholding reprimand of lawyer who wrote letters to Chief Immigration Judge complaining about the veracity and integrity of another immigration judge before whom the lawyer had appeared several times), with *In re Green*, 11 P.3d 1078 (Colo.2000) (lawyer who wrote letters to a judge calling him a racist and a bigot was merely stating an opinion protected by the First Amendment, and thus beyond the reach of discipline). Do the ethics rules prohibiting false extrajudicial criticisms of judges apply to lawyers acting as pro se litigants? See *Notopoulos v. Statewide Grievance Comm.*, 277 Conn. 218, 890 A.2d 509 (2006) (yes).

7. *Civil claim by person damaged by extrajudicial statement.* While litigators have an absolute privilege to defame others in the course of a judicial proceeding, *see* section 4 *infra*, a lawyer's *extrajudicial* statements may give rise to a cause of action for defamation. See, e.g., *Kennedy v. Zimmermann*, 601 N.W.2d 61 (Iowa 1999) (lawyer made statement to a newspaper reporter that his client's previous lawyer had "breach[ed] her ethical duties" and was "negligent").

D. The Advocate–Witness Rule

IN THE MATTER OF ESTATE OF WATERS
Supreme Court of Delaware, 1994.
647 A.2d 1091.

HOLLAND, Justice:

This is an appeal from a decision of the Court of Chancery in an action challenging the will of Elizabeth Waters ... [Waters' granddaughter, Clare Trent, was left only a remainder interest and challenged the will on two grounds: that Waters lacked testimonial capacity and that the will was the product of undue influence by Waters' cousin, Lillian Young, who was left a life estate. The Court of Chancery found the challenge to the will was without merit and that the will had been properly admitted to probate. Trent filed this direct appeal.]

[At the time the will was drafted, Waters was elderly, suffering from cancer, and disabled from strokes. Waters' relatives began exhibiting "a high degree of hostility" among themselves. Young and members of her family "decided that Waters should execute a will. Specifically, they wanted Waters' will to provide Young with a place to live for the rest of her life." (Waters' major asset was a house.)]

Young's sister, Maxine Young, contacted an attorney, Brian P. Murphy. Murphy was informed that Waters was in poor physical health and that she wanted to make a will leaving her house to Lillian Young for life and, on her death, to Trent. Murphy prepared a will according to Maxine Young's instructions and without direct contact with Waters.

[Murphy later went to Waters' home to have the will executed.] Murphy met Waters for the first time when he arrived at her home with the will. Waters was in her bedroom, attended by a visiting hospice nurse. Murphy testified that Lillian Young was present, as were others. Lillian Young testified that she was not present when the will was executed. . . . Murphy told Waters that he had prepared a will for her. Murphy explained to Waters, in summary fashion, that it would leave "all [her] estate, both personal and real, of every kind and description, and wheresoever situated, including [her] home situated at 118 East Anderson Street, Middletown, New Castle County, Delaware" to Young for life. He also explained that the property would pass to Trent on Young's death. Waters made a gesture with her head when Murphy asked if this was what she wanted her will to say.

[Murphy testified before the Master presiding over the probate proceedings to his belief that "in his opinion, Waters had testamentary capacity at the time the will was signed, based on his observations at this meeting." Murphy also represented the Waters estate in the will contest proceedings, including these appeals.]

When the Court of Chancery reviewed the Master's Final Report and the exceptions to it, the court summarized the central role of Murphy's testimony before the Master as follows:

> The critical question is whether Waters had testamentary capacity when she signed the will. The neighbors and relatives who testified were not present on that occasion. The two subscribing witnesses, Murphy and Tracey [the nurse], provided the only direct evidence as to Waters' condition on the day she executed her will.

The Court of Chancery ultimately declined to follow the recommendation in the Master's Final Report. It held that the will Murphy prepared had been properly admitted to probate. When Trent appealed, Murphy continued to represent the Waters' estate. . . .

Following oral argument, this Court [acting sua sponte] directed the parties to supplement the record with regard to why Murphy was permitted to testify on a contested matter and simultaneously remain as the trial attorney for the Waters' estate. . . .

It is a well-established ethical principle that, "in general a lawyer who represents a client in a litigated matter may not also appear therein as a witness, either for or against the client." Geoffrey C. Hazard, Jr. & W. William Hodes, *The Law of Lawyering: A Handbook on the Model Rules of Professional Conduct* 678 (2d ed. 1993). The Delaware Rules of Professional Conduct are patterned after the ABA Model Rules of Professional Conduct. The current Delaware ethical provision which circumscribes the propriety of a trial advocate also serving as a witness is Rule 3.7(a):

> A lawyer *shall not act as advocate at a trial* in which the lawyer is likely to be a necessary witness except where:
>
> > (1) the testimony relates to an uncontested issue;
> >
> > (2) the testimony relates to the nature and value of legal services rendered in the case; or
> >
> > (3) disqualification of the lawyer would work substantial hardship on the client. (emphasis added).

Rule 3.7(a) superseded Disciplinary Rules 5–101(B) and 5–102(A) of the former Delaware Lawyers' Code of Professional Responsibility. . . . [B]oth Delaware and the ABA Model Rule 3.7(a) continue "the traditional ban against an advocate also appearing as a witness in a case which he or she is handling on behalf of a client," albeit in a form more carefully tailored than its predecessors, DR 5–101(B) and DR 5–102 of the Code of Professional Responsibility.

The duty of a witness to state the objective truth when testifying is fundamentally different from the duty of a trial advocate to represent his or her client zealously within the bounds of the law. The personal credibility of a witness is always at issue and often subjected to vigorous cross-examination for purposes of impeachment. A trial advocate may not vouch for the credibility of a witness or state a personal belief in the merit of his or her client's position. Del.R.Prof.C. 3.4(e).

In fact, one of the rationales for prohibiting the dual lawyer-witness situation in a contested proceeding is to prevent confusion by the trier of fact with regard to the separate roles of an advocate and a witness. That rationale is explained as follows:

> Combining the roles of advocate and witness can prejudice the opposing party and can involve a conflict of interest between the lawyer and client.

The opposing party has proper objection where the combination of roles may prejudice that party's right in the litigation. A witness is required to testify on the basis of personal knowledge, while an advocate is expected to explain and comment on evidence given by others. It may not be clear whether a statement by an advocate-witness should be taken as proof or as an analysis of the proof.

Delaware and Model Rules of Professional Conduct Rule 3.7 (commentary).

"The interest of the opposing party protected by Rule 3.7 is parallel to that protected by Rule 3.4(e), which forbids an advocate from voicing personal opinions about the merits of a cause." Geoffrey C. Hazard, Jr. & W. William Hodes, *The Law of Lawyering: A Handbook on the Model Rules of Professional Conduct* 680 (2d ed. 1993). Rule 3.7 and Rule 3.4(e) both prohibit the mixing of advocacy and testimony. *Id.* There are multiple threats to the integrity of the judicial proceedings if a trial advocate also testifies as a trial witness regarding a contested issue, e.g., (i) the attorney may either be accused of distorting the truth for the client's benefit or testifying truthfully to the client's detriment; (ii) the attorney may, perhaps even inadvertently, interject unsworn testimony into the cross-examination of other witnesses; (iii) the attorney may be called upon by other evidence to argue his or her own credibility to the trier of fact; (iv) the attorney may, in effect, give "unsworn" testimony during arguments to the trial judge and/or jury.

Under the facts of this case, the centrality of Murphy's testimony to the contested issues of undue influence and testamentary capacity mandated his withdrawal as trial attorney. Del.R.Prof.C. 1.16(a)(1); 3.4(e); and 3.7. Unlike other members of the Delaware Bar confronted by the same ethical obligation in the past, Murphy failed to recognize his duty as a lawyer/witness to withdraw, even after opposing counsel called it to his attention. That is why trial judges have the power to disqualify trial counsel, when necessary, to preserve the integrity of the adversary process in the actions before them.

The Court of Chancery had full power to control the parties and counsel to ensure the fairness of the proceedings. It was plain error to permit Murphy to undermine the integrity of the adversary process by participating as a trial attorney in a proceeding in which he was a central witness on the contested issues being adjudicated. The judgment of the Court of Chancery is REVERSED. This matter is remanded for a new trial. The Clerk is directed to send a copy of this opinion to the Office of Disciplinary Counsel.

Notes

1.   The advocate-witness rule, like many rules dealing with the trial process, can be enforced either by the tribunal in the course of the litigation or by a disciplinary authority after the fact. In the context of the advocate-witness rule, if the court finds a violation it normally disqualifies the lawyer from continuing as advocate. If an advocate should have withdrawn but did not, the mandatory withdrawal provisions of Rule 1.16(a)(1) can be applied as a matter of discipline, since the continuing representation will have resulted in violation of Rule 3.7.

2.   As the case indicates, the advocate-witness rule is well entrenched and widely accepted. See Restatement § 108.

3.   Do you see how the advocate-witness rule relates to the rule forbidding a lawyer from stating personal opinions or asserting personal knowledge of facts during the trial? See *Cerros v. Steel Technologies, Inc.*, 398 F.3d 944 (7th Cir. 2005). Why doesn't the standard jury instruction that the lawyer's statements are not evidence suffice to cure any problems that might arise in the absence of such rules?

4.   *Client waiver of rule?* Can a client give consent to having his lawyer represent him at trial and also act as a witness in the trial? Given the interests protected by the rules, what do you think? See *State v. Vanover*, 559 N.W.2d 618 (Iowa 1997).

5.   *What does "disqualified" mean?* In *Anderson Producing Inc. v. Koch Oil Co.*, 929 S.W.2d 416 (Tex.1996), a lawyer learned that he would probably be called as a witness at the trial in which he was going to participate. He made the decision to work "behind the scenes," drafting pleadings, engaging in settlement negotiations, and assisting with trial strategy. Was this proper? The court of appeals thought not, but the Texas Supreme Court reversed, holding that the advocate-witness rule was not violated on those facts.

6.   *Lawyers serving as expert witnesses.* Lawyers sometimes serve as expert witnesses. The rules we have seen in this section prohibit a lawyer-expert from also serving as an advocate in the same matter. How can a lawyer serve in this role at all, then? According to an ABA Formal Opinion, a lawyer retained to testify as an expert does not thereby establish a client-lawyer relationship with the party who hires him or her. But the lawyer-expert should clarify this role at the outset of the employment agreement, and must maintain the party's confidences. ABA Formal Op. 97–407 (1997).

§ 3.   CLIENT PERJURY

PEOPLE v. DePALLO

Court of Appeals of New York, 2001.
96 N.Y.2d 437, 754 N.E.2d 751, 729 N.Y.S.2d 649.

Wesley, J.

This case calls upon us to clarify a defense attorney's responsibilities when confronted with the dilemma that a client intends to commit perjury.

Defendant and his accomplices executed a calculated attack on a 71–year-old man, ransacking his home, stabbing him repeatedly with a knife and scissors, and finally bludgeoning him to death with a shovel. Defendant's blood was found at the scene and on the victim's clothing. Defendant's fingerprint was also discovered in the home and, upon arrest, he made several incriminating statements placing him at the scene of the crime. Defendant also insisted on making a statement during pre-trial proceedings in which he admitted that he had forced one of his accomplices to participate in the crime under threat of death.

At trial, defense counsel noted at a sidebar that he had advised defendant that he did not have to testify and should not testify, but if he did, he should do so truthfully. Defendant confirmed counsel's statements to the court but insisted on testifying. Defense counsel elicited defendant's direct testimony in narrative form. Defendant testified that he was home the entire evening of the crime, and that his contrary statements to the police were induced by promises that he could return home. During the prosecutor's cross-examination, defense counsel made numerous objections.

After both sides rested, defense counsel addressed the court in Chambers, outside the presence of defendant and the prosecutor. Counsel stated:

> "prior to the [defendant's] testimony, I informed the Court that * * * the defendant was going to take the witness stand, and that he had previously told me he was involved in this homicide. Although I did not get into details with him, I don't know exactly what his involvement was, but he had stated to me that he was there that night, he had gotten at least that far.

> "Knowing that, I told the defendant I cannot participate in any kind of perjury, and you really shouldn't perjure yourself. But, he, you know, dealing with him is kind of difficult and he was insistent upon taking the stand. He never told me what he was going to say, but I knew it

was not going to be the truth, at least to the extent of him denying participation.''

The court then noted that counsel had complied with the procedures for such circumstances as outlined in *People v. Salquerro,* 107 Misc.2d 155, 433 N.Y.S.2d 711, *affd.* 92 A.D.2d 1090, 460 N.Y.S.2d 971 *lv. denied* 59 N.Y.2d 977, 466 N.Y.S.2d 1038, 453 N.E.2d 562. During summations, defense counsel did not refer to defendant's trial testimony. Defendant was convicted of two counts of second degree murder (intentional and felony murder based on the burglary), two counts of first degree robbery, two counts of first degree burglary, and one count of second degree robbery. The Appellate Division affirmed, rejecting defendant's claims that he was denied effective assistance of counsel when his attorney disclosed the perjured testimony to the court and that the ex parte conference was a material stage of trial. A Judge of this Court granted leave to appeal, and we now affirm.

The ethical dilemma presented by this case is not new. Defense attorneys have confronted the problem of client perjury since the latter part of the 19th century when the disqualification of criminal defendants to testify in their own defense was abolished by statute in federal courts and in most states, including New York in 1869. A lawyer with a perjurious client must contend with competing considerations—duties of zealous advocacy, confidentiality and loyalty to the client on the one hand, and a responsibility to the courts and our truth-seeking system of justice on the other. Courts, bar associations and commentators have struggled to define the most appropriate role for counsel caught in such situations (*compare* Wolfram, *Client Perjury,* 50 S. Cal. L. Rev. 809 [1977] [emphasizing the truth-seeking function of the judicial system] *with* Freedman, *Professional Responsibility of the Criminal Defense Lawyer: The Three Hardest Questions,* 64 Mich. L. Rev. 1469 [1966] [arguing that attorney's duty of confidentiality is paramount]).

Notwithstanding these ethical concerns, a defendant's right to testify at trial does not include a right to commit perjury (*see, United States v. Dunnigan,* 507 U.S. 87, 96, 113 S.Ct. 1111, 122 L.Ed.2d 445; *Harris v. New York,* 401 U.S. 222, 225, 91 S.Ct. 643, 28 L.Ed.2d 1), and the Sixth Amendment right to the assistance of counsel does not compel counsel to assist or participate in the presentation of perjured testimony (*see, Nix v. Whiteside,* 475 U.S. 157, 173, 106 S.Ct. 988, 89 L.Ed.2d 123). In light of these limitations, an attorney's duty to zealously represent a client is circumscribed by an ''equally solemn duty to comply with the law and standards of professional conduct * * * to prevent and disclose frauds upon the court'' (*id.,* at 168–169, 106 S.Ct. 988). The United States Supreme Court has noted that counsel must first attempt to persuade the client not to pursue the unlawful course of conduct. If unsuccessful, withdrawal from representation may be an appropriate response, but when confronted with the problem during trial, as here, an "attorney's revelation of his client's perjury to the court is a professionally responsible and acceptable response" (*id.*, at 170, 106 S.Ct. 988).

This approach is consistent with the ethical obligations of attorneys under New York's Code of Professional Responsibility. DR 7–102 (codified at 22 NYCRR 1200.33) expressly prohibits an attorney, under penalty of sanctions, from knowingly using perjured testimony or false evidence (DR 7–102[a][4]); knowingly making a false statement of fact (DR 7–102[a][5]); participating in the creation or preservation of evidence when the attorney knows, or it is obvious, that the evidence is false (DR 7–102[a][6]); counseling or assisting the client in conduct the lawyer knows to be illegal or fraudulent (DR 7–102[a][7]); and knowingly engaging in other illegal conduct (DR 7–102 [a][8]; *see also*, EC 7–26). Additionally, DR 7–102(b)(1) mandates that "[a] lawyer who receives information clearly establishing that * * * [t]he client has, in the course of the representation, perpetrated a fraud upon a * * * tribunal shall promptly call upon the client to rectify the same, and if the client refuses or is unable to do so, *the lawyer shall reveal the fraud to the affected * * * tribunal*, except when the information is protected as a confidence or secret" (emphasis added).

In accordance with these responsibilities, defense counsel first sought to dissuade defendant from testifying falsely, and indeed from testifying at all. Defendant insisted on proceeding to give the perjured testimony and, thereafter, counsel properly notified the court (*see, People v. Salquerro*, 107 Misc.2d 155, 433 N.Y.S.2d 711, *supra; see also, People v. Campos*, 249 A.D.2d 237, 672 N.Y.S.2d 680 [counsel properly informed the court about defendant's confidential plan to have counsel participate in laying a false foundation for a speedy trial application], *lv. denied* 92 N.Y.2d 923, 680 N.Y.S.2d 464, 703 N.E.2d 276).[1]

The intent to commit a crime is not a protected confidence or secret (*see, Nix, supra*, 475 U.S., at 174, 106 S.Ct. 988 [attorney's duty of confidentiality does not extend to a client's announced plans to engage in criminal conduct]; *see also*, DR 4–101[c][3] [22 NYCRR 1200.19] [a lawyer may reveal the intention of his client to commit a crime]). Moreover, in this case defense counsel did

---

1. Counsel's decision to disclose is in accord with standards announced by courts in other jurisdictions, bar associations and commentators (*see, e.g., Hinds v. State Bar*, 19 Cal.2d 87, 119 P.2d 134; *Thornton v. United States*, 357 A.2d 429 [D.C.], *cert. denied* 429 U.S. 1024, 97 S.Ct. 644, 50 L.Ed.2d 626; *State v. Henderson*, 205 Kan. 231, 468 P.2d 136; *In re King*, 7 Utah 2d 258, 322 P.2d 1095; *State v. Berrysmith*, 87 Wash.App. 268, 944 P.2d 397; ABA Annotated Model Rules of Professional Conduct, rule 3.3, comments 7–11; ABA Committee on Ethics & Professional Responsibility, Formal Opn. 87–353 [1987]; ABA Informal Opn. 1314 [1975]; Restatement [Third] of Law Governing Lawyers § 120[2], comment *i*; Wolfram, *Client Perjury, supra; cf.,* Freedman, *The Three Hardest Questions, supra*).

not reveal the substance of any client confidence as defendant had already admitted at a pre-trial hearing that he had forced one of his accomplices to participate in the crime under threat of death.[2]

Finally, defendant contends that his counsel should have sought to withdraw from the case. However, substitution of counsel would do little to resolve the problem and might, in fact, have facilitated any fraud defendant wished to perpetrate upon the court. We agree with *Salquerro* that withdrawal of counsel could present other unsatisfactory scenarios which ultimately could lead to introduction of the perjured testimony in any event or further delay the proceedings (*see, Salquerro, supra,* 107 Misc.2d, at 157–158, 433 N.Y.S.2d 711).

In this case, defendant was allowed to present his testimony in narrative form to the jury. The remainder of defense counsel's representation throughout the trial was more than competent. The lawyer's actions properly balanced the duties he owed to his client and to the court and criminal justice system; "[s]ince there has been no breach of any recognized professional duty, it follows that there can be no deprivation of the right to assistance of counsel" (*Nix, supra,* 475 U.S., at 175, 106 S.Ct. 988; *see also, People v. Baldi,* 54 N.Y.2d 137, 151–152, 444 N.Y.S.2d 893, 429 N.E.2d 400). . . .

Accordingly, the order of the Appellate Division should be affirmed.

Notes

1. *What is perjury?* Title 18 U.S.C. § 1621(1) states that "whoever . . . having taken an oath . . . that he will testify, declare, depose or certify truly . . . , willfully and contrary to such oath states or subscribes any material matter which he does not believe to be true . . . is guilty of perjury." The federal statute provides for a penalty of up to five years imprisonment. Note that the rules against a lawyer's assisting a client in putting on false evidence or testimony apply even if perjury is not literally present, as when the client makes a false statement but lacks the intent to lie. See Restatement § 120, comment *d*.

2. *Basic prohibitions.* The Restatement says that a lawyer may not "knowingly counsel or assist a witness to testify falsely" or "offer false evidence," or offer any evidence "as to an issue of fact known by the lawyer to be false." Restatement § 120(1). Model Rule 3.3(a)(3), remember, states that a lawyer "shall not knowingly offer evidence the lawyer knows to be false." Model Rule 3.3(b) says that if a lawyer represents a

---

2. We do not have occasion to address whether a similar disclosure in the course of a bench trial would be appropriate or implicate any due process concerns (*see, Lowery v. Cardwell,* 575 F.2d 727, 730 [9th Cir.] [disclosure of defendant's perjury to court deprived defendant of fair trial during bench trial where judge, not jury, was factfinder]; *see also,* Restatement [Third] of Law Governing Lawyers § 120, comment *i, supra*).

client in an adjudicative proceeding and "knows that a person intends to engage, is engaging or has engaged in criminal or fraudulent conduct relating to the proceeding shall take reasonable remedial measures, including, if necessary, disclosure to the tribunal." How does a lawyer "know" such things? Is reasonable suspicion enough? Compare MR 1.0(f) (defining "knows") with MR 1.0(i) & (j) (defining "reasonably believes" and "reasonably should know"); see Restatement § 120, comment *c* ("A lawyer should not conclude that testimony is or will be false unless there is a firm factual basis for doing so. Such a basis exists when facts known to the lawyer or the client's own statements indicate to the lawyer that the testimony or other evidence is false."); *Commonwealth v. Mitchell*, 438 Mass. 535, 781 N.E.2d 1237 (2003) (counsel must have a "firm basis in objective fact" that the client is going to commit perjury in order to invoke the rules on client perjury; proved here because the defendant had admitted to the lawyer he had committed the murders, but planned to deny it on the stand); *State v. McDowell*, 272 Wis.2d 488, 681 N.W.2d 500 (2004) ("Absent the most extraordinary circumstances, the knowledge requirement is satisfied only by the client's express admission of intent to testify untruthfully.")

3. How did the lawyer in *DePallo* know that his client was going to commit perjury on the stand before he did it? Is it possible that the client was lying earlier when he admitted involvement in the murder, and was now telling the truth?

4. *Reasonable remedial measures.* What should a lawyer do when faced with a client or a friendly witness who intends to offer false evidence? Both the comments to Model Rule 3.3 and to Restatement § 120 go into excruciating detail. First, with an important exception for criminal defendants, discussed more fully in Note 5 below, a lawyer can simply refuse to put on testimony or evidence he reasonably believes is false, even if he does not know it to be false. So if a friendly witness or a client in a civil case appears to be ready to lie, the lawyer can and should simply refuse to call them as witnesses. See MR 3.3, comment [9]; Restatement § 120, comment *i*. Any client who intends to lie on the stand should be counseled by the lawyer not to do so. MR 3.3, comment [6]; Restatement § 120, comment *g*. If the client promises not to lie but gets on the stand and does it anyway, then what? First, the lawyer should call a recess and try to persuade the client to recant. MR 3.3, comment [10]; Restatement § 120, comment *h*. If this does not work, the lawyer must take further remedial measures. The lawyer may seek to withdraw, if the court permits and withdrawal will remove the effect of the false testimony. *Id*. But where this act will not remove the effect of the false testimony (as it often will not), the lawyer must reveal the client's perjury to the tribunal or the opposing party. *Id*. The lawyer's revelation will, of course, have serious ramifications for the client. But as the Restatement puts it, "preservation of the integrity of the forum is a superior interest." Restatement § 120, comment *b*.

5. *Reasonable remedial measures: Criminal defendants.* Things are more complicated when the client intending to lie is a criminal defen-

dant, although the bottom line is the same. The client makes the decision whether or not to testify, and has a constitutional right to offer self-defense evidence. *Rock v. Arkansas*, 483 U.S. 44, 107 S.Ct. 2704, 97 L.Ed.2d 37 (1987); see also Restatement 120, comment *i*. Thus while a lawyer should still try to convince the client not to lie, the lawyer's arsenal of threats is not the same as in a civil case. Further, withdrawal from representation may not be a viable option in a criminal case, since courts often do not allow withdrawal in mid-trial. *Id.* Most jurisdictions agree, however, that even in the criminal context, if a client takes the stand and lies, the lawyer has a duty to inform the tribunal or the adversary of the false testimony. *Id.*; MR 3.3 comment [12]. The leading case on this issue, *Nix v. Whiteside*, 475 U.S. 157, 106 S.Ct. 988, 89 L.Ed.2d 123 (1986), held that a client's Sixth Amendment rights were not violated by his lawyer's threat to reveal his perjury to the court, implicitly recognizing such revelation as a proper course of action. Judges must take care not to assume the criminal defendant is going to lie just because he cannot produce corroborating witnesses. See, e.g., *United States v. Midgett*, 342 F.3d 321 (4th Cir. 2003) (vacating conviction where judge took defense counsel's request to withdraw as proof positive that defendant intended to lie, then advised defendant that he could either testify on his own behalf or have a lawyer, but not both).

6. *Reasonable remedial measures: The narrative solution.* Some jurisdictions do not require (or may not allow) a lawyer to reveal a criminal client's perjury, and instead authorize the lawyer to allow the client to testify in a "narrative" fashion. When the narrative is employed, the lawyer "asks only a general question about the events, provides no guidance through additional questions, and does not refer to the false evidence in subsequent argument." Restatement § 120, comment *i*. Jurisdictions that allow this include New York and California. See *DePallo*, *supra*, and *People v. Guzman*, 45 Cal.3d 915, 755 P.2d 917, 248 Cal.Rptr. 467 (1988). Is the narrative solution a good one? Should a lawyer who allows the client to testify in a narrative fashion inform the court or the adversary if the narrative itself is false? If the lawyer does not do so, does this solution strike a good balance between the client's right to testify and the lawyer's duties to the court?

7. *Notice to the client.* What if a lawyer begins his examination of his client in the normal fashion, then, upon hearing testimony he believes to be false, shifts to narrative questioning? Is this deficient performance under *Strickland*? See *Wisconsin v. McDowell*, 272 Wis.2d 488, 681 N.W.2d 500 (2004).

8. *Settings for the narrative solution.* Should the narrative solution be available only for a *jury* trial? How would you balance the interests involved in reaching your conclusion? See *People v. Andrades*, 4 N.Y.S.3d 355, 795 N.Y.S.2d 497, 828 N.E.2d 599 (2005).

9. *Duties of prosecutors.* Prosecutors have an especially weighty responsibility to avoid presenting false testimony or evidence at trial. A prosecutor has a duty to correct false evidence whenever it appears. A

defendant's conviction will be reversed if the prosecutor presents false evidence and there is a reasonable likelihood that the evidence could have affected the jury's verdict. See *Morris v. Ylst*, 447 F.3d 735 (9th Cir. 2006).

10. *Lying in depositions.* The rules prohibiting putting on false evidence also apply to testimony given in depositions. A lawyer is more likely to be allowed to withdraw from the representation if a client insists on lying in a deposition, since the trial has not started. This may give the lawyer more leverage with the client during counseling to tell the truth. A lawyer who allows a client to lie in a deposition and fails to take remedial measures may be subject to severe disciplinary sanctions. See, e.g., *In re Corizzi*, 803 A.2d 438 (D.C.2002) (disbarment for lawyer who directed clients to lie in depositions).

§ 4. CIVIL CLAIMS BY ADVERSARIES

SHELDON APPEL CO. v. ALBERT & OLIKER

Supreme Court of California, 1989.
47 Cal.3d 863, 765 P.2d 498, 254 Cal.Rptr. 336.

ARGUELLES, Justice.

Albert & Oliker (A & O), a law firm, appeals from a judgment entered against it in a malicious prosecution action. . . .

I

[Three of A & O's clients (collectively CKM) collectively agreed to sell an apartment building to Sheldon Appel Co. Sheldon Appel's stated plan was to convert the building to condominium units and sell the units individually. The agreement was that CKM would receive cash, plus a percentage of the gross sales receipts attributable to the sale of the condos. Shortly after the close of escrow, CKM learned that Sheldon Appel was offering to sell the building for a lump sum, which would result in a quick profit for Sheldon Appel, but far less money flowing to CKM. CKM consulted A & O, and a complaint was filed against Sheldon Appel, seeking a declaration of rights and the imposition of an equitable lien on the property. A & O also recorded a notice of lis pendens on the property on CKM's behalf.]

[About six weeks later, Sheldon Appel's motion to expunge the notice of lis pendens was granted. Eventually, all of the causes of action in CKM's lawsuit were terminated in favor of Sheldon Appel. Meanwhile, Sheldon Appel abandoned its bulk sale plan and began to sell individual condominium units. When Sheldon Appel failed to pay monies to CKM, A & O filed a new action on CKM's behalf seeking damages for breach of contract. Sheldon Appel responded by filing a cross-complaint against CKM and A & O for malicious prosecution, alleging that both had "knowingly asserted an untenable lien claim and recorded an impermissible lis pendens to force it to sell individual units."]

[The trial court severed the breach of contract action from the malicious prosecution claim. The contract claim proceeded to trial first and CKM won, obtaining a judgment of $720,000. The malicious prosecution claim then went to trial. The jury awarded Sheldon Appel $82,000 in compensatory damages and $1 million in punitive damages. A & O appealed, and a divided Court of Appeal affirmed the compensatory damages award.]

II

The common law tort of malicious prosecution originated as a remedy for an individual who had been subjected to a maliciously instituted criminal charge, but in California, as in most common law jurisdictions, the tort was long ago extended to afford a remedy for the malicious prosecution of a civil action. Under the governing authorities, in order to establish a cause of action for malicious prosecution of either a criminal or civil proceeding, a plaintiff must demonstrate "that the prior action (1) was commenced by or at the direction of the defendant and was pursued to a legal termination in his, plaintiff's, favor; (2) was brought without probable cause; and (3) was initiated with malice." (*Bertero v. National General Corp.* (1974) 13 Cal.3d 43, 50, 118 Cal.Rptr. 184, 529 P.2d 608; Rest.2d Torts, §§ 653–681B.) . . .

Although the malicious prosecution tort has ancient roots, courts have long recognized that the tort has the potential to impose an undue "chilling effect" on the ordinary citizen's willingness to report criminal conduct or to bring a civil dispute to court, and, as a consequence, the tort has traditionally been regarded as a disfavored cause of action. (See, e.g., *Babb v. Superior Court* (1971) 3 Cal.3d 841, 847, 92 Cal.Rptr. 179, 479 P.2d 379; cf. *Jaffe v. Stone* (1941) 18 Cal.2d 146, 159–160, 114 P.2d 335.)[5] In a number of other states, the disfavored status of the tort is reflected in a requirement that a plaintiff demonstrate some "special injury" beyond that ordinarily incurred in defending a lawsuit in order to prevail in a malicious prosecution action. (See *O'Toole v. Franklin* (1977) 279 Or. 513, 569 P.2d 561, 564, fn. 3 [listing 17 states adhering to special-injury rule]; *Friedman*

5. The disfavored status of the tort originated in the context of malicious prosecution actions brought by individuals who had been charged with a criminal offense, and stemmed from the important public policy of encouraging the reporting of suspected crimes by ordinary citizens. (See *Bertero v. National General Corp.,* supra, 13 Cal.3d 43, 53, 118 Cal.Rptr. 184, 529 P.2d 608.) Although that particular concern is not implicated when the focus of the malicious prosecution action is a prior civil suit, it is similarly important "that an individual be free to protect personal rights by resort to the courts without the threat of a countersuit for damages in the event the suit is unsuccessful" (Harper et. al., The Law of Torts (2d ed. 1986) § 4.2, p. 408), and courts have generally been sensitive to the need to carefully limit tort liability in the context of malicious prosecution of a civil proceeding, as well as when the focus of the action is a prior criminal charge.

v. Dozorc (1981) 412 Mich. 1, 312 N.W.2d 585, 596 [applying special-injury rule].) Even in jurisdictions, like California, which do not impose a special-injury requirement, the elements of the tort have historically been carefully circumscribed so that litigants with potentially valid claims will not be deterred from bringing their claims to court by the prospect of a subsequent malicious prosecution claim.

In recent years, however, the large volume of litigation filed in American courts has become a matter of increasing concern, and in some quarters it has been suggested that a reassessment of the traditional "disfavored" status of the malicious prosecution tort, and a relaxation of some of the traditional elements of the tort, may be in order.

A number of legal commentators have examined the merits of permitting more liberal use of malicious prosecution actions against litigants and their attorneys as a means of combating groundless litigation. Most of the academic commentators have concluded that expansion of the malicious prosecution tort is not a promising remedy for the problem. The courts of several other states have recently addressed this same question and, in thoughtful opinions, have rejected attempts to broaden the application of the tort, refusing to extend the scope of malicious prosecution liability.

After reviewing the competing policy considerations, we agree with those decisions and commentaries which have concluded that the most promising remedy for excessive litigation does not lie in an expansion of malicious prosecution liability. As the Supreme Court of Michigan has recently noted, "In seeking a remedy for the excessive litigiousness of our society, we would do well to cast off the limitations of a perspective which ascribes curative power only to lawsuits." (*Friedman v. Dozorc,* supra, 312 N.W.2d at p. 600.) While the filing of frivolous lawsuits is certainly improper and cannot in any way be condoned, in our view the better means of addressing the problem of unjustified litigation is through the adoption of measures facilitating the speedy resolution of the initial lawsuit and authorizing the imposition of sanctions for frivolous or delaying conduct within that first action itself, rather than through an expansion of the opportunities for initiating one or more additional rounds of malicious prosecution litigation after the first action has been concluded. In recent years, the Legislature has taken several steps in this direction, enacting legislation to facilitate the early weeding out of patently meritless claims and to permit the imposition of sanctions in the initial lawsuit— against both litigants and attorneys—for frivolous or delaying conduct. (See, e.g., Code Civ.Proc., §§ 437c, 1038, 128.5, 409.3.) Because these avenues appear to provide the most promising remedies for the general problem of frivolous litigation, we do not believe it advisable to abandon or relax the traditional limitations on malicious prosecution recovery. This general perspective informs our analysis of the more specific questions presented by this case, to which we now turn. . . .

III

A. *Role of Court and Jury in the Probable Cause Determination*

A & O's initial and broadest contention is that the trial court committed a fundamental error in effectively leaving the determination of the probable cause issue to the jury rather than resolving that question itself. We conclude that the objection is well taken.

As noted above, in a malicious prosecution action, the plaintiff, in addition to establishing that the prior action was terminated in its favor, must prove both (1) that the prior action was brought without probable cause and (2) that the action was initiated with malice.

The "malice" element of the malicious prosecution tort relates to the subjective intent or purpose with which the defendant acted in initiating the prior action, and past cases establish that the defendant's motivation is a question of fact to be determined by the jury. By contrast, the existence or absence of probable cause has traditionally been viewed as a question of law to be determined by the court, rather than a question of fact for the jury. . . .

An important policy consideration underlies the common law rule allocating to the court the task of determining whether the prior action was brought with probable cause. The question whether, on a given set of facts, there was probable cause to institute an action requires a sensitive evaluation of legal principles and precedents, a task generally beyond the ken of lay jurors, and courts have recognized that there is a significant danger that jurors may not sufficiently appreciate the distinction between a merely unsuccessful and a legally untenable claim. To avoid improperly deterring individuals from resorting to the courts for the resolution of disputes, the common law affords litigants the assurance that tort liability will not be imposed for filing a lawsuit unless *a court* subsequently determines that the institution of the action was without probable cause. If the court determines that there was probable cause to institute the prior action, the malicious prosecution action fails, whether or not there is evidence that the prior suit was maliciously motivated. . . .

B. *Objective or Subjective Nature of Probable Cause Element*

. . . [T]he "probable cause" element in the malicious prosecution tort plays a role quite distinct from the separate "malice" element of the tort. Whereas the malice element is directly concerned with the *subjective* mental state of the defendant in instituting the prior action, the probable cause element calls on the trial court to make an objective determination of the "reasonableness" of the defendant's conduct, i.e., to determine whether, on the basis of the facts known to the defendant, the institution of the prior action was legally tenable. The resolution of that question of law calls for the application of an *objective* standard to the facts on which the defendant acted. (See generally Dobbs, *Belief and Doubt in Malicious Prosecution and Libel* (1979) 21 Ariz. L.Rev. 607.) Because the malicious prosecution tort is intended to protect an individual's interest "in freedom from unjustifiable and unreasonable litigation" (see 1 Harper et al., The Law of Torts, supra, § 4.2, p. 407), if the trial court determines that the prior action was objectively reasonable, the plaintiff has failed to meet the threshold requirement of demonstrating an absence of probable cause and the defendant is entitled to prevail. . . .

The importance of the distinction between the defendant's knowledge of facts and his subjective assessment of tenability was made clear by Chief Justice Taft of the United States Supreme Court in explaining the nature of the probable cause element of the analogous tort of wrongful arrest: "The want of probable cause . . . is measured by the state of the defendant's *knowledge*, not by his *intent*. It means the absence of probable cause known to the defendant when he instituted the suit. But the standard applied to defendant's consciousness is external to it. The question is not whether *he* thought the facts to constitute probable cause, but whether *the court* thinks they did." (*Director General v. Kastenbaum* (1923) 263 U.S. 25, 27–28, 44 S.Ct. 52, 53, 68 L.Ed. 146 emphasis added.)

When there is a dispute as to the state of the defendant's knowledge and the existence of probable cause turns on resolution of that dispute, *Franzen* [*v. Shenk* (1923)], 192 Cal. 572, 221 P. 932, and similar cases hold that the jury must resolve the threshold question of the defendant's factual knowledge or belief. Thus, when, as in *Franzen,* there is evidence that the defendant may have known that the factual allegations on which his action depended were untrue, the jury must determine what facts the defendant knew before the trial court can determine the legal question whether such facts constituted probable cause to institute the challenged proceeding. As Chief Justice Taft's explanation of the probable cause element indicates, however, the jury's factual inquiry into the defendant's belief or knowledge is not properly an inquiry into "whether [the defendant] thought the facts to constitute probable cause"; when the state of the defendant's factual knowledge is resolved or undisputed, it is the court which decides whether such facts constitute probable cause or not.

Accordingly, when, as in this case, the facts known by the attorney are not in dispute, the probable cause issue is properly determined by the trial court under an objective standard; it does not include a determination whether the attorney subjectively believed that the prior claim was legally tenable.

Lest there be any confusion, however, we strongly emphasize that our conclusion in this regard does not by any means suggest that an attorney who institutes an action which he does not believe is legally tenable is free from the risk of liability for malicious prosecution. If the trial court concludes that the prior action was not objectively tenable, evidence that the defendant attorney did not subjectively believe that the action was tenable would clearly be relevant to the question of malice. Inasmuch as an attorney who does not have a good faith belief in the tenability of an action will normally assume that a court is likely to come to the same conclusion, the malicious prosecution tort will continue to deter attorneys from filing actions which they do not believe are legally tenable. . . .

C. *Irrelevance of Attorney Research to Probable Cause*

[California case law suggests that] a malicious prosecution plaintiff may establish a lack of probable cause simply by showing that its former adversary's attorney failed to perform reasonable legal research or factual investigation before filing a claim on his client's behalf. In the present case, the lower courts apparently relied on these precedents to conclude that because there was a dispute in the evidence as to the extent and adequacy of the legal research conducted by A & O prior to the filing of the earlier action, there was a crucial factual issue to be submitted to the jury on the probable cause element.

[This reasoning] is not only fundamentally incompatible with the objective nature of the probable cause determination, but it is also at odds with a consistent line of California decisions which have made clear that an attorney's duty of care runs primarily to his own client rather than to the client's adversary, and which— on the basis of important policy considerations—have precluded the adversary from maintaining a negligence cause of action against its opponent's attorney. (See, e.g., *Goodman v. Kennedy* (1976) 18 Cal.3d 335, 344, 134 Cal.Rptr. 375, 556 P.2d 737; *Norton v. Hines,* supra, 49 Cal.App.3d 917, 923, 123 Cal.Rptr. 237.) Allowing inadequate research to serve as an independent basis for proving the absence of probable cause on the part of an attorney would tend to create a conflict of interest between the attorney and client, tempting a cautious attorney to create a record of diligence by performing extensive legal research, not for the benefit of his client, but simply to protect himself from his client's adversaries in the event the initial suit fails. . . .

[I]f the trial court concludes that, on the basis of the facts known to the defendant, the filing of the prior action was objectively reasonable, the court has necessarily determined that the malicious prosecution plaintiff was not subjected to an unjustified lawsuit. When the court has made such a determination, there is no persuasive reason to allow the plaintiff to go forward with its tort action even if it can show that its adversary's attorney did not perform as thorough an investigation or as complete a legal research job as a reasonable attorney may have conducted. Permitting recovery on such a basis would provide the plaintiff with a windfall; since the prior action was objectively tenable, the plaintiff could properly have been put to the very same burden of defense if its adversary had simply hired more thorough counsel.

Of course, as with the question of the defendant's subjective belief in the tenability of the claim, if the trial court determines that the prior action was not objectively tenable, the extent of a defendant attorney's investigation and research may be relevant to the further question of whether or not the attorney acted with malice. We conclude, however, that the adequacy of an attorney's research is not relevant to the probable cause determination....

IV

As we have explained, the trial court in this case erred in submitting the probable cause issue to the jury, because this element of the malicious prosecution tort is always properly determined by the court.... A number of early cases, discussing the probable cause issue in relation to a claim of a malicious prosecution of a criminal charge, defined probable cause as "a suspicion founded upon circumstances sufficiently strong to warrant a reasonable man in the belief that the charge is true." In the context of an action alleging malicious prosecution of a prior civil suit, however, it has long been recognized that it is not "true charges" but rather legally tenable claims for relief that the law seeks to protect.

In addressing the somewhat related question as to the appropriate standard for determining the frivolousness of an appeal in *In re Marriage of Flaherty* (1982) 31 Cal.3d 637, 183 Cal.Rptr. 508, 646 P.2d 179, we concluded that an appeal could properly be found frivolous only if "any reasonable attorney would agree that the appeal is totally and completely without merit." In arriving at that standard, we reasoned that "any definition [of frivolousness] must be read so as to avoid a serious chilling effect on the assertion of litigants' rights.... Counsel and their clients have a right to present issues that are arguably correct, even if it is extremely unlikely that they will win...."

... Applying the appropriate probable cause standard to the facts of this case, we conclude that ... the lien claim pursued by A & O, although not ultimately successful, was legally tenable and thus that there was probable cause to support both the lien claim and the lis pendens. At the time the lien claim was filed, there was at least one prior California decision which had suggested that a vendor's lien, under Civil Code section 3046, might well be available to protect the interests of a seller of real property under facts somewhat comparable to the circumstances in this case and, in addition, there were a variety of decisions which had recognized the right of a court to impose an equitable lien on property—even in the absence of an express contractual security provision—to effectuate the intent of the parties or to prevent unjust enrichment. (See generally 3 Witkin, Summary of Cal.Law (9th ed. 1987) Security Transactions in Real Property, § 17, p. 530 and cases cited.) Although the trial court in the prior action evidently concluded that the past decisions should not be applied or extended to afford CKM a lien on the property in this case and accordingly expunged the lis pendens, in light of both the existing authorities and the leeway a litigant must be given to argue for an evolution of legal precedents, we conclude that the lien claim interposed by A & O was legally tenable. Accordingly, we conclude that the prior action was not instituted without probable cause.

V

The judgment of the Court of Appeal is reversed, and the case is remanded with directions to order the entry of judgment in favor of A & O on the malicious prosecution claim.

Notes

1. *Malicious prosecution.* As you can see from the case, the tort action for malicious prosecution (sometimes called "wrongful use of civil proceedings") is not a particularly strong remedy for an adversary in litigation to use against a lawyer. See Restatement (Second) of Torts § 674 (describing elements). Why would this be so? What, if anything, would be wrong with giving an adversary an effective, easy-to-prove tort remedy against an opposing lawyer? Does a party aggrieved by frivolous pleadings or vexatious actions have other adequate remedies?

2. *Malicious prosecution: A continuing duty.* In *Zamos v. Stroud*, 32 Cal.4th 958, 87 P.3d 802, 12 Cal.Rptr.3d 54 (2004), the court held that a lawyer may be liable for malicious prosecution for continuing to prosecute a suit he later discovers to lack probable cause. Does this continuing duty conception represent a good policy judgment, or should the court have limited the tort to situations where the case was "initiated with malice," to quote *Sheldon Appel*?

3. *Malicious prosecution: Favorable termination of proceedings.* One element of the malicious prosecution claim is that the proceedings terminated on the merits in the plaintiff's favor. This usually presents no conceptual difficulties. But what if the underlying case ended because of a ruling on the parol evidence rule? Is that "on the merits?" The court in *Casa Herrera, Inc. v. Beydoun*, 32 Cal.4th 336, 83 P.3d 497, 9 Cal.Rptr.3d 97 (2004), held that it was, disapproving an earlier Court of

Appeal decision to the contrary. What about an underlying case that ended with a ruling that the plaintiffs lacked standing? The court in *Hudis v. Crawford*, 125 Cal.App.4th 1586, 24 Cal.Rptr.3d 50 (2005), said that was *not* a favorable termination on the merits. What if a case does not go to a final judgment at all, but rather settles. Can that satisfy the "favorable termination on the merits" requirement? See *Toste Farm Corp. v. Hadbury, Inc.*, 798 A.2d 901 (R.I. 2002) (no).

4. *Reliance on client's information*. What if a lawyer prepares a complaint based on information given by the client, and that information turns out not to be true? If the facts as alleged are believed by the lawyers to be true, and the claims based on those facts are objectively tenable, does the adversary state a claim for malicious prosecution under the standards set forth in *Sheldon Appel*? See *Swat-Fame, Inc. v. Goldstein*, 101 Cal.App.4th 613, 124 Cal.Rptr.2d 556 (2002).

5. *Abuse of process*. Abuse of process is a separate tort in most jurisdictions, but like malicious prosecution, it is also extremely hard to prove. It generally requires three elements: (1) legal process; (2) use of that process in an improper or unauthorized manner; and (3) damages. See, e.g., *Wilson v. Hayes*, 464 N.W.2d 250 (Iowa 1990). The second element is the difficult one, because it requires that the plaintiff prove that the defendant used the legal process primarily for some impermissible or illegal motive. *Id.* As explained in the Restatement of Torts, "The usual case of abuse of process is some form of extortion, using the process to put pressure upon the other to compel him to pay a different debt or to take some other action or refrain from it." Restatement (Second) of Torts § 682, comment *b*.

6. A few states have merged the torts of malicious prosecution and abuse of process into a single new tort with distinct elements. See, e.g., *Yost v. Torok*, 256 Ga. 92, 344 S.E.2d 414 (1986) (new tort of "abusive litigation"); *DeVaney v. Thriftway Marketing Corp.*, 124 N.M. 512, 953 P.2d 277 (1997) (new tort of "malicious abuse of process"). Such new torts typically are no easier to establish than their component-part torts used to be.

7. *Negligence claims by adversaries*. Could a lawyer be sued by an adversary in litigation for negligently causing economic loss because of litigation tactics? Why would courts frown on such a theory? See, e.g., *Clark v. Druckman*, 218 W.Va. 427, 624 S.E.2d 864 (2005); *Garcia v. Rodey, Dickason, Sloan, Akin & Robb, P.A.*, 106 N.M. 757, 750 P.2d 118 (1988).

8. *Claims based on ethics rules violations*. Could an adversary sue a lawyer for damages for violating the ethics rules? Why might this not be allowed? See *Baxt v. Liloia*, 155 N.J. 190, 714 A.2d 271 (1998); *Stanley v. Richmond*, 35 Cal.App.4th 1070, 41 Cal.Rptr.2d 768 (1995).

NOTE: PRIVILEGES AND IMMUNITIES

The absolute privilege to defame. In virtually all states, a lawyer is granted an absolute privilege to utter defamatory statements in connection with judicial proceedings. Restatement § 57(1). This privilege protects the lawyer—along with witnesses and other participants in judicial proceedings and "quasi-judicial" proceedings—not only from suits for defamation, but also from related causes of action based on communicative acts. See, e.g., *Loigman v. Township Committee of Township of Middletown*, 185 N.J. 566, 889 A.2d 426 (2006) (applying privilege to sequestration proceedings before an ALJ in connection with a civil service appeal, barring civil rights claims based on state and federal law); *Rusheen v. Cohen*, 37 Cal.4th 1048, 128 P.3d 713, 39 Cal.Rptr.3d 516 (2006) (privilege bars claim for abuse of process where suit was based on lawyer's act of executing on a default judgment); *Price v. Armour*, 949 P.2d 1251 (Utah 1997) (privilege bars claim for intentional interference with business relations). The privilege protects communications preliminary to a reasonably anticipated proceeding. See Restatement § 57(1)(a); *Messina v. Krakower*, 439 F.3d 755 (D.C. Cir. 2006) (privilege bars claim for defamation based on letter sent to plaintiff and third party before the commencement of a suit). The point of the privilege is usually said to be to safeguard lawyers from subsequent tort suits, which promotes the zealous protection of clients' interests without the fear of having to defend their actions in later civil suits. See *Ingalsbe v. Stewart Agency, Inc.*, 869 So.2d 30 (Fla. App. 2004). Is the litigation privilege too protective of overzealous litigators? *See* Paul T. Hayden, *Reconsidering the Litigator's Absolute Privilege to Defame*, 54 Ohio St. L. J. 985 (1993). Don't lawyers have to foresee other potential proceedings (such as disciplinary actions) if they conduct litigation in a malicious or overzealous manner?

Based on the policies behind the privilege, there are limits to its sweep. It has been held not to apply to bar a suit for fraud, where a lawyer knowingly made misstatements about insurance coverage to an adversary in order to justify an insurance payment of $120,000 when a judgment totaled three times as much. *Shafer v. Berger, Kahn, Shafton, Moss, Figler, Simon & Gladstone*, 107 Cal.App.4th 54, 131 Cal.Rptr.2d 777 (2003) ("The litigation privilege is not a license to deceive an injured party who steps into the shoes of the insured."). And the statement must be made "in connection with" a judicial proceeding. While most courts construe this requirement quite broadly, many are reluctant to extend the privilege to extrajudicial statements by lawyers. See, e.g., *Bochetto v. Gibson*, 580 Pa. 245, 860 A.2d 67 (2004) (lawyer's transmittal of legal malpractice complaint to a freelance reporter not privileged because the act was outside the regular course of judicial proceedings); *Williams v. Kenney*, 379 N.J.Super. 118, 877

A.2d 277 (2005) (lawyer's letter sent to reporter's employer on behalf of lawyer's client was not privileged since it was unconnected to a judicial proceeding and sent to a person with no connection to the proceeding).

Prosecutorial immunity. Government prosecutors are granted an absolute immunity from civil suits, as long as they are acting within the scope of their duties as advocates. *Imbler v. Pachtman*, 424 U.S. 409, 96 S.Ct. 984, 47 L.Ed.2d 128 (1976) (prosecutor immune from civil suit for damages under § 1983 based on initiation and prosecution of criminal case); *Kalina v. Fletcher*, 522 U.S. 118, 118 S.Ct. 502, 139 L.Ed.2d 471 (1997) (same); *Buckley v. Fitzsimmons*, 509 U.S. 259, 113 S.Ct. 2606, 125 L.Ed.2d 209 (1993) ("acts undertaken by a prosecutor preparing for the initiation of judicial proceedings or for trial, and which occur in the course of his role as an advocate for the State, are entitled to the protections of absolute immunity"). This immunity protects prosecutors from claims based on federal or state law. *Shmueli v. City of New York*, 424 F.3d 231 (2d Cir. 2005). A prosecutor retains only a qualified immunity when performing administrative functions, or "investigative functions normally performed by a detective or police officer." *Kalina*, supra; see also, e.g., *Genzler v. Longanbach*, 410 F.3d 630 (9th Cir. 2005) (prosecutor had only qualified immunity while engaged in "police-type investigative work," rather than advocacy function). The qualified immunity protects a defendant from liability unless his conduct violates clearly established statutory or constitutional rights of which a reasonable person would have known. *Harlow v. Fitzgerald*, 457 U.S. 800, 102 S.Ct. 2727, 73 L.Ed.2d 396 (1982). Only when a prosecutor "acts without any colorable claim of authority" does he lose all immunity. *Barr v. Abrams*, 810 F.2d 358 (2d Cir. 1987).

§ 5. HANDLING TANGIBLE EVIDENCE

MORRELL v. STATE

Supreme Court of Alaska, 1978.
575 P.2d 1200.

RABINOWITZ, Justice.

Clayton Morrell brings this appeal from his conviction, after trial by jury, on one count of kidnapping, a single count of assault with intent to commit rape, and eight counts of forcible rape....

Morrell ... contends that the superior court's decision to admit Exhibit XXX (the kidnapping plan) deprived him of a fair trial because the exhibit was obtained in a manner which infringed upon his right to effective assistance of counsel. After Morrell's arrest, Stephen Cline of the Public Defender Agency was appointed to represent Morrell. About a month after his appointment, on

June 21, 1975, Cline received a telephone call from John Wagner, a friend of Morrell's who had been living in Morrell's home with Morrell's consent while Morrell awaited trial. At Morrell's suggestion, Wagner had cleaned out one of Morrell's vehicles and had found a legal pad on which had been written what appeared to be a kidnapping plan. Wagner asked Cline to come to the Morrell residence to see what he had found, and Cline did so.

Wagner asked Cline to take possession of the legal pad, which Cline also did. Shortly thereafter, Cline showed the papers to Morrell, who explained that he had sketched the plan in response to a television report of an earlier kidnapping in Fairbanks. A man named McCracken, who looked somewhat like Morrell and who drove a truck nearly identical to the one driven by Morrell, had been charged with the earlier kidnapping by the time Morrell was arrested. McCracken was also represented by the Public Defender Agency.

Cline, who was unsure what to do with the papers, contacted both the Alaska Bar Association and the American Bar Association for advice. The Ethics Committee of the Alaska Bar Association gave Cline an advisory opinion on the matter.

The opinion advised Cline to return the papers to Wagner, to explain to Wagner the law on concealment of evidence, and to withdraw from the case if it later became obvious to Cline that a violation of ethical rules would result. Cline testified that he decided to return the legal pad to Wagner and to withdraw from the case at approximately the same time. However, he was not able to reach Wagner until a few days after July 31, when he was relieved by the court of his obligation to defend Morrell.

Cline testified that when he called to tell Wagner that he intended to return the pad, Wagner at first indicated that he did not want to take it back. Cline said that he helped Wagner arrange the transfer to the police because he wanted Wagner to be able to return to his pipeline job without delay but that he assisted with the transfer only after it became clear that Wagner intended to turn the evidence over to the police. Cline stated that following his conversation with Wagner, he called the police. After ascertaining that Wagner had already requested police officers to come to his home to pick up some evidence, Cline requested that the dispatcher send one of the investigators assigned to the Morrell case. Cline was told that this would not be possible.

Wagner, on the other hand, testified that it had been Cline's idea to contact the police and that Cline had made the contact with the police to arrange the transfer. Both Cline and Wagner testified that Wagner had received the papers from Cline before turning them over to the troopers. Both men were at the Morrell home when the troopers arrived. The legal pad was resting on the hood of one of Morrell's vehicles, and Wagner initialed the pad before giving it to the troopers indicating that it was he who was relinquishing custody of the papers to the troopers.

Cline testified that he had given Wagner a copy of the statute governing concealment of evidence. He apparently would not discuss the meaning or applicability of the statute with Wagner, however. He did testify that he specifically refused to give Wagner advice intended either to encourage or to discourage Wagner from turning the evidence over to the police. After denial of a motion to suppress, the papers and a handwriting analysis which linked Morrell to the papers were introduced in evidence at trial.

Appellant argues that the actions of his former attorney, Stephen Cline, deprived him of his right to effective assistance of counsel. He contends that when Cline obtained knowledge of and possession of the kidnapping plan, he had no affirmative duty to come forward with the evidence nor to assist Wagner in carrying out his decision to turn the evidence over to the police. Morrell further urges that the only way to have cured the denial of his right to counsel would have been to suppress the evidence obtained as a result. He maintains that the superior court's refusal to suppress the kidnapping plan deprived him of a fair trial.

As Morrell notes, authority in this area is surprisingly sparse. The existing authority seems to indicate, however, that a criminal defense attorney has an obligation to turn over to the prosecution physical evidence which comes into his possession, especially where the evidence comes into the attorney's possession through acts of a third party who is neither a client of the attorney nor an agent of a client. After turning over such evidence, an attorney may have either a right or a duty to remain silent as to the circumstances under which he obtained such evidence, but Morrell presents no authority which establishes that a criminal defendant whose attorney chooses to testify regarding to these matters is denied effective assistance of counsel.

Most of the decisions which discuss the situation in question involve bar disciplinary proceedings or contempt proceedings against the attorney for refusing to answer questions or to turn over evidence. In State v. Olwell, 64 Wash.2d 828, 394 P.2d 681 (1964), an order holding an attorney in contempt was reversed. The attorney had refused to comply with a subpoena duces tecum or answer questions at a coroner's inquest concerning a knife owned by a client. The Washington Supreme Court assumed for purposes of its decision that the attorney had obtained the knife in question as a result of a confidential communication with his client. The court stated that if the evidence had been obtained from a third party with whom no attorney-client relationship existed, communications concerning the knife would not be privileged.

The court in Olwell held that incriminating objects delivered to a criminal defense attorney by his client may be withheld by the attorney for a reasonable time to help the attorney prepare his case, and then they must be given to the prosecution. In addition, the court held that in order to protect the attorney-client relationship, the prosecution must not reveal the source of such evidence in the presence of the jury when it is introduced at trial. In discussing the scope of this limited privilege, the court stated that to be protected as a privileged communication at all, the objects obtained by the attorney must have been delivered to the attorney by the client or have been acquired as a direct result of information communicated by the client and not merely have been obtained by the attorney while acting in that capacity for the client. In short, the Olwell rule requires a criminal defense attorney to turn over to the prosecution physical evidence that the attorney obtains from his client. This rule requires the defense attorney to avoid giving to investigating or prosecuting authorities any information concerning the source of the evidence or the manner in which it was obtained. [Citing Anderson v. State, 297 So.2d 871 (Fla.App.1974) and Dyas v. State, 539 S.W.2d 251 (Ark.1976).] Finally, if the evidence is obtained from a non-client third party who is not acting as the client's agent, even the privilege to refuse to testify concerning the manner in which the evidence was obtained is inapplicable.

In People v. Lee, 3 Cal.App.3d 514, 83 Cal.Rptr. 715 (1970), a district attorney obtained a search warrant for a pair of bloodstained shoes held by a judge pursuant to an agreement between the district attorney and the public defender. The judge and the two attorneys had agreed that the judge would hold the shoes pending a judicial determination of the proper disposition of the shoes. The public defender later testified at his client's trial that he had received the shoes from his client's wife and that he had delivered the shoes to the judge.

In both the Lee case and the case at bar a criminal defendant sought suppression of evidence delivered by his attorney to the authorities. The attorney obtained the evidence not from his client, but from a person with whom his client had a close personal relationship. Further, the attorney testified at the defendant's trial concerning the circumstances under which he obtained the evidence.

The court in Lee held that the attorney-client privilege does not give an attorney the right to withhold evidence. The court stated that it would be an abuse of a lawyer's duty of professional responsibility to knowingly take possession of and secrete instrumentalities of a crime. (The shoes were an instrumentality because the defendant had allegedly kicked the victim in the head.) In dicta, the court noted that although a client's delivery of evidence to the attorney may be privileged, the object itself does not become privileged. Thus, the California court held that seizure of the shoes by warrant was proper and that the objection to introduction of the shoes as evidence was properly overruled.

Further, the Lee court held that the attorney-client privilege did not cover the trial testimony of the attorney concerning the circumstances under which he obtained the shoes because he received the shoes from his client's wife rather than from his client. . . .

Also of significance is In re Ryder, 263 F.Supp. 360 (E.D.Va. 1967), aff'd 381 F.2d 713 (4th Cir.1967). Ryder involved a proceeding to determine whether an attorney should be suspended or disbarred. The attorney had taken possession from his client of stolen money and a sawed-off shotgun, knowing that the money was stolen and that the gun had been used in an armed robbery. The attorney intended to retain the property until after his client's trial and then to return the money to its rightful owner.

The client in Ryder had put the money and the gun in his safe deposit box. The attorney, knowing that the money in the box was marked and disbelieving his client's story about how the client had acquired the money, went to the bank to transfer the money to his own safe deposit box. Upon opening the client's box, the attorney discovered the shotgun and transferred both the money and the gun to his own box. The court stated in dicta that the attorney's state of mind when he transferred the evidence demonstrated sufficient knowledge to fall within the statute prohibiting knowing concealment of stolen property.

The court in Ryder suspended the attorney, holding that his actions did not fall within the protection of the attorney-client privilege. . . .

From the foregoing cases emerges the rule that a criminal defense attorney must turn over to the prosecution real evidence that the attorney obtains from his client. Further, if the evidence is obtained from a non-client third party who is not acting for the client, then the privilege to refuse to testify concerning the manner in which the evidence was obtained is inapplicable. We think the foregoing rules are sound, and we apply them in reaching our resolution of the effective assistance-of-counsel issue in the case at bar.

. . . [T]he cases disciplining attorneys for failing to turn over evidence or upholding denials of motions to suppress evidence turned over by attorneys do not rest alone on the notion that an attorney who does not turn over such evidence may be guilty of a crime. The cases cited are also based on the proposition that it would constitute unethical conduct for an attorney an officer of the court to knowingly fail to reveal relevant evidence in a criminal case.

We believe that Cline would have been obligated to see that the evidence reached the prosecutor in this case even if he had obtained the evidence from Morrell. His obligation was even clearer because he acquired the evidence from Wagner, who made the decision to turn the evidence over to Cline without consulting Morrell and therefore was not acting as Morrell's agent.

Since Cline was obligated to see that the evidence reached the prosecutor, Morrell cannot have been deprived of effective assistance of counsel by Cline's decision to return the evidence to Wagner. Further, Cline's efforts to aid Wagner's transfer of the evidence to the police appear to have been within the scope of Cline's obligation. Cline could have properly turned the evidence over to the police himself and would have been obliged to do so if Wagner had refused to accept the return of the evidence.[17]

One additional aspect of this issue remains for discussion. As was noted earlier, the Ethics Committee of the Alaska Bar Association gave Cline an advisory opinion as to what to do with the questioned legal pad. The opinion advised Cline to return the subject papers to Wagner, to explain to Wagner the law on concealment of evidence,[18] and to withdraw from the case if it later became obvious to Cline that a violation of ethical rules would result from his continued representation of Morrell. On June 6, 1977, the Board of Governors of the Alaska Bar Association adopted Ethics Opinion 76–7 which embodied the advice the Ethics Committee had earlier given Cline. The opinion also stated, however, that Cline would be ethically obligated not to reveal the existence of the physical evidence "unless required to do so by statute." The Bar Association declined to render an opinion as to the applicability of AS 11.30.315 or other state law.

We think Cline followed the advice of the Bar Association in relation to his dealings with Wagner. It also appears to us that Cline could have reasonably concluded that AS 11.30.315 required him to reveal the existence of the physical evidence; and thus, although he affirmatively involved himself in the revelation of the

---

17. The only remaining question is whether Cline's testimony concerning the Wagner incident was within the attorney-client privilege and, if it was, whether the testimony deprived Morrell of his rights to effective assistance of counsel and to a fair trial. While the Olwell rule might have imposed a duty on Cline to remain silent as to these matters if Cline had obtained the evidence from Morrell, the acquisition of incriminating evidence from a non-client third party who is not acting as a client's agent falls outside the attorney-client privilege. Cline could not have claimed that the attorney-client privilege precluded him from testifying as to his acquisition of the evidence from Wagner. Therefore, Morrell

cannot have been deprived of effective assistance of counsel by Cline's testimony.

18. AS 11.30.315 provides:

Destroying, altering or concealing evidence. A person who wilfully destroys, alters or conceals evidence concerning the commission of a crime or evidence which is being sought for production during an investigation, inquiry or trial, with the intent to prevent the evidence from being discovered or produced, is guilty of a misdemeanor and upon conviction is punishable by imprisonment for not more than one year, or by a fine of not more than $1,000, or by both.

evidence's existence, he did follow the advice of the Bar Association as it dealt with his obligation to preserve his client's secrets.

Assuming Ethics Opinion 76–7 is a correct statement of the law, whether Cline rendered effective counsel then turns on whether he could reasonably have concluded that AS 11.30.315 required him to reveal the existence of the evidence. Otherwise, the opinion states that he had an ethical obligation not to reveal the evidence. AS 11.30.315 makes it a crime to wilfully destroy, alter or conceal evidence concerning the commission of a crime or evidence which is being sought for production during an investigation, inquiry or trial, with the intent to prevent the evidence from being discovered or produced. While statutes which address the concealing of evidence are generally construed to require an affirmative act of concealment in addition to the failure to disclose information to the authorities, taking possession of evidence from a non-client third party and holding the evidence in a place not accessible to investigating authorities would seem to fall within the statute's ambit. Thus, we have concluded that Cline breached no ethical obligation to his client which may have rendered his legal services to Morrell ineffective. . . . *Affirmed.*

Notes

1. *Ethics rules.* Model Rule 3.4(a) prohibits unlawfully obstructing another's access to evidence or unlawfully altering, destroying or concealing any document or other material having potential evidentiary value. The rule also prohibits a lawyer from counseling another to do any of these things. California's Rule 5–220 prohibits a lawyer from suppressing "any evidence" that the lawyer "has a legal obligation to reveal or to produce." New York's DR 7–102(a)(3) [22 NYCRR 1200.33] forbids a lawyer to "conceal or knowingly fail to disclose that which the lawyer is required by law to reveal." On their face, these rules incorporate by reference other laws of more specific applicability. As *Morrell* suggests, most states do have laws forbidding altering, destroying or concealing evidence. See Restatement §§ 118–120.

2. *Criminal defense counsel's duty to turn over evidence.* A comment to Model Rule 3.4 states that "Applicable law may permit a lawyer to take temporary possession of physical evidence of client crimes for the purpose of conducting a limited examination that will not alter or destroy material characteristics. In such a case, applicable law may require the lawyer to turn the evidence over to the police or other prosecuting authority. . . . " MR 3.4, comment [2]. *Morrell* and the cases it cites (including *Olwell, Lee* and *Ryder*) are among the leading cases. The Restatement, citing the same cases and other "scattered decisions," provides that a lawyer may take possession of physical evidence of a client crime for a time reasonably necessary to examine it, but after that "must notify prosecuting authorities of the lawyer's possession of the evidence or turn the evidence over to them." Restatement § 119. A

comment cautions that if a lawyer takes possession of contraband or other evidence of client crime for any other purpose, the lawyer may be subjected to the risk of prosecution as an accessory after the fact. *Id.*, comment *b*.

3.   In *Commonwealth v. Stenhach*, 356 Pa.Super. 5, 514 A.2d 114 (1986), two young public defenders were appointed to represent a defendant in a murder trial. The client told them to recover a rifle stock used in the murder, and the lawyers complied. The lawyers did not turn the rifle stock over to prosecutors until ordered to do so by the court during the trial. After the client's conviction, the two lawyers were indicted under Pennsylvania statutes for hindering prosecution, tampering with evidence, conspiracy, and criminal solicitation. A jury convicted both of them on numerous counts. On appeal, the court held that their retention of the rifle stock was not proper, but reversed their convictions because the statutes were overbroad as applied to criminal defense lawyers.

4.   *Stolen goods.* If a lawyer comes into possession of goods that have been stolen by the client from another person, can the lawyer simply give the goods back to the victim? The Restatement, citing numerous cases, says yes. See Restatement § 45, comment *f*. The comment notes that if a lawyer knowingly retains stolen property, he is "helping the thief conceal them from their proper owner, which is a crime," and that if the lawyer returns such goods to the client-thief, "[t]he same would be true." *Id.* If the lawyer does return the goods, he need not name the thief, although a court might require disclosure. *Id.*

5.   *Information about the location of evidence.* What if a client tells the lawyer where evidence of a crime is located, but does not himself bring it to the lawyer? Can the lawyer go look at it? Bring it in and examine it? Must the lawyer inform the authorities after doing either? There are not many cases, but they tend to be both dramatic and famous. In *People v. Belge*, 83 Misc.2d 186, 372 N.Y.S.2d 798 (Co.Ct. 1975), *aff'd*, 41 N.Y.2d 60, 359 N.E.2d 377, 390 N.Y.S.2d 867 (1976), the client, during discussion of an insanity defense in a murder case, admitted to having murdered three other people and gave the lawyers information about where to find one of the bodies. Using this information, lawyer Belge found the body, inspected it, and ascertained that it was indeed the person his client had told him about. The lawyer did not disclose the location of the body to anyone until it was revealed during the trial (for the other murder) to establish the insanity defense. Lawyer Belge was then indicted for violating sections of the state Public Health Law requiring that dead bodies be buried properly and that people with knowledge of the death of a person must report it to authorities. The court dismissed the indictment, holding that the information about the location of the bodies was privileged. Thus indicting the lawyer for failure to disclose the information was not proper.

In *People v. Meredith*, 29 Cal.3d 682, 631 P.2d 46, 175 Cal.Rptr. 612 (1981), the client, on trial for murder, told his lawyer that he had burned the victim's wallet and put it in a trash can. That communication, the court said, was privileged. But the lawyer sent an investigator to get the wallet, and the investigator brought the wallet back to the lawyer's office. (The lawyer later turned the wallet over to the prosecutor.) The court held that once the lawyer has possession of such evidence, having removed it from its original location, the statutory privilege "does not bar revelation of the original location or condition of the evidence in question." Thus the trial court's decision to admit the investigator's testimony about where he found the wallet, over an objection of privilege, was not error. The court noted with approval that the trial court did not require the investigator to disclose that he was working for the defense lawyer when he found the wallet. The clear suggestion in the case: defense lawyers should leave evidence where they find it.

6. *Convincing the client to reveal criminal evidence.* Is it proper for a lawyer to convince a client to reveal criminal evidence? In *Wemark v. State*, 602 N.W.2d 810 (Iowa 1999), the client told his lawyers where he had hidden the knife he had used to kill his wife. The lawyers convinced the client to tell a medical expert where to find the weapon, in part by telling him that they might have to reveal the fact themselves. After the client was convicted, he claimed that the lawyers had provided ineffective assistance because of their coaxing to reveal the location. Rejecting the appeal, the Iowa Supreme Court opined that the lawyers had a duty *not* to tell the authorities about the location of the weapon, as long as they left it undisturbed. Their decision to talk the client into disclosing it, since that decision was based on an erroneous view of their duty, was not proper. But even if they had disclosed the location themselves, it would not have prejudiced the client since the evidence against him was overwhelming. Thus his *Strickland* claim failed.

7. *Spoliation of evidence.* In a few jurisdictions, destruction of evidence may give rise to a tort claim, called spoliation. See, e.g., *Holmes v. Amerex Rent–A–Car*, 710 A.2d 846 (D.C. 1998). The tort is designed to compensate a plaintiff whose prospective economic advantage—the ability to bring a case and win money—has been damaged by willful or negligent destruction of evidence. See David Bell, et al., *Let's Level the Playing Field*, 29 Ariz. St. L. J. 769 (1997) (reporting that a survey of litigators showed half of them thought that evidence destruction was a "frequent" or "regular" problem). Of course, destroying evidence can lead to other sanctions as well, from criminal prosecution for obstruction of justice to having the court instruct the jury that an inference may be drawn that the absent evidence would be adverse to the spoliator. See, e.g., *West v. Goodyear Tire & Rubber Co.*, 167 F.3d 776 (2d Cir.1999). Most states have rejected an independent tort of spoliation, usually on the ground that it creates "potentially endless litigation over a speculative loss." *Timber Tech Engineered Building Prods. v. Home Ins. Co.*, 118 Nev. 630, 55 P.3d 952 (2002) (collecting cases from many jurisdictions). California adopted the spoliation tort in 1984 only to reverse course over a decade later and hold that no such tort action should be allowed. See *Temple Community Hospital v. Superior Court*, 20 Cal.4th 464, 84 Cal.Rptr.2d 852, 976 P.2d 223 (1999).

8. What if a plaintiff's lawyer negligently destroys evidence and the defendant claims that its ability to defend was prejudiced? Can the defendant sue for spoliation? In *Hewitt v. Allen Canning Co.*, 321 N.J.Super. 178, 728 A.2d 319 (1999), the plaintiff sued the manufacturer, distributor and retailer of a can of spinach that allegedly contained a grasshopper. The plaintiff brought the can to his lawyer's office; when the can began to smell the lawyer had it thrown away. The defendants, learning of the destruction of the evidence, sought leave to file a third-party complaint against the plaintiff's lawyer for spoliation. Held, such a suit cannot be maintained because of the disruption it would cause to the client-lawyer relationship. The lawyer simply did not owe a tort duty to the defendants to preserve evidence. The proper remedy, said the court, was a discovery sanction.

§ 6. LITIGATION COUNSELING AND NEGOTIATION ETHICS

A. Counseling About Dispute Resolution Process Options

A lawyer advising a client must, as we saw in Chapter 4, counsel the client about the "means by which the client's objectives are to be accomplished." MR 1.4(a)(2); see also MR 1.2(a). In a litigated matter, this counseling should include informing the client about any appropriate dispute resolution processes, including alternatives to court adjudication. See MR 2.1, comment [5] ("when a matter is likely to involve litigation, it may be necessary under Rule 1.4 to inform the client of forms of dispute resolution that might constitute reasonable alternatives to litigation").

Most "litigated" matters do not end with a final court judgment. Over nine in ten civil cases end in a settlement, which is simply an agreement reached by the parties after negotiation. *Negotiation* itself, then, can be seen as a form of alternative dispute resolution, or ADR. Indeed, negotiation is by far the most common form of ADR. Most litigators negotiate more than they argue before juries. Negotiation is also the most flexible alternative, although partially constrained by two powerful forces: the other party and the law. A fantastic solution will remain inchoate if the other party cannot be convinced that it is also fantastic (or at least acceptable) from her perspective, also. And the law both constrains some solutions—for example, an agreement between the parties to something illegal under the law, such as housing discrimination, will not be enforceable—and casts a shadow over the negotiating process by influencing what the lawyers believe is viable and desirable in a negotiated agreement. Thus while a negotiated agreement can go beyond a remedy a court could order, competent lawyers will never enter into negotiations without knowing what a court *could* order, and likely *would* order, if the matter went to a judge for a final decision.

If negotiation reaches an impasse, then another method of ADR might be appropriate. ***Mediation*** is a form of facilitated negotiation in which a neutral third party (the mediator) works to help the parties reach a negotiated agreement. The mediator does not—at least in a pure form of mediation—make a decision, although some mediators do offer an evaluation of the merits as part of the process of helping the parties reach an agreement. ***Arbitration***, the other major form of ADR, also involves the use of a neutral third party (the arbitrator, or a panel of arbitrators). Unlike mediation, however, in arbitration the third party actually makes a decision. The arbitrator's goal is not to help the parties reach an agreement, but rather to give the parties a relatively fast decision (compared to a trial) on the merits. Arbitration is usually a binding process (typically because the parties have agreed to be bound), and appeals from an arbitral decision are quite limited.

There are many other forms of ADR, virtually all of which are variations or combinations of the three major forms (negotiation, mediation and arbitration) mentioned above. Since ADR is often consensual (unless, of course, it is mandated by court rule or by contract), the very process of dispute resolution itself can become the subject of a negotiation between disputing parties. Creative litigators can use negotiating skills to place their clients in appropriate processes within which to obtain their expressed goals. This is part and parcel of lawyering as "problem solving." See Carrie Menkel–Meadow, *Toward Another View of Legal Negotiation: The Structure of Problem Solving*, 31 UCLA L. Rev. 754 (1984). In short, lawyers who are knowledgeable about process options are more likely to have genuinely satisfied clients whose goals have been satisfied.

Is every case a candidate for ADR? No. Court adjudication has some advantages that may make it indispensable in some matters, and each form of ADR also has significant disadvantages for particular cases. A party who wants to set a precedent for the benefit of others should prefer court adjudication to any form of ADR, which will not set a precedent. A party who has a very strong case on the law might not want to agree to an arbitration proceeding, in which the arbitrator usually does not have to follow the law and cannot be reversed for making legal errors. See, e.g., *Wilko v. Swan*, 346 U.S. 427, 74 S.Ct. 182, 98 L.Ed. 168 (1953) (legal error is not a ground for vacating an arbitral award under the Federal Arbitration Act, although "manifest disregard" of legal rules might supply a ground for vacating), *overruled on other grounds, Rodriguez de Quijas v. Shearson/American Express*, 490 U.S. 477, 109 S.Ct. 1917, 104 L.Ed.2d 526 (1989); *George Watts & Son, Inc. v. Tiffany & Co.*, 248 F.3d 577 (7th Cir.2001) ("manifest disregard" means the award requires the parties to violate the law). Furthermore, some forms of ADR might not be available at all for one simple reason: most forms require the parties to agree to pursue the process itself. That is, you may think that voluntary mediation would be a great option for your client, but if the adversary does not agree, you are not going to be able to test your theory.

Increasingly, in many jurisdictions, the parties in a litigated matter *must* pursue ADR before going to trial. These forms of "court-annexed" ADR are controversial, but now widespread in many states. Mandatory mediation is a common form of court-annexed ADR. Two federal statutes have rapidly changed the ADR landscape in federal courts. In 1990, Congress passed the Civil Justice Reform Act, which required district courts to consider formal methods "to refer appropriate cases to alternative dispute resolution programs." 28 U.S.C. § 473(a). By mid-decade over half of the federal districts had put ADR procedures, most often court-annexed mediation, in place. The 1998 Alternative Dispute Resolution Act went even further, requiring district courts to offer at least one ADR program and authorizing them to require parties to go into mediation or "early neutral evaluation." 28 U.S.C. § 625.

Given the explosion in ADR in recent years, should state ethics rules specifically *mandate* ADR counseling in litigated matters? The Model Rules' direct suggestion that ADR counseling "may be necessary" is just that: a suggestion, not a mandatory rule. See MR 2.1, comment [5]. A few states have adopted more explicit ethics rules on the topic, but all fall short of mandating ADR counseling. See, e.g., Colo. Rule 2.1 ("In a matter involving or expected to involve litigation, a lawyer should advise the client of alternative forms of dispute resolution which might reasonably be pursued to attempt to resolve the legal dispute or to reach the legal objective sought."); Ga. Rule 3–107, EC 7–5 ("a lawyer has a duty to inform the client of forms of dispute resolution which might constitute reasonable alternatives to litigation"). Look back at Model Rule 1.2 and 1.4. Can those rules be read to *require* ADR counseling in litigated matters in which ADR is a viable option? If you think such a reading is plausible, then does a rule like Colorado's actually *weaken* that duty? See Robert F. Cochran, Jr., *Professional Rules and ADR: Control of Alternative Dispute Resolution under the ABA Ethics 2000 Commission Proposal and Other Professional Responsibility Standards*, 28 Fordham Urb. L. J. 895, 905 (2001).

Lawyers as third-party neutrals. Lawyers often serve as arbitrators or mediators in purely private or court-annexed proceedings. There is nothing improper about this, of course. But where the parties are unrepresented by lawyers, misunderstandings about the lawyer-neutral's role may arise. Especially where such an unrepresented party is unsophisticated, the lawyer-neutral may have to go into some detail about the difference between a lawyer acting as such and a lawyer acting as a neutral facilitator or decisionmaker. See MR 2.4 & comment [3]; see also *Furia v.*

Helm, 111 Cal.App.4th 945, 4 Cal.Rptr.3d 357 (2003) (lawyer-mediator who represents one of the two parties must be careful not to breach duties to either party; court did not address propriety of mediating at all under those circumstances). Lawyers who have a conflict of interest should fully disclose its nature and its ramifications and seek consent before agreeing to mediate a dispute.

B. Counseling Clients About Settlement

Because the vast majority of litigated cases terminate in a negotiated settlement, a litigator must prepare a client early for that eventuality. Inexperienced or ineffectual lawyers make promises that cannot be kept and thereby create dashed expectations, with predictable results on client satisfaction. In the words of a recent ABA report, "Early discussion of the option of pursuing settlement may help the client to develop reasonable expectations and to make better informed decisions about the course of the dispute. These early discussion may also reduce the risk of clients second-guessing their attorneys' strategies if they ultimately settle after paying substantial legal fees." ABA Section of Litigation, *Ethical Guidelines for Settlement Negotiations*, Guideline 3.1.1, Committee Notes at 7–8 (August 2002) ("*ABA Ethical Settlement Guidelines*").

Can a lawyer initiate settlement discussions without consulting the client first? The Restatement opines that "normally a lawyer has authority to initiate or engage in settlement discussions, although not to conclude them." Restatement § 22, comment *c*. The better practice, however, is probably to never initiate settlement negotiations without talking to the client about it first. ABA Ethical Settlement Guidelines, Guideline 3.1.2.

Reaching a settlement. A lawyer cannot finalize a settlement without the client's authorization. Restatement § 22, comment *c*. Of course, a client may give the lawyer settlement authority, including an authorization to settle a case within a set range of dollar amounts. *Id.* If such authorization has been given, the client is bound by any settlement reached within its terms. *Id.* When a lawyer acts without authorization, the settlement might be binding if a third party acts under a reasonable belief that the lawyer has the apparent authority to bind the client. *Id.*, § 27. This occurs when the client has manifested to a third person that the lawyer is empowered to act in the matter. *Id.*, comment *b*. (This is simply a rule of agency, not a special "law of lawyering." *Id.*) If that occurs, however, the client can sue the lawyer for legal malpractice or breach of fiduciary duty, or both, and the lawyer can be disciplined. *Id.*, comment *f*.

Aggregate settlements. Model Rule 1.8(g) provides that a lawyer who represents two or more clients should not enter into an aggregate settlement affecting those clients unless each client gives informed written consent. Informed consent in this context requires that the lawyer disclose "the existence and nature of all the claims or pleas involved and of the participation of each person in the settlement." *Id.* The rule is designed to prevent lawyers from favoring one client over another in settlement negotiations, and from subordinating the interests of one client to the interests of others. See ABA Formal Op. 06–438 (2006).

C. The Ethics of Negotiation

1. *Duties Owed to Adversaries*

KENTUCKY BAR ASSOCIATION v. GEISLER

Supreme Court of Kentucky, 1997.
938 S.W.2d 578.

The Board of Governors of the Kentucky Bar Association [hereinafter KBA], as a result of charges instigated against respondent, Maria T. Geisler of Louisville, found her guilty of violating SCR 3.130–4.1 by failing to divulge the fact of her client's death to opposing counsel prior to entering into and consummating settlement negotiations. Neither the KBA nor the respondent requested review of this case. However, this Court, on its own motion, elected to review the question of whether the respondent's actions were within the scope of SCR 3.130–4.1.

The critical facts in the present case involve respondent's filing of a civil action on behalf of Milton F. McNealy for injuries he sustained when he was struck by an automobile while walking along a street in Louisville, Kentucky on November 26, 1993. Subsequent to the filing of the initial complaint, defendant's counsel, P. Kevin Ford, filed a notice to take the deposition of McNealy. Respondent contacted Ford and told him that McNealy was physically unable to give a deposition since he was in very poor health. Consequently, the deposition of McNealy was never taken.

McNealy died on January 26, 1995. Shortly thereafter respondent contacted Ford and stated that her client wanted to settle the case and asked him to forward an offer of a settlement. After an exchange of offers and counter-offers, a settlement was reached on February 9, 1995. On February 23, 1995, McNealy's son, Joe, was duly appointed as the administrator of his father's estate. Ford eventually forwarded the settlement documents along with a settlement check to respondent on March 13, 1995. On March 22, 1995, Ford received back the settlement documents which had been executed by Joe. Upon receipt of the signed documents, Ford learned for the first time of McNealy's death. Ford took no further action to bring the court's attention to the settlement documents that were signed by the Administrator, but instead, sent the agreed order of dismissal to the circuit court which was signed and entered by the court. No appeal was taken.

Thereafter, Ford filed a bar complaint against respondent on May 5, 1995 due to her failure to advise Ford that her client, McNealy, had passed away during the settlement negotiation period of January 26, 1995 through February 9, 1995. The chair of the inquiry tribunal of the KBA charged respondent with violating SCR 3.130–4.1 for failing to divulge the fact of her client's death to opposing counsel prior to entering into and consummating settlement negotiations. After submission to the Board of Governors, the Board determined that respondent was guilty of the charge and recommended to this Court that it issue a private reprimand and a public opinion against an unnamed attorney for the benefit of other members of the KBA.

In its recommendation to this Court, the KBA noted that there is no KBA Ethics Opinion on point with this matter and no Kentucky case law dealing directly with this issue. However, the American Bar Association Standing Committee on Ethics and Professional Responsibility [hereinafter ABA], squarely addressed this issue when it issued Formal Opinion 95–397 entitled, "Duty to Disclose Death of Client."

Deciding that counsel has the duty to disclose the death of her client to opposing counsel and to the court when the counsel next communicates with either, the ABA specifically stated in its opinion:

> When a lawyer's client dies in the midst of the settlement negotiations of a pending lawsuit in which the client was the claimant, the lawyer has a duty to inform opposing counsel and the Court in the lawyer's first communications with either after the lawyer has learned of the fact.

The ABA's opinion further addressed the question of whether an attorney even has authority to act when her client dies. The opinion determined that prior to death, a lawyer acts on behalf of an identified client. When the death occurs, however, the lawyer ceases to represent that identified client. The ABA maintained that any subsequent communication to opposing counsel with respect to the matter would be the equivalent of a knowing, affirmative misrepresentation should the lawyer fail to disclose the fact that she no longer represents the previously identified client.

Basically, the ABA determined that a lawyer must inform her adversary of the death of her client in her first communication with the adversary after she has learned of that fact. Likewise, the lawyer must also inform her adversary, in the same communication, that the personal representative, if one has been appointed, of her former client is accepting the outstanding settlement offer. Thus, the ABA concluded that a failure to disclose the death of a client is tantamount to making a false statement of material fact within the meaning of Model Rule 4.1(a) (the precursor to our SCR 3.130–4.1).

... [R]espondent contends that she did have a duty to disclose "facts" or "evidence." Respondent asserts, however, that an attorney is typically not required to affirmatively reveal evidence that is unknown and potentially helpful to the adverse party. Respondent further maintains that McNealy's death had no significant bearing on the ultimate settlement that was achieved, and that Ford did not oppose the settlement even after it was revealed that McNealy was dead. Finally, respondent contends that Ford knew McNealy had been in poor health and that McNealy's death was a matter of public record reported in the daily newspaper. Respondent argues that she felt she had an ethical duty not to volunteer information about her client's passing. Thus, respondent maintains that is was Ford's own fault to have mistakenly believed that McNealy was alive at the time the settlement was negotiated, because if Ford had wanted to know whether McNealy was dead, all he had to do was ask respondent about it.

Kentucky's SCR 3.130–4.1 specifically provides: "In the course of representing a client a lawyer shall not knowingly make a false statement of material fact or law to a third person." This Court recently considered the application of that rule in *Mitchell v. Kentucky Bar Assoc.,* Ky., 924 S.W.2d 497 (1996). That case involved a public administrator of an estate who admitted that he had lied to two heirs by falsely stating that an action to determine ownership of some property had been filed, when in fact, no such action had been taken. The respondent in *Mitchell,* after offering extensive mitigating evidence, including the fact that the heirs' interest had not been impaired, received a public reprimand.

Moreover, in *Virzi v. Grand Trunk Warehouse & Cold Storage Co.,* 571 F.Supp. 507 (E.D.Mich.1983), the federal district court, relying on Model Rule 4.1 held that a plaintiff's attorney had a duty to disclose the death of her client. The circumstances in that case are strikingly similar to the case at bar in that:

> [H]ere, plaintiff's attorney did not make a false statement regarding the death of the plaintiff. He was never placed in a position to do so because during the two weeks of settlement negotiations defendants' attorney never thought to ask if plaintiff was still alive. Instead, in hopes of inducing settlement, plaintiff's attorney chose not to disclose plaintiff's death.

Virzi at 511. Ultimately, the *Virzi* court came down on the side of disclosure stating:

> This Court feels that candor and honesty necessarily require disclosure of such a significant fact as the death of one's client. Opposing counsel does not have to deal

with his adversary as he would deal in the marketplace. Standards of ethics require greater honesty, greater candor, and greater disclosure, even though it might not be in the interest of the client or his estate.

Thus, we hold that the respondent's failure to disclose her client's death to opposing counsel amounted to an affirmative misrepresentation in violation of our SCR 3.130–4.1. While the comments to SCR 3.130–4.1 do indicate that there is no duty to disclose "relevant facts," those same comments go on to state that:

A misrepresentation can occur if the lawyer incorporates or affirms a statement of another person that the lawyer knows is false. Misrepresentations can also occur by failure to act.

Consequently, respondent cannot reasonably argue that her failure to reveal this critical piece of information constituted ethical conduct within the framework of SCR 3.130–4.1.

Furthermore, respondent's argument that the burden of correcting the mistaken belief that her client was alive should be placed on Ford, is incorrect. Attorneys in circumstances similar to those at bar operate under a reasonable assumption that the other attorney's client, whether a legal fiction or in actual flesh, actually exists and, consequently, that opposing counsel has authority to act on their behalf. Here, respondent obtained authority to act on the behalf of Joe, the administrator, but not McNealy, once he passed away. Basically, when the offer was made after McNealy's death, respondent had no authority to act on his behalf. Despite this fact, respondent proceeded to settle the case under the guise that she still had the authority to do so on behalf of McNealy. Her letters to Ford clearly imply this. Accordingly, this Court cannot go so far as to say that such conduct was ethical under the circumstances and within SCR 3.130–4.1.

It should be noted, that this Court fails to understand why guidelines are needed for an attorney to understand that when their client dies, they are under an obligation to tell opposing counsel such information. This seems to be a matter of common ethics and just plain sense. However, because attorneys such as respondent cannot discern such matters and require written guidelines so as to figure out their ethical convictions, this Court adopts the ruling of ABA Opinion 95–397.

[Public reprimand ordered. Respondent ordered to pay the costs of this action.]

Notes

1. Kentucky's ethics rule, applied in *Geisler*, is in accord with MR 4.1. A comment explains that the rule requiring truth-telling "refers to

statements of fact," and whether something is considered a "statement of fact" depends on the setting. MR 4.1, comment [2]. Specifically, the comment continues, "Under generally accepted conventions in negotiation, certain types of statements are not taken as statements of material fact." *Id*. Such statements as "estimates of price or value placed on the subject of a transaction and a party's intentions as to an acceptable settlement of a claim" are in this category. *Id*; see also ABA Formal Op. 06–439 (2006) (lawyers may not make false statements of material fact, but may exaggerate the strengths of their factual or legal positions without violating MR 4.1). According to the Restatement, the line separating fair from foul can be ascertained by asking "whether it is reasonably apparent that the person to whom the statement is addressed would regard the statement as one of fact," an assessment which "depends on the circumstances in which the statement is made." Restatement § 98, comment *c*. Relevant circumstances include such things as "the plausibility of the statement on its face," "the phrasing of the statement," and "the known negotiating practices of the community in which both are negotiating." *Id*. Does this all mean that a lawyer negotiating with another lawyer is free to lie about his client's position on an acceptable settlement? If so, is that problematic? Do lawyers expect the truth to be spoken in negotiations on such matters?

2. State ethics rules often prohibit lawyers from engaging in conduct involving dishonesty, fraud, deceit or misrepresentation. MR 8.4(c). California's State Bar Act says that every attorney has a duty "[t]o employ, for the purpose of maintaining the causes confided to him such means only as are consistent with truth." Cal. Bus. & Prof. Code § 6068(d). Are such provisions applicable to negotiation? Are they drafted too broadly to be meaningful at all?

3. *Tactics: Liability for fraud.* Courts have allowed fraud claims where a lawyer has lied in negotiations to induce a lower settlement of a claim. See, e.g., *Siegel v. Williams*, 818 N.E.2d 510 (Ind.App. 2004); *Matsuura v. E.I. du Pont de Nemours & Co.*, 102 Hawai'i 149, 73 P.3d 687 (2003).

4. *Tactics: Threatening criminal or disciplinary charges.* The Model Code, in DR 7–105, prohibited lawyers from presenting or threatening to present criminal charges "solely to obtain an advantage in a civil matter." This is still the rule in a few states, including New York. See N.Y. DR 7–105(a) [22 NYCRR 1200.36]. California also has such a rule, even more broadly drafted: "A member shall not threaten to present criminal, administrative, or disciplinary charges to obtain an advantage in a civil dispute." Cal. Rule 5–100(A). The Model Rules contain no such provision. The Restatement, in a comment, suggests that a lawyer's statements in negotiation may be constrained by "the criminal law of extortion." Restatement § 98, comment *f*. How could a threat to present criminal charges against an adversary during settlement negotiations in a civil case be considered "extortion?" Cf. *Flatley v. Mauro*, 39 Cal.4th 299, 46 Cal.Rptr.3d 606, 139 P.3d 2 (2006) (holding that a lawyer's threats to an entertainer to publicize an alleged rape of the lawyer's

client unless the entertainer paid $1 million within a short period of time was extortion as a matter of law). In Wisconsin State Bar Comm. on Prof. Ethics, Formal Op. E–01–01 (2001), the ethics committee interpreted its disciplinary rule (identical to DR 7–105) to allow a lawyer to inform another person that his conduct might violate the criminal law. In the same opinion, the committee said that a lawyer could warn an opposing lawyer that a disciplinary complaint was going to be filed. What makes a threat unethical, said the committee, is the "unspoken suggestion" that the conduct would not be reported, in exchange for a favorable civil settlement.

5. *Tactics: Restricting the right to practice law.* Can a defense lawyer properly present a plaintiff with a settlement offer containing a clause that prohibits the plaintiff's lawyer from representing future clients against the defendant? See MR 5.6(b); DR 2–108; Cal. Rule 1–500(A). Why would a defendant want to be able to offer such a deal? Why might it be prohibited? See ABA Formal Op. 93–371 (1993).

2. Secret Settlements

In general, settlements are private agreements. Accordingly, there is nothing wrong with a defendant seeking, and a plaintiff agreeing to, a confidentiality provision under which neither party discloses the terms of the settlement to the outside world. See ABA Section of Litigation, Ethical Guidelines for Settlement Negotiations, Guideline 4.2.6, at 47 (August 2002). The parties sign an agreement and notify the court that it should enter a dismissal of the action, and no one hears any more about it.

But there are some limitations to the general rule. A few states have statutes or court rules that disallow secret settlements in particular cases. For example, Florida's "Sunshine in Litigation Act" (first passed in 1990) provides that "[a]ny portion of an agreement or contract which has the purpose or effect of concealing a public hazard, any information concerning a public hazard, or any information which may be useful to members of the public in protecting themselves from injury which may result from the public hazard, is void, contrary to public policy, and may not be enforced." Fla. Stat. Ann. § 69.081(4). The term "public hazard" is defined as "an instrumentality, including but not limited to any device, instrument, person, procedure, product, or a condition of a device, instrument, person, procedure or product, that has caused and is likely to cause injury." *Id.*, § 69.081(2). Further, the statute provides that no court shall enter an order or judgment which has the purpose of concealing a public hazard or "any information which may be useful to members of the public in protecting themselves from injury which may result from the public hazard." *Id.*, § 69.081(3). The statute grants standing to contest any agreement, contract, order or judgment to "[a]ny substantially affected person, including but not limited to representatives of the news media." *Id.*, § 69.081(6).

Should states forbid secret settlements in cases involving public health and safety? Many thoughtful people think so. See, e.g., Richard Zitrin, *The Fault Lies in the Ethics Rules*, Nat'l L.J., July 9, 2001, at A25 (arguing that states should adopt an ethics rule that would prevent lawyers from restricting the availability to the public of information that directly concerns a "substantial danger to the public health or safety"); Nicole Schultheis, *Court Secrecy: A Continuing National Disgrace*, 28:2 Litigation 29 (Winter 2002) (criticizing secret settlements in products liability litigation, citing many other articles on the topic). In light of the well-publicized problems with Firestone tires, more states have begun to consider passing "sunshine laws" similar to Florida's. See Rebecca A. Womeldorf & William S.D. Cravens, *More Sunshine Laws Proposed*, Nat'l L.J., November 12, 2001, at B14.

Critics of ethics rules or laws that restrict secret settlements argue that such provisions will make settlements less likely, thus clogging court dockets and increasing legal costs. A number of other issues remain cloudy. Proponents promise to continue to press state legislatures and bar groups to adopt restrictions on secret settlements.

If you are practicing in a state that does not bar or restrict secret settlements, what are your options if the defendant in your plaintiff client's products liability action offers a generous financial statement in return for your client's agreement to keep all information in the case secret?

Can a defense lawyer ethically ask a plaintiff to agree to a settlement that restricts the plaintiff's lawyer from using any of the information obtained in the case in another case against the same defendant? See MR 5.6(b); ABA Formal Op. 00–417 (2000).

Could a lawyer agree to refrain from reporting misconduct by opposing counsel as a condition of settlement of the client's claim? The ABA Settlement Guidelines, citing MR 8.3(a) and DR 1–103(A), give a negative answer. ABA Section of Litigation, Ethical Guidelines for Settlement Negotiations, Guideline 4.2.3, at 44 (August 2002). One caveat: A lawyer may agree not to report misconduct that, under the applicable rules, would not be subject to the duty to report. *Id.* at 45. Would this mean that in California, Georgia, or Massachusetts, three states without a mandatory reporting duty, there would be no restriction on agreeing to a settlement containing a "no misconduct report" provision? See Cal. Rule 1–500(B). If a defendant offers a generous financial settlement in an agreement that contains such a clause, should the plaintiff's lawyer recommend against accepting it? On what grounds?

3. Settlements Conditioned on Waiver of Attorneys' Fees

EVANS v. JEFF D.

Supreme Court of the United States, 1986.
475 U.S. 717, 106 S.Ct. 1531, 89 L.Ed.2d 747.

Justice STEVENS delivered the opinion of the Court.

The Civil Rights Attorney's Fees Awards Act of 1976 (Fees Act) provides that "the court, in its discretion, may allow the prevailing party ... a reasonable attorney's fee" in enumerated civil rights actions. 42 U.S.C. § 1988.... In this case, we consider the question whether attorney's fees *must* be assessed when the case has been settled by a consent decree granting prospective relief to the plaintiff class but providing that the defendants shall not pay any part of the prevailing party's fees or costs. We hold that the District Court has the power, in its sound discretion, to refuse to award fees.

I

The petitioners are the Governor and other public officials of the State of Idaho responsible for the education and treatment of children who suffer from emotional and mental handicaps. Respondents are a class of such children who have been or will be placed in petitioners' care.

On August 4, 1980, respondents commenced this action by filing a complaint against petitioners in the United States District Court for the District of Idaho. The factual allegations in the complaint described deficiencies in both the educational programs and the health care services provided respondents. These deficiencies allegedly violated the United States Constitution, the Idaho Constitution, four federal statutes, and certain provisions of the Idaho Code. The complaint prayed for injunctive relief and for an award of costs and attorney's fees, but it did not seek damages.

On the day the complaint was filed, the District Court entered two orders, one granting the respondents leave to proceed *in forma pauperis,* and a second appointing Charles Johnson as their next friend for the sole purpose of instituting and prosecuting the action. At that time Johnson was employed by the Idaho Legal Aid Society, Inc., a private, nonprofit corporation that provides free legal services to qualified low-income persons. Because the Idaho Legal Aid Society is prohibited from representing clients who are capable of paying their own fees, it made no agreement requiring any of the respondents to pay for the costs of litigation or the legal services it provided through Johnson. Moreover, the special character of both the class and its attorney-client relationship with Johnson explains why it did not enter into any agreement covering the various contingencies that might arise during the course of settlement negotiations of a class action of this kind.

Shortly after petitioners filed their answer, and before substantial work had been done on the case, the parties entered into settlement negotiations. [The parties reached a partial settlement on October 14, 1981.] The stipulation provided that each party would bear its "own attorney's fees and costs thus far incurred." The District Court promptly entered an order approving the partial settlement. [Negotiations on the treatment claims broke down, however, and the case was set for trial.]

In March 1983, one week before trial, petitioners presented respondents with a new settlement proposal. As respondents themselves characterize it, the proposal "offered virtually all of the injunctive relief [they] had sought in their complaint." The Court of Appeals agreed with this characterization, and further noted that the proposed relief was "more than the district court in earlier hearings had indicated it was willing to grant." As was true of the earlier partial settlement, however, petitioners' offer included a provision for a waiver by respondents of any claim to fees or costs. Originally, this waiver was unacceptable to the Idaho Legal Aid Society, which had instructed Johnson to reject any settlement offer conditioned upon a waiver of fees, but Johnson ultimately determined that his ethical obligation to his clients mandated acceptance of the proposal. The parties conditioned the waiver on approval by the District Court.

After the stipulation was signed, Johnson filed a written motion requesting the District Court to approve the settlement "except for the provision on costs and attorney's fees," and to allow respondents to present a bill of costs and fees for consideration by the court. At the oral argument on that motion, Johnson contended that petitioners' offer had exploited his ethical duty to his clients—that he was "forced," by an offer giving his clients "the best result [they] could have gotten in this court or any other court," to waive his attorney's fees.[6] The District Court, however, evaluated the waiver in the context of the entire settlement and rejected the ethical underpinnings of Johnson's argument. Explaining that although petitioners were "not willing to concede

---

6. Johnson's oral presentation to the District Court reads in full as follows:

"In other words, an attorney like myself can be put in the position of either negotiating for his client or negotiating for his attorney's fees, and I think that that is pretty much the situation that occurred in this instance.

"I was forced, because of what I perceived to be a result favorable to the plaintiff class, a result that I didn't want to see jeopardized by a trial or by any other possible problems that might have occurred. And the result is the best result I could have gotten in this court or any other court and it is really a fair and just result in any instance and what should have occurred years earlier and which in fact should have been the case all along. That result I didn't want to see disturbed on the basis that my attorney's fees would cause a problem and cause that result to be jeopardized."

that they were obligated to [make the changes in their practices required by the stipulation], ... they were willing to do them as long as their costs were outlined and they didn't face additional costs," it concluded that "it doesn't violate any ethical considerations for an attorney to give up his attorney fees in the interest of getting a better bargain for his client[s]." Accordingly, the District Court approved the settlement and denied the motion to submit a costs bill. . . .

The Court of Appeals ... invalidated the fee waiver and left standing the remainder of the settlement; it then instructed the District Court to "make its own determination of the fees that are reasonable" and remanded for that limited purpose. . . .

II

... The options available to the District Court were essentially the same as those available to respondents: it could have accepted the proposed settlement; it could have rejected the proposal and postponed the trial to see if a different settlement could be achieved; or it could have decided to try the case. The District Court could not enforce the settlement on the merits and award attorney's fees anymore than it could, in a situation in which the attorney had negotiated a large fee at the expense of the plaintiff class, preserve the fee award and order greater relief on the merits. The question we must decide, therefore, is whether the District Court had a duty to reject the proposed settlement because it included a waiver of statutorily authorized attorney's fees.

That duty, whether it takes the form of a general prophylactic rule or arises out of the special circumstances of this case, derives ultimately from the Fees Act rather than from the strictures of professional ethics. Although respondents contend that Johnson, as counsel for the class, was faced with an "ethical dilemma" when petitioners offered him relief greater than that which he could reasonably have expected to obtain for his clients at trial (if only he would stipulate to a waiver of the statutory fee award), and although we recognize Johnson's conflicting interests between pursuing relief for the class and a fee for the Idaho Legal Aid Society, we do not believe that the "dilemma" was an "ethical" one in the sense that Johnson had to choose between conflicting duties under the prevailing norms of professional conduct. Plainly, Johnson had no *ethical* obligation to seek a statutory fee award. His ethical duty was to serve his clients loyally and competently.[14]

14. Generally speaking, a lawyer is under an ethical obligation to exercise independent professional judgment on behalf of his client; he must not allow his own interests, financial or otherwise, to influence his professional advice. ABA, Model Code of Professional Responsibility EC 5–1, 5–2 (as amended 1980); ABA, Model Rules of Professional Conduct 1.7(b), 2.1 (as amended 1984). Accordingly, it is argued that an attorney is required to evaluate a settlement offer on the basis of his client's inter-

Since the proposal to settle the merits was more favorable than the probable outcome of the trial, Johnson's decision to recommend acceptance was consistent with the highest standards of our profession. The District Court, therefore, correctly concluded that approval of the settlement involved no breach of ethics in this case.

The defect, if any, in the negotiated fee waiver must be traced not to the rules of ethics but to the Fees Act.[15] Following this tack, respondents argue that the statute must be construed to forbid a fee waiver that is the product of "coercion." They submit that a "coercive waiver" results when the defendant in a civil rights action (1) offers a settlement on the merits of equal or greater value than that which plaintiffs could reasonably expect to achieve at trial but (2) conditions the offer on a waiver of plaintiffs' statutory eligibility for attorney's fees. Such an offer, they claim, exploits the ethical obligation of plaintiffs' counsel to recommend settlement in order to avoid defendant's statutory liability for its opponents' fees and costs.[16]

... [O]n the facts of record in this case, we are satisfied that the District Court did not abuse its discretion by approving the fee waiver.

III

The text of the Fees Act provides no support for the proposition that Congress intended to ban all fee waivers offered in connection with substantial relief on the merits.... The statute and its legislative history nowhere suggest that Congress intended to forbid *all* waivers of attorney's fees—even those insisted upon

est, without considering his own interest in obtaining a fee; upon recommending settlement, he must abide by the client's decision whether or not to accept the offer, see Model Code of Professional Responsibility EC 7-7 to EC 7-9; Model Rules of Professional Conduct 1.2(a).

15. Even state bar opinions holding it unethical for defendants to request fee waivers in exchange for relief on the merits of plaintiffs' claims are bottomed ultimately on § 1988. See District of Columbia Bar Legal Ethics Committee, Op. No. 147, reprinted in 113 Daily Wash.L.Rep. 389, 394–395 (1985); Committee on Professional and Judicial Ethics of the New York City Bar Association, Op. No. 82–80, p. 1 (1985); *id.,* at 4–5 (dissenting opinion); Committee on Professional and Judicial Ethics of the New York City Bar Association, Op. No. 80–94, reprinted in 36 Record of N.Y.C.B.A. 507, 508–511 (1981); Grievance Commission of Board of Overseers of the Bar of Maine, Op. No. 17, reprinted in Advisory Opinions of the Grievance Commission of the Board of

Overseers of the Bar 69–70 (1983). For the sake of completeness, it should be mentioned that the bar is not of one mind on this ethical judgment. See Final Subcommittee Report of the Committee on Attorney's Fees of the Judicial Conference of the United States Court of Appeals for the District of Columbia Circuit, reprinted in 13 Bar Rep. 4, 6 (1984) (declining to adopt flat rule forbidding waivers of statutory fees)....

16. See Committee on Professional and Judicial Ethics of the New York City Bar Association, Op. No. 80–94, reprinted in 36 Record of N.Y.C.B.A., at 508 ("Defense counsel thus are in a uniquely favorable position when they condition settlement on the waiver of the statutory fee: they make a demand for a benefit which the plaintiff's lawyer cannot resist as a matter of ethics and which the plaintiff will not resist due to lack of interest"). Accord, District of Columbia Bar Legal Ethics Committee, Op. No. 147, reprinted in 113 Daily Wash. L.Rep., at 394.

by a civil rights plaintiff in exchange for some other relief to which he is indisputably not entitled—anymore than it intended to bar a concession on damages to secure broader injunctive relief. Thus, while it is undoubtedly true that Congress expected fee shifting to attract competent counsel to represent citizens deprived of their civil rights, it neither bestowed fee awards upon attorneys nor rendered them nonwaivable or nonnegotiable; instead, it added them to the arsenal of remedies available to combat violations of civil rights, a goal not invariably inconsistent with conditioning settlement on the merits on a waiver of statutory attorney's fees.

In fact, we believe that a general proscription against negotiated waiver of attorney's fees in exchange for a settlement on the merits would itself impede vindication of civil rights, at least in some cases, by reducing the attractiveness of settlement.... Most defendants are unlikely to settle unless the cost of the predicted judgment, discounted by its probability, plus the transaction costs of further litigation, are greater than the cost of the settlement package. If fee waivers cannot be negotiated, the settlement package must either contain an attorney's fee component of potentially large and typically uncertain magnitude, or else the parties must agree to have the fee fixed by the court. Although either of these alternatives may well be acceptable in many cases, there surely is a significant number in which neither alternative will be as satisfactory as a decision to try the entire case.

The adverse impact of removing attorney's fees and costs from bargaining might be tolerable if the uncertainty introduced into settlement negotiations were small. But it is not. The defendants' potential liability for fees in this kind of litigation can be as significant as, and sometimes even more significant than, their potential liability on the merits....

The unpredictability of attorney's fees may be just as important as their magnitude when a defendant is striving to fix its liability.... It is ... not implausible to anticipate that parties to a significant number of civil rights cases will refuse to settle if liability for attorney's fees remains open, thereby forcing more cases to trial, unnecessarily burdening the judicial system, and disserving civil rights litigants. Respondents' own waiver of attorney's fees and costs to obtain settlement of their educational claims is eloquent testimony to the utility of fee waivers in vindicating civil rights claims. We conclude, therefore, that it is not necessary to construe the Fees Act as embodying a general rule prohibiting settlements conditioned on the waiver of fees in order to be faithful to the purposes of that Act.

IV

... What the outcome of this settlement illustrates is that the Fees Act has given the victims of civil rights violations a powerful weapon that improves their ability to employ counsel, to obtain access to the courts, and thereafter to vindicate their rights by means of settlement or trial. For aught that appears, it was the "coercive" effect of respondents' statutory right to seek a fee award that motivated petitioners' exceptionally generous offer. Whether this weapon might be even more powerful if fee waivers were prohibited in cases like this is another question,[34] but it is in any event a question that Congress is best equipped to answer. Thus far, the Legislature has not commanded that fees be paid whenever a case is settled. Unless it issues such a command, we shall rely primarily on the sound discretion of the district courts to appraise the reasonableness of particular class-action settlements on a case-by-case basis, in the light of all the relevant circumstances. In this case, the District Court did not abuse its discretion in upholding a fee waiver which secured broad injunctive relief, relief greater than that which plaintiffs could reasonably have expected to achieve at trial.

The judgment of the Court of Appeals is reversed. *It is so ordered.*

Justice BRENNAN, with whom Justice MARSHALL and Justice BLACKMUN join, dissenting.

Ultimately, enforcement of the laws is what really counts. It was with this in mind that Congress enacted the Civil Rights Attorney's Fees Awards Act of 1976, 42 U.S.C. § 1988 (Act or Fees Act). Congress authorized fee shifting to improve enforcement of civil rights legislation by making it easier for victims of civil rights violations to find lawyers willing to take their cases. Because today's decision will make it more difficult for civil rights plaintiffs to obtain legal assistance, a result plainly contrary to Congress' purpose, I dissent. . . .

[B]y awarding attorney's fees Congress sought to attract competent counsel to represent victims of civil rights violations. Congress' primary purpose was to enable "private attorneys general" to protect the public interest by creating economic incentives for lawyers to represent them. The Court's assertion that the Fees Act was intended to do nothing more than give individual victims of civil rights violations another remedy is thus at odds with the whole thrust of the legislation. Congress determined that

---

34. We are cognizant of the possibility that decisions by individual clients to bargain away fee awards may, in the aggregate and in the long run, diminish lawyers' expectations of statutory fees in civil rights cases. If this occurred, the pool of lawyers willing to represent plaintiffs in such cases might shrink, constricting the "effective access to the judicial process" for persons with civil rights grievances which the Fees Act was intended to provide. H.R.Rep. No. 94–1558, p. 1 (1976). That the "tyranny of small decisions" may operate in this fashion is not to say that there is any reason or documentation to support such a concern at the present time. Comment on this issue is therefore premature at this juncture. We believe, however, that as a practical matter the likelihood of this circumstance arising is remote.

the public as a whole has an interest in the vindication of the rights conferred by the civil rights statutes over and above the value of a civil rights remedy to a particular plaintiff.[4]

... It seems obvious that allowing defendants in civil rights cases to condition settlement of the merits on a waiver of statutory attorney's fees will diminish lawyers' expectations of receiving fees and decrease the willingness of lawyers to accept civil rights cases. Even the Court acknowledges "the possibility that decisions by individual clients to bargain away fee awards may, in the aggregate and in the long run, diminish lawyers' expectations of statutory fees in civil rights cases." The Court tells us, however, that "[c]omment on this issue" is "premature at this juncture" because there is not yet supporting "documentation." The Court then goes on anyway to observe that "as a practical matter the likelihood of this circumstance arising is remote."

I must say that I find the Court's assertions somewhat difficult to understand.... [N]umerous courts and commentators have recognized that permitting fee waivers creates disincentives for lawyers to take civil rights cases and thus makes it more difficult for civil rights plaintiffs to obtain legal assistance.

But it does not require a sociological study to see that permitting fee waivers will make it more difficult for civil rights plaintiffs to obtain legal assistance. It requires only common sense. Assume that a civil rights defendant makes a settlement offer that includes a demand for waiver of statutory attorney's fees. The decision whether to accept or reject the offer is the plaintiff's alone, and the lawyer must abide by the plaintiff's decision. See, *e.g.,* ABA, Model Rules of Professional Conduct 1.2(a) (1984); ABA, Model Code of Professional Responsibility EC 7–7 to EC 7–9 (1982).[8] As a formal matter, of course, the statutory fee belongs to the plaintiff, and thus technically the decision to waive entails a sacrifice only by the plaintiff. As a practical matter, however, waiver affects only the lawyer. Because "a vast majority of the victims of civil rights violations" have no resources to pay attorney's fees, H.R.Rep. 1, lawyers cannot hope to recover fees from the plaintiff and must depend entirely on the Fees Act

4. The Court seems to view the options as limited to two: either the Fees Act confers a benefit on attorneys, a conclusion which is contrary to both the language and the legislative history of the Act, or the Fees Act confers a benefit on individual plaintiffs, who may freely exploit the statutory fee award to their own best advantage. It apparently has not occurred to the Court that Congress might have made a remedy available to individual plaintiffs primarily for the benefit of the *public*....

8. The attorney is, in fact, obliged to advise the plaintiff whether to accept or reject the settlement offer based on his independent professional judgment, and the lawyer's duty of undivided loyalty requires that he render such advice free from the influence of his or his organization's interest in a fee. See, *e.g.,* ABA, Model Code of Professional Responsibility EC 5–1, EC 5–2, DR 5–101(A) (1982); ABA, Model Rules of Professional Conduct 1.7(b), 2.1 (1984). Thus, counsel must advise a client to accept an offer which includes waiver of the plaintiff's right to recover attorney's fees if, on the whole, the offer is an advantageous one....

for compensation.[10] The plaintiff thus has no real stake in the statutory fee and is unaffected by its waiver. Consequently, plaintiffs will readily agree to waive fees if this will help them to obtain other relief they desire.[11] As summed up by the Legal Ethics Committee of the District of Columbia Bar:

> "Defense counsel ... are in a uniquely favorable position when they condition settlement on the waiver of the statutory fee: They make a demand for a benefit that the plaintiff's lawyer cannot resist as a matter of ethics and one in which the plaintiff has no interest and therefore will not resist."

Of course, from the lawyer's standpoint, things could scarcely have turned out worse. He or she invested considerable time and effort in the case, won, and has exactly nothing to show for it. Is the Court really serious in suggesting that it takes a study to prove that this lawyer will be reluctant when, the following week, another civil rights plaintiff enters his office and asks for representation? Does it truly require that somebody conduct a test to see that legal aid services, having invested scarce resources on a case, will feel the pinch when they do not recover a statutory fee?

And, of course, once fee waivers are permitted, defendants will seek them as a matter of course, since this is a logical way to minimize liability. Indeed, defense counsel would be remiss *not* to demand that the plaintiff waive statutory attorney's fees. A lawyer who proposes to have his client pay more than is necessary to end litigation has failed to fulfill his fundamental duty zealously to represent the best interests of his client. Because waiver of fees does not affect the plaintiff, a settlement offer is not made less attractive to the plaintiff if it includes a demand that statutory fees be waived. Thus, in the future, we must expect settlement offers routinely to contain demands for waivers of statutory fees.

The cumulative effect this practice will have on the civil rights bar is evident. It does not denigrate the high ideals that motivate many civil rights practitioners to recognize that lawyers are in the business of practicing law, and that, like other business people, they are and must be concerned with earning a living. The conclusion that permitting fee waivers will seriously impair the ability of civil rights plaintiffs to obtain legal assistance is embarrassingly obvious.

---

10. Nor can attorneys protect themselves by requiring plaintiffs to sign contingency agreements or retainers at the outset of the representation. ... [N]one of the parties has seriously suggested that civil rights attorneys can protect themselves through private arrangements. After all, Congress enacted the Fees Act because ... it found such arrangements wholly inadequate.

11. This result is virtually inevitable in class actions where, even if the class representative feels sympathy for the lawyer's plight, the obligation to represent the interests of absent class members precludes altruistic sacrifice. In class actions on behalf of incompetents, like this one, it is the lawyer himself who must agree to sacrifice his own interests for those of the class he represents.

Because making it more difficult for civil rights plaintiffs to obtain legal assistance is precisely the opposite of what Congress sought to achieve by enacting the Fees Act, fee waivers should be prohibited.... This is simply straightforward application of the well-established principle that an agreement which is contrary to public policy is void and unenforceable.

This all seems so obvious that it is puzzling that the Court reaches a different result.... Each individual plaintiff who waives his right to statutory fees in order to obtain additional relief for himself makes it that much more difficult for the next victim of a civil rights violation to find a lawyer willing or able to bring *his* case. As obtaining legal assistance becomes more difficult, the "benefit" the Court so magnanimously preserves for civil rights plaintiffs becomes available to fewer and fewer individuals, exactly the opposite result from that intended by Congress....

... It is to be hoped that Congress will repair this Court's mistake. In the meantime, other avenues of relief are available. The Court's decision in no way limits the power of state and local bar associations to regulate the ethical conduct of lawyers. Indeed, several Bar Associations have already declared it unethical for defense counsel to seek fee waivers. See Committee on Professional Ethics of the Association of the Bar of the City of New York, Op. No. 82–80 (1985); District of Columbia Legal Ethics Committee, Op. No. 147. Such efforts are to be commended and, it is to be hoped, will be followed by other state and local organizations concerned with respecting the intent of Congress and with protecting civil rights.

In addition, it may be that civil rights attorneys can obtain agreements from their clients not to waive attorney's fees. Such agreements simply replicate the private market for legal services (in which attorneys are not ordinarily required to contribute to their client's recovery), and thus will enable civil rights practitioners to make it economically feasible—as Congress hoped—to expend time and effort litigating civil rights claims....

Notes

1. The majority holds that the statutory entitlement to fees belongs to the client, not the lawyer. This makes it easier, perhaps, for the majority to decide that the lawyer had no right to interfere with the client's decision to waive fees, and indeed acted consistently "with the highest standards of our profession" in recommending acceptance of the settlement agreement. Does the majority opinion place lawyers in these cases in a position in which their interests conflict with the client's interests? How might it?

2. Do you think a lawyer would be behaving ethically if he tried to convince the client not to accept a settlement offer conditioned on a fee

waiver? What could the lawyer say? Could he ethically stress his own interests? Could he ethically stress the interests of other similarly situated clients? Of society?

3.   Could a private lawyer protect himself from the *Jeff D.* situation by entering into an agreement with the client, perhaps at the beginning of the representation, under which the client agrees not to accept any settlement conditioned on a waiver of fees? Does such an agreement embody a fundamental conflict of interest?

4.   Could a lawyer provide in the retainer agreement that any fee owed will be paid from the proceeds of the client's recovery? See MR 1.5(c).

5.   Is Justice Brennan right that lawyers for defendants in future cases will be ethically bound to seek a waiver of fees? If this practice became widespread, might it produce the kind of problem the majority notes and dismisses in footnote 34 as a "remote" possibility? In *Willard v. City of Los Angeles*, 803 F.2d 526 (9th Cir.1986), the plaintiffs settled a civil rights action in exchange for a lump sum, which included all attorneys' fees potentially recoverable under § 1988. They nonetheless moved for an award of attorneys' fees, arguing that the settlement was unenforceable. The district court denied the motion. The Ninth Circuit affirmed, citing *Jeff D.*, but said that a settlement waiving fees might be unenforceable if the governmental unit had a "statute, policy, or practice requiring waiver of fees as a condition of settlement or … has vindictively sought to deter attorneys from bringing civil rights suits." Later, in *Bernhardt v. County of Los Angeles*, 279 F.3d 862 (9th Cir.2002), the plaintiff alleged that the County of Los Angeles had for years been following just such a policy, offering civil rights plaintiffs lump sum settlements that waived statutory fees. This, the plaintiff alleged, interfered with her implicit right to an attorney to pursue a civil rights claim. The district court dismissed *sua sponte* for lack of standing. Without deciding the merits, the appeals court held that the plaintiff had standing to pursue the allegation. On remand, the plaintiff sought a preliminary injunction against the alleged policy, which the district court denied. The Ninth Circuit reversed, finding there were "serious questions going to the merits" and that the other requirements of injunctive relief were met. *Bernhardt v. Los Angeles County*, 339 F.3d 920 (9th Cir. 2003). The trial court should have issued a narrowly-tailored injunction to prevent the County from using a lump-sum settlement policy in her particular case, alleged by the plaintiff to be an obstacle to her obtaining trial counsel. *Id.*

6.   Could states make it unethical for defense lawyers to seek fee waivers? Should states do so? On what grounds?

§ 7. ADVANCING LITIGATION COSTS

STATE EX REL. OKLAHOMA
BAR ASS'N v. SMOLEN

Supreme Court of Oklahoma, 2000.
17 P.3d 456.

HODGES, J.

Complainant, the Oklahoma Bar Association, alleged one count of misconduct warranting discipline against respondent attorney, Donald E. Smolen (Respondent). The complaint alleged that Respondent had violated rule 1.8(e) of the Oklahoma Rules of Professional Conduct (ORPC), Okla. Stat. tit. 5, ch. 1, app. 3–A (1991) (prohibition against providing financial assistance to a client in connection with pending or contemplated litigation). . . .

During Respondent's representation of Mr. Miles in a case before the Workers' Compensation Court, Respondent loaned Mr. Miles $1,200. The check to Mr. Miles recited that the money was for travel expenses. Respondent admitted that the true purpose of the loan was for living expenses because Mr. Miles' home had been destroyed by fire. Without the loan, Mr. Miles indicated he would have to move to Indiana and would be unable to continue his medical treatment or make court appearances. At the time of the loan, Mr. Miles was receiving temporary total disability benefits of $426.00 a week from which Respondent's attorney fee was subtracted. Mr. Miles received $384.00 a week before loan payments.

Respondent's loan to Mr. Miles was interest free and without penalty or cost other than the amount of the principle. Mr. Miles was to repay the loan at $100.00 a week from his temporary total disability benefits. Mr. Miles made three $100.00 payments on the loan. One of the payments was returned to Mr. Miles resulting in his paying only $200.00 on the loan. Respondent agreed to forego further repayment until final settlement of the Workers' Compensation case.

When Mr. Miles became involved in other legal matters, he sought an attorney to handle the additional matters together with the workers' compensation claim. After learning of Mr. Miles search for a new attorney, Respondent terminated the attorney-client relationship with Mr. Miles. Thereafter, Mr. Miles hired Mr. Elias to represent him. During mediation over a fee dispute between Mr. Miles and Mr. Elias, the Tulsa County Bar Association learned of Respondent's loan and reported Respondent's conduct to the Oklahoma Bar Association.

Respondent admits the loan to Mr. Miles is not an isolated incident. He testified that he had consulted lawyers whose opinions are well respected in legal ethics, and it was their belief that

Respondent's conduct would not violate rule 1.8(e). Respondent admits that his actions violate the express language of rule 1.8(e). However, Respondent submits that he has not violated the intent of rule 1.8(e), and that rule 1.8(e) unconstitutionally treats clients who need humanitarian loans differently than clients who receive advances of litigation expenses and court costs.

ANALYSIS

Rule 1.8(e) of the ORPC under which Respondent was [previously] disciplined in 1992 for giving financial assistance to clients, provided:

> While representing a client in connection with contemplated or pending litigation, a lawyer shall not advance or guarantee financial assistance to a client, except that a lawyer may advance or guarantee the expenses of litigation, including court costs, expenses of investigation, expenses of medical examination, and costs of obtaining and presenting evidence, provided the client remains ultimately liable for such expenses.

Based on the Model Rules adopted by the American Bar Association, rule 1.8(e) was amended in 1993 to provide:

> A lawyer shall not provide financial assistance to a client in connection with pending or contemplated litigation, except that a lawyer may advance court costs and expenses of litigation, the repayment of which may be contingent on the outcome of the matter.

The primary change under the Model Rules is that the repayment of litigation expenses and court costs may be contingent on the outcome of the case. Both the 1992 and 1993 versions of rule 1.8(e) unambiguously prohibit a lawyer from advancing living expenses to clients. In this case, Respondent advanced funds for living expenses to be repaid from the client's worker's compensation benefits, an action admittedly prohibited by rule 1.8(e).

Most authorities prohibit a lawyer from providing financial assistance to clients for living expenses during representation. In 1991, a draft of a provision of the Restatement of Law would have allowed a lawyer to make or guarantee a loan to a client "if the loan [was] needed to enable the client to withstand delay in litigation that otherwise might unjustly induce the client to settle or dismiss a case because of financial hardship rather than on the merits." However, in 1996 the American Law Institute Council decided the rule was ill-advised, and, in 1998, the provision was removed. The final draft of the Restatement would not allow a lawyer to make or guarantee a loan to a client except for litigation expenses and court costs. . . .

Twenty-nine states have adopted the current version of ABA Model Rule 1.8(e) which allows repayment of litigation costs to be contingent on the outcome of the case but forbids advances for living expenses. Fourteen other states follow the ABA Model Code of Professional Responsibility, adopted in 1969, or a version of the Model Rules or Model Code that requires the client remain liable for litigation expenses and court costs and prohibits advances for living expenses. Only eight states explicitly allow lawyers to advance or guarantee loans to clients for living expenses: Alabama, California, Louisiana, Minnesota, Mississippi, Montana, North Dakota, and Texas.

Only one state has refused to discipline a lawyer for advancing funds to clients for living expenses during representation. In *Louisiana State Bar Ass'n v. Edwins,* [329 So.2d 437 (La.1976)] the Louisiana State Supreme Court stated that advancing money to an indigent client for necessary living expenses during representation did not violate the Louisiana rules of legal ethics. Even though the *Edwins* court questioned the constitutionality of the rule, the court based its conclusion on a finding that the conduct did not violate the rule's intent. The lawyer in *Edwins* was disciplined for making advances which were not based on the client's needs. In *In re K.A.H.,* [967 P.2d 91 (Alaska 1998)] the Alaska Supreme Court held the rule did not unconstitutionally deny or interfere with the client's access to the courts. Further, no court has invalidated rule 1.8(e) based on a constitutional infirmity.

We have has previously disciplined lawyers for providing financial assistance to clients for purposes other than litigation expenses and court costs. Several other courts addressing the question have also imposed discipline on lawyers for like conduct. In *Mississippi Bar v. Attorney HH,* [671 So.2d 1293 (Miss.1995)] the Mississippi Supreme Court expressed its concern that allowing a lawyer to advance funds to a client for living expenses would "generate unseemly bidding wars for cases and inevitably lead to further denigration of our civil justice system."

A.   Intent of the Rule

Respondent admits violating rule 1.8(e) but argues that he should not be disciplined because he did not violate the intent of the rule. What Respondent in reality requests is that we adopt an exception to the rule that allows attorneys to make loans to clients for necessary living expenses after the attorney-client relationship is established.

The rule against attorneys providing financial assistance to clients for living expenses is based on the common-law prohibitions against practice of champerty and maintenance.[35] The evils

---

35. .... Champerty is "[a] bargain by a stranger with a party to a suit, by which such third person undertakes to carry on the litigation at his own cost and risk, in

associated with champerty and maintenance intended to be prevented by rule 1.8(e)'s prohibition are: (1) clients selecting a lawyer based on improper factors, and (2) conflicts of interest, including compromising a lawyer's independent judgment in the case and creating the potentially conflicting roles of the lawyer as both lawyer and creditor with divergent interests.

Respondent argues that he advanced the funds only after the attorney-client relationship was established with repayment to be made from benefits which had already been awarded, and the loan was for humanitarian purposes. Thus, he posits that the evils of champerty and maintenance are absent here and that he should not be disciplined because he did not violate the intent of the rule. We reject this argument as have most other states. First, Mr. Miles' workers' compensation claim had not been completely resolved. He was receiving only temporary benefits at the time Respondent made the loan, and, at least, a potential settlement regarding permanent disability remained pending. Second, it would be unrealistic to conclude that even if Respondent does not publicize that he makes loans to clients for living expenses, potential clients would not learn of Respondent's practice from existing and past clients. Thus, potential clients may base their decision to retain Respondent on improper inducements. The fact that the loan was for humanitarian purposes may be a mitigating factor. Nonetheless, Respondent violated rule 1.8(e).

Given that the Restatement and the ABA have rejected the same exception tendered by Respondent and an overwhelming number of courts have also declined to adopt Respondent's proposed exception, we also decline to make the ad hoc exception to rule 1.8(e) advocated by Respondent. We are not unsympathetic to the plight of litigants. However, because of the potential ethical problems which can arise from a lawyer advancing clients money for living expenses, the explicit prohibition against such conduct in the Oklahoma Rules of Professional Conduct, we believe Respondent should be disciplined.

B. *Constitutionality*

Respondent asserts that rule 1.8(e) is invalid because it does not treat similarly situated classes of litigants equally. The Fourteenth Amendment to the United States Constitution provides: "No State shall make or enforce any law which shall . . . deny to any person within its jurisdiction the equal protection of the laws." This same prohibition is present in article 2, section 7 of the Oklahoma Constitution. The two classes of clients proposed by

consideration of receiving, if successful, a part of the proceeds or subject sought to be recovered." Black's Law Dictionary 209 (5th ed.1979). "Maintenance" is "[a]n officious intermeddling in a suit which in no way belongs to one, by maintaining or assisting either party, with money or otherwise, to prosecute or defend it." *Id.* at 860.

Respondent are those who need advances for living expenses and those who need advances for litigation costs.

The deferential rational basis test is applied in constitutional challenges based on the equal protection clause when the classification is not based upon an inherently suspect characteristic or jeopardizes a fundamental right.... Assuming for purposes of argument that the two classes posed by Respondent are similarly situated, rule 1.8(e)'s disparate treatment of advances for litigation expenses and court costs and advances for all other expenses is based on legitimate goals and reflects the differences in living expenses and litigation expenses and court costs. First, litigation expenses and court costs are directly related to the actual litigation. Living and other expenses are not. Second, litigation expenses and court costs are within a lawyer's expertise. Other expenses of clients are not considered part of a lawyer's expertise. Third, it is a lawyer's duty to advise his client on which litigation expenses and court costs are necessary for the litigation. It is not generally the lawyer's duty to advise his clients as to what other expenses are necessary. Fourth, a lawyer generally pays the litigation expenses and costs directly to the provider. In the case of other expenses, the lawyer generally would give the money to the client, and there would be no guarantee that the money would be utilized for the loan's intended purpose.

We agree with the drafters of the Restatement and the ABA Model Rules that a rule allowing lawyers to make loans to clients for reasons other that advancing litigation expenses and court costs is ill-advised. Because of the potentially inherent abuses in allowing lawyers to make loans to clients for reasons other than litigation expenses and court costs, the divergent treatment is rationally related to a legitimate goal of protecting clients and maintaining the integrity of the Bar. Respondent has failed to show that rule 1.8(e) is unconstitutional....

CONCLUSION

Based on respondent attorney Donald E. Smolen's violation of rule 1.8(e) of the Oklahoma Rules of Professional Conduct, he is suspended from the practice of law for sixty days and is ordered to pay the costs of these proceedings in the amount of $583.15.

Notes

1. Model Rule 1.8(e) prohibits a lawyer from providing "financial assistance to a client in connection with pending or contemplated litigation," with two exceptions: (1) a lawyer may advance court costs and expenses of litigation, the repayment of which may be contingent on the outcome of the matter; and (2) a lawyer representing an indigent client may pay court costs and expenses of behalf of the client. *Accord*, Restatement § 36. As explained in *Smolen*, this rule does not authorize a

lawyer's payment of a litigation client's living expenses or medical costs. Should it do so? Do you accept the court's statement of the rationale behind this limitation?

2. *Advancing living expenses to indigents.* Almost all states prohibit advancing living and medical expenses to all clients, even indigent ones. Should an exception be made for indigent clients? Louisiana's Rule 1.8(e), as adopted in 2006, makes such an exception when a client is in "necessitous circumstances," following earlier precedent that allowed advancing minimal living expenses to needy clients for humanitarian purposes. See *Louisiana State Bar Ass'n v. Edwins*, 329 So.2d 437 (La. 1976). Isn't advancing living expenses to a poor client an act worthy of praise rather than condemnation? In *Cleveland Bar Ass'n v. Nusbaum*, 93 Ohio St.3d 150, 753 N.E.2d 183 (2001), the client had been seriously injured in a motorcycle accident. The lawyer advanced him $26,000 for living expenses while he handled the lawsuit. The court acknowledged the fact that the client was "not harmed but helped by the loans," and noted that the grievance was filed not by the client but by the lawyer's ex-wife. But because Ohio DR 5–103(B) forbids advancing such costs, the lawyer was publicly reprimanded.

3. *Constitutionality.* The court in *Smolen* held, in accord with all others, that the ethics rules prohibiting the lawyer's payment of a litigation client's living and medical expenses do not violate the equal protection clause. Might these restrictions violate the right to access to courts, by preventing poor people from effectively asserting their legal rights? This argument too has thus far met with no success. See, e.g., *In re K.A.H.*, 967 P.2d 91 (Alaska 1998).

4. California's Rule 4–210(A)(2) prohibits a lawyer from "directly or indirectly" paying "the personal or business expenses of a prospective or existing client," with some rather large exceptions: the rule explicitly does not prohibit a lawyer (1) with client consent, from paying such expenses to "third persons from funds collected or to be collected for the client as a result of the representation"; or (2) after the employment has commenced, "from lending money to the client upon the client's promise in writing to repay such loan." Any such loan would have to comply with the rule on business transactions with clients, Rule 3–300. Is this rule preferable to the Model Rule? Is it better for clients who need money for personal or medical expenses while awaiting the outcome of a case in which such expenses are sought as an element of damages?

5. A few other states explicitly allow a lawyer to advance medical and living expenses to litigation clients after the employment has commenced. See Ala. Rule 1.8(e)(3) (allowing lawyer to advance "emergency financial assistance"); Miss. Rule 1.8(e) (allowing lawyer to advance "reasonable and necessary" medical and living expenses); Tex. Rule 1.8(d) (allowing lawyer to advance "reasonably necessary medical and living expenses").

6. A few states explicitly allow a lawyer to guarantee a bank loan to a client when such funds are needed "to withstand delay in litigation

that would otherwise put substantial pressure on the client to settle a case because of financial hardship rather than on the merits." Minn. Rule 1.8(e)(3); Mont. Rule 1.8(e)(3); N.D. Rule 1.8(e)(3). Is such a provision a good idea?

7. *Bank lines of credit.* As we have seen, state ethics rules allow lawyers to advance litigation costs to clients. But these costs can be quite large, leaving small firms at a competitive disadvantage. Can law firms go to a bank to borrow money to advance to clients, and pass the interest charges along to the clients? Most states have said yes to this arrangement, as long as the client has consented in writing, the lawyer has no financial interest in the lender, and the interest charges are those actually incurred. See, e.g., Ohio Supreme Court Ethics Op. 2001–3; Ariz. State Bar Comm. on Rules of Prof. Conduct, Op. 2001–07; *Chittenden v. State Farm Mut. Auto. Ins. Co.*, 788 So.2d 1140 (La.2001) (citing other states' approval of such arrangements).

8. *Litigation-finance companies.* Ethics rules restrictions on lawyers' advancing funds to litigation clients leaves many clients in a tough position. Even if they retain counsel on a contingent fee, and the lawyer advances litigation costs, they may not have enough money to pay their living expenses and as a result may be forced to enter in to a fast settlement or even to abandon their case completely. In response to this situation, private companies have recently sprung up to advance money to litigants (most commonly plaintiffs in personal injury suits), the repayment of which is contingent on prevailing in the case. If the plaintiff wins a settlement or judgment, the loan must be repaid, often as a percentage of the recovery—an amount which may be much more than the amount of the original loan. If the plaintiff wins nothing, then the loan need not be repaid at all. This practice, sometimes called "non-recourse funding" or "future settlement financing," is not illegal, according to most courts. See, e.g., *Saladini v. Righellis*, 426 Mass. 231, 687 N.E.2d 1224 (1997) (holding that a financier's agreement to advance funds to a litigant on a contingency basis is enforceable, abrogating the common-law doctrines of champerty, barratry and maintenance). But not all agree. See. e.g., *Rancman v. Interim Settlement Funding Corp.*, 99 Ohio St.3d 121, 789 N.E.2d 217 (2003) (contract making repayment of funds advanced to a party in a pending case void as champerty and maintenance "because it gives a nonparty an impermissible interest in a suit, impedes the settlement of the underlying case, and promotes speculation in lawsuits").

Private litigation funding is controversial for several reasons, including high interest rates and the potential for interference with the client-lawyer relationship. *How could a litigation-finance company interfere with the client-lawyer relationship?* In *Weaver, Bennett & Bland, P.A. v. Speedy Bucks, Inc.*, 162 F.Supp.2d 448 (W.D.N.C.2001), the litigation finance company advanced $200,000 to the Weaver law firm's client, based on the client's promise to pay a minimum of $600,000 if she prevailed in her lawsuit. Neither the company nor the client told the law firm about this arrangement. The defendant in that underlying lawsuit offered a $1 million settlement, which the client rejected because such an amount was insufficient to pay both the finance company and the Weaver firm's contingent fee. The case went to trial and the plaintiff lost. Upon learning of the finance company's contract, the Weaver firm sued the company for tortious interference with contract, fraud, and unfair trade practices. The firm sought more than $325,000 in damages, claiming that the finance contract's onerous repayment terms cost the firm its contingent fee it would have earned had the client accepted the $1 million settlement offer. The finance company moved to dismiss. *Held*, motion denied; the law firm's complaint stated claims on all causes of action.

Chapter 8

ADVERTISING AND SOLICITATION

§ 1. ADVERTISING

IN RE R. M. J.

Supreme Court of the United States, 1982.
455 U.S. 191, 102 S.Ct. 929, 71 L.Ed.2d 64.

Justice POWELL delivered the opinion of the Court.

The Court's decision in *Bates v. State Bar of Arizona*, 433 U.S. 350, 97 S.Ct. 2691, 53 L.Ed.2d 810 (1977), required a re-examination of long-held perceptions as to "advertising" by lawyers. This appeal presents the question whether certain aspects of the revised ethical rules of the Supreme Court of Missouri regulating lawyer advertising conform to the requirements of *Bates*.

I

As with many of the States, until the decision in *Bates*, Missouri placed an absolute prohibition on advertising by lawyers.[1] After the Court's invalidation of just such a prohibition in *Bates*, the Committee on Professional Ethics and Responsibility of the Supreme Court of Missouri revised that court's Rule 4 regulating lawyer advertising. The Committee sought to "strike a midpoint between prohibition and unlimited advertising," and the revised regulation of advertising, adopted with slight modification by the State Supreme Court, represents a compromise. Lawyer

---

1. Prior to the 1977 revision, Rule 4 provided in pertinent part:

"(A) A lawyer shall not prepare, cause to be prepared, use, or participate in the use of, any form of public communication that contains professionally self-laudatory statements calculated to attract lay clients; as used herein, 'public communication' includes, but is not limited to, communication by means of television, radio, motion picture, newspaper, magazine, or book.

"(B) A lawyer shall not publicize himself, his partner, or associate as a lawyer through newspaper or magazine advertisements, radio or television announcements, display advertisements in city or telephone directories, or other means of commercial publicity, nor shall he authorize or permit others to do so in his behalf . . . " Mo.Sup.Ct.Rules Ann., Rule 4, DR 2–101, p. 63 (Vernon 1981) (historical note).

579

advertising is permitted, but it is restricted to certain categories of information, and in some instances, to certain specified language.

Thus, part B of DR 2–101 of the Rule states that a lawyer may "publish ... in newspapers, periodicals and the yellow pages of telephone directories" 10 categories of information: name, address and telephone number; areas of practice; date and place of birth; schools attended; foreign language ability; office hours; fee for an initial consultation; availability of a schedule of fees; credit arrangements; and the fixed fee to be charged for certain specified "routine" legal services.[3] Although the Rule does not state explicitly that these 10 categories of information or the 3 indicated forms of printed advertisement are the only information and the only means of advertising that will be permitted, that is the interpretation given the Rule by the State Supreme Court and the Advisory Committee charged with its enforcement.

In addition to these guidelines, and under authority of the Rule, the Advisory Committee has issued an addendum to the Rule providing that if the lawyer chooses to list areas of practice in his advertisement, he must do so in one of two prescribed ways. He may list one of three general descriptive terms specified in the Rule—"General Civil Practice," "General Criminal Practice," or "General Civil and Criminal Practice." Alternatively, he may use one or more of a list of 23 areas of practice, including, for example, "Tort Law," "Family Law," and "Probate and Trust Law." He may not list both a general term and specific subheadings, nor may he deviate from the precise wording stated in the Rule. He may not indicate that his practice is "limited" to the listed areas and he must include a particular disclaimer of certification of expertise following any listing of specific areas of practice.

Finally, one further aspect of the Rule is relevant in this case. DR2–102 of Rule 4 regulates the use of professional announcement cards. It permits a lawyer or firm to mail a dignified "brief professional announcement card stating new or changed associates or addresses, change of firm name, or similar matters." The Rule, however, does not permit a general mailing; the announcement cards may be sent only to "lawyers, clients, former clients, personal friends, and relatives."

II

Appellant graduated from law school in 1973 and was admitted to the Missouri and Illinois Bars in the same year. After a

---

3. The 10 listed "routine" services are: an uncontested dissolution of marriage; an uncontested adoption; an uncontested personal bankruptcy; an uncomplicated change of name; a simple warranty or quitclaim deed; a simple deed of trust; a simple promissory note; an individual Missouri or federal income tax return; a simple power of attorney; and a simple will. The Rule authorizes the Advisory Committee to approve additions to this list of routine services.

short stint with the Securities and Exchange Commission in Washington, D.C., appellant moved to St. Louis, Mo., in April 1977, and began practice as a sole practitioner. As a means of announcing the opening of his office, he mailed professional announcement cards to a selected list of addressees. In order to reach a wider audience, he placed several advertisements in local newspapers and in the yellow pages of the local telephone directory.

The advertisements at issue in this litigation appeared in January, February, and August 1978, and included information that was not expressly permitted by Rule 4. They included the information that appellant was licensed in Missouri and Illinois. They contained, in large capital letters, a statement that appellant was "Admitted to Practice Before THE UNITED STATES SUPREME COURT." And they included a listing of areas of practice that deviated from the language prescribed by the Advisory Committee—*e.g.*, "personal injury" and "real estate" instead of "tort law" and "property law"—and that included several areas of law without analogue in the list of areas prepared by the Advisory Committee—*e.g.*, "contract," "zoning & land use," "communication," "pension & profit sharing plans." In addition, and with the exception of the [yellow pages] advertisement appearing in August 1978, appellant failed to include the required disclaimer of certification of expertise after the listing of areas of practice.

[In November 1979, the Advisory Committee charged appellant with "unprofessional conduct," specifically charging him with publishing three advertisements that listed areas of law unapproved by the Advisory Committee, that listed the courts in which appellant was admitted to practice, and, in the case of two of the advertisements, that failed to include the required disclaimer of certification. He was also charged with sending announcement cards in violation of DR 2–102(A)(2).] In response, appellant argued that, with the exception of the disclaimer requirement, each of these restrictions upon advertising was unconstitutional under the First and Fourteenth Amendments. In a disbarment proceeding, the Supreme Court of Missouri upheld the constitutionality of DR 2–101 of Rule 4 and issued a private reprimand. . . .

III

In *Bates v. State Bar of Arizona*, 433 U.S. 350, 97 S.Ct. 2691, 53 L.Ed.2d 810 (1977), the Court considered whether the extension of First Amendment protection to commercial speech announced in *Virginia Pharmacy Board v. Virginia Citizens Consumer Council*, 425 U.S. 748, 96 S.Ct. 1817, 48 L.Ed.2d 346 (1976), applied to the regulation of advertising by lawyers. The *Bates* Court held that indeed lawyer advertising was a form of commercial speech, protected by the First Amendment, and that "advertising by attorneys may not be subjected to blanket suppression."

More specifically, the *Bates* Court held that lawyers must be permitted to advertise the fees they charge for certain "routine" legal services. The Court concluded that this sort of price advertising was not "inherently" misleading, and therefore could not be prohibited on that basis. The Court also rejected a number of other justifications for broad restrictions upon advertising including the potential adverse effect of advertising on professionalism, on the administration of justice, and on the cost and quality of legal services, as well as the difficulties of enforcing standards short of an outright prohibition. None of these interests was found to be sufficiently strong or sufficiently affected by lawyer advertising to justify a prohibition.

But the decision in *Bates* nevertheless was a narrow one. The Court emphasized that advertising by lawyers still could be regulated. False, deceptive, or misleading advertising remains subject to restraint, and the Court recognized that advertising by the professions poses special risks of deception—"because the public lacks sophistication concerning legal services, misstatements that might be overlooked or deemed unimportant in other advertising may be found quite inappropriate in legal advertising." The Court suggested that claims as to quality or in-person solicitation might be so likely to mislead as to warrant restriction. And the Court noted that a warning or disclaimer might be appropriately required, even in the context of advertising as to price, in order to dissipate the possibility of consumer confusion or deception. "[T]he bar retains the power to correct omissions that have the effect of presenting an inaccurate picture, [although] the preferred remedy is more disclosure, rather than less."

In short, although the Court in *Bates* was not persuaded that price advertising for "routine" services was necessarily or inherently misleading, and although the Court was not receptive to other justifications for restricting such advertising, it did not by any means foreclose restrictions on potentially or demonstrably misleading advertising. Indeed, the Court recognized the special possibilities for deception presented by advertising for professional services. The public's comparative lack of knowledge, the limited ability of the professions to police themselves, and the absence of any standardization in the "product" renders advertising for professional services especially susceptible to abuses that the States have a legitimate interest in controlling.

Thus, the Court has made clear in *Bates* and subsequent cases that regulation–and imposition of discipline–are permissible where the particular advertising is inherently likely to deceive or where the record indicates that a particular form or method of advertising has in fact been deceptive. . . .

Commercial speech doctrine, in the context of advertising for professional services, may be summarized generally as follows: Truthful advertising related to lawful activities is entitled to the protections of the First Amendment. But when the particular content or method of the advertising suggests that it is inherently misleading or when experience has proved that in fact such advertising is subject to abuse, the States may impose appropriate restrictions. Misleading advertising may be prohibited entirely. But the States may not place an absolute prohibition on certain types of potentially misleading information, *e.g.*, a listing of areas of practice, if the information also may be presented in a way that is not deceptive. Thus, the Court in *Bates* suggested that the remedy in the first instance is not necessarily a prohibition but preferably a requirement of disclaimers or explanation. Although the potential for deception and confusion is particularly strong in the context of advertising professional services, restrictions upon such advertising may be no broader than reasonably necessary to prevent the deception.

Even when a communication is not misleading, the State retains some authority to regulate. But the State must assert a substantial interest and the interference with speech must be in proportion to the interest served. *Central Hudson Gas & Electric Corp. v. Public Service Comm'n*, 447 U.S. 557, 563–564, 100 S.Ct. 2343, 2350, 65 L.Ed.2d 341 (1980).[15] Restrictions must be narrowly drawn, and the State lawfully may regulate only to the extent regulation furthers the State's substantial interest. Thus, in *Bates*, the Court found that the potentially adverse effect of advertising on professionalism and the quality of legal services was not sufficiently related to a substantial state interest to justify so great an interference with speech.

IV

We now turn to apply these generalizations to the circumstances of this case.

The information lodged against appellant charged him with four separate kinds of violation of Rule 4: listing the areas of his

---

15. See *Central Hudson Gas & Electric Corp. v. Public Service Comm'n*, 447 U.S., at 566, 100 S.Ct., at 2351:

"In commercial speech cases, then, a four-part analysis has developed. At the outset, we must determine whether the expression is protected by the First Amendment. For commercial speech to come within that provision, it at least must concern lawful activity and not be misleading. Next, we ask whether the asserted governmental interest is substantial. If both inquiries yield positive answers, we must determine whether the

regulation directly advances the governmental interest asserted, and whether it is not more extensive than is necessary to serve that interest."

As the discussion in the text above indicates, the *Central Hudson* formulation must be applied to advertising for professional services with the understanding that the special characteristics of such services afford opportunities to mislead and confuse that are not present when standardized products or services are offered to the public.

practice in language or in terms other than that provided by the Rule, failing to include a disclaimer, listing the courts and States in which he had been admitted to practice, and mailing announcement cards to persons other than "lawyers, clients, former clients, personal friends, and relatives." Appellant makes no challenge to the constitutionality of the disclaimer requirement, and we pass on to the remaining three infractions.

Appellant was reprimanded for deviating from the precise listing of areas of practice included in the Advisory Committee addendum to Rule 4. The Advisory Committee does not argue that appellant's listing was misleading. The use of the words "real estate" instead of "property" could scarcely mislead the public. Similarly, the listing of areas such as "contracts" or "securities," that are not found on the Advisory Committee's list in any form, presents no apparent danger of deception. Indeed, ... in certain respects appellant's listing is more informative than that provided in the addendum. Because the listing published by the appellant has not been shown to be misleading, and because the Advisory Committee suggests no substantial interest promoted by the restriction, we conclude that this portion of Rule 4 is an invalid restriction upon speech as applied to appellant's advertisements.

Nor has the Advisory Committee identified any substantial interest in a rule that prohibits a lawyer from identifying the jurisdictions in which he is licensed to practice. Such information is not misleading on its face. Appellant was licensed to practice in both Illinois and Missouri. This is factual and highly relevant information particularly in light of the geography of the region in which appellant practiced.

Somewhat more troubling is appellant's listing, in large capital letters, that he was a member of the Bar of the Supreme Court of the United States. The emphasis of this relatively uninformative fact is at least bad taste. Indeed, such a statement could be misleading to the general public unfamiliar with the requirements of admission to the Bar of this Court. Yet there is no finding to this effect by the Missouri Supreme Court. There is nothing in the record to indicate that the inclusion of this information was misleading. Nor does the Rule specifically identify this information as potentially misleading or, for example, place a limitation on type size or require a statement explaining the nature of the Supreme Court Bar.

Finally, appellant was charged with mailing cards announcing the opening of his office to persons other than "lawyers, clients, former clients, personal friends and relatives." Mailings and handbills may be more difficult to supervise than newspapers. But again we deal with a silent record. There is no indication that an inability to supervise is the reason the State restricts the potential audience of announcement cards. Nor is it clear that an absolute prohibition is the only solution.... There is no indication in the record of a failed effort to proceed along such a less restrictive path. See *Central Hudson Gas & Electric Corp. v. Public Service Comm'n*, 447 U.S., at 566 ("we must determine whether the regulation ... is not more extensive than is necessary to serve" the governmental interest asserted).

In sum, none of the three restrictions in the Rule upon appellant's First Amendment rights can be sustained in the circumstances of this case. There is no finding that appellant's speech was misleading. Nor can we say that it was inherently misleading, or that restrictions short of an absolute prohibition would not have sufficed to cure any possible deception. We emphasize, as we have throughout the opinion, that the States retain the authority to regulate advertising that is inherently misleading or that has proved to be misleading in practice. There may be other substantial state interests as well that will support carefully drawn restrictions. But although the States may regulate commercial speech, the First and Fourteenth Amendments require that they do so with care and in a manner no more extensive than reasonably necessary to further substantial interests. The absolute prohibition on appellant's speech, in the absence of a finding that his speech was misleading, does not meet these requirements.

Accordingly, the judgment of the Supreme Court of Missouri is *Reversed*.

Notes

1. In *In re R.M.J.*, Justice Powell helpfully summarizes the Supreme Court's lawyer advertising jurisprudence, beginning with the landmark case of *Bates v. State Bar of Arizona*. Before *Bates* was decided (1977), most states enforced an absolute prohibition on advertising. *Bates* struck down such a prohibition in a case involving a newspaper advertisement that listed set fees for some routine legal services. Clearly, similarly broad prohibitions would now be held to violate free speech rights. But the organized bar, both at the national and state levels, continues to believe that some restrictions on lawyer advertising are needed. Based on the discussion in *R.M.J.*, what kinds of restrictions will pass constitutional muster? Does the Court's jurisprudence on this issue–especially its use of the analysis from *Central Hudson*–strike a good balance between the interests implicated?

2. *Sophisticated marketing. Bates* radically changed law firm marketing strategies. While small firms and solo practitioners run advertisements on the sides of buses, in TV guides, and on late-night television, larger firms typically spend big money on marketing consultants to conduct more sophisticated campaigns. See Mark Ballard, *The Little Ad That Changed Everything*, Nat'l L.J., Sept. 23, 2002, at A1. Some large firms have now engaged in substantial television advertising, something that would have been unimaginable just a few years ago. *See* Martha

Neil, *Learning How to Ad*, ABA J., Oct. 2001, at 42 (discussing the growth of big-firm marketing consultancy and describing $3.5 million TV ad campaign by Brobeck, Phleger & Harrison). Does advertising in the media help the public? Does it harm the legal profession?

3. *Current ethics rules.* Ethics rules on lawyer advertising are subject to revision each time the Supreme Court speaks on the issue; obviously, the bar cannot maintain any rule that the Court declares unconstitutional. The Model Rules on advertising, which immediately after *Bates* were among the longest in the entire set, are now fairly streamlined. See MR 7.1 (prohibiting "false or misleading communication about the lawyer or the lawyer's services"); MR 7.2 (expressly allowing advertisements as long as Rules 7.1 and 7.3—on solicitation—are complied with). Several states maintain fairly detailed rules on the subject, often including examples of messages that will presumed to be misleading and those that will be presumed otherwise. In all states, the central focus remains on prohibiting false, deceptive or misleading statements. See, e.g., Tex. Rules 7.02, 7.04, 7.07; Cal. Rule 1–400; Cal. Bus. & Prof. Code §§ 6157 *et seq.*; Iowa rules 7.1–7.5 (2005). (As this book was going to press, New York was overhauling its advertising rules; the new rules will be found on the web site of the New York Courts at www.nycourts.gov/rules., if they are not in your current statutory supplement.)

4. *State consumer protection statutes.* Most states have consumer protection statutes that grant a cause of action to consumers for a defendant's unfair or deceptive trade practice. Might such a statute apply to misleading lawyer advertisements? See *Crowe v. Tull*, 126 P.3d 196 (Colo. 2006) (holding that lawyers may be liable for violations of Colorado Consumer Protection Act if their advertisements are deceptive); *Short v. Demopolis*, 103 Wash.2d 52, 691 P.2d 163 (1984) (holding that the "business aspects of the legal profession are legitimate concerns of the public which are properly subject to" Washington state's Consumer Protection Act).

5. *All the world's a stage.* Advertising is part and parcel of capitalism, of course, and a desire for financial gain leads to some humorous marketing techniques that continue to raise the eyebrows (and often the ire) of bar authorities. Television advertisements involving dramatizations provide the most colorful examples.

a. In *In re Pavilack*, 327 S.C. 6, 488 S.E.2d 309 (1997), a lawyer aired two television advertisements involving automobile accidents. As described by the court, "In one of the advertisements, an individual portraying a police officer summoned respondent by radio and asked him to come to the scene of the accident to determine who was at fault. The other advertisement places respondent at the scene of an accident directing the police officer to interview the occupants of the vehicle which rear-ended respondent's client." These were held to violate South Carolina's Rule 7.1(b), since they "imply that respondent has the ability to control a police officer's investigation.'' Pavilack was publicly reprimanded.

b. In *Farrin v. Thigpen*, 173 F.Supp.2d 427 (M.D.N.C.2001), two law firms (Farrin and Lewis & Daggett) and a production company challenged the constitutionality of a formal ethics opinion issued by the North Carolina State Bar in which the panel determined that a specific television advertisement was misleading, in violation of North Carolina's Rule 7.1. The advertisement at issue, called ''Strategy Session,'' used actor Robert Vaughn (of ''The Man From U.N.C.L.E.'' fame) as a spokesperson. The court described the ad as follows:

> The ad depicts a scene, which is viewed through blinds as if the viewer were looking into a window, which takes place in a conference room where three people, a woman and two men, are seated at a table. A fourth man dressed in a business suit, the ''senior man,'' the oldest person in the room, is seated on the edge of a credenza facing one of the men at the table, the ''junior man,'' who is coatless. There is a book or binder open in front of the junior man, and he is leaning back and turned to face the senior man. The other two individuals, both dressed in business suits, have their backs to the camera for the duration of the vignette and have no apparent role other than to listen to the junior man and senior man converse. In the background there is a large pad resting on an easel; a list is visible on it, but due to the short time it is displayed and its small print, it is not possible to discern the contents of the list.

> The vignette opens on that scene with a box of text (white type against a black background) superimposed that either states ''Insurance adjusters strategy session'' or ''Legal strategy session: insurance company,'' depending on whether it is Farrin's or Lewis and Daggett's ad. Beneath the box in much smaller, white letters imposed on the scene itself rather than in a black box appears the following disclaimer: ''Dramatization by actors. No specific result implied. Vaughn is a paid spokesperson for The Law Office of James Scott Farrin. Copr. 2000 Market Masters–Legal, A Resonance Co., Inc.'' [The Lewis & Daggett ad contained a similar disclaimer.] Daggett testified that the disclaimer for both ads was on the screen approximately four seconds.

> The camera focuses on the senior man alone, who asks the junior man, ''How do you suggest we handle *this* claim?'' The camera then pans to the junior man, who leans back slightly in his seat and replies, ''It's a large claim, a serious auto accident. We could try to deny it or delay, see if they'll crack.''

> The camera returns to the senior man's face, as he asks in a slower, more deliberate tone, ''Who's the lawyer representing the victim?'' As the senior man is speaking, the camera returns to a close-up of the junior man, who frowns slightly with a

reluctant expression. The camera again focuses on the senior man's face, his expression calm and his eyes looking downward as he awaits the answer. While the camera is on the senior man's face, the junior man's voice is heard saying slowly, "Lewis and Daggett." [The script used by Farrin is identical, except that the junior man and senior man replace "Lewis and Daggett" with "James Scott Farrin."]

The pace of the remainder of the vignette speeds up. A loud, metallic gong sounds immediately after the name of the firm is stated. Upon hearing the name, while the gong is sounding, the senior man's expression changes dramatically. His eyebrows shoot up and his eyes widen and shift from downward toward the junior man. The court finds that the senior man's expression would be characterized by a reasonable person as dismayed or alarmed. The camera returns to the junior man's face, while the senior man exclaims the name of the firm as a question, "Lewis and Daggett?" The junior man nods, his mouth in a grim line. The vignette ends with the camera back on the senior man's face as he says, "Let's settle this one." His mouth is also set into a grim line, and he looks away from the junior man and downward.

The camera then moves away to the second part featuring Vaughn, who looks into the camera in the direction of the viewer and says, "North Carolina insurance companies know the name Lewis and Daggett. If you've been injured in an auto accident, tell them *you mean business.*—Call Lewis and Daggett. 1–800–LAW–7777 right now." Vaughn points at the screen while he emphasizes the italicized words.

The court concluded that "[t]he 'Strategy Session' is not an accurate portrayal of the method employed by insurance adjusters or defense attorneys in determining whether to settle a case." It is entirely fictional, not truthful, and therefore not protected commercial speech at all. The court concluded further that the ad was inherently misleading, and thus violative of Rule 7.1, for two reasons: first, the portrayal of "the insurance industry constitutes a material misrepresentation of fact"; second, the ad "is likely to create an unjustified expectation that the lawyers advertised can obtain settlements based solely on their reputation and the insurance industry's fear of or reluctance to try a case against them."

The same advertisement and two others produced by the same national marketing firm were later found to be deceptive and misleading when used by a firm in Indiana. *In re Keller*, 792 N.E.2d 865 (Ind. 2003) (public reprimand upheld for firm's violation of Rules 7.1(d)(3) & (4)).

6. *"Self-laudatory" claims.* Many states explicitly prohibit "self-laudatory" claims, a phrase taken from DR 2–101(A) with a pedigree from Canon 27 (which condemned all advertising "and all other self-laudation" as "lower[ing] the tone of our profession"). Given constitu-

tional guidelines, most modern courts interpret such prohibitions to cover claims that are misleading because they create unjustified expectations or tout the quality of a lawyer's work in a manner that cannot be verified objectively.

a. In *Florida Bar v. Pape*, 918 So.2d 240 (Fla. 2005), a law firm displayed the image of a pit bull wearing a spiked collar and displayed the term "pit bull" as part of the firm's phone number ("1–800–PIT-BULL") in their advertisements. The Florida Bar filed complaints against the firm for violation of state rules 7.2(b)(3) (prohibiting statements characterizing the quality of a lawyer's services) and 7.2(b)(4) (prohibiting deceptive, misleading or manipulative visual or verbal depictions). The referee who first heard the case ruled against the bar, finding that pit bulls are "perceived as loyal, persistent, tenacious, and aggressive," qualities which are "objectively relevant" to choosing a lawyer. He also found that while the pit bull logo "describe[d] qualities of the respondent attorneys," it did not describe or characterize "the quality of the lawyer services" as prohibited by the rule. He further opined that the advertisement was protected speech under the First Amendment. The Florida Supreme Court reversed. "The rules [for lawyer advertising in Florida] are designed to permit lawyer advertisements that provide objective information about the cost of legal services, the experience and qualifications of the lawyer and law firm, and the types of cases a lawyer handles," the court said. The use of slogans and images violates the rules. Further, the "pit bull" logo and phone number do describe the quality of the lawyers, in violation of Rule 7.2(b)(3): "A courteous lawyer can be expected to be well mannered in court, a hard-working lawyer well prepared, and a 'pit bull' lawyer vicious to the opposition." The court found a violation of 7.2(b)(4) because the use of the pit bull image and name "would suggest to many persons not only that the lawyers can achieve results but also that they engage in a combative style of advocacy. The suggestion is inherently deceptive because there is no way to measure whether the attorneys in fact conduct themselves like pit bulls so as to ascertain whether this logo and phone number convey accurate information." Because the advertising device "connotes combativeness and viciousness without providing objectively verifiable factual information," it falls outside the protection of the First Amendment. The court concluded that "[w]ere we to approve the referee's finding, images of sharks, wolves, crocodiles, and piranhas could follow. For the good of the legal profession and the justice system, . . . this type of non-factual adverting cannot be permitted." Public reprimand was ordered.

b. In *In re Wamsley*, 725 N.E.2d 75 (Ind.2000), the lawyer placed his advertisement prominently on the back cover of the 1997 Indianapolis telephone directory. It included the following statements: "Best Possible Settlement . . . Least Amount of Time"; "My reputation, experience, and integrity result in most of our cases being settled without filing a complaint or lengthy trial"; and "I have helped thousands who have been seriously hurt or lost a loved one." The court found these statements violative of Indiana Rules 7.1(b) ("misleading, deceptive, self-laudatory and unfair" statements in advertising); 7.1(c)(3) (creating an unjustified expectation of a particular result); 7.1(d)(4) (offering a statement or opinion as to the quality of the services); and 7.1(d)(2) (offering statistical data or other information based on past performance and an implicit prediction of future success). A public reprimand was ordered. What about a Yellow Pages ad that uses the headline "INJURY EXPERTS," and says "WE ARE THE EXPERTS IN . . . " followed by a listing of three areas of law? Does the ad violate Rule 7.1? See *In re PRB Docket No. 2002.093*, 177 Vt. 629, 868 A.2d 709 (2005).

c. In *Iowa Supreme Court Board of Professional Ethics and Conduct v. Bjorklund*, 617 N.W.2d 4 (Iowa 2000), the lawyer's advertisement appeared in four monthly issues of a publication called "Movie Facts," which was handed out to movie theater patrons at at least four theaters in Iowa City. As described by the court, "The ad prominently displays Bjorklund's name and occupation as an attorney at law following the question, 'Have you been caught drinking and driving?' and the exclamation 'I can help!' " The ad also contained information about a book titled "Drunk Driving Defense: How to Beat the Rap," authored by Bjorklund. Bjorklund argued that the advertisement was intended to promote his book, not his practice, but the court concluded that the ad "does not offer the book for sale or necessarily promote the book as the source of help, but mainly refers to the book as a means to validate the ability of Bjorklund to help." The lawyer was publicly reprimanded for participating in the promulgation of an ad "which is self-laudatory, relates to the quality of the lawyer's legal services, and is not verifiable," in violation of Iowa DR–2–101(A).

7. *Client testimonials.* Many states ban client testimonials entirely. Others require disclaimers. Why might client testimonials be misleading? See, e.g., Conn. Bar Ass'n Comm. on Prof. Ethics, Informal Op. 01–07 (2001); Va. State Bar Standing Comm. on Lawyer Advertising and Solicitation, Op. 1750 (2001); Ohio S. Ct. Bd. of Comm'rs on Grievances and Discipline, Op. 2000–6 (2000). Are *all* such testimonials misleading, or do they give consumers useful information?

WALKER v. BOARD OF PROFESSIONAL RESPONSIBILITY OF THE SUPREME COURT OF TENNESSEE

Supreme Court of Tennessee, 2001.
38 S.W.3d 540.

DROWOTA, J.

The Code of Professional Responsibility requires attorneys who advertise with regard to any area of law but who are not certified in that area to include the following disclaimer in their advertisements: "Not certified as a (area of practice) specialist by the Tennessee Commission on Continuing Legal Education and Specialization." DR 2–101(C)(3). The appellant was not certified as a civil trial specialist (which when this case arose covered the area of divorce law) yet he specifically mentioned divorce law in certain ads, and in another ad he did not adhere to the exact wording of the required disclaimer. The Board of Professional Responsibility brought a disciplinary action against the appellant and, finding him in violation of DR 2–101(C)(3), issued a private reprimand. The appellant sought review of the Board's action in Chancery Court, which upheld the sanction. He now seeks further review in this Court, arguing for the reversal of the sanction on the ground that DR 2–101(C)(3) violates the First Amendment to the United States Constitution. We hold that this disclosure rule is constitutional and that the private reprimand may stand. . . .

Ted F. Walker (Walker), the plaintiff/appellant, is an attorney who maintains a divorce law practice in Nashville, Memphis, and Chattanooga. His practice focuses on uncontested divorces in which both parties agree to a settlement. Walker is not certified as a specialist in civil trial practice (which included divorce law) by the Tennessee Commission on Continuing Legal Education and Specialization. Certification, while not required to practice a particular area of law, is intended to enhance both the skills of attorneys licensed in Tennessee and "the ability of the citizens . . . to identify attorneys with special competence in particular areas of practice."

Over the years Walker has advertised his services by placing short ads in local newspapers. The Board of Professional Responsibility of the Supreme Court of Tennessee (Board), the defendant/appellee, became aware of these ads, believed they violated provisions of the Code of Professional Responsibility, and filed two petitions for discipline against Walker. . . .

PROCEDURAL HISTORY

In February 1995, Walker placed an advertisement for divorce services in the *Chattanooga News Free Press TV Magazine*. The ad was published over the week of February 12 through 18, 1995 and states in its entirety: "DIVORCE, BOTH PARTIES SIGN, $125 + COST, NO EXTRA CHARGES, Ted Walker, [address & telephone number]." On March 29, 1995, the Board's Disciplinary Counsel filed a complaint against Walker alleging that this advertisement listed divorce as a specific area of practice but did not include the disclaimer required by DR 2–101(C) of the Code of Professional Responsibility. . . . In his response to the complaint, Walker argued that his advertisement fully complied with the United States Supreme Court's decision in *Bates v. State Bar of Arizona*, 433 U.S. 350, 97 S.Ct. 2691, 53 L.Ed.2d 810 (1977) and that "the law, as set out by the United States Supreme Court, is governing over a conflicting law by the Tennessee Supreme Court." After an exchange of correspondence with the Disciplinary Counsel, Walker apparently agreed to change his advertisement to add the required disclaimer. [The Board issued and Informal Admonition and offered to close the file, but Walker requested a formal proceeding to challenge the rule.]

The Board filed a "Supplemental Petition for Discipline" on July 21, 1997. The supplemental petition alleged that a complaint file had been opened pertaining to two advertisements placed in *The Chattanooga Times* on February 9, 1997: one in the *Chattanooga TV Guide* and one in the Business Directory Section of the classified ads. The TV guide ad stated: "DIVORCE, BOTH PARTIES SIGN, $90.00 + COURT COSTS $89.50, No 'Extra' Charges, TED WALKER, [phone number], Not certified as a specialist by the TN Commission on Certification and Specialization." The ad in the Business Directory Section was similar but did not contain the "not certified" statement. The Board's supplemental petition alleged that the ad in the *Chattanooga TV Guide* did not use "the precise language required by the Tennessee Supreme Court in quotation marks within Tenn. R.S.Ct. 8, DR 2–101(C)(2)(3), with no variations or abbreviations, an interpretation adopted by the Board in *Tennessee Formal Ethics Opinion 95–F–137*." The supplemental petition also alleged that the advertisement in the Business Directory Section "include[d] no mandatory disclosure of specialty certification whatsoever, as is required under DR 2–101(C)(3)." The petition further alleged that Walker did not comply with DR 2–101(F) (pertaining to filing copies of advertisements within three days of their publication) as to either of the ads.

[Both petitions were set for a hearing before a Board Hearing Committee. Walker agreed to enter a "no contest" plea and to a private reprimand for violating the rules as alleged, but was granted the right to appeal the judgment to attack the constitutionality of DR 2–101. The Chancery Court found against him, and the Court of Appeals transferred Walker's appeal directly to this Court.]

Analysis

Attorney Advertising and the First Amendment

We have never before addressed lawyer advertising, but we have squarely addressed a similar regulation of another profession. In *Douglas v. State,* 921 S.W.2d 180 (Tenn.1996), we upheld the constitutionality of an administrative rule requiring dentists who are not certified specialists but who advertise that they offer specialty services like orthodontics to disclose that their services "are being provided by a general dentist." *Douglas* is, of course, similar to the case before us, all the more so because the case law does not make distinctions among the professions. For example, in

Ibanez v. Florida Dep't of Bus. & Prof'l Regulation, 512 U.S. 136, 114 S.Ct. 2084, 129 L.Ed.2d 118 (1994), the United States Supreme Court relied heavily on attorney advertising cases although the regulation before it involved advertising by Certified Public Accountants (CPAs) and Certified Financial Planners. *See also Edenfield v. Fane,* 507 U.S. 761, 113 S.Ct. 1792, 123 L.Ed.2d 543 (1993) (involving the regulation of CPAs). Our opinion in *Douglas* also relied heavily on attorney advertising cases. Since the commercial speech standards recently discussed in *Douglas* apply here, and since the United States Supreme Court has not decided a "regulation of professions" commercial speech case after *Douglas,* we find that case to be highly relevant authority.

[The validity of commercial speech regulations is subject to intermediate scrutiny, under the *Central Hudson* test.] The regulation before us requires that whenever a lawyer advertises his services in a particular area of law for which certification is available in Tennessee, he must disclose in the ad whether he is certified. DR 2–101(C). Since Walker was not certified as a civil trial specialist (which then covered the area of divorce law) yet he specifically mentioned divorce law in his ads, the disciplinary rule mandates that his ads include the following language: "Not certified as a civil trial specialist by the Tennessee Commission on Continuing Legal Education and Specialization." DR 2–101(C)(3). This regulation does not prohibit or limit speech; instead it requires more speech by way of an explanatory disclaimer.

The fact that the regulation requires disclosure rather than prohibition tends to make it less objectionable under the First Amendment. Recognizing that the "bar retains the power to correct omissions that have the effect of presenting an inaccurate picture," the Court in *Bates* specifically noted that "the preferred remedy is more disclosure, rather than less." In *Douglas* we addressed the distinction between prohibition and disclosure. We discussed *Zauderer v. Office of the Disciplinary Counsel,* 471 U.S. 626, 105 S.Ct. 2265, 85 L.Ed.2d 652 (1985), in which the United States Supreme Court struck down an Ohio regulation prohibiting the use of illustrations in attorney ads, but upheld that state's regulation requiring an attorney who advertises her availability on a contingent-fee basis to disclose that clients are responsible for court costs. We noted that the First Amendment analysis in *Zauderer* was more forgiving of disclosure-type regulations and we quoted from that decision at length, parts of which we again recite:

> Appellant, however, overlooks material differences between disclosure requirements and outright prohibitions on speech.... Ohio has not attempted to prevent attorneys from conveying information to the public; it has only required them to provide somewhat more information than they might otherwise be inclined to pres-

ent.... Because the extension of First Amendment protection to commercial speech is justified principally by the value to consumers of the information such speech provides, appellant's constitutionally protected interest in *not* providing any particular factual information in his advertising is minimal....

In *Douglas* a principal question was whether the United States Supreme Court repudiated this disclosure analysis in *Ibanez*. The petitioner in *Douglas* pointed to language in *Ibanez* to support that contention, but we held that *Ibanez* should be interpreted to harmonize rather than conflict with *Zauderer*.... Thus, under current law–as announced in *Zauderer*–as long as the disclosure requirement is reasonably related to the state's interest in preventing deception of consumers, and not unduly burdensome, it should be upheld. Recent cases have also applied the less rigorous *Zauderer* standard when confronted with government regulations requiring disclosure of information. *See, e.g., Commodity Trend Serv., Inc. v. Commodity Futures Trading Comm'n,* 233 F.3d 981, 994 (7th Cir.2000) ("The government can impose affirmative disclosures in commercial advertising if these are reasonably related to preventing the public from being deceived or misled."); *Commodity Futures Trading Comm'n v. Vartuli,* 228 F.3d 94, 108 (2d Cir.2000); *Consolidated Cigar Corp. v. Reilly,* 218 F.3d 30, 54 (1st Cir.2000). Of course, the state must always meet its burden of justifying the need for regulation in the first place. The holding of *Douglas* simply recognizes that the Board's burden is lower than it would be had it prohibited Walker from advertising truthful information.

The Constitutionality of DR 2–101(C)(3)

The Board argues that Tennessee's interest in requiring non-certified attorneys who advertise specialty services to include a disclaimer in their ads is substantial: protecting consumers of legal services by allowing them to make informed judgments about which attorney to hire to handle their legal needs. We agree that this interest is substantial. As one court has put it, "the state, as part of its duty to regulate attorneys, has an interest in ensuring and encouraging the flow of helpful, relevant information about attorneys." *Mason,* 208 F.3d at 956; *see also Peel v. Attorney Registration and Disciplinary Comm'n,* 496 U.S. 91, 110 (1990)("Information about certification and specialties facilitates the consumer's access to legal services and thus better serves the administration of justice.").

Since the state's interest is substantial, the question is whether DR 2–101(C)(3) is reasonably related to promoting that interest. The record before this Court when the certification disclaimer rule was considered in 1993 reveals that the Commission on Continuing Legal Education ("Commission"), which petitioned this Court to adopt the rule, had the following concern: lawyers who were advertising specialties were actually obtaining far fewer Continuing Legal Education hours of training than leading practitioners in that specialty area who were not advertising.[2] This was problematic because an American Bar Association survey indicated that the public expected a lawyer who advertised in a particular area of law to have greater education in that area than other lawyers. The Commission thought the public would be better served if presented with a more accurate picture of an advertising lawyer's level of education.

The disclaimer rule the Commission advocated and this Court ultimately adopted promotes the Commission's legitimate goal by clearly and succinctly providing the public with information about the certification status of attorneys who advertise their services. This information will help a consumer identify which lawyers may have more experience and education in a particular area of law—knowledge which will help that consumer hire a lawyer to represent his interests. It is not contended, of course, that the disclaimer rule by itself provides all the useful information the public might wish to obtain; indeed, many attorneys advertise, and consumers will still have to make choices among attorneys with a similar certification status. But the information required by DR 2–101(C)(3) is one piece of information that will assist consumers in making those choices. The required disclaimer is therefore reasonably related to promoting the substantial interest of helping consumers to make informed judgments about which attorneys they should entrust with their legal needs.

Next, we must determine whether DR 2–101(C)(3) is unduly burdensome. The United States Supreme Court in *Ibanez* confronted a Florida Board of Accountancy rule that required a Certified Financial Planner who included a specialist designation on an advertisement to disclose, among other things, the requirements for recognition of the agency that certified her as a specialist. Although the Court concluded that the disclosure requirement was unconstitutional because the Florida Board had failed to justify the need for such regulation, it also noted that the disclosure requirement was too burdensome: "The detail required in the disclaimer currently described by the Board effectively rules out notation of the 'specialist' designation on a business card or letterhead, or in a yellow pages listing." In contrast to the detailed

---

2. The Commission conducted a survey comparing the number of continuing legal education hours earned per year by attorneys who advertised (Advertisers) with display ads in the yellow pages to hours earned by attorneys recognized as leading practitioners (LPs) in four areas of law: bankruptcy, criminal defense, domestic relations, and personal injury. The results were as follows: (1) in bankruptcy the LPs averaged 14.6 hours and the Advertisers averaged 4.1 hours; (2) in criminal defense the LPs averages 19.6 hours and the Advertisers averaged 2.2 hours; (3) in domestic relations the LPs averaged 8.7 hours and the Advertisers averaged 1.9 hours; and (4) in personal injury the LPs averaged 16.2 hours and the Advertisers averaged 6 hours.

disclaimer in *Ibanez,* the disclaimer required by DR 2–101(C)(3) is as short and free of burdensome detail as possible. It simply requires the following language: "Not certified as a (area of practice) specialist by the Tennessee Commission on Continuing Legal Education and Specialization." This statement does not require an attorney who advertises his skills to disclose anything more than the basic fact of his non-certification; no extraneous information or lengthy detail is required. We hold that the disclaimer here satisfies the constitutional standard....

Finally, Walker argues that even if the disclosure rule is constitutional, the State cannot require him to use the precise language listed in DR 2–101(C)(3). He argues that any statement that conveys the same meaning as the specific language in the disciplinary rule is sufficient. He claims that his disclaimer, which states that he was "not certified as a specialist by the Tennessee Commission on Certification and Specialization," meets this standard....

Walker argues that the United States Supreme Court's decision in *In re R.M.J.,* 455 U.S. 191, 102 S.Ct. 929, 71 L.Ed.2d 64 (1982) supports his position. We disagree. ... Unlike *R.M.J.,* where the attorney's advertisements could not have been misleading, we think that deviations from the specific wording of DR 2–101(C)(3) could lead to public confusion. The required disclaimer statement was worded in the most simple, direct fashion so that the public would have no difficulty understanding its meaning or comparing different attorney advertisements. This goal might easily be thwarted if attorneys were allowed to write their own disclaimer statements. Rather than focus on the intended message—that an attorney is not certified—a consumer would be forced to parse the meaning of different disclaimer statements, attempting to understand without any guidance why one attorney's disclaimer was different than another's.

The Board's interest in requiring uniform language is significant for another reason. Just as the absence of uniformity would require a consumer to compare many different disclaimer statements, so would the Board, and subsequently the courts, be forced to examine advertisement after advertisement in an effort to determine which attorneys substantially complied with DR 2–101(C)(3) and which attorneys fell somewhat short. This costly and inefficient task seems entirely unnecessary in light of the ease of complying with a uniform rule—especially one which is as short and free of burdensome detail as possible....

For the reasons discussed above, we affirm the Chancery Court's ruling that the disclaimer requirement of DR 2–101(C)(3) is constitutional....

Notes

1. *Certification of specialties.* Lawyer certification programs began to grow in popularity in the mid–1970s, sparked in part by a speech by Chief Justice Warren Burger in which he argued that specialized training and certification in trial advocacy was needed. See Warren E. Burger, *The Special Skills of Advocacy: Are Specialized Training and Certification of Advocates Essential to Our System of Justice?*, 42 Fordham L. Rev. 227 (1973). National certification groups, including the National Board of Trial Advocacy, were formed and many states developed specialization commissions.

2. *Communication of certified specialties and fields of practice.* Once certified specialty programs were in place, disciplinary authorities were faced with the issue of whether and to what extent lawyers could properly advertise their certified specialist status. Two cases went to the high court as challenges to the constitutionality of state bar restrictions on such statements. In *Peel v. Attorney Registration and Disciplinary Comm'n of Illinois*, 496 U.S. 91, 110 S.Ct. 2281, 110 L.Ed.2d 83 (1990), a lawyer stated on his letterhead that he was certified as a civil trial specialist by the National Board of Trial Advocacy. For this, he was publicly censured by the Illinois Supreme Court, which concluded that the statement was misleading as "tantamount to an implied claim of superiority of the quality of [his] legal services." But six members of the U.S. Supreme Court found the letterhead "neither actually nor inherently misleading," and reversed. "Disclosure of information such as that on petitioner's letterhead both serves the public interest and encourages the development and utilization of meritorious certification programs." Id. (plurality opinion by Justice Stevens). In *Ibanez v. Florida Dep't of Bus. & Prof'l Regulation*, 512 U.S. 136, 114 S.Ct. 2084, 129 L.Ed.2d 118 (1994), discussed in *Walker* above, the Court concluded that Florida could not constitutionally require a lawyer to add a lengthy disclaimer to her designation that she was a Certified Financial Planner.

Model Rule 7.4 allows a lawyer to "communicate the fact that the lawyer does or does not practice in particular fields of law," and to state that the lawyer is a specialist, as long as the lawyer complies with specific guidelines relating to the particular state's certification process.

3. *Mason v. Florida Bar*, 208 F.3d 952 (11th Cir.2000), was a successful constitutional challenge to the Florida Bar's requirement, pursuant to its rules prohibiting "self-laudatory" advertisements, that Mason place a disclaimer in his yellow pages advertisement in which he truthfully said that he had received Martindale–Hubbell's highest rating. The court rejected the state's argument that the rating was misleading without the disclaimer that it was based "exclusively on opinions expressed by confidential sources." Applying *Central Hudson*, the court held that the state simply did not prove that the advertisement posed a genuine threat of harm that would be addressed by the restriction.

4. *Firm names and letterheads.* As you can tell from the cases, letterheads can be an effective form of advertising, giving recipients of the lawyer's mail some useful information about the lawyer's qualifications. Model Rule 7.5 prohibits the use of letterheads or firm names that violate Rule 7.1, meaning letterheads or firm names that are "false or misleading." See also N.Y. DR 2–102; Cal. 1–400(A)(1) & (2). When would this occur? Could two lawyers who share office space but who are not otherwise associated call themselves "Smith and Jones?" Could a solo practitioner named Brown practice under the firm name "Lincoln, Herndon & Brown," where neither Lincoln nor Herndon were ever his partners? See MR 7.5(a) & (d) & comments [1] & [2]. A law firm may continue to use the name of a deceased partner in its firm name, but may not continue to use the name of a lawyer who is still in practice but in another firm. MR 7.5, comment [2]. Why would that be the rule? See Md. State Bar Ass'n Comm. on Ethics, Op. 00–03 (1999).

5. *Trade names.* Could a law firm call itself "American Tort Claims Advocates?" Or "Center for Debt Relief?" A number of state advertising rules prohibit the use of trade names as inherently deceptive, making lawyers subject to discipline for using such names. See, e.g., *Medina Cty. Bar Ass'n v. Baker*, 102 Ohio St.3d 260, 809 N.E.2d 659 (2004) (public reprimand ordered for lawyer's use of "Full Service Credit Center" and "The Center for Debt Relief," even where these names were used in conjunction with the lawyer's real name in signage and advertisements); *Rodgers v. Commission for Lawyer Discipline*, 151 S.W.3d 602 (Tex. App. 2004) (lawyer placed on two-year probated suspension for his use of "Accidental Injury Hotline" name in advertising, without mentioning the lawyer's name; lawyer also failed to register ads with the state bar as required). The Texas rule applied in *Rodgers* defines a trade name as "a name that is misleading as to ... identity." Tex. Rule 7.01(a). How would the trade names used in *Baker* and *Rodgers* be misleading as to identity?

6. *Branding and consumer confusion.* There is a modern trend for firms, especially big ones with long names (typically of now-deceased founding partners) to shorten the firm's name to one or two names. Paul, Hastings, Janofsky & Walker thus becomes Paul Hastings in its signage and in print advertisements. Skadden, Arps, Slate, Meagher & Flom becomes Skadden Arps, or simply Skadden. Could this trend produce firm names that are so similar to each other that consumers are confused about what firm they are dealing with? What if both firms have offices in the same cities? If that occurs, does a firm have a cause of action against the one using the shortened form, or vice versa? In one well-known case, Milwaukee-based Foley & Lardner began to refer to itself as simply *Foley*. Foley & Lardner expanded into Boston, the home turf of Foley Hoag, a 60–year-old firm. After seeing confusion over the names—including frequent misdirection of mail to *Foley* being sent to Foley Hoag, the latter firm sued in federal court for trademark infringement and violations of the Lanham Act, 15 U.S.C. § 1125(a) (prohibiting use of a misleading name or mark likely to cause confusion). The case

settled when Foley & Lardner agreed not to use a logo with the single word *Foley* without having *Foley & Lardner* "in close proximity and prominence." See G.M. Filisko, *A Different Foley Fracas*, A.B.A. J. eReport (Oct. 20, 2006). See also *Suisman, Shapiro, Wool, Brennan, Gray, & Greenberg, P.C. v. Suisman*, 2006 WL 387289 (D.Conn.) (granting summary judgment in Lanham Act case for firm whose use of *Suisman Shapiro* brand has developed secondary meaning, against a newer firm called Suisman & Shapiro; both firms are in New London, Connecticut); *Keaton and Keaton v. Keaton*, 842 N.E.2d 816 (Ind. 2006) (denying such relief on ground that plaintiff's *Keaton and Keaton, P.C.* brand did not have secondary meaning so as to prevent another firm named Keaton and Keaton from doing business in the same area).

§ 2. SOLICITATION

A. In–Person and Other Real–Time Solicitation

OHRALIK v. OHIO STATE BAR ASS'N

Supreme Court of the United States, 1978.
436 U.S. 447, 98 S.Ct. 1912, 56 L.Ed.2d 444.

Mr. Justice POWELL delivered the opinion of the Court.

In *Bates v. State Bar of Arizona*, 433 U.S. 350, 97 S.Ct. 2691, 53 L.Ed.2d 810 (1977), this Court held that truthful advertising of "routine" legal services is protected by the First and Fourteenth Amendments against blanket prohibition by a State. The Court expressly reserved the question of the permissible scope of regulation of "in-person solicitation of clients—at the hospital room or the accident site, or in any other situation that breeds undue influence–by attorneys or their agents or 'runners.'" Today we answer part of the question so reserved, and hold that the State— or the Bar acting with state authorization—constitutionally may discipline a lawyer for soliciting clients in person, for pecuniary gain, under circumstances likely to pose dangers that the State has a right to prevent.

I

Appellant, a member of the Ohio Bar, lives in Montville, Ohio. Until recently he practiced law in Montville and Cleveland. On February 13, 1974, while picking up his mail at the Montville Post Office, appellant learned from the postmaster's brother about an automobile accident that had taken place on February 2 in which Carol McClintock, a young woman with whom appellant was casually acquainted, had been injured. Appellant made a telephone call to Ms. McClintock's parents, who informed him that their daughter was in the hospital. Appellant suggested that he might visit Carol in the hospital. Mrs. McClintock assented to the idea, but requested that appellant first stop by at her home.

During appellant's visit with the McClintocks, they explained that their daughter had been driving the family automobile on a local road when she was hit by an uninsured motorist. Both Carol and her passenger, Wanda Lou Holbert, were injured and hospitalized. In response to the McClintocks' expression of apprehension that they might be sued by Holbert, appellant explained that Ohio's guest statute would preclude such a suit. When appellant suggested to the McClintocks that they hire a lawyer, Mrs. McClintock retorted that such a decision would be up to Carol, who was 18 years old and would be the beneficiary of a successful claim.

Appellant proceeded to the hospital, where he found Carol lying in traction in her room. After a brief conversation about her condition, appellant told Carol he would represent her and asked her to sign an agreement. Carol said she would have to discuss the matter with her parents. She did not sign the agreement, but asked appellant to have her parents come to see her.[2] Appellant also attempted to see Wanda Lou Holbert, but learned that she had just been released from the hospital. He then departed for another visit with the McClintocks.

On his way appellant detoured to the scene of the accident, where he took a set of photographs. He also picked up a tape recorder, which he concealed under his raincoat before arriving at the McClintocks' residence. Once there, he re-examined their automobile insurance policy, discussed with them the law applicable to passengers, and explained the consequences of the fact that the driver who struck Carol's car was an uninsured motorist. Appellant discovered that the McClintocks' insurance policy would provide benefits of up to $12,500 each for Carol and Wanda Lou under an uninsured-motorist clause. Mrs. McClintock acknowledged that both Carol and Wanda Lou could sue for their injuries, but recounted to appellant that "Wanda swore up and down she would not do it." The McClintocks also told appellant that Carol had phoned to say that appellant could "go ahead" with her representation. Two days later appellant returned to Carol's hospital room to have her sign a contract, which provided that he would receive one-third of her recovery.

In the meantime, appellant obtained Wanda Lou's name and address from the McClintocks after telling them he wanted to ask her some questions about the accident. He then visited Wanda Lou at her home, without having been invited. He again concealed his tape recorder and recorded most of the conversation with Wanda Lou. After a brief, unproductive inquiry about the facts of the accident, appellant told Wanda Lou that he was representing Carol and that he had a "little tip" for Wanda Lou: the McClin-

2. Despite the fact that appellant maintains that he did not secure an agreement to represent Carol while he was at the hospital, he waited for an opportunity when no visitors were present and then took photographs of Carol in traction.

tocks' insurance policy contained an uninsured-motorist clause which might provide her with a recovery of up to $12,500. The young woman, who was 18 years of age and not a high school graduate at the time, replied to appellant's query about whether she was going to file a claim by stating that she really did not understand what was going on. Appellant offered to represent her, also, for a contingent fee of one-third of any recovery, and Wanda Lou stated "O. K."[4]

Wanda's mother attempted to repudiate her daughter's oral assent the following day, when appellant called on the telephone to speak to Wanda. Mrs. Holbert informed appellant that she and her daughter did not want to sue anyone or to have appellant represent them, and that if they decided to sue they would consult their own lawyer. Appellant insisted that Wanda had entered into a binding agreement. A month later Wanda confirmed in writing that she wanted neither to sue nor to be represented by appellant. She requested that appellant notify the insurance company that he was not her lawyer, as the company would not release a check to her until he did so. Carol also eventually discharged appellant. Although another lawyer represented her in concluding a settlement with the insurance company, she paid appellant one-third of her recovery in settlement of his lawsuit against her for breach of contract.

Both Carol McClintock and Wanda Lou Holbert filed complaints against appellant with the Grievance Committee of the Geauga County Bar Association. [The Bar Association referred the grievance to the State Bar. The Board of Commissioners on Grievances and Discipline found that appellant violated two provisions of the Ohio Code of Professional Responsibility: DR 2–103(A), which provides that "A lawyer shall not recommend employment, as a private practitioner, of himself, his partner, or associate to a non-lawyer who has not sought his advice regarding employment of a lawyer," and DR 2–104(A), which provides that "A lawyer who has given unsolicited advice to a layman that he should obtain counsel or take legal action shall not accept employment resulting from that advice, except that ... [a] lawyer may accept employment by a close friend, relative, former client (if the advice is germane to the former employment), or one whom the lawyer reasonably believes to be a client."] The Board rejected appellant's defense that his conduct was protected under the First and Fourteenth Amendments. The Supreme Court of Ohio

---

4. Appellant told Wanda that she should indicate assent by stating "O.K.," which she did. Appellant later testified: "I would say that most of my clients have essentially that much of a communication.... I think most of my clients, that's the way I practice law." In explaining the contingent-fee arrangement, appellant told Wanda Lou that his representation would not "cost [her] anything" because she would receive two-thirds of the recovery if appellant were successful in representing her but would not "have to pay [him] anything" otherwise.

adopted the findings of the Board,[10] reiterated that appellant's conduct was not constitutionally protected, and increased the sanction of a public reprimand recommended by the Board to indefinite suspension.... We now affirm the judgment of the Supreme Court of Ohio.

II

The solicitation of business by a lawyer through direct, in-person communication with the prospective client has long been viewed as inconsistent with the profession's ideal of the attorney-client relationship and as posing a significant potential for harm to the prospective client. It has been proscribed by the organized Bar for many years.[11] Last Term the Court ruled that the justifications for prohibiting truthful, "restrained" advertising concerning "the availability and terms of routine legal services" are insufficient to override society's interest, safeguarded by the First and Fourteenth Amendments, in assuring the free flow of commercial information. *Bates*, 433 U.S., at 384, 97 S.Ct., at 2709; see *Virginia Pharmacy Board v. Virginia Citizens Consumer Council*, 425 U.S. 748, 96 S.Ct. 1817, 48 L.Ed.2d 346 (1976). The balance struck in *Bates* does not predetermine the outcome in this case. The entitlement of in-person solicitation of clients to the protection of the First Amendment differs from that of the kind of advertising approved in *Bates,* as does the strength of the State's countervailing interest in prohibition.

A

Appellant contends that his solicitation of the two young women as clients is indistinguishable, for purposes of constitutional analysis, from the advertisement in *Bates*. Like that advertisement, his meetings with the prospective clients apprised them of their legal rights and of the availability of a lawyer to pursue their claims. According to appellant, such conduct is "presumptively an exercise of his free speech rights" which cannot be curtailed in the absence of proof that it actually caused a specific harm that the State has a compelling interest in preventing. But in-person solicitation of professional employment by a lawyer does not stand on a par with truthful advertising about the availability and terms of routine legal services, let alone with forms of speech more traditionally within the concern of the First Amendment.

Expression concerning purely commercial transactions has come within the ambit of the Amendment's protection only recently. In rejecting the notion that such speech "is wholly outside the protection of the First Amendment," *Virginia Pharmacy*,

---

10. The Board found that Carol and Wanda Lou "were, if anything, casual acquaintances" of appellant ...

11. An informal ban on solicitation, like that on advertising, historically was linked to the goals of preventing barratry, champerty, and maintenance....

supra, at 761, 96 S.Ct., at 1825, we were careful not to hold "that it is wholly undifferentiable from other forms" of speech. We have not discarded the "common-sense" "distinction between speech proposing a commercial transaction, which occurs in an area traditionally subject to government regulation, and other varieties of speech.... [We] have afforded commercial speech a limited measure of protection, commensurate with its subordinate position in the scale of First Amendment values, while allowing modes of regulation that might be impermissible in the realm of noncommercial expression...."

In-person solicitation by a lawyer of remunerative employment is a business transaction in which speech is an essential but subordinate component. While this does not remove the speech from the protection of the First Amendment, as was held in *Bates* and *Virginia Pharmacy,* it lowers the level of appropriate judicial scrutiny.

As applied in this case, the Disciplinary Rules are said to have limited the communication of two kinds of information. First, appellant's solicitation imparted to Carol McClintock and Wanda Lou Holbert certain information about his availability and the terms of his proposed legal services. In this respect, in-person solicitation serves much the same function as the advertisement at issue in *Bates*. But there are significant differences as well. Unlike a public advertisement, which simply provides information and leaves the recipient free to act upon it or not, in-person solicitation may exert pressure and often demands an immediate response, without providing an opportunity for comparison or reflection. The aim and effect of in-person solicitation may be to provide a one-sided presentation and to encourage speedy and perhaps uninformed decisionmaking; there is no opportunity for intervention or counter-education by agencies of the Bar, supervisory authorities, or persons close to the solicited individual. The admonition that "the fitting remedy for evil counsels is good ones" is of little value when the circumstances provide no opportunity for any remedy at all. In-person solicitation is as likely as not to discourage persons needing counsel from engaging in a critical comparison of the "availability, nature, and prices" of legal services, it actually may disserve the individual and societal interest, identified in *Bates,* in facilitating "informed and reliable decisionmaking."

It also is argued that in-person solicitation may provide the solicited individual with information about his or her legal rights and remedies. In this case, appellant gave Wanda Lou a "tip" about the prospect of recovery based on the uninsured-motorist clause in the McClintocks' insurance policy, and he explained that clause and Ohio's guest statute to Carol McClintock's parents. But neither of the Disciplinary Rules here at issue prohibited appellant from communicating information to these young women about their legal rights and the prospects of obtaining a monetary recovery, or from recommending that they obtain counsel. DR 2–104(A) merely prohibited him from using the information as bait with which to obtain an agreement to represent them for a fee. The Rule does not prohibit a lawyer from giving unsolicited legal advice; it proscribes the acceptance of employment resulting from such advice.

Appellant does not contend, and on the facts of this case could not contend, that his approaches to the two young women involved political expression or an exercise of associational freedom, "employ[ing] constitutionally privileged means of expression to secure constitutionally guaranteed civil rights." *NAACP v. Button,* 371 U.S. 415, 442, 83 S.Ct. 328, 343, 9 L.Ed.2d 405 (1963); see *In re Primus,* 436 U.S. 412, 98 S.Ct. 1893, 56 L.Ed.2d 417.... A lawyer's procurement of remunerative employment is a subject only marginally affected with First Amendment concerns. It falls within the State's proper sphere of economic and professional regulation. While entitled to some constitutional protection, appellant's conduct is subject to regulation in furtherance of important state interests.

B

The state interests implicated in this case are particularly strong. In addition to its general interest in protecting consumers and regulating commercial transactions, the State bears a special responsibility for maintaining standards among members of the licensed professions. "The interest of the States in regulating lawyers is especially great since lawyers are essential to the primary governmental function of administering justice, and have historically been 'officers of the courts.'" *Goldfarb v. Virginia State Bar,* 421 U.S. 773, 792, 95 S.Ct. 2004, 2016, 44 L.Ed.2d 572 (1975). While lawyers act in part as "self-employed businessmen," they also act "as trusted agents of their clients, and as assistants to the court in search of a just solution to disputes."

As is true with respect to advertising, see *Bates, supra,* 433 U.S., at 371, it appears that the ban on solicitation by lawyers originated as a rule of professional etiquette rather than as a strictly ethical rule. "[T]he rules are based in part on deeply ingrained feelings of tradition, honor and service. Lawyers have for centuries emphasized that the promotion of justice, rather than the earning of fees, is the goal of the profession." Comment, A Critical Analysis of Rules Against Solicitation by Lawyers, 25 U.Chi.L.Rev. 674 (1958) (footnote omitted). But the fact that the original motivation behind the ban on solicitation today might be considered an insufficient justification for its perpetuation does not detract from the force of the other interests the ban continues to serve. While the Court in *Bates* determined that truthful, restrained advertising of the prices of "routine" legal services would not have an adverse effect on the professionalism of lawyers, this was only because it found "the postulated connection between advertising and the erosion of *true professionalism* to be severely strained." The *Bates* Court did not question a State's interest in maintaining high standards among licensed professionals. Indeed, to the extent that the ethical standards of lawyers are linked to the service and protection of clients, they do further the goals of "true professionalism."

The substantive evils of solicitation have been stated over the years in sweeping terms: stirring up litigation, assertion of fraudulent claims, debasing the legal profession, and potential harm to the solicited client in the form of overreaching, overcharging, underrepresentation, and misrepresentation. The American Bar Association, as *amicus curiae,* defends the rule against solicitation primarily on three broad grounds: It is said that the prohibitions embodied in DR 2–103(A) and 2–104(A) serve to reduce the likelihood of overreaching and the exertion of undue influence on lay persons, to protect the privacy of individuals, and to avoid situations where the lawyer's exercise of judgment on behalf of the client will be clouded by his own pecuniary self-interest.[19]

We need not discuss or evaluate each of these interests in detail as appellant has conceded that the State has a legitimate and indeed "compelling" interest in preventing those aspects of solicitation that involve fraud, undue influence, intimidation, overreaching, and other forms of "vexatious conduct." We agree that protection of the public from these aspects of solicitation is a legitimate and important state interest.

III

Appellant's concession that strong state interests justify regulation to prevent the evils he enumerates would end this case but for his insistence that none of those evils was found to be present in his acts of solicitation. He challenges what he characterizes as the "indiscriminate application" of the Rules to him and thus attacks the validity of DR 2–103(A) and DR 2–104(A) not facially, but as applied to his acts of solicitation. And because no allegations or findings were made of the specific wrongs appellant concedes would justify disciplinary action, appellant terms his solicitation "pure," meaning "soliciting and obtaining agreements from Carol McClintock and Wanda Lou Holbert to represent each of them," without more. Appellant therefore argues that we must

---

19. A lawyer who engages in personal solicitation of clients may be inclined to subordinate the best interests of the client to his own pecuniary interests. Even if unintentionally, the lawyer's ability to evaluate the legal merit of his client's claims may falter when the conclusion will affect the lawyer's income. A valid claim might be settled too quickly, or a claim with little merit pursued beyond the point of reason. These lapses of judgment can occur in any legal representation, but we cannot say that the pecuniary motivation of the lawyer who solicits a particular representation does not create special problems of conflict of interest.

decide whether a State may discipline him for solicitation *per se* without offending the First and Fourteenth Amendments.

We agree that the appropriate focus is on appellant's conduct. And, as appellant urges, we must undertake an independent review of the record to determine whether that conduct was constitutionally protected. But appellant errs in assuming that the constitutional validity of the judgment below depends on proof that his conduct constituted actual overreaching or inflicted some specific injury on Wanda Holbert or Carol McClintock. His assumption flows from the premise that nothing less than actual proved harm to the solicited individual would be a sufficiently important state interest to justify disciplining the attorney who solicits employment in person for pecuniary gain.

Appellant's argument misconceives the nature of the State's interest. The Rules prohibiting solicitation are prophylactic measures whose objective is the prevention of harm before it occurs. The Rules were applied in this case to discipline a lawyer for soliciting employment for pecuniary gain under circumstances likely to result in the adverse consequences the State seeks to avert. In such a situation, which is inherently conducive to overreaching and other forms of misconduct, the State has a strong interest in adopting and enforcing rules of conduct designed to protect the public from harmful solicitation by lawyers whom it has licensed.

The State's perception of the potential for harm in circumstances such as those presented in this case is well founded. The detrimental aspects of face-to-face selling even of ordinary consumer products have been recognized and addressed by the Federal Trade Commission, and it hardly need be said that the potential for overreaching is significantly greater when a lawyer, a professional trained in the art of persuasion, personally solicits an unsophisticated, injured, or distressed lay person. Such an individual may place his trust in a lawyer, regardless of the latter's qualifications or the individual's actual need for legal representation, simply in response to persuasion under circumstances conducive to uninformed acquiescence. Although it is argued that personal solicitation is valuable because it may apprise a victim of misfortune of his legal rights, the very plight of that person not only makes him more vulnerable to influence but also may make advice all the more intrusive. Thus, under these adverse conditions the overtures of an uninvited lawyer may distress the solicited individual simply because of their obtrusiveness and the invasion of the individual's privacy, even when no other harm materializes. Under such circumstances, it is not unreasonable for the State to presume that in-person solicitation by lawyers more often than not will be injurious to the person solicited.

The efficacy of the State's effort to prevent such harm to prospective clients would be substantially diminished if, having proved a solicitation in circumstances like those of this case, the State were required in addition to prove actual injury. Unlike the advertising in *Bates,* in-person solicitation is not visible or otherwise open to public scrutiny. Often there is no witness other than the lawyer and the lay person whom he has solicited, rendering it difficult or impossible to obtain reliable proof of what actually took place. This would be especially true if the lay person were so distressed at the time of the solicitation that he could not recall specific details at a later date. If appellant's view were sustained, in-person solicitation would be virtually immune to effective oversight and regulation by the State or by the legal profession, in contravention of the State's strong interest in regulating members of the Bar in an effective, objective, and self-enforcing manner. It therefore is not unreasonable, or violative of the Constitution, for a State to respond with what in effect is a prophylactic rule.

On the basis of the undisputed facts of record, we conclude that the Disciplinary Rules constitutionally could be applied to appellant.... Under our view of the State's interest in averting harm by prohibiting solicitation in circumstances where it is likely to occur, the absence of explicit proof or findings of harm or injury is immaterial. The facts in this case present a striking example of the potential for overreaching that is inherent in a lawyer's in-person solicitation of professional employment. They also demonstrate the need for prophylactic regulation in furtherance of the State's interest in protecting the lay public. We hold that the application of DR 2–103(A) and 2–104(A) to appellant does not offend the Constitution.

Accordingly, the judgment of the Supreme Court of Ohio is *Affirmed.*

Notes

1. *Rules prohibiting "real-time" solicitation.* Soliciting clients in person, or on the telephone, or in real time electronically, is prohibited, with only narrow exceptions. MR 7.3(a). The exceptions are when the person contacted (1) is a lawyer; or (2) has a family, close personal, or prior professional relationship with the lawyer. This prohibition is thought to be necessary to prevent "undue influence, intimidation, and over-reaching." MR 7.3, comment [1]. Did Ohralik's behavior in the case above reflect those evils?

California's anti-solicitation rule has been written to last: it prohibits solicitation, unless the lawyer has a family or prior professional relationship with the person, "unless the solicitation is protected from abridgement by the Constitution of the United States or by the Constitution of the State of California." Cal. Rule 1–400(C).

2. *Prohibited forms of "solicitation."* Prohibited solicitation is defined categorically as seeking employment from a prospective client when a significant motive for the lawyer's doing so is the lawyer's pecuniary gain. MR 7.3(a). Is a lawyer not prohibited, then, from soliciting legal work from persons when pecuniary gain is not a significant motive? The Supreme Court allowed this form of contact in *In re Primus*, 436 U.S. 412, 98 S.Ct. 1893, 56 L.Ed.2d 417 (1978). In *Primus*, the Court held that a lawyer who engages in solicitation as a form of protected political association generally may not be disciplined without proof of actual wrongdoing that the State constitutionally may proscribe. The lawyer in the case, who was a legal consultant for a non-profit organization and a cooperating lawyer with the ACLU, met with a group of women who had been sterilized, allegedly under duress. The South Carolina Supreme Court upheld the lawyer's reprimand for improper solicitation. But the Supreme Court, saying that "her actions were undertaken to express personal political beliefs and to advance the civil-liberties objectives of the ACLU, rather than to derive financial gain," found her activity constitutionally-protected and thus not sanctionable by the State. See also ABA Formal Op. 148 (1935) (Canons' ban on solicitation "was never aimed at a situation . . . in which a group of lawyers announce that they are willing to devote some of their time and energy to the interests of indigent citizens whose constitutional rights are believed to be infringed").

3. *Prohibited methods.* Even if a particular *form* of client-getting is not categorically prohibited, the lawyer must not use prohibited *methods* of client-getting. For example, it would violate the rules if a lawyer approached potential clients in a pro bono case (thus not off limits under *Primus*), using false or misleading information (MR 7.1), or using coercion or duress (MR 7.3(b)(2)), or where the potential clients had previously expressed a desire not to be contacted by the lawyer (MR 7.3(b)(1)).

4. *Vendor booths.* Could a lawyer purchase a vendor booth at a professional conference or seminar, in hopes of being approached by prospective clients? Would the fact that persons at such a meeting are generally sophisticated make such a plan ethical? See Maryland State Bar Ass'n Comm. on Ethics, Op. 2004–29 (2004) (while the plan might not be a "per se" violation of the rules, no lawyer at the booth may initiate contact with any prospective client; the sophistication of the would-be clients is irrelevant, since the lawyer could not gauge that accurately).

5. *Internet solicitation.* The anti-solicitation rules treat real-time electronic communication, and telephone communication, the same as in-person solicitation. This means that a lawyer cannot solicit prospective clients on the internet, such as via "chat rooms." See, e.g., Florida Bar Standing Comm. on Advertising, Op. A–00–1 (2000); Virginia Advertising Op. A–0110 (1998); W.Va. Ethics Op. 98–03 (1998); Utah Ethics Op. 97–10 (1997); Mich. Informal Ethics Op. RI–276 (1996). Cf. Cal. State Bar

Standing Comm. On Prof'l Resp. and Conduct, Op. No. 2004–166 (2004) (opining that communicating with a mass-disaster victim in a chat room is not a prohibited "solicitation" under Cal. Rule 1–400(B), although it is improper under Rule 1–400(D)(5) because it is a communication that intrudes or causes duress). Should telephone calls and internet communications be lumped in with in-person solicitation? Or are phone calls and internet communications more like mail solicitation, which, as we will see in the next section, is treated more leniently?

6. *Web sites.* Virtually every large law firm now has a web site. Is a web site a solicitation? Or an advertisement? State Bar of California Formal Op. No. 2001–155 (2001), says that a web site is an "advertisement" and a "communication," but is not a "solicitation." Many states have adopted specific rules on web sites to clarify their relationship to existing solicitation and advertising rules. See, e.g., Fla. Bar Rule 4–7.6 ("Computer-assisted communications"); Miss. Rule 7.2 & 7.5.

7. *Prepaid legal plans.* Model Rule 7.3 (d) allows a lawyer to participate in a prepaid or group legal plan that itself solicits memberships or subscriptions for the plan. The lawyer cannot do the solicitation. *Id.,* comment [8]. Another comment to the same rule allows a lawyer to contact "representatives of organizations or groups that may be interested in establishing a group or prepaid legal plan," since such a communication is not directed to a prospective client but rather to a fiduciary seeking legal services for others. *Id.,* comment [6].

8. *Getting clients by purchasing a law practice.* As mentioned in Note 5 above, Model Rule 7.2 forbids a lawyer from giving anything of value to a person for recommending another's services, with some exceptions; the third one listed in the Rule is that a lawyer may "pay for a law practice in accordance with rule 1.17." MR 7.2(b)(3). Rule 1.17 allows a lawyer to buy another lawyer's practice, or sell a law practice to another lawyer, if the seller complies with a number of conditions, including that the seller ceases to engage in the practice of law (at least in the area of law sold), notice is given to all affecting clients, and extra fees are not charged to clients by reason of the sale. See also Cal. Rule 2–300 (similar to Model Rule, with more detail on certain matters); N.Y. DR 2–111 [22 NYCRR 1200.15–a](similar to California rule). Such sales most commonly occur when a lawyer retires from practice.

9. *"Pay to play."* Lawyers have sometimes made political contributions in hopes of obtaining legal business. The ABA in 2000 adopted Model Rule 7.6, to prohibit that practice if the contribution is made "for the purpose of obtaining or being considered" for "a government legal engagement or an appointment by a judge." The rule is aimed at conduct that would not be considered illegal bribery. See *id.,* comment [6].

THE FLORIDA BAR v. BARRETT

Supreme Court of Florida, 2005.
897 So.2d 1269.

PER CURIAM.

We have for review a referee's report regarding alleged ethical breaches by attorney David A. Barrett.... We approve the referee's findings of fact and recommendations as to guilt. For the reasons explained below, we decline to approve the recommended sanction of a one-year suspension and instead disbar Barrett.

I. FACTS

The Florida Bar filed a complaint against respondent David A. Barrett, alleging numerous counts of misconduct involving two unethical schemes to solicit clients. After a multiple-day hearing, the referee issued a report making the following findings and recommendations.

Barrett was the senior partner and managing partner in the Tallahassee law firm of Barrett, Hoffman, and Hall, P.A. In approximately January 1993, Barrett hired Chad Everett Cooper, an ordained minister, as a "paralegal." Although Cooper had previously worked for a law firm in Quincy, Florida, Cooper's primary duty at Barrett's law firm was to bring in new clients. As Cooper testified, Barrett told him to "do whatever you need to do to bring in some business" and "go out and . . . get some clients." Cooper was paid a salary averaging $20,000 and, in addition to his salary, yearly "bonuses" which generally exceeded his yearly salary. In fact, Cooper testified that Barrett offered him $100,000 if he brought in a large case.

To help Cooper bring in more personal injury clients to the law firm, Barrett devised a plan so that Cooper could access the emergency areas of a hospital and thus be able to solicit patients and their families. In order to gain such access, Barrett paid for Cooper to attend a hospital chaplain's course offered by Tallahassee Memorial Hospital.

In approximately March of 1994, Molly Glass's son was critically injured when he was struck by an automobile while on his bicycle. While her son was being treated in the intensive care unit at Tallahassee Memorial Hospital, Cooper met the Glass family. Cooper, who dressed in "clothing that resembled a pastor," identified himself to the family as a chaplain and offered to pray with them. Thereafter, Cooper gave a family member of Molly Glass the business card of attorney Eric Hoffman, one of the partners in Barrett's law firm, and suggested that the family call the firm. Neither Barrett nor Cooper knew Molly Glass prior to Cooper's solicitation at the hospital. After her son died, Molly Glass retained Barrett's law firm in a wrongful death action. A settlement was negotiated, and she was pleased with the result until May of 1999, when she read a newspaper article about improper solicitation of clients and realized that Cooper's actions in the hospital constituted inappropriate solicitation. The referee specifically found that Cooper was Barrett's agent at the time that Cooper solicited Molly Glass and that Barrett ordered the conduct and ratified it by paying Cooper a salary and bonuses.

In April 1994, Cooper referred his friend, Terry Charleston, to Barrett's law firm. Charleston was an automobile accident victim whose injuries left him a quadriplegic. After the case was settled for over $3 million, Cooper was paid a bonus that year of $47,500. Barrett attempted to justify the extremely large bonus, contending that the bonus was based on personal services, pastoral services, and companionship that Cooper provided to Charleston. The referee rejected this explanation, finding that Barrett lied about the reason for the bonus. Instead, the referee found that Barrett gave Cooper the bonus for bringing in the case, and thus Barrett engaged in an illegal fee-splitting plan.

On September 19, 1997, Barrett, who had the ultimate authority for hiring and firing in his law firm, fired Cooper. In the words of Barrett's now-deceased partner, Eric Hoffman, Barrett fired Cooper because "it was getting pretty hot and he was afraid that everyone would get caught." However, even after Cooper was fired, his relationship with Barrett did not end.

While Cooper obtained accident reports and solicited patients for a chiropractor, he also continued to solicit clients for Barrett. After the patients were seen by the chiropractor, the accident reports were forwarded to Barrett's law partner, Hoffman. Cooper was paid $200 for each client who was brought into the law firm. The referee specifically found that Barrett knew about this scheme and that he ratified the conduct of Hoffman and Cooper. Barrett micromanaged the office, especially the finances, and personally signed the checks to Cooper in the amount of $200 per client for soliciting eight clients. Moreover, Barrett inquired as to whether there was insurance coverage before authorizing the firm's checks written to Cooper for soliciting clients. In addition to Molly Glass, the referee found that Barrett improperly solicited twenty-one other clients in violation of the Rules of Professional Conduct.

Finally, in May 1996, Barrett sent Cooper to Miami and Chicago in order to solicit clients as a result of the Value Jet airplane crash in the Everglades. Although Barrett denied any knowledge about this, his own business records show that $974.24 was paid for Cooper's travel expenses. The referee found that Barrett's testimony regarding this matter was not credible. While neither solicitation resulted in clients for Barrett's firm, the referee concluded these were inappropriate solicitation attempts directed by Barrett.

Based on the above factual findings, the referee found that Barrett was guilty of violating the following sections of the Rules Regulating the Florida Bar: 4–5.l(c)(1) (responsibilities of a partner); 4–5.3(b)(3)(A) (responsibilities regarding nonlawyer assistants); 4–5.4(a)(4) (sharing fees with nonlawyers); 4–7.4(a) (solicitation); 4–8.4(a) (violating or attempting to violate the rules of professional conduct); 4–8.4(c) (engaging in conduct involving deceit); and 4–8.4(d) (engaging in conduct in connection with the practice of law that is prejudicial to the administration of justice).... [After considering aggravating and mitigating factors,] the referee recommended that Barrett be suspended from the practice of law for one year and be ordered to pay the Bar's costs.

The Florida Bar appeals to this Court, contending that we should increase the discipline to disbarment. Respondent cross-appeals.... Since Barrett challenges both the findings of fact and the recommended discipline, we address the cross-appeal first.

II. ANALYSIS

Findings of Fact

... Barrett challenges numerous aspects of the referee's findings of fact, contending that the Bar did not prove his misconduct by clear and convincing evidence.... The objecting party carries the burden of showing that the referee's findings of facts are clearly erroneous. Barrett cannot satisfy this burden by simply pointing to contradictory evidence when there is also competent, substantial evidence in the record that supports the referee's findings.... Because competent, substantial evidence in the record supports the referee's findings, we adopt the findings of fact and further approve without further discussion the referee's recommendation that Barrett be found guilty of violating the above rules.

Discipline

Both parties appeal the recommended discipline of a one-year suspension. Barrett argues that a twenty-day suspension is appropriate based on previous solicitation cases. The Bar argues that the appropriate discipline for such egregious ethical misconduct is disbarment. We agree with the Bar.

When reviewing a referee's recommended discipline, this Court's scope of review is broader than that afforded to the referee's findings of fact because this Court has the ultimate responsibility to determine the appropriate sanction. In determining a proper sanction, the Court will take into consideration the three purposes of lawyer discipline.

First, the judgment must be fair to society, both in terms of protecting the public from unethical conduct and at the same time not denying the public the services of a qualified lawyer as a result of undue harshness in imposing penalty. Second, the judgment must be fair to the respondent, being sufficient to punish a breach of ethics and at the same time encourage reformation and rehabilitation. Third, the judgment must be severe enough to deter others who might be prone or tempted to become involved in like violations.

Florida Bar v. Lord, 433 So.2d 983, 986 (Fla.1983) (emphasis omitted). . . .

Our cases involving unethical solicitation of clients have imposed a wide variety of discipline depending on the specific facts of each case. *See, e.g., Florida Bar v. Wolfe,* 759 So.2d 639 (Fla.2000) (one-year suspension); *Florida Bar v. Weinstein,* 624 So.2d 261 (Fla.1993) (disbarment); *Florida Bar v. Stafford,* 542 So.2d 1321 (Fla.1989) (six-month suspension); *Florida Bar v. Sawyer,* 420 So.2d 302 (Fla.1982) (eighteen-month suspension); *Florida Bar v. Gaer,* 380 So.2d 429 (Fla.1980) (public reprimand). Moreover, the Standards authorize either disbarment or suspension in such circumstances, depending on the amount of harm or potential harm caused and on whether the conduct was intentional versus knowing.

Barrett argues that he should receive the same discipline (a twenty-day suspension) ordered in two previous unpublished decisions that involved improper solicitations. He further alleges that discipline is completely unwarranted because the facts of the case do not support that Barrett was responsible for the improper schemes. The referee found that Barrett was responsible for the misconduct based on findings that he personally directed some of the solicitations and because he ratified all of the misconduct. As addressed above, these findings are supported by competent, substantial evidence.

We find that the facts of this case are substantially similar to those in the case of *Weinstein.* In *Weinstein,* the attorney personally solicited a critically injured patient in his hospital room, using lies and deception to gain entrance into the room. Further, the attorney gave false or misleading testimony under oath regarding his improper solicitations. We stated that

in-person solicitation of a [critically injured] patient in a hospital room, accompanied by lying to health-care personnel, [is] one of the more odious infractions that a lawyer can commit; his conduct brings his profession into disrepute and reduces it to a caricature. Disbarment is the appropriate sanction in the aggravated circumstances of this case.

Similarly, Barrett used deception to gain access to hospital patients by paying for Cooper to complete a hospital chaplain's course and sending him under the guise of providing spiritual comfort to people in their most needy time, when at the time Cooper was an attorney's employee being paid to obtain clients. Barrett then changed his scheme when "it was getting pretty hot," instead relying on Cooper to obtain clients while he worked for a chiropractor. His schemes resulted in twenty-two improperly solicited clients. Additionally, Barrett also engaged in an illegal fee-splitting plan with Cooper. The conduct in this case is clearly as egregious as the conduct in *Weinstein*. Moreover, this is not a situation where Barrett failed to realize his actions were wrong; he engaged in the conduct intentionally and then fired Cooper when he became concerned about the possibility of being caught. As this Court has held, when an attorney "affirmatively engages in conduct he or she knows to be improper, more severe discipline is warranted." *Florida Bar v. Wolfe,* 759 So.2d 639, 645 (Fla. 2000).

Finally, the instant case had substantial aggravating circumstances, including that (1) Barrett engaged in this type of improper solicitations based on a selfish motive to obtain clients; (2) the improper solicitations were a part of organized schemes that lasted for years; (3) multiple offenses occurred, including two different schemes which led to at least twenty-two improper solicitations; (4) Barrett lied to the referee during the proceedings; (5) one of the victims was especially vulnerable and in fact retained Barrett's law firm only because she was angry that somebody else had tried to take advantage of her during a time in which she was clearly preoccupied with her son's critical injuries; and (6) Barrett had substantial experience in the practice of law. While the referee did find that mitigating circumstances applied, these pale by comparison to the aggravating circumstances in this case. Any discipline less than disbarment is far too lenient based on the amount and type of misconduct which occurred here and would not fulfill the three purposes of lawyer discipline.

In sum, members of The Florida Bar are ethically prohibited from the solicitation of clients in the manner engaged in by Barrett. The Court expects that its rules will be respected and followed. This type of violation brings dishonor and disgrace not only upon the attorney who has broken the rules but upon the entire legal profession, a burden that all attorneys must bear since it affects all of our reputations. Moreover, such violations harm people who are already in a vulnerable condition, which is one of the very reasons these types of solicitations are barred. Therefore, this Court will strictly enforce the rules that prohibit these improper solicitations and impose severe sanctions on those who commit violations of them.

III. CONCLUSION

We approve the referee's findings of fact and recommendations as to guilt, but we decline to approve the recommended discipline of a one-year suspension and instead disbar respondent. Accordingly, David A. Barrett is hereby disbarred from the practice of law in the State of Florida. The disbarment will be effective thirty days from the date this opinion is filed so that Barrett can close out his practice and protect the interests of existing clients. If Barrett notifies this Court in writing that he is no longer practicing and does not need the thirty days to protect existing clients, this Court will enter an order making the disbarment effective immediately. Barrett shall accept no new business after this opinion is filed. [Costs of $16,156.67 assessed against Barrett.]

It is so ordered.

Notes

1. *Discipline for using runners and cappers.* In most states, lawyers may not pay others to send them legal work, with narrow exceptions that include paying for the costs of advertisements or paying fees to a qualified referral service. MR 7.2(b); N.Y. DR 2–103(b). This basic prohibition reflects the profession's longstanding condemnation of the use of "runners" and "cappers," persons paid by lawyers to solicit business. See ABA Canon 28; Cal. Bus. & Prof. Code § 6151 (defining terms). The Supreme Court in *Ohralik*, in a footnote not reprinted in this book, commented that "[a]lthough our concern in this case is with solicitation by the lawyer himself, solicitation by a lawyer's agents or runners would present similar problems." See Ohio S. Ct. Bd. of Comm'rs on Grievances and Discipline, Op. 99–5 (1999)(lawyers may not pass out brochures at fairs or church festivals, and may not use others to do the same).

Disciplinary sanction for using runners and cappers is usually severe, as you might glean from *Barrett*. See, e.g., *In re Robbins*, 276 Ga. 124, 575 S.E.2d 501 (2003) (disbarment for giving a paralegal a 25 percent cut of fees to employ runners to go out and find personal injury clients); *In re Barnes*, 275 Ga. 812, 573 S.E.2d 80 (2002) (three-year suspension for paying a paralegal firm to refer cases); *In re Goff*, 837 So.2d 1201 (La. 2003) (nine-month suspension ordered, while noting that "the baseline sanction for respondent's misconduct is disbarment"); *In re Grand*, 778 So.2d 580 (La. 2001) (disbarment).

2. *Effect on contracts.* California law specifically provides that any contract secured through the services of a runner or a capper is void. Cal. Bus. & Prof. Code § 6154(a). See also *Trotter v. Nelson*, 684 N.E.2d 1150 (Ind.1997) (an agreement requiring the payment of money to a non-attorney for referring clients to a lawyer is void as against public policy).

3. *Soliciting clients using coercion or duress.* Coercion or duress is present if a client's emotional, physical or mental state prevents him or her from making a reasonable judgment about whether or not to use the

lawyer's services. See, e.g., *Falanga v. State Bar of Georgia*, 150 F.3d 1333 (11th Cir.1998) (upholding constitutionality of in-person solicitation rules as applied to lawyers who approach unsophisticated, injured or distressed lay people); *In re Ravich, Koster, Tobin, Oleckna, Reitman & Greenstein*, 155 N.J. 357, 715 A.2d 216 (1998)(reprimanding law firm for renting recreational vehicle, posting numerous advertisements on it, and parking it near victims of a gas line explosion at an apartment complex, pursuant to rule forbidding solicitation of clients with emotional, physical or mental vulnerabilities).

B.   Solicitation by Mail

SHAPERO v. KENTUCKY BAR ASS'N

Supreme Court of the United States, 1988.
486 U.S. 466, 108 S.Ct. 1916, 100 L.Ed.2d 475.

Justice BRENNAN announced the judgment of the Court and delivered the opinion of the Court as to Parts I and II and an opinion as to Part III in which Justice MARSHALL, Justice BLACKMUN, and Justice KENNEDY join.

This case presents the issue whether a State may, consistent with the First and Fourteenth Amendments, categorically prohibit lawyers from soliciting legal business for pecuniary gain by sending truthful and nondeceptive letters to potential clients known to face particular legal problems.

I

In 1985, petitioner, a member of Kentucky's integrated Bar Association, see Ky.Sup.Ct. Rule 3.030 (1988), applied to the Kentucky Attorneys Advertising Commission for approval of a letter that he proposed to send "to potential clients who have had a foreclosure suit filed against them." The proposed letter read as follows:

> "It has come to my attention that your home is being foreclosed on. If this is true, you may be about to lose your home. Federal law may allow you to keep your home by *ORDERING* your creditor [*sic*] to *STOP* and give you more time to pay them.

> "You may call my office anytime from 8:30 a.m. to 5:00 p.m. for *FREE* information on how you can keep your home.

> "Call *NOW,* don't wait. It may surprise you what I may be able to do for you. Just call and tell me that you got this letter. Remember it is *FREE,* there is *NO* charge for calling."

The Commission did not find the letter false or misleading. Nevertheless, it declined to approve petitioner's proposal on the

ground that a then-existing Kentucky Supreme Court Rule prohibited the mailing or delivery of written advertisements "precipitated by a specific event or occurrence involving or relating to the
addressee or addressees as distinct from the general public."
Ky.Sup.Ct. Rule 3.135(5)(b)(i).[2] The Commission registered its
view that Rule 3.135(5)(b)(i)'s ban on targeted, direct-mail advertising violated the First Amendment—specifically the principles
enunciated in *Zauderer v. Office of Disciplinary Counsel of Supreme Court of Ohio,* 471 U.S. 626, 105 S.Ct. 2265, 85 L.Ed.2d 652
(1985)—and recommended that the Kentucky Supreme Court
amend its Rules. Pursuing the Commission's suggestion, petitioner petitioned the Committee on Legal Ethics (Ethics Committee)
of the Kentucky Bar Association for an advisory opinion as to the
Rule's validity. Like the Commission, the Ethics Committee, in an
opinion formally adopted by the Board of Governors of the Bar
Association, did not find the proposed letter false or misleading,
but nonetheless upheld Rule 3.135(5)(b)(i) on the ground that it
was consistent with Rule 7.3 of the American Bar Association's
Model Rules of Professional Conduct (1984).

　　On review of the Ethics Committee's advisory opinion, the
Kentucky Supreme Court felt "compelled by the decision in *Zauderer* to order [Rule 3.135(5)(b)(i)] deleted, and replaced it with
the ABA's Rule 7.3, which provides in its entirety:

> " 'A lawyer may not solicit professional employment from
> a prospective client with whom the lawyer has no family
> or prior professional relationship, by mail, in-person or
> otherwise, when a significant motive for the lawyer's
> doing so is the lawyer's pecuniary gain. The term 'solicit'
> includes contact in person, by telephone or telegraph, by
> letter or other writing, or by other communication direct-
> ed to a specific recipient, but does not include letters
> addressed or advertising circulars distributed generally to
> persons not known to need legal services of the kind
> provided by the lawyer in a particular matter, but who
> are so situated that they might in general find such
> services useful.' "

　　The court did not specify either the precise infirmity in Rule
3.135(5)(b)(i) or how Rule 7.3 cured it. Rule 7.3 like its predecessor, prohibits targeted, direct-mail solicitation by lawyers for
pecuniary gain, without a particularized finding that the solicitation is false or misleading. We granted certiorari to resolve whether such a blanket prohibition is consistent with the First Amend-

---

2.　Rule 3.135(5)(b)(i) provided in full:

"A written advertisement may be sent or
delivered to an individual addressee only
if that addressee is one of a class of
persons, other than a family, to whom it
is also sent or delivered at or about the
same time, and only if it is not prompted
or precipitated by a specific event or occurrence involving or relating to the addressee or addressees as distinct from the
general public."

ment, made applicable to the States through the Fourteenth Amendment, and now reverse.

II

Lawyer advertising is in the category of constitutionally protected commercial speech. The First Amendment principles governing state regulation of lawyer solicitations for pecuniary gain are by now familiar: "Commercial speech that is not false or deceptive and does not concern unlawful activities ... may be restricted only in the service of a substantial governmental interest, and only through means that directly advance that interest." Since state regulation of commercial speech "may extend only as far as the interest it serves," state rules that are designed to prevent the "potential for deception and confusion ... may be no broader than reasonably necessary to prevent the" perceived evil. *In re R.M.J.,* 455 U.S. 191, 203, 102 S.Ct. 929, 937, 71 L.Ed.2d 64 (1982).

In *Zauderer,* application of these principles required that we strike an Ohio rule that categorically prohibited solicitation of legal employment for pecuniary gain through advertisements containing information or advice, even if truthful and nondeceptive, regarding a specific legal problem. We distinguished written advertisements containing such information or advice from in-person solicitation by lawyers for profit, which we held in *Ohralik v. Ohio State Bar Assn.,* 436 U.S. 447, 98 S.Ct. 1912, 56 L.Ed.2d 444 (1978), a State may categorically ban....

Our lawyer advertising cases have never distinguished among various modes of written advertising to the general public. Thus, Ohio could no more prevent Zauderer from mass-mailing to a general population his offer to represent women injured by the Dalkon Shield than it could prohibit his publication of the advertisement in local newspapers. Similarly, if petitioner's letter is neither false nor deceptive, Kentucky could not constitutionally prohibit him from sending at large an identical letter opening with the query, "Is your home being foreclosed on?," rather than his observation to the targeted individuals that "It has come to my attention that your home is being foreclosed on." The drafters of Rule 7.3 apparently appreciated as much, for the Rule exempts from the ban "letters addressed or advertising circulars distributed generally to persons ... who are so situated that they might in general find such services useful."

The court below disapproved petitioner's proposed letter solely because it targeted only persons who were "known to need [the] legal services" offered in his letter, rather than the broader group of persons "so situated that they might in general find such services useful." Generally, unless the advertiser is inept, the latter group would include members of the former. The only reason to disseminate an advertisement of particular legal services among those persons who are "so situated that they might in general find such services useful" is to reach individuals who *actually* "need legal services of the kind provided [and advertised] by the lawyer." But the First Amendment does not permit a ban on certain speech merely because it is more efficient; the State may not constitutionally ban a particular letter on the theory that to mail it only to those whom it would most interest is somehow inherently objectionable.

The court below did not rely on any such theory. Rather, it concluded that the State's blanket ban on all targeted, direct-mail solicitation was permissible because of the "serious potential for abuse inherent in direct solicitation by lawyers of potential clients known to need specific legal services." By analogy to *Ohralik*, the court observed:

> "Such solicitation subjects the prospective client to pressure from a trained lawyer in a direct personal way. It is entirely possible that the potential client may feel overwhelmed by the basic situation which caused the need for the specific legal services and may have seriously impaired capacity for good judgment, sound reason and a natural protective self-interest. Such a condition is full of the possibility of undue influence, overreaching and intimidation."

Of course, a particular potential client will feel equally "overwhelmed" by his legal troubles and will have the same "impaired capacity for good judgment" regardless of whether a lawyer mails him an untargeted letter or exposes him to a newspaper advertisement–concededly constitutionally protected activities–or instead mails a targeted letter. The relevant inquiry is not whether there exist potential clients whose "condition" makes them susceptible to undue influence, but whether the mode of communication poses a serious danger that lawyers will exploit any such susceptibility.

Thus, respondent's facile suggestion that this case is merely "*Ohralik* in writing" misses the mark. In assessing the potential for overreaching and undue influence, the mode of communication makes all the difference. Our decision in *Ohralik* that a State could categorically ban all in-person solicitation turned on two factors. First was our characterization of face-to-face solicitation as "a practice rife with possibilities for overreaching, invasion of privacy, the exercise of undue influence, and outright fraud." Second, "unique difficulties," would frustrate any attempt at state regulation of in-person solicitation short of an absolute ban because such solicitation is "not visible or otherwise open to public scrutiny." Targeted, direct-mail solicitation is distinguishable from the in-person solicitation in each respect.

Like print advertising, petitioner's letter—and targeted, direct-mail solicitation generally—"poses much less risk of over-reaching or undue influence" than does in-person solicitation. Neither mode of written communication involves "the coercive force of the personal presence of a trained advocate" or the "pressure on the potential client for an immediate yes-or-no answer to the offer of representation." Unlike the potential client with a badgering advocate breathing down his neck, the recipient of a letter and the "reader of an advertisement . . . can 'effectively avoid further bombardment of [his] sensibilities simply by averting [his] eyes,'" *Ohralik, supra,* 436 U.S., at 465, n. 25. A letter, like a printed advertisement (but unlike a lawyer), can readily be put in a drawer to be considered later, ignored, or discarded. In short, both types of written solicitation "convey[y] information about legal services [by means] that [are] more conducive to reflection and the exercise of choice on the part of the consumer than is personal solicitation by an attorney." Nor does a targeted letter invade the recipient's privacy any more than does a substantively identical letter mailed at large. The invasion, if any, occurs when the lawyer discovers the recipient's legal affairs, not when he confronts the recipient with the discovery.

Admittedly, a letter that is personalized (not merely targeted) to the recipient presents an increased risk of deception, intentional or inadvertent. It could, in certain circumstances, lead the recipient to overestimate the lawyer's familiarity with the case or could implicitly suggest that the recipient's legal problem is more dire than it really is. Similarly, an inaccurately targeted letter could lead the recipient to believe she has a legal problem that she does not actually have or, worse yet, could offer erroneous legal advice.

But merely because targeted, direct-mail solicitation presents lawyers with opportunities for isolated abuses or mistakes does not justify a total ban on that mode of protected commercial speech. See *In re R.M.J.,* 455 U.S., at 203. The State can regulate such abuses and minimize mistakes through far less restrictive and more precise means, the most obvious of which is to require the lawyer to file any solicitation letter with a state agency, giving the State ample opportunity to supervise mailings and penalize actual abuses. The "regulatory difficulties" that are "unique" to in-person lawyer solicitation—solicitation that is "not visible or otherwise open to public scrutiny" and for which it is "difficult or impossible to obtain reliable proof of what actually took place"—do not apply to written solicitations. . . .

III

The validity of Rule 7.3 does not turn on whether petitioner's letter itself exhibited any of the evils at which Rule 7.3 was directed. Since, however, the First Amendment overbreadth doctrine does not apply to professional advertising, see *Bates,* 433 U.S., at 379–381, we address respondent's contentions that petitioner's letter is particularly overreaching, and therefore unworthy of First Amendment protection. In that regard, respondent identifies two features of the letter before us that, in its view, coalesce to convert the proposed letter into "high pressure solicitation, overbearing solicitation," which is not protected. First, respondent asserts that the letter's liberal use of underscored, uppercase letters (*e.g.,* "Call *NOW,* don't wait"; "it is *FREE,* there is *NO* charge for calling") "fairly shouts at the recipient . . . that he should employ Shapero." Second, respondent objects that the letter contains assertions (*e.g.,* "It may surprise you what I may be able to do for you") that "stat[c] no affirmative or objective fact," but constitute "pure salesman puffery, enticement for the unsophisticated, which commits Shapero to nothing."

The pitch or style of a letter's type and its inclusion of subjective predictions of client satisfaction might catch the recipient's attention more than would a bland statement of purely objective facts in small type. But a truthful and nondeceptive letter, no matter how big its type and how much it speculates can never "shou[t] at the recipient" or "gras[p] him by the lapels," as can a lawyer engaging in face-to-face solicitation. The letter simply presents no comparable risk of overreaching. And so long as the First Amendment protects the right to solicit legal business, the State may claim no substantial interest in restricting truthful and nondeceptive lawyer solicitations to those least likely to be read by the recipient. . . .

The judgment of the Supreme Court of Kentucky is reversed, and the case is remanded for further proceedings not inconsistent with this opinion.

It is so ordered.

[The dissenting opinion of Justice O'CONNOR, with whom THE CHIEF JUSTICE and Justice SCALIA joined, is reprinted in Chapter 1, § 1. *Re-read that opinion now.*]

FLORIDA BAR v. WENT FOR IT, INC.

Supreme Court of the United States, 1995.
515 U.S. 618, 115 S.Ct. 2371, 132 L.Ed.2d 541.

Justice O'CONNOR delivered the opinion of the Court.

Rules of the Florida Bar prohibit personal injury lawyers from sending targeted direct-mail solicitations to victims and their relatives for 30 days following an accident or disaster. This case asks us to consider whether such Rules violate the First and Fourteenth Amendments of the Constitution. We hold that in the circumstances presented here, they do not.

I

In 1989, the Florida Bar (Bar) completed a 2–year study of the effects of lawyer advertising on public opinion. After conducting hearings, commissioning surveys, and reviewing extensive public commentary, the Bar determined that several changes to its advertising rules were in order. In late 1990, the Florida Supreme Court adopted the Bar's proposed amendments with some modifications. Two of these amendments are at issue in this case. Rule 4–7.4(b)(1) provides that "[a] lawyer shall not send, or knowingly permit to be sent, ... a written communication to a prospective client for the purpose of obtaining professional employment if: (A) the written communication concerns an action for personal injury or wrongful death or otherwise relates to an accident or disaster involving the person to whom the communication is addressed or a relative of that person, unless the accident or disaster occurred more than 30 days prior to the mailing of the communication." Rule 4–7.8(a) states that "[a] lawyer shall not accept referrals from a lawyer referral service unless the service: (1) engages in no communication with the public and in no direct contact with prospective clients in a manner that would violate the Rules of Professional Conduct if the communication or contact were made by the lawyer." Together, these Rules create a brief 30–day blackout period after an accident during which lawyers may not, directly or indirectly, single out accident victims or their relatives in order to solicit their business.

[In March 1992, G. Stewart McHenry and his lawyer referral service, Went For It, Inc., sought declaratory and injunctive relief in federal district court, challenging Rules 4–7.4(b)(1) and 4–7.8(a) as violative of the First and Fourteenth Amendments.] McHenry alleged that he routinely sent targeted solicitations to accident victims or their survivors within 30 days after accidents and that he wished to continue doing so in the future. Went For It, Inc., represented that it wished to contact accident victims or their survivors within 30 days of accidents and to refer potential clients to participating Florida lawyers. . . .

[The parties filed cross-motions for summary judgment. The trial court referred these motions to a Magistrate Judge, who concluded that "the Bar had substantial government interests, predicated on a concern for professionalism, both in protecting the personal privacy and tranquility of recent accident victims and their relatives and in ensuring that these individuals do not fall prey to undue influence or overreaching." He recommended that the Bar's motion be granted. The District Court rejected this recommendation and entered summary judgment for the plaintiffs. The Eleventh Circuit affirmed.] The panel noted, in its conclusion, that it was "disturbed that *Bates* and its progeny require the decision" that it reached. We granted certiorari, and now reverse.

II

A

[The Court reviewed the history of constitutional protection of lawyer advertising, beginning with *Bates*.] It is now well established that lawyer advertising is commercial speech and, as such, is accorded a measure of First Amendment protection. Such First Amendment protection, of course, is not absolute.... [W]e engage in "intermediate" scrutiny of restrictions on commercial speech, analyzing them under the framework set forth in *Central Hudson Gas & Elec. Corp. v. Public Serv. Comm'n of N.Y.,* 447 U.S. 557, 100 S.Ct. 2343, 65 L.Ed.2d 341 (1980). Under *Central Hudson,* the government may freely regulate commercial speech that concerns unlawful activity or is misleading. Commercial speech that falls into neither of those categories, like the advertising at issue here, may be regulated if the government satisfies a test consisting of three related prongs: First, the government must assert a substantial interest in support of its regulation; second, the government must demonstrate that the restriction on commercial speech directly and materially advances that interest; and third, the regulation must be " 'narrowly drawn.' "

B

"Unlike rational basis review, the *Central Hudson* standard does not permit us to supplant the precise interests put forward by the State with other suppositions." The Bar asserts that it has a substantial interest in protecting the privacy and tranquility of personal injury victims and their loved ones against intrusive, unsolicited contact by lawyers.... This interest obviously factors into the Bar's paramount (and repeatedly professed) objective of curbing activities that "negatively affec[t] the administration of justice." Because direct-mail solicitations in the wake of accidents are perceived by the public as intrusive, the Bar argues, the reputation of the legal profession in the eyes of Floridians has suffered commensurately. The regulation, then, is an effort to protect the flagging reputations of Florida lawyers by preventing them from engaging in conduct that, the Bar maintains, " 'is universally regarded as deplorable and beneath common decency because of its intrusion upon the special vulnerability and private grief of victims or their families.' "

We have little trouble crediting the Bar's interest as substantial. On various occasions we have accepted the proposition that "States have a compelling interest in the practice of professions within their boundaries, and ... as part of their power to protect the public health, safety, and other valid interests they have broad power to establish standards for licensing practitioners and regulating the practice of professions." *Goldfarb v. Virginia State Bar,* 421 U.S. 773, 792, 95 S.Ct. 2004, 2016, 44 L.Ed.2d 572 (1975). Our precedents also leave no room for doubt that "the protection of potential clients' privacy is a substantial state interest." ...

Under *Central Hudson's* second prong, the State must demonstrate that the challenged regulation "advances the Government's interest 'in a direct and material way.' " That burden, we have explained, " 'is not satisfied by mere speculation or conjecture; rather, a governmental body seeking to sustain a restriction on commercial speech must demonstrate that the harms it recites are real and that its restriction will in fact alleviate them to a material degree.' " In *Edenfield,* the Court invalidated a Florida ban on in-person solicitation by certified public accountants (CPA's). We observed that the State Board of Accountancy had "present[ed] no studies that suggest personal solicitation of prospective business clients by CPA's creates the dangers of fraud, overreaching, or compromised independence that the Board claims to fear." ...

The direct-mail solicitation regulation before us does not suffer from such infirmities. The Bar submitted a 106–page summary of its 2–year study of lawyer advertising and solicitation to the District Court. That summary contains data—both statistical and anecdotal—supporting the Bar's contentions that the Florida public views direct-mail solicitations in the immediate wake of accidents as an intrusion on privacy that reflects poorly upon the profession. As of June 1989, lawyers mailed 700,000 direct solicitations in Florida annually, 40% of which were aimed at accident victims or their survivors. A survey of Florida adults commissioned by the Bar indicated that Floridians "have negative feelings about those attorneys who use direct mail advertising." Fifty-four percent of the general population surveyed said that contacting persons concerning accidents or similar events is a violation of privacy. A random sampling of persons who received direct-mail advertising from lawyers in 1987 revealed that 45% believed that direct-mail solicitation is "designed to take advantage of gullible or unstable people"; 34% found such tactics "annoying or irritating"; 26% found it "an invasion of your privacy"; and 24% reported that it "made you angry." Significantly, 27% of direct-mail recipients reported that their regard for the legal profession and for the judicial process as a whole was "lower" as a result of receiving the direct mail.

The anecdotal record mustered by the Bar is noteworthy for its breadth and detail. With titles like "Scavenger Lawyers" (The Miami Herald, Sept. 29, 1987) and "Solicitors Out of Bounds" (St. Petersburg Times, Oct. 26, 1987), newspaper editorial pages in Florida have burgeoned with criticism of Florida lawyers who send targeted direct mail to victims shortly after accidents. The study summary also includes page upon page of excerpts from complaints of direct-mail recipients. For example, a Florida citizen described how he was " 'appalled and angered by the brazen attempt' " of a law firm to solicit him by letter shortly after he was injured and his fiancee was killed in an auto accident. Another found it " 'despicable and inexcusable' " that a Pensacola lawyer wrote to his mother three days after his father's funeral. Another described how she was " 'astounded' " and then " 'very angry' " when she received a solicitation following a minor accident. Still another described as " 'beyond comprehension' " a letter his nephew's family received the day of the nephew's funeral. One citizen wrote, " 'I consider the unsolicited contact from you after my child's accident to be of the rankest form of ambulance chasing and in incredibly poor taste.... I cannot begin to express with my limited vocabulary the utter contempt in which I hold you and your kind.' "

In light of this showing—which respondents at no time refuted, save by the conclusory assertion that the Rule lacked "any factual basis,"—we conclude that the Bar has satisfied the second prong of the *Central Hudson* test.... After scouring the record, we are satisfied that the ban on direct-mail solicitation in the immediate aftermath of accidents ... targets a concrete, nonspeculative harm.

In reaching a contrary conclusion, the Court of Appeals determined that this case was governed squarely by *Shapero v. Kentucky Bar Assn.*, 486 U.S. 466, 108 S.Ct. 1916, 100 L.Ed.2d 475 (1988). Making no mention of the Bar's study, the court concluded that " 'a targeted letter [does not] invade the recipient's privacy any more than does a substantively identical letter mailed at large. The invasion, if any, occurs when the lawyer discovers the recipient's legal affairs, not when he confronts the recipient with the discovery.' " In many cases, the Court of Appeals explained, "this invasion of privacy will involve no more than reading the newspaper."

While some of *Shapero*'s language might be read to support the Court of Appeals' interpretation, *Shapero* differs in several fundamental respects from the case before us. First and foremost, *Shapero*'s treatment of privacy was casual. Contrary to the dissent's suggestions, the State in *Shapero* did not seek to justify its regulation as a measure undertaken to prevent lawyers' invasions of privacy interests. Rather, the State focused exclusively on the special dangers of overreaching inhering in targeted solicitations. Second, in contrast to this case, *Shapero* dealt with a broad ban on *all* direct-mail solicitations, whatever the time frame and whoever the recipient. Finally, the State in *Shapero* assembled no evidence attempting to demonstrate any actual harm caused by targeted direct mail. The Court rejected the State's effort to justify a prophylactic ban on the basis of blanket, untested assertions of undue influence and overreaching. Because the State did not make a privacy-based argument at all, its empirical showing on that issue was similarly infirm.

We find the Court's perfunctory treatment of privacy in *Shapero* to be of little utility in assessing this ban on targeted solicitation of victims in the immediate aftermath of accidents. While it is undoubtedly true that many people find the image of lawyers sifting through accident and police reports in pursuit of prospective clients unpalatable and invasive, this case targets a different kind of intrusion. The Bar has argued, and the record reflects, that a principal purpose of the ban is "protecting the personal privacy and tranquility of [Florida's] citizens from crass commercial intrusion by attorneys upon their personal grief in times of trauma." The intrusion targeted by the Bar's regulation stems not from the fact that a lawyer has learned about an accident or disaster (as the Court of Appeals notes, in many instances a lawyer need only read the newspaper to glean this information), but from the lawyer's confrontation of victims or relatives with such information, while wounds are still open, in order to solicit their business. In this respect, an untargeted letter mailed to society at large is different in kind from a targeted solicitation; the untargeted letter involves no willful or knowing affront to or invasion of the tranquility of bereaved or injured individuals and simply does not cause the same kind of reputational harm to the profession unearthed by the Bar's study. . . .

[T]he harm targeted by the Bar cannot be eliminated by a brief journey to the trash can. The purpose of the 30–day targeted direct-mail ban is to forestall the outrage and irritation with the state-licensed legal profession that the practice of direct solicitation only days after accidents has engendered. The Bar is concerned not with citizens' "offense" in the abstract, but with the demonstrable detrimental effects that such "offense" has on the profession it regulates. Moreover, the harm posited by the Bar is as much a function of simple receipt of targeted solicitations within days of accidents as it is a function of the letters' contents. Throwing the letter away shortly after opening it may minimize the latter intrusion, but it does little to combat the former. . . .

Passing to *Central Hudson*'s third prong, we examine the relationship between the Bar's interests and the means chosen to serve them. With respect to this prong, the differences between commercial speech and noncommercial speech are manifest. In *Fox*, we made clear that the "least restrictive means" test has no role in the commercial speech context. What our decisions require, instead, "is a 'fit' between the legislature's ends and the means chosen to accomplish those ends, a fit that is not necessarily perfect, but reasonable; that represents not necessarily the single best disposition but one whose scope is 'in proportion to the interest served,' that employs not necessarily the least restrictive means but . . . a means narrowly tailored to achieve the desired objective." . . .

Respondents levy a great deal of criticism ... at the scope of the Bar's restriction on targeted mail. "[B]y prohibiting written communications to all people, whatever their state of mind," respondents charge, the Rule "keeps useful information from those accident victims who are ready, willing and able to utilize a lawyer's advice." This criticism may be parsed into two components. First, the Rule does not distinguish between victims in terms of the severity of their injuries. According to respondents, the Rule is unconstitutionally overinclusive insofar as it bans targeted mailings even to citizens whose injuries or grief are relatively minor. Second, the Rule may prevent citizens from learning about their legal options, particularly at a time when other actors–opposing counsel and insurance adjusters–may be clamoring for victims' attentions. Any benefit arising from the Bar's regulation, respondents implicitly contend, is outweighed by these costs.

We are not persuaded by respondents' allegations of constitutional infirmity. We find little deficiency in the ban's failure to distinguish among injured Floridians by the severity of their pain or the intensity of their grief. Indeed, it is hard to imagine the contours of a regulation that might satisfy respondents on this score.... Unlike respondents, we do not see "numerous and obvious less-burdensome alternatives" to Florida's short temporal ban. The Bar's rule is reasonably well tailored to its stated objective of eliminating targeted mailings whose type and timing are a source of distress to Floridians, distress that has caused many of them to lose respect for the legal profession.

Respondents' second point would have force if the Bar's Rule were not limited to a brief period and if there were not many other ways for injured Floridians to learn about the availability of legal representation during that time. Our lawyer advertising cases have afforded lawyers a great deal of leeway to devise innovative ways to attract new business. Florida permits lawyers to advertise on prime-time television and radio as well as in newspapers and other media. They may rent space on billboards. They may send untargeted letters to the general population, or to discrete segments thereof. There are, of course, pages upon pages devoted to lawyers in the Yellow Pages of Florida telephone directories.... These ample alternative channels for receipt of information about the availability of legal representation during the 30–day period following accidents may explain why, despite the ample evidence, testimony, and commentary submitted by those favoring (as well as opposing) unrestricted direct-mail solicitation, respondents have not pointed to—and we have not independently found—a single example of an individual case in which immediate solicitation helped to avoid, or failure to solicit within 30 days brought about, the harms that concern the dissent. In fact, the record contains considerable empirical survey information suggesting that Floridians have little difficulty finding a lawyer when they need one. Finding no basis to question the commonsense conclusion that the many alternative channels for communicating necessary information about attorneys are sufficient, we see no defect in Florida's regulation.

III

Speech by professionals obviously has many dimensions. There are circumstances in which we will accord speech by attorneys on public issues and matters of legal representation the strongest protection our Constitution has to offer. This case, however, concerns pure commercial advertising, for which we have always reserved a lesser degree of protection under the First Amendment. Particularly because the standards and conduct of state-licensed lawyers have traditionally been subject to extensive regulation by the States, it is all the more appropriate that we limit our scrutiny of state regulations to a level commensurate with the " 'subordinate position' " of commercial speech in the scale of First Amendment values.

We believe that the Bar's 30–day restriction on targeted direct-mail solicitation of accident victims and their relatives withstands scrutiny under the three-pronged *Central Hudson* test that we have devised for this context. The Bar has substantial interest both in protecting injured Floridians from invasive conduct by lawyers and in preventing the erosion of confidence in the profession that such repeated invasions have engendered. The Bar's proffered study, unrebutted by respondents below, provides evidence indicating that the harms it targets are far from illusory. The palliative devised by the Bar to address these harms is narrow both in scope and in duration. The Constitution, in our view, requires nothing more.

The judgment of the Court of Appeals, accordingly, is *Reversed.*

Justice KENNEDY, with whom Justice STEVENS, Justice SOUTER, and Justice GINSBURG join, dissenting.

Attorneys who communicate their willingness to assist potential clients are engaged in speech protected by the First and Fourteenth Amendments.... The Court today undercuts this guarantee in an important class of cases and unsettles leading First Amendment precedents, at the expense of those victims most in need of legal assistance. With all respect for the Court, in my view its solicitude for the privacy of victims and its concern for our profession are misplaced and self-defeating, even upon the Court's own premises.

I take it to be uncontroverted that when an accident results in death or injury, it is often urgent at once to investigate the occurrence, identify witnesses, and preserve evidence. Vital interests in speech and expression are, therefore, at stake when by law an attorney cannot direct a letter to the victim or the family explaining this simple fact and offering competent legal assistance. Meanwhile, represented and better informed parties, or parties who have been solicited in ways more sophisticated and indirect, may be at work. Indeed, these parties, either themselves or by their attorneys, investigators, and adjusters, are free to contact the unrepresented persons to gather evidence or offer settlement. This scheme makes little sense. As is often true when the law makes little sense, it is not first principles but their interpretation and application that have gone awry. . . .

I

As the Court notes, the first of the *Central Hudson* factors to be considered is whether the interest the State pursues in enacting the speech restriction is a substantial one. The State says two different interests meet this standard. The first is the interest "in protecting the personal privacy and tranquility" of the victim and his or her family. As the Court notes, that interest has recognition in our decisions as a general matter; but it does not follow that the privacy interest in the cases the majority cites is applicable here. The problem the Court confronts, and cannot overcome, is our recent decision in *Shapero v. Kentucky Bar Assn.,* 486 U.S. 466, 108 S.Ct. 1916, 100 L.Ed.2d 475 (1988). In assessing the importance of the interest in that solicitation case, we made an explicit distinction between direct, in-person solicitations and direct-mail solicitations. *Shapero,* like this case, involved a direct-mail solicitation, and there the State recited its fears of "overreaching and undue influence." We found, however, no such dangers presented by direct-mail advertising. . . .

To avoid the controlling effect of *Shapero* in the case before us, the Court seeks to declare that a different privacy interest is implicated. As it sees the matter, the substantial concern is that victims or their families will be offended by receiving a solicitation during their grief and trauma. But we do not allow restrictions on speech to be justified on the ground that the expression might offend the listener. On the contrary, we have said that these "are classically not justifications validating the suppression of expression protected by the First Amendment." And in *Zauderer v. Office of Disciplinary Counsel of Supreme Court of Ohio,* 471 U.S. 626, 105 S.Ct. 2265, 85 L.Ed.2d 652 (1985), where we struck down a ban on attorney advertising, we held that "the mere possibility that some members of the population might find advertising . . . offensive cannot justify suppressing it. The same must hold true for advertising that some members of the bar might find beneath their dignity." . . .

In the face of these difficulties of logic and precedent, the State and the opinion of the Court turn to a second interest: protecting the reputation and dignity of the legal profession. The argument is, it seems fair to say, that all are demeaned by the crass behavior of a few. The argument takes a further step in the *amicus* brief filed by the Association of Trial Lawyers of America. There it is said that disrespect for the profession from this sort of solicitation (but presumably from no other sort of solicitation) results in lower jury verdicts. In a sense, of course, these arguments are circular. While disrespect will arise from an unethical or improper practice, the majority begs a most critical question by assuming that direct-mail solicitations constitute such a practice. The fact is, however, that direct solicitation may serve vital purposes and promote the administration of justice, and to the extent the bar seeks to protect lawyers' reputations by preventing them from engaging in speech some deem offensive, the State is doing nothing more (as *amicus* the Association of Trial Lawyers of America is at least candid enough to admit) than manipulating the public's opinion by suppressing speech that informs us how the legal system works. The disrespect argument thus proceeds from the very assumption it tries to prove, which is to say that solicitations within 30 days serve no legitimate purpose. This, of course, is censorship pure and simple; and censorship is antithetical to the first principles of free expression.

II

Even were the interests asserted substantial, the regulation here fails the second part of the *Central Hudson* test, which requires that the dangers the State seeks to eliminate be real and that a speech restriction or ban advance that asserted state interest in a direct and material way. The burden of demonstrating the reality of the asserted harm rests on the State. Slight evidence in this regard does not mean there is sufficient evidence to support the claims. Here, what the State has offered falls well short of demonstrating that the harms it is trying to redress are real, let alone that the regulation directly and materially advances the State's interests. . . .

It is telling that the essential thrust of all the material adduced to justify the State's interest is devoted to the reputational concerns of the Bar. It is not at all clear that this regulation advances the interest of protecting persons who are suffering trauma and grief, and we are cited to no material in the record for that claim. . . .

III

The insufficiency of the regulation to advance the State's interest is reinforced by the third inquiry necessary in this analysis. Were it appropriate to reach the third part of the *Central Hudson* test, it would be clear that the relationship between the Bar's interests and the means chosen to serve them is not a reasonable fit. The Bar's rule creates a flat ban that prohibits far more speech than necessary to serve the purported state interest. Even assuming that interest were legitimate, there is a wild disproportion between the harm supposed and the speech ban enforced. It is a disproportion the Court does not bother to discuss, but our speech jurisprudence requires that it do so. ...

There is ... simply no justification for assuming that in all or most cases an attorney's advice would be unwelcome or unnecessary when the survivors or the victim must at once begin assessing their legal and financial position in a rational manner. With regard to lesser injuries, there is little chance that for any period, much less 30 days, the victims will become distraught upon hearing from an attorney. It is, in fact, more likely a real risk that some victims might think no attorney will be interested enough to help them. It is at this precise time that sound legal advice may be necessary and most urgent.

Even as to more serious injuries, the State's argument fails, since it must be conceded that prompt legal representation is essential where death or injury results from accidents. The only seeming justification for the State's restriction is the one the Court itself offers, which is that attorneys can and do resort to other ways of communicating important legal information to potential clients. Quite aside from the latent protectionism for the established bar that the argument discloses, it fails for the more fundamental reason that it concedes the necessity for the very representation the attorneys solicit and the State seeks to ban. The accident victims who are prejudiced to vindicate the State's purported desire for more dignity in the legal profession will be the very persons who most need legal advice, for they are the victims who, because they lack education, linguistic ability, or familiarity with the legal system, are unable to seek out legal services.

The reasonableness of the State's chosen methods for redressing perceived evils can be evaluated, in part, by a commonsense consideration of other possible means of regulation that have not been tried. Here, the Court neglects the fact that this problem is largely self-policing: Potential clients will not hire lawyers who offend them. And even if a person enters into a contract with an attorney and later regrets it, Florida, like some other States, allows clients to rescind certain contracts with attorneys within a stated time after they are executed. The State's restriction deprives accident victims of information which may be critical to their right to make a claim for compensation for injuries. The telephone book and general advertisements may serve this purpose in part; but the direct solicitation ban will fall on those who most need legal representation: for those with minor injuries, the victims too ill informed to know an attorney may be interested in their cases; for those with serious injuries, the victims too ill informed to know that time is of the essence if counsel is to assemble evidence and warn them not to enter into settlement negotiations or evidentiary discussions with investigators for opposing parties. One survey reports that over a recent 5–year period, 68% of the American population consulted a lawyer. The use of modern communication methods in a timely way is essential if clients who make up this vast demand are to be advised and informed of all of their choices and rights in selecting an attorney. The very fact that some 280,000 direct-mail solicitations are sent to accident victims and their survivors in Florida each year is some indication of the efficacy of this device. Nothing in the Court's opinion demonstrates that these efforts do not serve some beneficial role. . . .

IV

It is most ironic that, for the first time since *Bates v. State Bar of Arizona,* the Court now orders a major retreat from the constitutional guarantees for commercial speech in order to shield its own profession from public criticism. Obscuring the financial aspect of the legal profession from public discussion through direct-mail solicitation, at the expense of the least sophisticated members of society, is not a laudable constitutional goal. There is no authority for the proposition that the Constitution permits the State to promote the public image of the legal profession by suppressing information about the profession's business aspects. If public respect for the profession erodes because solicitation distorts the idea of the law as most lawyers see it, it must be remembered that real progress begins with more rational speech, not less. . . . The image of the profession cannot be enhanced without improving the substance of its practice. The objective of the profession is to ensure that "the ethical standards of lawyers are linked to the service and protection of clients."

Today's opinion is a serious departure, not only from our prior decisions involving attorney advertising, but also from the principles that govern the transmission of commercial speech. The Court's opinion reflects a new-found and illegitimate confidence that it, along with the Supreme Court of Florida, knows what is best for the Bar and its clients. Self-assurance has always been the hallmark of a censor. That is why under the First Amendment the public, not the State, has the right and the power to decide what ideas and information are deserving of their adherence. "[T]he general rule is that the speaker and the audience, not the government, assess the value of the information presented." By validating Florida's rule, today's majority is complicit in the Bar's censorship. For these reasons, I dissent from the opinion of the Court and from its judgment.

Notes

1. How does the majority in *Went For It* distinguish *Shapero*? Are the two cases distinguishable? Does *Went For It* represent a significant departure from *Shapero*, as the dissent charges?

2. Do you agree with Justice Kennedy that the majority in *Went For It* elevates a concern for the reputation of the bar over more important societal interests?

3. *Criminalization of forms of solicitation.* Many states have criminalized certain forms of solicitation by lawyers. Are such laws constitutional, or do they sweep too broadly and with too much force? It depends, of course, on the statute and the state's arguments. Compare *Chambers v. Stengel*, 256 F.3d 397 (6th Cir.2001) (upholding constitutionality of Kentucky statute that criminalizes solicitation of accident victims within 30 days of an accident), with *State v. Bradford*, 787 So.2d 811 (Fla. 2001)(statute criminalizing solicitation of motor vehicle tort claims or claims for personal injury protection auto insurance benefits held unconstitutional because of overbreadth) and *Anderson Courier Service v. State*, 104 S.W.3d 121 (Tex.App.2003) (law criminalizing the use of certain accident report information obtained from governmental agencies for solicitation of pecuniary gain held unconstitutional abridgement of free speech).

Chapter 9

JUDICIAL ETHICS

Judges play a central role in our society in general, let alone in the life of lawyers and the law. This is the best answer to the question, "If I'm not going to be a judge, then why study judicial ethics?" Of course, you might well become a judge, or you might find yourself defending or prosecuting one. If you are a litigator you will certainly appear before them. This chapter provides an introduction to some of the most important aspects of the various rules that govern judicial behavior, both official and unofficial. First, we see cases and rules restricting judges in their function as judges. Second, we see the permissible limits on extra-judicial conduct. And third, we will look at some of the important issues relating to the selection of judges, including the free speech rights of persons running for elected judicial office.

Judges, like lawyers, may be disciplined by the jurisdiction in which they work. The ABA Model Code of Judicial Conduct (hereinafter "Judicial Code") has been adopted by most states as the disciplinary code for judges in their jurisdiction. The ABA first adopted Canons of Judicial Ethics in 1924. The federal Judicial Conference of the United States adopted standards for federal judges in the 1960s. After the development of the Model Code of Professional Responsibility (for lawyers) in 1970, the ABA went to work on a new model Judicial Code. It was first promulgated in 1972, then substantially revised in 1990. It is the 1990 Code (as amended through the years) that most states follow at this time, and citations in this chapter are to this Judicial Code, as amended through 2005.

In 2003, the ABA appointed a Joint Commission to Evaluate the Model Code of Judicial Conduct. That commission completed a complete draft set of revised rules in late 2005 and was continuing to receive comments on it as this book was being completed. One proposed change in the new judicial code is in format. While Canons would remain as titles, rules under them would address particular conduct that is clearly prohibited, followed by comments, much like the structure of the Model Rules for lawyers.

Substantively, the proposed rules (as of fall, 2006) are not radically different from the Model Code, although there are several new proposed rules, on such matters as a judge's independently investigating the facts of a case (prohibited), gifts to judges, acceptance of travel reimbursements, and charitable activities. Proposed rules on judges' political activities—the subject of section 3 of this Chapter—are structured differently than in the current Code, setting up different rules for judicial candidates in partisan elections, candidates in nonpartisan elections, and judges in retention elections.

The revised Judicial Code—called the ABA Model Rules of Judicial Conduct—may have been approved by the ABA House of Delegates as you read this. Of course, just like the ABA Model Rules for lawyers, any new set of rules will have legal effect only when adopted by particular states, meaning that the current Model Code will remain the basic template in place in the states for some years to come. The full text of the ABA Model Rules, and up-to-date information about promulgation and adoption, is available on the website of the ABA.

§ 1. JUDICIAL FUNCTIONS

QUERCIA v. UNITED STATES

Supreme Court of the United States, 1933.
289 U.S. 466, 53 S.Ct. 698, 77 L.Ed. 1321.

Mr. Chief Justice HUGHES delivered the opinion of the Court.

Petitioner was convicted of violating the Narcotic Act. 26 U.S.C. §§ 692, 705 (26 USCA §§ 692, 705). The conviction was affirmed by the Circuit Court of Appeals, and this court granted certiorari.

Reversal is sought upon the ground that the instructions of the trial court to the jury exceeded the bounds of fair comment and constituted prejudicial error. After testimony by agents of the government in support of the indictment, defendant testified, making a general denial of all charges. His testimony is not set forth in the record. Defendant's motion for a direction of verdict and requests for rulings substantially to the same effect were denied. The court instructed the jury concerning the rules as to presumption of innocence and reasonable doubt, and stated generally that its expression of opinion on the evidence was not binding on the jury and that it was their duty to disregard the court's opinion as to the facts if the jury did not agree with it. The court ruled as matter of law that if the jury believed the evidence for the government, it might find the defendant guilty. The court then charged the jury as follows:

And now I am going to tell you what I think of the defendant's testimony. You may have noticed, Mr. Foreman and gentlemen, that he wiped his hands during his testimony. It is rather a curious thing, but that is almost always an indication of lying. Why it should be so we don't know, but that is the fact. I think that every single word that man said, except when he agreed with the Government's testimony, was a lie.

Now, that opinion is an opinion of evidence and is not binding on you, and if you don't agree with it, it is your duty to find him not guilty.

To this charge the defendant excepted.

In a trial by jury in a federal court, the judge is not a mere moderator, but is the governor of the trial for the purpose of assuring its proper conduct and of determining questions of law. In charging the jury, the trial judge is not limited to instructions of an abstract sort. It is within his province, whenever he thinks it necessary, to assist the jury in arriving at a just conclusion by explaining and commenting upon the evidence, by drawing their attention to the parts of it which he thinks important, and he may express his opinion upon the facts, provided he makes it clear to the jury that all matters of fact are submitted to their determination. Sir Matthew Hale thus described the function of the trial judge at common law: 'Herein he is able, in matters of law emerging upon the evidence, to direct them; and also, in matters of fact to give them a great light and assistance by his weighing the evidence before them, and observing where the question and knot of the business lies, and by showing them his opinion even in matter of fact; which is a great advantage and light to laymen.' Hale, History of the Common Law, 291, 292. Under the Federal Constitution the essential prerogatives of the trial judge as they were secured by the rules of the common law are maintained in the federal courts.

This privilege of the judge to comment on the facts has its inherent limitations. His discretion is not arbitrary and uncontrolled, but judicial, to be exercised in conformity with the standards governing the judicial office. In commenting upon testimony he may not assume the role of a witness. He may analyze and dissect the evidence, but he may not either distort it or add to it. His privilege of comment in order to give appropriate assistance to the jury is too important to be left without safeguards against abuses. The influence of the trial judge on the jury 'is necessarily and properly of great weight' and 'his lightest word or intimation is received with deference, and may prove controlling.' This court has accordingly emphasized the duty of the trial judge to use great care that an expression of opinion upon the evidence 'should be so given as not to mislead, and especially that it should not be one-sided'; that 'deductions and theories not warranted by the evidence should be studiously avoided.' Starr v. United States, 153 U.S. 614, 626, 14 S.Ct. 919, 923, 38 L.Ed. 841; Hickory v. United States, 160 U.S. 408, 421–423, 16 S.Ct. 327, 332, 40 L.Ed. 474. He may not charge the jury 'upon a supposed or conjectural state of facts, of which no evidence has been offered.' United States v. Breitling, 20 How. 252, 254, 255, 15 L.Ed. 900. It is important that hostile comment of the judge should not render vain the privilege of the accused to testify in his own behalf. Thus, a statement in a charge to the jury that 'no one who was conscious of innocence would resort to concealment,' was regarded as tantamount to saying 'that all men who did so were necessarily guilty,' and as magnifying and distorting 'the proving power of the facts on the subject of the concealment.' Hickory v. United States, supra. And the further charge that the proposition that 'the wicked flee when no man pursueth, but the innocent are as bold as a lion,' was 'a self-evident proposition' which the jury could 'take * * * as an axiom, and apply it' to the case in hand, was virtually an instruction that flight was conclusive proof of guilt. Such a charge 'put every deduction which could be drawn against the accused from the proof of concealment and flight, and omitted or obscured the converse aspect'; it 'deprived the jury of the light requisite to safely use these facts as means to the ascertainment of truth.' Id. So where the trial judge, in referring to the defendant's story of self-defense, said, 'All men would say that. No man created would say otherwise when confronted by such circumstances,' this court held that the comment practically deprived the defendant of the benefit of his testimony. 'It was for the jury to test the credibility of the defendant as a witness, giving his testimony such weight under all the circumstances as they thought it entitled to, as in the instance of other witnesses, uninfluenced by instructions which might operate to strip him of the competency accorded by the law.' Allison v. United States, supra. Similarly, where no testimony had been offered as to the previous character of the accused, it was prejudicial error for the trial court to comment unfavorably upon his general character.

In the instant case, the trial judge did not analyze the evidence; he added to it, and he based his instruction upon his own addition. Dealing with a mere mannerism of the accused in giving his testimony, the judge put his own experience, with all the weight that could be attached to it, in the scale against the accused. He told the jury that 'wiping' one's hands while testifying was 'almost always an indication of lying.' Why it should be so, he was unable to say, but it was 'the fact.' He did not review the evidence to assist the jury in reaching the truth, but in a sweeping denunciation repudiated as a lie all that the accused had said in his own behalf which conflicted with the statements of the government's witnesses. This was error and we cannot doubt that it was highly prejudicial.

Nor do we think that the error was cured by the statement of the trial judge that his opinion of the evidence was not binding on the jury and that if they did not agree with it they should find the defendant not guilty. His definite and concrete assertion of fact, which he had made with all the persuasiveness of judicial utterance, as to the basis of his opinion, was not withdrawn. His characterization of the manner and testimony of the accused was of a sort most likely to remain firmly lodged in the memory of the jury and to excite a prejudice which would preclude a fair and dispassionate consideration of the evidence.

The judgment must be reversed. It is so ordered.

Notes

1. *Impartiality and the appearance of impartiality.* Several provisions of the Judicial Code are bottomed on the notion that a judge must decide cases impartially. See generally Judicial Code Canons 2 & 3 (2002). But actual impartiality, or the absence of actual bias or prejudice, is not enough: The Judicial Code states that judges shall avoid even the appearance of impropriety in all their activities. See *id.*, Canon 2. The key inquiry here is whether a reasonable person would perceive an impairment in the judge's ability to carry out his or her responsibilities with "integrity, impartiality and competence." *Id.*, Canon 2A, commentary [2]. Why this focus on "the appearance" of impropriety, as opposed to "actual" impropriety only? If lawyers are not generally held to this high a standard—and they are not in most states—why should judges? See *id.*, Canon 1, commentary.

2. *Quercia* is an oft-cited case on the limits of a judge's commentary on evidence during a jury trial. As the case indicates, judges can comment on the evidence at trial, but must do so with some care to avoid the appearance of partiality. See *United States v. Hefferon*, 314 F.3d 211 (5th Cir.2002) (holding that judge's comment to defense counsel that his assertions were unsupported by the evidence "did not have a significant effect on the jury and did not give the appearance of partiality"). Would it be proper "commentary" for a judge to "emit a 'raspberry'" to indicate disbelief of a witness? See *Spruance v. Commission on Judicial Qualifications*, 13 Cal.3d 778, 532 P.2d 1209, 119 Cal.Rptr. 841 (1975). Why is commentary on the evidence allowed at all? Should prudent judges avoid such conduct entirely?

3. Does your analysis of the question above turn on your view of the trial judge's proper role? What does Chief Justice Hughes think is the proper role?

4. *Questioning witnesses.* Trial judges are also authorized to question witnesses at trial, although once again they must take care not to appear biased in doing so. See Fed. R. Evid. 614(b) ("The court may

interrogate witnesses, whether called by itself or by a party.") There is nothing wrong with a judge asking questions to clarify testimony, expedite the trial, and maintain courtroom decorum. See, e.g., *Logue v. Dore*, 103 F.3d 1040 (1st Cir.1997). But courts have recognized that "cross-examination of a witness by the trial judge is potentially more impeaching than such an examination conducted by an adversary attorney. The judge, by his office, carries an imprimatur of impartiality and credibility in the eyes of the jury." *United States v. Godwin*, 272 F.3d 659 (4th Cir.2001)(criticizing judge's extensive questioning but affirming convictions because of the lack of timely objections by defense counsel).

5. *Curative instructions.* The Court in *Quercia* found deficient the judge's attempt to cure the harm caused by his comments by further instructing the jury that they were free to disagree with his perspective. But modern courts often hold that curative instructions remove the problems created by judicial commentary. In *Navellier v. Sletten*, 262 F.3d 923 (9th Cir.2001), for example, the trial judge, in the presence of the jury, commented that defendant might have committed perjury during his testimony. When the defendant's lawyer objected, the judge told the jury to disregard his comment. On appeal, the conviction was affirmed: "[E]ven if the comment could be considered prejudicial, any prejudice was cured by the court's contemporaneous instruction and the final jury instructions, which stressed that the jurors were the sole judge of the facts." See also *United States v. James*, 576 F.2d 223 (9th Cir.1978) (judge commented to the jury that all the elements of the offense had been established, then added that the jury was the final arbiter of the facts; conviction affirmed). Do you think curative instructions are effective in this context?

6. *The "extrajudicial source" factor.* Can a party prove that a judge is biased, or has the appearance of being biased, merely by pointing to adverse rulings in the case? The clear answer is no. See, e.g., *Liteky v. United States*, 510 U.S. 540, 114 S.Ct. 1147, 127 L.Ed.2d 474 (1994); *State v. Stockert*, 684 N.W.2d 605 (N.D. 2004). Why might that not be sufficient? See, e.g., *Henderson v. G & G Corp.*, 582 So.2d 529 (Ala.1991); *Williams v. Williams*, 812 So.2d 352 (Ala.Civ.App.2001).

7. *Commendation or criticism of jurors.* Would it be proper for a judge to tell a jury after its verdict that he agreed with them? Would it be proper for the judge to tell the jury that he did not? See Judicial Code Canon 3B(10).

NOTE: REMEDIES

There are a number of distinct remedies for judicial misconduct—or the appearance of bias or partiality—deriving from a number of sources.

First, a judgment (or part of one, such a remedial order) may be reversed, as we saw in *Quercia*. See also *Tesco American, Inc. v.*

Strong Industries, Inc., ___ S.W.3d ___, 2006 WL 662740 (Tex.) (ordering reversal of appellate decision when appellate justice should have recused himself). In rare cases, such a reversal may be required because misconduct or bias causes a denial of due process, as we will see *infra* in the *Aetna* case.

Second, a judge may be disqualified from presiding over a case. Two federal statutes address recusal of federal judges. Title 28 U.S.C. § 455 requires a federal judge to "disqualify himself in any proceeding in which his impartiality might reasonably be questioned." Title 28 U.S.C. § 144 provides that whenever a party in a trial court proceeding files a proper affidavit stating that the judge has a "personal bias or prejudice either against him or in favor of any adverse party, such judge shall proceed no further therein, but another judge shall be assigned to hear such proceeding." At the state level, rules are generally similar or identical to those contained in the federal law, and may be found either in the state's judicial ethics code, statutes, court rules, or rules of procedure. See, e.g., Tex. Civ. Proc. Rule 18b (2003); Mich. Court Rule 2.003 (2003); Judicial Code Canon 3E (all similar to § 455). A ruling on a motion to disqualify a judge is appealable by the losing party, although the judge has no standing to challenge an order removing her from a case. See *Curle v. Superior Court*, 24 Cal.4th 1057, 16 P.3d 166, 103 Cal.Rptr.2d 751 (2001)(reasoning that allowing such an appeal where neither party wants it causes unnecessary delay).

Third, a judge is subject to discipline for misconduct on or off the bench. All states have a state judicial commission charged with disciplining judges pursuant to the state's judicial ethics code. The Judicial Code contains five Canons covering judicial functions; extra-judicial functions; and political activities. Discipline can range from private admonition to removal from office. See, e.g., *Moore v. Judicial Inquiry Comm'n*, 891 So.2d 848 (Ala. 2004) (removal of Chief Justice of the Alabama Supreme Court for willfully disobeying a federal court order to remove a tablet depicting the Ten Commandments from the state Judicial Building); *Inquiry Concerning a Judge*, 275 Ga. 404, 566 S.E.2d 310 (2002) (removal of judge for incompetence). In the federal system, Congress has authorized judicial councils in each federal circuit to perform this disciplinary function. 28 U.S.C. §§ 331 *et seq.* A number of sanctions are available against federal judges pursuant to the judicial council system, from private censure to a recommendation for impeachment by Congress and removal from office. 28 U.S.C. § 372.

Fourth, a judge is subject to criminal liability just as is any other citizen. *Ex parte Virginia*, 100 U.S. (10 Otto) 339, 25 L.Ed. 676 (1880). But there is an absolute immunity from civil liability for official judicial acts, even where the acts themselves are improper. See, e.g., *Pierson v. Ray*, 386 U.S. 547, 87 S.Ct. 1213, 18

L.Ed.2d 288 (1967); *Stump v. Sparkman*, 435 U.S. 349, 98 S.Ct. 1099, 55 L.Ed.2d 331 (1978). Civil immunity attaches even where the judge's conduct is criminal, such as where the judge has accepted bribes. See, e.g., *Sherman v. Almeida*, 747 A.2d 470 (R.I.2000) (affirming dismissal of civil case for failure to state a claim, citing judicial immunity).

INQUIRY CONCERNING A JUDGE
(IN RE SHELDON SCHAPIRO)

Supreme Court of Florida, 2003.
845 So.2d 170.

PER CURIAM.

We review the recommendation of the Judicial Qualifications Commission (JQC) that Judge Sheldon Schapiro be disciplined. In a stipulation with the JQC, Judge Schapiro admits engaging in inappropriate behavior in court that is unbecoming a member of the judiciary, brings the judiciary into disrepute, and impairs the citizens' confidence both in the integrity of the judicial system and in Judge Schapiro as a judge.

The stipulation, which quotes the notice of formal charges directed to Judge Schapiro, sets forth the facts as follows:

Charge No. 1—In violation of Canon 1, Canon 2A, and Canon 3B(4), in approximately 1996, you chastised an attorney, Joseph Dawson, for allegedly speaking in your courtroom by stating, "Why do I always have to treat you like a school child?" or words to that effect. When Mr. Dawson responded that you routinely treat everyone in your courtroom like a school child, you ordered him out of the courtroom. Since that time, Mr. Dawson has routinely sought your recusal and you have granted those requests.

Charge No. 2—In violation of Canon 1, Canon 2A, and Canon 3B(4), in May, 1998, you ordered Denise Neuner, an assistant state attorney, to appear before you and try a criminal case although Ms. Neuner had previously contacted your chambers to explain she had a severe medical condition and had been ordered by her physician to bed rest because of the possibility she might have pneumonia.

Charge No. 3—In violation of Canon 1, Canon 2A, and Canon 3B(4), in approximately March or April 1998, you attempted to force Greg Rossman, an assistant state attorney, to try a case that was assigned to another assistant state attorney. When Mr. Rossman responded that the practice of the State Attorney's Office was for each assistant to try only his or her own cases, you proceeded to scream at Mr. Rossman and tell him that the case in question was a "nothing case," which he should be prepared to try with no advance preparation. You further admonished Mr. Rossman by making the following sarcastic remarks:

> THE COURT: All right, you want to waste my time, there will come a time I warn you, when I'm going to be tied up in something and you will have a speedy pending and my time will not be available. You are squandering the Court's time.

Charge No. 4—In violation of Canon 1, Canon 2A, and Canon 3B(4), you have routinely berated and unnecessarily embarrassed attorneys for allegedly talking in your courtroom when those attorneys were either not talking at all or speaking in appropriately low tones of voice concerning legitimate business of the court (e.g. state attorneys and defense counsel conferring with one another concerning plea negotiations), as evidenced by the following examples:

a. You chastised and unnecessarily raised your voice at Ginger Miranda, an assistant public defender, as she attempted to confer with her client who was a prisoner in custody. Specifically, you said to Ms. Miranda, "Psst. Hey you. I'm sick and tired of the noise you make in my courtroom" or words to that effect. When Ms. Miranda explained that she was trying to discuss a plea offer with her client, you continued to berate her. Ms. Miranda then apologized to which you sarcastically replied, "Oh yeah, you're sorry," or words to that effect.

b. In approximately September, 2000, as Deborah Carpenter, an assistant public defender, was waiting in open court for her case to be called, another public defender began speaking with her. You then said, "Ms. Carpenter, if you say one more word, I'm going to have you removed from the courtroom" or words to that effect. When the other assistant public defender interceded and stated, "Judge, I'm sorry, it was me," you ignored her statement and responded, "I don't want to hear another word out of you Ms. Carpenter" or words to that effect.

c. On another occasion, you ordered Bradley Weissman, an assistant state attorney, to leave the courtroom because you believed he was talking, although Mr. Weissman was not talking.

d. In a similar episode, during the summer of 1999, you had previously ordered everyone in the courtroom to be quiet. Dennis Siegel, an assistant state attorney, was among the attorneys in the courtroom at the time. You then turned to Mr. Siegel and said, "Mr. Siegel, I told you to be quiet" or words to that effect. Mr. Siegel responded that he had not been talking. Despite his denial, you continued to insist that you saw Mr. Siegel talking. . . .

Charge No. 6—In violation of Canon 1, Canon 2A, and Canon 3B(4), several years ago, as a criminal defense attorney was making an argument in a sexual battery case, you cut him off and said, "Do you know what I think of your argument?" or words to that effect, at which time you pushed a button on a device that simulated the sound of a commode flushing.

Charge No. 7—In violation of Canon 1, Canon 2A, and Canon 3B(4), in a case involving a defendant driving with a suspended driver's license approximately four years ago, Louis Pironti, an assistant public defender at the time, advised you during a sidebar conference that he might need a continuance in order to secure an expert witness. The sidebar was held in a small room behind the bench commonly known as the woodshed among attorneys familiar with your courtroom (hereinafter "backroom"). Instead of simply denying the motion, you became agitated and responded by saying to Mr. Pironti, "You're going to try this mother fu__ing case." You then returned to the bench and threw the docket down on a desk.

Charge No. 8—In violation of Canon 1, Canon 2A, Canon 3B(4), and Canon 3B(5), approximately 4 1/2 years ago, as Shari Tate, a female assistant state attorney, was arguing a motion to revoke bond, you summoned Ms. Tate to the backroom behind your bench and told her that she needed to emulate the style of male attorneys when addressing the court because male attorneys did not get as emotional about their cases as the female attorneys did. As a result of this experience, Ms. Tate advised you that she would never go to the backroom with you again without a court reporter being present.

Charge No. 9—In violation of Canon 1, Canon 2A, and Canon 3B(4), in another incident involving Ms. Tate when she was eight months pregnant, she was hospitalized because of pregnancy complications on the third day of a trial over which you presided. As a result of her hospitalization, Ms. Tate requested a continuance of the trial. You denied the continuance and further advised Ms. Tate that she should get another prosecutor from her office to complete the trial. When Ms. Tate advised your chambers that "substituting" counsel was not feasible in that no other assistant state attorney was familiar enough with the case to step in her place, you, or your chambers, advised Ms. Tate that if she were not in court the following morning, you would dismiss the case. As a result, Ms. Tate left the hospital against her doctor's orders in order to complete the trial before you.

Charge No. 10—In violation of Canon 1, Canon 2A, and Canon 3B(4), in 1999, you presided over a bond hearing where a motorcyclist had killed a child and left the scene. The child's mother and neighbor came to the bond hearing, which was approximately two days after the incident and before the child was buried. After you made a preliminary determination that the defendant was entitled to bond, the assistant state attorney advised you that the mother of the victim was present and wanted to address the court. You responded by saying, "What do I need to hear from the mother of a [deceased] kid for? All she will tell me is to keep the guy in custody and never let him out" or words to that effect. The victim's mother heard your sarcastic remarks and was then afraid to address the court.

Charge No. 11—In violation of Canon 1, Canon 2A, and Canon 3B(4), you have fallen into a general pattern of rude and intemperate behavior by needlessly interjecting yourself into counsel's examinations of witnesses; embarrassing and belittling counsel in court; and questioning the competence of counsel by making remarks such as, "What, are you stupid?"

[Based on these violations, the JQV recommended the following discipline: (1) public reprimand; (2) participation in sensitivity training supervised by a "qualified health care provider"; and (3) a public apology "to the citizens of Broward County."]

We agree with the JQC's determination that Judge Sheldon Schapiro has violated the Code of Judicial Conduct. We conclude that Judge Schapiro has clearly undermined the public's confidence in and respect for both the integrity of the judicial system and Judge Schapiro as a judge. These violations are extreme in their seriousness, in their number, and in the length of time over which they occurred. To undermine public confidence and respect by such serious violations strikes at the very roots of an effective judiciary, for those who are served by the courts will not have confidence in and respect for the courts' judgments if judges engage in this egregious conduct. Were it not for Judge Schapiro's efforts to participate in behavioral therapy, this Court would have sanctioned Judge Schapiro in a substantially more severe manner. Judge Schapiro is expressly notified that if his efforts do not consistently continue as agreed to in the stipulation, this Court will severely sanction Judge Schapiro's misconduct.

In view of the stipulation and the ongoing treatment program, we approve the recommendation of a public reprimand and a continual treatment program but also order Judge Schapiro to, within thirty days of the filing of this opinion, write and mail personal letters of apology to those individuals identified in the above-quoted portion of the stipulation. Judge Schapiro is directed to appear before this Court for the administration of a public reprimand on June 4, 2003, at 9 a.m. Judge Schapiro shall pay the costs of these proceedings.

It is so ordered.

Notes

1. Judicial Code Canon 3B(3) requires a judge to maintain order and decorum in proceedings. Canon 3B(4), cited by the court in *Schapi-*

ro, requires a judge to be "patient, dignified and courteous" to all persons with whom the judge deals in an official capacity. Why is this kind of civility thought to be so important in judicial ethics? Does it have anything to do with what we expect of lawyers? See MR 3.4 (fairness to opposing party and counsel), 3.5 (impartiality and decorum of the tribunal); 4.4 (respect for the rights of third persons); 8.4(d) (prohibiting engaging in conduct that is prejudicial to the administration of justice).

2. Judicial Code Canon 1, also cited by the court, requires a judge to participate in establishing, maintaining and enforcing high standards of conduct, and to personally observe those standards. Canon 2A requires a judge to "act at all times in a manner that promotes public confidence in the integrity and impartiality of the judiciary." A judge may be found to violate these provisions by making improper remarks in open court. In *In re Inquiry Concerning a Judge (In re Hill)*, 357 N.C. 559, 591 S.E.2d 859 (2003), a lawyer was arguing a motion when the judge interrupted her and "demanded her personal opinion about a legal issue. When attorney [Larsen] declined to express such an opinion, [the judge] engaged in unwarranted, unprovoked personal and professional criticism ... , accusing her of being insensitive and heartless and suggesting she was an incompetent attorney." Ordering censure, the court found that the judge had engaged in conduct prejudicial to the administration of justice in violation of North Carolina Code of Judicial Conduct Canons 1, 2A, and 3A(3) [numbered 3B(3) in the Model Judicial Code]. See also *In re Hart*, 7 N.Y.3d 1, 849 N.E.2d 946, 816 N.Y.S.2d 723 (2006) (censuring judge for holding litigant in summary contempt in apparent response to litigant's counsel's attempts to make a record about an out-of-court incident involving the judge and the litigant).

3. Given the number of incidents of misconduct, should Judge Schapiro have been removed from office, rather than simply reprimanded? See *Fletcher v. Commission on Judicial Performance*, 19 Cal.4th 865, 968 P.2d 958, 81 Cal.Rptr.2d 58 (1998) (removing judge from office for "a persistent pattern of misconduct that reflects a lack of judicial temperament"). And what do you think of the mandatory apology order? If you were one of the people who received such an apology, how would it make you feel?

4. *The recusal remedy.* In *In re Blake*, 912 So.2d 907 (Miss. 2005), a judge reacted with apparently-unprovoked "anger and vitriol" toward a lawyer (Robinson) for failure to produce an expert witness at a particular time, then continued to berate him at various times during the case, apparently with little or no justification. The Mississippi high court, ruling on Robinson's writ of mandamus to recuse the judge in seven pending cases and all future cases in which Robinson appeared as counsel, could find nothing in the record that "demonstrated the slightest disrespect or insult from Robinson directed toward the court." Indeed, "[t]he record provides no justification whatsoever for Judge Green's animosity and sarcasm toward Robinson. We recognize and endorse a trial judge's duty to control the courtroom.... However, the professional obligations of dignity, respect and decorum is not limited to

counsel.... [J]udges and lawyers are not required to like each other. They are, however, required to maintain a reasonable level of respect, decorum and professional courtesy." Finding that the judge's conduct "would lead a reasonable person to question whether the judge would have a personal bias or prejudice concerning the lawyer's client," the court granted the lawyer's request to have the judge recused from each of the seven cases the lawyer had pending before Judge Green. It refused, however, to grant prospective recusal.

5. *Performance of duties without bias or prejudice.* Judicial Code Canon 3B(5) requires a judge to perform duties without manifesting bias or prejudice, including bias based on race, gender, religion, national origin, disability, age, sexual orientation or socioeconomic status. Canon 3B(6) places judges under a mandatory duty to require lawyers to refrain from manifesting any such bias or prejudice. The commentary to Canon 3B(5) explains that these duties are corollary to the larger duty to refrain from activities that bring the judiciary into disrepute or that create an appearance of unfairness in performing judicial functions.

6. *The absent judge.* A judge has a duty to perform the duties of office, which of course means being in the courtroom during proceedings. Cf. Judicial Code Canon 3A, 3B(1). "The presence of and supervision by a Judge constitutes an integral component of the right to a jury trial." *People v. Toliver*, 89 N.Y.2d 843, 652 N.Y.S.2d 728, 675 N.E.2d 463 (1996) (absence from judge during voir dire denies criminal defendant the right to a fair trial, warranting reversal of conviction, even where defense counsel did not object at the time).

7. *The (allegedly) sleeping judge.* Is a sleeping judge tantamount to an absent judge? The cases say no. In *People v. Degondea*, 3 A.D.3d 148, 769 N.Y.S.2d 490 (2003), the record showed no objection by defense counsel to the alleged judicial somnolence, but on appeal of a conviction the defendant mounted such a claim, citing the "absent judge" cases in support of his argument for reversal of his murder conviction. A trial judge (not the one allegedly sleeping) granted the motion to vacate judgment, but the appeals court reversed and reinstated the conviction. The court concluded that a claim that a judge was sleeping, where no objection was made on the record, "is subject to dispute by its very nature, inasmuch as it focuses on the judge's subjective state of mind, a matter subject to proof only by indirect and circumstantial evidence, aside from the judge's recollection.... As this case illustrates, a claim of judicial somnolence or inattention is readily generated by the inherently biased interpretations of ambiguous evidence by the defendant, his family and his trial counsel." Any such claim, held the court, is waived if there was no objection by defense counsel at the time. In any event, there was insufficient proof here that the judge, who admittedly "sometimes presided with his eyes closed and his head tilted back," was asleep at all. Even where the judge was asleep (or presumed so), courts often require proof of prejudice before granting relief. See *United States v. White*, 589 F.2d 1283 (5th Cir. 1979) (trial judge admittedly fell asleep during defense counsel's opening argument; held, not prejudicial error

given the judge's explanation to the jury of his ill health); *Hummel v. State*, 617 N.W.2d 561 (Minn. 2000) (petitioner failed to prove prejudice under *Strickland* for counsel's alleged ineffective assistance in not waking allegedly sleeping judge; argument was first raised nine years after the trial).

8. *Reporting misconduct.* Judicial Code Canon 3D(1) requires a judge who has knowledge that another judge has committed a Code violation that raises a substantial question as to that other judges fitness for office to inform appropriate authorities. If a judge receives information indicating a "substantial likelihood" of such misconduct, the judge "should take appropriate action," which according to the Commentary may include direct communication with the other judge in question. Canon 3D(2) is a similar reporting rule, requiring a judge to inform appropriate authorities, or take other appropriate action, about misconduct by lawyers. Many disciplinary complaints about lawyer misconduct originate with judges who have witnessed the misconduct. These rules are corollary to MR 8.3, the duty of lawyers to report the misconduct of other lawyers. Recall that in MR 8.3, however, that duty exists only where disclosure would not violate the lawyer's confidentiality duty under MR 1.6. Judges are under no such limitation.

AETNA LIFE INSURANCE CO. v. LAVOIE

Supreme Court of the United States, 1986.
475 U.S. 813, 106 S.Ct. 1580, 89 L.Ed.2d 823.

Chief Justice BURGER delivered the opinion of the Court.

The question presented is whether the Due Process Clause of the Fourteenth Amendment was violated when a justice of the Alabama Supreme Court declined to recuse himself from participation in that court's consideration of this case.

I

This appeal arises out of litigation concerning an insurance policy issued by appellant covering appellees Margaret and Roger Lavoie. [Aetna Life & Casualty Co. refused to pay the entire amount of Mrs. Lavoie's medical bills, concluding that the length of her hospitalization for tests was "unnecessary." The Lavoies sued, seeking payment of the claim and punitive damages for bad-faith refusal to pay a valid claim. The trial court dismissed the bad faith claim. On appeal, the Alabama Supreme Court reversed and remanded. On remand, the trial court found for the Lavoies on their coverage claim, but against them on the bad-faith claim. The Alabama Supreme Court again reversed the judgment on the bad-faith claim.] On remand, appellees' bad-faith claim was submitted to a jury. The jury awarded $3.5 million in punitive damages. The trial judge denied appellant's motion for judgment n.o.v. or, alternatively, for remittitur.

The Alabama Supreme Court affirmed the award in a 5-to-4 decision. An unsigned *per curiam* opinion expressed the view of five justices that the evidence demonstrated that appellant had acted in bad faith. The court interpreted its prior opinions as not requiring dismissal of a bad-faith-refusal-to-pay claim even where a directed verdict against the insurer on the underlying claim was impossible. The opinion also clarified the issue of whether a bad-faith suit could be maintained where the insurer had made a partial payment of the underlying claim. Although earlier opinions of the court had refused to allow bad-faith suits in such circumstances, partial payment was not dispositive of the bad-faith issue. The court also rejected appellant's argument that the punitive damages award was so excessive that it must be set aside.

Chief Justice Torbert, joined by Justice Beatty, dissented; Justice Maddox, joined by Justice Shores, also dissented, concluding that the case was controlled by the court's earlier decision in *National Savings Life Ins. Co. v. Dutton,* 419 So.2d 1357 (1982), because there was an arguable reason for appellant's refusal to pay the claim.

The court's opinion was released on December 7, 1984; on December 21, 1984, appellant filed a timely application for rehearing. On February 14, 1985, before its application had been acted on, appellant learned that while the instant action was pending before the Alabama Supreme Court, Justice Embry, one of the five justices joining the *per curiam* opinion, had filed two actions in the Circuit Court for Jefferson County, Alabama, against insurance companies. Both of these actions alleged bad-faith failure to pay a claim. One suit arose out of Maryland Casualty Company's alleged failure to pay for the loss of a valuable mink coat; the other suit, which Justice Embry brought on behalf of himself and as a representative of a class of all other Alabama state employees insured under a group plan by Blue Cross–Blue Shield of Alabama (including, apparently, all justices of the Alabama Supreme Court), alleged a willful and intentional plan to withhold payment on valid claims. Both suits sought punitive damages.

On February 21, 1985, appellant filed two motions in the Alabama Supreme Court, challenging Justice Embry's participation in the court's December 7, 1984, decision and his continued participation in considering appellant's application for rehearing. The motion also alleged that all justices on the court should recuse themselves because of their interests as potential class members in Justice Embry's suit against Blue Cross. On March 8, 1985, the court unanimously denied the recusal motions. The brief order stated that each justice had voted individually on the matter of whether he should recuse himself and that each justice had voted not to do so. At the same time, by a 5–to–4 division, the court denied appellant's motion for rehearing.

Chief Justice Torbert wrote separately, explaining that although his views had not been influenced by his possible membership in the putative class alleged in Justice Embry's suit against Blue Cross, he was nonetheless notifying the Clerk of the court where that suit was pending not to permit him to be included in the alleged class. Justice Maddox also wrote separately, taking similar action.

On March 20, 1985, appellant obtained a copy of the transcript of Justice Embry's deposition, taken on January 10, 1985, in connection with his Blue Cross suit. The deposition revealed that Justice Embry had authored the *per curiam* opinion in this case over an 8–or 9–month period during which his civil action against Blue Cross was being prosecuted. Justice Embry also stated that, during that period, he had received "leads" from people with regard to his bad-faith action against Blue Cross and that he put them in touch with his attorney. Finally, Justice Embry revealed frustration with insurance companies. For example, when asked if he had ever had any difficulty with processing claims, Justice Embry retorted: "[T]hat is a silly question. For years and years."

Appellant moved for leave to file a second application for rehearing based on the deposition, but that motion was denied. Appellant filed an appeal with this Court, and Justice POWELL, as Circuit Justice, granted appellant's application for a stay of the judgment below pending this Court's disposition of the appeal. Shortly thereafter, Justice Embry's suit against Blue Cross was settled by stipulation of the parties. In the stipulation, Blue Cross recognized that "some problems have occurred in the past and is determined to minimize them in the future." Justice Embry received $30,000 under the settlement agreement on a basic compensatory claim of unspecified amount; a check for that sum was deposited by his attorney directly into Justice Embry's personal account. . . .

III

A

Appellant contends Justice Embry's general hostility towards insurance companies that were dilatory in paying claims, as expressed in his deposition, requires a conclusion that the Due Process Clause was violated by his participation in the disposition of this case. The Court has recognized that not "[a]ll questions of judicial qualification . . . involve constitutional validity. Thus matters of kinship, personal bias, state policy, remoteness of interest, would seem generally to be matters merely of legislative discretion." *Tumey v. Ohio*, 273 U.S. 510, 523, 47 S.Ct. 437, 441, 71

L.Ed. 749 (1927). Moreover, the traditional common-law rule was that disqualification for bias or prejudice was not permitted. See, *e.g., Clyma v. Kennedy,* 64 Conn. 310, 29 A. 539 (1894). As Blackstone put it, "the law will not suppose a possibility of bias or favour in a judge, who is already sworn to administer impartial justice, and whose authority greatly depends upon that presumption and idea." The more recent trend has been towards the adoption of statutes that permit disqualification for bias or prejudice. See *Berger v. United States,* 255 U.S. 22, 31, 41 S.Ct. 230, 232, 65 L.Ed. 481 (1921) (enforcing statute disqualifying federal judges in certain circumstances for personal bias or prejudice). See also ABA Code of Judicial Conduct, Canon 3C(1)(a) (1980) ("A judge should disqualify himself ... where he has a personal bias or prejudice concerning a party"). But that alone would not be sufficient basis for imposing a constitutional requirement under the Due Process Clause. We held in *Patterson v. New York,* 432 U.S. 197, 201–202, 97 S.Ct. 2319, 2322–2323, 53 L.Ed.2d 281 (1977) (citations omitted), that

> "it is normally within the power of the State to regulate procedures under which its laws are carried out ... and its decision in this regard is not subject to proscription under the Due Process Clause unless it offends some principle of justice so rooted in the traditions and conscience of our people as to be ranked as fundamental."

We need not decide whether allegations of bias or prejudice by a judge of the type we have here would ever be sufficient under the Due Process Clause to force recusal. Certainly only in the most extreme of cases would disqualification on this basis be constitutionally required, and appellant's arguments here fall well below that level. Appellant suggests that Justice Embry's general frustration with insurance companies reveals a disqualifying bias, but it is likely that many claimants have developed hostile feelings from the frustration in awaiting settlement of insurance claims. Insurers, on their side, have no easy task, especially when trying to evaluate whether certain medical diagnostic tests or prolonged hospitalization were indicated. In turn, the physicians and surgeons, whether impelled by valid medical judgment or by apprehension as to future malpractice claims—or some combination of the two—similarly face difficult problems. Appellant's allegations of bias and prejudice on this general basis, however, are insufficient to establish any constitutional violation.

B

The record in this case presents more than mere allegations of bias and prejudice, however. Appellant also presses a claim that Justice Embry had a more direct stake in the outcome of this case. In *Tumey,* while recognizing that the Constitution does not reach every issue of judicial qualification, the Court concluded that "it certainly violates the Fourteenth Amendment ... to subject [a person's] liberty or property to the judgment of a court the judge of which has a direct, personal, substantial, pecuniary interest in reaching a conclusion against him in his case."

More than 30 years ago Justice Black, speaking for the Court, reached a similar conclusion and recognized that under the Due Process Clause no judge "can be a judge in his own case [or be] permitted to try cases where he has an interest in the outcome." *In re Murchison*, 349 U.S. 133, 136, 75 S.Ct. 623, 625, 99 L.Ed. 942 (1955). He went on to acknowledge that what degree or kind of interest is sufficient to disqualify a judge from sitting "cannot be defined with precision." Nonetheless, a reasonable formulation of the issue is whether the "situation is one 'which would offer a possible temptation to the average ... judge to ... lead him not to hold the balance nice, clear and true.' "

Under these prior holdings, we examine just what factors might constitute such an interest in the outcome of this case that would bear on recusal. At the time Justice Embry cast the deciding vote and authored the court's opinion, he had pending at least one very similar bad-faith-refusal-to-pay lawsuit against Blue Cross in another Alabama court. The decisions of the court on which Justice Embry sat, the Alabama Supreme Court, are binding on all Alabama courts. We need not blind ourselves to the fact that the law in the area of bad-faith-refusal-to-pay claims in Alabama, as in many other jurisdictions, was unsettled at that time, as the court's close division in deciding this case indicates. When Justice Embry cast the deciding vote, he did not merely apply well-established law and in fact quite possibly made new law; the court's opinion does not suggest that its conclusion was compelled by earlier decisions. Instead, to decide the case the court stated that "it is first necessary to review the policy considerations, elements, and instructive guide posts set out by this court in earlier case law." And in another case the court acknowledged that "the tort of bad faith refusal to pay a valid insurance claim is in the embryonic stage, and the Court has not had occasion to address every issue that might arise in these cases."

The decision under review firmly established that punitive damages could be obtained in Alabama in a situation where the insured's claim is not fully approved and only partial payment of the underlying claim had been made. Prior to the decision under review, the Alabama Supreme Court had not clearly recognized any claim for tortious injury in such circumstances; moreover, it had affirmatively recognized that partial payment was evidence of good faith on the part of the insurer. The Alabama court also held that a bad-faith-refusal-to-pay cause of action will lie in Alabama even where the insured is not entitled to a directed verdict on the underlying claim, a conclusion that at the least clarified the thrust of an earlier holding. Finally, the court refused to set aside as excessive a punitive damages award of $3.5 million. The largest punitive award previously affirmed by that court was $100,000, a figure remitted from $1.1 million as "obviously the result of passion and prejudice on the part of the jury."

All of these issues were present in Justice Embry's lawsuit against Blue Cross. His complaint sought recovery for partial payment of claims. Also the very nature of Justice Embry's suit placed in issue whether he would have to establish that he was entitled to a directed verdict on the underlying claims that he alleged Blue Cross refused to pay before gaining punitive damages. Finally, the affirmance of the largest punitive damages award ever (by a substantial margin) on precisely the type of claim raised in the Blue Cross suit undoubtedly "raised the stakes" for Blue Cross in that suit, to the benefit of Justice Embry. Thus, Justice Embry's opinion for the Alabama Supreme Court had the clear and immediate effect of enhancing both the legal status and the settlement value of his own case. . . .

We also hold that his interest was " 'direct, personal, substantial, [and] pecuniary.' " *Ward, supra,* 409 U.S., at 60, 93 S.Ct., at 83 (quoting *Tumey v. Ohio,* 273 U.S., at 523, 47 S.Ct., at 441). Justice Embry's complaint against Blue Cross sought "compensatory damage for breach of contract, inconvenience, emotional and mental distress, disappointment, pain and suffering" in addition to punitive damages for himself and for the class. Soon after the opinion of the Alabama Supreme Court in this case was announced, Blue Cross paid Justice Embry what he characterized in an interview as "a tidy sum," to settle the suit. Records lodged with this Court show that Justice Embry received $30,000, which was deposited by his attorney directly into Justice Embry's personal account. . . . [This] "tidy sum" that Justice Embry received directly is sufficient to establish the substantiality of his interest here.

We conclude that Justice Embry's participation in this case violated appellant's due process rights as explicated in *Tumey, Murchison,* and *Ward.* We make clear that we are not required to decide whether in fact Justice Embry was influenced, but only whether sitting on the case then before the Supreme Court of Alabama " 'would offer a possible temptation to the average . . . judge to . . . lead him to not to hold the balance nice, clear and true.' " *Ward,* 409 U.S., at 60, 93 S.Ct., at 83 (quoting *Tumey v. Ohio, supra,* 273 U.S., at 532, 47 S.Ct., at 444). The Due Process Clause "may sometimes bar trial by judges who have no actual bias and who would do their very best to weigh the scales of justice equally between contending parties. But to perform its high function in the best way, 'justice must satisfy the appearance of justice.' " *Murchison,* 349 U.S., at 136, 75 S.Ct., at 625 (citation omitted).

C

Appellant has challenged not only the participation of Justice Embry in this case but also the participation of all the other justices of the Alabama Supreme Court, or at least the six justices who did not withdraw from Justice Embry's class action against Blue Cross, claiming that they also have an interest in this case. Such allegations do not constitute a sufficient basis for requiring recusal under the Constitution. In the first place, accepting appellant's expansive contentions might require the disqualification of every judge in the State. If so, it is possible that under a "rule of necessity" none of the judges or justices would be disqualified. See *United States v. Will,* 449 U.S. 200, 214, 101 S.Ct. 471, 480, 66 L.Ed.2d 392 (1980).

More important, while these justices might conceivably have had a slight pecuniary interest, we find it impossible to characterize that interest as " 'direct, personal, substantial, [and] pecuniary.' " ... At some point, "[t]he biasing influence ... [will be] too remote and insubstantial to violate the constitutional constraints." *Marshall v. Jerrico, Inc.,* 446 U.S. 238, 243, 100 S.Ct. 1610, 1614, 64 L.Ed.2d 182 (1980). Charges of disqualification should not be made lightly. See *Rooker v. Fidelity Trust Co.,* 263 U.S. 413, 44 S.Ct. 149, 68 L.Ed. 362 (1923). We hold that there is no basis for concluding these justices were disqualified under the Due Process Clause.

D

Having concluded that only Justice Embry was disqualified from participation in this case, we turn to the issue of the proper remedy for this constitutional violation. Our prior decisions have not considered the question whether a decision of a multimember tribunal must be vacated because of the participation of one member who had an interest in the outcome of the case. Rather, our prior cases have involved interpretations of statutes with provisions concerning this question, disqualifications of the sole member of a tribunal. Some courts have concluded that a decision need not be vacated where a disqualified judge's vote is mere surplusage. But we are aware of no case, and none has been called to our attention, permitting a court's decision to stand when a disqualified judge casts the deciding vote. Here Justice Embry's vote was decisive in the 5–to–4 decision and he was the author of the court's opinion. Because of Justice Embry's leading role in the decision under review, we conclude that the "appearance of justice" will best be served by vacating the decision and remanding for further proceedings. Appellees have not contended that, upon a finding of disqualification, this disposition is improper.

III

We underscore that our decision today undertakes to answer only the question of under what circumstances the Constitution requires disqualification. The Due Process Clause demarks only the outer boundaries of judicial disqualifications. Congress and the states, of course, remain free to impose more rigorous standards for judicial disqualification than those we find mandated here today. . . .

The judgment of the Supreme Court of Alabama is vacated, and the case is remanded for further proceedings not inconsistent with this opinion.

[Concurring opinions omitted.]

Notes

1. *Financial conflicts of interest.* Financial conflicts of interest produce a particular kind of appearance of bias or partiality, and may of course produce actual bias. The Model Judicial Code therefore instructs judges that they must keep informed about their own personal financial interests and make reasonable efforts to keep informed about those of their immediate family (spouse and minor children). Judicial Code Canon 3E(2). See also 28 U.S.C. § 455(c) (same). A judge has a duty to disqualify herself from a case in which she or an immediate family member (spouse and children at home) has an economic interest in either the subject matter of the case, or in a party to the case, that could be substantially affected by the outcome. *Id.*, Canon 3E(1)(c); 28 U.S.C. § 455(b)(4). See *Liljeberg v. Health Services Acquisition Corp.*, 486 U.S. 847, 108 S.Ct. 2194, 100 L.Ed.2d 855 (1988) (upholding order disqualifying judge who sat on university board of trustees, when case before him would have significant financial impact on the university). *Aetna* is a leading case concerning judicial conflict due to a personal financial interest in the outcome of a case. As you can see from that case, such a conflict can rise to the level of a due process violation. See also *Bracy v. Gramley*, 520 U.S. 899, 117 S.Ct. 1793, 138 L.Ed.2d 97 (1997) (due process violated where judge was predisposed to rule against defendants who did not bribe him, in order to hide the fact that he ruled in favor of defendants who did bribe him).

2. *Curing a financial conflict.* In the federal system, if it comes to the judge's attention "after substantial time has been devoted to the matter" that the judge or an immediate family member has a financial interest in a party (other than an interest that could be substantially affected by the outcome), recusal is not required if the judge or family member divests himself or herself of the interest that provides the grounds for the judge's disqualification. 28 U.S.C. § 455(f). The Model Judicial Code provides that a judge may disclose a financial conflict to the parties and ask them to consider whether to waive the disqualification. Judicial Code Canon 3F. If the parties and lawyers unanimously agree to a waiver, the judge may conduct the proceeding. *Id.*

3. *Personal conflicts because of blood or marriage relationships.* An appearance of bias or partiality may also arise where a judge is related

by blood or marriage to a party, a witness, or a lawyer in the proceeding, and recusal may be appropriate under such a circumstance. See Canon 3E(1)(d); 28 U.S.C. § 455(b)(5). Recusal is required only where the judge is related to a lawyer of record; thus disqualification is not appropriate merely where the judge is related to a lawyer who works in the same office as a lawyer of record. See *State v. Harrell*, 199 Wis.2d 654, 546 N.W.2d 115 (1996) (judge whose wife was an assistant district attorney in the same county as the prosecutor in the criminal case before him did not have to recuse himself). One caveat: A personal relationship may also produce a financial conflict of interest. For example, if a judge's spouse is an equity partner in a law firm representing a party before the judge, and the firm stands to benefit financially from the outcome of the case, recusal may be required under the rules cited here and in Note 1 above. What if a lawyer attempts to force recusal by associating a relative of the judge as co-counsel? See *Grievance Adm'r v. Fried*, 456 Mich. 234, 570 N.W.2d 262 (1997) ("It is unethical conduct for a lawyer to tamper with the court system or to arrange disqualifications, selling the lawyer's family relationships rather than professional services."); Cf. *In re Bell-South Corp.*, 334 F.3d 941 (11th Cir. 2003) (denying mandamus relief from trial judge's disqualification of law firm, one partner in which was the judge's nephew, which had been deliberately retained in order to force judge's recusal).

4. *Conflicts with former law clerks.* There is no specific provision in the Judicial Code concerning a judge's recusal on the ground that one of the lawyers for a party in a case used to be the judge's law clerk. Of course, the more general rules on disqualification, Canon 3E(1) and (2), would apply, where such a fact might call the judge's impartiality into question, or where the judge has a personal bias or prejudice relating to the former law clerk. See *Comparato v. Schait*, 180 N.J. 90, 848 A.2d 770 (2004) (holding that recusal was not warranted where there was nothing in the record to indicate that the former law clerk's current representation of the defendant "has caused the judge to be predisposed to rule against plaintiff on any future question").

5. *Conflicts created by prior legal career.* What if the judge served as a lawyer in the case now before her? Or what if the judge used to work as a lawyer with a lawyer now arguing before her? Does that create an appearance of partiality requiring recusal? See Judicial Code Canon 3E(1)(b); 28 U.S.C. § 455(b)(2); *Tesco American, Inc. v. Strong Industries, Inc.*, ___ S.W.3d ___, 2006 WL 662740 (Tex.).

6. *Conflicts created by former client-lawyer relationship.* What if the lawyers for one party in a case before the judge had represented the judge in previous matters? Does that require recusal? See *Dodson v. Singing River Hospital System*, 839 So.2d 530 (Miss. 2003) (relying on Canons 3C and 3E, ordering recusal).

7. *Conflicts created by prior litigation with a party.* No rule requires a judge to recuse himself simply because he was previously involved in litigation with one of the parties. See, e.g., *Del Vecchio v.*

Illinois Dept. of Corrections, 31 F.3d 1363 (7th Cir. 1994) (en banc); *United States v. Watson*, 1 F.3d 733 (8th Cir. 1993). Why would this be true? If there were such a rule, do you see the potential for abusive "judge shopping?" See *In re Taylor*, 417 F.3d 649 (7th Cir. 2005).

8. *Personal knowledge of facts.* A judge must disqualify himself if the judge has personal knowledge of disputed evidentiary facts. Judicial Code Canon 3E(1)(a); 28 U.S.C. § 455(b)(1). In *In re Wilkins*, 780 N.E.2d 842 (Ind.2003), Justice Rucker voluntarily recused himself from hearing the appeal of a lawyer's disciplinary sanction for improper criticism of judges in a brief to the court, in violation of Indiana Professional Conduct Rule 8.2(a), which forbids a lawyer from making a statement "that the lawyer knows to be false or with reckless disregard as to its truth or falsity concerning the qualifications or integrity of a judge." Justice Rucker, before being elevated to the Supreme Court, had sat on the appellate panel that had drawn the lawyer's improper criticism. While Justice Rucker stated that he could in fact remain impartial, he recused himself "out of an abundance of caution" because of the possibility that his impartiality could be questioned.

What if a judge simply makes comments before the trial showing he has knowledge of "facts" about the parties that relate to the matter being litigated—even if the "facts" may not be correct? Should this force the judge to recuse himself? See *Mihm v. American Tool*, 11 Neb.App. 543, 664 N.W.2d 27 (2003) (recusal required where judge made unilateral comments in workers' compensation case about the defendant's prospects of continuing to do business in the state in the future; defense counsel protested that there was no evidence supporting judge's statements).

9. *Confidential knowledge.* What if a judge gained knowledge about the case in a confidential mediation and now presides over the trial? Is recusal required? In *Enterprise Leasing Co. v. Jones*, 789 So.2d 964 (Fla.2001), the parties were engaged in a personal injury action. Their attempt to reach a resolution through mediation failed. During litigation, the parties were asked at a pretrial conference whether they had attempted mediation. The plaintiff—in violation of a Florida statute making confidential all information presented in a court-ordered mediation process—not only said "yes" but also told the trial judge what the defendant's highest settlement offer had been. The defendant moved to disqualify the judge. Both the trial court and the intermediate appeals court denied that motion. Because no stay had been entered, the trial continued during this process, and during jury deliberations the parties settled the underlying case. The disqualification motion then landed in the Florida Supreme Court, which affirmed. Citing cases from several jurisdictions holding the same way, the Court said it could "see no compelling reason to treat a trial court's knowledge of inadmissible information in the mediation context any differently from the other situations presented every day where judges are asked to set aside their personal knowledge and rule based on the evidence presented by the parties at the trial or hearing." The court recognized a "presumption

disfavoring prejudice or bias on the part of a judge," at least in this particular context.

10. *Recusal from contempt proceedings.* If a judge issues an order to show cause why a lawyer should not be held in criminal contempt for improper conduct in the judge's presence during a proceeding, can that same judge preside at the contempt trial or hearing? The answer is yes, unless the contemptuous behavior involves "disrespect toward or criticism of a judge." See Fed. Rules of Crim. Proc. 42(a)(3); *United States v. Ortlieb*, 274 F.3d 871 (5th Cir.2001) (holding that a lawyer's response of "Ah, shit" in response to an adverse ruling, followed by his statement "You know and I know that that's an improper ruling," was not a criticism of the judge and thus did not disqualify the judge from presiding over the criminal contempt proceeding based on those comments).

11. *Negotiating for a job.* Is it improper for a judge to negotiate for employment with a party or lawyer for a party in a matter being adjudicated before him? Not surprisingly, the Model Rules—and judges who are members of a state bar are subject to that state's ethics rules for lawyers—say yes. MR 1.12(b). See, e.g., *Pepsico, Inc. v. McMillen*, 764 F.2d 458 (7th Cir.1985) (recusal required where headhunter working on judge's behalf contacted law firm representing parties appearing before him). What about a law clerk to that same judge? The same Rule allows a law clerk to negotiate about a job with a party or lawyer participating in a case before the judge, but requires the clerk to tell the judge about the situation. *Id.* Should the rules be stricter on law clerks? Why not disqualify law clerks from working on cases involving law firms with which they are actively seeking employment after their clerkship ends? Of course, many judges do enforce such a policy, even if the Rules do not impose it.

12. *Negotiating for private judging jobs.* California is not alone in having a booming "private judging" industry, but it is most certainly the industry leader. Judges who leave the bench to work for ADR firms offering this form of private arbitration services can expect to make many times their government incomes; indeed the estimated annual income of a "top-tier" retired judge acting as a private arbitrator is $1 million. See Eric Berkowitz, *Is Justice Served?*, West [Los Angeles Times Magazine] (Oct. 22, 2006), at 20, 24. In response to these market forces, the California legislature amended the Civil Procedure Code to provide for mandatory disqualification of a judge whenever the judge "has a current arrangement concerning prospective employment or other compensated service as a dispute resolution neutral, or is participating in, or, within the last two years has participated in, discussions regarding prospective employment or service as a dispute resolution neutral, or has been engaged in such employment or service," and such arrangement or discussion was with a party to the proceeding, or the matter before the judge "includes issues relating to the enforcement of either an agreement to submit a dispute to an alternative dispute resolution process or an ward or other final decision by a dispute resolution neutral," or the

judge directs the parties to participate in an ADR process in which the neutral is a person or entity with whom the judge has made contact about prospective employment, or the judge will select an ADR neutral, and among those available for selection is a person or entity with whom the judge has made such contact. Cal. Code Civ. Proc. § 170.1(a)(8)(A) (2005). Is such a law sufficient to remove an appearance of bias? Should the Judicial Conduct Code simply bar judges from taking positions as private judges after leaving the bench?

UNITED STATES v. MICROSOFT CORP.

United States Court of Appeals, District of Columbia Circuit, 2001.
253 F.3d 34.

PER CURIAM:

Microsoft Corporation appeals from judgments of the District Court finding the company in violation of §§ 1 and 2 of the Sherman Act and ordering various remedies.... [On appeal, Microsoft argues, inter alia,] that the trial judge committed ethical violations by engaging in impermissible *ex parte* contacts and making inappropriate public comments on the merits of the case while it was pending....

* * *

Canon 3A(6) of the Code of Conduct for United States Judges requires federal judges to "avoid public comment on the merits of [ ] pending or impending" cases. Canon 2 tells judges to "avoid impropriety and the appearance of impropriety in all activities," on the bench and off. Canon 3A(4) forbids judges to initiate or consider *ex parte* communications on the merits of pending or impending proceedings. Section 455(a) of the Judicial Code requires judges to recuse themselves when their "impartiality might reasonably be questioned." 28 U.S.C. § 455(a).

All indications are that the District Judge violated each of these ethical precepts by talking about the case with reporters. The violations were deliberate, repeated, egregious, and flagrant. The only serious question is what consequences should follow. Microsoft urges us to disqualify the District Judge, vacate the judgment in its entirety and toss out the findings of fact, and remand for a new trial before a different District Judge. At the other extreme, plaintiffs ask us to do nothing. We agree with neither position.

A. The District Judge's Communications with the Press

Immediately after the District Judge entered final judgment on June 7, 2000, accounts of interviews with him began appearing in the press. Some of the interviews were held after he entered final judgment. *See* Peter Spiegel, *Microsoft Judge Defends Post-*

trial Comments, FIN. TIMES (London), Oct. 7, 2000, at 4; John R. Wilke, *For Antitrust Judge, Trust, or Lack of It, Really Was the Issue—In an Interview, Jackson Says Microsoft Did the Damage to Its Credibility in Court,* WALL ST. J., June 8, 2000, at A1. The District Judge also aired his views about the case to larger audiences, giving speeches at a college and at an antitrust seminar.

From the published accounts, it is apparent that the Judge also had been giving secret interviews to select reporters before entering final judgment—in some instances long before. The earliest interviews we know of began in September 1999, shortly after the parties finished presenting evidence but two months before the court issued its Findings of Fact. *See* Joel Brinkley & Steve Lohr, *U.S. vs. Microsoft: Pursuing a Giant; Retracing the Missteps in the Microsoft Defense,* N.Y. TIMES, June 9, 2000, at A1. Interviews with reporters from the *New York Times* and Ken Auletta, another reporter who later wrote a book on the Microsoft case, continued throughout late 1999 and the first half of 2000, during which time the Judge issued his Findings of Fact, Conclusions of Law, and Final Judgment. *See id.*; Ken Auletta, *Final Offer,* THE NEW YORKER, Jan. 15, 2001, at 40. The Judge "embargoed" these interviews; that is, he insisted that the fact and content of the interviews remain secret until he issued the Final Judgment. . . .

The published accounts indicate that the District Judge discussed numerous topics relating to the case. Among them was his distaste for the defense of technological integration—one of the central issues in the lawsuit. . . . Reports of the interviews have the District Judge describing Microsoft's conduct, with particular emphasis on what he regarded as the company's prevarication, hubris, and impenitence. In some of his secret meetings with reporters, the Judge offered his contemporaneous impressions of testimony. . . . He also provided numerous after-the-fact credibility assessments. He told reporters that Bill Gates' "testimony is inherently without credibility" and "[i]f you can't believe this guy, who else can you believe?" BRINKLEY & LOHR, U.S. v. MICROSOFT 278; Brinkley & Lohr, N.Y. TIMES; *see also* Auletta, THE NEW YORKER, at 40. As for the company's other witnesses, the Judge is reported as saying that there "were times when I became impatient with Microsoft witnesses who were giving speeches." "[T]hey were telling me things I just flatly could not credit." Brinkley & Lohr, N.Y. TIMES. . . .

According to reporter Auletta, the District Judge told him in private that, "I thought they [Microsoft and its executives] didn't think they were regarded as adult members of the community. I thought they would learn." AULETTA, WORLD WAR 3.0, at 14. . . . The Judge apparently became, in Auletta's words, "increasingly troubled by what he learned about Bill Gates and couldn't get out of his mind the group picture he had seen of Bill Gates and Paul

Allen and their shaggy-haired first employees at Microsoft." The reporter wrote that the Judge said he saw in the picture "a smart-mouthed young kid who has extraordinary ability and needs a little discipline. I've often said to colleagues that Gates would be better off if he had finished Harvard."

The District Judge likened Microsoft's writing of incriminating documents to drug traffickers who "never figure out that they shouldn't be saying certain things on the phone." Brinkley & Lohr, U.S. v. Microsoft 6; Brinkley & Lohr, N.Y. Times. He invoked the drug trafficker analogy again to denounce Microsoft's protestations of innocence . . .

The District Judge also secretly divulged to reporters his views on the remedy for Microsoft's antitrust violations. On the question whether Microsoft was entitled to any process at the remedy stage, the Judge told reporters in May 2000 that he was "not aware of any case authority that says I have to give them any due process at all. The case is over. They lost." Brinkley & Lohr, N.Y. Times. . . .

In February 2000, four months before his final order splitting the company in two, the District Judge reportedly told *New York Times* reporters that he was "not at all comfortable with restructuring the company," because he was unsure whether he was "competent to do that." A few months later, he had a change of heart. . . . The Judge recited a "North Carolina mule trainer" story to explain his change in thinking from "[i]f it ain't broken, don't try to fix it" and "I just don't think that [restructuring the company] is something I want to try to do on my own" to ordering Microsoft broken in two:

> He had a trained mule who could do all kinds of wonderful tricks. One day somebody asked him: "How do you do it? How do you train the mule to do all these amazing things?" "Well," he answered, "I'll show you." He took a 2–by–4 and whopped him upside the head. The mule was reeling and fell to his knees, and the trainer said: "You just have to get his attention."

Brinkley & Lohr, U.S. v. Microsoft 278. The Judge added: "I hope I've got Microsoft's attention."

B. Violations of the Code of Conduct for United States Judges

The Code of Conduct for United States Judges was adopted by the Judicial Conference of the United States in 1973. It prescribes ethical norms for federal judges as a means to preserve the actual and apparent integrity of the federal judiciary. . . . While some of the Code's Canons frequently generate questions about their application, others are straightforward and easily understood. Canon 3A(6) is an example of the latter. In forbidding federal judges to comment publicly "on the merits of a pending or impending action," Canon 3A(6) applies to cases pending before any court, state or federal, trial or appellate. *See* Jeffrey M. Shaman et al., Judicial Conduct and Ethics § 10.34, at 353 (3d ed.2000). As "impending" indicates, the prohibition begins even before a case enters the court system, when there is reason to believe a case may be filed. An action remains "pending" until "completion of the appellate process." Code of Conduct Canon 3A(6) cmt.; Comm. on Codes of Conduct, Adv. Op. No. 55 (1998).

The Microsoft case was "pending" during every one of the District Judge's meetings with reporters; the case is "pending" now; and even after our decision issues, it will remain pending for some time. The District Judge breached his ethical duty under Canon 3A(6) each time he spoke to a reporter about the merits of the case. Although the reporters interviewed him in private, his comments were public. Court was not in session and his discussion of the case took place outside the presence of the parties. He provided his views not to court personnel assisting him in the case, but to members of the public. And these were not just any members of the public. Because he was talking to reporters, the Judge knew his comments would eventually receive widespread dissemination.

It is clear that the District Judge was not discussing purely procedural matters, which are a permissible subject of public comment under one of the Canon's three narrowly drawn exceptions. He disclosed his views on the factual and legal matters at the heart of the case. His opinions about the credibility of witnesses, the validity of legal theories, the culpability of the defendant, the choice of remedy, and so forth all dealt with the merits of the action. It is no excuse that the Judge may have intended to "educate" the public about the case or to rebut "public misperceptions" purportedly caused by the parties. *See* Grimaldi, Wash. Post; *Microsoft Judge Says He May Step down from Case on Appeal*, Wall St. J., Oct. 30, 2000. If those were his intentions, he could have addressed the factual and legal issues as he saw them—and thought the public should see them—in his Findings of Fact, Conclusions of Law, Final Judgment, or in a written opinion. Or he could have held his tongue until all appeals were concluded.

Far from mitigating his conduct, the District Judge's insistence on secrecy—his embargo—made matters worse. Concealment of the interviews suggests knowledge of their impropriety. Concealment also prevented the parties from nipping his improprieties in the bud. Without any knowledge of the interviews, neither the plaintiffs nor the defendant had a chance to object or to seek the Judge's removal before he issued his Final Judgment.

Other federal judges have been disqualified for making limited public comments about cases pending before them. *See In re Boston's Children First,* 244 F.3d 164 (1st Cir.2001); *In re IBM Corp.,* 45 F.3d 641 (2d Cir.1995); *United States v. Cooley,* 1 F.3d 985 (10th Cir.1993). Given the extent of the Judge's transgressions in this case, we have little doubt that if the parties had discovered his secret liaisons with the press, he would have been disqualified, voluntarily or by court order.

In addition to violating the rule prohibiting public comment, the District Judge's reported conduct raises serious questions under Canon 3A(4). That Canon states that a "judge should accord to every person who is legally interested in a proceeding, or the person's lawyer, full right to be heard according to law, and, except as authorized by law, neither initiate nor consider *ex parte* communications on the merits, or procedures affecting the merits, of a pending or impending proceeding." CODE OF CONDUCT Canon 3A(4).

What did the reporters convey to the District Judge during their secret sessions? By one account, the Judge spent a total of ten hours giving taped interviews to one reporter. AULETTA, WORLD WAR 3.0, at 14 n.*. We do not know whether he spent even more time in untaped conversations with the same reporter, nor do we know how much time he spent with others. But we think it safe to assume that these interviews were not monologues. Interviews often become conversations. When reporters pose questions or make assertions, they may be furnishing information, information that may reflect their personal views of the case. The published accounts indicate this happened on at least one occasion. Ken Auletta reported, for example, that he told the Judge "that Microsoft employees professed shock that he thought they had violated the law and behaved unethically," at which time the Judge became "agitated" by "Microsoft's 'obstinacy'." It is clear that Auletta had views of the case. As he wrote in a *Washington Post* editorial, "[a]nyone who sat in [the District Judge's] courtroom during the trial had seen ample evidence of Microsoft's sometimes thuggish tactics."

The District Judge's repeated violations of Canons 3A(6) and 3A(4) also violated Canon 2, which provides that "a judge should avoid impropriety and the appearance of impropriety in all activities." Canon 2A requires federal judges to "respect and comply with the law" and to "act at all times in a manner that promotes public confidence in the integrity and impartiality of the judiciary." The Code of Conduct is the law with respect to the ethical obligations of federal judges, and it is clear the District Judge violated it on multiple occasions in this case. The rampant disregard for the judiciary's ethical obligations that the public witnessed in this case undoubtedly jeopardizes "public confidence in the integrity" of the District Court proceedings.

Another point needs to be stressed. Rulings in this case have potentially huge financial consequences for one of the nation's largest publicly-traded companies and its investors. The District Judge's secret interviews during the trial provided a select few with inside information about the case, information that enabled them and anyone they shared it with to anticipate rulings before the Judge announced them to the world. Although he "embargoed" his comments, the Judge had no way of policing the reporters. For all he knew there may have been trading on the basis of the information he secretly conveyed. The public cannot be expected to maintain confidence in the integrity and impartiality of the federal judiciary in the face of such conduct.

C. *Appearance of Partiality*

The Code of Conduct contains no enforcement mechanism. The Canons, including the one that requires a judge to disqualify himself in certain circumstances, *see* CODE OF CONDUCT Canon 3C, are self-enforcing. There are, however, remedies extrinsic to the Code. One is an internal disciplinary proceeding, begun with the filing of a complaint with the clerk of the court of appeals pursuant to 28 U.S.C. § 372(c). Another is disqualification of the offending judge under either 28 U.S.C. § 144, which requires the filing of an affidavit while the case is in the District Court, or 28 U.S.C. § 455, which does not. Microsoft urges the District Judge's disqualification under § 455(a): a judge "shall disqualify himself in any proceeding in which his impartiality might reasonably be questioned." The standard for disqualification under § 455(a) is an objective one. The question is whether a reasonable and informed observer would question the judge's impartiality.

"The very purpose of § 455(a) is to promote confidence in the judiciary by avoiding even the appearance of impropriety whenever possible." *Liljeberg v. Health Servs. Acquisition Corp.*, 486 U.S. 847, 865, 108 S.Ct. 2194, 100 L.Ed.2d 855 (1988). As such, violations of the Code of Conduct may give rise to a violation of § 455(a) if doubt is cast on the integrity of the judicial process. . . .

While § 455(a) is concerned with actual and apparent impropriety, the statute requires disqualification only when a judge's "impartiality might reasonably be questioned." Although this court has condemned public judicial comments on pending cases, we have not gone so far as to hold that every violation of Canon 3A(6) or every impropriety under the Code of Conduct inevitably destroys the appearance of impartiality and thus violates § 455(a).

In this case, however, we believe the line has been crossed. . . . Judges who covet publicity, or convey the appearance that they do, lead any objective observer to wonder whether their judgments are being influenced by the prospect of favorable coverage in the media. Discreet and limited public comments may not compromise a judge's apparent impartiality, but we have little doubt that the District Judge's conduct had that effect. Appearance may be all there is, but that is enough to invoke the Canons and § 455(a)....

D. Remedies for Judicial Misconduct and Appearance of Partiality

1. Disqualification

Disqualification is mandatory for conduct that calls a judge's impartiality into question. *See* 28 U.S.C. § 455(a). Section 455 does not prescribe the scope of disqualification. Rather, Congress "delegated to the judiciary the task of fashioning the remedies that will best serve the purpose" of the disqualification statute. *Liljeberg,* 486 U.S. at 862, 108 S.Ct. 2194.

At a minimum, § 455(a) requires prospective disqualification of the offending judge, that is, disqualification from the judge's hearing any further proceedings in the case. Microsoft urges retroactive disqualification of the District Judge, which would entail disqualification antedated to an earlier part of the proceedings and vacatur of all subsequent acts.... [We] conclude that the appropriate remedy for the violations of § 455(a) is disqualification of the District Judge retroactive only to the date he entered the order breaking up Microsoft. We therefore will vacate that order in its entirety and remand this case to a different District Judge, but will not set aside the existing Findings of Fact or Conclusions of Law (except insofar as specific findings are clearly erroneous or legal conclusions are incorrect).... [F]ull retroactive disqualification is unnecessary to protect Microsoft's right to an impartial adjudication. The District Judge's conduct destroyed the appearance of impartiality. Microsoft neither alleged nor demonstrated that it rose to the level of actual bias or prejudice. There is no reason to presume that everything the District Judge did is suspect....

[Affirmed in part, reversed in part, and remanded in part.]

Notes

1. *Public comment on pending cases.* Why must a judge refrain from public comments about pending cases? Doesn't society benefit from the kind of information that the trial judge in Microsoft gave to reporters? Is the real problem one of timing rather than the content of the speech? See Judicial Code Canon 3B(9); *In re Boston's Children First,* 244 F.3d 164 (1st Cir.2001) (judge should have recused herself from case after making statements to the press about it; in a high-profile case, public attention to comments may create appearance of impropriety).

2. *The appearance of personal bias.* Part of the problem with the comments in *Microsoft* is that they demonstrated a personal bias, or

apparent personal bias, against Bill Gates and Microsoft itself. See Judicial Code Canon 3B(5). If the trial judge had made his comments from the bench, do you think Microsoft would have had grounds to disqualify him? Cf. *United States v. Doe*, 348 F.3d 64 (2d Cir. 2003) (resentencing of convicted criminal defendant required where judge's sentence appeared to have been motivated out of annoyance with prosecutor's failure to make a specific recommendation about the sentence). Was the fact that the judge hid his views from the parties during trial therefore yet another problem?

3. *Personal beliefs or friendships.* What if a judge's personal beliefs or even friendships would influence a ruling, or would appear to? Should the judge voluntarily recuse himself before making any such ruling? See *Cleveland Bar Ass'n v. Cleary*, 93 Ohio St.3d 191, 754 N.E.2d 235 (2001) (former judge suspended from practice for six months for having offered a criminal defendant probation if she agreed to have a baby rather than have an abortion, where the judge opposed abortion); *United States v. Tucker*, 78 F.3d 1313 (8th Cir.1996) (criminal case against Arkansas Governor Jim Guy Tucker ordered reassigned to different judge because of an appearance of impropriety created by judge's friendship with President and Mrs. Clinton "and the Clintons' connection to Tucker"); *In re Starr*, 986 F.Supp. 1144 (E.D.Ark.1997) (four federal district judges recused themselves from case accusing Independent Counsel Kenneth Starr of conflicts of interest in his investigation of Whitewater matter, on the grounds that "We are friends of the Clintons, and they are the targets of the Independent Counsel."). Is the recusal decision different for a Justice of the United States Supreme Court? Why might it be? See *Cheney v. United States District Court*, 541 U.S. 913, 124 S.Ct. 1391, 158 L.Ed.2d 225 (2004) (Scalia, J., sitting as single Justice).

4. *The judge's religious views.* Does membership in a particular church, or adherence to particular religious views, require recusal in particular cases? The clear answer is no–recusal or disqualification of a judge cannot be based on "assumptions about a judge's beliefs" as opposed to "outward manifestations and reasonable inferences drawn therefrom" that prove that a reasonable person would harbor doubts about the judge's impartiality. *In re McCarthey*, 368 F.3d 1266 (10th Cir. 2004); see also *Bryce v. Episcopal Church*, 289 F.3d 648 (10th Cir. 2002). Were courts to rule otherwise, they would run up against Article VI, Clause 3 of the U.S. Constitution, which provides that "no religious Test shall ever be required as a Qualification to any Office or public Trust under the United States." As Justice Stevens put it in his concurrence in *United States v. Lee*, 455 U.S. 252, 102 S.Ct. 1051, 71 L.Ed.2d 127 (1982), if judges were required to disclose the firmness of their religious beliefs, we flirt with entering the constitutionally-prohibited realm of "evaluating the relative merits of differing religious claims."

5. *Ex parte contacts.* A judge is permitted to have ex parte contacts on non-substantive matters (such as scheduling), and may with the parties' consent have ex parte meetings in connection in settlement talks. See Judicial Code Canon 3B(7). But with those and some other

narrow exceptions, a judge is forbidden to have substantive conversations about a pending or impending case with persons outside the presence of all parties unless authorized to do so by law. *Id.* Why would this be? See *In re Kensington Int'l Ltd.*, 368 F.3d 289 (3d Cir. 2004) (judge's ex parte meetings with "neutral advisors" who simultaneously served as advocates in an unrelated case caused judge's disqualification from several cases). Are you convinced by the *Microsoft* court's description of the problems created by the trial judge when he spoke to reporters in private?

§ 2.   EXTRA–JUDICIAL ACTIVITIES

IN RE INQUIRY OF BROADBELT

Supreme Court of New Jersey, 1996.
146 N.J. 501, 683 A.2d 543.

PER CURIAM.

This appeal concerns whether a sitting municipal court judge may appear on television to comment on cases pending in other jurisdictions. After the matter was referred to the Advisory Committee on Extrajudicial Activities, the Committee issued Opinion No. 13–95, which disapproved of Judge Broadbelt's appearances on "Court TV" and "Geraldo Live" as a commentator. We granted review.

I

The facts are undisputed. Petitioner, Evan W. Broadbelt, has been a municipal court judge since 1982 and serves five municipalities in Monmouth and Ocean counties. A well-respected municipal judge, Judge Broadbelt appeared on "Court TV" in excess of fifty times since 1992 to serve as a guest commentator. Since November 1994, Judge Broadbelt appeared on CNBC on three occasions to provide guest commentary on the "O.J. Simpson case," *People v. Simpson,* No. BA097211 (Cal.Super.Ct.1995). He also appeared on a local television program in 1994 to discuss generally the jurisdiction and procedures of the municipal courts. Judge Broadbelt did not receive compensation for any of those television appearances.

In December 1994, Judge Lawrence M. Lawson, A.J.S.C., requested that all municipal court judges notify the Assignment Judge before making any television appearances. After twice giving Judge Broadbelt permission to appear on "Geraldo Live," Judge Lawson, on March 20, 1995, withdrew his approval and requested that Judge Broadbelt refrain from appearing on television. After Judge Broadbelt noted his disagreement with Judge Lawson's decision, Judge Lawson referred the issue to the Advisory Committee on Extrajudicial Activities (Committee). That Committee, which is appointed by this Court, accepts inquiries about extrajudicial activities from a judge or this Court. After an oral decision, the Committee issued Opinion No. 13–95, pursuant to *Rule* 1:18A–4, and determined that Judge Broadbelt's activities did not conform with Canon 2 of the Code of Judicial Conduct (Code) and Guideline IV.C.1. of the Guidelines for Extrajudicial Activities for New Jersey Judges....

II

Although not the focus of the Committee's determination, we first consider whether Judge Broadbelt's commentary violated Canon 3A(8) [In the Model Code, this provision is contained in Canon 3A(6)]. Canon 3 provides that judges "should perform the duties of judicial office impartially and diligently." Extrajudicial duties should not encroach on or conflict with those duties. Canon 3A(8) of the Code provides:

> A judge should abstain from public comment about a pending or impending proceeding in any court and should require similar abstention on the part of court personnel subject to the judge's direction and control. This subsection does not prohibit judges from making public statements in the course of their official duties or from explaining for public information the procedures of the court.

... We find the Canon to be clear and unambiguous: a judge should not comment on pending cases in any jurisdiction. By prohibiting judges from commenting on pending cases in *any* court, we avoid the possibility of undue influence on the judicial process and the threat to public confidence posed by a judge from one jurisdiction criticizing the rulings or technique of a judge from a different jurisdiction.

We conclude that Judge Broadbelt should not have commented on pending cases from any jurisdiction. Moreover, we are persuaded that Judge Broadbelt's commentary on pending cases on "Court TV" and on "Geraldo Live" was inappropriate and had the potential to compromise the integrity of the judiciary in New Jersey....

III

We also determine whether Judge Broadbelt's conduct violated Canon 2B. Canon 2 states that a judge "should avoid impropriety and the appearance of impropriety in all activities." Canon 2B forbids a judge from "lend[ing] the prestige of office to advance the private interests of others.... " The Commentary to Canon 2B states:

> Public confidence in the judiciary is eroded by irresponsible or improper conduct by judges. A judge must avoid all impropriety and appearance of impropriety and must

expect to be the subject of constant public scrutiny. A judge must therefore accept restrictions on personal conduct that might be viewed as burdensome by the ordinary citizen and should do so freely and willingly.

Judge Broadbelt argues that his appearance on commercial television programs to discuss pending cases is neither governed by nor violative of Canon 2B. The Advisory Committee insists that the judge's conduct violated Canon 2B because his regular television appearances allowed the prestige of his judicial office to advance the private interests of commercial television.

Our case law does not address this issue directly. None of our decisions concerning Canon 2 relate to a judge's appearance on a commercial television program. In *In re Santini,* 126 *N.J.* 291, 597 *A.*2d 1388 (1991), we found that a municipal court judge violated Canon 2 and *Rule* 1:15–1(b) when he telephoned another municipal court judge concerning his client's arrest on a warrant for failure to appear at a zoning hearing. We noted that a judge must not use his office to advance the private interest of others, nor should he convey or permit others to convey the impression that he is in a special position to exert influence. *See also In re Anastasi,* 76 *N.J.* 510, 514, 388 *A.*2d 620 (1978) (holding that judge should not be voluntary character witness for friend applying for racing license because to do so lends prestige of judicial office to advance private interest of another). . . .

The purpose of Canon 2B is to protect the independence and integrity of the judiciary. That a judge may not lend the prestige of judicial office to advance the private interests of others is well settled. However, the question whether a judge lends the prestige of office to a television program merely by appearing on that program is more difficult to answer. A number of factors must be taken into account: the frequency with which the judge appears on the program, the intended audience, the subject matter, and whether the program is commercial or non-commercial. In general, a judge should avoid appearing on either commercial or non-commercial programs when the judge's association with that program compromises the independence and integrity of the judiciary.

In the instant case, Judge Broadbelt's regular appearances on commercial television violated Canon 2B. Because of the frequency of Judge Broadbelt's appearances, Judge Broadbelt became regularly identified with the program, thereby lending it the prestige of his judicial office.

Not every television appearance by a judge on commercial television will be improper, or will create the appearance of impropriety. For example, it might be permissible for a municipal court judge to make an isolated appearance on public television to comment on the role of municipal court judges in the judiciary.

Similarly, a one-time appearance by a Superior Court judge on a commercial television program dealing with the benefits and disadvantages of televising civil trials might be permissible. However, a judge's regular weekly appearance on a television program, whether the program was commercial or non-commercial, to comment on recent court decisions in New Jersey clearly would be improper....

IV

The final Canon involved in this case is Canon 4. Canon 4 states that a judge "may engage in activities to improve the law, the legal system, and the administration of justice." It further provides:

> A judge, subject to the proper performance of judicial duties, may engage in the following quasi-judicial activities if in doing so the judge does not cast doubt on the judge's capacity to decide impartially any issue that may come before the court and provided the judge is not compensated therefor:
>
> A. A judge may speak, write, lecture, and participate in other activities concerning the law, the legal system, and the administration of justice.
>
> B. A judge may teach concerning the law, the legal system, and the administration of justice.

Petitioner insists that his conduct is governed and permitted by Canon 4 because it is extrajudicial in nature and constitutes teaching about the judicial system. The Committee argues that the judge's conduct is not subject to review solely under Canon 4 because it is extrajudicial in nature; rather, the conduct is to be examined under each of the canons to determine its propriety....

We have no doubt that Petitioner Broadbelt's commentary was informative and educational. Nevertheless, conduct that is violative of another canon is not excused because it appears to be authorized by Canon 4. Although Petitioner's conduct may have included teaching about the law, the legal system, and the administration of justice, that conduct is not permitted if it violates another canon. Accordingly, because Petitioner's conduct violated Canons 3A(8) and 2B, Canon 4 does not excuse it.

V

Finally, we address the constitutional question whether placing restrictions on a judge's speech violates the First Amendment. A judge does not relinquish his or her First Amendment rights on ascending to the bench. However, limitations may be placed on a judge's First Amendment rights. In analyzing a judge's right to speak freely, courts have employed different constitutional standards: the *Pickering* public-employee balancing test, the strict-scrutiny test, and the hybrid *Pickering*/strict-scrutiny test. In addition, commentators have advocated that courts apply the *Gentile v. State Bar of Nevada*, 501 *U.S.* 1030, 111 *S.Ct.* 2720, 115 *L.Ed.*2d 888 (1991) middle-tier scrutiny standard to regulate judicial speech. Erwin Chemerinsky, *Is it the Siren's Call?: Judges and Free Speech While Cases are Pending*, 28 *Loy. L.A. L.Rev.* 831, 842 (1995). . . .

Although we believe that the imposition of restrictions on a judge's free speech rights would probably pass constitutional muster under any of those standards, we find most appropriate the *Gentile/Hinds* standard. Under that standard, the regulation of a judge's speech will be upheld if it furthers a substantial governmental interest unrelated to suppression of expression, and is no more restrictive than necessary. Avoiding material prejudice to an adjudicatory proceeding is one example of a governmental interest sufficient to uphold restrictions on a judge's speech. The preservation of the independence and integrity of the judiciary and the maintenance of public confidence in the judiciary—the interests underlying Canons 3A(8) and 2B—are obviously interests of sufficient magnitude to sustain those Canons under the *Gentile /Hinds* standard, and we are satisfied that the restrictions on a judge's speech imposed by those Canons are no greater than necessary. Accordingly, we uphold the constitutionality of their application to Petitioner.

VI

As modified by this opinion, we affirm Opinion No. 13–95 of the Advisory Committee on Extrajudicial Activities.

Notes

1. *Television and newspaper commentary.* Do you agree that Judge Broadbelt's television commentary was "inappropriate and had the potential to compromise the integrity of the judiciary in New Jersey?" In *United States v. Cooley*, 1 F.3d 985 (10th Cir.1993), a federal district judge who had issued an order preventing abortion protesters from blocking a clinic, and then learned that the protesters planned to violate his order, appeared on "Nightline" and said "these people are breaking the law." The appeals court ordered him disqualified from the case on the ground that his television appearance created an appearance of partiality. The court concluded that "it unavoidably created the appearance that the judge had become an active participant in bringing law and order to bear on the protesters, rather than remaining as a detached adjudicator." Was this the problem in *Broadbelt*? Was there a problem at all in *Broadbelt*? Is the Canon restricting public comment on pending cases too broadly applied in that case?

2. Judicial Code Canon 4, discussed in *Broadbelt*, does authorize a number of extra-judicial activities, such as teaching and lecturing about

the legal system. The central thrust of Canon 4, however, is to restrict extra-judicial activities. Judges must conduct themselves off the bench in a way that does not call their impartiality into question, demean the judicial office, or interfere in any other way with the performance of their job. *Id.*, Canon 4A. This means that a number of specific activities are either prohibited entirely or severely curtailed. See *id.*, Canon 4C(1) (limiting appearing at a public hearing or consulting with an executive or legislative body or official); Canon 4C(2) (forbidding appointments to governmental positions on matters other than improvement of the law or the legal system); Canon 4C(3) (restricting service as an officer, director, trustee or non-legal advisor to an organization); Canon 4D (restricting financial and business dealings that either create apparent conflicts or appear to exploit the judge's position, including limitations on the receipt of gifts); Canon 4E (restricting fiduciary activities); Canon 4F (forbidding service as a mediator or arbitrator unless expressly authorized by law to do so); Canon 4G (forbidding a judge from practicing law).

3. *Sanctionable personal conduct related to judicial functions.* As noted above, judges may be sanctioned for personal conduct that calls into doubt the judge's capacity to perform judicial functions properly. Some of the cases deal with conduct that relates to the misuse of judicial power, or at least to conduct closely related to the performance of judicial activities. For example, in *In re Judicial Disciplinary Proceedings Against Crawford*, 245 Wis.2d 373, 629 N.W.2d 1 (2001), a judge was suspended for 75 days for attempting to coerce the chief judge into changing an administrative order regulating court hours by threatening to accuse the chief judge, his family and his chief administrator of professional misconduct. Other cases deal with misuse of the prestige of judicial office for personal gain, a violation of Canon 2B. See, e.g., *In re Mosley*, 120 Nev. 908, 102 P.3d 555 (2004) (judge improperly used judicial letterhead in two letters to the principals at his child's school). Still others deal with situations where the judge's conduct calls into question the judge's core honesty, integrity, or impartiality. See, e.g., *In re Jones*, 255 Neb. 1, 581 N.W.2d 876 (1998) (judge removed from office for, among other things, making a death threat to another judge); *In re Inquiry Concerning a Judge (In re Robertson)*, 277 Ga. 831, 596 S.E.2d 2 (2004) (elected judge removed from office for falsely swearing in a candidate affidavit that he had never been convicted of a felony involving moral turpitude); *In re Ellender*, 889 So.2d 225 (La. 2004) (judge suspended for one year for appearing in public, at a Halloween party, wearing an afro wig, black face makeup, and prison jumpsuit).

4. *Sanctionable personal conduct unrelated to judicial functions.* Sanctioning judges for personal conduct that does not have much of a connection to the judicial function is more controversial, but it does occur. Often, such cases do involve some demonstrated disrespect for the law, so in that sense they are related to the cases in Note 3 above. For example, In *In re Williams*, 169 N.J. 264, 777 A.2d 323 (2001), a judge was suspended without pay for three months after she got involved in altercations at a restaurant and tavern with a man with whom she had

previously had a romantic relationship, then gave misleading information to the police department about the incident. In *In re Gilbert*, 469 Mich. 1224, 668 N.W.2d 892 (2003), a judge was suspended without pay for three months for smoking marijuana at a Rolling Stones concert. In *Harris v. Smartt*, 311 Mont. 507, 57 P.3d 58 (2002), a justice of the peace was suspended without pay through the end of his term, effectively removing him from office, when a fellow judge found pornography on his office computer. Subsequently a man came forward and alleged that the justice had smoked marijuana with him and made unwanted sexual advances towards him. These latter allegations were never substantiated. A dissenting judge in the disciplinary action called the majority's sanction "misguided in several respects," arguing that the justice's privacy rights were violated and that any proven misconduct had nothing to do with his ability to perform judicial functions. The argument that the justice's conduct diminishes the public's esteem of the judiciary, the dissenter said, "shows a certain detachment from reality. Only judges and a few members of the bar are so deluded that they think the public expects more of them in the conduct of their personal lives than they expect of other people.... God protect us from the wrath of the righteous." Should personal misconduct that does not rise to the level of criminality be off-limits for discipline?

5. *Consensual romantic relationships.* Judges have also been sanctioned for engaging in consensual romantic relationships with the wrong people. See, e.g., *In re Flanagan*, 240 Conn. 157, 690 A.2d 865 (1997) (judge publicly reprimanded for having engaged in consensual sexual relationship with a married court reporter, on the ground that such conduct damages public confidence in the integrity of the judiciary); *In re Gerard*, 631 N.W.2d 271 (Iowa 2001) (judge suspended for 60 days without pay for engaging in secret intimate relationship with assistant county attorney who appeared before him on a daily basis). Are these two cases distinguishable? Should discipline have been imposed in either one?

6. *Accepting gifts and travel expenses.* Judicial Code Canon 4D(5) prohibits judges from accepting gifts, bequests, or loans from anyone, except for particular situations listed in the rule (such things as ordinary social hospitality; gifts from relatives or friends for some special occasion such as weddings, anniversaries, or birthdays; and loans from lending institutions, on the same terms and based on the same criteria as loans to other applicants, are not prohibited). Another exception is for "an invitation to the judge and the judge's spouse or guest to attend a bar-related function or an activity devoted to the improvement of the law, the legal system or the administration of justice." Canon 4D(5)(a). Canon 4H allows a judge to receive compensation and reimbursement of expenses for any permitted extra-judicial activities as long as the source of such payments "does not give the appearance of influencing the judge's performance of judicial duties or otherwise give the appearance of impropriety."

§ 3.   ELECTIONS AND POLITICAL ACTIVITY

REPUBLICAN PARTY OF MINNESOTA v. WHITE

Supreme Court of the United States, 2002.
536 U.S. 765, 122 S.Ct. 2528, 153 L.Ed.2d 694.

Justice SCALIA delivered the opinion of the Court.

The question presented in this case is whether the First Amendment permits the Minnesota Supreme Court to prohibit candidates for judicial election in that State from announcing their views on disputed legal and political issues.

I

Since Minnesota's admission to the Union in 1858, the State's Constitution has provided for the selection of all state judges by popular election. Minn. Const., Art. VI, § 7. Since 1912, those elections have been nonpartisan. Since 1974, they have been subject to a legal restriction which states that a "candidate for a judicial office, including an incumbent judge," shall not "announce his or her views on disputed legal or political issues." Minn.Code of Judicial Conduct, Canon 5(A)(3)(d)(i) (2000). This prohibition, promulgated by the Minnesota Supreme Court and based on Canon 7(B) of the 1972 American Bar Association (ABA) Model Code of Judicial Conduct, is known as the "announce clause." Incumbent judges who violate it are subject to discipline, including removal, censure, civil penalties, and suspension without pay. Lawyers who run for judicial office also must comply with the announce clause. Minn. Rule of Professional Conduct 8.2(b) (2002) ("A lawyer who is a candidate for judicial office shall comply with the applicable provisions of the Code of Judicial Conduct"). Those who violate it are subject to, *inter alia,* disbarment, suspension, and probation.

In 1996, one of the petitioners, Gregory Wersal, ran for associate justice of the Minnesota Supreme Court. In the course of the campaign, he distributed literature criticizing several Minnesota Supreme Court decisions on issues such as crime, welfare, and abortion. A complaint against Wersal challenging, among other things, the propriety of this literature was filed with the Office of Lawyers Professional Responsibility, the agency which, under the direction of the Minnesota Lawyers Professional Responsibility Board, investigates and prosecutes ethical violations of lawyer candidates for judicial office. The Lawyers Board dismissed the complaint; with regard to the charges that his campaign materials violated the announce clause, it expressed doubt whether the clause could constitutionally be enforced. Nonetheless, fearing that further ethical complaints would jeopardize his ability to practice law, Wersal withdrew from the election. In 1998, Wersal ran again for the same office. Early in that race, he sought an advisory opinion from the Lawyers Board with regard to whether it planned to enforce the announce clause. The Lawyers Board responded equivocally, stating that, although it had significant doubts about the constitutionality of the provision, it was unable to answer his question because he had not submitted a list of the announcements he wished to make.

Shortly thereafter, Wersal filed this lawsuit in Federal District Court against respondents, [officers of the Lawyers Board and of the Minnesota Board on Judicial Standards,] seeking, *inter alia,* a declaration that the announce clause violates the First Amendment and an injunction against its enforcement. . . . Other plaintiffs in the suit, including the Minnesota Republican Party, alleged that, because the clause kept Wersal from announcing his views, they were unable to learn those views and support or oppose his candidacy accordingly. The parties filed cross-motions for summary judgment, and the District Court found in favor of respondents, holding that the announce clause did not violate the First Amendment. Over a dissent by Judge Beam, the United States Court of Appeals for the Eighth Circuit affirmed. We granted certiorari.

II

Before considering the constitutionality of the announce clause, we must be clear about its meaning. Its text says that a candidate for judicial office shall not "announce his or her views on disputed legal or political issues."

We know that "announc[ing] . . . views" on an issue covers much more than *promising* to decide an issue a particular way. The prohibition extends to the candidate's mere statement of his current position, even if he does not bind himself to maintain that position after election. All the parties agree this is the case, because the Minnesota Code contains a so-called "pledges or promises" clause, which *separately* prohibits judicial candidates from making "pledges or promises of conduct in office other than the faithful and impartial performance of the duties of the office,"—a prohibition that is not challenged here and on which we express no view.

There are, however, some limitations that the Minnesota Supreme Court has placed upon the scope of the announce clause that are not (to put it politely) immediately apparent from its text. The statements that formed the basis of the complaint against Wersal in 1996 included criticism of past decisions of the Minnesota Supreme Court. One piece of campaign literature stated that "[t]he Minnesota Supreme Court has issued decisions which are marked by their disregard for the Legislature and a lack of common sense." It went on to criticize a decision excluding from evidence confessions by criminal defendants that were not tape-recorded, asking "[s]hould we conclude that because the Supreme Court does not trust police, it allows confessed criminals to go free?" It criticized a decision striking down a state law restricting welfare benefits, asserting that "[i]t's the Legislature which should set our spending policies." And it criticized a decision requiring public financing of abortions for poor women as "unprecedented" and a "pro-abortion stance." Although one would think that all of these statements touched on disputed legal or political issues, they did not (or at least do not now) fall within the scope of the announce clause. The Judicial Board issued an opinion stating that judicial candidates may criticize past decisions, and the Lawyers Board refused to discipline Wersal for the foregoing statements because, in part, it thought they did not violate the announce clause. The Eighth Circuit relied on the Judicial Board's opinion in upholding the announce clause, and the Minnesota Supreme Court recently embraced the Eighth Circuit's interpretation, *In re Code of Judicial Conduct*, 639 N.W.2d 55 (Minn.2002).

There are yet further limitations upon the apparent plain meaning of the announce clause: In light of the constitutional concerns, the District Court construed the clause to reach only disputed issues that are likely to come before the candidate if he is elected judge. The Eighth Circuit accepted this limiting interpretation by the District Court, and in addition construed the clause to allow general discussions of case law and judicial philosophy. The Supreme Court of Minnesota adopted these interpretations as well when it ordered enforcement of the announce clause in accordance with the Eighth Circuit's opinion.

It seems to us, however, that—like the text of the announce clause itself—these limitations upon the text of the announce clause are not all that they appear to be. First, respondents acknowledged at oral argument that statements critical of past judicial decisions are *not* permissible if the candidate also states that he is against *stare decisis*. Thus, candidates must choose between stating their views critical of past decisions and stating their views in opposition to *stare decisis*. Or, to look at it more concretely, they may state their view that prior decisions were erroneous only if they do not assert that they, if elected, have any power to eliminate erroneous decisions. Second, limiting the scope of the clause to issues likely to come before a court is not much of a limitation at all. One would hardly expect the "disputed legal or political issues" raised in the course of a state judicial election to include such matters as whether the Federal Government should end the embargo of Cuba. Quite obviously, they will be those legal or political disputes that are the proper (or by past decisions have been made the improper) business of the state courts. And within that relevant category, "[t]here is almost no legal or political issue that is unlikely to come before a judge of an American court, state or federal, of general jurisdiction." *Buckley v. Illinois Judicial Inquiry Bd.*, 997 F.2d 224, 229 (C.A.7 1993). Third, construing the clause to allow "general" discussions of case law and judicial philosophy turns out to be of little help in an election campaign. At oral argument, respondents gave, as an example of this exception, that a candidate is free to assert that he is a " 'strict constructionist.' " But that, like most other philosophical generalities, has little meaningful content for the electorate unless it is exemplified by application to a particular issue of construction likely to come before a court—for example, whether a particular statute runs afoul of any provision of the Constitution. Respondents conceded that the announce clause would prohibit the candidate from exemplifying his philosophy in this fashion. Without such application to real-life issues, all candidates can claim to be "strict constructionists" with equal (and unhelpful) plausibility.

In any event, it is clear that the announce clause prohibits a judicial candidate from stating his views on any specific nonfanciful legal question within the province of the court for which he is running, except in the context of discussing past decisions—and in the latter context as well, if he expresses the view that he is not bound by *stare decisis*.

Respondents contend that this still leaves plenty of topics for discussion on the campaign trail. These include a candidate's "character," "education," "work habits," and "how [he] would handle administrative duties if elected." Indeed, the Judicial Board has printed a list of preapproved questions which judicial candidates are allowed to answer. These include how the candidate feels about cameras in the courtroom, how he would go about reducing the caseload, how the costs of judicial administration can be reduced, and how he proposes to ensure that minorities and women are treated more fairly by the court system. Whether this list of preapproved subjects, and other topics not prohibited by the announce clause, adequately fulfill the First Amendment's guarantee of freedom of speech is the question to which we now turn.

III

As the Court of Appeals recognized, the announce clause both prohibits speech on the basis of its content and burdens a category of speech that is "at the core of our First Amendment freedoms"—speech about the qualifications of candidates for public office. The Court of Appeals concluded that the proper test to be applied to determine the constitutionality of such a restriction is what our cases have called strict scrutiny; the parties do not dispute that this is correct. Under the strict-scrutiny test, respondents have the burden to prove that the announce clause is (1) narrowly tailored, to serve (2) a compelling state interest. In order for respondents to show that the announce clause is narrowly tailored, they must demonstrate that it does not "unnecessarily circumscrib[e] protected expression." *Brown v. Hartlage,* 456 U.S. 45, 54, 102 S.Ct. 1523, 71 L.Ed.2d 732 (1982).

The Court of Appeals concluded that respondents had established two interests as sufficiently compelling to justify the announce clause: preserving the impartiality of the state judiciary and preserving the appearance of the impartiality of the state judiciary. Respondents reassert these two interests before us, arguing that the first is compelling because it protects the due process rights of litigants, and that the second is compelling because it preserves public confidence in the judiciary. Respondents are rather vague, however, about what they mean by "impartiality." ...

A

One meaning of "impartiality" in the judicial context—and of course its root meaning—is the lack of bias for or against either *party* to the proceeding. Impartiality in this sense assures equal application of the law. That is, it guarantees a party that the judge who hears his case will apply the law to him in the same way he applies it to any other party. This is the traditional sense in which the term is used. See Webster's New International Dictionary 1247 (2d ed.1950) (defining "impartial" as "[n]ot partial; esp., not favoring one more than another; treating all alike; unbiased; equitable; fair; just"). It is also the sense in which it is used in the cases cited by respondents and *amici* for the proposition that an impartial judge is essential to due process.

We think it plain that the announce clause is not narrowly tailored to serve impartiality (or the appearance of impartiality) in this sense. Indeed, the clause is barely tailored to serve that interest *at all,* inasmuch as it does not restrict speech for or against particular *parties,* but rather speech for or against particular *issues.* To be sure, when a case arises that turns on a legal issue on which the judge (as a candidate) had taken a particular stand, the party taking the opposite stand is likely to lose. But not because of any bias against that party, or favoritism toward the other party. *Any* party taking that position is just as likely to lose. The judge is applying the law (as he sees it) evenhandedly.

B

It is perhaps possible to use the term "impartiality" in the judicial context (though this is certainly not a common usage) to mean lack of preconception in favor of or against a particular *legal view.* This sort of impartiality would be concerned, not with guaranteeing litigants equal application of the law, but rather with guaranteeing them an equal chance to persuade the court on the legal points in their case. Impartiality in this sense may well be an interest served by the announce clause, but it is not a *compelling* state interest, as strict scrutiny requires. A judge's lack of predisposition regarding the relevant legal issues in a case has never been thought a necessary component of equal justice, and with good reason. For one thing, it is virtually impossible to find a judge who does not have preconceptions about the law. . . . Indeed, even if it were possible to select judges who did not have preconceived views on legal issues, it would hardly be desirable to do so. "Proof that a Justice's mind at the time he joined the Court was a complete *tabula rasa* in the area of constitutional adjudication would be evidence of lack of qualification, not lack of bias." The Minnesota Constitution positively forbids the selection to courts of general jurisdiction of judges who are impartial in the sense of having no views on the law. Minn. Const., Art. VI, § 5 ("Judges of the supreme court, the court of appeals and the district court shall be learned in the law"). And since avoiding judicial preconceptions on legal issues is neither possible nor desirable, pretending otherwise by attempting to preserve the "appearance" of that type of impartiality can hardly be a compelling state interest either.

C

A third possible meaning of "impartiality" (again not a common one) might be described as open-mindedness. This quality in a judge demands, not that he have no preconceptions on legal issues, but that he be willing to consider views that oppose his preconceptions, and remain open to persuasion, when the issues arise in a pending case. This sort of impartiality seeks to guarantee each litigant, not an *equal* chance to win the legal points in the case, but at least *some* chance of doing so. It may well be that impartiality in this sense, and the appearance of it, are desirable in the judiciary, but we need not pursue that inquiry, since we do not believe the Minnesota Supreme Court adopted the announce clause for that purpose.

Respondents argue that the announce clause serves the interest in open-mindedness, or at least in the appearance of open-mindedness, because it relieves a judge from pressure to rule a certain way in order to maintain consistency with statements the judge has previously made. The problem is, however, that statements in election campaigns are such an infinitesimal portion of the public commitments to legal positions that judges (or judges-to-be) undertake, that this object of the prohibition is implausible. Before they arrive on the bench (whether by election or otherwise) judges have often committed themselves on legal issues that they must later rule upon. More common still is a judge's confronting a legal issue on which he has expressed an opinion while on the bench. Most frequently, of course, that prior expression will have occurred in ruling on an earlier case. But judges often state their views on disputed legal issues outside the context of adjudication—in classes that they conduct, and in books and speeches. Like the ABA Codes of Judicial Conduct, the Minnesota Code not only permits but encourages this. See Minn.Code of Judicial Conduct, Canon 4(B) (2002) ("A judge may write, lecture, teach, speak and participate in other extra-judicial activities concerning the law ... "); Minn.Code of Judicial Conduct, Canon 4(B), Comment. (2002) ("To the extent that time permits, a judge is encouraged to do so ... "). That is quite incompatible with the notion that the need for open-mindedness (or for the appearance of open-mindedness) lies behind the prohibition at issue here.

The short of the matter is this: In Minnesota, a candidate for judicial office may not say "I think it is constitutional for the legislature to prohibit same-sex marriages." He may say the very same thing, however, up until the very day before he declares himself a candidate, and may say it repeatedly (until litigation is pending) after he is elected. As a means of pursuing the objective of open-mindedness that respondents now articulate, the announce clause is so woefully underinclusive as to render belief in that purpose a challenge to the credulous....

IV

There is an obvious tension between the article of Minnesota's popularly approved Constitution which provides that judges shall be elected, and the Minnesota Supreme Court's announce clause which places most subjects of interest to the voters off limits. (The candidate-speech restrictions of all the other States that have them are also the product of judicial fiat.) The disparity is perhaps unsurprising, since the ABA, which originated the announce clause, has long been an opponent of judicial elections. That opposition may be well taken (it certainly had the support of the Founders of the Federal Government), but the First Amendment does not permit it to achieve its goal by leaving the principle of elections in place while preventing candidates from discussing what the elections are about....

The Minnesota Supreme Court's canon of judicial conduct prohibiting candidates for judicial election from announcing their views on disputed legal and political issues violates the First Amendment. Accordingly, we reverse the grant of summary judgment to respondents and remand the case for proceedings consistent with this opinion.

It is so ordered.

Justice O'CONNOR, concurring.

I join the opinion of the Court but write separately to express my concerns about judicial elections generally. Respondents claim that "[t]he Announce Clause is necessary ... to protect the

State's compelling governmental interes[t] in an actual and perceived ... impartial judiciary." I am concerned that, even aside
from what judicial candidates may say while campaigning, the
very practice of electing judges undermines this interest.

We of course want judges to be impartial, in the sense of
being free from any personal stake in the outcome of the cases to
which they are assigned. But if judges are subject to regular
elections they are likely to feel that they have at least some
personal stake in the outcome of every publicized case. Elected
judges cannot help being aware that if the public is not satisfied
with the outcome of a particular case, it could hurt their reelec-
tion prospects. Even if judges were able to suppress their awareness of the potential electoral consequences of their decisions and
refrain from acting on it, the public's confidence in the judiciary
could be undermined simply by the possibility that judges would
be unable to do so.

Moreover, contested elections generally entail campaigning.
And campaigning for a judicial post today can require substantial
funds. See Schotland, Financing Judicial Elections, 2000: Change
and Challenge, 2001 L.Rev. Mich. State U. Detroit College of Law
849, 866 (reporting that in 2000, the 13 candidates in a partisan
election for 5 seats on the Alabama Supreme Court spent an
average of $1,092,076 on their campaigns); American Bar Associa-
tion, Report and Recommendations of the Task Force on Lawyers'
Political Contributions, pt.2 (July 1998) (reporting that in 1995,
one candidate for the Pennsylvania Supreme Court raised
$1,848,142 in campaign funds, and that in 1986, $2,700,000 was
spent on the race for Chief Justice of the Ohio Supreme Court).
Unless the pool of judicial candidates is limited to those wealthy
enough to independently fund their campaigns, a limitation unrelated to judicial skill, the cost of campaigning requires judicial
candidates to engage in fundraising. Yet relying on campaign
donations may leave judges feeling indebted to certain parties or
interest groups. See Thomas, National L. J., Mar. 16, 1998, p. A8,
col. 1 (reporting that a study by the public interest group Texans
for Public Justice found that 40 percent of the $9,200,000 in
contributions of $100 or more raised by seven of Texas' nine
Supreme Court justices for their 1994 and 1996 elections "came
from parties and lawyers with cases before the court or contributors closely linked to these parties"). Even if judges were able to
refrain from favoring donors, the mere possibility that judges'
decisions may be motivated by the desire to repay campaign
contributors is likely to undermine the public's confidence in the
judiciary.

Minnesota has chosen to select its judges through contested
popular elections instead of through an appointment system or a
combined appointment and retention election system.... In doing
so the State has voluntarily taken on the risks to judicial bias

described above. As a result, the State's claim that it needs to significantly restrict judges' speech in order to protect judicial impartiality is particularly troubling. If the State has a problem with judicial impartiality, it is largely one the State brought upon itself by continuing the practice of popularly electing judges.

Justice KENNEDY, concurring.

. . . There is general consensus that the design of the Federal Constitution, including lifetime tenure and appointment by nomination and confirmation, has preserved the independence of the federal judiciary. In resolving this case, however, we should refrain from criticism of the State's choice to use open elections to select those persons most likely to achieve judicial excellence. States are free to choose this mechanism rather than, say, appointment and confirmation. By condemning judicial elections across the board, we implicitly condemn countless elected state judges and without warrant. Many of them, despite the difficulties imposed by the election system, have discovered in the law the enlightenment, instruction, and inspiration that make them independent-minded and faithful jurists of real integrity. . . .

These considerations serve but to reinforce the conclusion that Minnesota's regulatory scheme is flawed. By abridging speech based on its content, Minnesota impeaches its own system of free and open elections. The State may not regulate the content of candidate speech merely because the speakers are candidates. . . .

Justice STEVENS, with whom Justice SOUTER, Justice GINSBURG, and Justice BREYER join, dissenting.

. . . The Court's disposition rests on two seriously flawed premises—an inaccurate appraisal of the importance of judicial independence and impartiality, and an assumption that judicial candidates should have the same freedom " 'to express themselves on matters of current public importance' " as do all other elected officials. Elected judges, no less than appointed judges, occupy an office of trust that is fundamentally different from that occupied by policymaking officials. Although the fact that they must stand for election makes their job more difficult than that of the tenured judge, that fact does not lessen their duty to respect essential attributes of the judicial office that have been embedded in Anglo–American law for centuries.

There is a critical difference between the work of the judge and the work of other public officials. In a democracy, issues of policy are properly decided by majority vote; it is the business of legislators and executives to be popular. But in litigation, issues of law or fact should not be determined by popular vote; it is the business of judges to be indifferent to unpopularity. . . .

Justice GINSBURG, with whom Justice STEVENS, Justice SOUTER, and Justice BREYER join, dissenting.

Whether state or federal, elected or appointed, judges perform a function fundamentally different from that of the people's elected representatives. . . .

The ability of the judiciary to discharge its unique role rests to a large degree on the manner in which judges are selected. The Framers of the Federal Constitution sought to advance the judicial function through the structural protections of Article III, which provide for the selection of judges by the President on the advice and consent of the Senate, generally for lifetime terms. Through its own Constitution, Minnesota, in common with most other States, has decided to allow its citizens to choose judges directly in periodic elections. But Minnesota has not thereby opted to install a corps of political actors on the bench; rather, it has endeavored to preserve the integrity of its judiciary by other means. Recognizing that the influence of political parties is incompatible with the judge's role, for example, Minnesota has designated all judicial elections nonpartisan. And it has adopted a provision, here called the Announce Clause, designed to prevent candidates for judicial office from "publicly making known how they would decide issues likely to come before them as judges." . . . I do not agree with [the Court's] unilocular, "an election is an election," approach. Instead, I would differentiate elections for political offices, in which the First Amendment holds full sway, from elections designed to select those whose office it is to administer justice without respect to persons. Minnesota's choice to elect its judges, I am persuaded, does not preclude the State from installing an election process geared to the judicial office. . . .

Judges are not politicians, and the First Amendment does not require that they be treated as politicians simply because they are chosen by popular vote. Nor does the First Amendment command States who wish to promote the integrity of their judges in fact and appearance to abandon systems of judicial selection that the people, in the exercise of their sovereign prerogatives, have devised. . . . Accordingly, I would affirm the judgment of the Court of Appeals for the Eighth Circuit.

Notes

1. *The history of electing judges.* Federal judges are appointed (pursuant to Constitutional directive), not elected. But at the state level, judicial elections have a long history. Georgia was the first state to elect judges, beginning in 1812. The populism of the Jacksonian era fueled a trend, and by the Civil War era, most states chose their judges in partisan elections. By all accounts these elections were often hotly

contested. See Berkson, *Judicial Selection in the United States: A Special Report*, 64 Judicature 176 (1980). Today, over three-fifths of the states pick some or all of their general-jurisdiction and appellate judges in popular elections, although most of these are non-partisan. In addition, just over a dozen states now employ a modified election method (often called the "Missouri Plan," after the first state that used it) in which at least some of their judges are appointed, then after some number of years on the bench appear on the ballot unopposed, with voters choosing simply to retain them or not. For an interesting perspective on retention elections, written by a former California Supreme Court Justice who lost one, see Joseph Grodin, *Developing a Consensus of Constraint: A Judge's Perspective on Judicial Retention Elections*, 61 S. Cal. L. Rev. 1969 (1988).

2. The ABA has long taken the position that allowing the general public to choose judges is a bad idea, a view reflected in a comment to the current Judicial Code. See Judicial Code Canon 5C(2), commentary ("merit selection of judges is a preferable manner in which to select the judiciary"). In 2003, the ABA House of Delegates adopted a commission report calling for a system in which governors would appoint judges from a pool of candidates reviewed and approved by a neutral commission. Judges would then serve until they reach a particular age, with no re-selection at all. Do you share Justice O'Connor's (and the ABA's) misgivings about selecting judges by popular vote? What do you think of the 2003 ABA recommendation? Or should state judges be appointed for life, as are Article III federal judges? For a critical look at the issues raised by the popular election of judges, see Stephen P. Croley, *The Majoritarian Difficulty: Elective Judiciaries and the Rule of Law*, 62 U. Chi. L.Rev. 689 (1995).

3. *The history of restrictions on judicial campaign speech.* Restrictions of the kind challenged and overturned in *White* first appeared early in the last century. The ABA's first code of judicial conduct, adopted in 1924, said: "A candidate for judicial position . . . should not announce in advance his conclusions of law on disputed issues to secure class support. . . . " ABA Canon of Judicial Ethics 30 (1924). When *White* arose, all but four states—Idaho, Michigan, North Carolina and Oregon—had adopted some version of the "announce clause." Do you believe the announce clause serves a compelling government interest? What interest?

4. Judicial Code Canon 5, as amended in 2003 after the *White* decision, still contains a number of restrictions on judicial participation in political activity. These restrictions purport to apply to judges and candidates for judicial office, either elected or appointed. See Judicial Code, Canon 5E. They restrict what judges and judicial candidates can say and do in connection with campaigns for office, by expressly authorizing certain kinds of activities in Canon 5B and 5C and forbidding everything else in Canon 5A. Canon 5C(2) sets forth a number of restrictions on fundraising.

5. Judicial Code Canon 3B(10), added in 2003, prohibits a judge from "making pledges, promises or commitments that are inconsistent with the impartial performance of the adjudicative duties of the office" with respect to "cases, controversies or issues that are likely to come before the court." Canon 5A(3)(d), as amended in 2003, prohibits a candidate for judicial office from making "pledges, promises or commitments" with respect to "cases, controversies or issues that are likely to come before the court ... that are inconsistent with the impartial performance of the adjudicative duties of the office." Does *White* call the constitutionality of these provisions into doubt, or do these rule stand on a firmer footing than the "announce clause?" See *North Dakota Family Alliance, Inc. v. Bader*, 361 F.Supp.2d 1021 (D.N.D. 2005) (holding unconstitutional the state's "pledges or promises" clause and its "commit" clause, in light of *White*).

6. *White* did not deal with the constitutionality of state judicial code rules patterned on Judicial Code Canons 5A and 5B that prohibit judges or candidates for judicial appointment or elective office from soliciting campaign contributions and from engaging in partisan activities such as attending political gatherings. But those provisions, commonly called the "solicit" clause and the "partisan activities" clause, may be the next to fall. See *Republican Party of Minnesota v. White*, 416 F.3d 738 (8th Cir. 2005) (en banc) (on remand from Supreme Court's decision, declaring Minnesota's "solicitation" and "partisan activities" clauses unconstitutional violations of judges rights to free speech and free association, respectively); *Kansas Judicial Watch v. Stout*, 440 F.Supp.2d 1209 (D. Kan. 2006) (holding unconstitutional Kansas's "pledges and promises," "commit," and "solicit" clauses).

7. *False campaign speech.* In *In re Chmura*, 461 Mich. 517, 608 N.W.2d 31 (2000), a district court judge challenged the constitutionality of a Michigan judicial conduct rule that prohibited a candidate for judicial office from participating in the use of "any form of public communication that the candidate knows or reasonably should know is false, fraudulent, misleading [or] deceptive." The judge was the subject of a complaint by the state Judicial Tenure Commission, which alleged that he violated that rule by allowing his campaign committee to distribute four fliers that described, in colorful language, the judge's record and positions on some political issues (including his opposition to former Detroit Mayor Coleman Young). The Michigan Supreme Court agreed with Judge Chmura that the challenged provision was facially unconstitutional because of overbreadth, and narrowed its construction to prohibit only a candidate's knowingly or recklessly disregarding the truth or falsity of a public communication. The case was remanded to the Judicial Tenure Commission for reconsideration in light of the narrowed construction.

8. *Political opposition as conflict of interest.* In *Joiner v. Joiner*, 2005 WL 2805566 (Tenn. App.), a trial judge ruled that the lawyer for one of the parties before him should be disqualified from trying any cases in the Fourth Circuit Court because of the lawyer's announced

intention to run against him in the next general election. In making this ruling, the judge said the lawyer "voluntarily" created this "running-for-election conflict." Two questions: (1) Should the judge recuse himself from cases involving this lawyer? (2) Should the lawyer be disqualified from representing any clients in the Fourth Circuit Court, even where the particular judge was not presiding? What do you see as the key public interests involved in answering these questions?

9. *Campaign contributions as conflicts of interest.* Must a judge recuse herself if one of the parties or lawyers in a case before her has contributed to her election campaign? Not necessarily. See, e.g., *MacKenzie v. Super Kids Bargain Store, Inc.*, 565 So.2d 1332 (Fla.1990) ("that a litigant has made a legal campaign contribution to the political campaign of the trial judge ... without more, is not a legally sufficient ground" for disqualification); *City of Las Vegas Downtown Redevelopment Agency v. Eighth Judicial District Court*, 116 Nev. 640, 5 P.3d 1059 (2000) (judge's receipt of campaign contributions from casinos that stood to benefit from the outcome of the case did not constitute proper grounds for disqualification; court ordered judge to preside over the case after he had recused himself). When might a campaign contribution create an appearance of partiality? In *Pierce v. Pierce*, 39 P.3d 791 (Okla.2001), a judge presiding over a divorce case had accepted campaign contributions in the maximum allowed amount from both the husband's lawyer and that lawyer's father. Further, that lawyer had solicited funds for the judge's campaign during the pendency of the case. On those facts, the Supreme Court concluded, the plaintiff proved that the trial judge should have been disqualified.

10. *Public financing of judicial campaigns.* Justice O'Connor's concurrence in *White* provides some recent data on the amount of money spent in judicial elections—almost $3 million on the Ohio Chief Justice race in 1986; close to $10 million by Texas Supreme Court Justices ten years later. Not surprisingly, the amounts continue to go up. Data from 2005 show that in Alabama, candidates for the Supreme Court had spent $41 million in elections since 1993; in Texas, in the same time period, candidates for the Supreme Court spent $27 million. Special interest groups, many of them self-styled "pro-life" and "tort reform" groups, are responsible for much of the spending on television commercials. See Amanda Bronstad, *Cash is flowing in judicial elections*, 29:6 Nat'l L. J. (Oct. 9, 2006), at 1. Contested judicial elections, especially partisan elections, can get particularly nasty, with judicial candidates (and the aforementioned special-interest groups) running "attack ads" that often accuse sitting judges of such things as turning violent criminals loose on the streets. See Terry Carter, *Mud and Money: Judicial Elections Turn to Big Bucks and Nasty Tactics*, A.B.A.J. (Feb. 2005), at 40, 42.

Does this situation erode public confidence in the judiciary's competence and impartiality? Many think so. In 2002, North Carolina became the first state to provide public funding for all appellate and supreme court judicial candidates. Funding comes from a check-off on income tax forms and from voluntary $50 contributions from lawyers, made at the time they renew their licenses. N.C. Gen. Stat. §§ 163–278 *et seq.* (2002). Several states are considering similar legislation. Do you think this will help avoid some of the problems that Justice O'Connor identifies in her opinion in *White*? Will it improve public perception of the impartiality of the elected judiciary?

11. New York's system for nominating and electing trial judges, in place since 1921, in which political party members elected convention delegates who then selected judicial nominees, was struck down as unconstitutional in *Lopez Torres v. New York State Board of Elections*, 462 F.3d 161 (2d Cir. 2006). The court found the system violated judicial candidates' First Amendment rights of association and was not narrowly tailored to serve any compelling state interest. Evidence showed that "through a byzantine and onerous" network of regulations used in areas where one party controlled matters, New York had transformed a *de jure* election system into a *de facto* appointment system.

12. *Seeking election after removal from office.* Can a judge who is removed from office by the state judicial disciplinary authorities later run for election to judicial office? A number of states have constitutional provisions, statutes or rules that explicitly say no. See, e.g., Cal. Const. Art. IV, § 18(d); Wash. Const. Art. IV, § 31(5); N.Y. Const. Art. VI, § 22(h). In *Kentucky Judicial Conduct Comm'n v. Woods*, 25 S.W.3d 470 (Ky.2000), a judge had been removed by the Judicial Conduct Commission for misconduct (including displaying a handgun in court and generally engaging in "judicial tyranny"). When he publicly announced he would himself run as a candidate in the special election being held to pick his successor, the Commission brought an action to declare him ineligible to run. The court, even in the absence of the kind of provision or law referenced above, found in favor of the Commission. Prohibiting the removed judge from running for judicial office, at least during the remainder of the current term of judges in the affected district, was necessary to preserve the Commission's authority to remove a judge for misconduct.

Index

References are to pages

ABA
See *American Bar Association*

ABUSE OF PROCESS
elements of, 539
immunity from claims of, 540–41
malicious prosecution, compared to, 539

ABUSIVE LITIGATION TACTICS
See *Advocacy, Frivolous Claims and Arguments, Overzealous Advocacy, Sanctions*

ACCREDITATION
See *Legal Education*

ADMINISTRATIVE AGENCY PRACTICE
advocacy rules on, 507
by non-lawyers, 54
federal agencies, 65

ADMISSION TO PRACTICE
See *Bar, Admission to*

ADR
See *Alternative Dispute Resolution*

ADVANCING LITIGATION COSTS
bank lines of credit, 577
constitutionality of restrictions, 574–75, 576
litigation finance companies, 577–78
living expenses, 572–74, 576
medical expenses, 576
restrictions on, 571–78
state variations on, 576–77

ADVERSARY SYSTEM
abuses of, *see Advocacy; Criminal Practice; Frivolous Claims and Arguments; Ineffective Assistance of Counsel; Overzealous Advocacy; Sanctions; Trial Misconduct*
constitutional rules and, 121–32, 482–83
criminal defense counsel and, 121–45, 479, 482
critiques of, 477–83
ineffective assistance of counsel, 121–45
judges, role in, 634–39
lawyers, role in, 477–83
loyalty and, 479–82
prosecutors and, 482–83
role of judges in, 634–39

ADVERSARY SYSTEM—Cont'd
role of lawyers in, 477–83
search for truth in, 477–83
truth and, 477–83
work-product immunity and, 160–64

ADVERTISING
areas of practice, 579–85, 590–97
branding of firm names, 598–99
client testimonials in, 590
consumer protection statutes and, 586
ethics rules on, 586
letterheads, 598
firm names, 598
First Amendment and, 2–11, 579–99
prices for services, 2–5
professionalism and, 2–11, 579–99
self-laudatory claims, 588–90, 597–98
specialization, 590–97
television dramatizations, 586–88
trade names, 598
trademark infringement, 598–99
web sites, 609

ADVOCACY
See also *Advocate-Witness Rule; Frivolous Claims and Arguments; Overzealous Advocacy; Sanctions; Trial Misconduct*
adverse authority, duty to cite, 491, 503–07
advocate-witness rule, 520–24
asserting personal knowledge of facts, 501, 524
candor in, 503–07
client perjury, 525–31
criminal defense counsel and, 482, 525–31
improper, sanctions for, 483–503
improper influence over decision-makers, 507–08
overzealous, 493–503
prosecutors and, 482–83, 501–02, 519
Rule 11 sanctions, 483–93
sanctions for improper, 483–503
skills, 483
zealous, 482

ADVOCATE-WITNESS RULE
Generally, 520–24
client waiver of, 524
expert witnesses and, 524

†